Gale Library of Daily Life

American Civil War

Gale Library of Daily Life

American Civil War

VOLUME 2

Steven E. Woodworth

EDITOR

GALE
CENGAGE Learning™

Detroit • New York • San Francisco • New Haven, Conn • Waterville, Maine • London

Gale Library of Daily Life
American Civil War

Steven E. Woodworth, Editor

Project Editor: Angela Doolin

Editorial: Mark Drouillard, Andrea Fritsch, Carly S. Kaloustian, Brad Morgan, Darcy L. Thompson, Ken Wachsberger

Rights Acquisition and Management: Beth Beaufore, Barb McNeil, Jackie Jones, Kelly Quin

Imaging: Lezlie Light

Product Design: Pamela A. Galbreath

Composition: Evi Seoud

Manufacturing: Drew Kalasky

Library of Congress Cataloging-in-Publication Data

American Civil War / Steven E. Woodworth, editor.
p. cm. -- (Gale library of daily life)
Includes bibliographical references and index.
ISBN-13: 978-1-4144-3009-6 (set)
ISBN-13: 978-1-4144-3010-2 (vol. 1)
ISBN-13: 978-1-4144-3011-9 (vol. 2)
1. United States--History--Civil War, 1861-1865--Social aspects. 2. United States--Social life and customs--1775-1865. 3. United States--Social conditions--To 1865. 4. Confederate States of America--Social life and customs. 5. Confederate States of America--Social conditions. 6. United States--History--Civil War, 1861-1865--Sources. I. Woodworth, Steven E.

E468.9.A46 2008
973.7'1--dc22 2007047017

Gale
27500 Drake Rd.
Farmington Hills, MI 48331-3535

ISBN-13: 978-1-4144-3009-6 (set) ISBN-10: 1-4144-3009-4 (set)
ISBN-13: 978-1-4144-3010-2 (vol. 1) ISBN-10: 1-4144-3010-8 (vol. 1)
ISBN-13: 978-1-4144-3011-9 (vol. 2) ISBN-10: 1-4144-3011-6 (vol. 2)

This title is also available as an e-book.
ISBN-13: 978-1-4144-3012-6 ISBN-10: 1-4144-3012-4
Contact your Gale representative for ordering information.

Printed in the United States of America
2 3 4 5 6 7 12 11 10 09 08

Contents

VOLUME 2

A Chronology of the Civil War

1858

August–October

Incumbent U.S. senator Stephen A. Douglas of Illinois and challenger Abraham Lincoln hold a series of debates. Douglas maintains that he does not care about slavery and is content to let the people in each western territory "vote it up, or vote it down." Lincoln counters that slavery is a moral wrong and should not be allowed to spread.

1859

October 16

Abolitionist John Brown leads nineteen men in a raid on the U.S. armory at Harper's Ferry, Virginia (now West Virginia). Ten of the raiders are killed. Brown and seven others are captured.

December 2

John Brown is hanged at Charlestown, Virginia, for murder, conspiring with slaves to rebel, and for treason against Virginia, though he had never been a citizen of that state.

1860

February 27

Abraham Lincoln delivers a speech at the Cooper Union in New York City, arguing that the goal of the Republican Party—preventing the further spread of slavery—is consistent with the thinking of the Founding Fathers.

May 3

The Democratic National Convention, meeting in Charleston, South Carolina, breaks up when Southern delegates use convention rules to block the nomination of the majority's choice, Stephen A. Douglas.

May 9

Southerners who had formerly belonged to the defunct Whig and Know-Nothing parties meet in Baltimore, Maryland, to form the Constitutional Union Party and nominate John Bell of Tennessee for president.

May 16

Abraham Lincoln wins the presidential nomination of the Republican National Convention, meeting in Chicago.

June 18

The Democrats meet again in Baltimore, Maryland, but Southern delegates walk out when the majority rejects their demand for a federal slave code for the territories. The remaining delegates nominate Douglas.

June 28

Southern delegates who had bolted the Democratic convention meet in Richmond, Virginia, and nominate Vice President John C. Breckinridge of Kentucky.

November 6

In the presidential election, Lincoln wins a majority of the electoral vote and a plurality of the popular vote.

November 10

The South Carolina legislature authorizes a special convention to consider the question of the state's secession. Both of South Carolina's U.S. senators resign their seats and leave Washington.

December 20

The South Carolina convention, meeting in Charleston, adopts an ordinance of secession.

1861

January 9

The unarmed steamer *Star of the West* attempts to enter Charleston Harbor carrying supplies and reinforcements for Fort Sumter, but Rebel cannon opens fire and forces it to turn back. Union gunners within Fort Sumter do not return fire.

Mississippi secedes.

January 10

Florida secedes.

January 11

Alabama secedes.

January 19

Georgia secedes.

January 26

Louisiana secedes.

February 1

Texas secedes.

February 8

A convention of the seceded states, meeting in Montgomery, Alabama, adopts a constitution for the new Confederate States of America.

February 9

The convention in Montgomery elects Jefferson Davis as president of the Confederate States.

February 11

Davis leaves his plantation in Mississippi to travel to Montgomery for his inauguration.

Abraham Lincoln leaves Springfield, Illinois, to travel to Washington for his inauguration.

February 18

Jefferson Davis is inaugurated president of the Confederacy.

March 4

Lincoln is inaugurated.

April 6

Lincoln informs South Carolina governor Francis Pickens that U.S. ships will attempt to resupply Fort Sumter with food only and will not insert reinforcements unless resistance is made.

April 11

Brig. Gen. P. G. T. Beauregard, commander of the Confederate forces around Charleston, demands the surrender of Fort Sumter.

April 12

When Fort Sumter's commander, Maj. Robert Anderson, refuses Beauregard's order to surrender, Confederate guns open fire on the fort.

April 13

Fort Sumter is surrendered.

April 15

Lincoln calls on the states to muster 75,000 volunteers to put down the rebellion—the first of many calls for troops.

April 17

Virginia secedes.

April 19

A proslavery mob attacks Massachusetts militia passing through Baltimore on their way to Washington.

May 6

Arkansas and Tennessee secede.

May 20

North Carolina secedes.

June 10

A small force of Federal troops advancing from Fort Monroe meet defeat at Big Bethel, Virginia.

June 18

Lincoln signs legislation creating the United States Sanitary Commission, an organization tasked with coordinating the efforts of civilians who desire to aid Union soldiers by serving as volunteers in hospitals or by providing food, clothing, or other items.

July 21

A Federal army advancing from Washington toward the new Rebel capital at Richmond, Virginia, meets a humiliating defeat near a stream known as Bull Run.

July 27

Lincoln gives command of the Union troops in Virginia to Maj. Gen. George B. McClellan.

August 10

Union and Confederate troops clash at Wilson's Creek, Missouri, resulting in another Confederate victory.

August 28

Union naval forces capture Fort Hatteras on the North Carolina coast.

October 21

A Union reconnaissance probe suffers a disastrous defeat at Balls Bluff, Virginia, leading to the creation of the Congressional Join Committee on the Conduct of the War.

November 7

Union naval forces capture Port Royal Sound on the South Carolina coast.

November 8

Capt. Charles Wilkes of the U.S.S. *San Jacinto* stops the British mail steamer *Trent* and removes Confederate envoys James M. Mason and John Slidell, who had been bound for Europe. The incident creates a severe diplomatic crisis between the United States and Great Britain.

November 15

The national committee of the Young Men's Christian Association organizes the United States Christian Commission for the purpose of bringing comfort and Christian witness to the men of the Union armies.

1862

February 6

Union forces led by Brig. Gen. Ulysses S. Grant and Flag Officer Andrew H. Foote capture Fort Henry, in Tennessee, opening the Tennessee River to Union incursion as far south as northern Alabama.

February 8

Union amphibious forces capture Roanoke Island on the coast of North Carolina.

February 16

Grant strikes again, this time capturing Fort Donelson, Tennessee, and 15,000 prisoners and opening the Cumberland River all the way to Nashville. Along with the surrender of Fort Henry, this marks the most important turning point of the war.

March 7–8

A Union army under the command of Samuel R. Curtis defeats Confederates at the Battle of Pea Ridge in Arkansas.

April 6–7

A Confederate army commanded by Albert Sidney Johnston attacks Grant's Union army in what becomes known as the Battle of Shiloh, near the Tennessee River in the southern part of that state. Johnston is killed and Grant is victorious.

April 25

A Union fleet commanded by David G. Farragut captures New Orleans.

May 5

McClellan's Union army, advancing on Richmond from the east, fights and wins the Battle of Williamsburg, Virginia.

May–June

The small Confederate army of Thomas J. "Stonewall" Jackson wages a successful campaign in the Shenandoah Valley of Virginia, distracting Union attention from McClellan's campaign near Richmond.

May 31

The Confederate army defending Richmond, commanded by Gen. Joseph E. Johnston, attacks McClellan's army at what comes to be called the Battle of Fair Oaks (or the Battle of Seven Pines). The attack is a failure. Johnston is wounded and replaced by Robert E. Lee.

June 6

Union naval forces capture Memphis, Tennessee.

June 25–July 1

In a series of fierce attacks known as the Seven Days' Battles, Lee forces McClellan to withdraw from the outskirts of Richmond to Harrison's Landing on the James River, twenty-five miles away.

July 22

Lincoln reads the Emancipation Proclamation to his cabinet. Secretary of State William H. Seward suggests he delay public announcement of the proclamation until after the next Union victory, so that it will not be interpreted as an act of desperation.

August 28–30

Lee defeats the Union army of Maj. Gen. John Pope at the Second Battle of Bull Run.

September 17

Having crossed the Potomac River into Maryland, Lee's army faces its Union antagonist, this time once again under the command of McClellan, along Antietam Creek. The badly outnumbered Confederates narrowly escape destruction, and Lee finds that he has no choice but to retreat back into Virginia.

September 22

Lincoln publicly issues the preliminary Emancipation Proclamation: "That on the first day of January in the year of our Lord, one thousand eight hundred and sixty-three, all persons held as slaves, within any state, or designated part of a state, the people whereof shall then be in rebellion against the United States shall be then, thenceforward, and forever free."

October 3–4

Union forces under the overall command of Ulysses S. Grant defeat Earl Van Dorn's Confederate army at the Battle of Corinth, Mississippi.

October 8

The Union army commanded by Don Carlos Buell defeats Braxton Bragg's Confederate army at the Battle of Perryville, Kentucky.

November 4

The Democrats make significant gains in the mid-term Congressional elections.

November 7

For the last time, Lincoln removes the dawdling McClellan from command of the Union army in the East.

December 13

McClellan's successor, Ambrose Burnside, leads the Army of the Potomac to defeat at the Battle of Fredericksburg. Lee is once again victorious.

December 21

Confederate cavalry destroys Grant's supply depot at Holly Springs, Mississippi, forcing him to give up his attempt to reach the Confederate fortress of Vicksburg from the rear.

December 29

William T. Sherman leads a direct Union frontal assault on Vicksburg and suffers a severe defeat at the Battle of Chickasaw Bayou.

December 31

Union General William S. Rosecrans, the successor of Buell, clashes with Bragg's army at the Battle of Stone's River. Rosecrans wins a victory by the narrowest of margins.

1863

January 1
Lincoln issues the final Emancipation Proclamation: "I do order and declare that all persons held as slaves within said designated States, and parts of States, are, and henceforward shall be free."

March 3
Lincoln signs legislation setting up federal conscription.

April 2
In the so-called Richmond "Bread Riot," citizens of the Confederate capital, including many women, riot, complaining of lack of food but engaging in much looting of non-food items.

April 30
Grant's army lands on the east bank of the Mississippi River below Vicksburg and begins a rapid campaign to get at the Confederate fortress from the rear.

May 1–4
The Army of the Potomac, now under the command of Joseph Hooker, meets another humiliating defeat at the Battle of Chancellorsville, Virginia, though the battle results in the wounding of Stonewall Jackson.

May 10
Jackson dies.

May 14
Grant captures Jackson, Mississippi, and turns toward Vicksburg.

May 16
Grant defeats Confederate general John C. Pemberton in the Battle of Champion's Hill, fought between Jackson and Vicksburg.

May 18
Grant bottles up Pemberton and his 30,000 Confederate troops inside the Vicksburg defenses and lays siege to the fortress.

June 16
Lee's army once again crosses the Potomac into Maryland.

June 27
Lincoln removes Hooker as commander of the Army of the Potomac and appoints Maj. Gen. George G. Meade in his place.

July 1–3
Once again the eastern armies meet in a bloody but inconclusive clash. This time they fight in Pennsylvania, at Gettysburg. After the battle, Lee, who has gotten the worse of the encounter, has to retreat back into Virginia. Within a few weeks the armies are back in their pre-campaign positions, as has been the case with all of the other major campaigns east of the Appalachians.

July 4
In a stunning blow to the Confederacy, Pemberton surrenders Vicksburg and 30,000 troops to Grant. Within days the entire Mississippi River is under Union control, and the Confederacy is severed from its three westernmost states, Louisiana, Arkansas, and Texas.

July 13
Large mobs in New York City, including many Irish immigrants, riot against the draft, committing numerous atrocities against African Americans.

September 9
Union troops occupy Chattanooga, Tennessee.

September 10
Union troops take Little Rock, Arkansas.

September 18–20
In northwestern Georgia, Bragg's Confederate army, heavily reinforced by other Southern forces, attacks Rosecrans's advancing Union army and defeats it at the Battle of Chickamauga. Rosecrans retreats into Chattanooga, and Bragg virtually besieges him there.

October 13
In a widely watched election, Ohio voters resoundingly reject antiwar Democratic gubernatorial candidate Clement L. Vallandigham in favor of prowar Republican John Brough.

October 16

Lincoln gives Grant command of all Union armies west of the Appalachians, including Rosecrans's besieged force at Chattanooga.

October 27

Grant, having gone to Chattanooga in person, successfully reopens a supply line to the besieged army there.

November 23–25

Grant trounces Bragg in the Battle of Chattanooga, capturing dozens of cannon and thousands of prisoners. Bragg's battered army retreats to Dalton, Georgia, where Davis will soon replace Bragg with Joseph E. Johnston.

December 8

Lincoln issues his Proclamation of Amnesty and Reconstruction, offering pardons to low-ranking Rebels willing to take an oath of future loyalty to the United States.

1864

March 9

Lincoln makes Grant a lieutenant general, the highest rank in the Union army, and gives him command over all of the nation's armies.

April 12

Confederate troops under the command of Nathan Bedford Forrest massacre surrendering Union troops, many of them African American, at Fort Pillow, on the Mississippi River in Tennessee.

May 5–6

Grant's grand offensive begins. Grant accompanies the Army of the Potomac, still under the direct command of Meade, as it advances and tangles inconclusively with Lee's Confederates in the Battle of the Wilderness.

May 7

Sherman, now commanding the western Union armies, begins to advance from Chattanooga toward Atlanta.

May 8–21

Grant and Lee clash again at Spotsylvania Court House, ten miles closer to Richmond. As with the Battle of the Wilderness, casualties are appalling.

June 1–3

Grant and Lee meet yet again at Cold Harbor, Virginia, just outside Richmond. Once again fighting results in high casualties and no decisive outcome, but Grant is now scarcely ten miles from the center of Richmond.

June 8

The Republican Party, now styling itself the National Union Party, convenes in Baltimore and nominates Lincoln for a second term.

June 15

Sliding his army around behind Richmond, Grant strikes at Petersburg, nexus of the rail lines entering the Confederate capital from the south. Lee counters and a deadlock ensues, with both sides gradually extending their trench lines.

June 27

Sherman suffers a setback in his advance toward Atlanta, losing several thousand men in an unsuccessful attack on Kennesaw Mountain. Not long after, he finds a way to get around the mountain and its defenders, and his advance continues.

July 4

Congress adjourns, leaving the Wade-Davis Bill for Lincoln to sign. Instead, he pocket-vetoes it, believing its conditions for the reconstruction of the rebellious states are too harsh.

July 20

John Bell Hood, who had replaced Johnston as commander of the Confederate army in Georgia, attacks Sherman on the outskirts of Atlanta, in what comes to be known as the Battle of Peachtree Creek. Sherman's Federals prevail.

July 22

Hood attacks again, triggering the Battle of Atlanta. Again Sherman's men are victorious.

July 28

For the third time in eight days Hood launches a major attack on Sherman. Again Sherman wins, but he cannot get quite enough leverage to pry Hood out of Atlanta. Here, as at Richmond and Petersburg, deadlock ensues.

August 5

U.S. naval forces under the command of Rear Admiral David G. Farragut successfully take control of Mobile Bay, on the Gulf coast of Alabama, closing it as a port for blockade-runners.

August 23

Lincoln privately writes that he does not believe he will be reelected. The Democratic assertion that the war is a failure seems to be resonating with the voters.

August 31

The Democratic National Convention, meeting in Chicago, nominates George B. McClellan.

September 2

Sherman's troops march into Atlanta after forcing Hood's Confederates to evacuate. The Democrats' antiwar platform suddenly looks very foolish.

October 19

Union troops operating in the Shenandoah Valley under the command of Philip H. Sheridan administer a crushing defeat to the Confederate army of Jubal A. Early at the Battle of Cedar Creek.

November 8

Voters in the North give Lincoln a resounding victory at the polls in reelecting him for a second term.

November 16

Sherman sets out from Atlanta on the March to the Sea.

December 13

Sherman's army makes contact with Union naval forces near Savannah, having completed the March to the Sea.

December 15–16

Hood's Confederate army, which had slipped around into Tennessee, is routed by a Union army commanded by George H. Thomas.

December 21

Sherman's troops occupy Savannah following the retreat of the Confederate garrison.

1865

January 15

Union amphibious forces capture Fort Fisher, effectively closing Wilmington, North Carolina, as the last Confederate port open for blockade-runners.

January 31

The U.S. House of Representatives approves the Thirteenth Amendment, banning slavery throughout the United States. Already approved by the Senate, the amendment heads to the states for ratification.

Jefferson Davis, with the prompt approval of the Confederate senate, appoints Robert E. Lee commander of all Confederate armies.

February 1

Sherman's army marches north from Savannah, crossing into South Carolina, aiming to march across that state and North Carolina to join Grant in Virginia and finish off Lee.

February 3

Lincoln and Seward meet with three Confederate emissaries on board the steamer *River Queen* in Hampton Roads, just off Fort Monroe, Virginia, to discuss possible peace terms. Lincoln is prepared to make concessions but will not accede to the Confederates' non-negotiable demand that their states be treated as an independent nation.

February 17

Sherman's troops march into Columbia, South Carolina. That night the city burns, though it remains unclear whether the fires were set by Sherman's men, retreating Confederates, newly freed slaves, escaped prisoners of war, or all or some combination of the above.

March 19–21

Joseph E. Johnston, now commanding Confederate troops in the Carolinas, makes a desperate attempt to stop Sherman at the Battle of Bentonville, North Carolina, but is forced to withdraw. Sherman's army moves on inexorably.

April 1

At the Battle of Five Forks, a detachment of Grant's forces led by Philip H. Sheridan crushes Lee's western flank, gravely endangering the continued flow of supplies to Lee's army and Richmond.

April 2

Grant launches a predawn assault along the entire length of his lines, and the Confederate defenses crumble. Lee's troops resist just long enough to allow the Confederate government to flee Richmond, then make their own escape.

April 3

Union troops occupy Richmond while most of Grant's forces continue to pursue Lee's fleeing army west of the city.

April 6

Grant's leading units catch up with the rear of Lee's column and defeat it at the Battle of Sayler's Creek, capturing 8,000 Confederates —about a third of the men Lee has left.

April 9

Lee meets with Grant at Appomattox Court House, Virginia, and surrenders what is left of the Army of Northern Virginia.

April 14

In a formal ceremony, Robert Anderson, now a retired brigadier general, raises over Fort Sumter the flag he had lowered there four years and one day earlier.

That evening Lincoln is assassinated by pro-Confederate actor John Wilkes Booth while attending a performance of the play *Our American Cousin* at Ford's Theater in Washington.

April 18

Sherman and Johnston sign a preliminary agreement for the surrender of Johnston's army. A truce is maintained until the surrender is finalized eight days later.

April 26

Union cavalry catches up with John Wilkes Booth and an accomplice in rural Virginia. Booth refuses to surrender and is fatally shot.

May 4

Confederate Gen. Richard Taylor surrenders the forces of his Department of Alabama, Mississippi, and East Louisiana.

May 10

Union cavalry captures the fleeing Jefferson Davis near Irwinville, Georgia.

May 12

The last skirmish of the war is fought at Palmito Ranch, Texas.

May 26

Confederate Gen. Simon B. Buckner formally surrenders the remaining Confederate troops still at large west of the Mississippi.

Gale Library of Daily Life

American Civil War

Health and Medicine

■ Health and Medicine Overview

Twenty-first-century Americans are likely to react with horror when reading about or—worse still—seeing graphic depictions of medicine as it was practiced during the Civil War. For those who have grown up taking for granted the best medical care history has yet known, the standards of care and the level of ignorance of Civil War medical men are indeed a shocking contrast. Yet the physicians of the mid-nineteenth century were not fools, and the surgeons of the Civil War armies were not—for the most part, at least—uncaring and incompetent quacks. During the war years, dedicated medical personnel applied themselves diligently to repairing the damage war had wrought and made real progress in that direction. On the civilian front, throughout the nineteenth century the medical profession made steady progress in combating the many ills to which human flesh is heir, and a measure of its success can be seen in steadily rising average life expectancies.

For the average modern student of the war the limitations of Civil War medicine are perhaps most vividly pictured by the typical army surgeon's medical instrument kit, in which the most prominent object was a large bone saw. Surgeons of the day plied such saws actively in cutting through bones as part of the operation of amputating a limb. Amputations were appallingly common during the war, and numerous accounts of major battles tell of steadily growing piles of severed limbs outside the field hospitals where the surgeons were hard at work. Adding to the horror of the scene, supplies of anesthesia might well run out before the midway point of a major battle, and subsequent amputations were performed with the aid of several burly male nurses pinioning the screaming patient to the operating table.

The prevalence of amputation was not, however, entirely a factor of medical incompetence. Civil War rifles fired large slugs, usually about 0.58 of an inch in diameter, made of soft lead. Traveling at low velocity, such a slug would carry bits of soiled clothing with it into the body, starting the process of infection at the moment of wounding. Upon striking a bone, the slug would flatten and shatter the bone rather than pierce it cleanly. The resulting mass of splintered bone and mangled flesh would present severe challenges even to modern surgeons trying to save a limb. Even if the bone could be set, the infection that often followed such a wound often proved fatal to the patient, and the only way to be sure of removing all of the infection was to remove the area of damage. Numerous accounts tell of wounded soldiers who steadfastly refused amputation only to die of gangrene or blood poisoning several weeks later. Generally for a shattered limb, amputation was the only reasonable treatment and proved to be a life-saving one in many cases.

That amputation was not more effective than it was in saving life was due to what was probably the greatest shortcoming of the Civil War medical profession: an all but complete ignorance of germs and of antiseptic practices. Surgeons did not realize that they were spreading infection by using unsterilized instruments in one operation after another. Often during a major battle, Civil War surgeons came to look more like butchers than physicians, wiping their bone saws on their aprons before starting the next amputation. Infection of the stump could often follow and sometimes proved fatal. Still, odds of survival were better for amputees than for those with shattered limbs who refused the procedure.

Civilians, of course, rarely had to face the horrors of amputation. Yet disease could and frequently did carry off Americans of any age group living in any part of the country, and medical care could be as inadequate on the home front as it was on the battle fronts. Cholera and typhoid were common and deadly diseases throughout the United States during this period. It was typhoid that took the life of Lincoln's favorite son, Willie, in February 1862. Small pox was not yet extinct and still took many lives, as did a host of other maladies. Doctors did what they could, but the medicines of the day could be as bad as—or worse than—the diseases they were supposed to

THE CONQUEST OF PAIN

One of the most noteworthy medical advances of the nineteenth century—the discovery and use of reliable general anesthetics—took place in the 1840s, less than two decades before the Civil War. Prior to the introduction of ether and chloroform, surgery (including dental extractions) and childbirth were dreaded ordeals.

Chloroform, also known as methyl trichloride, was discovered in 1831 by Samuel Guthrie (1782–1848), an American physician, and rediscovered independently in 1832 by Eugène Soubiran, a French chemist, and Justus von Liebig, a German professor. Guthrie's method of synthesizing chloroform was relatively simple; it involved mixing chlorinated lime with whiskey. The compound was known locally as "Guthrie's sweet whiskey." Diethyl ether, first synthesized by the German Valerius Cordus in 1540, was known to have anesthetic properties but was not used in surgery until 1842. In March of that year, Crawford Long (1815–1878), a physician practicing in Georgia, used ether to anesthetize a patient in order to remove a cancerous tumor from his neck. Ether was also used in the mid-1840s for dental surgery.

The most important use of both anesthetics from the standpoint of the civilian population in those last years before the Civil War, however, was the relief of pain in childbirth. Dr. Long began to use ether to help women in childbirth shortly after his successful 1842 operation; in fact, when he died in 1878, he was on his way home after delivering a baby.

The use of either anesthetic to ease the pain of delivery was controversial in the 1840s, however. Dr. Long was accused of witchcraft by some Southerners and of disturbing the natural order by others. Many people interpreted Genesis 3:16 as implying that easing the pain of childbirth by administering anesthesia is contrary to God's will. When the Scottish obstetrician James Young Simpson (1811–1870) first administered chloroform to a woman in childbirth, he was criticized by some conservative clergy. The debate over the moral legitimacy of obstetrical anesthesia, however, was effectively ended in 1853, when Dr. John Snow (1813–1858)—a devout churchgoer—administered chloroform to Queen Victoria for the birth of her youngest son, Prince Leopold. Thereafter, women on both sides of the Atlantic were able to benefit from the use of anesthesia during delivery.

Neither drug was ideal, however. Ether is highly flammable and is easily ignited by an open flame, a spark, or even a hot metal surface. It also frequently causes nausea and vomiting when the patient recovers consciousness. Its chief advantage over chloroform is that it has a higher margin of safety (that is, the difference between a therapeutic and a toxic dose is greater). Chloroform, while nonflammable, requires a skilled anesthesiologist, as it is relatively easy to give a patient an overdose. In addition, chloroform has been known to cause liver damage and abnormal heart rhythms leading to death. Both compounds have been largely replaced by halothane, sevoflurane, and other modern inhaled anesthetics; nevertheless, for civilians and soldiers alike during the Civil War, these first general anesthetics were truly "wonder drugs."

REBECCA J. FREY

BIBLIOGRAPHY

Keys, Thomas E. The History of Surgical Anesthesia. *Rev. ed. New York: Dover Press, 1963.*

Radford, Ruby L. Prelude to Fame: Crawford Long's Discovery of Anaesthesia. *Los Altos, CA: Geron-X, 1969.*

cure. Many mid-nineteenth-century medicines were purgatives, since the medical wisdom of the day held that sickness might be cured by purging impurities from the system. Among the worst was mercury calomel, which was not only a diuretic but also a poison. Mid-nineteenth-century medical men were not oblivious to the fact that the calomel they prescribed did not necessarily produce the desired results in many of their patients, so they took the logical step and began prescribing much larger doses.

Not all of the doctors' ministrations were harmful though. Quinine is an example of a Civil War era medicine that was actually somewhat effective against malaria, although doctors prescribed it fairly freely for many sorts of diseases against which it had no discernable effect. Medical authorities also strove to design and build hospitals that were both comfortable and healthy for the sick and wounded soldiers and made great advances in the quality of hospital care. The giant Chimborazo Hospital in Richmond was the largest and most dramatic example, but a number of northern hospitals established during the war were at least equally good. Most physicians took their duties very seriously and worked steadily throughout the war years to improve the quality of their care. The experience gained by surgeons during the Civil War brought important improvements to both military and civilian medicine in the years that followed. Nevertheless, medical care presents one of the most striking contrasts between the everyday life of the mid-nineteenth century and that of the early twenty-first.

Steven E. Woodworth

■ Battlefield Wounds

Civil War combat was up close and personal. Because of the relatively limited range of the weapons used and the inability to accurately observe enemy formations from any great distance, most fighting was done within a few hundred yards of the opposition. As a result, munitions retained their maximum ability to deliver horrific damage to the human body.

The threat of injury in some sort of military action was an almost daily reality for most troops. Soldiers faced wounds or death from three distinct classes of weapons: small arms (pistols, shotguns, rifles, muskets, and carbines), artillery, and edged weapons (swords, sabers, and bayonets). Each presented its own unique threat to a serviceman's body, though the degree of their lethality and the damage they could inflict varied due to a host of factors. The injuries caused by these weapons ranged from minor to serious, disabling, or fatal. They also had a psychological impact on both the victim and those witnessing his distress.

Wounds from Small Arms Fire

According to statistics in the multivolume *Medical and Surgical History of the War of the Rebellion*, published by the U.S. government between 1870 and 1888, the vast majority of battlefield wounds, 88 percent to be precise, were caused by rifle or musket fire. Pistol or shotgun rounds were responsible for 9 percent of the wounds recorded at field hospitals.

Twelve percent of gunshot wounds were caused by the .69-caliber smoothbore musket round, whereas 76 percent were inflicted by the more common .58-caliber "Minié" bullet (commonly, but incorrectly, called a *ball*), used in the rifled muskets of both armies. Between 1863 and 1865 fewer smoothbores were in use than was the case in 1861 and 1862. Hence, the number of injuries caused by .69-caliber rounds decreased dramatically, while those inflicted by Minié bullets rose. Both smoothbore and rifled muskets propelled a soft lead projectile at a relatively slow muzzle velocity. While both could kill, the Minié bullet caused infinitely greater damage than the round .69-caliber musket ball because of its conical shape.

According to Confederate surgeon Deering Roberts, smoothbore musket balls "caused many fractures in bones on the extremities" (Bollet 2002, p. 148). The Minié bullet's effect on its victim, however, was usually much worse because the soft lead bullet tended to flatten and distort when it hit, greatly magnifying its potential for damage. "The shattering, splintering, and splitting of a long bone by the impact of the minie ... ball," Roberts recorded, was "both remarkable and frightful" (Bollet 2002, p. 148). A surgical textbook published during the war also spoke of the "frightful traces of devastation" left by Minié bullets (Bollet 2002, p. 146). In his memoir, *The Surgeon and the Hospital in the Civil War* (1987), Albert G. Hart noted that the rifled musket and Minié bullet combined to vastly increase the striking power of projectiles, resulting in "more dangerous wounds." Whereas a smoothbore round might be deflected from a thigh bone "with no serious injury," a Minié bullet "under similar conditions might not only fracture, but crush two or three inches of the bone" (p. 34). The fact that a high percentage of wounds treated by field hospitals had been caused by Minié bullets and musket balls indicates that small arms fire was generally not immediately fatal. Indeed, there are many examples of men shot through the head who lingered for hours or days before they died.

Where a man was hit could make a huge difference to his chances for survival. According to the *Medical and Surgical History* (1870–1888, vol. 3, p. 392), wounds to the chest or abdomen were either immediately fatal or led quickly to death; they were responsible for 51 percent of battlefield deaths but only 18 percent of recorded wounds. Injuries to the head and neck accounted for 42 percent of those killed in action, but a mere 11 percent of wounds. Hits to the legs or feet killed only 5 percent of those who died in battle, but on average produced 35 percent of a battle's wounded, whereas injuries to the arms or hands were responsible for 3 percent of battlefield fatalities and 36 percent of wounds. In most cases, therefore, small arms fire wounded, rather than killed.

The majority of men struck by small arms fire experienced similar sensations. In his memoir, *Fighting for the Confederacy* (1989), artilleryman Edward Porter Alexander recalled being hit by a sharpshooter's bullet during the siege of Petersburg, Virginia (June, 1864 to April, 1865). Ricocheting off "hard ground," the bullet flew upward and struck the colonel in the left shoulder, going under his shoulder bones and "lodging in the muscle behind." Alexander felt his arm go numb, but "no real pain" (p. 445). E. D. Patterson recalled being struck by a bullet at very close range in the Battle of Frayser's Farm, June 30, 1862. "I fell forward across my gun, my left arm useless falling under me," he reported. However, Patterson "did not at the moment feel any pain, only a numbness all over my body. I felt as if someone had given me an awful jar, and fell as limber as a drunken man. I could not even tell where I was hit" (Wiley 1971 [1943], pp. 265–266).

For most men, the first instinct after being hit was to determine the nature and extent of their wounds. In a memoir entitled *Recollections of a Private Soldier in the Army of the Potomac* (1887), Frank Wilkeson recalled that wounded men "almost always tore their clothing away from their wounds, so as to see them and to judge of their character" (p. 204). Long experience made veterans "exceedingly accurate judges" of wounds and they could quickly tell whether an injury was fatal or not. Wounds from bullets, therefore, generally afforded men the opportunity to evaluate their chances of survival. Those injured by other weapons were often not so lucky.

Wounds from Artillery Fire

Fragments from exploding shells accounted for 12 percent of all wounds treated at field hospitals, whereas grapeshot or canister rounds were responsible for 1 percent of the total (*Medical and Surgical History*,

Injured Union soldiers housed in a hospital railroad car, February 27, 1864. Wounded soldiers did not always receive medical treatment on the battlefield or in field hospitals. Only those who did not die immediately, did not die before they could be reached by medical aid, or those without fatal wounds saw hospitals, such as this railroad car. *The Art Archive/Culver Pictures/The Picture Desk, Inc.*

1870–1888, vol. 3, p. 696). The small percentage of wounds resulting from artillery fire appears at first to make a case for the ineffectiveness of cannon on the Civil War battlefield. Close examination of after-action reports published in the *Official Records of the War of the Rebellion*, and of regimental histories, memoirs, and diaries, leads to a different conclusion, however.

Official statistics reflect only those wounds treated at field hospitals. Men who were killed outright on the battlefield, who succumbed to their wounds before reaching medical aid, or who were considered to have mortal wounds upon reaching a hospital, were not recorded as wounded but rather as killed in action. For understandable reasons, no effort was made to officially determine the cause of death for these men. Thus, the nature and cause of their wounds never became part of the statistical record.

In his *Civil War Medicine* (2002), Alfred Bollet points out that it is highly likely that artillery munitions—shells, grapeshot, and canister—accounted for a high percentage of fatal wounds on the battlefield (p. 84). The reasoning behind this assumption is easily understood: Civil War artillery was most effective in a defensive role. At great distances, field pieces fired solid shot (the stereotypical solid cast-iron round cannon ball) or exploding shells. Solid shot was intended to break down fortifications and structures, but could also be useful against tightly massed bodies of troops. A twelve-pound iron ball hurtling into the bodies of unprotected men would often cause crushing injuries that were quickly fatal. Shells, on the other hand, were designed to explode and throw jagged metal fragments in all directions, intending to inflict injuries and death over a wide area.

Although shell fuses sometimes proved faulty and ordnance occasionally failed to explode or fragment satisfactorily, shellfire generally killed rather than wounded. Examples of lethal shell explosions are readily found. In a skirmish near Stevensburg, Virginia, in October 1863, a shell fired from a Confederate cannon exploded among a group of Union troops. The shell ripped off the top of one victim's head, killing him instantly. Another quickly bled to death when a piece of shell ruptured an artery in his thigh. A third Federal was so badly torn apart by the explosion that his bowels and part of his spine protruded from his body. This final victim, although mortally wounded, was not killed instantly. The dying man begged his enemies for water and pleaded for them to shoot him and end his misery. Indeed, wounds from artillery fire were generally more gruesome than those caused by other means. Frank Wilkeson reported that the most horrific wound he ever saw was the result of an exploding shell. A Federal soldier, lying face down to obtain cover, was struck by a shell fragment that tore the flesh off both thighs, "exposing the bones." The soldier bled to death within minutes (Wilkeson 1887, p. 205).

Solid shot could be just as deadly. During the Mine Run Campaign, of November 26 to December 1, 1863, several men were killed when solid shot burrowed into the ground beneath their prone position. Although not a mark was found on their bodies, they had been killed by concussions. Wounds caused by grapeshot and canister were almost universally fatal. Considered close-range ordnance, grapeshot and canister were specially designed as antipersonnel weapons. Grapeshot consisted of "nine cast-iron balls of varying sizes" held between wooden plates that were secured together by "a vertical rod with nuts on each end" (*Medical and Surgical History*, 1870–1888, vol. 3, p. 697). Canister was a tin can filled with two dozen or so round musket balls. When either type of ammunition was fired, cannon became, in essence, huge shotguns. The wooden plates or tin can came apart, allowing the balls to spray over a wide area. Remnants of the plates, rod, nuts, and tin can also became projectiles. Effective up to a range of several hundred yards, a well-placed canister round could cover an area dozens of yards wide and deep. Men caught in its blast often received multiple wounds simultaneously and were sometimes all but obliterated by the impact. An eyewitness to the Battle of Franklin, of November 30, 1864, for example, described the terrible destruction caused by a Federal gunner firing off his cannon: "Like a huge thunder bolt that awful roar and flash went blasting through that crowd of men, annihilating scores. Arms, legs and mangled trunks were torn and thrown in every direction" (McDonough and Connelly 1983, p. 114).

Few men hit by grapeshot or canister survived to reach a field hospital. It is this that accounts for the fact that only a tiny percentage of reported wounds were recorded as having been caused by artillery projectiles. By contrast, bountiful evidence of deaths inflicted by these weapons can be found in the testimony of men who survived the war.

Wounds from Edged Weapons

Swords, sabers, and bayonets were responsible for only a minuscule number of wounds treated by surgeons—no more than 0.4 percent of the total (Bollet 2002, p. 84). Despite its widespread portrayal in works of art, fiction, and film, hand-to-hand combat was relatively rare in the Civil War. The effectiveness of small arms and artillery fire meant rival bodies of troops seldom came close enough to fight with bayonets or clubbed muskets—and one side or the other usually gave way before the moment of contact was reached. Nonetheless, such combat did on occasion take place, and when it did, witnesses or survivors were quick to recall its vicious finality.

Injuries from the swords carried by officers were indeed rare. The officer's sword was more a badge and tool of rank than a combat weapon. In close action an officer was more apt to use his pistol, and hence wounds or deaths from swords were quite unusual. Sabers, used almost exclusively by cavalry, were more formidable weapons, although mounted troops tended to prefer firearms to edged weapons in combat. When sabers were used, the very nature of a cavalry melee worked against their lethalness. Two men dueling with each other on moving horses generally slashed with their sabers rather than trying to stab. The result was seldom fatal, as the saber was designed to be a stabbing, not a cutting, weapon. The cuts about the face, hands, and arms that were most typical could be painful, but seldom proved fatal and often did not even require a visit to a surgeon.

Bayonets and clubbed muskets were another story. Rare though bayonet fighting was, when it did occur it was incredibly savage. "It would be impossible to picture that scene in all of its horrors," one Union colonel recalled of a bayonet fight. "I saw a Confederate... thrust one of our men through with the bayonet, and before he could draw his weapon from the ghastly wound, his brains were scattered on all of us that stood near, by the butt of a musket swung with terrific force" (McDonough and Connelly 1983, p. 117). Little wonder that wounds inflicted in this kind of combat almost invariably proved fatal and thus sent few men to hospitals.

Effect of Wounds on Morale

Death and wounds inflicted on the battlefield had a psychological as well as a physical impact. Men unaccustomed to the realities of combat were shaken by their first exposure to the brutal damage or death inflicted by a wide variety of weapons. A sudden wave of casualties in the ranks of a green unit could lead it to flee to the rear. Sometimes, the death of an admired leader, or simply a single particularly gruesome wound, could cause a military formation to break apart. However, even in their first combat, most soldiers absorbed the horror around them and continued to perform their duty. Caught up in circumstances and influenced by the odd mixture of emotions that overcome men in battle, they kept fighting. In the aftermath of their initial combat, however, most soldiers recoiled at the evidence of the damage inflicted by rival armies.

AMBROSE BIERCE'S "CHICKAMAUGA"

Ambrose Bierce's short story "Chickamauga" (1889) contains horrifying descriptions of the injuries inflicted on soldiers and civilians alike during the Civil War, as the following excerpt shows. Bierce (1842–1914?) works these descriptions into a plotline full of irony: A little boy wanders off into the woods to play soldier, falls asleep in the forest, and wakes up after dark to have his innocent childish notions of soldiering destroyed by the realities of war:

> One sunny autumn afternoon a child strayed away from its rude home in a small field and entered a forest unobserved. It was happy in a new sense of freedom from control, happy in the opportunity of exploration and adventure.... The [boy's father] loved military books and pictures and the boy had understood enough to make himself a wooden sword, though even the eye of his father would hardly have known it for what it was.... [B]ack at the little plantation, where white men and black were hastily searching the fields and hedges in alarm, a mother's heart was breaking for her missing child. Hours passed, and then the little sleeper rose to his feet....
>
> A thin, ghostly mist rose along the water. It frightened and repelled him; instead of recrossing, in the direction whence he had come, he turned his back upon it, and went forward toward the dark inclosing wood. Suddenly he saw before him a strange moving object which he took to be some large animal-a dog, a pig—he could not name it; perhaps it was a bear....Before it had approached near enough to resolve his doubts he saw that it was followed by another and another. To right and to left were many more; the whole open space about him was alive with them-all moving toward the brook....
>
> He now approached one of these crawling figures from behind and with an agile movement mounted it astride. The man sank upon his breast, recovered, flung the small boy fiercely to the ground as an unbroken colt might have done, then turned upon him a face that lacked a lower jaw-from the upper teeth to the throat was a great red gap fringed with hanging shreds of flesh and splinters of bone. The unnatural prominence of nose, the absence of chin, the fierce eyes, gave this man the appearance of a great bird of prey crimsoned in throat and breast by the blood of its quarry. The man rose to his knees, the child to his feet. The man shook his fist at the child; the child, terrified at last, ran to a tree near by, got upon the farther side of it and took a more serious view of the situation. ...
>
> Shifting his position, [the child's] eyes fell upon some outbuildings which had an oddly familiar appearance, as if he had dreamed of them. He stood considering them with wonder, when suddenly the entire plantation, with its inclosing forest, seemed to turn as if upon a pivot. His little world swung half around; the points of the compass were reversed. He recognized the blazing building as his own home!
>
> For a moment he stood stupefied by the power of the revelation, then ran with stumbling feet, making a half-circuit of the ruin. There, conspicuous in the light of the conflagration, lay the dead body of a woman—the white face turned upward, the hands thrown out and clutched full of grass, the clothing deranged, the long dark hair in tangles and full of clotted blood. The greater part of the forehead was torn away, and from the jagged hole the brain protruded, overflowing the temple, a frothy mass of gray, crowned with clusters of crimson bubbles—the work of a shell.
>
> The child moved his little hands, making wild, uncertain gestures. He uttered a series of inarticulate and indescribable cries-something between the chattering of an ape and the gobbling of a turkey—a startling, soulless, unholy sound, the language of a devil. The child was a deaf mute.
>
> Then he stood motionless, with quivering lips, looking down upon the wreck.

REBECCA J. FREY

SOURCE: Collected Works of Ambrose Bierce, Vol. 2: In the Midst of Life: Tales of Soldiers and Civilians. *New York and Washington: Neale Publishing Company, 1909, pp. 46–57.*

In his *The Life of Johnny Reb* (1971), the historian Bell Irvin Wiley traces a common evolution in the way soldiers responded to combat. One Georgian's reaction to his first battle at Gaines' Mill on June 27, 1862, was typical of those new to fighting. Recalling "friends falling on both sides dead and mortally wounded," he found it "impossible to express" his feelings "when the fight was over and I saw what was done." Viewing the battlefield he admitted "the tears came ... free, oh that I never could behold such a sight again to think of it among civilized people killing one another like beasts" (Wiley 1971 [1943], p. 32). Continued exposure to the hardships of soldiering and the realities of battle quickly transformed men into veterans, however. Before long they took death and wounds, even those of close friends and comrades, in stride. "I saw the body [of a man killed the previous day]," wrote Private Henry Graves, "and a horrible sight it was. Such sights do not affect me as they once did. I can not describe the change nor do I know when it took place, yet I know that there is a change for I look on the carcass of a man now with pretty much such feeling as I would do were it a horse or hog" (Wiley 1971 [1943], p. 35).

At Vicksburg, John T. Sibley saw a shell tear off the arm of a soldier standing nearby, and noted the lack of reaction among the men in his unit. "I am astonished at my own indifference, as I never pretended to be brave; it distresses me at times when I am cool and capable of reflection to think how indifferent we become in the hour of battle when our fellowmen fall around us by scores" (Wiley 1971 [1943], p. 35). Union Captain Francis Donaldson, recalling childhood games in which he and his brother aped the "indifference" of famous military commanders to the "work of death" going on about them, remarked: "I little thought then that my attempts at being funny would ever be recalled to mind so vividly as they were at Gettysburg," where two fellow officers "were shot down on either side [of] me, [one] killed outright, and to view with actual indifference an occurrence that at any other time would have horrified me" (Donaldson 1998, p. 322).

Troops quickly hardened to the business of war. They viewed wounds and death as part of their trade and came to look upon them analytically. Such detachment, however, could never completely inure a soldier to the wounding or death of a dear friend or family member. Nor could it remove from his mind the fear of being maimed, disfigured, or left wounded on the field of battle without aid or assistance.

BIBLIOGRAPHY

Alexander, Edward Porter. *Fighting for the Confederacy: The Personal Recollections of General Edward Porter Alexander*. Ed. Gary W. Gallagher. Chapel Hill: University of North Carolina Press, 1989.

Bollet, Alfred Jay. *Civil War Medicine: Challenges and Triumphs*. Tucson, AZ: Galen Press, 2002.

Cozzens, Peter. *The Darkest Days of the War: The Battles of Iuka and Corinth*. Chapel Hill: University of North Carolina, 1997.

Donaldson, Francis Adams. *Inside the Army of the Potomac: The Civil War Experiences of Captain Francis Adams Donaldson*, ed. J. Gregory Acken. Mechanicsburg, PA: Stackpole Books, 1998.

Hart, Albert G. *The Surgeon and the Hospital in the Civil War*. Palmyra, VA: Old Soldier Books, 1987.

McDonough, James Lee, and Thomas Connelly. *Five Tragic Hours: The Battle of Franklin*. Knoxville: University of Tennessee Press, 1983.

The Medical and Surgical History of the War of the Rebellion (1861–1865), Surgical Section, Vol. 3. Prepared under the direction of Surgeon General Joseph K. Barnes. Washington, DC: Government Printing Office, 1870–1888.

Wiley, Bell Irvin. *The Life of Johnny Reb: The Common Soldier of the Confederacy*. New York: Bobbs-Merrill, 1943. Reprint, Baton Rouge: Louisiana State University Press, 1971.

Wilkeson, Frank. *Recollections of a Private Soldier in the Army of the Potomac*. New York: G. P. Putnam's Sons, 1887.

Jeffrey William Hunt

■ Field Hospitals

FIELD HOSPITALS: AN OVERVIEW

No other part of the battlefield represented such an odd mixture of hope and terror as the field hospital. The writings of veterans almost universally picture it as a place to be feared and avoided if at all possible. To the men who survived the conflict, hospitals presented a gruesome compendium of the horrors of the war, second only to the sight of torn, bloated, lifeless bodies on the field of battle. Yet the field hospital's staff, medicines, facilities, and surgeons were the only hope desperately wounded men had to save life and limb.

It was predictable that there would be contradictory views of the hospital. Only there could wounded soldiers find relief from their pain, comfort and assistance in their weakened and helpless condition, and life-saving surgery and medical care. At the same time, however, the hospital was a site of agony and misery—the place where men with mangled limbs, bleeding bodies, torn flesh, blinded eyes, and worse, were brought together. It was the spot where overworked doctors hurriedly examined and probed painful wounds; where, all too often, surgeons used their instruments to amputate shattered and infected limbs. Field hospitals were facilities where mortally wounded men were given a few comforts and set aside to die. They were in short a concentration of the vilest aftereffects of battle.

The common perception of Civil War hospitals and surgeons was generally quite negative during the conflict. Time did little to alter that point of view and, in fact, did much to reinforce it. The disorganized and grossly inadequate efforts made by both Union and Confederate medical departments at the start of the war were widely reported in newspapers of the day. However, both sides were able to rapidly improve the standard of care delivered to sick and wounded soldiers alike. This remarkable advance in battlefield medical

HOSPITAL TRAINS

The Civil War was the first railroad war. Both sides used trains to move troops and supplies to the front and transport sick and wounded men to general hospitals located throughout the North and South. Initially, ordinary boxcars were used to haul patients. These cars had no provisions for the feeding, care, or comfort of wounded soldiers, who endured journeys lasting hours, and sometimes days, without medical attention or basic necessities. The agony and misery such trips entailed was extreme, provoking demands for change.

The industry-poor Confederacy could do little to remedy such problems. The North, with facilities for building locomotives and railway cars, developed hospital trains. Specially designed "ambulance cars" were built, each containing space for thirty hospital litters, suspended three high from stanchions by rubber straps. The litters, complete with mattresses and pillows, swung gently, preventing the pain previously caused by any movement of the trains. Each car had a seating area and a fully stocked pantry. A stove heated the cabin. Kitchen and dining cars accompanied the ambulance cars, as did sleeping cars for doctors and nurses staffing the train. The locomotive and tender were painted bright red, and *U.S. Hospital Train* was emblazoned in large red letters on every car. These trains provided all the facilities of an efficient and well-regulated hospital. Sick and injured troops were never without food, water, comfort, or medical care while being carried to their destination.

JEFFREY WILLIAM HUNT

SOURCE: *Bollet, Alfred Jay.* Civil War Medicine: Challenges and Triumphs. *Tucson, AZ: Galen Press, 2002.*

practices saved many lives before the war was over (Bollet 2002, p. xiii).

But improvements and innovations seldom made headlines and largely went unnoticed. The horror, fear, and sadness surrounding even an efficiently run and effective field hospital kept most veterans from seeing or understanding the vast change for the better made by dedicated doctors, surgeons, officers, and administrators. Postwar memoirs and regimental histories are full of stories of needless amputations conducted without anesthesia. Also prevalent are tales of incompetent surgeons, indifferent doctors, callous nurses or stretcher-bearers, and half-trained medical students conducting unnecessary surgery on injured soldiers simply to gain experience (Bollet 2002, p. xiii).

Perception vs. Reality

The attitude of many soldiers toward the men who worked in field hospitals, and toward what went on in them, is abundantly clear in an account given by a Union officer wounded during the May 23 to July 9, 1863, siege of Port Hudson, Louisiana:

> The surgeons used a large Cotton Press for the butchering room & when I was carried into the building and looked around I could not help comparing the surgeons to fiends.... [A]ll around on the ground lay wounded men; some of them shrieking, some cursing & swearing & some praying; in the middle of the room was some 10 or 12 tables just large enough to lay a man on; these were used as dissecting tables & they were covered with blood; near & around the tables stood the surgeons with blood all over them & by the side of the tables was a heap of feet, legs & arms. (Wiley 1952, p. 148)

The bloody mass of waiting wounded, the tables, the appearance of the surgeons, and the agony of the injured were, of course, very real. But the words this injured soldier used to describe what he saw—"butchering," "fiends," "dissecting"—reveal all too well how he perceived those who were about to save his life. His point of view was hardly unusual. For people unaccustomed to the sight of mass casualties gathered together, or the instruments and operations of surgeons, revulsion and horror were common reactions. Wounds, after all, are horrific to look at; suffering is difficult to hear or see, and the methods used by doctors and surgeons to treat major wounds must, of necessity, sometimes cause pain. The very tools used to repair and heal—probes, saws, scalpels, needles—were enough to make most witnesses shudder, especially if they did not fully understand what was being done or why. Any modern person who has felt ill at ease while staring at medical instruments in a doctor or dentist's office has had a similar, although certainly less intense, experience.

Furthermore, field hospitals posed dangers that were unrecognized at the time. The Civil War was fought just prior to the discovery of bacteria and their role in causing infections, and the development of methods of sterilization used to prevent the transmission of disease from cross-contamination.

One Federal surgeon, looking back on the war from the vantage point of 1918, was amazed at the ignorant practices employed between 1861 and 1865:

> We operated in old blood-stained and often pus-stained coats....We used un-disinfected instruments from un-disinfected plush-lined cases, and still worse, used marine sponges which had been used in prior pus cases and had been only washed in tap water. If a sponge or an instrument fell on the floor it was washed and squeezed in a basin of tap water and used as if it were clean. Our silk to tie blood vessels was un-disinfected....The silk with which we sewed up all wounds was un-disinfected. If there was any difficulty threading the needle we moistened it with...bacteria-laden saliva, and rolled it between bacteria-infected

> fingers. We dressed wounds with clean but undisinfected sheets, shirts, tablecloths, or other old soft linen rescued from the family ragbag. We had no sterilized gauze dressing, no gauze sponges.... We knew nothing about antiseptics and therefore used none. (Wiley 1952, p. 148)

Little wonder then, that wounds frequently became infected even after successful operations. Very often, injured men who survived the trip from the battlefield to the field hospital and underwent life-saving procedures died weeks or months later from the unrecognized bacteria that caused gangrene, tetanus, and other complications.

Nonetheless, field hospitals saved many more lives than they took. Fortunate to be working, for the most part, on healthy young men, inured to hardship by a soldier's life, surgeons and doctors ministered to a population with a better than average likelihood of healing and recovering. If infection could be avoided, and the wound was at all survivable, medical personnel usually managed to save life, if not limb.

Supplies

At the war's outset, the typical surgeon used his own personal instruments, usually brought into service from prewar private practice. He was authorized by the government to purchase and use whatever medicines or supplies he thought appropriate. Hospital stewards in every regiment carried a medical knapsack, which was similar in shape and size to the pack carried by infantrymen and worn in identical fashion. Union hospital steward Charles Johnson recalled that this knapsack contained such emergency supplies as "bandages, adhesive plaster, needles, artery forceps, scalpels, spirits of ammonia, brandy, chloroform and ether" (Commager 1973 [1950], pp. 195–196).

The type and quantity of supplies and medicines at the field hospital was constrained by the necessity of mobility. The number of wagons and ambulances assigned to a hospital was finite, and care had to be taken not to overload vehicles that would be pulled by mules or horses over rough and difficult roads. The standard stock of medicines in a field hospital consisted of "opium, morphine, Dover's powder, quinine, rhubarb, Rochelle salts, castor oil, sugar of lead, tannin, sulphate of copper, sulphate of zinc, camphor, tincture of opium, tincture of iron, tincture opii, camphorate, syrup of squills, simple syrup" and a wide variety of alcohol (Commager 1973 [1950], p. 195). Most medicines were compounded in liquid or powdered form. Few pills were available, so powders were typically mixed with water and drunk by the patient. Precise measurements were not made and surgeons simply apportioned the amount of medicine they thought necessary (Commager 1973 [1950], p. 195).

The resulting lack of uniformity in supplies, instruments, and medicines proved a logistical nightmare. Combined with the widely varying levels of experience and skill found among surgeons and stewards, it also frequently resulted in poor or indifferent care for the sick and wounded. By late 1862, however, changes born of experience and good leadership began to address these concerns.

Among the many vital improvements made by Jonathan Letterman, medical director of the Army of the Potomac from July 1862 to January 1864, was standardization of equipment and medicines for field hospitals. Letterman developed a thoroughly modern system of evacuating wounded from the battlefield, totally reformed the organization and staffing of field hospitals, and established standardization in the army's Medical Department.

Letterman introduced a standard medical kit for each doctor, equipped with exactly the same instruments, arranged in precisely the same fashion (Freemon 2001, p. 75). He also oversaw the adoption of the *Autenrieth Wagon*—a specially designed supply wagon that carried a standard set of surgical instruments and medicines, arranged to provide immediate and unfettered access in time of need. Because every wagon was identically organized, packed, and equipped, any surgeon could find exactly what he needed from any such wagon, regardless of the unit to which it belonged (Bollet 2002, pp. 244–245). These reforms, first instituted in the Army of the Potomac, were later extended to all Union armies and replicated as much as possible by the Confederates.

Organization

One of the greatest challenges facing Union and Confederate medical departments was the problem of how best to utilize their resources. Every regiment was entitled to a surgeon, an assistant surgeon, and one hospital steward. The latter carried out the same function as the military medic or corpsman of the twentieth and twenty-first centuries. Surgeons held officer's commissions, while the steward was equivalent in rank to a sergeant. Special duty men, drawn from regimental ranks, would do the odd jobs—cooking, drawing water, and so on—necessary for the hospital to function. All were responsible to the regimental commander. The titles of these men were sometimes deceptive, however. The term *surgeon* was applied to any officer assigned medical duties, even if he did not have surgical experience. Many "surgeons" were simply doctors, of varying educational background and experience, and some were mere medical students (Freemon 2001, p. 41).

Nonetheless, the medical personnel assigned to a regiment were the primary source of care in camp and aid on the battlefield. As their unit moved toward battle, they selected a sheltered spot behind the lines on which

Surgical tent at Gettysburg, Pennsylvania, 1863. In their attempts at repairing battle-wounded soldiers, surgeons operating in field hospitals often labored long hours under grisly conditions. Wounded soldiers who survived amputation surgery often succumbed to infections contracted through the use of unsanitary medical equipment. *Hulton Archive/Getty Images.*

to establish the regimental field hospital. If at all possible, the site chosen was near a source of water—either a stream or well—and beyond the range of small arms fire, if not always artillery fire. Houses or barns, if available, were often requisitioned for use by the surgeons. Such structures supplemented the meager four tents allotted to reach regimental hospital by army regulations: two small tents for the officers, one small kitchen tent, and one hospital tent capable of holding eight cots (Commager 1973 [1950], p. 194).

At the beginning of the conflict every hospital was marked by a red flag. By early 1864, however, a yellow flag with a large green *H* painted or sewn on it was the standard banner used to designate the presence of a field hospital. These flags helped walking wounded, ambulances, and litter-bearers find the facility, and hopefully kept the enemy from firing on it (Bollet 2002, p. 218).

The assistant surgeon, accompanied by the steward with his knapsack, followed closely behind the battle line. Their job was to establish a field dressing station as near to the firing line as practicable, where they would provide first aid and immediate emergency care. Here wounded men received initial treatment to stop bleeding, splint fractures, and relieve pain, usually through the administration of opiates.

The assistant surgeon was also responsible for making initial triage decisions—determining the order by which wounded were taken to the regimental hospital, based on the severity of their wounds. Lightly wounded men had their injuries dressed and were either sent back to the firing line or ordered rearward under their own power. Badly hurt men whose lives might be saved by immediate surgery were assigned first priority for transportation by ambulance or stretcher-bearers. Those believed to have mortal wounds were made comfortable and set aside to die. If they did not die, they would be sent to the hospital when resources and time allowed (Bollet 2002, pp. 100–101).

The regimental hospital system, used by both sides in the first year of the war, proved wasteful and inefficient. It required great redundancy in supplies and equipment and proved problematic on the battlefield. Even in a large engagement, a significant number of surgeons and stewards would be idle when their unit was not involved in combat, even as the small staffs of other hospitals were being overwhelmed by a flood of casualties. The wide range of skill levels among surgeons meant that the quality of care provided was uneven at best. Some regimental hospitals refused to treat wounded not from their own command, and there was an almost total lack of coordination among the field hospitals, as well as between the field hospitals and the large general hospitals in rear areas.

Once again it was Jonathan Letterman who developed the answer to seemingly intractable problems. His solution was to concentrate medical supplies and personnel in division hospitals. The elimination of regimental hospitals allowed for the pooling of surgeons and doctors (Freemon 2001, p. 75). The division hospitals were better staffed and equipped and became the primary field unit of the medical departments of North and South, although there were a few brigade-level hospitals, especially in the Rebel armies. The typical division hospital was run by a surgeon-in-chief, who was one of the most experienced surgeons at the facility. He directed the activities of three operating surgeons and nine assistant surgeons. There was also an officer who oversaw the provision of food and shelter for staff and patients; he worked under the direction of the surgeon-in-chief, as did the enlisted men assigned duty as nurses (Bollet 2002, pp. 106–107).

The best surgeons were attached to division or brigade hospitals, where they were tasked with performing surgical procedures assigned on the basis of skill and experience. Military rank was irrelevant in these assignments. As a result, a soldier would have the services of the man best suited to deal with his particular injury. Surgeons of lesser abilities staffed the dressing stations behind the battle lines, administering emergency aid and conducting first-level triage. Almost all surgery, however, was performed at the brigade or division level (Freemon 2001, p. 46).

Medical equipment and supplies were also issued on the brigade or division level. The average Union division hospital was issued eighteen wagons, including four Autenrieth wagons, twenty-two hospital tents, and sufficient surgical instruments, equipment, medicines, and other supplies to care for 7,000 to 8,000 casualties at one time (Coggins 1962, p. 116).

This equipment was in addition to the emergency medical supplies maintained at the regimental level, as well as the regimental ambulances. When the Medical Corps' Ambulance Service was created by the U.S. Congress on March 11, 1864, the number of ambulances assigned to each regiment was fixed according to the unit's strength. A regiment with 500 or more troops would be allowed three ambulances; a command of 200 men or less was worthy of a single vehicle. Additional ambulances were assigned to corps headquarters and would be sent to whatever divisional field hospital needed them most (Bollet 2002, p. 105).

The hallmark of Letterman's organizational system was concentration of resources and flexibility. Letterman's system began in the Army of the Potomac and soon spread to all Federal forces. To the extent possible given the South's lack of industrial capacity—which created shortages of purpose-built ambulances, Autenrieth wagons, tents, medicines, surgical instruments, and so on—Confederate armies also copied Letterman's design. As might be expected, many of the ambulances and much of the equipment used by the Rebel medical services was captured from the enemy (Coggins 1962, p. 117).

Letterman's reforms made a world of difference and vastly improved both the quality and speed of battlefield medical care. Combined with the development of specialized military vehicles and a well-organized system to evacuate wounded from the front lines to the dressing stations, then to the field hospital and finally rearward to general hospitals, the reorganization of medical services

HOSPITAL SHIPS

Both North and South used waterways to evacuate sick and wounded during the Civil War. Early in the conflict, efforts to utilize ships for medical purposes proved chaotic and haphazard. Civilian craft, under contract to each army's quartermaster corps, were used to evacuate patients. Often captains commanding these vessels, and the quartermasters who controlled them, made medical duties a low priority. Injured men were sometimes left to languish on vessels for days before beginning their journey to a hospital. Ships used to transport casualties lacked medical staff, military discipline, organization, adequate food, supplies, and facilities of any kind to care for or treat their patients.

Public outcry in response to these facts produced rapid change. The U.S. Army and U.S. Navy both purchased vessels to act solely as hospital ships. The United States Sanitary Commission and the Western Sanitary Commission did the same. Even the Confederacy managed to designate some of its limited floating stock for a hospital role. By 1863, specially designed hospital ships were in operation in every theater of war.

The biggest and best ships were literally floating hospitals, outfitted with hundreds of regular hospital beds organized into wards; operating rooms; and quarters for a full complement of surgeons, doctors and nurses. They also came equipped with bathrooms, laundries, steam-powered fans to circulate air below decks, elevators for moving patients between decks, gauze blinds to protect passengers from smoke or embers spewed by a ship's stacks, and even cold water produced by passing water in pipes through ice chests to faucets located conveniently about the vessel. These ships saved many lives and alleviated much suffering wherever they sailed.

JEFFREY WILLIAM HUNT

BIBLIOGRAPHY

Bollet, Alfred Jay. Civil War Medicine: Challenges and Triumphs. *Tucson, AZ: Galen Press, 2002.*

Freemon, Frank R. Gangrene and Glory: Medical Care during the American Civil War. *Madison, NJ: Fairleigh Dickinson University Press, 2001.*

and the development of brigade and division field hospitals made for a revolution in military medicine. European armies were quick to take note and soon copied these American innovations. The system of battlefield medical care developed between 1862 and 1865 remained standard both in the United Sates and Europe until after World War II (Bollet 2002, p. 107).

No matter how helpful in saving lives Letterman's innovations were, however, they could not erase the damage caused by ignorance of bacteria and of the importance of sterilizing medical instruments, bandages, dressings, sheets, and hands. Such ignorance cost hundreds, if not thousands of men their lives. No amount of organization could have prevented the heart-rending agony, fear, courage, stoicism, and sadness that were all too often seen at field hospitals. Despite this, the tireless efforts of overworked surgeons and medical staff, who scarcely took a moment to eat or sleep so long as injured men suffered, made the field hospital an example of inspiring selflessness and the highest devotion to duty.

BIBLIOGRAPHY

Bollet, Alfred Jay. *Civil War Medicine: Challenges and Triumphs.* Tucson, AZ: Galen Press, 2002.

Coggins, Jack. *Arms and Equipment of the Civil War.* Garden City, NY: Doubleday, 1962.

Commager, Henry Steele. *From the Battle of Gettysburg to Appomattox.* Vol. 2 of *The Blue and the Gray.* Indianapolis, IN: Bobbs-Merrill, 1950. Reprint, New York: Mentor, 1973.

Freemon, Frank R. *Gangrene and Glory: Medical Care during the American Civil War.* Madison, NJ: Fairleigh Dickinson University Press, 2001.

Wiley, Bell Irvin. *The Life of Billy Yank: The Common Soldier of the Union.* Indianapolis, IN: Bobbs-Merrill, 1952.

Jeffrey William Hunt

COMRADES AND THE AMBULANCE CORPS

Civil War battles were incredibly bloody affairs. Every large engagement produced tens of thousands of casualties in the span of one to three days. Wounded numbering in the thousands presented a challenge of enormous proportions to both Union and Confederate Armies. The dictates of humanity as well as military necessity required the prompt evacuation and medical treatment of wounded soldiers. From the medical standpoint, the motivation was to save life and limb, as well as to ease pain and suffering. From a military perspective, maintenance of morale and manpower were the critical factors. Troops fought better if they believed prompt and adequate care would be delivered to them if wounded. The evacuation of stricken soldiers removed an unnerving distraction for men still locked in combat. In addition, men whose lives were saved and bodies repaired by hospitals could be sent back to the ranks once their wounds healed.

Both North and South entered the war utterly unprepared to deal with the flood of wounded men streaming from the battlefield. Previous conflicts provided little guidance, as they had produced nothing like the scale of casualties typical of the Civil War. The frontier experience of the small regular army provided even less preparation for officers faced with the need to evacuate and care for large numbers of wounded.

An Inadequate Approach

Past experience, however, was the only guide available. As Frank Freemon points out in his 2001 book, *Gangrene and Glory: Medical Care during the American Civil War*, the initial medical organization of Northern and Southern armies was based on regulations of the prewar United States military (p. 28). Control of ambulances and medical evacuation fell under the authority of the Quartermaster Corps. The ambulances, of which there were only a few, were used to haul supplies to the battlefield and were driven by civilian contractors. Once emptied of cargo, they would be available to carry wounded.

Each regiment was responsible for providing its own stretcher-bearers. In his 1988 book *Soldiers Blue and Gray*, James Robertson observes that commanders were unlikely to assign their best men to such duties. The standard pool from which stretcher-bearers were drawn was the regimental band. Generally, there were not enough musicians available, so various men deemed poor soldiers would be called on to round out details. Stretchers were not supplied to regiments, and thus makeshifts of every sort—from blankets to house doors—were pressed into service (Robertson 1988, 160).

In his book *Civil War Medicine* (2002), Dr. Alfred Bollet explains that the shortcomings of this system were apparent as early as the battle of First Bull Run (First Manassas) on July 21, 1861. Civilian drivers, exhibiting little desire to risk their lives, fled the field or stayed far to the rear. Quartermasters often commandeered ambulances to move ammunition or other equipment, making them unavailable to evacuate the wounded (Bollet 2002, pp. 103, 117). The relative handful of stretcher-bearers available were quickly overwhelmed or failed to do their duty (Robertson 1988, p. 160).

Injured soldiers had only limited options if no ambulance or stretcher-bearers reached them. If still mobile, they could leave the field under their own power and attempt to reach a field hospital. Such attempts were risky, however. Unaided movement could aggravate wounds or cause additional injury. Loss of blood or shock could quickly overcome the victim, leading to his collapse, sometimes in a spot where he might remain

Ambulatory Union soldier casualties. The early carnage of Civil War battles found both Union and Confederate armies unprepared to handle the large number of casualties. In order to devote more men to fighting, military commanders eventually dedicated the task of removing the wounded from the battlefield to the expressly-created ambulance corps. *National Archives/Time Life Pictures/Getty Images.*

unnoticed for hours or days, if he were noticed at all—a situation that could prove fatal.

The second option was to be helped from the field by unwounded or lightly wounded comrades. This was a much safer method of evacuation, as it ensured assistance and care (no matter how minimal) all the way to a field hospital. Helping a wounded friend was a natural impulse. Soldiers often served alongside members of their family or prewar community, and shared emotional connections borne of common sacrifice and service. Men were inclined to go to the aid of a friend in distress—and doing so, incidentally, also provided them with an honorable excuse for leaving the zone of danger. From a military standpoint, however, this form of assistance was the worst system imaginable, as it removed healthy men from the firing line, thus significantly multiplying the effect of casualties.

The final option for men too badly hurt to move on their own, and unlucky enough to fall out of reach or view of comrades, was to lie on the field until the fighting ended. In this circumstance an injured man had no one to provide aid, except, perhaps, a nearby soldier who shared his fate. For soldiers without food, medical aid, or sometimes even water, the odds of survival grew worse with each passing hour on the battlefield.

The experience of Major John Haskell during the battle of Gaines' Mill, on June 27, 1862, provides a graphic example of the difficulties wounded men faced early in the war. Haskell was leading an attack when an artillery projectile smashed his right shoulder and virtually ripped off his arm. Unconscious for an unknown length of time, Haskell awakened to find his arm "wrapped around" the blade of his sword in a "most remarkable manner" (Haskell 1960, p. 34). On sitting up, Haskell passed out. Awakening a second time, he managed to separate the remnant of his arm from his sword. Stuffing the injured limb into the breast of his coat, Haskell got up and started for the rear, using a flagstaff as a crutch.

On his way, the major heard a close friend crying for help. Finding the man lying in a ravine and shot through the lungs, Haskell held up his shattered arm, explaining he could not help. Seeing a nearby soldier, the major ordered him to aid his friend. Accomplishing this, Haskell continued rearward, but did not get far before falling down. Weak from loss of blood, he was unable to get back up. Luckily, a fellow officer saw his distress, dismounted, put Haskell on his horse, and took him to a surgeon who provided first aid and sent Haskell to a field hospital via ambulance (Haskell 1960, pp. 34–36).

Encapsulated in this account are all the perils a wounded man faced early in the war. No stretcher-bearers were present to evacuate Haskell or his wounded comrade. One man was too badly wounded to move on his own, while Haskell's efforts to reach the rear alone

THE FATHER OF BATTLEFIELD MEDICINE

Jonathan Letterman (1824–1872) was born in Canonsburg, Pennsylvania, the son of a local surgeon. He graduated from Jefferson Medical College in 1849 and became an assistant surgeon in the Army Medical Department that same year.

In the 1850s Letterman was assigned to various military campaigns in Florida (against the Seminole Indians), New Mexico Territory (against the Apaches), and California (against the Utes). Letterman returned East at the beginning of the Civil War. He was named medical director of the Department of West Virginia in May 1862 and medical director of the entire Army of the Potomac just one month later. General George McClellan (1826–1885) gave Letterman, now a major, full permission to reorganize the army's medical service as seemed best to him. Letterman introduced a series of forward first aid stations at the battle of Antietam in 1862 as well as the practice of triage (sorting the wounded into categories in order to focus treatment on those most likely to survive). At the battle of Gettysburg in July 1863 Letterman created a large field hospital on the grounds of a local farmer to treat Confederate as well as Union wounded left behind after the three-day battle. The hospital was named Camp Letterman in his honor. Members of the U.S. Sanitary Commission visited Camp Letterman to bring supplies and help transport the more severely wounded to permanent hospitals elsewhere. One member of the commission reported that Letterman gave soldiers from both armies the best care he could: "The surgeon in charge of our camp, with his faithful dresser and attendants, looked after all their wounds, which were often in a most shocking state, particularly among the rebels. Every evening and morning they were dressed. Often the men would say, 'That feels good, I haven't had my wound so well dressed since I was hurt'" (Camp Letterman General Hospital). Letterman's system was so successful that it was established by an act of Congress in March 1864 for all Union armies in the field.

Letterman moved to San Francisco after the war and worked in the veterans' hospital at the Presidio. Saddened by the death of his wife in 1867, he died a few years later at the relatively young age of 48. In 1911 the hospital at the Presidio was named Letterman General Hospital to commemorate his work. Letterman was buried in Arlington National Cemetery; his epitaph reads, "Medical Director of the Army of the Potomac, June 23, 1862 to December 30, 1863, who brought order and efficiency into the Medical Service and who was the originator of modern methods of medical organization in armies" ("Jonathan K. Letterman").

REBECCA J. FREY

BIBLIOGRAPHY

"Camp Letterman General Hospital." Voice of Battle: Gettysburg National Military Park Virtual Tour. Available from http://www.nps.gov/.

"Jonathan K. Letterman." Arlington National Cemetery. http://www.arlington cemetery.net/.

ultimately failed. Stragglers and friends provided the only assistance. The ambulance that finally evacuated the major was found well to the rear of the firing line. In all likelihood, Haskell would not have survived if he had fallen somewhere outside the view of his passing comrade.

The inadequacy of this haphazard system was obvious. Nonetheless, it continued in the eastern Union Army until the late summer of 1862, and in the western Federal army until early 1863. Fortunately for the hundreds of thousands of men destined to be wounded in the middle and latter stages of the conflict, change eventually came.

The Letterman System

By mid-1862, voices advocating change and modernization of medical evacuation services were heard in both the North and South. The man who brought about those changes for the Union was Jonathan Letterman, who became the medical director of the Army of the Potomac in late June 1862. Letterman urged the creation of a dedicated ambulance corps, equipped with its own wagons, ambulances, tents, and supplies, and staffed by personnel specifically detailed and trained for the job of evacuating and caring for the wounded. Vehicles, equipment, and personnel would be under the sole authority of medical officers and could not be interfered with by anyone. Major General George B. McClellan, commander of the Army of the Potomac, instantly saw merit in Letterman's proposal and ordered its implementation (Bollet 2002, pp.103–105).

By the battle of Antietam (Sharpsburg) on September 17, 1862, Letterman's ambulance corps had begun to take the field. Although not fully staffed, equipped, or trained, it performed well. The battle of Fredericksburg, on December 13, 1862, was the first full test of the "Letterman System." In a single day of combat, 9,028 Union soldiers were wounded. Within just twenty-four hours of the end of the fighting, virtually every wounded man had been removed from the battlefield and taken to a field hospital (Bollet 2002, p. 125).

So effective was the new method of evacuation that Surgeon General William Hammond urged its adoption by all Union armies. Inexplicably, the War Department and General-in-Chief's office rejected the proposal. The logic of what Letterman was doing, however, could not be denied, and commanders of other Northern armies replicated his system. At the same time, Confederate armies, urged on by Dr. Hunter McGuire of the Army of Northern Virginia, were putting in place a system virtually identical to Letterman's. On March 11, 1864, the U.S. Congress passed legislation creating the Medical Corps' Ambulance Service, and requiring the army to adopt Letterman's system everywhere (Bollet 2002, pp. 105–106).

Inevitable Horrors

Although the new ambulance corps made an enormous difference, it could not solve all the problems or prevent all the terrors associated with removing injured soldiers from the battleground. Even trained stretcher-bearers were not always able or eager to evacuate wounded from a battlefield swept by enemy fire. Generally in a hurry to get out of danger, they tended to move quickly, which did little for the comfort or safety of an injured man on a litter. Major battles producing heavy casualties in short periods of time could still overwhelm the ability of stretcher-bearers to promptly remove or even find wounded men, especially in the hilly, heavily wooded terrain typical of most engagements.

At the beginning of the war the only ambulances available were two-wheeled carts or ordinary wagons. Lacking springs, these vehicles, often moving over unpaved and rutted country roads, provided a jarring and extraordinarily painful ride for wounded men. New four-wheeled ambulances with springs came into use by late 1862. They provided greater comfort but were always in short supply. In the aftermath of any large engagement, there were never enough purpose-built vehicles to transport the wounded and anything that rolled was pressed into service. The results were often heart-rending, especially for an army forced into a lengthy retreat.

No better example of this sad reality can be found than in the aftermath of the battle of Gettysburg. During its retreat, the Army of Northern Virginia was forced to transport 8,500 badly wounded soldiers over a hundred miles back to Virginia. There were not enough ambulances to do the job, so every available vehicle was utilized. The resulting misery endured by the wounded was grimly predictable and altogether too common in the annals of Civil War battles.

Brigadier General John Imboden was given the job of protecting the fifteen-mile-long procession of wagons and ambulances carrying the wounded southward. His vivid description of what the injured endured is one of the most memorable accounts of the horrors associated with the evacuation of the wounded:

> From almost every wagon for many miles issued heart-rending wails of agony. For four hours I hurried forward ... and in all that time I was never out of hearing of the groans and cries of the wounded and dying. Scarcely one in a hundred had received adequate surgical aid, owing to the demands on the hard-working surgeons from still worse cases that had to be left behind. Many of the wounded ... had been without food for thirty-six hours. Their torn and bloody clothing, matted and hardened, was rasping the tender, inflamed, and still oozing wounds. Very few of the wagons had even a layer of straw in them, and all were without springs. The road was rough and rocky. ... The jolting was enough to have killed strong men.... From nearly every wagon as the teams trotted on, urged by whip and shout, came such cries and shrieks as these: "O God! Why can't I die?" "My God! Will no one have mercy and kill me?" "Stop! Oh! For God's sake stop just for one minute; take me out and leave me to die on the roadside." "I am dying! I am dying! My poor wife, my dear children, what will become of you?"
>
> Some were simply moaning; some were praying, and others uttering the most fearful oaths and execrations that despair and agony could wring from them; while the majority, with a stoicism sustained by sublime devotion to the cause they fought for, endured without complaint unspeakable tortures, and even spoke words of cheer and comfort to their unhappy comrades of less will or more acute nerves.... No help could be rendered to any of the sufferers. No heed could be given to any of their appeals. Mercy and duty to the many forbade the loss of a moment in the vain effort then and there to comply with the prayers of the few. On! On! We *must* move on.... There was no time even to fill a canteen of water for a dying man; for, except the drivers and the guards, all were wounded and utterly helpless in that vast procession of misery. (McDonald 1907, pp. 318–319)

It was a scene that no witness could ever forget. "During this one night," Imboden wrote, "I realized more of the horrors of war than I had in all the preceding years" (McDonald 1907, p. 319).

BIBLIOGRAPHY

Bollet, Alfred Jay. *Civil War Medicine: Challenges and Triumphs.* Tucson, AZ: Galen Press, 2002.

Freemon, Frank R. *Gangrene and Glory: Medical Care during the American Civil War.* Madison, NJ: Fairleigh Dickinson University Press, 2001.

Haskell, John Cheves. *The Haskell Memoirs*, ed. Gilbert E. Govan and James W. Livingood. New York: Putnam, 1960.

McDonald, James Joseph. *Life in Old Virginia*, ed. J. A. C. Chandler. Norfolk, VA: The Old Virginia Publishing Co. (Inc.), 1907.

Robertson, James I., Jr. *Soldiers Blue and Gray.* Columbia: University of South Carolina Press, 1988.

Jeffrey William Hunt

TRIAGE AND SURGERY

Brigadier-General Gladden of South Carolina, at the Battle of Shiloh in 1863, had his left arm shattered by a cannon ball. As William Stevenson, a volunteer for the

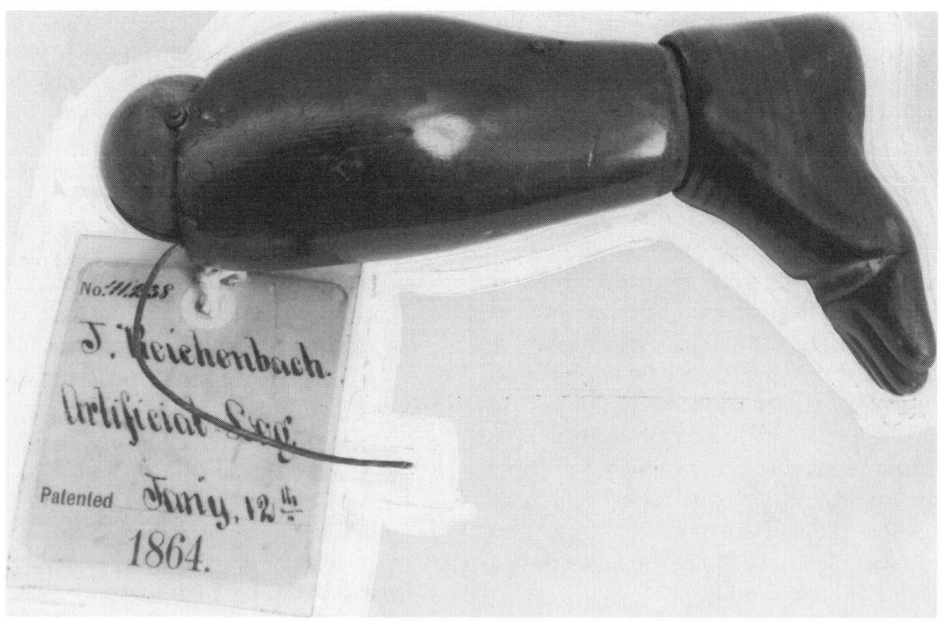

An artificial leg patented on January 12, 1864. With thousands of soldiers losing arms and legs during Civil War fighting, demand for artificial limbs increased greatly, inspiring inventors to develop and patent better medical devices. *Hulton Archive/Getty Images.*

Confederacy, recalled in his 1862 book *Thirteen Months in the Rebel Army: Being a Narrative of Personal Adventures in the Infantry, Ordnance, Cavalry, Courier, and Hospital Services*…:

> Amputation was performed hastily by his staff-surgeon on the field; and then, instead of being taken to the rear for quiet and nursing, he mounted his horse, against the most earnest remonstrances of all his staff, and continued to command. On Monday, he was again in the saddle, and kept it during the day; on Tuesday, he rode on horseback to Corinth, twenty miles from the scene of action, and continued to discharge the duties of an officer. On Wednesday, a second amputation, near the shoulder, was necessary. Against the remonstrances of personal friends, and the positive injunctions of the surgeons, he persisted in sitting up in his chair… till Wednesday afternoon, when lockjaw seized him, and he died in a few moments. (pp. 179–180)

Albeit heroic, death often befell those who survived surgery in the Civil War. Initially, both sides of the conflict were ill-prepared to handle mass casualties, and at the onset of the war there were 113 surgeons in the U.S. Army, of which twenty-four joined the Confederate army and three were dismissed for disloyalty. By the end of the war more than 12,000 surgeons had served in the Union army and nearly 3,200 in the Confederate army.

Triage

Although infection was yet to be understood, battlefield surgical conditions were far from primitive. Medical staff assessed the wounded in a system of triage. Soldiers brought in with head, chest, or stomach wounds were considered the least likely to survive; they were given morphine and water to ease their pain as they waited to die. This allowed doctors who were stretched to their limits (after the Battle of Gettysburg on July 1, 1863, the ratio of patients to doctors was nearly 300 to 1), to attend to the soldiers who could be saved. As a result, those slightly wounded and considered beyond help were set aside.

Amputation

Even in the early twenty-first century, many misconceptions persist about battlefield surgery during the Civil War. It is often thought that the injured soldier received inadequate treatment, an untrained surgeon giving him a doubtful glance before concluding amputation was the only solution—without anesthetic—only to have the patient die after surgery from "surgical fevers," such as deadly septicemia or gangrene. Contrary to this popular belief, however, amputation was not the first course of action. Surgeons took great care not to amputate, oftentimes causing greater harm than good. George Worthington Adams quotes William Williams Keen, a renowned surgeon of the war and West Point military cadet, in his 1985 book *Doctors in Blue: The Medical History of the Union Army in the Civil War*, where Keen stated, "I have no hesitation in saying that far more lives were lost in refusal to amputate than by amputation" (p. 163).

British and American civilian surgeon observers also felt that too few amputations were done, resulting in deaths that could have been prevented if amputation was chosen. William M. Caniff, professor of surgery at the University of Victoria College in Toronto, published in the British medical journal *Lancet* on February 28, 1863, and reprinted by Alfred J. Bollet in his 2004 article "The Truth About Civil War Surgery" that, "Although a strong advocate of conservative surgery... I became convinced that upon the field amputation was less frequently resorted to than it should be; that while in a few cases the operation was unnecessarily performed, in many cases it was omitted when it afforded the only chance of recovery" (p. 27).

When amputation was the chosen course of action, surgeons had a choice of performing a "flap" operation (which was the preferred method by the end of the war) or the circular procedure that left a small area open, prone to infection. The "operator," wielding his bone saw (thus the moniker of "Sawbones" attributed to Civil War doctors) would saw through the bone of the limb to be amputated. The arteries were then tied off using sutures of horsehair, silk, or cotton threads. After the bleeding was controlled, the surgeon scraped the freshly cut bone smooth so it would not damage the skin to be sewn shut. In the "flap" procedure, the extra skin would then be sewn shut and a small hole would be left for drainage. Finally, the appendage would be set in isinglass plaster and bandaged.

As an alternative to amputation, surgeons on both sides of the war tried using a medical technique called excision, or resection. Wherever bone was damaged, the broken pieces were removed from the limb in the hopes that the healthy bone would reattach itself. Many soldiers, however, preferred to have prosthetics attached to an amputated limb rather than have a poorly functioning limb that was shortened. Excisions also resulted in higher mortality rates than did amputations.

Infection

Infection ran rampant under the poor sanitary conditions of the camps. Hospital gangrene threatened to infect even the simplest cut and resulted in severe pain and fever for the patient, and the formation of pus at the wound site—the foul smell that pervaded the hospitals of the time. Where amputation was afforded, the threat of infection persisted. Often soldiers would not make it to the surgical theater for many days after being wounded. Surgeons at the time thought it was imperative to operate within the first day of receiving the wound to avoid the period during which infection could set in. Within a few days "laudable pus" would often appear, which doctors at the time believed was how clean tissue replaced itself within the body; in actuality, healthy tissue was already undergoing decomposition. William Stevenson noted in his 1862 book *Thirteen Months in the Rebel Army*: "On account of exposures, many wounds were gangrenous when the patients reach the hospital. In these cases delay was fatal, and an operation almost equally so, as tetanus often followed speedily. Where amputation was performed, eight out of ten died" (p. 177).

Operations at the time were disease-ridden from beginning to end. Everything the surgeons used was unsanitary. The operating table, tools—literally everything—was pus- and blood-laden. Between surgeries, tools were cleansed in nothing more than cold water; if surgical forceps or an incision knife was dropped on the floor, it too would be cleaned in the same water. Wounds were often wrapped in unsterilized, wet bandages. Although germs were not fully understood at the time, medical staff did have sterilizers such as bichloride of mercury, sodium hypochlorite, and carbolic acid. The error in reasoning occurred when disinfectant was used after infection had already set in.

Anesthesia

Anesthesia was introduced to the medical community in 1846. Thus, most surgeries during the Civil War were carried out under anesthesia. There is a record in the United States Surgeon-General's Office 1879 publication *Medical and Surgical History of the War of the Rebellion*, however, in which, at the Battle of Iuka in September 1862, 254 casualties were operated on without the use of anesthetic, the single largest such documented case. Chloroform and ether were the types of anesthetics used. Usually a cloth was placed over the face of the patient and a few drops were placed on the cloth as the patient breathed in the fumes. Chloroform was usually preferred to ether because of ether's explosive chemical properties.

By War's End

Despite the lack of preparation, Union surgeons treated more than 400,000 wounded men—about 245,000 of them for gunshot or artillery wounds—and performed at least 40,000 operations. Less complete Confederate records show that fewer surgeons treated a similar number of patients. Oftentimes, soldiers were operated on by surgeons of the opposing forces. Thomas Ellis, a Union surgeon, gives an account of a Confederate major from a North Carolina regiment in his 1863 book *Leaves from the Diary of an Army Surgeon; or, Incidents of Field, Camp, and Hospital Life*: "The major was shot in the thigh, fracturing the bone very badly and rendering amputation necessary, he thanked us for our attention stating that he had not expected such kind treatment at our hands" (p. 76). In the 1862 article "Surgeon at Work," *Harper's Weekly* reported, "Arteries are tied, ligatures and tourniquets applied, flesh wounds hastily dressed, broken limbs set, and sometimes, where haste is essential, amputations performed within sight and sound of the cannon. Of all officers the surgeon is often the one who requires most nerve and most courage" (p. 439).

According to the United States Sanitary Commission's 1869 work *Sanitary Memoirs of the War of the Rebellion*, "The whole number of casualties during the forty-eight months of the war, among 2,480,000 white soldiers, was 858,000. The total number of deaths in the same service was about 250,000, making the ratio of deaths to the whole number of casualties as 100 to 343" (p. 9). The surgeons on both sides did well to keep the men of the nation alive for without them, untold numbers would have perished, making Reconstruction for a war-weary nation nearly impossible.

BIBLIOGRAPHY

Adams, George Worthington. *Doctors in Blue: The Medical History of the Union Army in the Civil War.* Dayton, OH: Press of Morningside, 1985.

Bollet, Alfred J. "The Truth About Civil War Surgery." *Civil War Times* 43, no. 4 (2004): 27–33, 56.

Coco, Gregory A. *Gettysburg, The Aftermath of a Battle.* Gettysburg, PA: Thomas Publications, 1995.

Ellis, Thomas T. *Leaves from the Diary of an Army Surgeon; or, Incidents of Field, Camp, and Hospital Life.* New York: J. Bradburn, 1863.

Stevenson, William G. *Thirteen Months in the Rebel Army: Being a Narrative of Personal Adventures in the Infantry, Ordnance, Cavalry, Courier, and Hospital Services....* New York: A. S. Barnes and Burr, 1862.

"Surgeon at Work." *Harper's Weekly* 6, no. 289 (1862): 439.

United States Sanitary Commission. *Sanitary Memoirs of the War of the Rebellion, v. 2, Investigations in the Military and Anthropological Statistics of American Soldiers.* Cambridge, MA: Riverside Press, 1869.

United States Surgeon-General's Office. *The Medical and Surgical History of the War of the Rebellion, 1861–1865.* Washington. U.S. Government Printing Office, 1870.

Anurag Biswas

EVACUATION HOSPITALS

During the Civil War years, 1861 through 1865, hundreds of hospitals, including evacuation hospitals—those situated far from the battlefields, often in larger cities—became important scenes for dealing with the thousands of injured or ill soldiers. In addition to the common problems soldiers endured, like bullet wounds and gangrene, many people fell ill with infectious diseases unrelated to battlefield wounds, such as typhoid fever or dysentery, and required hospitalization. In the early 1860s, links between health and sanitation were poorly understood, and there was not yet knowledge of antiseptic principles or an understanding of the spread of bacteria and germs. Also, anesthesia was becoming widely used, but still largely experimental. The emerging role of hospitals and health care professionals in dealing with large numbers of people requiring treatment, pushed the hospital system forward during this historical military and medical period. In April 1861 the people of the United States and the new Confederate States of America found themselves unprepared for the fierce and bloody struggle that awaited them. The shocking realization that the war would not be short was accompanied by another epiphany: The wounded were piling up, and the hospitals of the time were severely inadequate.

The medical system as it existed, including the establishment of hospitals, faced a myriad of challenges, including the accommodation of thousands of wounded soldiers. Before the war, most people who became ill had been accustomed to home care. With home care more common, hospital buildings were rare before the war. In fact, the early causalities of the war during the fall and winter of 1861, created the need for several buildings to be used as hospitals, as there were not adequate numbers already established; churches, courthouses, barns, stores, warehouses, and multiple other buildings became interim hospitals (Cunningham 1958, p. 45). One account from Private David Holt of the Sixteenth Mississippi Regiment, details the early limitations of these temporary hospitals from his observations in Bedford County, Virginia:

> This old one-story freight station had been converted into the receiving room of a temporary hospital, and the ward for the wounded and very sick was a long shack about ten feet high at the eaves with a shingle roof and the ground for a floor. I never went into the ward, but Milton [a hospital worker] said there were not enough cots and some of the sick and wounded lay on the floor. He also said it was hotter than the hinges of hell. (Cockrell and Ballard 1995, p. 106)

Also contributing to the problems was the common medical doctrine of the time that recovery from disease or injury in large hospitals tended to take longer than in the preferred small private hospitals. Large public hospitals were thought to be full of "tainted air which fills the wards and ... enfeebles the nervous system," leading to new diseases and slower healing of wounds ("Military Hygiene," November 5, 1861, n.p.). The notion that mortality rates were higher inside hospitals than outside them meant that there were very few large hospitals built at the time. Soldiers often preferred to be treated at camp at the temporary or mobile field hospitals. They feared the unfamiliarity of the hospitals that were located far from the battlegrounds in the cities. Rumors and first-hand accounts from patients, frequently reported lack of organization in hospitals, crowded corridors, shortages of medical supplies, and minimal individualized attention for patients. (Rutkow 2005, p. 152). Private houses were thought to be more hygienic.

Wolfe Street Hospital, Alexandria, VA. Prior to the Civil War, physicians thought it healthier for the sick and injured to recover at home. However, faced with large numbers of soldiers distant from their homes, both Union and Confederate armies began building hospitals where wounded soldiers could convalesce for an extended period of time. *© Medford Historical Society Collection/Corbis.*

An "Ancient and Fossilized" Medical System

After the Battle of Bull Run (known as the First Battle of Manassas by the Confederate forces) on July 21, 1861 the casualties began to mount. Because existing hospitals could not deal with the numbers, military evacuation hospitals were set up in buildings intended for other purposes: "[P]ublic buildings, school-houses, churches, hotels, warehouses, factories, and private dwellings" became the treatment centers for sick and wounded soldiers from all over the country (Otis 1865, p. 152). On August 3, 1861, there were 945 sick and wounded soldiers in the five hospitals in Washington, DC; many were divided among the hospitals improvised at Miss English's Seminary and the Columbia College buildings, not to mention the House and Senate Chambers in the Capitol Building ("Sick and Wounded Soldiers," August 8, 1861). However, these buildings were still insufficient in size, supplies, toilet facilities, ventilation, and heating. The *New York Times* (July 27, 1861) noted less than a week after the Battle of Bull Run that "we are inexpressibly pained to learn from Washington that very inadequate provision has been made by the regular authorities, for the proper care of the wounded in the late battle. . . . [S]ome of our gallant soldiers, for want of hospital garments, even yet lie sweltering in their bloody uniforms, festering with fever and maddened with thirst." The Medical Department's preparations were "ancient and fossilized" and only adequate for a force of "less than fifteen thousand men" (n.p.). Clearly, new measures had to be taken. Plans on both sides varied widely over time and place.

Confederate Hospitals

In the South, soldiers were not always sent to division hospitals. According to Confederate medical department regulations, the sick and wounded were to be "sent to the hospitals representing their respective states," unless their sickness or wounds were too severe and another hospital was closer (Confederate States of America War Department 1863, p. 56).

By 1862, more hospitals were being built, but there were still too few to take care of the soldiers needing treatment and long-term care. However, positive changes persisted throughout the years of the Civil War; by 1863, many more hospitals had been created. Hospitals in Richmond, Virginia had the best reputation and were thought of as the medical center for the Confederacy (Cunningham 1958, p. 50).

On October 11, 1861, Chimborazo, the most well-known Confederate hospital, opened in Richmond, Virginia. The hospital was located on the edge of Richmond, which allowed convenient access to York River Railroad. Chimborazo had room for approximately 8,000 patients, and it eventually became regarded as the best hospital in the North and the South. Chimborazo Hospital grew its own food, and even had around two hundred cows and a herd of goats on its hospital farm.

Union Hospitals

The Saterlee Hospital in Philadelphia, developed by William Hammond after he became the Surgeon General in

April of 1862, exemplified the grand visions held for a nationwide military hospital system. The structure had twenty-eight pavilions, with room for well over a thousand patients. "With barbershops, laundries, a pharmacy, and smoking rooms, the complex was a city unto itself, and following further additions, by war's end bed capacity reached an amazing 3,519" (Rutkow 2005, p. 157). Another Union hospital, Mower U.S. General Hospital, was constructed by architect John McArthur Jr. in Philadelphia, in the city's Chestnut Hill area. Named after an Army surgeon, Thomas Mower, the hospital was in operation from 1863 to 1865. During those years, it treated over 20,000 patients, most of whom were Union soldiers. Saterlee and Mower U.S. General were two of several hospitals that became established in Philadelphia. In fact, by 1865, there were twenty-seven hospitals in the city (Adams 1958, p. 155). Like the city of Washington, Philadelphia played a key role in the development of the hospital system.

In both the North and the South, a directory was created to present organized information about patients in over two hundred hospitals (Denney 1994, p. 12). The public was gaining both a familiarity with the hospital system, and experiencing the advancement of the American hospital system. By the end of the war in 1865, the United States' hospital system had undergone significant changes in the architecture, organization, and administration of hospitals, and laid the foundation for a better hospital system across the country.

New Plans, New Hospitals

Medical treatment of injured soldiers took place in a series of locations. After being stabilized, or if further care not available at the field hospital was needed, a wounded soldier was transported to a hospital camp or a division or regimental hospital (though this step was often skipped). From there the surviving soldier would be transported to a general hospital for extended care and convalescence. In 1864 the Union soldier Henry Meacham was wounded in the arm and underwent an amputation in a battlefield hospital before being taken to City Point Hospital for extensive care and convalescence: "We were treated well and had all the comforts that could be expected. Never but once while at City Point did I have occasion to find fault with my treatment . . . I had good care." After leaving City Point, Meacham was transferred to the Third Division Hospital near Alexandria, Virginia, and found it "very pleasant . . . ; the ground was kept neat and clean, and everything was neat about the building and tents. We were treated kindly" (Meacham 1869?, pp. 28–29).

In order to establish hospitals that were both sufficient in size and properly ventilated, many facilities were built according to the new "pavilion" model. Adelaide Smith described one of these, Fort Schuyler Hospital along the East River in New York, as being "formed like a wheel, the hub being headquarters and spokes extending into wards for patients" (Smith 1911, p. 31). Other pavilions were triangular in design, such as Lincoln

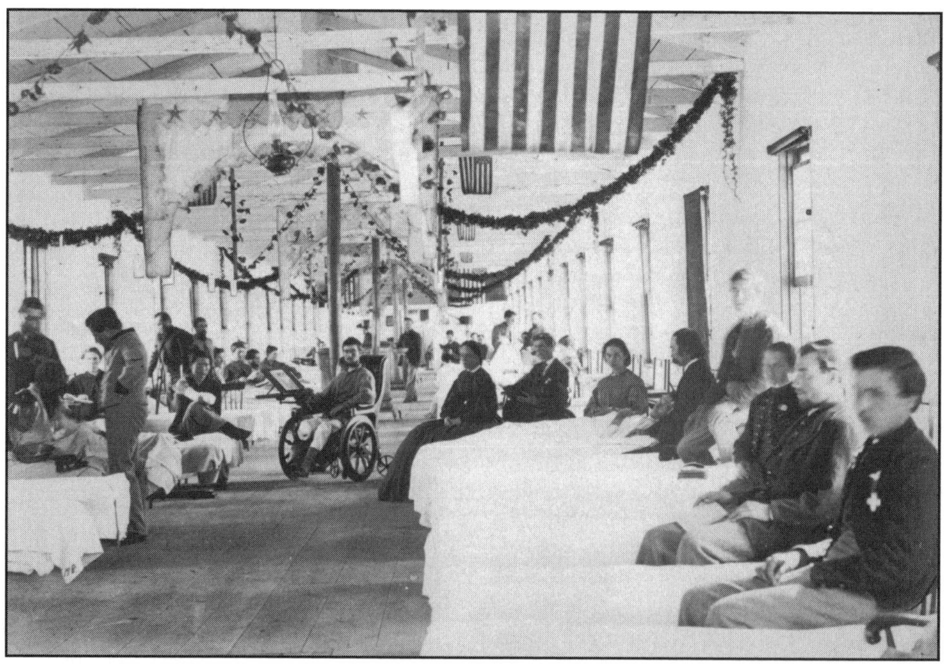

Ward in Armory Square Hospital, Washington, DC. Wounded soldiers recovered in newly built hospitals until their wounds healed enough to return home or to the front lines of conflict. *The Library of Congress.*

Hospital in Washington, DC. The pavilion plan allowed the assignment of different medical problems to separate buildings, which were no more than two stories in most cases.

With the larger buildings, design was an important consideration, and structures were created to foster more hygienic practices. For instance, there was an emphasis on incorporating fewer ninety-degree angles to prevent the accumulation of hard to clean dirt. These hospitals also featured ventilation refinements in the form of ridge-ventilated ceilings, which could be closed off during the winter, when shaft ventilation would substitute. According to the *New York Times*, the "ventilation of these buildings is their triumphant singularity, and, properly arranged, completely ignores contagion." The construction was such that each building "admits of the freshest circulation of air," allowing the wards to be cool and comfortable in the summer—forming a "seductive place for convalescing patients to lounge" (April 9, 1862, n.p.). These pavilion hospitals were commissioned in both the North and South—some with the wards directly connected to the central building, others with free-standing buildings. In July 1864, the Union Secretary of War, Edwin Stanton, issued official orders that all new military hospitals were to be built in the detached pavilion style with sixty beds per ward, and that no other buildings were to be used as hospitals unless inspected by the Medical Corps. These pavilion hospitals would feature dining rooms, kitchens, laundry facilities, quartermaster offices, storage areas for patients' effects, guardhouses, dead houses, housing for female nurses, operating rooms, stables, and a chapel (Otis 1865, pp. 153–154).

The new hospitals were built quickly and cheaply. They were supplied primarily through donations from citizens, without which the majority of hospitals would not have lasted. Throughout the summer of 1861 Northern and Southern newspapers published letters from military staff, war department officials, and private citizens calling for contributions and volunteers. Lists of contributed items were also printed in these newspapers. The war departments, the Northern Sanitary Commission, volunteer organizations, and independent hospitals also directly solicited more donations. This practice was especially commonplace in the South, where hospital supplies often ran low. However, the North was not without its needs. In October 1861, acknowledging the poor quality of hospital care in the North, the federal government made an appeal "to the loyal women of America." The authorities admitted that "lives [were] lost because the government cannot put the right thing in the right place at the right time." While the U.S. Sanitary Commission had been created to solve the problems, the commission still had to rely on voluntary contributions, which at that point numbered around sixty thousand articles (United States Sanitary Commission 1861, pp. 1–2).

Under the supervision of the Sanitary Commission, Northern hospitals underwent required inspections that examined "theoretically and practically all questions of diet and cooking [,] . . . climate, malaria and contagions, [and] ventilation" (*New York Times*, June 25, 1861). A questionnaire of 179 items was filled out by inspectors regarding the health of the patients and the environment of the hospital, with consideration given to such things as the latrines, soldiers' diets, the laundry, and hygiene (Bollet 2002, p. 225). After inspections, unfit hospitals would be reformed, "careless or ignorant officials" would be chastised or removed, and every hospital was made to adhere to the "uniformity of plans and harmony of action between the States" (*New York Times*, June 25, 1861).

General hospitals were built across the nation, both near the front lines and far away. By June 1865 the Union had 204 hospitals and the Confederates had created about 154. The majority of Northern hospitals were in and around Washington, DC, whereas in the South, though Richmond had many, hospitals were concentrated in several areas, as nearly all the fighting took place throughout the Southern states (Bollet 2002, p. 221–223).

Hospital Services

The evacuation or general hospitals, as well as the soldiers' homes, were intended to be places where sick and wounded soldiers could rest, recuperate, receive any needed medical attention, and prepare to return to either their regiment or, in the case of disabled soldiers, to their homes.

Over the course of the war, women became the backbone of Union and Confederate hospitals—as matrons, nurses, volunteers, or simply by making donations. Certainly, these women did not lack for patriotic fervor. A New York woman wrote directly to President Lincoln: "[W]ere I a man I would . . . fight in a moment. . . . [Being unable to,] I offer my services to nurse our wounded soldiers. I do not wish any pay for my services, but only to nurse the sick and wounded soldiers who are fighting for the rights of our glorious country" (*New York Herald*, April 22, 1861). In the South, many women were moved by the desire to contribute "to the comfort of the men who had been wounded in protecting their homes" (Stevenson 1862, p. 190). They volunteered for hospital duty in droves, and their effect on soldiers in hospitals was profound. William Stevenson, a Confederate wounded at Shiloh, found the hospital nearby to be in a state of chaos, with men going untreated, unskilled young surgeons wreaking havoc on bodies, and disease spreading—until the nurses arrived: "Their presence worked like a charm. Order emerged from chaos, and in a few hours all looked cleaner and really felt better, from the skill and industry of a few devoted women" (Stevenson 1862, pp. 177–178).

In her book *Hospital Days* (1870), Jane Stuart Woolsey noted that women nurses were of all sorts: "volunteers paid or unpaid; soldiers' wives or sisters who had come to see their friends, and remained without any clear commission or duties;... [and others] sent by state agencies or societies... [and] set adrift... without training or discipline ... or officers" (p. 43). Despite this lack of oversight, the air and tone of a hospital, according to Woolsey, would invariably improve within only a few days of the women's arrival. The character of many nurses was so stubborn that they would "gaily starve... [themselves] to feed a sick soldier... [and] cheerfully sacrifice time, ease and health, to the wants or whims of a wounded man" (Woolsey 1870, pp. 43–44).

At most general hospitals the first order of business was recuperation. Wounds and diseases were cared for by nurses and surgeons, who generally made rounds once a day. Volunteers read and wrote letters for the infirm. Many hospitals featured extensive grounds for walking, which aided in both physical and mental recovery. Meals were provided daily, as well as medicine, depending on availability. When it was time for a sick or wounded soldier to leave the hospital, either to return to his regiment or to return home, most hospitals offered assistance in procuring papers, pensions, transportation, and back pay. Some hospitals had cemeteries for those who did not recover.

In addition to general hospitals, specialty hospitals were created. Philadelphia's Turner's Lane Hospital catered to nerve injuries and neurological disorders. A Nashville hospital dealt with venereal diseases. A specialty hospital in Washington, DC, which was named the Desmarres Hospital after it was moved to Chicago in 1864, dealt with both eye and throat injuries and diseases, while the Confederacy opened an eye hospital in Athens, Georgia. Both sides responded to the immense need for orthopedic hospitals for soldiers with wounds or injuries to the extremities, as well as those who had lost limbs and needed prostheses (Bollet 2002, pp. 227–229).

Results

In a few short years, the medical situation on both sides had drastically improved. "Never before, in the history of the world," declared the Union medical officer George Alexander Otis, "was so vast a system of hospitals brought into existence in so short a time... [or] has the mortality rate in military hospitals been so small" (Otis 1865, p. 152). By 1865 it was realized that "the ill-ventilated barracks and private edifices... occupied as hospitals during the earlier part of the war" (Otis 1865, p. 87) were indeed only contributing to disease. The creation of the Sanitary Commission and the reforms it enacted, especially mandatory hospital inspections, helped pave the way for a new era of expectations for public hospitals. The designs of the pavilion hospitals influenced hospital architecture, and the creation of specialty hospitals continued beyond the war. While the majority of general hospitals closed after the war, the very idea of what a hospital is and what it should be had been forever altered in America.

BIBLIOGRAPHY

Adams, G.W. *Doctors in Blue.* Baton Rouge: Louisiana State University Press, 1958.

"The Army Hospitals at Washington." *New York Times,* August 13, 1861.

Bollet, Alfred J. *Civil War Medicine: Challenges and Triumphs.* Tucson, AZ: Galen Press, 2002.

Cockrell, T. D. and M. B. Ballard, eds. *A Mississippi Rebel in the Army of Northern Virginia: The Civil War Memoirs of Private David Holt.* Baton Rouge: Louisiana State University Press, 1995.

"Condition of Our Wounded." *New York Times,* July 27, 1861.

Confederate States of America. War Department. *Regulations for the Medical Department of the C.S. Army.* Richmond, VA: Ritchie & Dunnavant, 1863.

Cunningham, H. H. *Doctors in Gray, The Confederate Medical Service.* Baton Rouge: Louisiana State University Press, 1958.

Denney, R. E. *Civil War Medicine: Care & Comfort of the Wounded.* New York: Sterling Publishing Co., Inc., 1994.

"Health of the Army: The Sanitation Commission." *New York Times,* June 25, 1861.

"Local Military Matters." *New York Times,* July 10, 1861.

Meacham, Henry H. *The Empty Sleeve; or, The Life and Hardships of Henry H. Meacham, in the Union Army.* Springfield, MA: Author, 1869?.

"Military Hygiene." *North American and United States Gazette,* November 5, 1861.

Otis, George Alexander. *Reports on the Extent and Nature of the Materials Available for the Preparation of a Medical and Surgical History of the Rebellion.* Philadelphia: J. B. Lippincott, 1865.

"A Patriotic Lady Offers Her Services to Nurse the Wounded." *New York Herald,* April 22, 1861.

Rutkow, I. M. *Bleeding Blue and Gray: Civil War Surgery and the Evolution of American Medicine.* New York: Random House, 2005.

"Sick and Wounded Soldiers." (Letter to the editor.) *Washington, DC, Daily National Intelligencer,* August 8, 1861.

Smith, Adelaide W. *Reminiscences of an Army Nurse during the Civil War.* New York: Greaves Publishing Company, 1911.

Stevenson, William G. *Thirteen Months in the Rebel Army: Being a Narrative of Personal Adventures in the Infantry, Ordnance, Cavalry, Courier, and Hospital Services.* New York: A. S. Barnes & Burr, 1862.

United States Sanitary Commission. General Aid Society for the Army (Buffalo, NY). *Report of Delegates from the General Aid Society for the Army at Buffalo, N.Y.: To Visit the Government Hospitals, and the Agencies of the United States.* Buffalo, NY: Franklin Steam, 1862.

United States Sanitary Commission. *To the Loyal Women of America.* Washington, DC: Author, 1861.

"Ward's Island." *New York Times,* April 9, 1862.

Woolsey, Jane Stuart. *Hospital Days.* New York: D. Van Nostrand, 1870.

J. Douglas Tyson
Jenny Lagergren

■ Disease

During the Civil War more soldiers died as a result of disease than perished at the hands of the enemy. Disease caused roughly 65 percent of all deaths and left hundreds of thousands of additional soldiers permanently disabled. Such estimates do not account for the number of deaths that can be attributed to disease on the home front. Sick soldiers returning home or seeking care in general hospitals carried illness back to their communities, further adding to the devastation. Disease was truly an equal opportunity killer, striking rich and poor, black and white, and men and women indiscriminately. President Abraham Lincoln's (1809–1865) eleven-year-old son, William Wallace Lincoln, for example, died from typhoid fever in February 1862. Disease contributed to the war's unprecedented mortality rates while also exacting a heavy psychological burden on the sick, their caregivers and dependents, and the community at large. Likewise, disease crippled armies, reducing available manpower, and sometimes altered a commander's campaign strategy. Despite the war's heavy disease-related death toll the Civil War marked a period of steady improvement in mortality rates among soldiers. Fewer soldiers per capita died from disease during the Civil War than any other previous American war. Improvements in medical knowledge, medicine, facilities, and a general awareness of the need for proper sanitation contributed to this distinction, but despite those advances disease remained the war's principal killer.

Throughout history disease has been a constant companion of warfare. Wars typically involve armies filled with soldiers who are in constant close proximity to one another, human waste, animal waste, and who are subject to bouts of malnutrition, fatigue, depression, and unsanitary conditions. Most Civil War soldiers came from rural agrarian backgrounds. Farmers and laborers living in a rural setting are by the nature of their occupation relatively isolated from contact with large numbers of individuals. Their separation greatly reduced their exposure to various childhood and epidemic diseases. When those men enlisted in the military and were suddenly thrust into a highly concentrated setting, their immune systems were unprepared to guard against an onslaught of new bacteria and viruses.

Inadequate and often nonexistent physical examinations for recruits facilitated the spread of diseases among Civil War soldiers. Most men joined the military without an inspection, while those who were examined only received a cursory physical exam. A New Jersey volunteer described the scene of one examination:

> The company was drawn up in line on one side of the room and when a man's name was called he would step up to the doctor, who to him the following questions. Were you ever sick in your life, have you got the rheumatism, have you got varicose veins, and other questions of like matters, instead of finding out for himself by actual examination whether you had or not. If the questions were answered in the affirmative and he had no reason to doubt it, he would give us a thump on the chest, and if we were not floored nor showed any other sign of inconvenience, we were pronounced in good condition. (Robertson 1988, p. 147)

Without the benefit of proper physical examinations, both armies enlisted thousands of soldiers and sailors who were unfit for duty and were highly susceptible to disease.

The vast majority of soldiers contracted some form of disease during their first weeks of military service. Those first weeks of duty were a period of enormous physical and psychological adjustment. Physically, soldiers grew accustomed to a new diet and sleep routine. Psychologically, most soldiers combated homesickness that sometimes turned into prolonged bouts of depression. The average soldier was sick at least three times annually between 1861 and 1865. Approximately 5 percent of all soldiers diagnosed with a disease died as a result of that ailment or from mounting complications stemming from their original malady. For unknown reasons, soldiers serving in the western theatre suffered a higher disease mortality rate than their eastern counterparts. Additionally, African American soldiers reported a higher rate of disease and disease mortality than did white soldiers. Lackluster conditions, inadequate supplies, preexisting conditions, and overt racism possibly account for those higher numbers.

Childhood Diseases

The types of diseases contracted by soldiers can be divided into three main categories: childhood diseases, camp diseases, and epidemic diseases. Soldiers raised in rural areas usually had little exposure to childhood diseases such as chicken pox, measles, mumps, and whooping cough. The worst of these was measles. In the

Confederate general Joseph E. Johnston (1807–1891). During the Civil War, the mortality rate from disease outnumbered the rate from combat injuries. In an attempt to limit his troops' exposure to disease, Confederate General Joseph E. Johnston restricted civilian contact with his soldiers. *The Library of Congress.*

summer of 1861 measles struck several regiments in surgeon Legrand Wilson's brigade. More than two hundred men died from measles in his brigade that summer. With hundreds more inflicted the Confederates converted a neighboring tobacco warehouse into a measles hospital. "About one hundred sick men," wrote Wilson, as reprinted in Robertson's book, "crowded in a room sixty by one hundred feet in all stages of measles. The poor boys lying on the hard floor, with only one or two blankets under them, not even straw, and anything they could find for a pillow. Many sick and vomiting, many already showing the unmistakable signs of blood poisoning" (p. 149). Measles were so prevalent in the army that twentieth-century writers such as Margaret Mitchell (1900–1949) incorporated the disease into their fictionalized accounts of the war. In Mitchell's 1936 book *Gone With the Wind* heroine Scarlett O'Hara's first husband, Charles Hamilton, died from measles while in camp and prior to seeing battle. Mitchell's choice of disease was more than an act of literary convenience but instead a reflection of dozens of memoirs and diaries read by the Georgian author in preparation for writing the book. Childhood diseases frequently reduced a regiment's fighting strength by half before the unit ever fired a single volley toward the enemy.

Childhood diseases reappeared throughout the war. During the summer and fall of 1862 a second wave of childhood diseases spread throughout both armies, claiming the lives of hundreds and debilitating thousands. As late as winter 1865 diseases such as measles and chicken pox continued to plague both armies, even among veteran regiments.

Camp Diseases

Soldiers who survived bouts with childhood diseases also faced a number of camp diseases. Camp diseases were caused by a variety of factors, including poor sanitary conditions, vitamin deficient diets, inadequate shelter, contaminated drinking water, and insect infestations.

Union soldiers benefited from the work of organizations such as the United States Sanitary Commission, the Christian Commission, the Western Sanitary Commission, and the Young Men's Christian Association, whose combined efforts worked toward improving sanitary conditions. Their volunteers instructed soldiers and their commanders on the importance of maintaining both a hygienic body and campsite. The Confederacy never developed a similar network of sanitary crusaders. Their armies depended on staff surgeons and commanders to improve camp conditions. James M. McPherson reproduces the words of Robert E. Lee, commander of the Army of Northern Virginia, in his 2001 book *Ordeal by Fire*: "Our poor sick, I know suffer much, but they bring it on themselves by not doing what they are told. They are worse than children, for the latter can be forced" (p. 385).

Maintaining a sanitary camp was beyond the capabilities of most soldiers and commanders. Sites placed on low-lying land or flood plains were subject to sitting water. Soldiers often slept on the damp ground. In such a state of affairs soldiers caught a variety of respiratory ailments, including bronchitis and pneumonia. Charles Smedley relayed an example of such problems in his 1865 memoir *Life in Southern Prisons from the Diary of Corporal Charles Smedley*: "Last night was the coldest we have had for some time. My attack of bronchitis has extended far into the chest, and is going to bring on that terrible "army scourge" again" (p. 33). Bronchitis was accompanied by a persistent cough and chest pain. Once diagnosed, soldiers could spend as much as a month in the hospital before their lungs regained normal function. Under regular circumstances bronchitis was rarely fatal, but diseases of the respiratory system proved to be cyclical for Civil War soldiers. Within days after being released from the hospital soldiers again began experiencing inflammation of the bronchial tubes accompanied by an abrasive cough, muscle pain, and a bloody mucus discharge. For many, such discomforts were routine parts of the daily life of a Civil War soldier.

Large armies produced substantial amounts of human waste. Disposing of human excrement in a sanitary fashion required special planning, especially when armies were on the move. Soldiers frequently scraped out temporary latrines, also known as sinks, during short encampments. Such facilities provided no privacy and were usually located within close proximity to where soldiers ate, drank, and slept. Physicians did not understand the need to locate latrines a significant distance downstream from a camp's source of drinking water. Consequently, soldiers often drank water gathered within a few yards of their latrines. Feces contain high levels of bacteria. One poorly placed latrine could spread bacterial infections such as pneumonia and diarrhea throughout an entire company of soldiers with devastating effect. Soldiers held in prison camps experienced frightening conditions. About Andersonville, John Worrell Northrop recorded the following account in his 1904 book *Chronicles from the Diary of a War Prisoner in Andersonville and Other Military Prisons in the South in 1864*: "Men unable to go to the swampy sinks, have dug holes close by where they lay. The rains wash these away or overflow them, and the filthy contents are carried into our resting places" (p. 71). Northrop's description, though written while in prison, portrays similar conditions in thousands of military camps, where many soldiers paid scant attention to the devastating effects of improper sanitation.

Dietary deficiencies weakened soldiers' immune system and increased their susceptibility to certain types of disease. Soldiers' letters regularly complained about their substandard diet. They ate sparingly during a campaign and when they did manage to eat a sufficient number of calories, it usually consisted of meals rich in corn protein and saturated fat. Poor diet made soldiers prone to ailments such as diarrhea and dysentery. More soldiers suffered from chronic bouts of diarrhea during the war than of any other disease. Editor David P. Jackson published the words of ancestor Oscar Lawrence Jackson in the 1922 edition of *The Colonel's Diary*: "A great many of our men," Oscar Lawrence Jackson wrote, "suffered with diarrhea and some with fevers and our regiment gradually ran down in strength" (p. 57). Diarrhea confounded physicians, who struggled to find an effective treatment and remained uncertain about its principal causes. Cases of diarrhea and dysentery steadily increased throughout the war, whereas diagnoses of more fatal diseases such as typhoid fever slowly decreased. Private Peter W. Homer, 1st New Jersey Cavalry Regiment, Army of the Potomac, was admitted to the hospital in January 1863 after enduring a prolonged bout of typhoid aggravated by an "exhausting diarrhea, from ten to twelve thin watery evacuations daily," recounted George C. Rable in his 2002 book *Fredericksburg! Fredericksburg!* (p. 105). Homer, age twenty-six, died several weeks later after recovering from typhoid but eventually succumbing to successive bouts of diarrhea. Dietary deficiencies also caused such prominent and deadly diseases as scurvy and dyspepsia, but diarrhea was the most common.

A DEADLY TREATMENT

Surgeons in the Civil War operated under difficult conditions. Despite their heroic efforts, they often could not save their patients, who suffered from wounds and complications for which the surgeons lacked the proper medicines or technologies. Surgeons also routinely used practices that were more dangerous than helpful. For example, they often treated gunshot wounds by "hermetically sealing" the opening, a practice in which a wound was closed without removing the bullet. The practice was later all but condemned because of its nearly 100 percent mortality rate. George Alexander Otis's 1865 report on surgical procedure during the Civil War recorded only one soldier who made a full recovery after having his wound hermetically sealed. The passage below describes that soldier's treatment for a bullet wound:

> Corporal Peter Welker, Co., A., 1st U.S. Sharpshooters, was admitted July 30th, 1863, into Mount Pleasant Hospital, at Washington, having received, at Manassas Gap, July 23, 1863, a gunshot wound of the chest. The missile entered near the nipple, between the fourth and fifth ribs, traversed the lung, and emerged at the inferior border of the scapula, fracturing the sixth rib. Treatment: Opiates and stimulants, the wound being hermetically sealed. When admitted, the patient had much pain in his chest dyspacea. The latter increased almost to suffocation, and was accompanied by fever. On July 31st the posterior wound gave way, and a profuse discharge of clotted blood and purulent matter escaped. The next day the anterior wound was opened, and a pint of matter of similar character escaped, after which the patient became much better. He continued to improve until furloughed. On December 13th, 1863, when readmitted, he had entirely recovered. (Otis 1865, p. 22)

CARLY S. KALOUSTIAN

SOURCE: *Otis, George Alexander.* Reports on the Extent and Nature of the Materials Available for the Preparation of a Medical and Surgical History of the Rebellion. *Philadelphia: J. B. Lippincott, 1865. Available online from http://galenet.galegroup.com/servlet/.*

Epidemic Diseases

Soldiers weakened by the rigors of military service and protracted exposure to childhood and camp diseases were especially at risk to contract any one of a number of epidemic diseases. An epidemic disease differed from most camp diseases because of the rate of its expansion and the geographic size of its growth. Common Civil War epidemics included malaria, cholera, and small pox, but at times camp diseases such as diarrhea occurred in such widespread numbers that it too could be considered a disease of epidemic proportion. A vaccination existed for small pox but its supply was irregular and the results of the inoculation varied. Civilians constantly worried that approaching armies might introduce an epidemic into their community. Residents of Bartow County, Georgia, located in northwest Georgia, grew so concerned about the rate of small pox in the Army of Tennessee that several dozen families sought refuge at locations far removed from the army months prior to beginning phases of the Atlanta campaign. Army commanders also worried that civilians might transmit epidemic diseases to their forces. While in winter quarters at Dalton, General Joseph E. Johnston (1807–1891) issued firm orders restricting civilian access to his post, citing the risk of the spread of disease as a major factor. Meanwhile in Christiansburg, Virginia, located in southwest Virginia, conditions at Montgomery White Sulphur Springs Hospital reached near chaos as a small pox epidemic ravaged their soldier patients, staff, and the surrounding community. As conditions worsened the psychological and physical hardships imposed on the staff as a result of the disease created internal strife as commanders and their subordinates uncharacteristically sniped at one another, each blaming the other for their post's situation.

Malaria, like small pox, played a prominent role in the war's military history. Commanders serving in mosquito-infested areas had to account for malaria when planning their military campaigns. During the Peninsula campaign Union troop numbers were reduced dramatically by outbreaks of malaria. Gerald F. Linderman recounted the words of one Union soldier in his 1987 book *Embattled Courage: The Experience of Combat in the American Civil War*, that "at times one might sit in the door of his tent and see as many as six or seven funeral parties bearing comrades to their humble resting places.... Our army seemed on the point of annihilation from disease" (p. 116). As the Army of the Potomac approached the Confederate capital Richmond many of its regiments were missing as many as 75 percent of their men due to numerous outbreaks. Malaria rarely killed soldiers but did weaken their bodies, allowing accompanying illnesses such as diarrhea to become increasingly deadly. About 5 percent of soldiers who had malaria died, while more than half returned to active duty following a hospital stay or recuperation period that typically lasted for two or more weeks.

Small pox, malaria, influenza, yellow fever, cholera, and other forms of epidemic disease spread virtually uncontested throughout the war. Even when such diseases were not present, the mere threat of their arrival and dispersion was enough to have a tremendous psychological impact upon a soldier's psyche. Union soldiers such as Alfred Lewis Castleman saw the South as a land of epidemic diseases and some worried that this fact might provide the Confederates with a distinct advantage. Castleman wrote in his 1863 book *The Army of the Potomac, Behind the Scenes*, "They [Confederates] will then, I think, fall back on the Cotton States, luring us on to an enemy more formidable than their guns—rice swamps, hot weather, and yellow fever" (p. 110). Some Confederate civilians saw this as an advantage. In her 1911 book *The Journal of Julia LeGrand, New Orleans 1862–1863* Julia Ellen LeGrand Waitz reproduced this journal entry: "I feel that these insolent invaders with their bragging, should be conquered—come what will. Better to die than to be under their rule. The Yankees have established strict quarantine. The people of the town are frightening them terribly with tales about the yellow fever. We are compelled to laugh at the frequent amusing accounts" (p. 46).

Venereal and Behavioral Diseases

Venereal disease too struck numerous soldiers, embarrassing the infected and further reducing their side's effective fighting force. Such disease typically involved a plethora of symptoms including, but not limited to, painful urination, genital swelling, persistent rash, and genital bleeding. The surviving medical records of the Army of Tennessee indicate that no soldier died as a result of a venereal disease, but fewer than half of those infected returned to active duty. Camp followers, like prostitutes, transmitted venereal diseases such as gonorrhea, syphilis, and herpes to soldiers. This became such a problem for the Army of Tennessee that surgeons opened a venereal disease hospital in Kingston, Georgia. During winter 1863–1864, Army of Tennessee general Joseph E. Johnston received reports that many of his men at winter quarters in Dalton, Georgia, had been slipping south along the railroad to a house located on the northern bank of the Etowah River. There, the men were reportedly soliciting the services of a known prostitute, Mary Edwards. Eager to stop this behavior, Johnston ordered a detachment of cavalry to destroy Edwards' brothel. The horse soldiers attached chains to the building and pulled it off of its rock foundation, toppling it into the Etowah River. Enraged, Edwards wrote an angry letter to Georgia governor Joseph E. Brown protesting Johnston's actions. Brown, unaware of the details of the situation, forwarded her letter along with a few harsh words of his own to Johnston. Johnston curtly replied, defending his actions and claimed that women such as Edwards had "disabled more men than the enemy" through their illicit behavior.

A number of behavioral diseases also impacted the daily lives of Civil War soldiers, such as alcoholism and other forms of drug addiction. Most soldiers drank, but many developed severe alcohol problems. Alcohol provided soldiers with a release from the stressful toll of daily life. During periods of inactivity, such as winter quarters, alcohol relieved boredom and tempered feelings of homesickness. Jenkins Lloyd Jones, in his 1914 book *An Artilleryman's Diary*, notes from December 1864 when serving in Savannah, "Our camp is right by a liquor saloon, which is sold indiscriminately. Nearly all of a neighboring regiment are beastly drunk, and with their unearthly yells and maniac demonstrations are making the air hideous. Our own Battery also presents a sad sight. Last night—was helplessly drunk.... Oh, why will not out officers put a stop to this demoralization" (p. 280).

Soldiers recovering from battle wounds, particularly Union soldiers, frequently received pain relievers such as morphine and laudanum either during surgery or throughout their recuperation. Supplies of these painkillers were limited in the Confederacy due to the blockade and poor domestic production. Morphine and laudanum were highly addictive painkillers necessary, though not always available, to ease a soldier's pain during intensive surgical procedures such as amputations. Surgeons, however, also used these drugs as sleep aids. Wounded soldiers recovering in hospitals regularly received various assorted doses of morphine to induce sleep. Such usage over even a short period of several days was enough to produce a life-long addiction for many soldiers. Post bellum physicians further aggravated the problem through their continued over-reliance on those and other painkillers. Civil War veteran surgeon and post bellum physician Robert T. Ellett of Christiansburg, Virginia, for example, routinely prescribed morphine to patients experiencing difficulty sleeping or hypertension. For those affected, postwar drug addiction was a wartime legacy many soldiers carried with them for the rest of their lives.

The Civil War was a medical catastrophe. More soldiers died from disease than battle. Most physicians and surgeons had little understanding about the relationship between soldiers' physical environment and their state of health. Medical personnel treated the disease and not the patient, frequently conquering one only to lose to another enemy whose presence attracted less attention. If they must die, soldiers wanted to do so with their face to the enemy in a manner somehow befitting all the glories of war. Disease brought a slow painful death void of heroism, yet all too familiar for most soldiers.

BIBLIOGRAPHY

Castleman, Alfred Lewis. *The Army of the Potomac, Behind the Scenes: A Diary of Unwritten History: from the Organization of the Army ... to the Close of the Campaign in Virginia, about the First Day of January, 1863.* Milwaukee, WI: Strickland and Co., 1863.

Courtwright, David T. "The Hidden Epidemic: Opiate Addiction and Cocaine Use in the South, 1860–1920," *Journal of Southern History* 49, no. 1 (February 1983): 57–72.

Gone With the Wind. Directed by Victor Fleming. MGM Pictures, 1939.

Jackson, David P., ed. *The Colonel's Diary: Journals Kept before and during the Civil War by the Late Colonel Oscar L. Jackson of Newcastle, Pennsylvania, Sometime Commander of the 63rd Regiment O. V. I.* New Castle, PA: David P. Jackson, [1922].

Jones, Jenkins Lloyd. *An Artilleryman's Diary.* Madison: Wisconsin History Commission, 1914.

Linderman, Gerald F. *Embattled Courage: The Experience of Combat in the American Civil War.* New York: Free Press, 1987.

McPherson, James M. *Ordeal by Fire: The Civil War and Reconstruction.* 3rd ed. New York: McGraw-Hill, 2001.

Northrop, John Worrell. *Chronicles from the Diary of a War Prisoner in Andersonville and Other Military Prisons of the South in 1864* . Wichita, KS: J. W. Northrop, 1904.

Rable, George C. *Fredericksburg! Fredericksburg!* Chapel Hill: University of North Carolina Press, 2002.

Robertson, James I., Jr. *Soldiers Blue & Gray.* Columbia: University of South Carolina Press, 1988.

Shyrock, Richard H. "A Medical Perspective on the Civil War," *American Quarterly* 14, no. 2 (Summer 1962): 161–173.

Smedley, Charles. *Life in Southern Prisons from the Diary of Corporal Charles Smedley, of Company G, 90th Regiment Penn's Volunteers, Commencing a Few Days before the Battle of the Wilderness.* [Lancaster, PA:] Ladies' and Gentleman's Fulton Aid Society, 1865.

Waitz, Julia Ellen LeGrand. *The Journal of Julia LeGrand, New Orleans 1862–1863.* Richmond, VA: Everett Waddey Co., 1911.

Keith S. Hébert

Surgeons

When the U.S. Civil War began in April 1861, both the Union and Confederate sides were woefully underprepared to deal with the heavy flow of casualties that would soon result. New and ballistically advanced weaponry meant that an arm or leg bone could be easily shattered from a distance of several hundred yards. Many physicians of the era had been well trained at the medical schools that had sprung up in the first half of the nineteenth century, but their education rarely included the treatment of battlefield injuries.

AN AFRICAN AMERICAN SURGEON IN THE UNION ARMY

Cortlandt van Rensselaer Creed, M.D. (1833–1900), was the first black graduate of Yale and the first black person to receive a medical degree from an Ivy League university. Born in New Haven, Connecticut, Creed was the grandson of Prince Duplex, a soldier in the Revolutionary War who gained his freedom from slavery by serving in the Continental Army. Creed's mother, Vashti Duplex, was the first black schoolteacher in New Haven. His father, John William Creed, a native of the West Indies, worked as a Yale janitor but also built up a highly successful local catering business. Creed's parents were married by the Reverend Leonard Bacon, a professor of theology at Yale and an outspoken abolitionist.

Cortlandt Creed could not apply to Yale as an undergraduate because of his race; however, what was then known as the Medical Department of Yale College (now the School of Medicine of Yale University) was separate from the undergraduate school and accepted Creed when he applied in 1854. He completed his M.D. in 1857, submitting a dissertation on the circulation of the blood to fulfill the degree requirements. After graduation, Creed developed successful mixed-race practices in both New Haven and Brooklyn, New York. When the Civil War began in 1861, Creed offered his services as a field surgeon but was initially turned down because he was black. When Abraham Lincoln authorized the recruitment of black troops in 1863, however, Creed became acting surgeon of the 30th Regiment U.S.C. Infantry and served at the front until the end of the war in 1865. "On every side," he wrote, "we behold colored sons rallying to the sound of Liberty and Union" (Medical News Today).

Creed gained a considerable reputation after the war as an outstanding surgeon and medical examiner, being frequently mentioned in the New York Times as well as the local New Haven newspapers. When President James Garfield was shot in July 1881, Creed was consulted by surgeons in Washington to help locate the bullet in Garfield's body in order to remove it before infection could develop. X-ray machines did not yet exist and surgeons often found it difficult to find bullets within soft tissue. Garfield died of generalized blood poisoning two months after the shooting.

REBECCA J. FREY

BIBLIOGRAPHY

Creed, Cortlandt van Rensselaer. "Dissertation on the Blood." M.D. thesis, Yale Medical Department, 1857.

"Honoring First African American Alumnus." Yale Medicine (Autumn 2007): 50–51.

"Yale Celebrates 150th Anniversary of First African American Graduate." Medical News Today, May 31, 2007. Available online from http://www.medicalnewstoday.com/articles/72602.php.

Nor were these newly enlisted army doctors immune from the dangers of battle themselves—indeed, they were as much at risk of death or injury from enemy fire as were ordinary soldiers and officers. One surgeon, John H. Brinton, with a naval convoy near Belmont, Missouri, recalled that as he "stood on the front of our boat . . . I saw a puff of smoke afar off, and in a few seconds a huge projectile flew past us, and far above our heads." A second projectile that followed, he continued, "seemed to give birth to a black line, at first well up above the Mississippi, but gradually sinking as it came nearer. It seemed to making a bee-line for my eye, but fortunately changed its mind" (Brinton 1914, p. 72).

Dire Shortage of Doctors

About 1.5 million men served three-year stints in the Union Army, though an equal number served briefer three-month stints. The most accurate Confederate Army figures suggest a total force of 1.2 million, with two-thirds, or 800,000 men, serving a full three years (Heidler 2002, p. 373). Yet at the outset of the war there were only a handful of surgeons who were genuinely qualified as battlefield trauma specialists. To remedy this, civilian doctors were recruited to become field surgeons. These men left their positions at urban hospitals and medical schools, and their families, to serve in the Army as commissioned personnel.

Neither the War Department in Washington, DC, nor the one in Richmond, the Confederate capital, had adequate stockpiles of medical supplies at the onset of the conflict. In civilian life surgeons customarily carried their own instruments with them, a practice that continued in the field hospitals. These items included scalpels, bullet extractors, and clamps to stanch bleeding vessels. Surgeons also carried a supply of sewing needles and catgut to close wounds. The majority of battlefield wounds came from conical-shaped lead bullets known as *Minié balls*, which were fired from .58-caliber musket rifles; used by both sides, these bullets were ideal for shattering bones.

Primitive Conditions

Two types of hospitals were used during the Civil War: field hospitals, which were temporary and traveled with an Army division; and general hospitals, which were located further away from the battlefield. Railroad cars and river steamboats were also converted into medical-treatment facilities, especially in the North. The wounded would be carried by other soldiers to the surgical field stations after a retreat, or sometimes by local civilians recruited to help. A field station might be a tent or barn, but more often was simply a designated area out in the open, marked by a green flag to signify to enemy shooters that medical treatment was taking place.

At field hospitals, surgeons often used an ordinary wagon tailgate, or two barrels with a door stretched across, as an operating table. Nearby might be an Autenrieth medicine wagon, a four-wheeled vehicle that served as a mobile pharmacy and was stocked with medicines and surgical supplies. Chloroform, a liquid created by mixing chlorine and methane, had recently begun to replace ether as an anesthetic. Ether was a far more flammable compound, and thus potentially dangerous on the battlefield.

For injuries to the arms, legs, hands, and feet caused by Minié balls, amputation was the most commonplace procedure. While awaiting treatment, the injured soldier would be dosed with whiskey and, if it was available, opium, a powerful narcotic. Once he was brought to the operating table, anesthesia was administered via a rag soaked with chloroform or ether and placed over the nose and mouth. A surgical assistant would then begin counting aloud the passing seconds, which was done for two reasons: The patient would not be stunned into unconsciousness by chloroform or ether indefinitely, and recent medical advances showed that the quicker an operation was performed, the better the prognosis. Furthermore, the sooner a wound was closed up, the less chance there was of sepsis, or infection. The ideal surgery, according to common wisdom, lasted less than three minutes.

"The Veterans of a Hundred Fights"

A scalpel made the first incision, and arteries were tied off with oiled silk; a bone saw completed the amputation. Piles of severed limbs, especially during such major battles as Gettysburg and Chickamauga, were left in heaps at the roadside, or carried off by local farmers as pig feed. The stump was then doused with carbolic acid (also known as phenol), a strong disinfectant that also sped up the formation of scar tissue. Sanitary conditions, however, were still quite primitive. "We operated in old blood-stained and often pus-stained coats, the veterans of a hundred fights," wrote one surgeon, W. W. Keen, a half-century later. "We used undisinfected instruments from undisinfected plush-lined cases, and still worse, used marine sponges which had been used in prior pus cases and only washed in tap water" (Keen 1918, p. 24). Keen also recalled that

> silk to tie blood vessels was undisinfected. One end was left long hanging out of the wound and after three or four days was daily pulled to see if the loop on the blood vessel had rotted loose. When it came away, if a blood clot had formed and closed the blood vessel, well and good; if no such clot had formed then a dangerous "secondary" hemorrhage followed and not seldom was fatal. (Keen 1918, p. 24)

Wounds often became infected by gangrene, a type of tissue death that affects extremities when blood flow is restricted; this infection often then spread from the dead tissue to living tissue. Many firsthand reports written by those who worked in or visited military medical facilities noted that gangrene's particular stench was overwhelming.

At field hospitals, surgeons toiled under grueling conditions, bound to service by an Army rule that required them to remain at their post until every wounded soldier had received medical attention. Twenty-four-hour stretches at a field operating unit without food or rest were not uncommon, and there were reports of surgeons simply collapsing from exhaustion, then returning to work after their colleagues revived them. Hands rife with blisters and swollen feet were two of the most common signs of overwork for field doctors, but doctors were also subject to those infectious diseases that are estimated to have killed more Union and Confederate soldiers than bullets—namely, dysentery, typhoid fever, and malaria.

Field surgeons frequently had to cross enemy lines after control of territory had changed hands, in order to bring back their side's wounded. Doctor J. Franklin Dyer kept a journal during his three years with the 19th Massachusetts Infantry and wrote scores of letters home to his wife. One recounted a battle on the Potomac River, which concluded with a Confederate victory. The Confederate colonel informed Dyer's commanding officer that "a surgeon would be permitted to cross and attend to the wounded still remaining. On preparing to cross I was told by Colonel Burt [the Confederate officer] that I should be held as a prisoner, . . . [after which] I declined to cross. He was not well pleased and expressed a great desire to shoot me. He was unquestionably drunk" (Dyer 2003, pp. 7–8).

How-To Manuals

Surgeons were provided with some instructions on how to treat gunshot wounds, which were relatively rare in civilian life at the time. To Union doctors, U.S. Surgeon General William Alexander Hammond issued *Military, Medical, and Surgical Essays*, which contained crucial information on the treatment of battlefield injuries and on ways to to reduce the chance of infections from poor sanitary conditions at camp. Confederate physicians were similarly provided with J. Julius Chisholm's *Manual of Military Surgery*. The Confederacy, however, was at a dire disadvantage, despite the fact that several Army doctors based in Washington, DC, had fled the capital at the onset of war to serve in their native South and for its military. The South's medical resources were limited, and the situation only worsened as the war dragged on and supply lines were cut. John H. Worsham, a soldier with the 21st Regiment Virginia Infantry, was surprised "how the Confederacy got along with such a small variety of medicines, which consisted, in the field, almost entirely of blue powders, one kind of pills, and quinine" (Worsham 1912, p. 160).

The Surgeon-General's Office of the Confederate States of America even issued its field physicians an 1862 tome titled *General Directions for Collecting and*

Army doctors performing an amputation. Advancements in weaponry resulted in greater horrific injuries on the combat lines. The majority of doctors on both sides of the conflict had never faced such large scale carnage but soon learned how to expediently handle amputations and other operations under makeshift conditions. *Hulton Archive/Getty Images.*

Drying Medicinal Substances of the Vegetable Kingdom, which was a comprehensive guide to the plants of the Southern states and their various medicinal properties. The Confederate doctor Herbert M. Nash recalled

> the winter quarters of 1863–4, when the younger and men of the artillery of [General Alexander P.] Hill's corps, to which I was now attached, and nearly all of whom expected to return to college again if not killed in battle, sent to the University of Virginia for text-books, had regular hours for study when not engaged in military exercises, and at night by the light of fatted-pine torches (candles not to be had)... Mathematics and Latin and Greek authors were studied with deep interest under the supervision of our chaplain, himself a scholar of no mean pretensions. Joining these classes, I soon found that after a long neglect of the classics the effort to construe Horace was no easy task, especially while seated on a log, and by the light of a pine-knot. (Nash 1938 [1906], pp. 2–3)

Forerunner of the Army Medical Corps

Civil War doctors also treated the wounded at newly established general hospitals, located much farther away from the battlefield, such as Chimborazo Hospital in the Confederate capital of Richmond, which had 6,000 beds and was the largest military medical facility in North America at the time (*Medicine of the Civil War*, 1973, p. 5). In the North, Hammond, who took over as U.S. Surgeon General in April 1862, managed to implement several new procedures that comprised major advances in military medicine. These included an inspection system for hospitals—the guidelines of which were laid out in one section of the *Military, Medical, and Surgical Essays*—and the creation of a genuine ambulance corps for emergency medical care in wartime. Previously, when it became necessary to move large numbers of wounded or recovering men from field hospitals, the Army Quartermaster would commonly hire civilians to serve as drivers. But according to one Union doctor, Henry I. Bowditch, these drivers "were men of the lowest character, evidently taken from the vilest purlieus of Washington" (Bowditch 1863, n.p.).

Bowditch recalled that the drivers of the wagon train he traveled in were seemingly in no hurry to reach the wounded at Centreville; they frequently stopped to rest their horses, and after his own driver began falling asleep, Bowditch was forced to take the reins and drive through the night. Upon spotting a fruit orchard the next day, the drivers stole fruit from the trees. Finally, upon reaching the wounded, "the drivers did not feel it to be their duty to help the sufferers, but sulked, or swore, or laughed, as it pleased each" (1863, n.p.). Bowditch delivered a report on this state of affairs to the Boston Society for Medical Improvement on September 22, 1862. Not long afterward, his own son, a lieutenant, was wounded and died on the battlefield for lack of a stretcher and medical personnel to bring him to a field hospital.

U.S. Surgeon General Hammond and his second-in-command in Washington, Dr. Jonathan Letterman, were successful in winning approval for the creation of a legitimate Ambulance Corps, which was first deployed as a regular army unit at the Battle of Antietam. Its drivers were military personnel attached to the Medical Department of the Army of the Potomac, and as such subject to the strictest military discipline. The immediate improvement in treatment and casualty rates that resulted from their work led Congress to approve the Ambulance Corps Act of March 11, 1864, which established such units in all army divisions.

First Female Army Doctor

While women during the Civil War were almost entirely relegated to work as nurses, one notable woman did serve as an Army surgeon, though her military career was marked by controversy and a few instances of open hostility. Mary Edwards Walker was a native of Oswego, New York, and earned her M.D. from Syracuse Medical College in 1855. She was an advocate of women's rights and known for her habit of wearing men's trousers, which was a shocking sight for most at the time and considered an outrageous blurring of gender lines. At the outbreak of war, she traveled to Washington to work in a general hospital but was required to serve as a nurse, not a physician. In 1862 she traveled to Virginia battlefields and began treating the wounded, while formally requesting a military commission.

A year later, Walker was appointed the surgeon for a Union outfit positioned near Chattanooga, Tennessee—because her predecessor had died, and she was the nearest qualified surgeon. The regiment was fiercely opposed to having a woman doctor, and some members formally petitioned the Army to rescind her appointment. At one point, Walker was accused of spying for the Confederacy and was briefly detained as a prisoner of war, but in September of 1864 she finally won an Army commission that gave her a salary of $100 per month and made her the first commissioned female surgeon of the U.S. Army. She eventually won over many of the men, particularly because of her belief that many of the amputations performed were unnecessary. Walker was later awarded the Congressional Medal of Honor, but after her discharge in 1865 she was given a meager pension that was less than some veterans' widows received.

Medical Advances

Life-saving techniques were perfected by the surgeons who risked their lives to treat the wounded, and these advances were crucial to the development of modern medicine and trauma care. The estimated 500,000 injuries treated by doctors on both sides represented a massive, hands-on teaching experience that resulted in the development of new and more efficient surgical techniques and led to groundbreaking ideas about postoperative care (Smith 2001 [1962], p. 2). Indeed, the first federal medical research facility in the United States was established as a result of the war, when the Army Medical Museum began collecting scores of pathology specimens for investigative purposes. This facility later became the National Museum of Health and Medicine.

BIBLIOGRAPHY

Bowditch, Henry I. *A Brief Plea for an Ambulance System for the Army of the United States, As Drawn from the Extra Sufferings of the Late Lieut. Bowditch and a Wounded Comrade.* Boston: Ticknor & Fields, 1863.

Brinton, John H. *Personal Memoirs of John H. Brinton, Major and Surgeon U.S.V., 1861–1865.* New York: Neale Publishing Company, 1914.

Dyer, J. Franklin. *The Journal of a Civil War Surgeon*, ed. Michael B. Chesson. Lincoln: University of Nebraska Press, 2003.

Heidler, David Stephen, Jeanne T. Heidler, and David J. Coles. *Encyclopedia of the American Civil War: A Political, Social, and Military History.* New York: W. W. Norton, 2002.

Keen, W. W. "Military Surgery in 1861 and 1918." *Annals of the American Academy of Political and Social Science* 80: *Rehabilitation of the Wounded.* Philadelphia: American Academy of Political and Social Science, 1918.

Medicine of the Civil War. Bethesda, MD: National Library of Medicine, 1973. Available from http://www.nlm.nih.gov/.

Nash, Herbert M. "Some Reminiscences of a Confederate Surgeon." *Transactions of the College of Physicians of Philadelphia*, 3rd ser., no. 28 (1906): 122–144. Reprinted in College of Physicians of Philadelphia, *Transactions of the College of Physicians of Philadelphia*, 3rd series. Philadelphia: College of Physicians of Philadelphia, 1938.

Smith, George Winston. *Medicines for the Union Army: The United States Army Laboratories during the Civil War.* Madison, WI: American Institute of the History of Pharmacy, 1962, Reprint, Binghamton, NY: Haworth Press, 2001.

Worsham, John H. *One of Jackson's Foot Cavalry; His Experience and What He Saw during the War 1861–1865.* New York: Neale Publishing Company, 1912.

Carol Brennan

■ Nursing

NURSING: AN OVERVIEW

The Civil War was a watershed moment in the history of the American nursing profession. The war served as the primary impetus fueling an increasing demand for and recognition of the contributions of nurses as medical care providers. Prior to 1861, men dominated the newly developed nursing profession. During the war, the demand for nurses quickly outpaced the existing supply, providing women with opportunities to volunteer outside the home. By 1865 Americans no longer considered nursing to be a male occupation. And it was the wartime sacrifices of tens of thousands of women that made possible the profession's postbellum development.

Antebellum Nursing

The term *nurse* lacked any uniform definition during the antebellum period, due in part to deficiencies in nursing's professional development. Today, nursing is an occupation within the medical profession. Prior to the Civil War, the term *nurse* typically described someone who cared for children or was a wet nurse. Some excerpts from the "help wanted" advertisements published in the New York *Evening Post* in 1824 reflect such usage. For example, an advertisement placed on March 11, 1824, read: "A Nurse Wanted—wanted, a middle aged woman, capable of taking care of children. Apply at No. 77 Fulton Street." A similar advertisement in May 1824 read: "Wet Nurse: A Healthy young woman, with a good fresh breast of milk, wants a situation in the above capacity, in a respectable family. The most respectable references can be produced, as to character, ability, &c." In addition, Southern plantation households used similar language when referring to slaves who worked in the nursery.

Throughout American history, mothers and other female members of households traditionally worked within the home, where they attended to the bulk of their family's medical needs. While the use of male physicians increased during the antebellum period, mothers still exercised great authority, because patients by and large remained at home, and only rarely received care in a hospital. Many of the first female nurses to work outside the home were the spouses and daughters of male physicians, whom they routinely accompanied during house calls. These women served as an invaluable buffer between the male physician and the household's females, often working more as a source of comfort and support than as a medical care provider.

Several factors hampered the development of the antebellum nursing profession. Demand for nurses existed only in the nation's few hospitals. Such facilities were rare, except in such cities as New York, Boston, and Philadelphia. Gender-based expectations also inhibited the profession. Though by and large it was men who worked as nurses, nursing was still considered a feminine activity and was associated with mothers, not professionals. A lack of training and educational opportunities also limited the profession's development. Most nurses learned their skills through observation rather than as part of a regimented training program. Elizabeth Blackwell, the first woman to receive a medical degree in America, saw a need to develop such a program. In 1858 she started the nation's first nurses' training school at the New York Infirmary. Her efforts, however, were more reflective of her own feminist program than representative of any mass movement toward educating nurses.

Antebellum attitudes toward women and toward sex also hampered the profession's development. If nursing was conceived as a feminine activity, women were nonetheless considered poorly suited to serve as professional nurses. Antebellum women were seen by American culture as too weak, physically and emotionally, to endure the sight of blood. A female nurse, it was also believed, would be unable to control male patients. Perhaps most importantly, they would be exposed to the sight of male genitalia. While those prejudices were influential, the principal factor hampering the profession's development remained the lackluster demand for nursing, a reflection of the domestic nature of antebellum healthcare.

Florence Nightingale (1820–1910) and Mary Seacole (1805–1881), British nurses during the Crimean

War (1853–1856), directly influenced Civil War nursing. Nightingale's efforts to improve sanitary conditions for British soldiers in Scutari, Turkey, attracted international attention and directly influenced the duties of Civil War nurses. Her focus on sanitation was unprecedented. Like Nightingale, Mary Seacole—a woman of mixed racial ethnicity—nursed soldiers serving in frontline units and frequented the battlefields tending to the wounded. Both women were acclaimed by American newspapers, which printed many stories documenting their heroism. Those stories helped to recast the image of the nurse in the American imagination.

In 1860 Nightingale opened the Nightingale Training School at St. Thomas Hospital in London. That same year, she published *Notes on Nursing: What It Is, and What It Is Not.* This book served as the standard nursing text for decades. In it, Nightingale clearly defines nursing as women's work: "If, then, every woman must at some time or other of her life," she wrote, "become a nurse, *i.e.*, have charge of somebody's health, how immense and how valuable would be the produce of her united experience if every woman would think how to nurse" (Nightingale 1860, preface). The book also established a set of practical guidelines that defined nurses' distinctive role in providing health care. Nightingale fashioned nurses as sanitary crusaders and observers who monitored the health of men—duties that formed the daily life of Civil War nurses.

Civil War Nursing

Nurses, both male and female, have cared for wounded soldiers in every American war. During the Civil War, nurses worked in hospitals, on the battlefield, and in their homes. The war significantly altered the course of American nursing in two major ways. First, the carnage of the war created an unprecedented demand for nurses. This need made it possible for nursing to become a standard occupation within the American medical profession. Second, while the majority of wartime nurses were male, the contributions of thousands of female nurses helped alter the image of the professional nurse and changed American nursing from a male-dominated to a largely female profession. The Civil War set the stage for subsequent developments in the history of American nursing.

A myriad of factors motivated Americans to become nurses during the Civil War. "I long to be a man," wrote Louisa May Alcott, author of *Little Women* (1868–1869), who served as a Civil War nurse, "but as I can't fight, I will content myself with working for those who can" (Young 1996, p. 448). Judith White Brockenbrough echoed similar sentiments when she wrote: "We must do what we can for the comfort of our brave men. We must sew for them, knit for them, nurse the sick, keep-up the faint hearted, give them a word of encouragement in season and out of season" (McGuire 1889, p. 13).

Estimating the number of nurses who served during the Civil War is difficult, due to the destruction of Confederate Medical Department records, the large number of volunteer nurses, and the haphazard manner in which the military identified nurses. While an exact figure is impossible to provide, it has been estimated that there were as many as 400,000 Civil War nurses, though that number includes individuals who performed duties associated with but not directly related to nursing. During the war, the term *nurse* was associated with a variety of duties and types of individual. It did not by any means refer only to trained medical professionals. For example, both armies still referred to slave women charged with the care of children as nurses. Men whose work in the hospital involved such menial chores as chopping wood or transporting soldiers were often referred to as nurses. The word was also used for agents of the Sanitary Commission or Christian Commission, and for nuns from the Sisters of Mercy or Sisters of Charity. It might also be used to describe a person charged with caring for an ailing soldier within the privacy of their home, or a woman who accompanied her husband in camp, tending to the sick and wounded.

Some generalizations can be made about Civil War nurses. A majority were enlisted soldiers pressed into duty as nurses. While many soldiers fulfilled this assignment admirably, others did not. After the Battle of Shiloh, Union Army surgeon Robert Murray advocated for future use of fulltime nurses, a group that included a large number of women. Murray complained that wounded soldiers were "left partially attended to by an unwilling and forced detail of panic-stricken deserters from the battle-field" (*The War of the Rebellion*, ser. 1, vol. 10, p. 299). Soldier nurses were routinely accused of shirking the more dangerous duties of the frontline soldier. Both armies created strict regulations that governed who among the enlisted ranks would serve as nurses. While most regiments detailed active soldiers, male nurses in general hospitals tended to be convalescing soldiers recovering from their injuries.

There were several ways for women and men to become nurses. Some were mustered into service by the military and received payment for their work. Most women volunteered, either through local or national associations or by receiving permission from a commanding officer. The majority of female volunteers came from middle-class or upper-class social backgrounds, which enabled them to leave their homes for extended periods while others (servants, parents, or slaves) tended to their domestic affairs. These women usually earned no compensation. Still other women, and most men who worked as nurses, had their duties thrust upon them in ad hoc fashion, due to their proximity to a battlefield or field hospital.

The war significantly altered the development of the nursing profession. The entrance of women into nursing

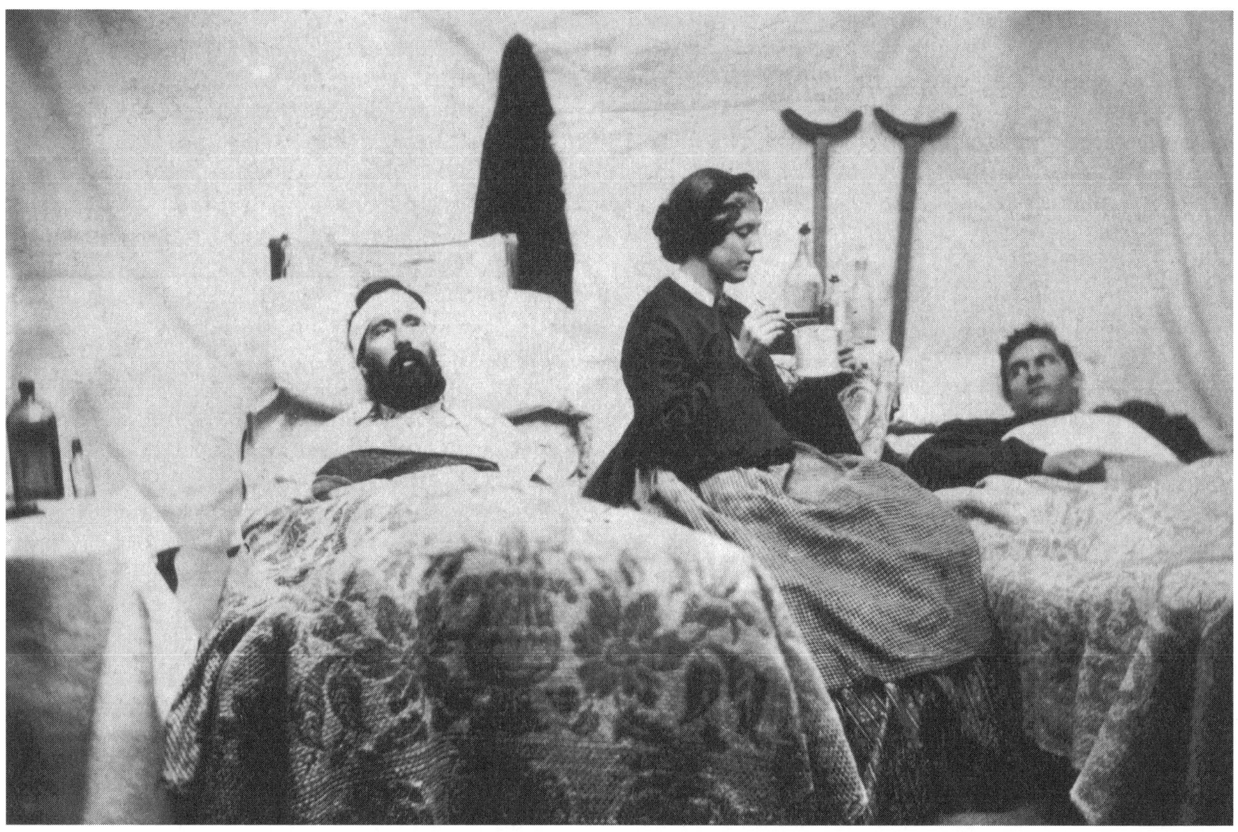

Nurse caring for wounded soldiers. As Civil War fighting created battle injuries on an unprecedented scale, nurses quickly demonstrated their value by tending to the sick. Though most of the nurses serving during the conflict were male, the thousands of women who proved themselves as capable volunteers established nursing as an acceptable field of employment for women after the war. *© Corbis.*

outside the home was a significant new development, even if men in the ranks comprised the majority of wartime nurses. Nonetheless, there continued to be resistance to female nurses. "It seems," wrote Kate Cumming, a volunteer nurse serving in the Confederate Army of Tennessee, "that surgeons entertain great prejudices against admitting ladies into the hospital in the capacity as nurses" (Cumming 1998 [1866], p. 12). "Hardly a surgeon of whom I can think received or treated them [women nurses] with even common courtesy," wrote volunteer nurse Georgeanna M. Woolsey (Bacon 2001 [1899], p. 142). "Government had decided that women should be employed, and the army surgeons—unable, therefore, to close the hospitals against them—determined to make their lives so unbearable that they should be forced in self-defense to leave" (Bacon 2001 [1899], p. 142).

If many surgeons initially saw female nurses as a potential threat to their authority, such objections grew increasingly less pronounced as women nurses proved their worth. In fact, some physicians strongly advocated their usage, or sought to recruit them. On May 14, 1861, a Georgia physician, H. L. Byrd, made an emotional plea in the Savannah *Daily Morning News* soliciting female nurses. "Every physician of experience," he wrote, "knows that much of his success depends upon the *nurse* who attends upon his patients in civil practice.... It is much more important that he should have an *educated nurse* upon the battle field."

Initially, both armies accepted female nurses with great reluctance and only under strict guidelines. In the Union Army, for example, the superintendent of women nurses, Dorothea Dix (1802–1887), established a set of criteria that women had to meet. "No woman under thirty years need apply to serve in government hospitals," wrote Dix. "All nurses are required to be very plain-looking women. Their dresses must be brown or black, with no bows, no curls, no jewelry, and no hoopskirts" (Young 1959, p. 61). On August 2, 1862, *Frank Leslie's Illustrated Newspaper* reported "that several young ladies of ... [Kingston, New York] volunteered as army nurses, but have been rejected on account of their good looks." Regulations also forbade female nurses from fraternizing with patients and frowned upon excessive physical contact.

The sights, sounds, and smells of Civil War hospitals were also major obstacles for many women. Civil War nurse Amanda Akin Stearns, who volunteered at the Armory Square Hospital in Washington, DC, described her initial trepidation: "I meekly followed through the long ward, unable to return the gaze of the occupants of twenty-six beds, to the table in the center, and with a sinking heart watched her [the matron] raise the head of a poor fellow in the last stages of typhoid, to give him a soothing draught. Could I ever do that? For once my courage failed" (Stearns 1909, p. 13). Cumming remembered that the "foul air from the mass of human beings at first made me giddy and sick, but I soon got over it" (Cumming 1998 [1866], p. 15). In 1864, after having served as a nurse, Georgeanna Woolsey warned women who aspired to become nurses that such work was inappropriate for "a delicate creature whose head is full only of the romance of the work" (Woolsey 1864, pp. 136–137).

The regimented daily life of a Civil War hospital helped nurses overcome the revulsion brought on by the sights, sounds, and smells they encountered. "My day begins early," wrote Emily Elizabeth Parsons; with "reveille at six, I must be up before to get the beds made, ward swept out, dressings attended to, and wounds unbandaged and washed ready for the surgeon's inspection" (Parsons 1984 [1880], pp. 18–21). Stearns described her hospital ward as a "solar system: every ward revolves around on its own axis" (Stearns 1909, p. 15). The daily work of female nurses mirrored the standards established by Nightingale's *Notes on Nursing*, as it was primarily focused on improving the sanitary conditions of a hospital and observing patients to better attend to their needs. Female nurses generally were not seen as medical care providers. They did dispense medicine, change bandages, and perform other medically related chores, but their daily tasks revolved more around sweeping floors, opening windows, circulating air, preparing meals, and consoling patients.

Sometimes, female nurses and the wounded soldiers they treated forged a unique bond. Many wounded soldiers arrived at a hospital scared and fearful of death. The hospital greeted them with putrid smells and gory sights that prevented a soldier from emotionally escaping the carnage of the battlefield. Numerous sources record that during periods of intense pain and fear, wounded soldiers in the field and in hospitals frequently called out for their mothers. Women thus were able to fill a role that men could not: surrogate mother. Elizabeth Comstock, a Union nurse, described a particularly touching encounter with one wounded soldier: "He opened his eyes, and, with an earnest appealing look at me, tried to speak. There was sufficient of memory and of reason left for him to remember his mother, and of sight to see that a woman stood beside him: and, mistaking me for his far-distant mother, he said 'Mother, I knew you would come'" (Comstock 1895, pp. 114–115). Louisa May Alcott recalled that wounded soldiers wanted a woman's touch: "I had forgotten that the strong man might long for the gentler tendance of a woman's hands," she wrote, "the sympathetic magnetism of a woman's presence" (Alcott 2004 [1863], p. 88).

Providing medical care for wounded enemy soldiers sometimes pitted a nurse's responsibilities against her national sympathies. Nurses usually acted in a professional manner, tending to the enemy's needs while privately displaying their prejudices. Union nurse Abby Hopper Gibbons recalled, "We have always observed that the Rebs make more noise when they are suffering than our men do" (Gibbons 1896–1897, p. 89). Nurses on both sides of the conflict tended to see the enemy as an inferior example of masculinity compared to their own soldiers. Overall, however, they treated enemy soldiers quite well, as evidenced by the writings of Union nurse and spy Sarah Emma Edmonds:

> [As] I looked upon...[the rebel soldier] in his helpless condition, I did not feel the least resentment, or entertain an unkind thought toward him personally, but looked upon him only as an unfortunate, suffering man, whose sad condition called forth the best feelings of my nature; and I longed to restore him to health and strength; not considering that the very health and strength I wished to secure for him would be employed against the cause which I espoused. (Edmonds 1865, p. 154)

Medical personnel attached to armies in the field also routinely exposed themselves to the additional risk of being captured by the enemy. During a battle, nurses did their best to move the wounded to the rear, where surgeons were stationed. Many enlisted nurses died while attempting such feats. During a retreat, they had to decide whether to flee with the army or remain behind and treat the wounded. When the Union Army fled from the battlefield at Chickamauga, blue-clad medical staff tending to the wounded at two field hospitals, Crawfish Springs and Cloud's Farm, remained and fell into enemy hands. Confederate forces removed all of the nurses from the two field hospitals, minus one who was allowed to remain to treat a wounded Confederate officer. When an unidentified medical staff member asked what could be done for a severely wounded Union sergeant, a Confederate officer reportedly replied, "Take the damn Yankee out and shoot him...[that] is the proper way of disposing of him" (*The War of the Rebellion,* ser. 2, vol. 6, pp. 567–568). Hundreds of enlisted nurses who remained behind during a retreat to care for the wounded became prisoners of war and had to endure the hardships of life in a Civil War prison camp.

The Civil War significantly altered the course of the nursing profession in America. Due to the actions of women nurses, nursing evolved into a female occupation following the war. The war enabled men to see and accept women as nurses. By the late nineteenth century, nursing schools existed throughout most of the country, providing women with educational opportunities. And, finally, individual acts of compassion and personal sacrifice on the part of Civil War nurses greatly improved the daily lives of hundreds of thousands of wounded soldiers. Nurses were a physical and emotional expression of what was good about humanity during a war that, at times, displayed the nation's most inhumane qualities. Nursing provided women with a way to contribute to the war effort, thereby adding their experiences and stories to a conflict otherwise dominated by male narratives.

BIBLIOGRAPHY

Alcott, Louisa May. *Hospital Sketches*, ed. Alice Fahs. New York: Bedford/St. Martin's, [1863] 2004.

Bacon, Georgeanna Woolsey, and Eliza Woolsey Howland, eds. *Letters of a Family during the War for the Union, 1861–1865.* 2 vols. New Haven, CT: Tuttle, Morehouse, & Taylor, 1899. Reprint, Roseville, MN: Edinborough Press, 2001.

Comstock, Elizabeth L. *Life and Letters of Elizabeth L. Comstock.* Compiled by Catherine Hare. Philadelphia: John C. Winston, 1895.

Culpepper, Marilyn Mayer, and Pauline Gordon Adams. "Nursing in the Civil War." *American Journal of Nursing* 88, no. 7 (1988): 981–984.

Cumming, Kate. *Kate: The Journal of a Confederate Nurse.* Ed. Richard Barksdale Harwell. Baton Rouge: Louisiana State University, 1998. (Orig. pub. in 1866 as *A Journal of Hospital Life in the Confederate Army of Tennessee.*)

Edmonds, Sarah Emma. *Nurse and Spy in the Union Army.* Hartford, CT: W. S. Williams, 1865.

Gibbons, Abby Hopper. *Life of Abby Hopper Gibbons: Told Chiefly through Her Correspondence.* 2 vols. Ed. Sarah Hopper Emerson. New York: G. P. Putnam's Sons, 1896–1897.

McGuire, Judith White Brockenbrough. *Diary of a Southern Refugee, during the War*, 3rd ed. Richmond, VA: J. W. Randolph & English, 1889.

Nightingale, Florence. *Notes on Nursing: What It Is, and What It Is Not.* New York: D. Appleton, 1860.

Parsons, Emily Elizabeth. *Civil War Nursing: Memoir of Emily Elizabeth Parsons.* Boston: Little, Brown, 1880. Reprint, New York: Garland, 1984.

Stearns, Amanda Akin. *The Lady Nurse of Ward E.* New York: Baker & Taylor, 1909.

The War of the Rebellion: A Compilation of the Official Records of the Union and Confederate Armies, 4 series. Washington, DC: Government Printing Office, 1880–1900.

Woolsey, Georgeanna [Georgeanna Woolsey Bacon]. *Spirit of the Fair.* New York: Metropolitan Sanitary Fair, 1864.

Young, Agatha [Agnes Brooks Young]. *The Women and the Crisis: Women of the North in the Civil War.* New York: McDowell & Obolensky, 1959.

Keith S. Hébert

ARMY NURSES

At the onset of the American Civil War in 1861, the U.S. Army Medical Bureau was unprepared for the staggering number of wounded the battlefields would produce over the next four years. There was a corps of trained physicians within the military, with a few doctors specializing in gunshot trauma, but no staff of trained nurses to care for patients. This lack held true in the Confederate states as well, which suffered from a more marked lack of resources and personnel. Regular-duty soldiers were often drafted to help army doctors, and scores of women volunteered as well.

Dorothea Dix

During the mid-nineteenth century, the word *nurse* had not yet come into its common usage to mean a professionally trained person who works in the medical field. Instead it was a term more loosely applied to anyone who helped another during a time of medical distress. There were no schools of nursing at the time; however, a British woman, Florence Nightingale (1820–1910), was working to establish professional guidelines and standards in England. Her work was becoming known in the United States as well. Nightingale shared her ideas with Dorothea Dix (1802–1887), a reformer from the Boston area, already famous for her efforts to improve the care of prisoners and the mentally ill over the previous two decades. Given Dix's reputation, war department officials named her the new superintendent of women nurses in June 1861.

This appointment would become the starting point for the first professional corps of nurses inside the U.S. military; however, Dix's stint as its supervisor was a controversial one. Clashing over entrance requirements with senior officials who wanted more male nurses, Dix firmly believed that women were better suited for the work and decreed that applicants must be at least thirty years of age. This stipulation, she believed, would keep the Army's nursing corps free from women who were seeking to meet a mate, because the age of thirty was considered well past the point of marital eligibility.

According to Ira M. Rutkow, there were between 3,000 and 5,000 women who served as volunteer nurses on both sides of the conflict (Rutkow 2005, p. 170). There were far more male nurses in service, however. Soldiers or recuperating patients were frequently drafted into service in both the field hospitals—which traveled with units and served as urgent-care facilities—and the general hospitals, located further away from the battle sites and designed for longer-term recuperative care. Rutkow estimates that the ratio of male to female nurses was five to one on both the Union and Confederate sides (Rutkow 2005, p. 172).

Long Shifts and Sleep Deprivation

One example of a soldier who was pressed into nursing duty was William Winters, who served with the 67th Indiana Volunteer Infantry Regiment. He was in his early thirties and a father of three when he enlisted, and kept a record of his service and wrote letters home to his wife that were published as *The Musick of the Mocking Birds, the Roar of the Cannon: The Civil War Diary and Letters of William Winters.* He was drafted into nursing service in early 1863 aboard a makeshift hospital boat on the Ohio River, the steamer *Fanny Bullitt.* "Today there has been four deaths in the different wards," he wrote. "I have but one in my ward as yet. [B]een very busy—have had no relief for 38 hours" (Winters 1998, n.p.). A few weeks later he wrote,

> I had just finished the last kind offices of friendship for Permenas Lick. I gave him his last dose of medicine and the last drink of water that he took on earth and closed his eyes in death. I nursed him for about a week or a little over and done all in my power, but it was of no avail. (Winters 1998, n. p.)

Like Winters, many male caregivers did the best job they could, but some army officials came to believe that women were better suited to such work. The director of a Confederate army hospital in Virginia issued a call for female nurses, asserting that soldier-nurses were "rough country crackers," many of whom were unable to distinguish "castor oil from a gun rod nor laudanum from a hole in the ground" (MacPherson 1998, p. 479). The Confederate States of America government, centered in Richmond, agreed. In September 1862 it enacted staffing guidelines for general hospitals and urged hiring "preference in all cases to females" (MacPherson 1998, p. 479).

Several women nurses distinguished themselves in general hospitals and on the battlefield. One of the more famous examples of the latter category was Mary Ann "Mother" Bickerdyke (1817–1901), who aided Union troops in the western theater. Bickerdyke, a native of Ohio, had more medical experience than most volunteer nurses, having supported herself as a practitioner of folk medicine in Galesburg, Illinois, before the war. When her community asked her to deliver supplies it had collected to a field hospital in Cairo, Illinois, she was so moved by the plight of the wounded that she immediately volunteered her services. Bickerdyke served with Union troops during the gory Battle of Vicksburg and was named chief of nursing by Ulysses S. Grant (1822–1885). She was reportedly the only woman another famous Union general, William T. Sherman (1820–1891), would permit inside his camps.

Perilously Close

Clara Barton (1821–1912), who would later gain fame as the founder of the American Red Cross, also distinguished herself as a war nurse. Her first forays came just days after the war broke out in April 1861, when she visited wounded men who were being housed in the U.S. Senate chamber, so great was the shortage of hospital beds in Washington. Barton soon devoted herself to the cause, and eventually served near the front lines. She described crossing the pontoon bridge across the Rappahannock River during the Battle of Fredericksburg in December 1862.

> An officer stepped to my side to assist me over… the end of the bridge. While our hands were raised in the act of stepping down, a piece of an exploding shell hissed through between us, just below our arms, carrying away a portion of both the skirts of his coat and my dress, rolling along the ground a few rods from us like a harmless pebble

BECOMING AN ARMY NURSE

Army Nurses faced many of the same hardships as the soldiers for whom they cared. Many of the women who joined the army as nurses had limited medical training. All cared for and comforted sick and dying soldiers, but they faced hardships beyond the battlefield. They performed jobs that many in society deemed inappropriate for their sex and, as a result, often faced social censure. Sarah Palmer describes this attitude in *The Story of Aunt Becky's Army-life* (1867):

> Standing firm against the tide of popular opinion; hearing myself pronounced demented-bereft of usual common sense; doomed to the horrors of an untended death-bed-suffering torture, hunger, and all the untold miseries of a soldier's fate; above the loud echoed cry, "It is no place for women," I think it was well that no one ever held a bond over me strong enough to restrain me from performing my plain duty, fulfilling the promise which I made my brothers on enlistment, that I would go with them down to the scene of conflict, and be near when sickness or the chances of battle threw them helpless from the ranks.
>
> I found it *was* a place for women… It was something to brave popular opinion, something to bear the sneers of those who loved their ease better than their country's heroes, and who could sit down in peace and comfort at home, while a soldier's rations, and a soldier's tent for months and years made up the sum of our luxurious life. (pp. 1–2)

CARLY S. KALOUSTIAN

SOURCE: *Palmer, Sarah A.* The Story of Aunt Becky's Army-life. *New York: J.F. Trow and Co., 1867.*

Clara Barton (1821–1912): war nurse and the founder of the Red Cross. Clara Barton was influenced to aid soldiers after her visit with the wounded, only days after the war began. She became dedicated to helping injured soldiers and eventually found herself near the front lines of battle. *National Archives and Records Administration.*

> into the water. The next instant a solid shot thundered over our heads, a noble steed bounded in the air, and, with his gallant rider, rolled in the dirt, not thirty feet in the rear! Leaving the kind-hearted officer, I passed on alone to the hospital. In less than a half-hour he was brought to me—dead. (Barton 1922, p. 217)

The Civil War marked the last time that the U. S. military went to war without a corps of trained nurses. In the Spanish-American War of 1898, Barton's Red Cross answered the Army's call for 700 nurses to assist its medical personnel in Cuba and the Philippines.

BIBLIOGRAPHY

Barton, William Eleazar. *The Life of Clara Barton: Founder of the American Red Cross.* Boston: Houghton Mifflin, 1922.

MacPherson, James M. *Battle Cry of Freedom: The Civil War Era.* New York: Oxford University Press, 1988.

Rutkow, Ira M. *Bleeding Blue and Gray: The Untold Story of Civil War Medicine.* New York: Random House, 2005.

Winters, William. *The Musick of the Mocking Birds, the Roar of the Cannon: The Civil War Diary and Letters of William Winters,* ed. Steven E. Woodworth. Lincoln: University of Nebraska Press, 1998.

Carol Brennan

VOLUNTEER NURSES

When President Abraham Lincoln issued a call for 75,000 volunteer soldiers on April 15, 1861, to help defend federal properties during the first weeks of the war, countless Union women also responded to the call for civilian help. Excluded from actual military service, Union women—and their Confederate sisters—volunteered as nurses despite the fact that most had little or no practical training. According to Ira M. Rutkow in *Bleeding Blue and Gray: The Untold Story of Civil War Medicine,* between three and five thousand women served as volunteer nurses on both sides of the conflict (2005, p. 170).

No Professional Nurses

The contemporary image conjured by the word "nurse"—a professionally trained person who works in the field of health care—was not used at the time of the Civil War. Instead it denoted anyone who helped another in distress; sometimes it referred to the wife of an officer who followed the regiment, or laundresses for army units who assumed nursing duties in times of need. The most common type of Civil War nurse, however, was a male soldier who was recovering from wounds himself but was more able-bodied than other patients. Rutkow places the ratio of male to female nurses at five to one on both sides of the battle (Rutkow 2005, p. 172).

There were no professional schools of nursing up through the 1850s; however, in 1860 Florence Nightingale (1820–1910), who had gained fame for the corps of nurses she trained to aid British troops during the Crimean War (1853–1856), published the first manual on nursing, which was widely read on both sides of the Atlantic. In *Notes on Nursing: What It Is and What It Is Not,* she reflected, "Every woman, or at least almost every woman . . . has, at one time or another of her life, charge of the personal health of somebody, whether child or invalid,—in other words, every woman is a nurse" (Nightingale 1860, p. 3).

Religious Women as Caregivers

The first wave of women who were recruited by military hospitals consisted of women from religious communities, both Protestant and Roman Catholic. In fact, Nightingale's only genuine training came from time

WALT WHITMAN, VOLUNTEER NURSE

While Walt Whitman (1819–1892) is far better known as a poet than as a nurse, some of his greatest poetry came out of his work as a volunteer nurse in wartime Washington. Because he was middle-aged when the war began, Whitman did not serve in the military during the Civil War; however, two of his brothers volunteered to fight on the Union side. Whitman's nursing work began when his brother George was wounded at the battle of Fredericksburg in December 1862. Whitman went to Falmouth, Virginia, to look for his brother and care for him. He originally meant to stay only a week and then return to Brooklyn, but decided that he could not leave the wounded soldiers that he saw while caring for George. Whitman had been working for various newspapers in New York City, but took a job in the Army Paymaster's Office in Washington in order to stay in the capital and visit the wounded. Whitman spent much of his salary from 1862 through 1865 on food or other small items for the soldiers he visited. He also wrote letters to the wounded men's loved ones, as many of the soldiers were illiterate or had had their arms amputated.

In 1865 Whitman published *Drum-Taps*, a collection of poems he wrote about his experiences as a nurse, tending to soldiers' emotional and physical wounds and listening to their memories of battle. The following is an excerpt from "The Wound-Dresser," a poem from *Drum-Taps* that was also included in later editions of *Leaves of Grass:*

> Bearing the bandages, water and sponge,
> Straight and swift to my wounded I go,
> Where they lie on the ground, after the battle brought in;
> Where their priceless blood reddens the grass, the ground;
> Or to the rows of the hospital tent, or under the roof'd hospital;
> To the long rows of cots, up and down, each side, I return;
> To each and all, one after another, I draw near-not one do I miss;
> An attendant follows, holding a tray-he carries a refuse pail,
> Soon to be fill'd with clotted rags and blood, emptied and fill'd again. . . .
> The hurt and wounded I pacify with soothing hand,
> I sit by the restless all the dark night-some are so young;
> Some suffer so much-I recall the experience sweet and sad;
> (Many a soldier's loving arms about this neck have cross'd and rested,
> Many a soldier's kiss dwells on these bearded lips).
> (Whitman 1914, pp. 241–244)

REBECCA J. FREY

BIBLIOGRAPHY

Price, Angel. "Whitman's Wartime Washington: Whitman's Drum Taps and Washington's Civil War Hospitals." Available from http://xroads.virginia.edu/.

Whitman, Walt. Leaves of Grass. *New York: Mitchell Kennerly, 1914.* (Drum-Taps *was often included in later editions of* Leaves of Grass).

spent at an exceptionally well-run hospital in Kaiserswerth, Germany, that was staffed by Lutheran deaconesses belonging to an order founded by Pastor Theodor Fliedner in 1836. In the United States, several communities of Roman Catholic sisters were already serving as nurses in urban hospitals. Confederate authorities requested that the Sisters of Charity in Emmitsburg, Maryland, come to Richmond to help care for the wounded. Initially, church authorities in the United States objected but were convinced of the contributions to the war effort the church could make. In Philadelphia, at the newly built Satterlee Hospital, Sister Mary Gonzaga, another Sister of Charity, supervised a team of forty nurses who came from across the United States to serve in the war effort. These lifetime members of Roman Catholic religious communities were actually preferred by hospital doctors over women from civilian life who volunteered as hospital nurses, for the latter had no experience and were far more likely to voice opinions and raise objections to treatment and care. The nuns, it was said, were far more docile and quite used to the hardships of life as a nurse (Rutkow 2005, p. 169).

Many civilian women who rushed to volunteer as nurses were answering the call issued by the Women's Central Association for Relief in New York City. The first women nurses came under the supervision of Dorothea Dix (1802–1887), a well-known reformer who had improved prison care and petitioned federal and state governments to establish mental hospitals over the past two decades. Dix was a no-nonsense, authoritarian figure and issued strict entrance requirements for the women who came to her headquarters on H Street in Washington, DC. They were barred from wearing curled hair, hoop skirts, or jewelry, and instructed to wear plain garments of black or brown cloth. Furthermore, Dix wanted them to be thirty years of age or older. Thirty was considered well past the limit of marital eligibility, and Dix believed that the rule would discourage women from volunteering as a way to look for husbands. But Dix soon fell out with Army officials and the executives of the U.S. Sanitary Commission, the organization that had begun training volunteer nurses, and was forced to relinquish much of her authority. As the demand for nurses increased after the first major battles in 1861, with

Michigan Soldiers' Relief Society at a Union field hospital Though men assumed the majority of nursing positions during the Civil War, the efforts of women filled an important role. Unable to enlist for combat, women volunteered to serve as nurses, establishing the occupation as a socially acceptable source of employment for females after war's end. *Hulton Archive/Getty Images.*

thousands of wounded needing urgent care, Dix's standards were ignored altogether.

A Turning Point for American Women

Northern and Southern women alike served as nurses in military facilities under the intense objections of many, from their families to Army doctors to the soldiers themselves, who were appalled by the idea of a woman seeing them incapacitated. In an era when not even the bare kneecaps of adults made public appearances in polite society, it was thought that women were ill-suited to handle the rigors of seeing bloody bandages, dealing with bedpans, and bathing patients. Yet most women were made of far sturdier material than the cultural taboos of the era made them out to be, and many rose to the challenge of the demanding, often gruesome work and the personal hardships that came with it.

One such woman was Hannah Ropes, who was nearing fifty when she enlisted as a nurse at a Washington hospital. Ropes came from a prominent Maine family; she had been active in the abolitionist movement and had worked in social reform efforts in New England. She wrote many letters to her grown daughter, Alice, who voiced hopes of joining her mother at the Union Hotel Hospital in Georgetown, but Ropes would not permit it. "It is no place for young girls. The surgeons are young and look upon nurses as their natural prey" (Rutkow 2005, p. 179). In the fall of 1862, Ropes was promoted to head nurse at Union Hotel Hospital, one of the first buildings in the federal capital to be converted for use as a hospital, but the immense building was poorly laid out and ill-suited for such use.

Louisa May Alcott's Experience

Life at Union Hotel Hospital was detailed by a 30-year-old journalist from Massachusetts who arrived as a volunteer nurse in December 1862. Louisa May Alcott (1832–1888) had yet to achieve the major fame she would earn for her semi-autobiographical tale of her three sisters and herself, *Little Women*. But she did gain some literary notice for her *Hospital Sketches*, written after she was forced to give up her 90-day stint early after contracting typhoid fever. In this 1863 work, Alcott wrote that on her third day on the job, the hundreds of wounded from the Battle of Fredericksburg arrived at dawn, but before she even saw her first battlefield wounds, "the first thing I met was a regiment of the vilest odors that ever assaulted the human nose" (Alcott 1885, p. 28).

Alcott wrote of the dreadfully unsanitary conditions at the hospital, and of the rats and lice that infested every floor. She shared a room with another nurse, which she described as well-ventilated thanks to its broken windows; their furniture consisted of a pair of iron beds with threadbare mattresses and "furnished with pillows in the last stages of consumption [tuberculosis]" as well as a fireplace too small to hold a log entirely (Alcott 1885, p. 61). "I tripped over it a dozen times a day, and flew up to poke it a dozen times at night. A mirror (let us be elegant!) of the dimensions of a muffin, and about as reflective, hung over a tin basin, blue pitcher, and a brace of yellow mugs" (Alcott 1885, p. 62). There was a closet for belongings, but it was already full, and "I always opened it with fear and trembling, owing to rats, and shut it in anguish of spirit" (Alcott 1885, p. 62).

Alcott and the other nurses were forced to abandon whatever task they were doing once the dinner bell was rung, for if they came late to the table, they sometimes found most of the food gone. The three daily meals

> ... consisted of beef, evidently put down for the men of [17]76; pork, just in from the street; army bread, composed of saw-dust and saleratus [baking soda]; butter, salt as if churned by Lot's wife; stewed blackberries, so much like preserved cockroaches, that only those devoid of imagination could partake thereof with relish; coffee, mild and muddy; tea: three dried huckleberry leaves to a quart of water flavored with lime also animated and unconscious of any approach to clearness. (Alcott 1885, p. 63)

Despite the hardships, Alcott tried to venture out every day for a walk—a young single woman, living alone in a large city where she had no family and no real constraints on her daily life, was a remarkably rare occurrence in this era—and was fascinated by the Southern blacks she saw for the first time in her life, whom she described as far different from "the respectable members of society I had known in moral Boston" (Alcott, 1885, p. 74). Slavery had been abolished in the federal capital district only the previous April with the Compensated Emancipation Act, which authorized payments to slaveholders in exchange for freeing them. The newly freed slaves continued to work for their former masters for the most part. Alcott wrote that she

> ... had not been there a week before the neglected, devil-may care expression in many of the faces about me, seemed an urgent appeal to leave nursing white bodies, and take some care for these black souls.... I liked them, and found that any show of interest or friendliness brought out the better traits which live in the most degraded and forsaken of us all. (Alcott 1885, p. 75)

Alcott remarked on the cheerful demeanor of blacks and obvious affection for their children, and noted that "the men and boys sang and whistled all day long ... as I listened, I felt that we never should doubt nor despair concerning a race which, through such griefs and wrongs, still clings to this good gift, and seems to solace with it the patient hearts that wait and watch and hope until the end" (Alcott 1885, p. 75).

A Strong-Willed Southern Nurse

Confederate women also took up nursing the wounded in sometimes hastily established hospitals. Felicia Grundy Porter was a well-known Tennessean who set up hospitals in Nashville and served as president of the Women's Relief Society of the Confederate States. Kate Cumming, a native of Scotland who had emigrated with her family first to Canada before settling in Mobile, Alabama, cared for the wounded at a Corinth, Mississippi, hospital that handled victims of the Battle of Shiloh. She was in her late twenties at the time, and served against the strenuous objections of her family. She first chronicled her experiences in an 1866 book, *A Journal of Hospital Life in the Confederate Army of Tennessee.* These passages were later revised for her 1895 title, *Gleanings from Southland: Sketches of Life and Manners of the People of the South before, during, and after the War of Secession, with Extracts from the Author's Journal.* In the final weeks of the war Cumming traveled with the Confederate Army of Tennessee in Georgia, and her journal recounts that she did not learn of the surrender of the Confederate forces on April 9, 1865, until eight days later. "The enemy did not come last night, but I expect they will honor us today," Cumming wrote on April 19. "We sat up all night in terror, starting at every sound" (Cumming 1895, p. 222). Later that evening, she watched from the balcony of the house where she was staying as Union troops destroyed railroad tracks. A few weeks later, she reacted strongly to news that President Andrew Jackson was planning to station federal troops in the vanquished Southern states. "What wound was ever healed by constant irritation?" she wrote. "If he wishes the South to live in peace and harmony with the North, it will never be done by oppression. History gives us no such examples" (Cumming 1895, pp. 235–236).

BIBLIOGRAPHY

Alcott, Louisa M. *Hospital Sketches and Camp and Fireside Stories.* Boston: Roberts Brothers, 1885.

Cumming, Kate. *Gleanings from Southland: Sketches of Life and Manners of the People of the South before, during, and after the War of Secession, with Extracts*

Medical supplies. Faced with staggering numbers of wounded soldiers, Civil War doctors and surgeons learned how to treat a wide variety of injuries by testing new techniques. Technologies such as sedatives, hypodermic syringes, and stethoscopes became widely used throughout the war, improving upon the medical care available to soldiers. *The Art Archive/Culver Pictures/The Picture Desk, Inc.*

from the Author's Journal. Birmingham, AL: Roberts & Son, 1895.

Nightingale, Florence. *Notes on Nursing: What It Is, and What It Is Not.* New York: D. Appleton and Company, 1860.

Rutkow, Ira M. *Bleeding Blue and Gray: The Untold Story of Civil War Medicine.* New York: Random House, 2005.

Carol Brennan

Recovery

When the Civil War began, the world was undergoing vast changes in medical knowledge. The old "heroic therapies" such as bleeding, cupping, and the use of leeches had fallen out of favor by 1860, and were being replaced with experimental (and not always successful or beneficial) medical treatments. Treating wounds and illnesses with medication had become common—opiates, stimulants, sedatives, diuretics, purgatives, and more were widely available and used. The first pills had been made in the early 1800s. The stethoscope and the hypodermic syringe were new. The use of anesthetics had begun in the 1840s; they allowed more extensive surgeries that previously had been impossible.

At the same time, the causes and transmission of diseases was a subject of debate. Vaccines and various treatments were still in their early stages. There was no understanding of microbiology, of the nature of germs and bacteria. Most epidemic diseases were blamed on "miasma" and "effluvia," unseen contagions that were in the air causing diseases and infections. Sanitation was in its very early stages, and the outrageously unhygienic surgical conditions were rarely blamed for their disastrous effects.

The war itself ushered in a new era in medical understanding at the expense of many lives. For a soldier recovering from a wound or struggling with an illness, Civil War medicine could be a blessing or a curse.

Anesthetics and General Medications

Anesthetics were widely used in both the North and the South for serious operations and for the treatment of painful wounds. The surgeon J. H. Brinton wrote of using chloroform on patients in a Nashville hospital: "when patients are first brought here it is often necessary to place them under the influence of chloroform while their wounds are being prepared, and obtund the pain caused by the remedies applied; afterward it is not refused them if the dressing is likely to be painful" (Barnes 1870–1888, vol. 3.2, p. 846). Although no exact number can be known, it is estimated that anesthetics were used in about 80,000 instances. Out of a group of nearly 9,000 cases cited in the *Medical and Surgical History of the War of the Rebellion*, chloroform was used 76.2 percent

PTSD AND THE CIVIL WAR SOLDIER

Posttraumatic stress disorder (PTSD) did not become a diagnostic category in American psychiatry until the third edition of the *Diagnostic and Statistical Manual of Mental Disorders* in 1980, after the condition had been studied systematically in veterans of the Vietnam War (1965–1975). Veterans of World Wars I (1914–1918) and II (1939–1945) were more likely to be diagnosed as suffering from "shell shock" or "traumatic war neurosis."

Until the early 2000s, however, no one had studied the mental and physical aftereffects of combat in Civil War veterans. In 2006 a team of researchers at the University of California, Irvine, published the results of their study of 17,700 Civil War veterans who had received standardized medical examinations over their postwar lifetimes by U.S. Pension Board surgeons. The results indicated that Civil War veterans suffered profoundly from posttraumatic stress, probably more so than veterans of later wars, for several reasons:

- The youth of Civil War soldiers. Between 15 and 20 percent of Union volunteers were between the ages of nine and seventeen. The researchers found that these young veterans were 93 percent more likely than the oldest soldiers (thirty-one or older) to experience both physical and psychiatric problems after the war, and to die at early ages.
- Loss of friends and family. Companies in Civil War armies were often made up of men from the same town, neighborhood, or extended family. This fact meant that a soldier whose company suffered heavy losses in battle was far more likely to grieve the loss of several close friends and relatives than his twentieth-century counterparts. Veterans from companies that lost large percentages of soldiers in battle were 51 percent more likely than other veterans to suffer heart attacks, stomach disorders, or mental illness after the war.
- The psychological impact of close-quarter or hand-to-hand combat, which was a common field tactic in the Civil War.

Psychiatry had not become a separate medical specialty at the time of the Civil War, although mental illnesses of various types were certainly recognized, and hospitals for the treatment of the mentally ill had existed in the United States since the early nineteenth century. In 1844 thirteen superintendents of what were then called insane asylums formed the Association of Medical Superintendents of American Institutions for the Insane. In 1921 the name changed to the American Psychiatric Association.

Civil War battlefield surgeons did not use terms such as "battle shock" or "PTSD" for posttraumatic symptoms in the soldiers they treated; instead, they used phrases such as "nervous disease" or "irritable heart syndrome" for psychiatric disorders resulting from combat stress. There was also a relatively new psychiatric hospital just for veterans—St. Elizabeths Hospital in Washington, DC. This institution had been founded by Congress in 1855 as the Government Hospital for the Insane, or GHI. Dorothea Dix (1802–1887), the social reformer whose work led to the foundation of the first public mental hospitals in Pennsylvania and North Carolina, was also responsible for the establishment of the GHI. Dix instructed the hospital to provide "the most humane and enlightened curative treatment of the insane of the Army, Navy, and District of Columbia" (The United States Congressional Serial Set 1855, p. 10).

The GHI provided psychiatric treatment for several hundred Union soldiers both before and after the war; many were eventually buried on its grounds. During the war soldiers were referred to the hospital after being evaluated by battlefield surgeons for malingering and deception. After the end of the war the increase in the number of mentally ill veterans led Congress to pass an act on July 13, 1866, that permitted the GHI to admit all men who had served as Union soldiers in the Civil War and were found insane within three years of discharge by reason of mental illness related to military service. Many of these veterans needed custodial care for the rest of their lives; Dr. Charles H. Nichols, the first superintendent of the hospital, saw to it that they received the best care possible at the time. He said, "The patriotic sacrifices of the military patients will always entitle them to our best endeavors to promote their comfort and their restoration to health" (Report of the Department of the Interior 1849, p. 174).

St. Elizabeths received its present name informally during the Civil War, as some soldiers who were treated there for physical injuries hesitated to use "Government Hospital for the Insane" for their return address when writing to loved ones back home. They called the hospital "St. Elizabeths" after the name given to its grounds by the original colonial landowner in 1663. Congress finally made the name change official in 1917.

REBECCA J. FREY

BIBLIOGRAPHY

Kanhouwa, Surya. "A Century of Pathology at Saint Elizabeths Hospital, Washington, DC." Archives of Pathology and Laboratory Medicine *121 (1997): 84–90.*

Pizarro, Judith, Roxane Cohen Silver, and JoAnn Prause. "Physical and Mental Health Costs of Traumatic War Experiences among Civil War Veterans." Archives of General Psychiatry *63 (2006): 193–200.*

Report of the Department of the Interior. Washington: United States Government Printing Office, 1849, p. 174.

The United States Congressional Serial Set. Washington: United States. Government Printing Office, 1855, p. 10.

of the time, ether in 14 percent, and a mixture of the two in 9.1 percent (p. 887). Chloroform was safer than ether, but both were toxic; as the Union surgeon C. J. Walton stated: "While I could not dispense with chloroform, I must protest against the extravagant and indiscreet use of it. It is a most potent agent, and should be used with the utmost caution" (Barnes 1870–1888, vol. 3.2, p. 888). Surgeons agreed that it should be used only as long as necessary, and then, "its administration should be discontinued . . . thereby avoiding . . . its toxical effect" (Barnes 1870–1888, vol. 3.2, p. 888). Both were carefully administered to soldiers by a cloth or sponge held over the nose and mouth. In the Southern army, where anesthetics could be harder to get, Surgeon J. J. Chisolm developed an inhaler that used less chloroform, and administered it directly into the nostrils via two nose pieces (Barnes 1870–1888, vol. 3.2, pp. 888–889).

Opium and morphine were seen as essential medications. They were available as pills or powder. Morphine could be injected as well, and small amounts of opium could be taken with alcohol in a solution called *laudanum* (Bollet 2002, pp. 238–239). Opiates seemed effective in treating a variety of symptoms, and so the drugs were liberally prescribed for everything from battlefield wounds to dysentery, and even for more common complaints such as headaches. It is estimated that the Union used about 10 million opium pills plus about 3 million ounces of opium powder and other opium mixed concoctions (Bollet 2002, p. 240). The Confederacy likewise prescribed opiates, but perhaps not as liberally: Because of the Union blockade, they were often hard to come by, so some Southerners turned to growing and harvesting their own poppies to create opium (Jackson 1863, pp. 103–104).

The use of antiseptics to prevent infections could not be relied on during the Civil War because general medical knowledge and practice at the time did not take sanitation into account. Surgeon W.W. Keen remembered that: "we used undisinfected instruments from undisinfected... cases, and still worse used marine sponges which had been used in prior pus cases and had been only washed in tap water" (Adams 1952, p. 125). Under such unsanitary conditions, a soldier recovering from surgery could expect infection to set in. However, antiseptics were available. Surgeons used "not only carbolic [acid], but many of the other chemicals that rank high as antiseptics" such as iodine, bromine, alcohol, and many other acids (Adams 1952, pp. 127–128). The problem was knowing exactly when to apply the treatment, and infected wounds usually had gone beyond repair before an antiseptic was applied.

Because of the often unsatisfactory effects of other medical treatments, proper diet became a treatment unto itself. Depending on the disease, each hospital made an effort to supply soldiers with food that would nourish them and aid in their recovery.

Common medical treatments included turpentine, ingested or applied to wounds and irritated skin; diaphoretics, including potassium nitrate, tartar emetic, and a combination of ipecac and opium called "Dover's powders," to induce sweating in order to cool fevers; calomel, a powder used as a purgative or laxative; and ipecac, which was prescribed heavily to induce vomiting. Many of the medicines were dangerous and toxic, such as the several compounds formed from mercury. Many were used irresponsibly, as when a patient suffering from dehydration might be given a diuretic.

Due to the Union blockade, obtaining certain medications was often difficult in the South. The *Regulations for the Medical Department of the C.S. Army* suggested more than sixty "Indigenous Remedies for Field Service and Sick in General Hospital." Among the items listed are hemlock and American hellebore as sedatives; and stimulants from parts of junipers, sassafras, lavender, and horsemint (CSA War Department 1863, p. 62). Citizens throughout the South were urged to grow and donate these indigenous plants to aid the Confederate army.

Perhaps one of the most used medications was quinine. An 1864 New Hampshire newspaper declared it "king of the medicines" ("Quinine and Its Substitutes," March 4, 1864), and it was so effective in treating malarial diseases that the *Daily Cleveland Herald* suggested "that every person who has a friend in the army send him a dollar's worth of quinine" to be drunk in coffee each morning so as to avoid "chronic diarrhea, fever and ague, and bilious fever" ("Quinine for the Army of the Potomac," July 22, 1864). Quinine was used far more frequently than any opiates, as it seemed to not only treat, but also to prevent malaria and reduce general fevers.

Medical Procedures

A soldier wounded on the field of battle had a long road ahead of him. His first stop would usually be a makeshift dressing station, where medical officers would check wounds for hemorrhaging, apply simple bandaging and tourniquets, and ply the soldier with either alcohol or opium or both to ease pain and forestall shock. A wound might either be plugged with lint, or have lint applied outside as a pad. His next stop would be a field hospital, where he would sit on the ground awaiting his turn to be seen. Attendants might prioritize those with treatable, but serious wounds, and treat those with lesser wounds—those with mortal wounds were regularly passed over in favor of more treatable wounds. Once upon the operating table, anesthetic would be administered, and wound-specific operations would begin.

General wound care sought to stop bleeding and seal the wound, to ease pain, and to stop infection. Wounds were packed with lint or sometimes sealed with a solution made of beeswax called *cerate*. "Astringents" applied to wounds would help blood clot (Bollet 2002, pp. 233–234). Ligation, an operation that involved tying off major arteries, was perfected during the war, and ligation of a vessel was lauded as a way to avoid amputation from gangrene. Wounds in which a bone was shattered might be excised instead of amputated by removing part of the destroyed bone, hoping that the bone would heal and bond over the break. However, recovery from such an operation was difficult, and usually resulted in a loss of function of the limb (Bollet 2002, p. 147).

Wounds to the head and torso were more likely to be mortal than wounds to the extremities. In a survey of 3,717 abdominal wounds, 87 percent were fatal (Barnes 1870–1888, vol. 2.2, p. 202), though when the

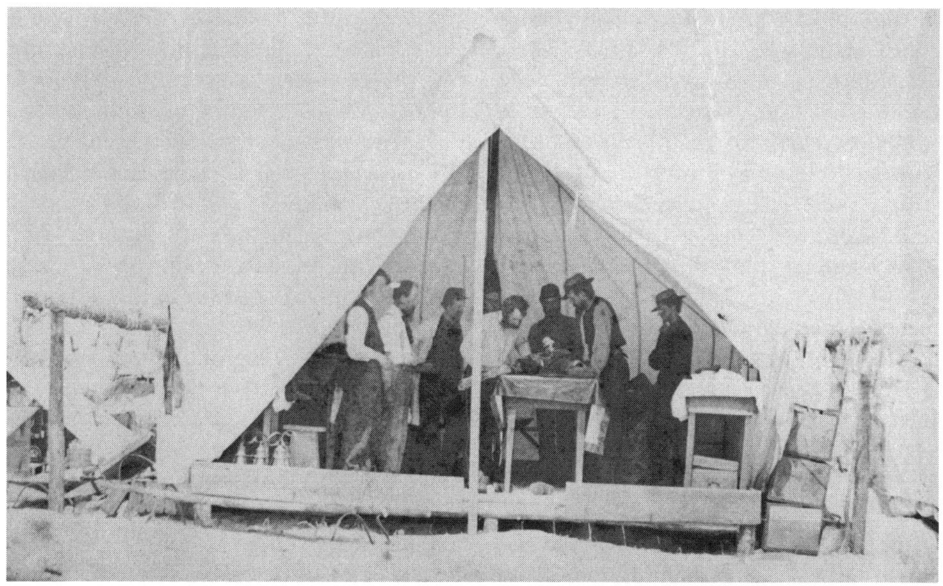

Setting a broken leg. Advances in medicine during the Civil War included the use of anesthetics, allowing for more efficient and complicated surgeries to treat war wounds. Chloroform-soaked cloths, as seen in the photograph, were placed over a patient's nose and mouth to temporarily induce unconsciousness and alleviate pain. © *Corbis*

intestines were not punctured, recovery was more likely. Head injuries did not fare much better: "Of one hundred and eighty-six cases of balls penetrating the cranial cavity, one hundred and one were fatal" (Barnes 1870–1888, vol. 1, p. 316). Operations to remove objects from the skull had about a 50 percent mortality rate, whereas cases where the object was left in had similar results. When deciding whether to attempt to save a probably mortally wounded man with a long, complicated, and dangerous surgery, or to save several men with treatable wounds, surgeons usually chose the welfare of the many over the one.

Injuries to the extremities comprised about 70 percent of the total injuries (Barnes 1870–1888, vol. 3, p. 691). When the bones of an extremity were shattered, or the tissue damaged beyond repair, amputation was the preferred treatment. Amputations were quick and usually successful, and anesthetic was almost always used. However, due to unsanitary operating and wound management conditions, infection was common, and there often were complications in recovering from the operation. Mortality rates increased in cases where the amputation was closer to the body trunk, and when there had been a long interval between injury and surgery.

Treating Diseases and Infections

Diseases of all kinds ran rampant through both armies. Out of a selection of 304,369 deaths cited in *Medical and Surgical History of the War of the Rebellion*, about 61 percent were caused by disease. The most common form of disease was diarrhea and dysentery. Although they did not have the highest mortality rate, they were the most widespread (the terms *diarrhea* and *dysentery* were often used to mean the same thing). The Union reported about 1,739,135 cases (Barnes 1870–1888, vol. 2.1, p. 2) and the Confederacy, though lacking an exact number, could also say that it was also the most common affliction (Bollet 2002, p. 284). Treating dysentery was not always easy. Assistant Surgeon James DeBrulen commented: "chronic diarrhea has been extremely common in the hospital, and in many cases so rebellious as to defy all modes of treatment we could devise" (Barnes 1870–1888, vol. 2.1, p. 42). In some stages, dysentery was curable, noted the surgeon William Wright, but in others it became "indominable [*sic*]: the cases in which a judicious course of treatment was pursued before emaciation" usually had favorable results; after emaciation had set in, most cases were fatal (Barnes 1870–1888, vol. 2.1, p. 62). There was little consensus on a cure, but doctors combated dysentery with nearly every medicine available: mercurials, opiates, and sulphate of copper, nitric acid, purgatives, Dover's powder, turpentine, mucilage, ipecac, quinine, bismuth, and many more. Opium and purgatives (laxatives) generally were the most relied upon. One doctor stated that "opiates and the ordinary astringents have been worse than useless," whereas another confidently stated that "I have used opium extensively... in combination with astringents" and had wonderful results. One agreed-upon treatment was a strict diet: "only bland and unirritating food" such as "milk, whey, eggs, mucilages, essence of beef, chicken soup" as well as a diet of fresh vegetables and peanuts (Barnes 1870–1888, vol. 2.1, p. 45). At Rock Island prison hospital patients were given beef tea and bromide of potassium, and out of 2,629 cases, only 159 died (Barnes 1870–1888, vol. 2.1, p. 53). Soldiers would be afflicted with dysentery for varying amounts of time. Private Joseph Westurn of New York fought the disease from July until December, continually relapsing and requiring a new treatment each time (Barnes 1870–1888, vol. 2.1, p. 46).

Nearly as widespread as dysentery were fevers. Malarial fevers sprang up yearly, especially in swampy areas, and were treated with multiple doses of quinine a day. Typhoid fevers were treated with turpentine and cold compresses, whereas the diarrhea that came with it was fought with opiates, Dover's powders, and other diaphoretics to lower the patient's body temperature.

Other than diseases, infections from wounds and operations plagued both armies. A wound received on the battlefield would be primed for infection from the start. Unsanitary surgical techniques propagated the problem. Surgeons did their best to remove foreign bodies from wounds, realizing the problems they caused. They would slough off infected tissue—not because they knew it bred infectious bacteria, but because they simply knew it was beneficial in some way. Hospital gangrene and erysipelas were constant fears. These infections spread through the body quickly and often led to secondary amputations, with high mortality rates. Doctors found bromine to be a successful treatment for gangrene later in the war, and the infection was mostly eradicated by the end of the war.

Getting Better

The evolution of medicine through the experience of war had a tremendous effect. For humanity in general, the Civil War ushered in the sanitary age of medicine and helped refine the prescription of medication and important surgical techniques. Surgeons' basic observations on the spread of diseases and infections would be validated by Joseph Lister's bacteriology work in 1865. Doctors experimented with new procedures such as plastic surgery, the treatment of chest, abdominal, and head wounds, and blood transfusions; all of these would continue to be perfected after the war. Experimenting with medications led to better understanding of appropriate use and dosage. Overall mortality rates fell drastically during the war, and would continue to do so afterwards as Americans, and the world, learned from the experience of the war.

BIBLIOGRAPHY

Adams, George W. *Doctors in Blue: The Medical History of the Union Army in the Civil War.* Baton Rouge: Louisiana State University Press, 1952.

Barnes, Joseph K. *Medical and Surgical History of the War of the Rebellion.* 3 vols. Washington, DC: Government Printing Office, 1870–1888.

Bollet, Alfred J. *Civil War Medicine: Challenges and Triumphs.* Tucson, AZ: Galen Press, 2002.

Confederate States of America War Department. *Regulations for the Medical Department of the C.S. Army.* Richmond, VA: Author, 1863.

Jackson, H. W. R. *The Southern Women of the Second American Revolution.* Atlanta, GA: Intelligencer Steampower Press, 1863.

Otis, George Alexander. *Reports on the Extent and Nature of the Materials Available for the Preparation of a Medical and Surgical History of the Rebellion.* Philadelphia: J.B. Lippincott, 1865.

"Quinine and Its Substitutes." *New Hampshire Statesman*, Concord, NH, March 4, 1864.

"Quinine for the Army of the Potomac." *Daily Cleveland Herald*, Cleveland, OH, July 22, 1864.

United States Sanitary Commission. *The Soldier's Friend.* Philadelphia: Author, 1865.

J. Douglas Tyson

■ Public Health and Sanitation

Public health and sanitation in America during the Civil War era was virtually nonexistent, but the efforts of reformers—many of whom worked to improve conditions in U.S. Army camps on the Union side—led to intensive clean-up efforts later in the nineteenth century. Military camps and hospitals were breeding grounds for many of the diseases that regularly felled urban populations, such as typhoid fever, cholera, and dysentery.

Deadly Miasmas

The medical community was woefully unaware of many of the basic tenets of public health and sanitation when the Civil War began in 1861. There was little knowledge about the causes of preventable diseases, and the correlation between germs and sickness had not yet been established by scientific observation and controlled experimentation. The commonly held belief at the time was that diseases are caused by vaporous exhalations known as miasmas, from a Greek word that means "pollution." Miasmas were associated with the rank odors of such things as sewer gas or piles of garbage.

The United States Sanitary Commission (USSC), a civilian organization founded in 1861 under the auspices of the federal government, was set up to inspect Union camps and hospitals and offer recommendations and guidelines to prevent infections and infectious diseases. Despite the commission's valiant efforts, the casualty numbers from the war paint a stark picture of how poor conditions were: The total number of war dead was an estimated 690,000, but only 240,000 of that number died from battlefield injuries; a staggering 425,000 were killed by such diseases and wound complications as typhoid fever and gangrene (Sutherland 1989, p. 19).

In civilian life, the death rates from preventable diseases were also high. Indoor plumbing was a rarity found usually in only the wealthiest households, and even then, the pipes were not always hooked up to municipal sewer systems, which were also still uncommon. When the sewer pipes were connected to a sewer system, they often emptied into the same water source that supplied local drinking water. Most households used either an outhouse or an "earth closet" located inside the house. The latter was a specially constructed wooden chamber with a seat; waste went into a galvanized metal tube, but once too much waste had accumulated, the drain would have to be cleaned out. Outhouses, often located in the same backyard where livestock animals were kept, were similarly constructed and these, too, would overflow. At night, most families relied on relieving themselves in the chamber pot, the contents of which would be tossed onto the street the next day.

Garbage collection was also a rarity in most communities. In some cases, cities allocated funds for this task, but corrupt local district leaders often took the money without hiring collectors. In upscale urban neighborhoods, where residents banded together to pay for private collection, garbage did not pile up to the point of making certain avenues impassable, as it did elsewhere.

Overcrowded Manhattan

New York City presented a particularly foul scenario. Immigration over the past two decades had brought an influx of new inhabitants to the city, many of whom were relegated to living in abject squalor. Multistory tenement buildings began to crop up, which housed dozens of people in one or two rooms with a single window overlooking a garbage-strewn airshaft. Each floor usually had a version of the earth closet, but no running water or indoor heating. Cholera and typhus outbreaks were common.

Typhus is a highly communicable disease, and the organisms (rickettsiae) that cause it are transmitted by lice living on the human body. Typhus should not be confused with typhoid fever, which is contracted from ingesting food or water contaminated with the feces of an already infected person; however, both diseases are equally swift-moving and often deadly. Cholera also results from poor sanitary conditions, and regular outbreaks occurred in the nineteenth-century United States every spring when passenger ships began dislodging new immigrants and travelers at the international ports of arrival. These diseases reached every quarter—even President Abraham Lincoln's eleven-year-old son Willie died of typhoid fever in February 1862—a personal loss from which neither Lincoln nor his wife ever fully recovered.

Frederick Law Olmsted (1822–1903), leader of medical volunteerism. Upon its creation in 1861, the United States Sanitary Commission organized the efforts of women, who brought clean bedding, food, and medical supplies to Union soldiers. Led by Frederick Law Olmsted, volunteers visited soldiers' campsites, offering medical care and sanitation instruction. *The Library of Congress.*

The decision to locate the federal capital in Washington had always been much maligned, for the city had been built on swampy land, which is known to be a breeding ground for mosquitoes, the carriers of deadly malaria.

Cities further south were usually even more dismally filthy, for the balmy weather only exacerbated the stench and the germ colonies that came from untreated sewage, garbage piles, and the waste droppings of horses.

Stephen Smith and the *Report of the Council of Hygiene and Public Health*

In the 1850s, the New York City physician Stephen Smith emerged as a prominent and tireless advocate for improved public health and sanitation. Early on, he was one of the few among the medical profession who recognized the link between the abominable living conditions of the poor and outbreaks of disease. A few years before the onset of the Civil War, Smith was appointed to supervise a quarantine facility on Roosevelt Island during a typhus outbreak in the city. When he realized that an extraordinary number of patients were coming from the same tenement building on East 22nd Street, he went to inspect the property himself. "The doors and windows were broken," he reported. "The cellar was partly filled with filthy sewage; the floors were littered with decomposing straw, which the occupants used for bedding. . . . The whole establishment was reeking with filth, and the atmosphere was heavy with the sickening odor of the deadly typhus, which reigned supreme in every room" (Rutkow 2005, p. 267).

In 1859 Smith founded the New York Sanitary Association, which worked to improve conditions in the city. He soon became known as a prominent Sanitarian, as public-health reformers were called. Some of his like-minded colleagues played a key role in the establishment of the United States Sanitary Commission (USSC). One of these fellow reformers was Frederick Law Olmsted, who resigned as New York City's parks commissioner to serve as executive director of the USSC. Smith also worked for the USSC, and served as acting assistant surgeon at a Union Army base at Fort Monroe, Virginia, during the war. Once back in civilian life, he refocused his efforts to clean up New York City, and established a commission that funded a groundbreaking 1864 sanitary survey of the island of Manhattan. He chaired the commission and sent physicians to inspect each of the thirty-one districts into which he divided the borough. The conditions these doctors found were so dreadful that the report of their findings, *Report of the Council of Hygiene and Public Health of the Citizens' Association of New York, upon the Sanitary Condition of the City*, caused a major public outcry. Its publication became the turning point for public health and sanitation efforts in New York City.

Smith's *Report* detailed horrendous overcrowding in the city, where about half a million people lived in a two-square-mile area (Rutkow 2005, p. 270). Some lived in tenements, but others who had their own plots of land raised hogs in their backyard and lived right next to manufacturing enterprises, in an era when zoning laws were nonexistent. One of Smith's inspectors wrote of "a sausage and fat-boiling establishment . . . [where the] heads and of animals are received . . . and the parts which can be profitably [used] are selected, while the rest is thrown upon the ground or buried[;] adjoining streets have no sewerage, and this building no drainage" (Rutkow 2005, p. 310). Another physician hired for the job visited a residence near Avenue B and Attorney Street, and found "two of the scrofulous children in that house on crutches. The grave has a strong claim upon others." The inspector noted several livery stables nearby, and remarked that "the prevalence and fatality of pulmonary diseases among horses in overcrowded and neglected stables is only equalled by the fatality of like maladies in the women and children of tenant-houses" (Rutkow 2005, p. 175).

Smith took his *Report* to Albany and testified before the New York state legislature. Finally, in 1866 a new Metropolitan Health Bill—part of it drafted by Smith—was enacted. Two years later, Smith became commissioner of the New York City Board of Health. The Metropolitan Health Bill was a groundbreaking piece of legislation that was widely copied by other cities in their efforts to curb disease outbreaks. Some of its most significant reforms included the removal of slaughterhouses to locations outside city limits, new health standards for the dairy industry, and the regular removal of horse droppings from city streets.

BIBLIOGRAPHY

Citizens' Association of New York. *Report of the Council of Hygiene and Public Health of the Citizens' Association of New York, upon the Sanitary Condition of the City.* New York: D. Appleton, 1865.

Rutkow, Ira M. *Bleeding Blue and Gray: The Untold Story of Civil War Medicine.* New York: Random House, 2005.

Smith, Stephen. *The City That Was.* New York: F. Allaben, 1911.

Sutherland, Daniel E. *The Expansion of Everyday Life, 1860–1876.* New York: Harper & Row, 1989.

Carol Brennan

■ United States Sanitary Commission

The United States Sanitary Commission (USSC) was a volunteer agency run under government auspices that sought to ensure the health and safety of Union Army soldiers during the American Civil War. It also collected donations of clothing, blankets, food, and medical supplies for military personnel, trained volunteer nurses, and ran a service that located lost or missing soldiers on behalf of their families. Commonly referred to as "the Sanitary" during its years of operation between 1861 and 1865, the USSC served as an umbrella organization for the scores of soldiers' aid societies formed at the local level. One volunteer, Katharine Prescott Wormeley, called it "the great artery which bears the people's love to the people's army" in her 1863 book, *The United States Sanitary Commission: A Sketch of Its Purposes and Its Work* (p. xv).

A Surge of Patriotism

When the war began in April 1861, a Chicago journalist and women's rights activist named Mary Livermore was in Boston visiting her ailing father. She was a committed abolitionist, as a result of an earlier job as a tutor on a

Virginia plantation, where she had been appalled by the treatment of slaves. She was also active in the Universalist religious movement; with her husband, a minister, she edited the Chicago-based Universalist newspaper, *New Covenant.* During her visit to Boston, Livermore was stirred by the patriotic fervor and outpourings of support she witnessed on the streets in the days following the declaration of war. One aspect of this was the hasty assembling of volunteer units in response to President Abraham Lincoln's request for 75,000 civilians to serve a three-month stint protecting federal property until regular troops could be mustered. In her 1888 memoir, *My Story of the War: A Woman's Narrative of Four Years Personal Experience*, Livermore reported that Boston's historic Fanueil Hall was the designated assembly point for these militias, who arrived from elsewhere in New England by train and "were escorted by crowds cheering vociferously" down residential and commercial streets where nearly every address displayed the U.S. flag (p. 90).

In New York City, affluent women met on April 25 to form the Women's Central Relief Association (WCRA), whose goal was to organize soldiers' aid efforts. Its founding members invited a prominent New York Unitarian minister, Dr. Henry W. Bellows, to participate, and Bellows soon traveled to Washington with a delegation of physicians. Their aim was to meet with government officials and formally define the WCRA's role in the war effort. Bellows soon decided, however, that a larger organization with a more overtly medical mission was necessary. His model for this new organization was the British Sanitary Commission, which had helped eliminate brucellosis—an infectious disease transmitted from livestock to humans—during the Crimean War of 1853–1856.

Henry W. Bellows (1814–1882). In 1861, a small group of wealthy women from New York looked to contribute to the war by providing aid to soldiers. Henry W. Bellows, a Unitarian minister, helped organize the group, which eventually evolved into the United States Sanitary Commission. *The Library of Congress.*

Military officials, however, were uneasy with the idea of an American sanitary commission, believing that civilian interference in Army camps would only prove problematic. Even President Lincoln warned that a USSC could become the proverbial "fifth wheel" in the war effort, but despite these reservations, he signed a bill authorizing its creation as an official government entity of unpaid volunteers on June 18, 1861. The president was convinced by USSC supporters that a centralized agency was the best way to placate the growing number of women asserting their intention to contribute to the war effort in a useful way. A Western Sanitary Commission under similar charter was organized three months later in September 1861, and headquartered in St. Louis, Missouri, in order to meet the needs of Union soldiers in that region of the country.

Leadership and Organization

The executive leadership of the USSC was entirely male. Its first executive secretary was a prominent New Yorker, the landscape architect Frederick Law Olmsted, who took a break from his post as commissioner of Central Park, which he had designed, to run the USSC. The WCRA was eventually subsumed into the USSC, but its first few months of collecting goods for soldiers—such as hospital gowns and bedding—proved extraordinarily fruitful at the first USSC collection depot in New York City.

The work of the volunteers was initially disorganized, but as one Mrs. Sherwood recalled years later in an article she wrote for the *New York Times*, Bellows was confident that blunders were an inevitable part of a new organization. "Dr. Bellows would say, as we told him of more boxes gone to the wrong place, 'let us go ahead and make more mistakes'" (May 28, 1898). Bellows soon began writing instruction pamphlets that were distributed to USSC auxiliaries; these dealt with such matters as the ideal way to pack and label shipments of clothing and blankets, and the proper method of making items like sanitary bandages.

Another key USSC figure was Louisa Lee Schuyler, who came from a prominent New York family. Schuyler was the great-granddaughter of the first Secretary of the

U.S. Treasury, Alexander Hamilton, and organized the WCRA's New York office, then went on to coordinate bandage-collection efforts in the city. In Chicago, the Northwestern auxiliary of the USSC was run by the aforementioned Livermore and Jane Hoge. Hoge was active in charitable work aiding the poor and immigrants in Chicago, and went on to serve as a volunteer nurse aboard hospital ships the USSC later created.

A Range of Volunteer Efforts

The volunteer efforts coordinated by the USSC took many forms. In the initial months of the war, for example, there was a call for Northern women to organize sewing circles to make hoods known as *havelocks.* These hoods were linen and were worn over a regulation uniform cap; they offered soldiers protection from both rain and sun. Fueling the demand for havelocks were worries that Union soldiers might suffer sunstroke in the Southern states, where the climate was considered dangerously tropical by Northerners. A veritable "havelock mania" raged across several states during the first year of the war. By May 20, some 1,100 of the cap covers had been sewn by the Ladies Havelock Association of New York City, according to a *New York Times* report from that day—but the headgear was later deemed useless, for it actually increased body temperature, and the mania died away.

Scores of Northern women also demonstrated their desire to contribute to the war effort by collecting lint for bandages. A *New York Times* article dated April 22, 1861, with the quaint title "Work for the Ladies," urged women's groups in churches to organize bandage-making crews. It also promised that such women would have allies: Recounting how women in Paris had made bandages for injured soldiers during the Paris Commune uprising of 1848, it declared, "[t]here are French ladies in this city who would gladly give their aid now to anything that may be undertaken here." Jane Woolsey, a young woman from an affluent New York City family, described the activity that ensued in a letter to a friend:

"The Sanitary." A volunteer organization committed to improving the physical well-being of Northern soldiers, the United States Sanitary Commission (USSC) coordinated the efforts of women looking to support the troops. In addition to providing extra supplies, the USSC also worked to improve hygiene in the army camps in hopes of limiting the spread of disease. *© Bettman/Corbis.*

"Inside the parlor windows the atmosphere has been very fluffy since Sumter, with lint-making and the tearing of endless lengths of flannel and cotton bandages and cutting out of innumerable garments" (Attie 1998, p. 35). Woolsey would go on to become a well-known pioneer in medical education thanks to her experiences as a volunteer nurse during the war.

Women who lived far from USSC offices also contributed. In her *New York Times* article, Mrs. Sherwood recalled the packages the USSC branches received from women around the country, often containing clothing and food that donors hoped would find their way to soldiers in need. One letter accompanying a donation read, "These clothes belonged to my poor Bob. He would have gone to war had he lived, but he died last Winter, and I send these clothes for some young man whom they may fit, and some jelly for the sick in the hospitals" (May 28, 1898).

Over time, a standard list of useful items was established and these items were packaged together in what became known as *Comfort Bags.* Bags contained such items as pen and paper, shaving supplies, and even needles and thread so that soldiers could repair their own uniforms. A miniature Bible or a small knife for woodcarving—a popular hobby at the time—might also be included. In his 1866 memoir, *Hospital Life in the Army of the Potomac,* Doctor William H. Reed recalled the arrival of one such shipment of Comfort Bags:

> In all my hospital experiences I have never seen anything which has given such real pleasure to the men. Those who were able to move gathered round the stoves in their wards, the cripples of all kinds crept up and sat up! on the adjoining beds, each waiting for his gift. As it was handed to him, he went to the bottom of it with the pleased curiosity of a little child searching the stocking for the gifts of Santa Claus on Christmas morning. (p. 151)

In a number of major cities, efforts to raise money to meet the USSC's needs periodically took the form of charity events known as *Sanitary Fairs.* These popular events were staged in Boston, Chicago, Baltimore, and New York. They featured booths with donated items for sale—including costly antiques and works of art—and gave those outside the USSC volunteer network a chance to contribute their support. The Fairs raised enormous sums for the USSC, which were used for administrative purposes, such as sending out field agents, or to train nurses, and also to assemble and distribute Comfort Bags, with the goal of providing one to each Union soldier every month.

Some of the work performed by USSC volunteers tapered off as the war dragged on and the enthusiasm of the first months waned. Reports of corruption occasionally surfaced, including claims that local farmers paid by the USSC to deliver donated supplies instead sold them to troops, or that unscrupulous Army officers took the Comfort Bags or other items for themselves. The USSC leadership launched internal investigations whenever such allegations arose, realizing that their mission depended heavily on the public's trust.

Hygiene Inspections

In addition to collecting supplies for soldiers through its local depots and volunteer workers, the USSC trained nurses and regularly sent experts to Union camps to inspect hygiene conditions. The agents—of whom Livermore was one—looked into sanitary practice at field hospitals and kitchens, ensured that latrines had been dug in a place where freshwater supplies could not become contaminated, and issued recommendations on how to improve conditions. In early 1863, reports began appearing in Northern newspapers that infectious diseases were killing far too many Union soldiers, and that this was directly attributable to unhygienic camp conditions. In response, the president of the Western Sanitary Commission, James Yeaton, sent a letter to the *New York Times* in which he reported on his visits to General William T. Sherman's corps after their defeat near Vicksburg, Mississippi, at the Battle of Chickasaw Bayou. Yeaton found that the incidence of sickness was not as dire as he expected, but did note that "the great danger to be apprehended is from the want of a proper vegetable diet. Symptoms of scurvy have already made their appearance, and it behooves friends at home to make prompt efforts to aid in remedying this." His letter urged readers to donate pickles, sauerkraut, and other canned fruits and vegetables (*New York Times,* March 22, 1863).

Hospital Ships

The USSC established hospital ships that plied the rivers and brought wounded Union soldiers from the areas near battlefields further north to safety and medical care. In her 1867 memoir *The Boys in Blue: Or, Heroes of the "Rank and File,"* Hoge recalled witnessing men being loaded onto the ships. "Many of these men were raving in the delirium of fever, fainting from exhaustion, or maddened with festering or undressed wounds, unamputated limbs, and raging thirst, which must be quenched before the removal could take place" (p. 67). Hoge also recounted the aftermath of the April 1862 Battle of Shiloh in southwestern Tennessee, which left more than 8,000 Union wounded. "The cabin floor of the hospital boat, where the operations were performed, ran in streams of blood, and legs and arms, as they were rapidly dismembered, formed a stack of human limbs" (p. 67).

The USSC Postal Service

Another division within the USSC located Union soldiers on behalf of their families. Though both Union and Confederate mail services worked remarkably well during the war, families sometimes waited months for a letter from a loved one in the field. To help locate missing soldiers, or determine if they had become a casualty of war, the USSC established a Hospital Directory that featured names of all Union soldiers recuperating in Washington, DC, hospitals. This directory eventually came to encompass all military medical facilities under the supervision of the War Department, and was one of the most costly expenditures of the USSC—but also the most priceless. In her 1863 book Wormely refers to the many heartbreaking inquiries the division received; one particular one provided the names and last-known whereabouts of two of the letter-writer's nephews, and concluded with the remark that "these are two out of fourteen nephews that I have no account of since the battle of Fredericksburg" (p. 235).

Aid to Newly Discharged Veterans

The last major fundraising effort for the USSC, a second Chicago Sanitary Fair, opened several weeks after the end of hostilities, and the funds raised were used to continue the USSC's work in aiding newly discharged veterans returning to civilian life. Those veterans who could not find their families or were permanently disabled came under the auspices of the Special Relief Department of the USSC. According to a *New York Times* report, this department's duties included investigating "the condition of discharged men who are assumed to be without means to pay the expense of going to their homes, and ... [furnishing] the necessary means where the man is found to be truly and really in need" (January 29, 1865).

One of the USSC's last significant efforts was the publication of a booklet titled *The Soldier's Friend*, which was distributed to Union soldiers. It listed the location of USSC branches and depots, as well as addresses for the newly created Soldiers' Homes, which offered returning soldiers a way station as they made their way back home—or refuge if they discovered there was no home left to which they could return. The booklet also featured valuable information on artificial limbs, back pay, and pensions. In this capacity, the USSC served in place of a national organization or agency to help veterans, the first of which came into existence in April 1866 as the Grand Army of the Republic, a fraternal organization for former Union soldiers. Only in 1921, following World War I, would a federal-level agency, the Veterans' Bureau, come into being to provide official federal assistance to those who had served their country.

The USSC disbanded in May 1866, a month after the Grand Army of the Republic was founded. Though prominent men served in its executive ranks, a tremendous amount of work was carried out by Livermore, Hoge, Woolsey, Schuyler, Wormeley, and countless other women. Many of them gained their first experience in financial and organizational administration, and went on to serve in the social-reform movements that gained momentum later in the century.

BIBLIOGRAPHY

Attie, Jeanie. *Patriotic Toil: Northern Women and the American Civil War.* Ithaca, NY: Cornell University Press, 1998.

"From City Point." *New York Times*, January 29, 1865.

"The Havelock Cap-Covers." *New York Times*, May 20, 1861.

Hoge, Jane [Mrs. A. H. Hoge]. *The Boys in Blue; Or, Heroes of the "Rank and File."* Chicago: C. W. Lilley, 1867.

Livermore, Mary A. *My Story of the War: A Woman's Narrative of Four Years Personal Experience as Field and Hospital Nurse in the Union Army.* Hartford, CT: A. D. Worthington, 1888.

Miller, Francis Trevelyan, and Robert Sampson Lanier, eds. *Prisons and Hospitals.* Vol. 7 of *The Photographic History of the Civil War.* New York: Review of Reviews, 1911.

Reed, William Howell. *Hospital Life in the Army of the Potomac.* Boston: W. V. Spencer, 1866.

"The Sanitary Condition of Gen. Grant's Army." *New York Times*, March 22, 1863.

Sherwood, Mrs. "Memories of 1861–64; The Sanitary Commission." *New York Times*, May 28, 1898.

"The Wants of the Western Sanitary Commission." *New York Times*, August 22, 1862.

"Work for the Ladies." *New York Times*, April 22, 1861.

Wormeley, Katharine Prescott. *The United States Sanitary Commission: A Sketch of Its Purposes and Its Work.* Boston: Little, Brown, 1863.

Carol Brennan

■ Sanitary Fairs

Despite their somewhat clinical-sounding name, sanitary fairs were lavish, well-attended charity events held in several major Northern cities with the goal of raising funds for the United States Sanitary Commission (USSC). This quasi-government organization, run mostly by volunteers, inspected Union Army camps and hospitals to ensure they were adhering to proper hygienic standards, and at the local level collected food, blankets, and medical supplies for soldiers fighting the Confederacy. These sanitary fairs, held between 1863 and 1865, were organized and run by the regional auxiliaries of the USSC and took place in Chicago, Boston, New York, and St. Louis. Altogether, the events collected an estimated \$2.7 million for the USSC. This figure was nearly half of the USSC's total revenues during its five years in operation, and its equivalent amount in twenty-first-century dollars is \$30 million (McCarthy 2003, p. 196).

There were some seven thousand local auxiliaries established after the start of the American Civil War in April 1861, and their active participants were among the most affluent and prominent women in each community (McCarthy 2003, p. 194). The sanitary fairs held in the larger Northern cities were well-attended and immensely successful charity events that became the focal point of an otherwise somber social season during the war years. There was an attempt, however, to make the goals of the USSC, and the sanitary fairs themselves, of interest to all who supported the Union cause. A press release issued to the clergy urged them to enjoin their congregations to participate. They were asked to issue a plea from their pulpits, calling on "every loyal and patriotic workingman, mechanic or farmer, who can make a pair of shoes or raise a barrel of apples... to contribute something that can be turned into money, and again from money into the means of ensuring the health and life of our national soldiers" (McCarthy 2003, p. 196).

Opposition to the USSC

The USSC's founding members modeled their organization in part on the British Sanitary Commission, which operated during the Crimean War of 1853–1856 and made immense strides in reducing disease outbreaks

Brooklyn Sanitary Fair, 1864. The Sanitary Fair was a project to benefit the United States Sanitary Commission, which gave supplies and health information to the troops during the Civil War. *The Art Archive/Museum of the City of New York/The Picture Desk, Inc.*

among British troops. Nonetheless, many politicians in Washington, along with top military brass, feared the meddling of self-appointed experts and opposed the USSC's offer to help the war effort; even President Abraham Lincoln warned that the Commission could become the proverbial "fifth wheel to the coach" (Miller 1911, p. 330). However, the surgeon general, Thomas Lawson, and War Secretary Simon Cameron both urged Lincoln to sign a June 18, 1861, proposal calling for the establishment of the USSC as an official government entity. The two men were part of a small contingent who believed it was wise to placate the growing number of Northern women who were eager to contribute to the war effort in a useful way.

Goals and Operations

The USSC operated on several levels. It trained volunteer nurses for field hospitals, and sent representatives to inspect army camps, field hospitals, and hospital ships to determine whether or not they maintained proper sanitary conditions. The volunteers also instructed camp kitchen personnel on food-safety issues and operated a post office service that located missing soldiers on behalf of their families. At the local level, sewing and knitting circles were organized to make uniforms, socks, gloves, and blankets for soldiers, and depots were established in cities and towns that accepted donations of both goods and money. The items collected by the USSC at these depots were either donated directly to soldiers or used for the sanitary fairs.

The goal of the sanitary fairs was to supply Union military personnel some of the basic necessities above and beyond what an already-overextended War Department could provide. One of their most significant contributions was the "comfort bag," assembled by USSC volunteers and distributed in the thousands to Union soldiers. These contained needles and thread, so that soldiers could repair their own uniforms, a miniature Bible, and a small knife for woodcarving—a popular hobby at the time—along with a comb, packets of coffee and sugar, and other incidentals that were gratefully received. "If the comfort bag contained no letter, with a stamped envelope, and blank sheet of paper added, its recipient was a little crestfallen," wrote Mary Livermore, head of the USSC Chicago auxiliary, in her 1888 memoir, *My Story of the War.* "The stationary was rarely forgotten. Folded in the sleeves of shirts, tucked in pockets, wrapped in handkerchiefs, and rolled in socks, were envelopes with stamps affixed, containing blank sheets of notepaper and usually a pencil was added. The soldiers expressed their need of stationary in almost every letter they wrote" (p. 140).

Fairs as Events

Livermore was a prominent journalist and women's rights activist who headed the USSC's Northwestern chapter in Chicago. She was instrumental in organizing the first sanitary fair, called the Northwestern Sanitary Fair, in October 1863. This event was notable for the $80,000 raised (in twenty-first century dollars, the equivalent of $1 million), part of which came from the sale of the original Emancipation Proclamation document (donated by President Lincoln), which fetched $3,000 at auction (Livermore 1888, p. 196). The document was destroyed just a few years later, however, during Chicago's notorious 1871 fire.

Other cities quickly copied Livermore's example. The Great Western Sanitary Fair in Cincinnati was held in December 1863, followed closely by a Boston event staged at the Boston Athenaeum that same month. The fairs' opening night galas quickly became eagerly anticipated social events, and wealthy families donated valuable items to be sold at auction. The Boston fair was notable for the sale of a painting by the Italian Renaissance painter Andrea del Sarto, donated by Peter Chardon Brooks, the son of Boston's first millionaire.

Civic pride and a confluence of wealth and power resulted in the New York Metropolitan Sanitary Fair topping the record for fundraising when its April 1864 event collected a stunning $2 million for the USSC (Silber 2005, p. 186). The New York fair was held at the since-demolished Palace Garden on 14th Street at Union Square, and its opening-day festivities included a military parade through the city and an opening address delivered by General John Adams Dix, who had stepped down from his position as U.S. Treasury Secretary when the war began. Dix told the crowd, according to a front-page article in the *New York Times*, that "our enemies abroad have said that the South ... [is] animated by the highest enthusiasm, and that we are comparatively cold and unmoved by the high motives of action. It is precisely the reverse; the contributions of the Northern people in treasure and blood have been voluntary offerings and sacrifices on the altar of their country" (April 5, 1864).

Among the Metropolitan Fair's most popular attractions was the Knickerbocker Kitchen, a temporary restaurant whose main novelty was the staff of socialites—from some of New York's oldest Dutch families, such as the Roosevelts—who waited on tables. The same *New York Times* front-page article also reported that three pickpockets were arrested on the first day of the Fair in the Palace Garden, and forced to parade through the crowd with a placard reading *Pickpocket* around their necks.

Baltimore, St. Louis, and Philadelphia all hosted sanitary fairs to raise money for Union soldiers and sailors over the course of 1864 and 1865. The final one, held in Chicago, opened on May 30, 1865, having already been planned by the time the war ended on April 9. Though the fairs were a quickly forgotten part of the war effort, for a generation of women who devoted their time and energy to them, they served as an invaluable introduction to the worlds of planning, organization, fundraising, financial administration, and outright commerce. The skills they learned would later be deployed in the burgeoning social

FREDERICK LAW OLMSTED, SANITARY COMMISSIONER AND CONSERVATIONIST

Frederick Law Olmsted (1822–1903) was one of a group of men involved with the work of the United States Sanitary Commission (USSC) and its sanitary fairs. By the early twenty-first century, however, he was better known as a landscape architect—he designed Central Park in New York City as well as many other famous parks and college campuses—and as an early conservationist than as a Civil War journalist and sanitary commissioner.

Olmsted was born in Hartford, Connecticut, the son of a well-to-do merchant. As a boy, Olmsted loved to explore the woods near his home, but had to give up plans for college when his eyes were damaged by exposure to poison sumac. Olmsted turned to agriculture and journalism, acquiring a farm on Staten Island in 1849 and taking a research journey through the South between 1852 and 1857 to write articles for the *New York Daily Times* (now *The New York Times*). Olmsted's articles for the *Times* were eventually collected into a set of volumes titled *Journeys and Explorations in the Cotton Kingdom of America*, first published in London in 1861. Olmsted's vivid first-person writing about the ills of slavery helped to shape public opinion in the North in the early months of the Civil War.

After returning from the South Olmsted turned his interest in gardening and landscape design to the development of Central Park in New York City. Olmsted envisioned the park as a space for enjoyment of nature that should be open to everyone. Although this concept of a "public" park seems obvious in the early 2000s, it was revolutionary in the late 1850s. Olmsted took a leave of absence from his work as director of Central Park to work for the USSC in 1861. In 1863, however, he was sent west to study the Mariposa mining estate in the Yosemite Valley and to manage it as a public park granted by Congress to the state of California. Two years later Olmsted drafted "Yosemite and the Mariposa Grove: A Preliminary Report, 1865," in which he set forth his vision of the national park as a place for all persons, not just the wealthy and powerful. Olmsted's view of nature as a source of spiritual and mental well-being was the basis of his determination to make this treasure freely available to all citizens. His 1865 report, available from the Yosemite Online Library, stated:

> It is a scientific fact that the occasional contemplation of natural scenes of an impressive character, particularly if this contemplation occurs in connection with relief from ordinary cares, change of air and change of habits, is favorable to the health and vigor of men . . . that it not only gives pleasure for the time being but increases the subsequent capacity for happiness and the means of securing happiness. . . .
>
> The enjoyment of the choicest natural scenes in the country and the means of recreation connected with them [have been] a monopoly, in a very peculiar manner, of a very few very rich people. The great mass of society, including those to whom it would be of the greatest benefit, is excluded from it. In the nature of the case private parks can never be used by the mass of the people in any country nor by any considerable number even of the rich, except by the favor of a few. . . .
>
> It was in accordance with . . . the duty of a Republican Government that Congress enacted that the Yosemite should be held, guarded and managed for the free use of the whole body of the people forever, and that the care of it, and the hospitality of admitting strangers from all parts of the world to visit it and enjoy it freely, should be a duty of dignity.

REBECCA J. FREY

BIBLIOGRAPHY

"The Evolution of the Conservation Movement, 1850–1920." The Library of Congress, May 3, 2002. Available from http://memory.loc.gov/.

Olmsted, Frederick Law. "Yosemite and the Mariposa Grove: A Preliminary Report, 1865." Yosemite Online Library. Available from http://www.yosemite.ca.us/.

Stevenson, Elizabeth. Park Maker: A Life of Frederick Law Olmsted. *New Brunswick, NJ: Transaction Publishers, 2000.*

reform and women's suffrage movements that gained steam in the decades following the war.

The recipients of the Sanitary Fair's efforts, the soldiers, were profoundly grateful to the USSC and the women who organized and staffed the fairs. Livermore, in her memoir, reprinted a letter from several wounded men who were recovering at a Memphis military hospital. The letter, addressed to "the Managers of the Northwestern Fair," asserted that its writers "are deeply grateful for the sympathy manifested towards us in words and deeds. We are cheered, comforted, and encouraged. . . . In the light of your smiles, and in this great earnest[ness] of your sympathy, we have an additional incentive never to relax our efforts for our native land, whose women are its brightest ornaments, as well as its truest patriots" (Livermore 1888, p. 460).

BIBLIOGRAPHY

"Art People." *New York Times*, April 5, 1985.

Livermore, Mary. *My Story of the War: A Woman's Narrative of Four Years Personal Experience as Field and Hospital Nurse in the Union Army.* Hartford, CT: A. D. Worthington, 1888.

"Luxury against Patriotism." *New York Times*, April 2, 1864, p. 6.

McCarthy, Kathleen D. *American Creed: Philanthropy and the Rise of Civil Society, 1700–1865.* Chicago: University of Chicago Press, 2003.

"Metropolitan Fair; The Grand Opening Yesterday." *New York Times*, April 5, 1864, p. 1.

Miller, Francis Trevelyan, and Robert Sampson Lanier, eds. *Prisons and Hospitals*. Vol. 7 of *The Photographic History of the Civil War*. New York: Review of Reviews, 1911.

Silber, Nina. *Daughters of the Union: Northern Women Fight the Civil War*. Cambridge, MA: Harvard University Press, 2005.

Vogel, Carol. "An Old Master Sold at Auction Raises Doubts." *New York Times*, February 17, 2000.

Carol Brennan

Civilian Health Care

For most of the nineteenth century, health care in the United States took place within the confines of the home. Physicians routinely paid visits to their patients to deliver diagnoses or to dispense treatments by the fireside. Only rarely were individuals treated in infirmaries. What few hospitals existed at the outbreak of the Civil War were typically considered the last refuge of the insane or fatally ill.

Soon after the onset of hostilities between the North and South, however, this situation changed, with many doctors soon finding their services in high demand on the battlefield. As a result, in-home medical care became harder for Americans to secure, especially in war-ravaged areas of the South. Still, as a percentage of the general population, the number of physicians remained high. Additionally, large numbers of midwives and folk healers—white and black alike—continued to provide care alongside their licensed counterparts.

Indeed, one of the chief impediments to civilian health care in the South during the Civil War was not a lack of medical practitioners but a lack of supplies. In particular, the Union blockade of Confederate ports prevented many much-needed medicines, deemed to be contraband during the conflict, from entering the region. With their already limited pharmacopeia continued shrinking in size, southerners began to seek alternative remedies in native medicinal plants.

Both lay and professional practitioners were aided in their attempts at alternative homeopathy by the 1863 publication of Francis P. Porcher's work *Resources of the Southern Fields and Forests, Medical, Economical, and Agricultural*. Written at the behest of the Confederate surgeon general, Porcher's book identified a number of indigenous plants that could serve as substitutes for many of the major refined pharmaceuticals of the age. Ultimately, *Resources of the Southern Fields and Forests* aided doctors and herbal healers, as portions of Porcher's work were widely reprinted throughout southern newspapers during the war. One southerner's description of the situation is recounted in Parthenia Antoinette Hague's 1888 work *A Blockaded Family: Life in Southern Alabama during the Civil War*: "the woods . . . were also our drug stores" (p. 46).

Beyond foraging through forests for alternative remedies, southerners also raised curatives in their own gardens. For instance, refined opium, one of the favored painkillers of the age, quickly came into short supply. Many citizens planted rows of poppies in their gardens to make opium. Such measures proved to be a very successful enterprise too. The homegrown products were just as effective as the ones that would have otherwise been purchased in stores and such individual production assured that pain relievers would be available when needed.

Regarding medical care for slaves on the home front, it remained similar to that of whites during the period. Physicians, who were typically kept on yearly retainer by an owner to attend their slaves, routinely traveled to the plantation to administer treatment either in the slave quarters or in the master's home. In these cases practitioners also faced a shortage of essential medications. For example, former slave Louis Hughes remembered in a 2005 reprint of his autobiography, *Thirty Years a Slave: From Bondage to Freedom, The Autobiography of Louis Hughes*, an instance during the war when he was treated for chills and fever. Since quinine was rare, he drank a tea made from lemon leaves. "I was treated in this manner," Hughes recounted, "to some advantage." He admitted that not all were so lucky however. While this makeshift remedy worked for him, the same "cannot always be said of all methods of treatment" (p. 73).

Aside from dealing with a dearth of pharmaceuticals, many doctors also had to manage their medical stores more closely. Not long after the outbreak of hostilities, Union and Confederate armies began appropriating existing supplies for military use. Basic items such as bandages and surgical implements quickly became scarce. For physicians on the home front, this situation only grew worse over time. While civilian aide agencies such as the United States Sanitary Commission emerged early in the war to assist in forwarding supplies to physicians on the battlefield, health care workers at home still had to scrounge for even the most rudimentary tools of their trade.

Notwithstanding the scarcity of pharmaceutical and medical supplies, civilian practitioners faced no shortage of sickness during the Civil War. Although spared the devastation of communicable diseases like typhus, measles, and whooping cough that spread rapidly through crowded, squalid military encampments, civilians in the South still suffered from high rates of infectious disease. The subtropical climate of certain portions of the region, for example, ensured that endemic ailments like malaria and yellow fever continued to wreak havoc. Moreover, chronic malnutrition compromised the immunity of many residents, creating conditions in which simple sicknesses could readily develop into deadly maladies. As for

MEDICINE'S INTERNAL CIVIL WAR: MAINSTREAM MEDICINE AND HOMEOPATHY

At the time of the Civil War, there were a number of different approaches to medicine in the United States, each having its own schools and curricula. It was not until the Flexner Report of 1910 that there was any attempt to standardize the training and certification of American physicians. What we now think of as mainstream or scientific medicine (sometimes called *allopathic medicine*) had a serious rival at the time of the Civil War-homeopathy. Homeopathy is now considered an alternative form of treatment and is used by only 2 percent of Americans, but in the 1860s, it was more popular in many areas of the country than mainstream medicine.

Homeopathy is a form of treatment in which the practitioner administers, in extremely dilute formulations, substances that would ordinarily cause symptoms similar to the patient's illness. For example, arsenic and belladonna, which cause fever in humans when given in large doses, are used by homeopaths in extremely small doses to treat fevers. The founder of homeopathy, a German chemist and physician named Samuel Hahnemann (1755–1843), experimented with minute doses of a wide range of plant and mineral compounds, believing they cured patients by stimulating the body's own vital force.

Although a commonplace modern criticism of homeopathy is that the remedies used are so diluted that they retain too little of the original substance to have any effect on the body, it is likely that their very mildness was one reason for the popularity of homeopathy in the United States from the 1830s to the 1860s. Mainstream medical practitioners often used bloodletting and dosed patients with such harmful compounds as calomel (mercurous chloride, used as a laxative). While some turned to folk remedies or Native American herbal treatments as alternatives to mainstream medicine, others were attracted to homeopathy because its practitioners had largely been educated in Europe. Immigrant homeopaths were often more highly educated than American allopathic physicians. The first American homeopath was Hans Gram, a Boston-born physician of Danish extraction who went to Europe to study homeopathy and returned to the United States to open a homeopathic practice in 1825. In less than a decade there were several schools of homeopathic medicine, the most famous of which was the Homeopathic Medical College of Philadelphia. In 1844 practitioners of homeopathy in the United States formed the American Institute of Homeopathy.

Orthodox or mainstream physicians began to oppose homeopathy in the early 1840s. The American Medical Association, founded in 1847, was organized at least in part to counteract the American Institute of Homeopathy. Oliver Wendell Holmes Sr. (1809–1894), a physician practicing in Boston, delivered two public lectures in 1842 on "Homeopathy and Its Kindred Delusions," in which he systematically mocked the underlying assumptions of homeopathy. When the Civil War began, the medical corps of the Union Army were dominated by allopathic doctors, and its examining boards routinely denied military commissions to homeopaths. This exclusion had the unfortunate side effect, however, of intensifying the shortage of experienced surgeons in the army, as many homeopaths in the 1860s had had more training in surgery than their mainstream medical counterparts.

REBECCA J. FREY

BIBLIOGRAPHY

Holmes, Oliver Wendell, Sr. "Homeopathy and Its Kindred Delusions." 1842. Available online from http://homeoint.org/cazalet/holmes/index.htm.

National Center for Complementary and Alternative Medicine (NCCAM). "Research Report: Questions and Answers about Homeopathy." Available online from http://nccam.nih.gov/health/homeopathy/.

Rutkow, Lainie W., and Ira M. Rutkow. "Homeopaths, Surgery, and the Civil War: Edward C. Franklin and the Struggle to Achieve Medical Pluralism in the Union Army." Archives of Surgery 139, no. 7 (2004): 785–791.

residents of the North, they too suffered from disease, especially the ever-present plague of urban life in the nineteenth century: tuberculosis.

There were numerous practical and epidemiological challenges civilian health care workers faced during the Civil War. In general, however, physicians, midwives, and folk healers continued to serve the American public without interruption, even if sometimes without necessary medicines and supplies in hand.

BIBLIOGRAPHY

Current, Richard N., ed. *Encyclopedia of the Confederacy*, vol. 2. New York: Simon and Schuster, 1993.

Flannery, Michael A. *Civil War Pharmacy: A History of Drugs, Drug Supply and Provision, and Therapeutics for the Union and Confederacy.* New York: Pharmaceutical Products Press, 2004.

Hague, Parthenia Antoinette. *A Blockaded Family: Life in Southern Alabama during the Civil War* [1888]. Bedford, MA: Applewood Books, [1995.]

Heidler, David S., and Jeanne T. Heidler, eds. *Encyclopedia of the American Civil War: A Political, Social and Military History.* New York: W.W. Norton and Co., 2000.

Hughes, Louis. *Thirty Years a Slave: From Bondage to Freedom, The Autobiography of Louis Hughes.* Montgomery, AL: NewSouth Books, 2002.

Porcher, Francis Peyre. *Resources of the Southern Fields and Forests, Medical, Economical, and Agricultural* [1863]. San Francisco: Norman Pub., 1991.

Rothstein, William G. *American Physicians in the Nineteenth Century: From Sects to Science.* Baltimore, MD: Johns Hopkins University Press, 1972.

Amy Crowson

Advances in Medicine

In a time before bacteriology and aseptic surgery were understood, before many of the technological advances of the twentieth century, Civil War doctors were making great advances in medicine, not only in battlefield techniques in caring for the injured, but also in medicine as a whole. Doctors practicing medicine and learning through trial by fire on the front lines of the Civil War took exceptional care of the wounded.

Advances in Medical Techniques and Understanding

For the first time in the United States, compiling a complete medical history was possible due to an accumulation of adequate records and detailed reports. This led to the publication of the Medical and Surgical History of the War of the Rebellion (1870), which was identified in Europe as the first major academic accomplishment in U.S. medicine (Blaisdell 1988, p. 1046). Thomas Ellis, an army surgeon during the Civil War, wrote, "Among the few benefits derived from the war, is the marked improvement in military surgery. Some of the surgeons; who now skillfully perform the necessary operations, and judiciously decline to amputate where a hope of saving the limb exists, were[,] at the commencement of the rebellion[,] inadequate to the positions they occupied" (1863, p. 231). Among advances in medical techniques there were modifications of surgical apparati and appliances, and doctors soon after the war learned about hospital gangrene, septicemia, and the effects of malnutrition, such as diarrhea. Although the use of anesthesia was not new at the time, during the war surgeons developed an inhaler for its administration; the previous method involved placing a chloroform or ether-doused rag over the face of the patient (Belferman 1996).

Over the course of the war, surgeons learned about treating head injuries and how to ligate arteries and better treat chest wounds, and they expanded their knowledge of spinal injuries. After the war, thermometers became widely available, as did stethoscopes, ophthalmoscopes, and hypodermic needles, which already had been widely used in Europe (Adams 1985, p. 176).

Infectious wounds proved to be the bane of both the Union and Confederate armies. The concept that cleanliness led to fewer complications was understood, but the reasons why were yet unknown. It was not until 1865 that Joseph Lister introduced antiseptic surgery. Prior to this, it was common for doctors to dig bullets and mortar fragments out with their bare fingers, sometimes using unsanitized instruments and employing only a quick rinse in cold water to rinse off the blood before moving on to the next patient (Belferman 1996).

Chronic diarrhea was a serious problem for both armies, and was responsible for more deaths than any other disease. Soldiers' rations consisted of dried beef or pork, coffee, and hard-tack biscuits that were often infested with weevils. Fresh fruits and vegetables were a luxury for a soldier. Malnutrition resulted in vitamin deficiencies. In turn, a vitamin-C deficiency led to scurvy and niacin deficiency led to pellagra. These conditions often caused skin infections, dementia, diarrhea, and sometimes, death (Bollet 2002, p. 87).

U.S. mortality rates from disease were about 65 per 1,000 for the troops that fought in the Civil War. Comparatively, mortality rates for U.S. troops fighting in the Mexican War of 1846 and those of the British troops in the Crimean War of 1854 were about 104 per 1,000 and 232 per 1,000 troops, respectively (Otis 1865, p. 93).

Medicines

Sarah Emma Edmonds, a nurse for the Union army, noted the "liberal distribution of quinine and blue pills, and sometimes a little eau de vie, to wash down the bitter drugs," given to the soldiers to cure a multitude of illnesses (1865, p. 282). Although morphine and quinine were plentiful and did much good, the "blue pill," calomel, and tartar emetic contained high levels of mercury and antimony, which led to heavy metal poisoning. This was such a problem that General William Hammond of the North forbade the use of mercurials, calomel, and tartar emetic by the end of the war.

Mercury was also the treatment of choice for syphilis, diarrhea, dysentery, and typhoid (Adams 1985, p. 154). Treatment included hourly administration of mercurous drugs, which often resulted in heavy metal poisoning of the patient. Ensuing symptoms included tongue swelling, bone necrosis, gangrene, loosening and loss of teeth, and excess salivation—anywhere from a pint to a quart a day was common.

Ambulance Corp

Ghastly accounts were told of men being left to die on the battlefield. In one instance, after the Battle of the Wilderness (May 5–7, 1864), so many men were wounded that they became lost in the brush and were not rescued. Then a fire erupted, burning to death hundreds of men. Henry Bowditch, a soldier in the Union army, beseeched Congress to arrange and equip an ambulance corp of detailed soldiers, similar to those that the English and French armies had at the time. Bowditch had lost many comrades in battles fought around Centreville, Virginia, and also

DENTISTRY IN THE CIVIL WAR

Dentistry in the United States had made a number of advances in the decades preceding the Civil War. Like veterinary medicine, dentistry had become a profession separate from general medicine and surgery in the nineteenth century. In the early part of the century most American dentists qualified for the profession by apprenticing themselves to established practitioners. The first independent school of dentistry in the United States, the Baltimore College of Dental Surgery, was established in 1840. By the time of the Civil War there were four American dental schools, all of them in the North. Southern as well as Northern dentists trained in these schools, and dentists on both sides used the same textbooks, *A Practical Treatise on Operative Dentistry* (1859) and *The Principles and Practice of Dental Surgery* (1863), both published in Philadelphia.

The American Dental Association (ADA), founded in 1859, was headquartered in New York City. Bitterness following the Civil War led Southern dentists to form their own professional organization, the Southern Dental Association, which did not rejoin the ADA until 1914.

The Confederacy established a separate dental corps to treat soldiers at the front. Dental surgeons in the Confederate Army were assigned to hospitals and combat regiments as medical surgeons. Union soldiers who did not have a dental corps either had to make do with local dentists in the towns where they were stationed, or request treatment from contract dentists hired by the Union Army or from dentists who had joined Union regiments as soldiers and were practicing dentistry unofficially.

Behind the lines Civil War dentists performed fillings and tooth extractions as well as instructing soldiers in basic oral hygiene. On the battlefield itself, injuries to the mouth and jaw were often treated by military surgeons as well as dentists, and instruments used to prepare teeth for fillings were part of many doctors' surgical field kits.

The dental textbooks in use in the early 1860s indicate that American dentists were knowledgeable about the advantages and drawbacks of different types of fillings. Unlike some of their European counterparts, they did not use lead to fill teeth because it was known to be dangerous to one's health. Gold was the preferred filling material because it was strong, easily placed in the tooth, and compatible with the body's tissues. Other dentists used an amalgam made of silver and tin. On the battlefield, dentists and surgeons used a mixture of zinc chloride and zinc oxide to make temporary fillings that could be replaced later with permanent ones.

Because of the Northern blockade, Southern dentists had difficulty obtaining gold for use in fillings during the war; there was only one dental supply company in Atlanta that was able to obtain gold for either civilian or military dentists. As the Confederate currency lost its value, the cost of a gold filling soared to $120—more than ten months' pay for a private in the Confederate Army.

Some information about Civil War dentistry has been obtained from the skulls of Confederate soldiers from the Battle of First Bull Run (1861) and the Battle of Glorieta Pass (1862) in New Mexico. The fillings in the soldiers' teeth were mostly gold, probably placed before the war, although one soldier had had his teeth filled with a mixture of mercury and tin. In another case the soldier's dentist had filled a tooth with thorium, not knowing that it is a radioactive material. He may have mistaken it for tin.

REBECCA J. FREY

BIBLIOGRAPHY

Asbell, Milton B. Dentistry: A Historical Perspective: Being a Historical Account of the History of Dentistry From Ancient Times, with Emphasis on the United States from the Colonial to the Present Period. *Bryn Mawr, PA: Dorrance and Co., [1988].*

Glenner, Richard A., and Willey, P. "Dental Filling Materials in the Confederacy," Journal of the History of Dentistry *46, no. 2 (July 1998): 71–75.*

had lost his son, a lieutenant with the First Massachusetts Cavalry. He remarked, "a wounded soldier is liable to be left to suffer, and die . . . on the battle-ground, without the least attention. . . . This happens, first, because Congress readily refuses to establish any definite and efficient Ambulance Corps in the armies of the Republic; and second, because the War Department declines to do anything in the premises" (1863, p. 6).

By the war's end, Jonathan Letterman, the medical director of the Union's Army of the Potomac, had developed a system for evacuating the wounded, and established ambulances and dedicated personnel for each regiment to take the wounded off the battlefield.

Hospitals

Initially, both the Union and the Confederacy thought the engagements between the two armies would be small, pitched battles. The country was unprepared when, in 1862, large-scale, devastating battles resulted in mass casualties. As the war raged, larger and better field hospitals developed. According to George Adams, regimental hospitals clustered together as brigade hospitals, with some differentiation of duty for the various medical officers; the chief surgeon of the brigade was in charge. Soon, brigade hospitals clustered into division hospitals, and 1864 saw the formation of corps hospitals. There the best surgeons would operate; another surgeon would be responsible for records, another for drugs, another for supplies, and yet another would treat the sick and lightly wounded (Adams 1981). Confederates developed the prototypes of mobile army surgical hospital (MASH) units as they fled before General William Tecumseh Sherman's advance (Belferman 1996).

At this time, female nurses were introduced to hospital care, and Catholic orders entered the hospital business. Nursing was elevated to a profession, with thousands of women working in hospitals for the first time. Civilians joined the Sanitary Commission, a soldiers' relief society that set the precedent for the development of the American Red Cross. By the last year of the war, in 1865, there were 204 Union general hospitals with beds for 136,894 patients (Adams 1981). The pavilion-style general hospitals were wood-built, clean, and had ample ventilation and sufficient bed space for eighty to one hundred patients; they became the model for large civilian hospitals over the next seventy-five years (Blaisdell 1988, pp. 1045–1046). Furthermore, specialist hospitals and departments to treat the specific problems of wartime soldiers appeared for the first time. The famous neurological hospital Turner's Lane was founded in Philadelphia, where W. W. Keen (1837–1932) is considered by some to have originated neurology in the United States. Silas Weir Mitchell (1829–1914) further advanced neurology by characterizing new syndromes of causalgia—triggered by nerve damage—and "phantom limb," and Jacob Da Costa (1833–1900) described "soldier's heart," the medical concept known today as posttraumatic stress disorder (PTSD) or "shell shock" (Bollet 2002, p. 363). The gains in medical knowledge during and immediately after the Civil War led to the development of a system of managing mass casualties that included the establishment of aid stations, field hospitals, and general hospitals. This system set the pattern for management of the wounded during World War I, World War II, and the Korean War (Blaisdell 1988, p. 1050).

In the Union army 30.5 percent of soldiers died during battle or from battle wounds; in the Confederate army the percentage was 36.4. Although the Civil War produced a high number of casualties, mortality rates due to direct combat and to disease both decreased. By the end of 1865 army doctors had set up large hospitals. The benefits of asepsis and general prevention of disease were better understood. The training of nurses became standardized. Medical professionals, soldiers, and civilians were also educated in issues of public health. Finally, the importance of specialization for certain diseases and the need for expanded laboratory studies were recognized (Adams 1985, p. 240).

BIBLIOGRAPHY

Adams, George W. "Fighting for Time." In *The Image of War, 1861–1865*, vol. 4, ed. William Davis. Garden City, NY: Doubleday, 1981. Available from http://www.civilwarhome.com/.

Adams, George Worthington. *Doctors in Blue: The Medical History of the Union Army in the Civil War.* Dayton, OH: Morningside, 1985.

Belferman, Mary. "On Surgery's Cutting Edge In Civil War: Medical 'Turning Point' Is Focus of New Museum." *Washington Post*, Washington, DC, June 13, 1996.

Blaisdell, F. W. "Medical Advances during the Civil War." *Archives of Surgical History* 123 (1988): 1045–1050.

Bollet, Alfred J. *Civil War Medicine: Challenges and Triumphs.* New York: Galen Press, 2002.

Bowditch, Henry I. *A Brief Plea for an Ambulance System for the Army of the United States, as Drawn from the Extra Sufferings of the Late Lieut. Bowditch and a Wounded Comrade.* Boston: Ticknor and Fields, 1863.

Edmonds, S. Emma E. *Nurse and Spy in the Union Army: Comprising the Adventures and Experiences of a Woman in Hospitals, Camps, and Battle-fields.* Hartford, CT: W. S. Williams, 1865.

Ellis, Thomas T. *Leaves from the Diary of an Army Surgeon, or, Incidents of Field, Camp, and Hospital Life.* New York: John Bradburn, 1863.

Marks, James Junius. *The Peninsular Campaign in Virginia, or, Incidents and Scenes on the Battle-fields and in Richmond.* Philadelphia: J. B. Lippincott, 1864.

Otis, George A. *Reports on the Extent and Nature of the Materials Available for the Preparation of a Medical and Surgical History of the Rebellion.* Philadelphia: J. B. Lippincott, 1865.

Anurag Biswas

Work and Economy

■ Work and Economy Overview

Even though the war was occupying the labors of the hundreds of thousands of young and middle-aged men who were serving as soldiers, the work of America had to go on. Scarcely more than ten percent of the American population served in the armies at any one time during the course of the war. Most Americans spent the war years at home, working at many familiar tasks and some unfamiliar ones.

Farming was still the occupation of a great many Americans in mid-nineteenth century, and in many ways its labor continued as it had before the outbreak of the conflict. Farmers still sowed and reaped, sheared sheep, milked cows, or slaughtered hogs as they had in peace time. But some things were different. In many parts of the South that anticipated the coming of the Union armies, as well as those parts of Pennsylvania visited by Robert E. Lee's Confederate army in 1863, farmers often saw their livestock confiscated, their fields trampled, and their food supplies depleted by hordes of hungry, hostile soldiers. A more subtle but no less painful loss was the destruction of fences. Most fences in the United States of the Civil War years were made of split rails with their ends crisscrossed to form zigzag fences five feet or more in height. This was necessary because farmers commonly let their livestock, especially hogs, run wild in the woods, and under the laws then prevailing, it was every farmer's responsibility to fence such animals out of the fields where they grew crops. If a farmer had no fence, his own and his neighbors' pigs would soon devour his crop as it stood in the field. Soldiers were always looking for good, dry, seasoned firewood, and the fence rails were perfect. When soldiers made a farmer's fence into "the watch fires of a hundred circling camps," that year's crop was most likely a loss.

For other farmers, the Civil War was a time of doing more with less. Many of the soldiers who filled the ranks of the armies were farm laborers, and their absence exacerbated America's chronic labor shortage and enhanced the desirability of labor-saving machines. From this was born the wisdom of Cyrus McCormick's decision to move his mechanical reaper business from his native Rockcastle County, Virginia, to Chicago, Illinois, a burgeoning rail hub smack in the middle of a vast expanse of the world's finest farmland. The war years saw vast increases in the use of McCormick's machine, as the mechanical reaper did the work of thousands of sturdy farm lads now shouldering rifles for the Union cause.

The South had never had much interest in machinery of any sort—save cotton gins—and certainly not mechanical reapers. After all, the South had slaves. Bondmen continued to perform much of the South's agricultural labor during the war, but their eagerness to escape at the first opportunity and their growing awareness that their days of unrequited toil were approaching an end made them an increasingly problematic source of labor for the flagging Confederacy.

By 1860, more Americans than ever before were employed in non-farm labor, and the war brought added stimulus for the growing industrialization that gave them their new types of work. Textile mills such as the pioneering facility in Lowell, Massachusetts, employed many "operatives," or factory workers, as they were then called, and many of those were young, unmarried women. Heavier industries, such as the foundries that made cannon, rails, or locomotives, employed exclusively male workers. The North had much more of both types of industry, with Richmond's Tredegar Iron Works being the only facility south of the Mason-Dixon Line that could make either a locomotive or a heavy cannon. During the course of the war, the Confederacy developed a small military-industrial base of its own, and many of the operatives in establishments making tents, uniforms, or even gunpowder, were women. Some of these were put out of work when Union armies destroyed their factories. Ulysses S. Grant on one occasion allowed each member of the female workforce of a

Confederate tent factory to take as much cloth as she could carry as a kind of severance package prior to the destruction of the establishment. William T. Sherman on another occasion had the entire workforce of a Confederate factory, all of them young women, shipped north of the Ohio River.

Wartime labor for many Southern women did not, however, involve factory work but rather many of the farm duties of an absent husband. This meant performing duties and assuming responsibilities a woman would not have ordinarily done in prewar days, but most of the women thus circumstanced seemed to have found it more of a burden than a liberation. Scores plied their fighting husbands with letters begging them to somehow get out of the army, get a furlough, or, in some cases, to desert their duties so as to come home and provide for their suffering families.

The situation in the North was less dire. A smaller percentage of Northern men went into the military, and the U.S. government was far more reliable in paying its soldiers. The Northern economy also remained sound enough that the money paid to the soldiers retained some, though by no means all, of its value, unlike the almost completely depreciated currency of the Confederacy. Nevertheless, many Northern women labored against severe hardship. The widow of one Illinois soldier, confined to her bed by sickness, lay on her back while knitting a pair of badly needed trousers for her teenaged son, on whose labor the family now depended for survival. Elsewhere in Illinois, in a small town a few miles from the Wisconsin line, boys in their young teens organized themselves into a sort of club known as the "sawbuck rangers," dedicated to sawing up a winter's supply of firewood for neighborhood families whose chief breadwinners were away in the army.

The work of Americans during the early 1860s differed according to their location in the country, their station in life, and the fortunes of war. For most, it was a time of increased labor to meet the demands of the wartime economy and the needs of their own families.

Steven E. Woodworth

■ Manufacturing

MANUFACTURING: AN OVERVIEW
Steven Barleen

NORTHERN MANUFACTURING
Steven Barleen

SOUTHERN MANUFACTURING
Steven Barleen

FACTORIES
Steven Barleen

ARMS MANUFACTURING
Carol Brennan

SHIPBUILDING
Jeffery Seymour

TEXTILES
Pamela L. Kester

MANUFACTURING: AN OVERVIEW

When the Civil War began in 1861, neither side in the conflict expected it to last very long. The South expected that due to the superiority of its fighting spirit it would defeat the North quickly on the battlefield and force it to recognize the independence of the Confederate States of America (McPherson 1988, pp. 316–317). Many people in the North were also eager for a brawl, expecting that with the Union's greater population and industrial capacity, it would quickly be able to make the South come to its senses (Foote 1958, pp. 50–60). As the next four years would demonstrate, however, both sides were grossly mistaken in their initial assessments of the other's ability to sustain the war, but in the long run the North was correct about its ability to overwhelm the states in rebellion. The North outstripped the South in manufacturing capacity and manpower, and while the Union struggled during the first few years of the conflict in coordinating its manufacturing resources, it was eventually able to meet all of its supply needs. The Confederacy, on the other hand, despite its attempts to develop a manufacturing base before and during the conflict, had an economy largely based on investment in slaveholding and land ownership (Luraghi 1978; Wright 1978; Genovese 1965). Even though the South desperately tried to marshal its manufacturing resources to supply its wartime needs, it simply lacked the manpower and manufacturing base to effectively counter the North's advantages in these areas.

An Unequal Contest

At the start of the conflict the manufacturing balance sheet between the North and the South was quite lopsided in favor of the Union. One historian notes that the North had 110,000 manufacturing establishments to the South's 18,000; the North had 1,300,000 industrial workers compared to the South's 110,000. Massachusetts alone produced over 60 percent more manufactured goods than all the Confederate states put together, Pennsylvania nearly twice as much, and New York more than twice as much (Foote 1958, p. 60). Another study demonstrates that the total value of manufactured goods in Virginia, Alabama, Louisiana, and Mississippi was less than $85 million while New York alone produced goods worth almost $380 million (Millett and Maslowski 1984, p. 164). Historian James McPherson points out the irony in this disproportion: while many in the South believed that cotton production would provide them with the wealth to fund their war, the states that grew the cotton possessed

Augusta Powder Works, Augusta, Georgia. Recognizing the greater manufacturing ability of its Northern opponent, the South nonetheless made great strides in closing this competitive advantage. Prior to the war's outset, Confederate states embarked on a furious, government-organized campaign to build factories, such as the Augusta Powder Works pictured here, to manufacture supplies rather than import them. *The Library of Congress*

only 6 percent of the nation's cotton manufacturing capacity (McPherson 1982, p. 23).

Furthermore, the states that remained within the Union had a better than ten-to-one advantage in the gross value of manufactured goods over the states that made up the Confederacy, with the latter producing only 7.4 percent of the nation's gross value of these goods (Tindall and Shi 1992, p. 642). The free states had 84 percent of the nation's capital invested in manufacturing in 1860. In such crucial industries as iron production, the South lagged far behind: During the year ending June 1, 1860, the Confederate states produced 36,790 tons of pig iron, while the figure for Pennsylvania alone was 580,049 tons (Millett and Maslowski 1984, p. 164). In other industries with a direct connection to warfare, the Northern states had 97 percent of the country firearms in 1860, 94 percent of its cloth, 93 percent of its pig iron, and more than 90 percent of its boots and shoes (McPherson 1988, 318).

Confederate manufacturers were at a considerable disadvantage because they had largely depended on Northern technological know-how to develop and run their industries, and many of these workers returned to the North at the start of hostilities. In addition, many of the mechanics who were Southern-born chose to seek glory in uniform rather than stay on the job in Southern manufactories (Dew 1966, pp. 90–91). Reflecting the problem in home-grown expertise, James McPherson estimates that the South had contributed only seven percent of the important inventions in the United States between 1790 and 1860 (McPherson 1982, p. 25). Furthermore, many of the South's industries were located in the Upper South close to coastal areas and were therefore always vulnerable to Union invasion (Millett and Maslowski 1984, p. 164).

Another great advantage for Northern manufacturers was the population base from which they drew their workers. In 1861 the North had twenty-two million people compared with 9 million in the Confederacy. Of the latter, three and a half million were slaves, and while the South increasingly tried to incorporate enslaved people into its manufacturing workforce as the war progressed, it found this a difficult endeavor (Tindall and Shi 1992, p. 642; Dew 1966, pp. 250–264). Not only did the North's population dwarf the South, the North was also more intensively engaged in industry at the outset of hostilities. Only forty percent of the Northern labor force worked in agriculture, while the slave states had 84 percent of their labor force occupied in farming. Consequently, the slave states had only ten percent of their population living in urban areas of 2,500 people or more, while the free states had 26 percent of their population living in such areas (McPherson 1982, p. 24).

The North's advantage in terms of population resulted from the steady flow of immigrants to the port cities of New York, Boston, and Philadelphia, from which many of them fanned out across the North to take manufacturing jobs in inland towns. This influx of workers did not cease during the war, with more than 800,000 new immigrants arriving between 1861 and 1865 (Millett and Maslowski 1984, p. 163).

The Southern Response

Statistics like these certainly give the impression that the South faced an uphill battle in meeting its manufacturing needs. While it certainly did struggle to meet its needs, it made a great effort to do so. Historian Raimondo Luraghi has argued that despite the omnipresent issue of states rights, the Confederate government took a decisive role in managing its industries through what might be called the first instance of forced industrialization through state socialism. The South's industrialization program had no equal until the rise of the Soviet Union in the early part of the twentieth century (Luraghi 1978, pp. 112–132). The authors of *Why the South Lost the Civil War* point to some of the ways in which the Confederacy brought its manufacturers under its control. One was conscription, which allowed the government to exempt skilled workers. The other was the

THE *SULTANA* DISASTER, APRIL 27, 1865

The explosion of the *Sultana*, a Mississippi River steamship transporting Union soldiers recently released from Confederate prison camps, in April 1865 was the greatest maritime disaster in United States history. It is estimated that more passengers on the *Sultana* lost their lives than on the *Titanic* in 1912.

The *Sultana* had been built in Cincinnati, Ohio, in 1862 for the cotton trade on the lower Mississippi. After 1864 the War Department commissioned the vessel for troop transport. On her last voyage, the *Sultana* left New Orleans on April 21, 1865, with livestock and about seventy-five cabin passengers bound for St. Louis, Missouri. The ship stopped at Vicksburg on April 24 to take on more passengers—Union soldiers recently released from prison camps at Andersonville and Cahaba. Although the *Sultana* had a legal capacity of 376 persons, more than 2,100 soldiers came aboard, filling every available space on the decks as well as the cabins. Many of these men had been severely weakened by wounds, malnutrition, and disease (Ambrose 2001).

The severe overcrowding helped set the stage for disaster. As the ship steamed north of Memphis, Tennessee, one of its poorly maintained boilers exploded at about 2 a.m. on the morning of April 27; two of the other boilers then followed. Many passengers were killed immediately by the blast; others were scalded by escaping steam or burned to death in the fire that engulfed the ship when hot coals from the exploding boilers set fire to the wooden decks. Still others drowned or perished from hypothermia after jumping into the cold waters of the Mississippi. For months after the disaster, bodies were found downstream as far as Vicksburg. Many victims were never recovered. About eight hundred people survived the initial explosion and fire, but three hundred of these died within a few days of severe burns or exposure. Estimates of the death toll range between 1,300 and 1,900.

It is thought that the boiler's explosion was the result of the *Sultana*'s careening; that is, as the overcrowded and top-heavy ship struggled around the bends in the Mississippi, she tilted from one side to the other. The four boilers were interconnected in such a way that the tilting caused water to flow out of the uppermost boiler on that side of the ship. Since fires were still burning underneath the boilers, the empty boiler would develop hot spots. When the ship tilted in the other direction, water would rush back into the empty boiler, turn at once into steam, and create a temporary surge in pressure. This effect of careening could be prevented by keeping high levels of water in the boilers; however, the *Sultana*'s boilers were leaky and one had been hastily and improperly repaired when the ship stopped at Vicksburg.

The *Sultana* disaster received surprisingly little press coverage at the time, most likely because the other events of April 1865—Robert E. Lee's (1807–1870) surrender, the end of the Civil War, and Abraham Lincoln's (1809–1865) assassination—were foremost in the public's attention. The tragedy was soon forgotten, though it cost nearly two thousand lives.

REBECCA J. FREY

BIBLIOGRAPHY

Ambrose, Stephen. "Remembering Sultana.*" National Geographic News, May 1, 2001. Available from http://news.nationalgeographic.com/.*

Potter, Jerry O. "Sultana: A Tragic Postscript to the Civil War." American History Magazine*, August 1998. Available from http://www.historynet.com/.*

Salecker, Gene Eric. Disaster on the Mississippi: The Sultana Explosion, April 27, 1865. *Annapolis, MD: Naval Institute Press, 1996.*

imposition of public domination over rail transportation. Thus the Confederate government in Richmond could force industrialists to do its bidding by denying them manpower or transportation (Beringer et al. 1986, p. 217). These authors then note that the government in Richmond also invested in manufacturing, establishing factories such as the Augusta Powder Works in Augusta, Georgia, which produced nitre (potassium nitrate, a chemical used to make gunpowder), lead, rifles, shoes, buttons, and other items. Moreover, this government-induced and controlled activity turned Southern cities into large industrial centers (Beringer et al. 1986, p. 217). Early in the short history of the Confederacy, the *New York Herald* reported on the frenetic pace of development that it saw occurring in the South:

> We perceive that the States of the Southern confederacy are bestirring themselves in the manufacturing line, with a view to provide for their own wants in those articles for which they were heretofore dependent upon New England. Cotton mills, shoe factories, yarn and twine manufactories are being put extensively into operation in Georgia and other States. An association of Southern merchants is busily engaged in locating sites for all kinds of factories, with the assistance of competent engineers, where the indispensable water power can be made available. In the neighborhood of Columbus, Georgia, there are already established cotton and woolen mills, a tan yard and a shoe factory, grist mills and saw mills, of the capacity and operations of which a description will be found in another column. In New Orleans there is a very large factory at work in manufacture of brogans, an article of immense consumption on plantations, and hitherto supplied by the factories of Lynn and other New England towns. It is evident that the Southern confederacy is straining every point to make itself independent of the North commercially as well as politically. (March 17, 1861, p. 4)

Besides largely being cut off from the importation of Northern goods, the North's blockade of the Southern coastline meant that items manufactured abroad would be severely curtailed as well. Early in the conflict, the government in Richmond tried to secure some necessary manufactured items from abroad. A Savannah, Georgia, newspaper reported on April 10, 1861, just a few days before shots were fired at Fort Sumter and only nine days before President Lincoln announced the blockade of Southern ports, that an American visiting a Prussian arms factory witnessed the manufactory of arms, where 60,000 rifles and 50,000 swords for the South were being produced (*Daily Morning News*, April 10, 1861, col. A). Whether this particular shipment of arms got through the blockade is unknown but it is likely that it did. Historians have estimated that despite the Union Navy's best efforts to maintain the blockade, the South exported at least a million bales of cotton and imported 600,000 rifles (McPherson 1982, p. 179). McPherson goes on to point out that while such large numbers may call the blockade's effectiveness into question, the blockade nevertheless cut the South's seaborne trade to less than a third of normal (McPherson 1982, p. 179). This impact meant that the Confederate government would have to get the most out of its own manufacturing base without being able to rely on help from abroad.

The most important manufacturing center of the Confederate States was in Richmond, where such factories as the Tredegar Iron Works provided the war effort with such essential items as cannons. The importance of Richmond's manufacturing establishments was one of the reasons that General Robert E. Lee sacrificed so much to prevent the city from falling under Union control (McPherson 1982, pp. 235–236). Other historians point out that while the South as a whole was largely agricultural, Virginia was a partial exception. "Virginians envisioned a Confederacy filled with large factories, teeming cities, and prosperous merchants ... Safely protected from more efficient Northern competitors, Virginia would give Southerners the industrial muscle they needed to sustain political independence" (Carlander and Majewski 2003, p. 335).

Early visions of turning the South into an independent manufacturing behemoth eventually came to naught. With a much smaller manufacturing base, the curtailing of imports due to the loss of trade with Northern states as well as the naval blockade, and the lack of an adequate supply of free labor for its manufactories, the South failed to develop an effective manufacturing base. The economic base of the South was weakened as the war continued. The real output of the Confederacy declined as many of the best workers left the factories for the army. The blockade cut the Confederacy off from the benefits of foreign trade, led to inefficient use of Southern labor, and compounded the difficulties of replacing worn-out or destroyed machinery. In addition, Union troops concentrated on destroying railroad equipment and entire factories and on cutting the supply lines of raw materials (Lerner 1955, pp. 20–40).

The Confederacy had simply started too far behind the Union in terms of manufacturing, and despite trying to catch up to the North, it faced too many obstacles to be successful. The antebellum South's planter economy was no match for the capitalist entrepreneurial spirit of the Northern manufacturers.

Northern Adjustments

Despite the North's advantages, however, it was unable to capitalize on them and overwhelm its weaker adversary early in the conflict. For the first few years of the war the South was able to take advantage of the North's inability to marshal its manufacturing resources. Initially, the North scrambled to meet its supply needs, even going abroad to import such essential items as rifles (Ransom 2006). For the Union the problem was not a lack of manufacturing facilities but a lack of coordination. During peacetime, manufacturers competed with one another and were not in business to cooperate. Moreover, most manufacturers in this period served local needs and did not ship their goods great distances or consider the needs of consumers in distant markets (Zunz 1990, pp. 12–15). Therefore military procurement officers had to encourage far-flung manufacturers to work together and pool their resources into large cooperative operations that met the military's needs. This wartime effort led to the development of a national market that linked distant consumers with manufacturers (Whitten and Whitten 2006, p. 5).

Even though effective coordination took some time, Northern producers were quick to see the money-making potential in supplying the needs of the Union Army and Navy. An article in the *Chicago Tribune* from the first year of the war illustrates some of the efforts taken by Midwestern manufacturers:

> Every day brings with it illustrations of the widespread activity caused by the preparations of the government for a long war. Passing through an alley ... we found it barricaded with packing boxes. The boxes are the work of a man who three months ago could hardly find any occupation. He is now making packing boxes for the government with all the hands he can employ ... The receipts of clothing at the arsenal are enormous. To inspect the operations is well worth a day's time. One single establishment delivers daily 3,000 shirts and 2,000 pairs of drawers; from another is received an equal number of hose ... The number of mills running solely upon army cloths and army flannel is becoming legion ... scarce a day passes in which some cotton mill is not altered into a woolen mill, and set at work upon cloth and flannel. (October 21, 1861, p. 2)

To meet the needs of the war, many Northern manufacturers converted their operations to allow them to make goods needed by soldiers. For example, the Amoskeag Manufacturing Company in Manchester, New Hampshire, at that time the largest textile manufacturer in the world, began making rifles (Hareven and Langenbach 1978, p. 10). The same newspaper article quoted above describes other wartime manufacturing conversions:

> Where hayforks and scythes took the attention of a manufacturer, sword blades and bayonets are produced instead. Brass turners have left off making faucets and door keys, and are doubling the product of their industry in making trappings for cavalry and the more delicate workmanship upon gun carriages, sword sheaths, &c. Trunk makers have taken to the fashioning of knapsacks, and men who once made carriages for the wealthy, are now making ambulances for the soldier. (October 21, 1861, p. 2)

What all this activity meant for cities like Chicago is described further in the *Tribune* article:

> The result is that the city is gradually becoming one vast workshop, and the hum of industry each day grows louder and louder. From the streets beggary has almost disappeared, and the demands upon the committee by the families of absent volunteers are daily diminishing from the abundance of employment offered to the industrious. The present war may pinch in some places, but it carries employment and comparative ease to others. (October 21, 1861, p. 2)

Despite the ambitions of Northern manufacturers to supply the military, however, many industries suffered economically during the initial months of the war due to the loss of their Southern customers and the accompanying sudden changes in market conditions. In fact, almost six thousand Northern businesses failed in the first year of the war, with financial losses totaling an estimated $178.5 million (Whitten and Whitten 2006, p. 8). Textile manufacturers suffered because of the loss of their cotton supply from Southern plantations, which resulted in a 74 percent drop in production (McPherson 1982, p. 372). Other manufacturers who suffered losses were iron producers, shoe manufacturers, and coal producers (McPherson 1982, p. 372). As manufacturers adjusted to wartime production needs, however, things began to turn around. The manufacturing index for the Union states alone rose to a level 13 percent higher by 1864 than that for the country as a whole in 1860 (McPherson 1982, p. 372). A Boston newspaper article describes the result of war production for Worcester, Massachusetts:

> The manufacturing interests of Worcester have been favorably affected by the war. Most of the establishments are in full operation. Most of the establishments are in full operation, many of them running over time, and with much more than the usual complement of hands, in the manufacture of articles worn by soldiers, or in making tools and machinery for the manufacture of those articles. (*Boston Daily Advertiser*, November 29, 1861, col. D)

With the boom in wartime profits, some manufacturers must have worried about the end of the war and the accompanying drop in military orders. A Mississippi newspaper article from 1863 reports the claims of a traveler just from the manufacturing districts of the North who reported that Northern manufacturers were doing so well that they callously did not want to see the war end: "All are making money by contract, working night and day, and are willing to pay three hundred dollars for substitutes out of their profits. Manufacturers make no complaint of their taxes. They feel none of the horrors of war, and care nothing about it" (*Natchez Daily Courier*, June 25, 1863, col. D).

The Civil War indeed proved to be a boon to Northern manufacturers, who supplied their nation with the tools of war needed to carry it to victory. The United States emerged from the conflict with a rapidly expanding manufacturing base that would in a few decades be the largest in the world. The 1860s was a period of transition for manufacturers from the small to mid-size manufactory to the large factories that would come to dominate American life. While these changes would have occurred without the Civil War, wartime necessities served to nationalize markets, increase cooperation between government and industry, and expand the size of manufacturing operations. The war speeded up the modernization of American industry but was not the cause of it (McPherson 1982, p. 373). Many veterans returned to their cities to join a new army: the legions of industrial workers that soon filled America's factories (Johnson 2003).

BIBLIOGRAPHY

Beringer, Richard, Herman Hattaway, Archer Jones, and William N. Still Jr. *Why the South Lost the Civil War.* Athens and London: University of Georgia Press, 1986.

Boston Daily Advertiser, November 29, 1861, Issue 128, col. D.

Carlander, Jay, and John Majewski. "Imagining A Great Manufacturing Empire: Virginia and the Possibilities of a Confederate Tariff." *Civil War History* 49, no. 4 (2003): 334–352.

Chicago Tribune, October 21, 1861, p. 2.

Daily Morning News (Savannah, GA), April 10, 1861, Issue 85; col. A.

Dew, Charles B. *Ironmaker to the Confederacy, Joseph R. Anderson and the Tredegar Iron Works.* New Haven, CT, and London: Yale University Press, 1966.

Foote, Shelby. *The Civil War, A Narrative: Fort Sumter to Perryville.* New York: Random House, 1958.

Genovese, Eugene D. *The Political Economy of Slavery.* New York: Vintage Books, 1965.

Hareven, Tamara K., and Randolph Langenbach. *Amoskeag, Life and Work in an American Factory-City.* New York: Pantheon Books, 1978.

Johnson, Russell L. *Warriors into Workers: The Civil War and the Formation of Urban-Industrial Society in a Northern City.* New York: Fordham University Press, 2003.

Lerner, Eugene. "Money, Prices, and Wages in the Confederacy, 1861–1865." *Journal of Political Economy* 63, no. 1 (1955): 20–40.

Luraghi, Raimondo. *The Rise and Fall of the Plantation South.* New York: New Viewpoints, 1978.

Maslowski, Peter, and Allan R. Millett. *For the Common Defense: A Military History of the United States of America.* New York: The Free Press, 1984.

McPherson, James M. *Battle Cry of Freedom: The Civil War Era.* New York: Oxford University Press, 1988.

McPherson, James M. *Ordeal by Fire: The Civil War and Reconstruction.* New York: Alfred A. Knopf, 1982.

Natchez (MS) *Daily Courier*, June 25, 1863, Issue 193, col. D.

New York Herald (NY), March 17, 1861, pg. 4; col. C.

Ransom, Roger L. Confederate States of America. *Historical Statistics of the United States,* Millennial Online, eds. Susan B. Carter, Scott Sigmund Gartner, Michael R. Haines, Alan L. Olmstead, Richard Stutch, and Gavin Wright. New York: Cambridge University Press, 2006.

Shi, David E., and George Brown Tindall. *America, A Narrative History,* 3rd ed. New York: W.W. Norton & Company, 1992.

Whitten, David O., and Bessie E. Whitten. *The Birth of Big Business in the United States, 1860–1914: Commercial, Extractive, and Industrial Enterprise.* Westport, CT: Praeger Publishers, 2006.

Wright, Gavin. *The Political Economy of the Cotton South: Households, Markets, and Wealth in the Nineteenth Century.* New York: W.W. Norton & Company, Inc., 1978.

Zunz, Oliver. *Making America Corporate, 1870–1920.* Chicago and London: The University of Chicago Press, 1990.

Steven Barleen

NORTHERN MANUFACTURING

At the beginning of the Civil War, neither side was prepared for the long, bloody struggle that lay ahead. The overwhelming superiority that the North enjoyed in its manufacturing capacity should have given it the clear advantage, but in 1861 the North's industries were not coordinated enough to efficiently supply the vast requirements of Northern armies. Furthermore, the majority of industries in the North were still small affairs, largely shops or mid-sized manufactories that primarily served local markets (Zunz 1990, p. 13). While there were many large factories as well, especially in textile manufacturing, where large factories with efficient modes of production had existed for some time, the widespread industrialization that would transform the country in the latter part of the nineteenth century was only in its beginning stages in most industries. For example, in Cincinnati in the 1850s, out of 1,259 manufactories only 21 employed more than hundred workers, while 1,207 establishments had less than fifty workers (Ross 1985, p. 80). Therefore, the Union government faced the task of coordinating disparate industries to produce maximum manufacturing efficiency in the service of its war machine. Over the four years of the war, government and manufacturers worked hand-in-hand to accomplish this goal, and in doing so paved the way both for victory and for the massive industries that would come to dominate much of American life in the decades following the conflict.

American inventor, Samuel Colt (1814–1862). In spite of early setbacks, Samuel Colt eventually persevered in his design and manufacture of a revolver with a reliable repeating feature. After the guns proved usable during the Mexican-American War, orders for the weapons increased, with Colt revolvers becoming a popular choice for both Union and Confederate troops. *Kean Collection/ Hulton Archive/Getty Images.*

Despite its need to organize and consolidate industrial production, the North's stronger manufacturing base still gave it an advantage over the South at the start of the war, an advantage it would maintain and increase throughout the conflict. The 1860 census shows that the total number of manufacturing establishments in the free states and territories was 108,573, while the states that would make up the Confederacy only counted 20,573 establishments. In terms of capital investment, the North had $840,802,835 invested in industry, whereas the South had only $95,922,489 invested in its industrial base ("Manufacturing in the Slave States"). The North also had a huge population advantage, which enabled it to simultaneously supply its factories with workers and its armies with soldiers. Because of its commitment to free labor and manufacturing, the North had for decades attracted large numbers of immigrants, with most workers coming through ports in New York, Philadelphia, and Boston and then fanning out throughout the Northeast, where they supplied manufacturing establishments with an ever increasing workforce pool (Wright 1978, pp. 121–125; Stott 1990, pp. 68–84). Even during the war, immigrants continued to arrive in large numbers: From 1861 to 1865, over 800,000 immigrants disembarked in the North (Millett and Maslowski 1984, p. 163). Southern factories, on the other hand, had to rely on a much smaller supply of white laborers, who were augmented by the numerous slaves hired out to Southern factories by their owners (Dew 1966).

The problem for the U.S. War Department was not a paucity of manufacturing establishments or workers, but the lack of coordination between the many manufacturing establishments, which were used to competing with one another and were often narrowly focused on local markets. With the fall of Fort Sumter, federal officials realized that they would need to move quickly to consolidate the North's disparate modes of production, transportation, and communication by having government agents work closely with manufacturers (Whitten and Whitten 2006, p. 5). The challenges they faced were vast. At the start of the conflict, basic needs such as armaments and uniforms could not adequately be supplied by the nation's manufacturing system. In October of 1861, M. C. Meigs, quartermaster-general to the secretary of war, lamented the "imperative demand for more army cloth than the present manufacturing resources of the North can furnish." The supply situation, Meigs asserted, was so bad that governors "daily complain that recruiting will stop unless clothing is sent in abundance and immediately to the various recruiting camps of regiments." Soldiers were reported to be "compelled to do picket duty in the late cold nights without overcoats, or even coats, wearing only the thin summer flannel clothing" (*Chicago Tribune*, October 31, 1861).

Besides its problems with uniforms, the North found arms manufacturers unable to supply its soldiers with the weapons of war. At the start of the conflict, the Northern states produced 97 percent of the nation's firearms at factories such as the New Haven Arms Factory (which would become the Winchester Repeating Arms Company after the war), the Springfield Armory, and the Colt Manufacturing Company. However, massive government orders for weapons could not be met without vastly expanding arms production (McPherson 1988, p. 318). In fact, during the first year of the conflict, the North had to import 80 percent of its firearms (Morris 2005, p. 54). The Comte de Paris, Louis Philippe Albert d'Orleans, who served on the staff of General McClellan, described the North's inability to adequately supply its armies with arms:

> The armory in Springfield had only the capacity for producing from ten to twelve thousand [weapons] yearly, and the supply could not be increased except by constructing new machines.... During the first year of the war the ordnance department succeeded in furnishing the various armies in the field, not counting what was left at the depots, one million two hundred and seventy-six thousand six hundred and eighty-six portable firearms (muskets, carbines, and pistols), one thousand nine hundred and twenty-six field or siege guns, twelve hundred pieces for batteries in position, and two hundred and fourteen million cartridges for small arms and cannon. (Commager 1973, p. 103)

However, the situation began to improve as the war dragged on: "In 1862," according to the Comte de Paris, "the Springfield manufactory delivered two hundred thousand rifles, while in the year 1863, during which there were manufactured two hundred and fifty thousand there, the importation of arms from Europe by the Northern States ceased altogether" (Commager 1973 [1950], p. 103).

The war was a boon to manufacturers. The DuPont Company, for example, massively expanded its operations to meet the military's voracious appetite for gunpowder, and emerged from the Civil War as the nation's largest manufacturer of gunpowder and other explosives (Zunz 1990, p. 16). Other companies expanded production rapidly as well, as the following notice in the *New Haven Daily Palladium* from May 19, 1865 testifies: "The Meriden Manufacturing Co. have a contract for five thousand breech-loading magazine carbines, Triplett's patent, for the State of Kentucky. The arms are to be finished in July, and the armory is run night and day."

The massive expansion of the arms industry, along with the growing demand for other products and parts made out of metal—from iron plates for warships, to railroad track, to horseshoes for army horses—greatly expanded the North's steel industry. The demand for military goods even prompted manufacturers to convert their operations. For example, the Amoskeag Manufacturing Company, the largest textile factory in the world, located in Manchester, New Hampshire, manufactured locomotives and rifles during the Civil War (Hareven and Langenbach 1978, p. 10).

Northern manufacturers also introduced several innovations. One of these was the repeating rifle, which allowed a soldier to fire several shots without reloading. According to the Comte de Paris, the rifle's reception by the troops was very favorable: "Many extraordinary instances have been cited of successful personal defence due to the rapidity with which this arm can be fired, and some Federal regiments of infantry which made a trial of it were highly pleased with the result" (Commager 1973 [1950], p. 104). John D. Billings, a member of the 10th Massachusetts battery of light artillery, recalled several other inventions produced by Northern manufacturers, such as the "combination knife-fork-and-spoon," the "water filterer," and the "fancy patent-leather haversack." One product that seems an essential for soldiers but, according to Billings, didn't catch on was an early form of the bulletproof vest:

> These ironclad warriors admitted that when panoplied for the fight their sensations were much as they might be if they were dressed up in an old-fashioned air-tight stove; still, with all the discomforts of this casing, they felt a little safer with it on than off in battle.... This seemed solid reasoning, surely; but, in spite of it all, a large number of these vests never saw Rebeldom. Their owners were subjected to such a storm of ridicule that they could not bear up under it.... [T]he ownership of one of them was taken as evidence of faint-heartedness. (Commager 1973 [1950], pp. 216–217)

A connection between manufacturers and the government had always existed in the United States, but the Civil War raised this connection to a new level. In the process, many manufacturers used their connections with government agents to secure manufacturing contracts that would make them rich. Many were able to stay home and let substitutes go do the fighting for them, because the 1863 Conscription Act allowed them to do so. A significant number of Civil War-era manufacturers and financiers, such as John Rockefeller, John Pierpont Morgan, Jay Gould, and Philip Armour, later went on to become the famous "robber barons" of the decades of rapid industrialization that followed the Civil War. An excellent case in point is J. P. Morgan, who as perhaps the most famous investment banker in American history became the archetype of the robber baron. Morgan, who got his start before the Civil War, and was well off before Fort Sumter, made a fortune during the war off of government manufacturing contracts.

Despite such corruption, and various road bumps and false starts, the North was able to use its superior manufacturing capacity, along with its vast numbers of workers and troops, to grind down the Confederate Army's ability to respond militarily to its invasion of the South. In 1865 Union armies marched in victory parades throughout the North to celebrate their efforts in preserving the Union. Northern manufacturers did not march in parades of their own, but they were also instrumental in their nation's victory as the suppliers of the instruments of war. Their efforts, too, laid the groundwork for the massive industrialization that was to follow, which by 1880 had transformed the United States into the world's foremost industrial power.

BIBLIOGRAPHY

Commager, Henry Steele, ed. *The Civil War Archive: The History of the Civil War in Documents.* New York: Bobbs-Merill, 1973.

Dew, Charles B. *Ironmaker to the Confederacy: Joseph R. Anderson and the Tredegar Iron Works.* New Haven: Yale University Press, 1966.

Dublin, Thomas. *Women at Work: The Transformation of Work and Community in Lowell, Massachusetts, 1826–1860.* New York: Columbia University Press, 1979.

Hareven, Tamera K., and Randolph Langenbach. *Amoskeag: Life and Work in an American Factory City.* New York: Pantheon Books, 1978.

Josephson, Matthew. *The Robber Barons: The Great American Capitalists, 1861–1901.* New York: Harcourt, Brace, 1934.

"Manufacturing in the Slave States: Establishments, Capital Invested, Product Value, and Employment, by State: 1860–1870" (Series Eh40-49). In *Historical Statistics of the United States: Millennial Edition*, ed. Susan B. Carter et al. New York: Cambridge University Press, 2006. Available online from http://hsus. cambridge.org/.

McPherson, James M. *Battle Cry of Freedom: The Civil War Era.* New York: Oxford University Press, 1988.

Millett, Allan R., and Peter Maslowski. *For the Common Defense: A Military History of the United States of America.* New York: Free Press; London: Collier Macmillan, 1984.

Morris, Charles R. *The Tycoons: How Andrew Carnegie, John D. Rockefeller, Jay Gould, and J. P. Morgan Invented the American Supereconomy.* New York: Times Books, 2005.

New Haven Daily Palladium, May 19, 1865.

"The Purchase of Cloth Abroad." *Chicago Tribune* October 31, 1861.

Ross, Steven J. *Workers on the Edge: Work, Leisure, and Politics in Industrializing Cincinnati, 1788–1890.* Los Angeles: Figueroa Press, 1985.

Stott, Richard B. *Workers in the Metropolis: Class, Ethnicity, and Youth in Antebellum New York City.* Ithaca, NY: Cornell University Press, 1990.

Whitten, David O., and Bessie E. Whitten. *The Birth of Big Business in the United States, 1860–1914: Commercial, Extractive, and Industrial Enterprise.* Westport, CT: Praeger Publishers, 2006.

Wright, Gavin. *The Political Economy of the Cotton South: Households, Markets, and Wealth in the Nineteenth Century.* New York: W. W. Norton, 1978.

Zinn, Howard. *A People's History of the United States.* New York: HarperCollins, 1980.

Zunz, Olivier. *Making America Corporate, 1870–1920.* Chicago and London: University of Chicago Press, 1990.

Steven Barleen

SOUTHERN MANUFACTURING

On April 14, 1861, after a short, bloodless battle, the Confederate States of America raised its flag over Fort Sumter, a coastal fortification in South Carolina, and in doing so initiated a war that its manufacturing base was ill equipped to deal with. One challenge among many for the Confederacy in the coming conflict was to make the best use of its much smaller manufacturing base in order to keep both the civilian population supplied with the necessities of life and the military supplied with the necessities of war. The manufacturing advantages of the North seemed overwhelming when compared to the South's largely agriculturally based economy, and yet many in the South were confident that their region could rise to the challenge and mobilize and equip an army that could successfully challenge the North, both on the field of battle and in the factory. In fact, some saw the arrival of conflict with their Northern neighbors as being a positive impetus for the development of the nascent Southern manufacturing base. For example, the June 1861 issue of the *Southern Cultivator* boldly proclaimed: "We notice with unfeigned pleasure the impetus which the secession movement has given to the manufacturing enterprises in the South. Old establishments are being remodeled, improved and enlarged, and new ones are springing up, while a much larger number still determined upon, are not yet, however, located" ("Southern Manufactures," 1861, p. 187).

Despite such optimism, the South began the conflict with a substantial disadvantage in terms of its industrial capabilities. In 1861, the United States was only a few decades away from becoming a global manufacturing superpower, but most of that incipient producing might was located in the North. The gross value of manufactured items produced in the states that made up the Union was more than ten times greater than the gross value of items manufactured in the states that made up the Confederacy, which collectively produced just 7.4 percent of the nations manufactured goods at the start of the war. Another stark statistic for the Confederacy was that the Union produced 97 percent of the nation's firearms (Tindall and Shi 1992, p. 642). The state of Massachusetts alone produced more industrial goods than all of the states of the Confederacy combined (McPherson 1982, p. 23). In terms of manpower for its manufacturing base, the North also clearly had the advantage: There were twenty-two million people in the states that made up the Union, whereas the Confederacy had a population of only nine million, with one-third of those being slaves (Tindall and Shi 1992, p. 642).

The reason for the South's distant position behind the North in manufacturing lay in a history of Southern investment in land and slaves, which had made the South largely rural in nature. At the start of the Civil War, the South had few cities of any size and the vast majority of its people lived in rural areas. Whereas around 35 percent of the population of New England and around 21 percent of the population of the Middle Atlantic States lived in urban areas, in the South only Virginia had an urban population that even came close to 10 percent of the state total, and the urban population of the South was less than 5 percent (Fox-Genovese 1988, pp. 74–76). The rural nature of the South,

Manufacturing differences between the North and South, 1860

	Number of manufacturing establishments	Percentage of the gross value of the nation's manufacturing goods	Percentage of nation's capital invested in manufacturing	Number of workers engaged in manufacturing	Total population
North	110,000	92.6	84	1,300,000	22,000,000
South	18,000	7.4	16	110,000	9,000,000*

*Out of the 9 million population figure, 3.5 million were slaves.

SOURCES: Foote, Shelby. *The Civil War, A Narrative: Fort Sumter to Perryville.* New York: Random House, 1958, p. 40. Tindall, George Brown and David E. Shi. *America, A Narrative History, Third Edition.* New York: W.W. Norton & Company, 1992, p. 642. Millett, Allan R. and Peter Maslowski. *For the Common Defense: A Military History of the United States of America.* New York: The Free Press, 1984, p. 164.

Manufacturing difficulties. The Civil War challenged the South's small manufacturing base to find ways to keep its civilians and soldiers supplied with military and agricultural necessities. *Illustration by GGS. Gale.*

Tredegar Iron Works, April 1865. An emphasis on producing cash crops for export in the South led to a manufacturing imbalance with the industrial North. Confederate leaders hoped, however, war would provide the impetus for the South to become more industrial and build more factories, such as the Tredegar Iron Works in Richmond, Virginia. *The Library of Congress.*

Southern methods of agriculture—which were labor-intensive and thus did not require as many manufactured farming instruments as were typically used on Northern and Western farms—and heavy investment of capital in land and slaves did not provide strong incentives for the establishment of a local industrial base.

Despite these stark figures, the South had a great deal of wealth that could have been put into manufacturing. Robert Fogel and Stanely Engerman in their seminal *Time on the Cross* (1974) point out that the South as an independent nation ranked fourth in the world in terms of wealth. The South's wealth, however, was based largely on the ownership of slaves and land, and with these two resources, the South became a major exporter of crops such as cotton, tobacco, rice, and indigo. An article in the October 12, 1861, edition of the Raleigh (North Carolina) *Daily Register* asserts that in 1860 the North exported slightly less than 98 million dollars worth of products, whereas the South exported around 219 million dollars worth. Unfortunately for the Confederacy's quartermasters, the South's exports could not be used to equip an army (Nicholson 1861).

Despite being well behind the North in manufacturing, several historians have concluded that Southern manufacturing deficiencies were not the chief cause of the South's ultimate defeat. The Civil War was still largely a low-technology conflict and Southern manufacturers in conjunction with government planners did a fairly good job of maintaining production throughout most of the war. Also, because it took so long for the North to coordinate the full capacity of its manufacturing base, Southern manufacturing deficiencies were not felt for some time as strongly as they might have been.

Despite the lack of urban centers and the structure of the Southern economy, several Southerners during the decades leading up to the Civil War had provided the region with a nascent industrial base. Historian Chad Morgan points out in his study of manufacturing in Georgia that during the 1850s, while the number of manufacturing establishments only increased from 1,527 to 1,890, the amount of money invested in these industries increased from $7,086,525 to $16,925,564 (2005, p. 10). According to the 1860 census, the total number of manufacturing establishments in what would be the Confederate states numbered 20,631, with the lead being taken by Virginia, home to more than 25 percent of these enterprises, followed by North Carolina, with nearly 4,000. The 1870 census indicates that the South had 33,360 manufacturing establishments, an increase of 62 percent over the course of the decade, despite the destruction brought to the South by Northern armies (Carter et al. 2006). The problem was that while the South was developing its industries, the North was developing its own faster, so that even though the South had 20 percent of the nation's industrial base in

1840, by 1860, despite a strong attempt by Southern industrialists to catch up, the South's share of the nation's manufacturing output was only 16 percent (Morgan 2005, p. 6).

From the beginning of the war, the government in Richmond encouraged manufacturing in two ways: It established direct state ownership of essential industries, especially ordnance and munitions production, and at the same time promoted private enterprise through the use of various incentives and penalties. These ranged from giving further contracts to businesses that produced according to Richmond's demands, to punitively taking over businesses that didn't meet the requirements set for them. Conscription, which passed the Confederate Congress on April 16, 1862, also aided the wartime manufacturing effort by allowing the government to exempt certain industrial workers from military service. Many patriotic Confederates declared their intention to meet the manufacturing demands of war in the face of the Northern blockade of the South's coasts. In November 1861, Jefferson Davis, president of the Confederacy, wrote optimistically of the South's ability to meet its logistical requirements, even if doing so might require its citizens to sacrifice:

> As long as hostilities continue the Confederate States will exhibit a steadily increasing capacity to furnish their troops with food, clothing, and arms. If they should be forced to forego many of the luxuries and some of the comforts of life, they will at least have the consolation of knowing that they are thus daily becoming more and more independent of the rest of the world. If in this process labor in the Confederate States should be gradually diverted from those great Southern staples which have given life to so much of the commerce of mankind into other channels, so as to make them rival producers instead of profitable customers, they will not be the only or even the chief losers by this change in the direction of their industry. (Davis 1906 [1861], p. 643)

Similarly, optimistic pronouncements came from many other quarters as well. An announcement concerning the production of gunpowder published in the September 14, 1861, edition of the Raleigh *Daily Register* proclaimed: "We are glad to see that North Carolina is taking the lead in the manufacture of this indispensable article in the prosecution of the war.... This company expects soon to be able to turn out one thousand kegs a day." And in an editorial titled "An Appeal to Planters," published in the March 19, 1862, Savannah (Georgia) *Daily Morning News*, the following is found: "We must not only have soldiers sufficient to prevent our gallant army from falling prey to superior numbers, but we must encourage domestic manufactures that shoes and clothing may be furnished for that army."

Despite the best efforts of Southern manufacturers and politicians to ensure that the war effort would be supplied, problems with supply abounded. In his 1907 memoir, Edward P. Alexander, who had served as chief of ordnance for the Army of Northern Virginia, recalled some of the logistical successes and failures. On the one hand, the Ordnance Bureau in Richmond was notable "for its success in supplying the enormous amount of ordnance material consumed during the war" (p. 54). On the other hand, the quality of at least some of the material produced by Southern manufacturers was questionable: "Our arsenals soon began to manufacture rifled guns, but they always lacked the copper and brass, and the mechanical skill necessary to turn out first-class ammunition" (p. 54). Through the capture of Northern guns, Alexander remarks, his soldiers were able to get the arms they needed, but "we were handicapped by our own ammunition until the close of the war" (p. 54). Colonel William Allan, who was the chief of ordnance of the Second Army Corp, recalled that in 1864 the Ordnance Department was not providing his men with enough nails and horseshoes. To compensate, he combed his units for blacksmiths and put them to work, producing what Richmond should have been providing him. However, this innovative plan was disrupted by a lack of iron. Allan responded by sending his own wagons and men to Richmond to obtain the iron from a manufacturer there. The story demonstrates obvious problems with Southern manufacturing and supply during the Civil War. In this case, the supply of raw materials was available but not the ability to turn them into manufactured products that could get to troops in the field.

Of course, a major problem the South faced in trying to keep its factories running stemmed from its need to supply its armies with soldiers while also supplying its manufacturing establishments with workers drawn from a population much smaller than its enemy's. Also, while the North gained over 800,000 immigrants between 1861 and 1865, the Confederacy not only did not see a gain in immigration during the war, it also lost many of its skilled workmen at the start of the conflict, as they returned to their homes in the North or donned Confederate uniforms (Dew 1966, pp. 228–264; Millett and Maslowski 1984, p. 163). As many as 750,000 men fought for the Confederacy, and this near total mobilization of young Southern white men inevitably translated into a shortage of industrial workers (Millet and Maslowski 1984, p. 163).

Despite starting the war well behind the North in terms of manufacturing capacity, the Confederacy made a strenuous effort to supply its needs. However, in the end Southern manufacturing was no match for the producing power and manpower of the Union.

BIBLIOGRAPHY

Alexander, Edward Porter. *Military Memoirs of a Confederate: A Critical Narrative*. New York: Charles Scribner's Sons, 1907.

Beringer, Richard E., Herman Hattaway, Archer Jones, and William N. Still Jr. *Why the South Lost the Civil War.* Athens: University of Georgia Press, 1986.

Beringer, Richard E., Herman Hattaway, Archer Jones, and William N. Still Jr. *The Elements of Confederate Defeat: Nationalism, War Aims, and Religion.* Athens: University of Georgia Press, 1988.

Boritt, Gabor S., ed., *Why the Confederacy Lost.* New York: Oxford University Press, 1992.

Carter, Susan B. et al., eds. "Manufacturing in the Slave States: Establishments, Capital Invested, Product Value, and Employment, by State: 1860–1870" (Series Eh40-49). *Historical Statistics of the United States: Millennial Edition.* Cambridge, U.K., and New York: Cambridge University Press, 2006. Available from http://hsus.cambridge.org/.

Commager, Henry Steele, ed. *The Civil War Archive: The History of the Civil War in Documents.* New York: Bobbs-Merill, 1973.

Davis, Jefferson Finis. "Letter from Jefferson Finis Davis, November 18, 1861." *A Compilation of the Messages and Papers of the Confederacy, Including the Diplomatic Correspondence, 1861–1865*, ed. James D. Richardson. Nashville, TN: United States Publishing Company, 1906.

Dew, Charles B. *Ironmaker to the Confederacy: Joseph R. Anderson and the Tredegar Iron Works.* New Haven and London: Yale University Press, 1966.

Fayetteville (NC) *Observer*, July 17, 1862.

Fogel, Robert William, and Stanley L. Engerman. *Time on the Cross: The Economics of American Negro Slavery.* New York and London: W. W. Norton, 1974.

Fox-Genovese, Elizabeth. *Within the Plantation Household: Black and White Women of the Old South.* Chapel Hill: University of North Carolina Press, 1988.

Genovese, Eugene. *The Political Economy of Slavery.* New York: Vintage Books, 1967.

J., H. H. "An Appeal to Planters." *Savannah* (GA) *Daily Morning News*, March 19, 1862.

Luraghi, Raimondo. *The Rise and Fall of the Plantation South.* New York: New Viewpoints, 1978.

McPherson, James M. *Ordeal by Fire: The Civil War and Reconstruction.* New York: Alfred A. Knopf, 1982.

Millett, Alan R., and Peter Maslowski. *For the Common Defense: A Military History of the United States of America.* New York: Free Press; London: Collier Macmillan, 1984.

Morgan, Chad. "The Public Nature of Private Industry in Confederate Georgia." *Civil War History* 50, no. 1 (2004): 27–46.

Morgan, Chad. *Planter's Progress: Modernizing Confederate Georgia.* Gainesville: University Press of Florida, 2005.

Nicholson, A. O. P. "The Southern Confederacy Its Commercial and Financial Independence." *Raleigh* (NC) *Daily Register.* October 12, 1861, Issue 82; col. A.

Raleigh (NC) *Daily Register.* September 14, 1861, Issue 74, col. C.

"Southern Manufactures," *Southern Cultivator (1843–1906).* Atlanta: June 1861; Vol. 19, Issue 6.

Tindall, George Brown, and David Shi. *America: A Narrative History*, 3rd ed. New York and London: W. W. Norton, 1992.

Whitten, David O., and Bessie E. Whitten. *The Birth of Big Business in the United States, 1860–1914: Commercial, Extractive, and Industrial Enterprise.* Westport, CT: Praeger Publishers, 2006.

Wilson, Harold S. *Confederate Industry: Manufacturers and Quartermasters in the Civil War.* Jackson: University of Mississippi Press, 2002.

Wright, Gavin. *The Political Economy of the Cotton South: Households, Markets, and Wealth in the Nineteenth Century.* New York: W. W. Norton, 1978.

Steven Barleen

FACTORIES

When the Civil War began in 1861, the large factory operation had not yet become the normal means of production in the United States. Instead, the 1860s were a transitional period between earlier forms of manufacturing and the factory system that would come to dominate the American landscape over the course of the decades to follow. While some industries, such as textiles and meatpacking, had already begun the transformation process from small shop and mid-sized manufactory to large factory, most industrial workers still labored in small manufacturing operations. These maintained a different rhythm and style of work than the factory system that would later transform the lives of workers and the landscapes of America's large cities and small towns.

Thus, most workers during the Civil War still worked in shops that reflected more traditional forms of manufacturing. For example, in New York City in 1860, small shops predominated in the metal trade: only fourteen out of fifty-eight establishments had more than ten workers (Stott 1990, p. 47). The smallness of shop operations meant that workers often labored alongside their supervisor, who was oftentimes the shop's owner. This individual was likely a skilled craftsman who had worked his way up in his profession to the point where he owned his own operation. The pace of work in such establishments was not regulated by the rhythm of machines, and labor was not usually subdivided into monotonous, simple tasks (Stott 1990, pp. 36–37).

One of the most important factors in the shift from small manufactories to large factories was the steam engine, which allowed factory owners to run larger and more complex machinery that could do the work

James Watt's steam engine. The invention of the steam engine allowed factory owners to run larger and more complex machinery. It fueled the shift from small shops to large factories. *Photograph by Philip Gendreau. © Bettmann/Corbis.*

previously done by several laborers. During the 1860s, around 50 percent of the country's manufacturing enterprises still relied on waterpower (Gutman 1977, p. 33). Waterpower fluctuated based on the amount of water available in streams or rivers, which rose and fell, and thus could limit the size and output of an industrial operation. Steam power, in contrast, promised a steady supply of energy, allowing costly work stoppages to be avoided. It also meant that there was no limit on the size of a manufacturing operation. The introduction of steam power also made it possible for a factory to be located anywhere, not just next to a river. Before the rise of steam power, the need to be positioned near a stream or river meant that many shops were located in rural areas, but with the rise of the steam engine these operations began to move to large cities and grow in scale (Hunter 1985, p. 104). The decade before the Civil War witnessed a massive growth in the use of steam power, and new industries using this technology sprung up. For example, in 1850 in Massachusetts, 43 percent of manufacturing operations used steam power, but by 1860, the percentage had increased to 56 percent (Hunter 1985, p. 110). This rise in the use of steam power directly contributed to the growth of American cities, with the accompanying rise of concentrated manufacturing establishments and the rapid growth of immigrant working-class populations that would fill the factories with workers. Between 1840 and 1880, the total U.S. population nearly tripled, the number of industrial workers more than quintupled, and capital investment increased more than eightfold (Hunter 1985, p. 112). Printing establishments provide an excellent example of how the steam engine enabled operations to grow to massive size. For example, just before the Civil War, the New York firm Harper's employed numerous workers with subdivided tasks, supervised by scores of foremen in a seven-story operation (Stott 1990, p. 50).

While the small shop and mid-sized manufactory were still dominant in American manufacturing at the start of the Civil War, many industries—such as meatpacking, textiles, and arms manufacturing—had begun to move toward the large factory model. Indeed, the textile mills that began springing up in Lowell, Massachusetts, during the 1820s can be considered the first modern factories. By the time of the Civil War, many of these were mechanized to an unprecedented degree, and employed large and highly regulated workforces of a thousand or more (Rodgers 1974, p. 20).

The rise of the factory system increasingly meant that artisans who had previously worked on a product from start to finish now found themselves either tending a machine or performing the same task all day, as managers sought to subdivide labor in an effort to create more efficient systems of production. While many think of the assembly line as originating with Henry Ford in the early part of the twentieth century, James Barrett (1987) points out that assembly line production was employed in the meatpacking industry well before Ford's Model T (p. 20). Whereas in a small butcher shop, a butcher performed every task in the processing of each animal, thereby requiring that butchering be done by a skilled craftsman, large meatpacking plants divided the slaughter of each animal among multiple workers along an assembly line that could be sped up at will by the foreman. Many other industries went through the same development from small shops where workers performed tasks by hand from start to finish, at their own pace, to factories where work was highly subdivided, regimented, and mechanized.

As the war began, both the North and South faced the necessity of putting hundreds of thousands of men under arms, while at the same time continuing to keep their factories running. This did not present as much of a difficulty for the North, with its large pool of immigrants, as it did for the South, with its much smaller white population and its large black population that consisted primarily of slaves living in rural areas. The Tredegar Iron Works in Richmond, Virginia, provides an excellent example of some of the unique difficulties that Southern factories encountered during the Civil War. By the time the Civil War began, Richmond was the most important center of iron production in the South, and the Tredegar Iron Works was the largest of the mills, employing over 1,500 workers (Dew 1966, p. 3). The start of the conflict meant that Tredegar would have to rapidly increase production to meet the needs of the Confederacy. However, Tredegar initially encountered problems in stepping up production due to several factors: First, a number of workers rushed to join the newly formed Confederate Army; second, immigration as a source of labor had dried up due to the war; and finally, many of the mechanics with manufacturing know-how who had been employed at Tredegar were from the North and returned home at the start of the war. To fill these gaps, the managers at Tredegar hired almost three times as many youths as they had the previous year, and they increased the number of slave workers to around 10 percent of the labor force (Dew 1966, pp. 90–91). By 1863, Tredegar's labor shortage had become so acute that its owners were forced to hire 113 black convicts (p. 253). With large numbers of slave workers, Tredegar's management also faced the constant problem of its workforce liberating itself by running away (p. 255). By 1864, even slave labor was in short supply, and slave owners were able to command higher and higher rates for the renting of their slaves. Tredegar found itself in a bidding war for the renting of slaves with other manufacturing interests and even the army itself, so that prices for renting slaves jumped from a low of $225 to as much as $400 in a short time. Additionally, federal raids throughout northern Virginia further reduced the supply of available labor (p. 259). Nonetheless, by the end of the war, Southern factories were almost completely dependent on slave labor. For example, during the last few months of the war, more than three-quarters of the workers at the Naval ordnance works at Selma were slaves (p. 263).

Southern factories were hampered throughout the war not only by labor shortages, but also by problems with the supply of resources needed for manufacturing war essentials. By contrast, the North was able to more-efficiently utilize its factories as the war progressed, a development that proved crucial to its eventual victory.

BIBLIOGRAPHY

Barrett, James R. *Work and Community in the Jungle: Chicago's Packinghouse Workers, 1894–1922.* Urbana and Chicago: University of Illinois Press, 1987.

Dew, Charles B. *Ironmaker to the Confederacy: Joseph R. Anderson and the Tredegar Iron Works.* New Haven and London: Yale University Press, 1966.

Dublin, Thomas. *Women at Work: The Transformation of Work and Community in Lowell, Massachusetts, 1826–1860.* New York: Columbia University Press, 1979.

Gutman, Herbert G. *Work, Culture, and Society in Industrializing America.* New York: Vintage Books, 1977.

Hareven, Tamara K., and Randolph Langenbach. *Amoskeag: Life and Work in an American Factory-City.* New York: Pantheon Books, 1978.

Hunter, Louis C. *Steam Power.* Vol. 2 of *A History of Industrial Power in the United States, 1780–1930.* Charlottesville: University Press of Virginia, 1985.

Morris, Charles R. *The Tycoons: How Andrew Carnegie, John D. Rockefeller, Jay Gould, and J. P. Morgan Invented the American Supereconomy.* New York: Times Books, 2005.

Rodgers, Daniel T. *The Work Ethic in Industrializing America, 1850–1920.* Chicago: University of Chicago Press, 1974.

Ross, Steven J. *Workers on the Edge: Work, Leisure, and Politics in Industrializing Cincinnati, 1788–1890.* Los Angeles: Figueroa Press, 1985.

Stott, Richard B. *Workers in the Metropolis: Class, Ethnicity, and Youth in Antebellum New York City.* Ithaca, NY, and London: Cornell University Press, 1990.

Steven Barleen

ARMS MANUFACTURING

The manufacturing of arms during the Civil War occurred mainly at two sites: the U.S. Government Arsenal in Springfield, Massachusetts, commonly known as the Springfield Armory, and—on the Confederate side—the Virginia Manufactory of Arms at Richmond, known as the Richmond Arsenal. Together these sites produced the majority of the shoulder-fired muskets used by soldiers in both armies during the four years of the war.

The Springfield Armory

The Springfield Armory's origins dated back to 1777, when a site once used for military training on the Connecticut River in southern Massachusetts began making gun carriages and cartridges. It became a major ammunition and weapons depot, and was a target of the 1787 Shays Rebellion, when a group of disgruntled farmers led by Daniel Shays attempted to seize control of the site and the state in order to prevent foreclosures on their land. The Springfield Armory began making muskets in 1795, after President George Washington decided that a domestic manufacturing site was necessary in order to reduce the fledgling nation's dependence on foreign-made firearms.

The nearby village of Springfield grew in size and wealth during the first half of the nineteenth century as the Springfield Armory's output expanded. Highly skilled gunsmiths, often German or Irish immigrants, were the most vital members of the workforce, but in 1819 a new lathe was developed that allowed relatively unskilled workers to mass-produce the muskets. The U.S. Ordnance Department's decision to foster the development of interchangeable parts for muskets led to several more innovations at Springfield, including an early example of an assembly-line system, in which individual workers—some skilled, some unskilled—made various parts of a product. The writer Henry Wadsworth Longfellow visited the armory, and the immense stockpiles of new weapons he saw prompted him to pen the 1843 antiwar poem "The Arsenal at Springfield."

Labor tensions arose at the Springfield Armory in the 1840s, prompting a Congressional investigation. Periodically, military control was imposed at the site in order to rein in workers who were determined to protect their job status and wages, which were extraordinarily high for the western Massachusetts area. Indeed, workers were paid so well that many remained there until retirement, and though the European-style apprentice system had long been officially abolished, many of them still managed to pass their jobs down to sons or other family members.

Military control resumed at the Springfield Armory in April 1861 when the Civil War began. Springfield became the sole federal armory after the site at Harpers Ferry, Virginia, was set ablaze by retreating federal troops at the onset of the war. The newly installed commandant at the Springfield Armory was Captain Alexander Dyer, who immediately required all workers to swear an oath of allegiance to the United States. Workers promised to "support, protect, and defend the Constitution and Government of the United States against all enemies ... and ... that [they would] well and faithfully perform all the duties which may be required ... by law" (Whittlesey, p. 158). Dyer also instituted two ten-and-a-half-hour shifts, making the site a near round-the-clock operation, along with a raft of new rules prohibiting loitering, smoking, reading, and casual conversation on the job.

A Target of Espionage and Sabotage In 1861 the Springfield Armory employed 350 men and produced 1,500 rifle-muskets per month (Wilson 2006, p. 119). In 1864 nearly 2,500 workers were employed at the Armory, and production that same year reached a peak of 250,000 (Hattaway 1997, p. 38). During the war, however, the Armory had a difficult time maintaining an adequate workforce, as smaller rifle-musket manufacturers began springing up in the city to answer the demand of the Ordnance Department, attracting workers who sought both more money and less draconian working conditions.

The Springfield Armory was an obvious target for Confederate spies. It was ringed by an iron fence and heavily guarded by a Union Army detachment. After the war's end, revelations surfaced that in 1864 two enemy agents, possibly men disguised in women's clothing, had succeeded in planting a grenade-like device in the extremely flammable armory—but the gunpowder-filled iron pellet failed to ignite. A massive fire earlier that same year, in July, was attributed to spontaneous combustion, and destroyed the milling shop and dozens of milling machines. Because tables and other pieces of furniture were saturated with oil due to the nature of rifle manufacturing, the building was extremely flammable; however, firefighters on staff prevented the conflagration from spreading to other buildings.

The Richmond Arsenal

The Confederate states entered the war at a serious disadvantage in respect to armament stores. The decision to locate the capital of the Confederacy at Richmond, Virginia, was partly due to the fact that it was the most industrialized city in the largely agrarian South. One of Richmond's most impressive plants was the massive Tredegar Iron Works, a privately owned foundry that had been making iron locomotive carriages and railroad tracks since the late 1830s. The city was also the site of the Richmond Armory and Arsenal, which had been in operation since the 1790s but operated at a far lower capacity than its Springfield counterpart. The Richmond site turned out an average of 2,130 muskets annually prior to war compared to the Massachusetts numbers of 1,500 muskets every month, but Confederate firepower increased with the help of machinery taken from the Union-sacked federal armory at Harpers Ferry (Bilby, 1996). The Richmond Arsenal began making the "C. S. Richmond," a .58-caliber musket that would be used by the majority of Confederate infantry.

Armory room. The outbreak of fighting in 1861 forced factories in the North and South to produce weaponry on a large scale. Since it was more industrialized than the South, the North quickly became the home to a number of gun manufacturers, notably in the state of Massachusetts. *Hulton Archive/Getty Images.*

Responsibility for finding a solution to the serious disadvantage created by the South's minimal supply of the raw materials and skilled artisans necessary for arms manufacturing fell to the Confederate Army's Ordnance Bureau chief, Josiah Gorgas. He ordered a massive material effort to be implemented: Church bells were taken down and melted to provide cannon-making material, and even the stills used by moonshine makers were seized for their copper parts, which were made into musket percussion caps. Because potassium nitrate was crucial to the production of gunpowder, Gorgas sent crews into Appalachian caves to collect saltpeter, its naturally occurring mineral form. He even decreed that chamber pots should be leached of organic nitrogen, a byproduct of human digestion.

The Tredegar Iron Works made cannons for the Confederate Army, and outfitted the South's first ironclad battleship, the C.S.S. *Virginia*; at the height of the war, it employed a thousand workers (Heidler, p. 1970). A natural target of enemy spies, it was guarded by the Tredegar Battalion, one of the Confederate side's home-guard units. Like the Richmond Arsenal, the Tredegar Works was forced to employ women and children as the war dragged on and labor shortages worsened; it also made use of slave labor. An article in the July 29, 1864, *Richmond Whig* reports the beating of a slave by the foreman of the arsenal's smithing shop, who whipped the man after he denied the accusations of other workers that he was stealing copper. The article focused not on the fact that a worker had been whipped, but on whether he had been excessively whipped, and if this punishment should be an issue for the local magistrate. "We do not advocate negro murder, or cruelty towards negroes, but certainly it is much better when negroes are caught stealing to thrash them soundly than to pester the courts with their cases," the newspaper opined (p. 2).

Spectacular and Tragic Explosions Rates of injury and even death were high at the Richmond Arsenal because of the dangerous nature of the work done there, and the large number of unskilled employees. Indeed, in July 1861 a respected scientist lost his life at the Confederate States Laboratory adjacent to the Arsenal: Joseph Laidley, a chemist working for the Confederate cause, reportedly walked into a building with a lit cigar, though this account was disputed even at the time. "The wooden out-building and the interior one in which the powder was manufactured, were found blown down, and many of the timbers wrenched, twisted and broken in a manner to show the almost inconceivable power of the powder," the *Richmond Dispatch* reported. "Mr. Laidley was found lying on his back, one of the most horrible objects of mutilated humanity which it is possible to conceive.... [N]othing remained to mark the features of a man, except a pair of whiskers and a portion of the neck" (July 4, 1861, p. 2).

A far deadlier explosion, which left forty-five women and children dead, occurred at the Confederate States Laboratory on March 13, 1863. A report published a week later in the *Daily Morning News* of Savannah, Georgia, recounted that victims jumped into the river with their clothes aflame, and a boy named Currie "had his clothing burned entirely off, and ran about crying, 'mother, mother!' He soon died." The paper attributed the fire's cause to "the ignition of a friction cannon primer." One of the employees, Mary Ryan, "was working taskwork, filling these [primers] on a board in which they were inserted. Instead of taking them from the board singly, she struck the board upon the bench in her haste to empty them, and the explosion of one of them by the concussion was the dire consequence" ("Explosion at the Confederate States Laboratory Works on Brown's Island," March 20, 1863).

As Union troops neared Richmond and the city was forced to evacuate, Confederate officials ordered troops to dump 25,000 rounds of artillery ammunition into the James River. Reportedly, they also ordered troops to set fire to the Richmond Arsenal, as well as other buildings—though some Virginians later disputed this account. The Tredegar Iron Works survived, but was consumed by flames a century later. The Springfield Arsenal continued to serve as a main supplier of rifles to the U.S. Army up until the Vietnam War.

BIBLIOGRAPHY

Bilby, Joseph G. *Civil War Firearms: Their Historical Background and Tactical Use and Modern Collecting and Shooting.* Cambridge, MA: Da Capo Press, 1996.

"Charged with Cruelty to a Negro." *Richmond Whig* (VA), July 29, 1864, p. 2.

"The Explosion at the Confederate States Laboratory Works on Brown's Island." *Daily Morning News* (Savannah, GA), March 20, 1863.

Hattaway, Herman. *Shades of Blue and Gray: An Introductory Military History of the Civil War.* Columbia: University of Missouri Press, 1997.

Heidler, David Stephen, Jeanne T. Heidler, and David J. Coles, eds. *Encyclopedia of the American Civil War: A Political, Social, and Military History.* New York: W. W. Norton, 2002.

"Horrible Catastrophe." *Richmond Dispatch* (VA), July 4, 1861, p. 2.

Whittlesey, Derwent Stainthorpe. *The Springfield Armory: A Study in Institutional Development.* Ph.D. diss., University of Chicago, 1920.

Wilson, Mark R. *The Business of Civil War: Military Mobilization and the State, 1861–1865.* Baltimore, MD: Johns Hopkins University Press, 2006.

Carol Brennan

SHIPBUILDING

When hostilities began after the bombardment of Fort Sumter in Charleston Harbor in April 1861, both sides of the conflict geared up for war. Each side faced different challenges in order to accomplish its goals. Interestingly, both sides had to build a navy from very little, but it was the Northern states that were able to outproduce the Southern ones.

The Confederacy

When the Confederate government was formed in February 1861, its new Congress established a Navy Department on February 21. Its biggest challenge was to build a serviceable fleet completely from scratch. Over the course of the war the Navy Department, headed by Secretary of the Navy Stephen R. Mallory (1813–1873), scrambled to accomplish a great deal with limited means. Furthermore, the Confederate Navy competed with the Army for resources and transportation. These issues plagued the Confederate Navy because President Jefferson Davis and most of the rest of the government tended to ignore the navy in favor of the army.

The Confederacy acquired ten ships by purchase or capture in 1861 that mounted only fifteen guns. After the central government in Richmond began to operate, the various Confederate states handed over another fourteen vessels. Mallory made an effort to buy and convert merchant vessels for conversion to military purposes, but this initial move was meant only as a temporary measure until new warships could be built. The South, however, had only two major shipbuilding facilities in operation at the outbreak of hostilities. The more famous of these was the Gosport Shipyard in Norfolk, Virginia, which had its name changed in 1862 to Norfolk Naval Shipyard after the Union recaptured the facility; the other was in Pensacola, Florida, and was primarily a coaling and refitting station. There were also a number of private shipyards in

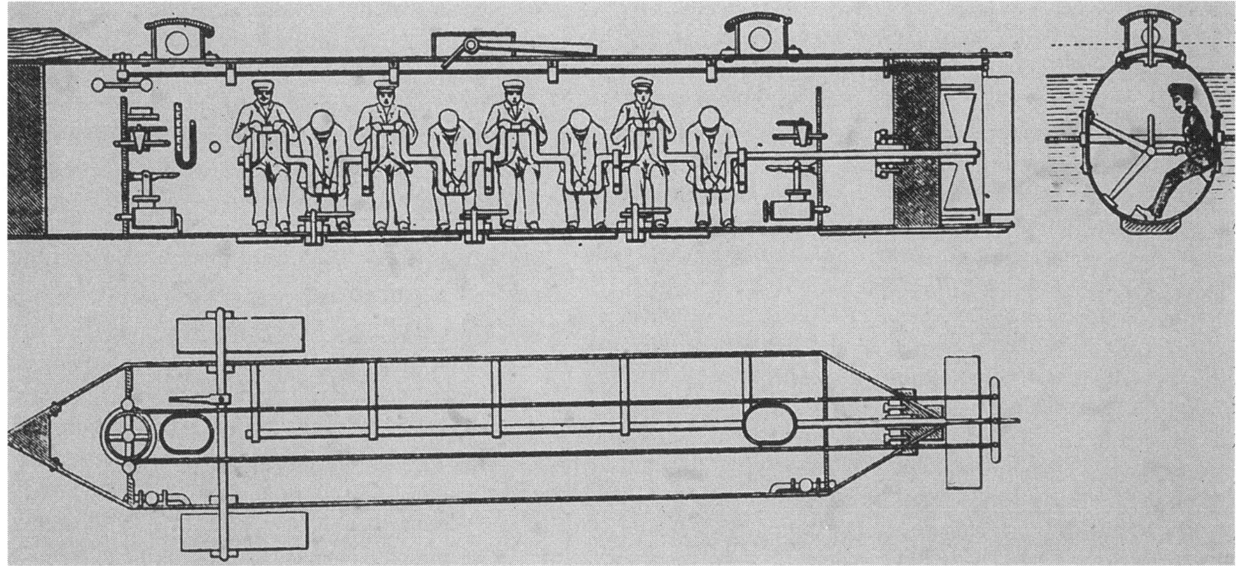

Diagram of the *H. L. Hunley.* Known as the first submarine to destroy an enemy ship, the Confederate vessel *H. L. Hunley* sank on its maiden voyage in 1864 after torpedoing the U.S.S. *Housatonic* in the Charleston Harbor. *Hulton Archive/Getty Images.*

the South, most of which were rather modest in size. The majority of these shipyards were in the coastal towns of the South; however, river towns like Columbus, Georgia, and Selma, Alabama, became focal points of ship construction as the war lengthened.

Secretary Mallory also sent agents abroad, particularly to Great Britain and France, to secure vessels of war from a variety of shipbuilders. The most famous of these vessels were the commerce raiders *Alabama*, *Florida*, and *Shenandoah*. These ships would wreak havoc on the shipping of the United States.

Unable to compete with Northern industrial capacity, Mallory believed that quality was better than quantity. In a letter to a congressman, the secretary stated that he regarded the "possession of an iron-armored ship as a matter of the first necessity. [The] inequality of numbers may be compensated by invulnerability: and thus not only does economy but naval success dictate the wisdom and expediency of fighting with iron against wood" (Still 1987, p. 8). Ironclad ships became the hope of the Confederate Navy against the Federal Navy. Congress allotted two million dollars for building ironclads. There were several facilities in the South able to produce or roll iron, but only eleven were large enough to produce enough for the navy's needs.

Another way to combat the might of the Union Navy was to offer letters of marque and reprisal, which allowed private citizens to be considered enemy combatants; if these private vessels sank or captured an enemy vessel, prize money would be awarded. Several types of ships were built by civilians in order to take advantage of the letters and possibly become wealthy. These vessels tended to be experimental in design. One ironclad, the *Manassas*, and the submarines, like the *H. L. Hunley*, fell into this category. Some citizens also built ships to be given to the navy to use. One instance of this was David S. Johnson, who built the gunboat *Chattahoochee* in Saffold, Georgia, along the lower Chattahoochee River. In all, between 1861 and 1865, Southern shipbuilders laid down 150 vessels. The competing interests of the Confederate government, the states, and private citizens hampered the overall effort to build enough warships.

The Union

At the time of Abraham Lincoln's inauguration, the United States Navy had ninety ships, of which forty-two were in commission. Most were stationed around the globe carrying out a variety of missions outside the United States. In the aftermath of Fort Sumter, Lincoln called for a blockade of Southern ports as part of the strategy to strangle the rebellious states into submission. With over three thousand miles of coastline, the Union needed more ships than it had in 1861. Within a year a vast construction program was under way. About 300 vessels were added to the Union Navy; these newer vessels started to make the blockade effective. By the end of the war, 418 vessels had been purchased, of which 313 were steamers. More than 200 other warships were built under contract, and over sixty of these were ironclads. These ships made the U.S. Navy one of the largest, most modern, and most powerful navies in the world.

The important shipyards in the North included: Philadelphia; Boston; New York City; Portsmouth, Maine; and the Navy Yard in Washington, DC. In addition, there were dozens of private shipbuilders on the coasts, the Great Lakes, and along the Mississippi and Ohio Rivers. The state of Pennsylvania alone could outproduce the entire South. While the *Merrimack* was slowly going through its transformation, the shipbuilders and iron makers in New York built the *Monitor* in about ninety days. The average price of a Union ironclad ended up being about $400,000.

As wide-ranging as were the designs of Confederate ships, Union ships were just as varied, if not more so. There were fast cruisers to chase down the commerce raiders the South unleashed, as well as ironclads, a submarine program, and river vessels. The most successful of the river vessels may have been the double-enders, which were capable of going up- or downriver without having to turn around.

The size of the Federal Navy tipped the scales in favor of the Union during the war. Mostly it was the effort of the fleets to not only blockade the Southern coastline, but also to be able to attack shore fortifications at various points in order to slowly reduce the capacity of the Confederate war effort.

Labor

Interestingly, Northern shipbuilders also had problems with a scarcity of labor like the South. Many shipyard workers joined the military for patriotic reasons. Others went into the Navy hoping to strike it rich with prize money made from captures. Later in the war, some shipyard workers were conscripted. In the South, hundreds of qualified carpenters, mechanics, ironworkers, and many other workers simply left because they were foreign-born and had no reason to support the rebellion. Those who were left volunteered for the army or were later drafted. The army was reluctant to allow these individuals to leave the land forces in order to resume their trade. As the war dragged on, the increasingly stringent draft measures continually reduced exemptions to the skilled workers the shipyards needed. The U.S. Navy Department worked better with the Union Army to deal with these issues than the Confederates ever did. In addition, Union shipyards were willing to hire black workers who had fled northward from the Confederate states.

Because of these manpower shortages and the need to complete the ships rapidly, wages for Northern workers tended to rise throughout the war. From late 1862, wages rose from $1.42 per day to $3.51 in March 1865 (Roberts 2002, p. 135.) Even so, labor strikes were fairly common in Eastern shipyards. New York City's shipbuilders suffered through a number of strikes late in 1862 and early in 1863, well before the draft riots of the latter year. The Boston Navy Yard shut down three times during 1863. Because of a tighter labor market, the Western shipyards experienced very few strikes.

Strikes were also common during the first year of the war for Southern shipbuilders. One strike occurred in New Orleans during November 1861, when the workers pushed for an increase in pay, which delayed the construction of several vessels. A more revealing episode came in 1864 at Selma, when Commander Catesby R. Jones (1821–1877) was threatened by his workers that they would strike if not given a wage of ten dollars a day because they had heard that the Atlanta shops were paying that price (Still 1987, p. 73).

The Confederate Navy tried a variety of ways to supplement the work that required completion. There were generous offerings of overtime pay. The Navy also shifted workers from one facility to another hoping to catch up on the backlog of work. A rivalry developed among these establishments for workmen, however, which hampered cooperation when it was needed the most. Eventually, this caused the Navy simply to take control over many of the works; even then, the deteriorating value of Confederate money exacerbated the problems. When one facility raised its wages, the other local producers would also have to raise their wages or lose their workers. Further compounding the production issue was that workers were organized into local defense units. Lieutenant Robert D. Minor (1821–1871), placed in charge of the ordnance works at Richmond, complained that his men were in the field and could not supply ammunition.

Eventually Southern shipbuilders followed the example of their Northern counterparts and put African Americans to work. A cross-section of free skilled and slave unskilled laborers worked in Southern shipyards. In the ordnance works of the navy in 1865, more than half the workers were African American (Still 1987, p. 69).

In the end a greater industrial capacity and a more stable workforce allowed the Union to build a much larger navy than the breakaway states. Even though the Confederate Navy had several successes, it was eventually restricted to fighting a defensive war, always responding to the initiatives of its Union counterpart. As the coastal cities fell to Union forces, the Confederates adapted as best they could, but in the end it was not enough. Even the commerce raiders, which greatly annoyed Yankee merchants, were only a nuisance to the Union's war effort.

BIBLIOGRAPHY

Canney, Donald L. *Lincoln's Navy: The Ships, Men and Organization, 1861–65.* Annapolis, MD: Naval Institute Press, 1998.

Hackemer, Kurt H. *The U.S. Navy and the Origins of the Military-Industrial Complex, 1847–1883.* Annapolis, MD: Naval Institute Press, 2001.

Luraghi, Raimondo. *A History of the Confederate Navy.* Annapolis, MD: Naval Institute Press, 1996.

Roberts, William H. *Civil War Ironclads: The U.S. Navy and Industrial Mobilization.* Baltimore, MD: Johns Hopkins University Press, 2002.

Still, William N., Jr. *Confederate Shipbuilding.* Columbia: University of South Carolina, 1987.

Jeffery Seymour

TEXTILES

In the years leading up to the U.S. Civil War, America's transition from an agricultural economy to a nation of industry accelerated. The nation's manufacturing centers, located primarily in Northern cities, were connected to labor markets, suppliers, and wholesalers by an ever-expanding network of roads, canals, rivers, and railroads. Remarking on the mountainous wooded landscape that housed much of the nation's industry, Thomas Kettell wrote in his tract *Southern Wealth and Northern Profits* that "the mountain torrents of New England have become motors, by which annually improving machinery has been driven" (Kettell 1860, p. 52).

A significant portion of the nation's industrial output consisted of textiles, a word that literally means "that which is woven." During the nineteenth century, textiles were chiefly made from five natural materials—hemp, flax, silk, wool, and cotton—or combinations thereof. Textile mills powered by water or coal sprang up in every Northern state, producing spun thread, yarn, ribbons, and a range of woven fabrics. While the production of these materials had been a household function at the start of the nineteenth century, by the 1830s, family self-sufficiency was relinquished in favor of inexpensive mass-produced goods.

Technological ingenuity drove the Anglo-American textile industry. Following the development of the power loom in England in 1784, William Horrocks engineered mechanized improvements in 1813. Other advancements in textile manufacture included the transition from water power to steam; the use of iron in the carding process; advances in the techniques of bleaching; and the development of the first synthetic dyes in 1856. In a related advance, Elias Howe patented the lock-stitch machine in 1846, and Isaac Merritt Singer did the same with the flying-shuttle machine in 1851. The Singer Sewing Machine Company, which sold machines on installment and provided free instructions to homemakers, quickly became the leader in the home sewing machine business.

Cotton Becomes King

Although the United States produced a variety of raw materials for textiles, cotton quickly eclipsed all others. An early industrialist named Samuel Slater (1768–1835) established one of the first U.S. cotton mills in Pawtucket, Rhode Island, in 1793, a year after Eli Whitney's cotton gin automated the process of separating cotton fibers from cotton seed. New England retained its concentration of textile mills up until the Civil War, producing almost 70 percent of the nation's total textile output by 1840. According to Treasury Department reports, by the 1850s, the Northern states manufactured five times as much cotton goods as the Southern states (Kettell 1860, p. 37).

Silk, another textile produced for both import and local consumption, was also made in the North. The invention of the Jacquard loom in France in 1804 sparked an increase in the use of this fiber. Boasting the region's leadership role in the U.S. silk industry, a Philadelphia newspaper was able to boast in 1858 that "from indisputable data ... textile fabrics are produced here on a scale which constitutes this city the great centre of that production for the whole United States" (*North American and U.S. Gazette,* March 5, 1858).

While the wool industry in the United States never achieved the export capacity of the cotton industry, it did keep pace with new technology and thus satisfied local demand. As Samuel Slater's biographer, George S. White, commented in 1836, England's leading position in the textile industry—particularly its share of the woolen market—might well be eclipsed by the United States, "where ingenuity and enterprise eminently mark the national character" (White 1836, p. 222).

Because of its versatility, raw cotton quickly established itself as one of the nation's primary exports. By 1834, the Southern cotton crop accounted for one-half the total cotton grown worldwide. Between 1835 and 1858, overseas demand—primarily from England—increased on average by 12.5 percent per year (Kettell 1860, p. 38); by 1860, cotton accounted for almost half of all U.S. exports. As an editorial in the *New York Herald* reported that same year, the Southern states exported four and a half bales of raw cotton, a quantity worth $25 million "before the merchant, the mariner, or the manufacturer had put a hand to it to double, triple and quadruple its value" (July 26, 1860, p. 4).

While U.S. cotton growers provided sufficient quantities of raw materials to keep factories in operation, quality also factored largely into the demand for Southern cotton. The highly desirable long-staple Sea Island cotton (with filaments of 1-1/8 inch in length and over) was grown only in Georgia, while New Orleans produced an especially soft and silky variety of cotton that could be had no where else. Goods produced in "the colonies" were "preferred to English, by reason of their superior texture; and also, that they shrunk much less in the process of printing," reported the *Boston Daily Advertiser,* quoting a London source (March 21, 1876).

England needed large amounts of raw materials in order to keep its urban industrial base growing. With regard to cotton, it found a source in the American South, and abolished import duties in order to make

Two sisters working at a sewing machine, circa 1864. While most of the cotton the United States produced was grown in the South, few textile mills existed there, leaving Southerners unable to turn raw material into cotton cloth. Consequently, women began making homespun cloth and using sewing machines, introduced in the late 1840s, to fashion apparel for the family. *London Stereoscopic Company/ Hulton Archive/Getty Images*

transatlantic trade more attractive. As a writer noted in the London *Times,* "the importation of cotton into this country [England] . . . is so large and so steady that we can steer our national policy by it; it is so important to us, that we should be reduced to embarrassment if it were suddenly to disappear" (Kettell 1860, p. 39).

Although cotton cultivation had been attempted—sometimes unsuccessfully—in India, Jamaica, Australia, China, and Africa, the quality of cotton grown in these areas proved to be inferior to that of the Southern United States. In addition, Southern growers had an efficient and cost-effective labor force: slaves. Ironically, while the slavery issue was hotly debated in the English

Parliament, and some called for a ban on anything other than "Free Labour Cotton"—cotton harvested without employing the "domestic institution" of slave labor—the country's demand was so great that none but slave labor could fulfill it. The year after England repealed its import duty on raw cotton, the country's demand for plantation-grown cotton fiber increased sixteen-fold (Kettell 1860, p. 41).

"The jump which the consumption of cotton in England has just made [following the repeal of the import duty] is but a single leap, which may be repeated indefinitely," the *Times* writer predicted. "There are a thousand millions of mankind upon the globe, all of whom can be most comfortably clad in cotton. Every year new tribes and new nations are added to the category of cotton wearers." With cotton such a "universal necessity," England "must continue to hope that the United States will be able to supply us in years to come with twice as much as we bought of them in years past" (Kettell 1860, p. 41). Although demand from England remained strong, the moral questions swirling around the slavery debate in Parliament cast a pall over trade relations with the Southern states.

Fashion Trends

Related to the increasing demand for U.S. textiles were developments in fashion. The years just prior to the U.S. Civil War saw the advent of the hoopskirt or cage crinoline, which was introduced in 1857. This marvel of engineering—a metal cage supported at the waist and ingeniously hinged to allow for movement and collapsibility—encouraged stylish women to wear ever-more voluminous skirts, some of which reached 15 feet in circumference. Silk taffetas in plaid and striped patterns, as well as iridescent or "shot" versions—available in ever-increasing combinations of vivid hues following the invention of synthetic coal tar dyes in 1856—also gained popularity among more affluent ladies (Tortora and Eubank 1998, p. 302).

Among men, a new demand for cotton came with the 1850s introduction of blue jeans, a garment made from heavy cotton denim devised by the German-born entrepreneur Levi Strauss (1829–1902) in San Francisco to address the needs of miners for sturdy work overalls during the California gold rush. Such other items of clothing for men as frock coats, trousers, and vests, were now factory-made and easier to obtain. Manufactured in standard sizes rather than made to order, some vests and trousers featured hidden buckles that allowed their fit to be adjusted, as well as manufactured hooks and eyes, snaps, and buttons (Tortora and Eubank 1998, p. 302).

While the South exported its luxurious long-staple cottons to overseas markets and Northern textile mills, the garments worn by the men, women, and children at work in the cotton fields were crafted of cheap, rough-textured cotton or wool obtained from manufacturers in Rhode Island or Europe. Most slaves were issued two outfits per year, one for warmer months and one for cooler weather. A coarse white homespun cloth frequently used in garments worn by slaves in both the South and in the West Indies became known as negro cloth (Bishop 1866, p. 339).

Textiles in the Union

The Southern states were a primary market for Northern manufactured goods prior to the outbreak of the Civil War. Of the $60 million worth of purchases estimated to have been made by Southern consumers in 1860, over a third consisted of boots and shoes, while textiles came in a close second (Kettell 1860, p. 60). "The shipowners and the manufacturers of New England, the merchants and mechanics of New York, and the manufacturers and miners of Pennsylvania and New Jersey, all draw no small portion of their daily wages and profits from the stream that rises in the cotton fields of the South," asserted a *New York Herald* editorial in the summer of 1860, addressing this trade between North and South (July 26, 1860, p. 4). The outbreak of the Civil War in 1861 interfered initially with this profitable trade. In addition to leaving Northern businesses holding trade losses totaling $300 million, the war disrupted the North's supply of raw cotton and labor (*Bangor Daily Whig & Courier*, July 7, 1864).

While Northern textile mills experienced a temporary setback in 1860, their initial losses were mitigated by the new orders that poured in from the Union Army. The Civil War generated an immediate and substantial demand for ready-to-wear uniforms. In the Union Army alone, over 1.5 million uniforms were required each year between 1861 and 1865, and the cloth for all these uniforms was a product of the Utica Steam Woolen Company, of upstate New York (Coates 2002, p. 103). Because textile mill machinery was already operated in large part by women, the transfer of men from the factories into the Union Army also affected wartime industrial output in the North far less than it did in the South.

In fact, the war accelerated the spread of mechanization and the efficiencies of the factory system. The number of sewing machines used by Northern factories doubled between 1860 and 1865, and shoe production increased as a result of the development of a machine for sewing the uppers to the soles (Depew 1895, p. 571). To supply the textiles needed for uniforms, tents, and other supplies, smugglers provided Southern cotton while wool came from New England and the Western states. To meet demand, Northern mills also turned to Britain and France, where English woolens and Egyptian and Indian cotton were readily available. This transatlantic trade was made easier because such Northern ports as New York City were already central to the textile export business, having eclipsed such Southern ports as Charleston years before.

Also affecting the Northern textile industry during wartime was the Morrill Act. A controversial measure supported by Northern Republicans and spearheaded by the Vermont congressman Justin Smith Morrill (1810–1898), the Act established a tariff wall designed to protect Northern industrial manufacturing from foreign competition. The Morrill tariff, which went into effect on April 1, 1861, imposed a protective tax of between twenty and fifty percent on imported silk, cotton, woolens, and iron. Although the tariff provoked some manufacturers in England to shift their support to the Confederacy, its impact was so minimal that two further tariffs were enacted during the war as a way to fund the war effort. Because of the favorable balance of trade resulting from the importation of raw cotton by the North, French and English markets continued to do business with the United States despite the costs on their products imposed by the Morrill tariff (*Boston Daily Advertiser*, March 21, 1876).

Textiles in the Confederacy

Textile manufacturing in the South, more specifically the manufacture of cotton fabrics, had increased dramatically during the 1850s. Such companies as the Charleston Cotton Manufacturing Company, which began business in the summer of 1850, inspired one business journal to note that "our Southern friends [seem] ... destined to become largely interested in fostering at home those branches of industry to which their great staple owes its importance and value" (*North American and United States Gazette,* July 2, 1850). Despite this expansion and the advocacy of such individuals as the South Carolina businessman William Green, the industry was still in its infancy when war broke out in 1861.

As Edward A. Pollard explained in his *The Lost Cause,* "the South entered the war with only a few insignificant manufactories of arms and materials of war and textile fabrics. She was soon to be cut off by an encircling blockade from all those supplies upon which she had depended" (Pollard 1866, p. 132). With President Abraham Lincoln's proclamation in April 1861, ordering naval commanders to blockade Southern ports, the importation of foreign goods to the South slowed dramatically. Apart from a small amount of goods smuggled in by blockade runners, Southern stores quickly found their shelves emptied of inventory.

The slogan "Cotton is king" reflects the heady exuberance of many in the South following the formation of the Confederacy on February 4, 1861. Representatives of the city of Columbus, Georgia, even published an open invitation to Northern "men of reason" in the *New York Herald.* While regretting that "circumstances have made it necessary to dissolve the government of the United States," the writers proclaimed that "the boasted shuck and hay trade of the Northern States dwindles into utter insignificance compared to this great staple," cotton. "We invite ... all the manufacturing and commercial men of the North, who are our friends, to leave the bleak republican North. Unite with us; make our homes your homes, and you shall share the prosperity and happiness in store for us" (April 9, 1861, p. 2).

Unfortunately for the residents of Columbus, Georgia, and elsewhere throughout the South, prosperity and happiness were not the end result of secession. Although the much-hated Morrill tariff applied only to Northern exports, the Confederate president Jefferson Davis's policy of free trade was undermined by the antislavery debates ongoing in England. Like England, Europe "entirely misapprehended the controversy between the Northern and Southern States of the Union," according to the London *Times* (March 5, 1861, p. 2). Observing the tensions between North and South only weeks before the firing upon Fort Sumter drew the new Confederate States of America into war, the *Times* writer maintained that "the slavery question ... has been merely introduced as a blind ... and the real point of contention lies in the national tariff." Southern interests, in fact, "have only one object, which is to get the highest price for the greatest quantity of cotton" (March 5, 1861, p. 2).

While the South had great quantities of cotton, it had few mills to process it, resulting in clothing shortages. Homespun clothes for civilians quickly became the norm. In order to reproduce anything even remotely resembling the crinoline, fashion-conscious Southern women relied on their wits and the textiles to be found in their homes to maintain their wardrobes. Like Scarlett O'Hara in Margaret Mitchell's 1936 novel *Gone with the Wind*, they made use of everything from window curtains to bed hangings. Skirts and blouses were cut from aprons, shawls, and other large spans of cloth, while sleeves became tighter so that new sleeves could be cut out of fuller existing sleeves. Kid gloves were replaced by silk or lace mitts, new hair ribbons were a rarity, and white summer dresses were no longer trimmed with French lace. Women also patched their clothing with scraps cut from discarded garments. As Elzey Hay wrote in *Godey's Lady's Book*, recalling Southern fashion during wartime, "Before the blockade was raised all learned to wear every garment to the very last rag that would hang on our backs" (Hay 1866, p. 32).

Perhaps fortunately, most American fashion magazines were published in such Northern cities as Philadelphia and Boston. With the circulation of these periodicals now restricted to the North, Southern women felt less pressure to conform to the latest styles. "We knew very little of the modes in the outer world," Hay recalled (Hay 1866, p. 32). "Now and then a [fashion magazine] ... would find its way through the blockade, and create a greater sensation than the last battle." According to Hay,

... the finest traveling dress I had during the war was a brown alpaca turned wrong side out, upside down, and trimmed with quillings [small rounded ridges in a piece of cloth] made from [an] umbrella cover. I will venture to say that no umbrella ever served so many purposes or was so thoroughly used up before. The whalebones served to stiffen corsets and the waist of a homespun dress, and the handle was given to a wounded soldier for a walking stick. (Hay 1866, p. 32)

As the supply of textiles continued to diminish throughout the South, prices correspondingly went up. In the bonnet market, for example, a well-connected milliner could pay the going rate for a simple bonnet, refashion it, and then sell it for four times her investment (Hay 1866). For the average Southern woman, however, wartime required a return to home industry. In addition to their own fashion needs, the wives and mothers of Confederate soldiers had to find a way to outfit their loved ones. Hand looms and spinning wheels were retrieved from attics, and the womenfolk set about transforming King Cotton into cloth. A popular song of the era, reportedly written by Carrie Belle Sinclair, captures the spirit of the times. "The homespun dress is plain, I know,/ My hat's palmetto, too; But then it shows what Southern girls/ for Southern rights will do," are some of the lyrics to "The Homespun Dress." "We scorn to wear a bit of silk,/ A bit of Northern lace,/ But make our homespun dresses up,/And wear them with a grace" (Silber and Silverman 1960, p. 68).

After the Reconstruction, in the New South Era, the cotton industry would resume its development, fueled by inexpensive water power, low taxation, and boosterism by the likes of Henry Grady. By 1880, over 14,000,000 acres were under cultivation in the South (Steele 1885, p. 306).

BIBLIOGRAPHY

Bishop, J. Leander. *A History of American Manufactures from 1608 to 1860.* 3 vols. Philadelphia: Edward Young & Co., 1866.

Coates, Earl J. *Don Troiani's Regiments and Uniforms of the Civil War.* Mechanicsburg, PA: Stackpole Books, 2002.

"Cotton and the Constitution: The Relations of Politics, Industry, and Trade." *New York Herald,* July 26, 1860, p. 4.

Depew, Chauncey M., ed. *One Hundred Years of American Commerce: A History of American Commerce by One Hundred Americans.* 2 volumes. New York: D.O. Haynes & Co., 1895.

"Factories at the South." *North American and United States Gazette,* July 2, 1850, p. B3.

Hay, Elzey. "Dress under Difficulties; or, Passages from the Blockade Experiences of Rebel Women." *Godey's Lady's Book,* July 1866, p. 32.

Kettell, Thomas Prentice. *Southern Wealth and Northern Profits, as Exhibited in Statistical Facts and Official Figures: Showing the Necessity of Union to the Future Prosperity and Welfare of the Republic.* New York: George W. & John A. Wood, 1860.

Letters from the 44th Regiment M.V.M.: A Record of the Experience of a Nine Months' Regiment in the Department of North Carolina in 1862–3. Boston: Boston Herald, 1863.

Lord, Daniel. *The Effect of Secession upon the Commercial Relations between the North and South,* 2nd ed. New York: New York Times, 1861.

"The Morrill Tariff in Europe." *Daily Morning News,* (Savannah, GA) March 27, 1861.

"Our Columbus Correspondence." *New York Herald,* April 9, 1861, p. 2.

Pollard, Edward A. *The Lost Cause: A New Southern History of the War of the Confederates,* 2nd edition. Chicago, IL: E.B. Treat & Co., 1890.

Silber, Irwin, and Jerry Silverman, compilers. *Songs of the Civil War.* New York: Columbia University Press, 1960.

Steele, Joel Dorman. *A Brief History of the United States.* New York: A.S. Barnes, 1885.

"Textile Fabrics: Their Production and Distribution." *North American and United States Gazette,* March 5, 1858, col. B.

"The Textile Trades: From the *London Hour.*" *Boston Daily Advertiser,* March 21, 1876.

Times (London, England), March 5, 1861, as reported in the *Daily (Savannah, GA) Morning News,* March 27, 1861.

Tortora, Phyllis, and Keith Eubank. *Survey of Historic Costume,* 3rd ed. New York: Fairchild Publications, 1998.

White, George S. *Memoir of Samuel Slater: The Father of American Manufactures,* 2nd ed. Philadelphia, PA: privately printed, 1836.

Pamela L. Kester

■ Agriculture

Fredonia Jane Davis, a Georgia farmwoman, wrote to her brother, a Confederate soldier, from her mother's farm in Decatur in 1862: "Ma had her wheat cut last week—it is not very good, therefore we will not eat much biscuit next year. The corn looks very well but we are deep in the grass. I expect we will have to let some of it go. We have tried to get help but can not" (Rasmussen 1965, p. 188). The Buttles family living in Wisconsin, in contrast, purchased a new cultivator in 1862, reducing the amount of physical labor required on their farm. The prior year they had built a new stable with the help of twenty neighbors despite low crop prices. The Buttles also bought a new horse in 1863 and cut their neighbor's wheat while he served in the army (Rasmussen 1965, p. 191).

The Civil War brought obvious disadvantages to the South when the Union blockade and military invasion disrupted agricultural production and markets. Similarly, Northern agriculture benefited from the price increases driven by wartime demand and the North's relatively secure borders. Historians disagree very little about these broad conclusions. They have, however, revealed fascinating details leading to more complex and informative explanations of the factors underlying the distinction between agriculture in the North and the South during the Civil War.

Early Farming

Antebellum agricultural science experienced a period of intense development resulting from soil exhaustion throughout the eastern United States. Colonial growth came less from labor than from the abundance of land available after Native Americans had been removed through disease and warfare. Cheap land encouraged poor conservation habits; most Americans simply moved to new soil when an area's productivity declined. Tobacco and corn, the two most abundant crops in the colonial period, made quick work of Eastern soils, draining them of essential nutrients in a matter of a few years. While population pressures induced New Englanders to begin conservation efforts in the late eighteenth century, however, the Southern colonies were not under similar pressure. The historian Sarah Phillips notes that Northern and mid-Atlantic farmers were diversifying their crops, using crop rotation, and adding livestock to provide manure for fertilizer, helping them to manage sustainable and settled farming practices (Phillips 2000, p. 802). Cheap Western (today's Midwest) land and its suitability for grain crops, which commanded high prices in the East, created new pressure for Northern agricultural improvements. During the 1830s and 1840s agricultural societies, journals, and education programs acquired new importance across the nation. Americans were responding to earlier destructive agricultural practices with significant effort.

Southern farms, like their Northern counterparts, had contributed to soil depletion. After cotton became a major cash crop in the South, the depletion rates rose even more quickly. Southern agrarians recognized the need for change. Soil exhaustion in the Upper South encouraged westward migration, which was intensified by the emphasis on short-staple cotton. With the migrating farmers went their slaves and capital. The farmers left behind called for better conservation and crop diversification; however, the constraints of and profits from slavery offered little incentive for such dramatic changes. As Phillips notes, Southern agricultural reformers like the planter Edmund Ruffin were unwilling to place reform above slavery. Ruffin said in one address, "I would not hesitate a moment to prefer the entire existing social, domestic, and industrial conditions of these slaveholding states, with all the now existing evils of indolence and waste, and generally exhausting tillage and declining fertility, to the entire conditions of any other country on the face of the globe" (Phillips 2000, p. 807). Choosing slavery over innovation kept both better soil conservation practices and mechanical innovations out of the South.

The problems for Southerners during the war were not limited to their lagging behind other regions in agricultural science. The huge investment made in growing short-staple cotton left the region dependent on the rest of the country for many agricultural products. This dependency was a significant contributor to the Confederacy's defeat and Southern agriculturalists knew it. A reporter for the *Southern Cultivator* remarked too late in 1861, "The absurdity of our importing Hay from Maine, Irish Potatoes from Nova Scotia, Apples from Massachusetts, Butter and Cheese from New York; Flour and Pork from Ohio, or Beef from Illinois, is apparent at a glance.... Let us at least show the world that we are AGRICULTURALLY INDEPENDENT" (Coulter 1927, pp. 4–5).

The extent of regional resistance to agricultural innovation before the war should not be exaggerated, however. Twenty years before open hostilities, there were Southerners who advocated reform through diversification. During the late 1840s Richard Peters experimented with varieties of cattle, sheep and goats. Perhaps his most significant success was breeding a goat for the production of acceptable mohair. Other Southern farmers worked to develop a commercial fruit industry, particularly peaches in South Carolina, Georgia, and Alabama, and apples in the Appalachian foothills (Bonner 1948, pp. 252–253). Although such efforts were relatively minor, they indicate that the South was capable of some changes.

Results of the War

When the war came both the North and the South faced new agricultural conditions and needs. Within the opening year of the war, Southern farm production was disrupted and failed to recover. The historian Eugene Lerner maintained in the late 1950s that the decline was severe. He noted that during the war the Southern horse population experienced a decline of 29 percent and that of cattle dropped by 32 percent, while the value of farm implements dropped 46 percent and the value of farms was reduced almost in half (Lerner 1959, p. 117). The South was in such disarray by the end of the conflict that there are no comprehensive data on the region's agricultural capacity in 1865. Fighting the war demanded the services of the men who had managed and labored on the farms. Even with efforts to rotate soldiers from the front to their homes during harvest season, the South's

"King Cotton Bound; or, The Modern Prometheus." After President Lincoln blockaded Southern ports, the Confederacy lost its primary source of revenue, exported cotton. Without a diversified agricultural base or income from the cotton trade, daily life in the South became difficult as common foodstuffs, such as grain, meat, and produce, became scarce. *HIP/Art Resource, NY.*

needs exceeded the capacity of the region to maintain both a standing army and a healthy agricultural system.

Garland Brinkley offered another approach to understanding the postwar decline in the productivity of Southern agriculture. He contended that a significant factor was the impact of diseases endemic in the region, specifically rampant infestations of hookworm. Brinkley noted, "Ubiquitous hookworm symptoms were reported by Confederate medical personnel even though they were unaware of hookworm itself" (Brinkley 1997, p. 119). The symptoms of the parasite's presence in humans include lethargy, anemia, vomiting, rash, and in extreme or repeated cases—juvenile cases in particular—a decline in mental capacity. Brinkley concluded that so many Southerners were infected during and after the war that the disease significantly reduced the region's capacity for agricultural production.

Historians have alternated between a theory of continuity and a theory of postbellum change in evaluating the effects of the war on agriculture. Paul Gates's 1965 book *Agriculture and the Civil War* helped establish one account of what happened. Gates argued that Northern and Midwestern farmers experienced less change from the war itself than from long-established economic trends, including the growth of cities, railroad development, and market shifts. Dairy production, for example, gained new life from faster trains, which could move dairy products into urban areas before they spoiled. Wheat production grew not so much from war needs but from rising European demand (Gates 1965, pp. 3–6).

When Gates examined agriculture in the South, he found that a steady decline in production contributed significantly to Southern defeat. The Confederate government attempted to direct agriculture across the Southern states in an unprecedented effort that the historian Raimondo Luraghi described as "state socialism" (Miller 1979, p. 436). The Confederate government tried solutions that undermined its social structure, including the impressment of slaves, as noted by the historian Bernard Nelson (p. 392). Attempts at the state and national level to restrict cotton planting in 1862 faced the commonsense observation that rising cotton prices would work against a policy of restriction. Profits won out over patriotism during the first full year of the war.

Focusing more on slavery, Gavin Wright's seminal work *The Political Economy of the Cotton South: Households, Markets, and Wealth in the Nineteenth Century* supported the theory that the Civil War brought about significant changes in Southern agriculture. Wright convincingly demonstrated that slavery limited agricultural development before the war and established an inflexible system ill suited to wartime. Prior to the war wealthy planters, unlike small farmers who had to maintain significant investments in subsistence production, could afford to make decisions about crops and labor management on the basis of prices for their products. In the postbellum era the same planters had little capital and few choices when they faced a decline in cotton demand. Wright maintained that the depressed world cotton market would have arrived regardless of the Civil War, but that the combination forced Southern cotton producers to gamble by raising production and thus further depressing prices. The result was the beginning of a long period of poverty and agricultural decline.

Similarly, historian John Otto contended that the devastation of the war required farmers to remake the agricultural system in the South. The war imposed new conditions, including higher labor costs, low capital reserves, and an inability to afford farm machinery. Labor organization was perhaps the most significant change. In cotton production most landowners after the war turned to forms of tenancy and sharecropping, while farmers growing other crops, particularly sugar in the Deep South, turned to wage labor.

It is difficult to sustain the argument that little changed in agriculture at the national level during the Civil War, particularly if one examines the efforts of the federal government. Congress passed four laws in 1862 that continue to shape American farming. The first, which was legislation creating the Department of Agriculture, may not have dramatically altered farm production during the war; however, the newly organized department began by printing annual reports encouraging innovations in crop science and mechanization. Within a few years the department was poised to become a world leader in agricultural research. The second enactment, the Homestead Act, helped encourage Western land development in the Great Plains region; combined with the Pacific Railway Act, the Homestead Act directed Americans toward productive agricultural expansion. Finally, the Morrill Land Grant College Act created institutions of higher learning with a focus on the agricultural sciences. Although there was no immediate benefit from this effort, it would help the United States become a leader in crop science.

Although the South found it difficult to modernize its agricultural practices for more than a generation after the war, Southern farmers and the entire nation faced a transformation in farming. Mechanization increasingly replaced hand labor and agricultural science dictated farming practices.

BIBLIOGRAPHY

Bagley, Jr., William Chandler. *Soil Exhaustion and the Civil War*. Washington, DC: American Council on Public Affairs, 1942.

Bonner, James C. "Advancing Trends in Southern Agriculture, 1840–1860." *Agricultural History* 22 (1948): 248–259.

Brinkley, Garland L. "The Decline in Southern Agricultural Output, 1860–1880." *The Journal of Economic History* 57 (March 1997): 116–138.

Coulter, E. Merton. "The Movement for Agricultural Reorganization in the Cotton South during the Civil War." *Agricultural History* 1 (1927): 3–17.

Gates, Paul W. *Agriculture and the Civil War*. New York: Alfred A. Knopf, 1965.

Lerner, Eugene M. "Southern Output and Agricultural Income, 1560–1880." *Agricultural History* 33 (1959): 117–125.

Luraghi, Raimondo. *The Rise and Fall of the Plantation South*. New York: New Viewpoints, 1978.

Miller, Randall M. "The Political Economy of the Cotton South: Households, Markets, and Wealth in the Nineteenth Century." *The History Teacher* 12 (May 1979): 435–437.

Nelson, Bernard H. "Confederate Slave Impressment Legislation, 1861–1865." *Journal of Negro History* 31 (1946): 392–410.

Otto, John Solomon. *Southern Agriculture during the Civil War Era, 1860–1880*. Westport, CT: Greenwood Publishing Group, 1994.

Phillips, Sarah T. "Antebellum Agricultural Reform, Republican Ideology, and Sectional Tension." *Agricultural History* 74 (2000): 799–822.

Rasmussen, Wayne D. "The Civil War: A Catalyst of Agricultural Revolution." *Agricultural History* 39 (1965): 187–195.

Wright, Gavin. *The Political Economy of the Cotton South: Households, Markets, and Wealth in the Nineteenth Century*. New York: W.W. Norton & Company, 1978.

David F. Herr

Shortages

Shortages during the Civil War touched soldiers and civilians alike. The citizens of the Confederate States were especially devastated by shortages: Civilian crops were appropriated for the military, livestock were stolen by the Union army, railroad and port blockades stopped precious supplies of food from reaching their destinations, and the passage of the Emancipation Proclamation took slaves out of the fields. To add insult to injury, hungry civilians had to contend with greedy merchants who used food as a source of speculative profit. It is little wonder that riots, generally referred to as "bread riots," swept across the South.

The Confederacy attempted to rectify the shortage situation in the South by encouraging farmers to replace cash crops like cotton and tobacco with food-bearing plants and grains. "[A]s long as the war lasts, let every man do all he can to raise and produce things that are required for food and clothing," insisted the *Southern Cultivator*; otherwise, "if we suffer for the necessaries of life it is our own fault" ("Planting in 1863," January/February 1863, p. 30). Following this "good, sound, practical common-sense advice" would mean that while farmers would lose money from not raising cash crops, "the present high prices will quickly be materially reduced" and widespread starvation would be halted (p. 30).

By 1863 food shortages had made it difficult for the Confederate States of America to provision its starving army. James A. Seddon, Jefferson Davis's secretary of war, recommended the appropriation of civilian foodstuffs to feed the soldiers. Seddon called on each county, parish, or ward to appoint a committee of three or more "discreet citizens" who would be charged with ascertaining "what amount of surplus corn and meat, whether bacon, pork or beef" could be supplied to the military (*New York Times*, April 19, 1863, p. 1). Such committees would be expected to fix prices, pay citizens for the materials appropriated by the government, and make sure those materials reached the nearest military quartermaster. Seddon's demand on the civilians of the South was taken as an encouraging sign in the North. Whereas "the President of the United States has not had to send a message to Congress on the danger of starvation[,] ... Jeff. Davis and his Secretary of War, Seddon have," declared the Boston *Independent*.

John Letcher (1813–1884). Lacking a diverse agricultural system and being forced to divert the limited food available to its troops, the South found feeding its civilian population difficult. Bread riots began to break out in the spring of 1863, the largest of which took place in Richmond, Virginia, and was only quieted when Governor John Letcher promised the all-female mob that more food would be distributed to them. *The Library of Congress.*

"[R]ebel authorities affirm that if they are vanquished it will be for want of food" (April, 23, 1863, p. 8).

Throughout the South, it was not only the military that suffered from a lack of food. According to the *Christian Inquirer*, for example, only the Union capture of New Orleans "saved this region from the starvation that was staring them in the face" (March 21, 1863, p. 2). In other Southern cities and towns, the hunger of civilian populations led to rioting and looting during 1863. Despite "the efforts of Confederate journals North and South to conceal the fact, or deprive it of its importance, no doubt remains that very serious *bread riots* have taken place," declared the *New York Times* ("Famine in the South," April 20, 1863, p. 4). "[W]omen have been leaders; and that fact alone proves that absolute hunger must be the cause" (p. 4).

The most famous of the bread riots took place in Richmond, Virginia—the capital of the Confederacy—on April 2, 1863. According to historian Alan Pell Crawford, these riots were the culmination of a series of factors. The quick rise of the population of Richmond after it became the Confederate capital, appropriation of food supplies by the military, hoarding of scarce foodstuffs by speculators, the destruction of valuable farmland throughout Virginia, and the diminishing value of Confederate money all made Richmond ripe for civil disturbance (Crawford 2002, pp. 21–23). To make matters worse, heavy snows during March made it difficult for rural farmers to get their produce to market.

Despite Jefferson Davis's command to send "nothing of the unfortunate disturbance of today over the wires for any purpose" (Crawford 2002, p. 26), news of the Richmond bread riot quickly reached Northern media outlets, which published a variety of somewhat contradictory accounts. The *New York Times* for April 8, 1863, quoted the eyewitness account of one Col. Stewart, a recently released prisoner of war. From his prison window Stewart saw "a great bread riot, in which about three thousand women were engaged, armed with clubs, guns and stones.... [They] broke open the Government stores and took bread, clothing and whatever else they wanted" ("Bread Riot in Richmond," p. 1). Also on April 8, the *New York Herald* weighed in on the significance of the riots: "Virginia is the most fruitful grain raising States in the South ... and if the want of food manifests itself in such a demonstrative fashion as to bring out a hungry mob of three thousand women into the streets of the capital, we can readily imagine how dire must be the distress existing in the other States" ("The Situation," p. 4). On April 9, 1863, the *New York Observer* reported that "the rioters were composed of about 8,000 women, who were armed with clubs, and guns and stones[;] ... they broke open government and private stores, and took bread, clothing, and whatever else they wanted" ("Bread Riot in Richmond," p. 118). The April 10 *New York Times* reported that neither Richmond's mayor nor General Winder could appease the crowd as it rioted through the streets; instead, Jefferson Davis himself had to be called on to quiet the rabble-rousers. Davis agreed to supply the rioters with "daily rations," after which the throng returned to their homes carrying their hard-won loot ("The Rebel Bread Riots," p. 1). According to the *Times*, a "renegade Confederate General ... publicly stated that from all the information in his possession he thought the Southern Confederacy might, possibly, hold out for three months under the present circumstances, but no longer, unless they obtained better means of procuring food and clothing.... [S]tarvation and insurrection is inevitable, unless relief is obtained" (p. 1).

The April 17, 1863, edition of the *New York Herald* described the riot as a "popular movement" in "consequence of the exorbitant prices" of food and materials in Richmond, and provided the fullest account ("Interesting from the South: 'The Food Question,'" p. 1). On the morning of April 2, before the riot, the paper reported, "a large meeting, composed principally of the wives and daughters of the working classes, was held in the African church, and a committee appointed to wait upon the Governor to request that articles of food should be sold at government rates" (p. 1). The women who met with Governor Letcher found no help forthcoming, so took matters into their own hands.

The riot began when "a body of females, numbering about three hundred, collected together and commenced helping themselves to bread, flour, meat, articles of clothing, &c," at which "the entire city was thrown into consternation" (p. 1). The women were not to be stopped: "[H]atchets and axes in the hands of women rendered desperate by hunger made quick work, and building after building was rapidly broken open" (p. 1). In response, the governor called out the city guard to help storeowners control the rioters; "a few individuals attempted to resist the women, but without success" (p. 1). Finally, the mayor read the crowd the Riot Act, but to little avail—"during the reading of that document a portion of the crowd suspended operations; but no sooner had the Mayor concluded than the seizure of provisions commence again more vigorously than before" (p. 1). Governor Letcher then addressed the masses and tried to shame them by "characterizing the demonstration as a disgrace and a stigma upon the city" (p. 1). It was not until the "arrest of about forty women, and the promise of the Governor to relieve the wants of the destitute" that the riot broke up, however (p. 1). In the end, "a large amount of bread and bacon was carried off, and all engaged in the riot succeeded in getting a good supply of provisions" (p. 1). In an effort to hide the true nature of events from Northern officials, "leading men of the city attempted to circulate the report that the women were 'Irish and Yankee hags,' endeavoring to mislead the public concerning the amount of loyal sentiment in the city" (p. 1). However, "the fact of ... [the rioters'] destitution and respectability was too palpable, and the authorities are forced to admit the conclusion that starvation alone incited the movement" (p. 1).

According to Crawford, the popular movement that led to the Richmond bread riots was begun when one Mary Jackson began discussing the practices of food speculators with her neighbors in the working-class neighborhood of Oregon Hill. Word soon spread of Mary Jackson's idea to confront the governor over the issue. A group met at the Belvidere Hill Baptist Church to put together a list of demands. When the governor tried to postpone a meeting with the women, they took to the streets, some of them armed with knives, hatchets, or guns. They marched down Capital Hill toward Main Street, where shops and the government commissary were located. Once they reached the shopping area, they broke into the commissary and smashed store windows, grabbing food and other supplies. Richmond's mayor and governor attempted to halt the progress of the throng but no headway was made until Jefferson Davis, president of the Confederacy, appeared on the scene. According to the memoirs of Varinda Davis, "the president told the mob that rioting was not the way to redress their grievances[;] ... such disorder ... would only make matters worse.... [I]t would discourage farmers from trying to bring their produce to town, further restricting access to food" (Crawford 2002, p. 24). Davis declared, "we do not desire to injure anyone ... but this lawlessness must stop.... I will give you five minutes to disperse, otherwise you will be fired upon" (Crawford 2002, p. 24). The crowd finally broke up, and arrests were made.

The Richmond riot resulted in pervasive unease and fear of further uprisings. Indeed, it was not the only April bread riot. The *New York Observer and Chronicle* of April 16, 1863, reports that "soldiers wives and others rose *en masse*" in Petersburg, Maryland, and "visiting the stores of the mercenary speculators who have been enriching themselves ... helped themselves forcibly to what they wanted, pitching out goods to the poor and needy as they went" (p. 126). In Atlanta, Georgia, "some fifteen or twenty women ... made an impressment of about 200 pounds of bacon belonging to private parties" (p. 126). Apparently, they first offered to purchase the bacon at government rates, but were met with denial so took the bacon instead. Rioters also rose in North Carolina that spring. The April 19, 1863, *New York Times* reported that near Raleigh, North Carolina, "a company of women, most of them soldiers' wives, went to the store of William Welsh[,] ... [where they] rolled out several barrels of molasses and divided it" ("Bread Riots in Raleigh, N.C.," p. 1). In Salisbury, North Carolina, another band of women appropriated flour, salt, and molasses from private owners and then divided their takings equally amongst themselves (p. 1).

The summer of 1863 proved quieter than the spring, but the troubles were not yet over. Mobile, Alabama saw two riots on September 4, 1863. Demonstrators holding banners that read "Bread or Blood" and "Bread and Peace" marched down Dauphine Street "armed with knives and hatchets," and broke "open the stores in their progress, ... taking for their use such articles of food or clothing as they were in urgent need of" ("The Bread Riot in Mobile," *New York Times*, October 1, 1863, p. 4). When ordered to halt the progress of the rioters, the Seventeenth Alabama regiment said they "would rather assist those starving wives, mothers, sisters and daughters of men who had been forced to fight in the battles of the rebellion" (p. 4). The mayor of Mobile halted the riot with promises and the women returned to their homes; "in the evening, however, the riot broke out again, more fiercely than ever" (p. 4).

Most Northern press coverage of Southern bread riots was sympathetic to the women who were forced into violence in order to feed and clothe themselves and their family members. Occasionally, however, a more mocking or censorious tone crept into reports. *Vanity Fair*, for example, noted that while "the 'Southern Chivalry' are fond of boasting that they are the best bred people in the world, ... they lately had ... the worst bread riots that ever the world heard of" ("Our View of It," May 2, 1863, p. 35). The same publication, reporting on a riot in Milledgeville, Georgia, involving "about three hundred women ... [who] pitched into a dry-goods store ... and seized ... fine goods," remarked that "the whole fray ... would naturally resolve itself into a bonnet-box—that is, in a pugilistic, not modistic, sense.... [W]hile one half of the Southern females is contending with the other half in wild rushes over a box of *ruches*, the proprietor might be enabled to call in the police and quell the row" ("The 'Wayward Sisters' Down South," May 9, 1863, p. 54).

Regardless of how the bread riots are conceived, the undeniable fact is that some Southerners were left with no other recourse but to loot in order to meet their basic survival needs. The Civil War was a "total war," aimed at and affecting civilians as well as soldiers. Southern rioting and looting illustrate just how well Union tactics to demoralize and starve the Confederate States of America succeeded.

BIBLIOGRAPHY

"Army Correspondence." *Christian Inquirer*, March 21, 1863.

"The Bread Riot in Mobile." *New York Times*, October 1, 1863.

"Bread Riot in Raleigh, N.C." *New York Times*, April 19. 1863.

"Bread Riot in Richmond." *New York Observer*, April 9, 1863.

"Bread Riot in Richmond." *New York Times*, April 8, 1863.

Crawford, Alan Pell. "Richmond's Bread Riot" *American History* 153, no. 4 (2002): 20–26.

"Domestic." *New York Observer and Chronicle*, April 16, 1863.

"Famine in the South." *New York Times*, April 20, 1863.

"General News." *Independent*, Boston April 23, 1863.

"Interesting from the South: 'The Food Question'; The Bread Riot in Richmond." *The New York Herald*, April 17, 1863.

"News of the Week." *Circular*, New York, January 10, 1861.

"Our View of It." *Vanity Fair*, May 2, 1863.

"Planting in 1863." *Southern Cultivator*, January/February 1863.

"The Rebel Bread Riots." *New York Times*, April 10, 1863.

Seddon, James A. "The Food Question." *New York Times*, April 19, 1863.

"The Situation." *The New York Herald*, April 8, 1863.

"The 'Wayward Sisters' Down South." *Vanity Fair*, May 9, 1863.

Micki Waldrop

Black Market

The underground economy—or *black market*, to use the term coined after World War I to describe illegal commodity exchange—often thrives during wartime as governments impose tighter restrictions, attempting to proscribe certain items or to limit trade between one side and the other. The U.S. Civil War was no exception.

The laissez-faire ideas that prevailed in the nineteenth century kept political leaders of the Union and the Confederacy from introducing regulations on consumer consumption of liquor and other substances. Despite taxes on virtually all commodities, the Union did not experience severe shortages or exorbitant prices during the war, and never imposed widespread rationing on its citizenry. Consequently, few Northerners ever encountered the underground economy.

In the South, however, the region's lack of industry and manufacturing, a poor transportation and distribution system, the Union blockade, disruptions caused by the Union army's penetration, and the Confederacy's own economic policies resulted in shortages of everything from shoes, leather, food, and salt to military arms and ammunition. As the war wore on, Southerners faced runaway inflation, widespread shortages, and, for some, the real possibility of starvation. Southern women, especially those left behind by Confederate soldiers, demanded government action. An observer of a riot in Richmond, Virginia, watched as crowds of mostly female Southerners armed with "clubs, axes, brooms, etc.," rushed "frantically up and down the street, crying for bread," and raided prisons, warehouses, and grocers for food in response to sky-high prices and government inaction (*Scioto Gazette*, October 25, 1865). Similar events also were reported in Richmond, Virginia; Mobile, Alabama; and Augusta, Georgia. Confederate states and cities sometimes responded with price controls or antimonopoly laws, which almost never succeeded.

In Richmond, for example, General John Winder (1800–1865) instituted price controls in spring 1862, but farmers and fishermen stopped selling their products at the stipulated prices, and the controls were rescinded within a month. Some merchants were punished if enough people complained that their prices had far exceeded the prescribed limit, or if they sold inferior provisions. In Mobile, Alabama, a trader who was convicted of violating the city's price controls was fined and jailed for three months. A Richmond butcher named Louis Frick was charged with selling "filthy and unsound meat" when one of his customers broke open a sausage Frick had sold him to discover "a number of puppy's claws," according to an account from the *Richmond Examiner* (reprinted in the *Cleveland Daily Herald*, October 3, 1863).

Probably the most widespread and profitable black-market activities involved the "contraband trade" with the enemy, and illegal speculation in cotton; these two sometimes were closely linked. Civilians in areas between the Union and Confederate armies often traded with the enemy. The Official Records of the War of the Rebellion note that in all areas of the South where Union forces penetrated, military officers complained of civilians engaged in illegal trade (U.S. War Department 1995). Southerners who found themselves in Union-occupied areas often continued to support the Confederacy by selling salt, coffee, shoes, leather, food, weapons, and ammunition to Confederate guerrillas, regular Confederate army units, or civilians.

In 1864, for example, the Eleventh Wisconsin Infantry surprised a boatload of men and women carrying supplies of coffee, salt, and a chest full of merchandise from Union-occupied Louisiana to outlying Confederate forces. In December of the same year the colonel of the Third Minnesota Infantry reported that between Memphis and rural Arkansas "an extensive contraband trade is carried on ... at enormous profits (such as a bale of cotton for a barrel of salt) to the parties at Memphis engaged in it," and concluded his report with a list of recently captured articles that included "10 barrels salt, 1 barrel pork, one-half barrel molasses" (U.S. War Department 1995, Vol. 51, p. 990). Union soldiers on garrison duty in occupied territory spent much of their time stopping illegal trade.

The Lincoln administration recognized fairly early in the war that the United States needed Southern cotton to supply Northern textile mills and to export to Great Britain. To restore the flow of cotton after secession, the administration devised a system overseen by Treasury Secretary Salmon P. Chase (1808–1873) to license individuals to trade Northern goods for Southern cotton and other agricultural products in areas that came under the Union flag. Unfortunately, as cotton prices skyrocketed, the temptations became too great for many soldiers, officers, and civilians, and corruption flourished. Unlicensed speculators flooded into areas controlled by the Union military, trading supplies or Union gold to Southerners for cotton. Jewish merchants were singled out by military officers for their participation in the illegal cotton trade. In late 1862 Ulysses S. Grant banned all Jewish traders from his theater of operations.

Chief Justice Salmon P. Chase (1808–1873). Needing to supply Northern textile factories with cotton and retain trade with the British, the Federal government devised a system of exchange with the South, managed by then Treasury Secretary Salmon P. Chase. *The Library of Congress.*

Soldiers often made fortunes trading or seizing cotton and selling it at a premium—often using government ships or wagons to transport it to markets in Memphis or New Orleans. The practice became so widespread among the military in the Mississippi River Valley that Lincoln appointed a special commission headed by General Irvin McDowell (1818–1885) to investigate. The commission exonerated General S. R. Curtis of using his position to obtain and sell cotton in violation of regulations, but the testimony confirmed the existence of a thriving and extremely profitable black market in cotton and supplies. Captain S. N. Wood of the Sixth Missouri Cavalry, for instance, admitted to making $20,000 in cotton speculation (*Chattanooga Daily Gazette*, July 10, 1864). The commission's final report was never made public.

In 1862 William T. Sherman (1820–1891) argued that the legal and illegal trades in cotton, supplies, and gold were prolonging the war: The "secessionists" who traded cotton to Northern speculators "had become so open in refusing anything but gold .... Without money ... they cannot get arms and ammunition of the English colonies;

Major General Irvin McDowell (1818–1885) of the federal army. Skyrocketing prices for cotton during the Civil War tempted many soldiers to sell confiscated bales to black-market traders. Disturbed by the practice among his own troops, President Abraham Lincoln assigned General Irvin McDowell to investigate reports of illegal cotton trade on the Mississippi River. *The Library of Congress.*

and without salt they cannot make bacon and salt beef. We cannot carry on war and trade with a people at the same time" (U.S. War Department 1995, Vol. 17, pp. 140–141). Despite the efforts of Sherman and other officials to curb illegal trade, where large profits or dire necessity existed, the underground economy continued to flourish throughout the Civil War.

BIBLIOGRAPHY

Chattanooga Daily Gazette, July 10, 1864.

Cleveland Daily Herald, October 3, 1863.

Cole, Garold L. *Civil War Eyewitness: An Annotated Bibliography of Books and Articles, 1955–1986.* Columbia: University of South Carolina Press, 1988.

Coulter, E. Merton. *The Confederate States of America, 1861–1865: A History of the South.* Vol. 7. Baton Rouge: Louisiana State University Press, 1962.

Fite, Emerson David. *Social and Industrial Conditions in the North during the Civil War.* New York: Macmillan, 1910.

Freehling, William W. *The South vs. the South: How Anti-Confederate Southerners Shaped the Course of the Civil War.* New York: Oxford University Press, 2002.

Gallman, J. Matthew. *The Civil War Chronicle.* New York: Gramercy, 2003.

Massey, Mary Elizabeth. *Ersatz in the Confederacy: Shortages and Substitutes on the Southern Homefront.* Columbia: University of South Carolina Press, 1993.

McPherson, James M. *Battle Cry of Freedom: The Civil War Era.* New York: Oxford University Press, 2003.

O'Connor, Thomas H. "Lincoln and the Cotton Trade." *Civil War History* 7, no. 1 (1961): 20–35.

Ramsdell, Charles. *Behind the Lines in the Southern Confederacy.* Baton Rouge: Louisiana State University Press, 1997.

Scioto Gazette, October 25, 1865.

Smith, George Winston, and Charles Judah. *Life in the North during the Civil War: A Source History.* Albuquerque: University of New Mexico Press, 1966.

Speyer, Ronald Jeffrey. "The McDowell Commission: February–July, 1863." Ph.D. diss., St. John's University, 1974.

U.S. War Department. *War of the Rebellion Official Records of the Union and Confederate Armies.* Series I. Wilmington, NC: Broadfoot Publishing, 1985.

Robert S. Shelton

■ Blockade and Blockade Running

The announcement of a blockade of the southeastern coastline of the North American continent was the second military proclamation made by President Abraham Lincoln in the opening days of the American Civil War, following his call for 75,000 men to suppress the Rebellion. It was in part a response to recent events at Fort Sumter, in Charleston Harbor, South Carolina. When Confederate batteries opened fire on the Union-held fort in April 1861, precipitating the Civil War, neither side foresaw a prolonged conflict, and thus neither government had a strategy for extended military and naval engagement. The action at Fort Sumter was to some degree a naval conflict, as the necessary supplies, military reinforcement, and proposed relief of the fort needed to come by sea to a military installation originally established to protect the city from coastal invasion. A small relief force was sent by sea from New York City, but arrived too late. Fort Sumter was forced to surrender on April 14.

The loss of Fort Sumter and the port of Charleston underscored for both sides the importance of coastal access. For the Union, an effective blockade now seemed essential. As part of the initial call to arms, President Lincoln announced the naval blockade of the enemy coastline on April 19. Almost immediately, potential conflicts with international law became apparent. The federal government did not recognize the Confederate States as a country, but as an organization of insurrectionists leading an illegal rebellion. If the Confederacy was not a country, then foreign nations could grant them neither official recognition nor aid. If this were the case, could the United States legally "blockade" its own coastline? Could such a blockade be construed as an implied recognition of the Confederacy as a nation? The matter was troubling for Gideon Welles, Lincoln's secretary of the navy. Welles believed that the proper action would be to close all Southern ports, a concentrated naval action that would place considerably fewer demands on the small naval force available at the current time and in the foreseeable future. However, Lincoln and his closest advisor in the cabinet, Secretary of State William Seward, believed that the blockade was imperative. They chose to ignore the issue of legality under international law, and instituted the blockade.

Welles readily complied with the official position. Initially, three blockading squadrons were created: the North Atlantic Squadron, the South Atlantic Squadron, and the Gulf Squadron. Just before Admiral David Farragut's capture of the city and port of New Orleans in 1862, however, the Gulf blockade force was divided into an East and a West Squadron, resulting in a total of four squadrons. The U.S. Navy, however, lacked the ships necessary to establish a true blockade. The enemy coastline ran from Virginia to Florida along the Atlantic Coast, north along the western coast of Florida, and west along the southern border on the Gulf of Mexico to the mouth of the Rio Grande, the border between Texas and Mexico. To institute a total blockade, the squadrons would need to cover more than 3,600 nautical miles of coastline with numerous tributaries that opened on navigable rivers. In the course of the war, approximately 1,300 ships attempted to elude the blockade; 1,000 or more did so successfully.

In 1861 the total strength of the U. S. Navy was ninety ships. Of that number only forty-two were in commission. Just twenty-four of the commissioned vessels were steam-powered, and eighteen of these were cruising in distant seas around the world, maintaining American presence and protecting commercial shipping. In the waters of the North Atlantic, only three steam-powered ships were available for blockade duty. To meet the immediate need, Welles began acquiring any available vessel that could mount a few guns and was sufficiently seaworthy to sail south along the coast of the Confederacy and help to establish the blockade. He also began an extensive shipbuilding and acquisition program that would, by 1864, increase the total number of ships from ninety to more than 670 (Simson 2001, pp. 53–54).

To implement the blockade effectively, Welles formed an advisory panel called the Blockade Strategy Board, charged with collecting and reviewing information pertaining to coastal surveys and charts, weather, tide and current conditions, and distances. A primary concern was the establishment at selected locations of refueling stations for blockading steamships. It was essential that a Union ship that might sight a blockade-runner have sufficient coal for the full head of steam needed for effective pursuit and capture. The board was an experienced and highly competent group, with scientific resources unavailable to the Confederacy.

Welles's first appointment was Alexander Dallas Bache, a great grandson of Benjamin Franklin. Bache was the superintendent of the U.S. Coast Survey, an independent agency charged with the responsibility of charting the North American coastline. In addition to Bache were Captain Samuel F. Du Pont and Commander Charles H. Davis, both active naval officers, Major J. G. Barnard of the Army Corps of Engineers, and the Assistant Secretary of the Navy, Gustavus Vasa Fox. The Board produced five reports at intervals throughout the summer of 1861. The first report of July 5 called for a secure refueling and supply depot to be established at Fernandina, a small town on Amelia Island just off the Atlantic coast of Florida at the mouth of the St. Marys River. The second report of July 13 suggested the establishment of refueling and supply stations at three locations on the coast of South Carolina: Bulls Bay, north of Charleston; St. Helena Sound, between Charleston and Savannah; and Port Royal Sound, slightly north of Savannah.

The third report of July 16 recommended that the area patrolled by the South Atlantic Blockading Squadron be divided into two parts. The coastline from Cape Henry, Virginia, to Cape Romain, South Carolina, a distance of 370 miles, would be the northern sector. The southern sector would extend 220 miles further south, from Cape Romain to St. Augustine, Florida. The northern sector was topographically different from the southern, and was largely comprised of barrier islands of sand that often altered with tides and currents. These barrier islands separated the inland rivers and sounds from the Atlantic, and were linked to the open sea by inlets that occurred at irregular geographic intervals. The Board proposed blocking these inlet channels with hulks, out-of service-ships that would be towed to the appropriate location and scuttled. Particular emphasis was placed on Hatteras Inlet at the southern end of the Outer Banks of North Carolina. The inlet provided access to both Albemarle Sound and Pamlico Sound, two of North Carolina's principal outlets to the sea.

The fourth report, delivered on July 26, cited the particular importance of the coast of Georgia, and of controlling the inland waterway from Savannah to the St. Marys River. The fifth and final report, received by Welles on August 9, concentrated on the Gulf of Mexico, beginning with the Florida Keys and placing particular emphasis

A captured blockade runner's vessel. Attempting to circumvent President Lincoln's blockade of Southern ports, private ship owners used small, fast-sailing ships to outrun Union naval patrols. Lacking a diverse industrial base, the Confederacy depended on blockade runners to export cotton to ports in the Caribbean and return with much needed war supplies. *MPI/Hulton Archive/Getty Images*

on the details of the coastal areas of New Orleans and Mobile Bay (Simson 2001, pp. 57–58).

Jefferson Davis, president of the newly formed Confederate States of America, attempted to counter the Union blockade by calling for privateers—nonmilitary, privately owned vessels—that would, with government authorization under what were termed *letters of marque*, attack and pillage enemy shipping. Davis's invoking of this kind of government-sanctioned piracy, which had already been outlawed by most of the maritime powers of Europe, was hasty and injudicious, but it underscored a serious deficiency in the Confederacy's power to wage war effectively: It had no navy.

Welles's counterpart, newly appointed Confederate Secretary of the Navy Stephen Mallory, realized that the South did not have the resources and industrial strength to build a navy that would compare in size to the North's, so he developed other priorities to combat the blockade and render it ineffective. Mallory had little faith in privateers, and quietly treated Davis's proclamation with benign neglect. He knew that history had shown that privateers had never proved decisive in winning any war. They were also civilian enterprises, not subject to naval discipline, and could not be relied upon to carry out established strategy. Mallory preferred instead the idea of commerce raiders—armed commercial ships that would avoid conventional naval engagement but were instead specifically charged with the mission of attacking the commercial shipping of the Northern states. He proposed to concentrate on New England shipping, reasoning that if the Confederacy could inflict sufficient damage on New England's maritime economy, the New England states would force the federal government to sue for peace.

Other priorities of Mallory's for building an effective navy included equipping all vessels fighting for the Confederacy with newly developed "rifled" guns, which were far more accurate than the more common smoothbore weapons, and experimenting with submarine warfare. His highest priority, however, was the production of the ironclad warship, the new naval weapon of the future. With a sufficient number of steam-powered ironclads, Mallory believed the Confederacy could break the blockade at will and even seize control of the North Atlantic. When Virginia's secession from the Union resulted in the Confederate seizure of the Federal shipyard at Norfolk and of the steam frigate, the U.S.S. *Merrimack*, Mallory took the opportunity to fulfill his highest priority. The *Merrimack* was converted into the Confederacy's first ironclad, the C.S.S. *Virginia* (newspapers in the North continued to identify the ship by its original name). In March 1862 at Hampton Roads, the *Virginia* inflicted the worst defeat ever suffered by the U.S. Navy prior to the Japanese attack at Pearl Harbor in World War II: Three ships were sunk, one was severely burned, and three others were run aground and left helpless. Three hundred men on the Union side were killed. Only the falling tide and the *Virginia*'s shallow draft and limited mobility prevented a greater disaster. On the second day of the battle, the *Virginia* fought to a draw with the Union ironclad, the U.S.S. *Monitor.* Ironclads would continue to be built and commissioned by both sides, but they would never prove decisive for the Confederacy in naval engagements. The outcome at Hampton Roads also made it clear that Confederate ironclads would not be able to destroy the Union blockade.

The Effects of the Blockade

Despite this disappointment, President Davis and many others in the South believed that the blockade would eventually be effectively destroyed by the European need for cotton, particularly that of Great Britain. Europe had become highly dependent on high-quality American Cotton. In 1840 the South produced 60 percent of the world's cotton. In the years just before the war, 80 percent of Great Britain's cotton came from the North American continent.

Nathaniel Dawson, a cotton grower, lamented in an 1862 letter to his fiancée, Elodie Todd, that the "largest cotton crop ever" sat in warehouses unable to move because of the blockade. In her reply, Ms. Todd prayed for "foreign aid in breaking the blockade," expressing the hope of many in the South (Sword 1999, p. 106).

For a time, Great Britain seemed strongly inclined to recognize the Confederacy, and intervene. Attempting to force the issue, the Confederacy began to severely restrict its cotton shipments—a strategy dubbed *King Cotton diplomacy.* The hope was that the denial of prized cotton would force Britain to use its naval power to open the blockade and restore European maritime trade with the Confederacy. The Confederate government called upon cotton growers to use the land to grow much needed food instead. In New Orleans, 2.5 million bales of cotton were burned. Geoffrey Ward (1990) cites a letter written on April 26 by a young Louisiana woman who witnessed the conflagration: "We went this morning to see the cotton burning—a sight never before witnessed and probably never again to be seen. Wagons, drays—everything that can be driven or rolled—were loaded with the bales and taken to burn on the commons" (p. 95). It was common belief that without American cotton, the economy of Great Britain could not survive. "The cards are in our hands!" declared the *Charleston Mercury*, and "we intend to play them out to the bankruptcy of every cotton factory in Great Britain and France for the acknowledgement of our independence" (Ward 1990, p. 94).

Although many of the Midland cloth mills in England were shut down as the blockade took effect, British mill owners had a surplus of American cotton purchased in 1860, and also began to look to cotton from India and Egypt to offset the eventual deficit. In the beginning, there was considerable sympathy for the Confederacy. The infamous Mason and Slidell affair of November 1861, in which the U.S.S. *San Jacinto* stopped the *Trent*, a British mail steamer, and took two Confederate diplomats, James Mason and John Slidell, as prisoners, greatly inflamed public opinion in London and other capitals of Europe. British diplomacy brought about their release before the end of the year. To many in positions of power in Great Britain, the Confederacy seemed a gallant enterprise, fighting for its independence and the preservation of a way of life dominated by landed gentry, a culture not unlike that of Great Britain. Officially, Great Britain asserted a political and imperial view that did not sympathize with geographic entities declaring independence, but it did nonetheless have a need for unrestricted cotton trade. It was also annoyed with the Federal Navy's growing presence in the North Atlantic in the exercise of the blockade. As Great Britain weighed the matter, certain events came together that made the British government decide to remain neutral: the failure of General Lee's Army of Northern Virginia to win decisive victories in the North after attempts at Antietam and Gettysburg, and the fall of Vicksburg and subsequent Union control of the Mississippi, which effectively split the states of the Confederacy. Finally, President Lincoln's Emancipation Proclamation (1863) eclipsed the states' rights issue by bringing the moral issue of slavery to the forefront. As a nation, Great Britain took great pride in its reputation as the naval power that had eliminated the transatlantic slave trade thirty years earlier.

Blockade Running

In the early years of the war, the blockade seemed to have little effect, as blockade-runners, the South's only connection to an outside world cut off by the cessation of maritime trade, seemed able to penetrate at will. The small ships that ran the Union Blockade were swift steamers with shallow drafts, streamlined vessels often

DAVID FARRAGUT: FIRST ADMIRAL OF THE U.S. NAVY

The naval battles of the Civil War generally receive less attention than the land campaigns, even though the Union blockade of the Confederacy and several naval engagements in the Gulf of Mexico and along the Mississippi were important factors in the outcome of the war.

The Union Navy was unprepared for war; it consisted of ninety ships of war, but only 42 were ready for active service in the spring of 1861. It had only 7600 sailors and 1467 officers in 1861, but by the end of the war, the Navy had 51,500 sailors and 7500 officers. The Union sailors included 18,000 African Americans (twelve of whom were women); unlike the Union Army, the Navy accepted black volunteers from the beginning of the Civil War. Lincoln's Secretary of the Navy, Gideon Welles, issued an order in September 1861 providing for the hiring of runaway slaves as seamen, firemen, or navy yard employees with full pay.

The Civil War was a turning point in the history of naval as well as land warfare. Prior to the 1840s, fighting ships around the world had been constructed largely of wood and powered by sail. The U.S. Navy was one of the earliest to recognize the importance of steam-powered vessels; in the twenty years before the Civil War, the Navy had largely replaced its older sailing vessels with steamships. Its fleet was the third most efficient in the world, surpassed only by the navies of England and France.

At the head of the Union Navy was David Farragut (1801–1870), the son of a Spanish merchant captain who had come to America in 1776 and served in the Revolutionary War. Farragut was born in Tennessee and settled in Virginia, but decided to remain in the Union Navy at the beginning of the Civil War. He had joined the Navy as a midshipman in 1810, when he was only nine years old. He served in the War of 1812; at the age of twelve, he was given command of a British ship captured by the *U.S.S Essex* and brought the captured vessel safely to port.

Farragut proved himself one of the ablest Union commanders of the Civil War. Given the *U.S.S Hartford* as his flagship, he took the port of New Orleans on April 29, 1862, an important morale boost for the Union. The Navy created a new rank for him, that of rear admiral, in July 1862. Prior to that time the Navy had used only the term flag officer in order to separate itself from the aristocratic traditions of European navies.

Farragut won another strategic victory for the Union at the Battle of Mobile Bay in August 1864. Mobile, Alabama, was the Confederacy's last remaining port on the Gulf of Mexico. The battle was the occasion for the quotation by which Farragut is still remembered. At the time of the Civil War, a torpedo was a naval mine placed in a harbor, not a self-propelled underwater weapon of the type used by twentieth-century submarines. When Farragut's fleet entered Mobile Bay, which had been heavily mined by the Confederate Navy, one of the Union ships struck one of the torpedoes and sank. The others began to pull back. Farragut asked the captain of one of the other ships what the trouble was. When told that it was torpedoes, Farragut replied, "Damn the torpedoes! Full speed ahead!" The rest of Farragut's fleet succeeded in entering the bay and forcing the surrender of the Confederate ships. After the victory of Mobile Bay, Farragut was promoted to vice admiral in December 1864 and to full admiral in July 1866, the first four-star commander in the history of the U.S. Navy.

REBECCA J. FREY

BIBLIOGRAPHY

Black Sailors: The Howard University Research Project. Available from http://www.itd.nps.gov/cwss/sailors_index.html.

Eicher, John H., and David J. Eicher. Civil War High Commands. Stanford, CA: Stanford University Press, 2001.

designed with innovative features such as collapsible funnels and masts that would enable them, if pursued, to reduce wind resistance and gain additional speed. The *Bermuda*, the first of these runners to get through the blockade, arrived in Savannah from Liverpool, England, on September 18, 1861. Its primary cargo consisted of four large pieces of artillery. In October the *Bermuda* departed for England, where it sold a cargo of prized cotton for a high profit (Norris 2000, p. 243). In addition to whatever cargo the blockade-runners brought, they also did much for the general morale of the people of the South. Mary Chestnut, the noted diarist of Confederate life on the home front, offered this succinct and somewhat poetic observation: "An iron steamer has run the blockade at Savannah. We raise our wilted heads like flowers after a shower" (Ward 1990, p. 166).

The standard pattern for a blockade-runner returning from a foreign port was to stop in Bermuda (a British possession), Havana, or one of the smaller ports in the Caribbean. Goods from Europe came in heavy merchant ships, which were able to transport large quantities. In the Caribbean ports the goods were transferred to the somewhat smaller, but decidedly faster, shallow draft blockade-runners. Some blockade-runners were lightly armed, but most were not armed at all. Under international law, the crew of a ship that returned fire while being lawfully pursued would be officially guilty of piracy and subject to hanging.

The independent blockade-runners, however, were not as patriotically motivated in their pursuit of the Confederate cause as commonly believed. Unlike the North, the South, with its largely agricultural economy, did not have the manufacturing base it needed to fight the kind of war it had undertaken. It had to import cannons, gunpowder, small arms and rifles, uniforms, and other things needed to meet the logistical needs

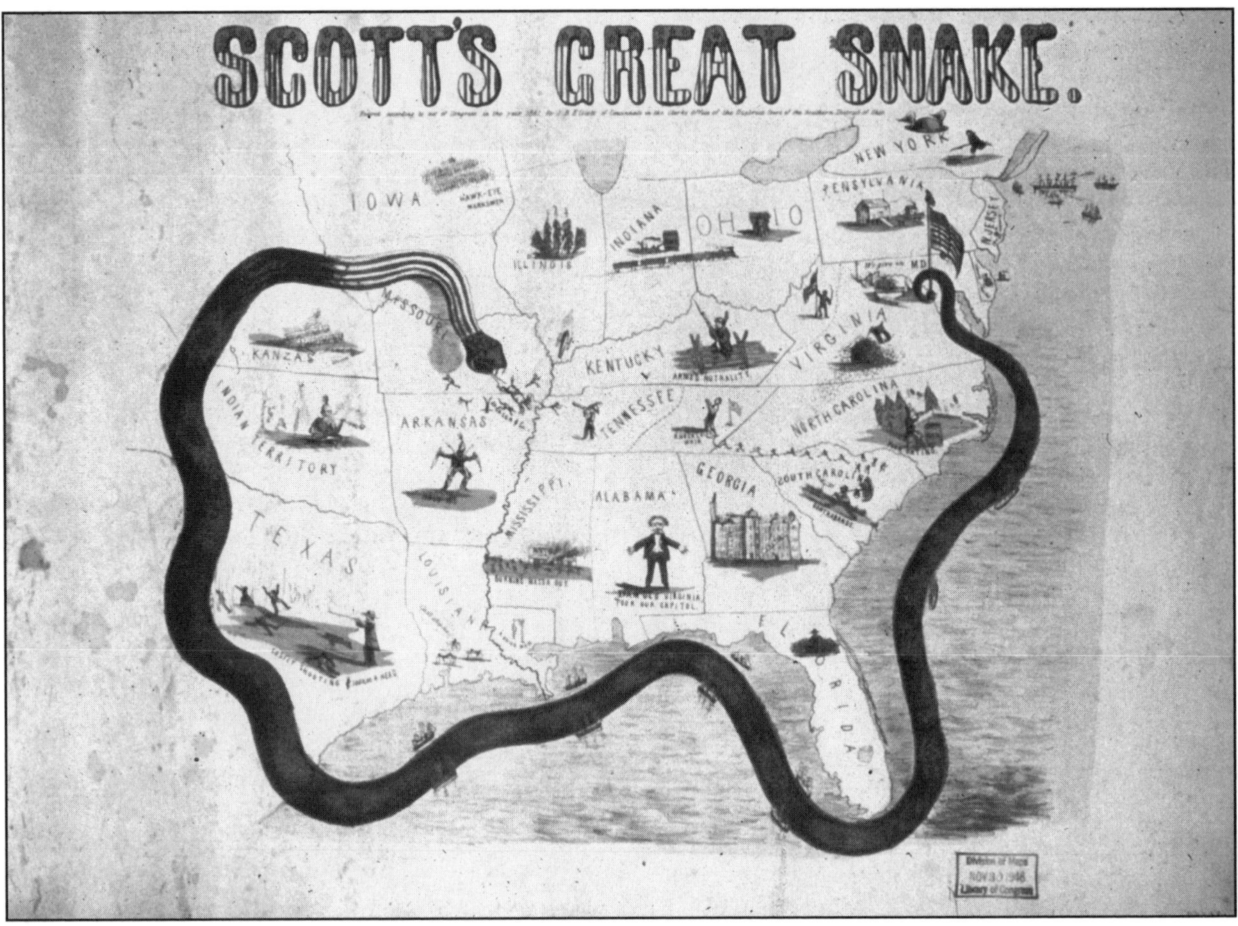

Scott's Great Snake. As part of Union strategy to crush the South, General-in-Chief Winfield Scott proposed to first blockade Southern sea ports, then take control of the Mississippi River, and eventually return east to defeat the Confederacy in their capital of Richmond, Virginia. *MPI/Hulton Archive/Getty Images.*

of a modern army. Cloth, medicine, and machinery were also much needed imports. The Confederate government commissioned merchant ships as blockade-runners, but the South was never a maritime power; it had nothing that even approximated a merchant fleet. Independent blockade-runners would often run the blockade with cargoes of prized cotton, but found it more profitable to bring back cigars from Havana, perfume and fine wines from France, and silks, soaps, spices, and other luxury items. Although generally recognized staples, such as books or stationery, were in short supply, luxury items were often readily available, albeit at very high prices.

Patriotic idealism aside, the law of supply and demand frequently led the South to circumvent the naval blockade in one way or another to get the things it desperately required. The South, for example, needed salt, necessary to preserve meat in the days before refrigeration, and salt came from the North. The South also needed medicines, surgical instruments, clothing, leather goods, and, to feed both the white populace and slaves in an agricultural economy largely given over to cotton and sugar production, it needed corn and pork. At the same time, the North still needed things from the South, such as cotton, sugar, rice, and tobacco. Despite the war, the North and the South carried on a brisk trade in basic commodities, to the decided advantage of Northern merchants.

This exchange of contraband goods developed in those Southern cities that came under Northern occupation. Nashville and Memphis, once the Union established control, were both depots through which Northern goods were shipped to the South. General William Tecumseh Sherman, who was in command in Memphis before his army moved toward Georgia, tried to stop the passage of contraband to the South, but was unsuccessful. Finding that many of the confiscated goods on the way to the South came from Cincinnati, he noted with some slight exaggeration that "Cincinnati furnishes more contraband goods than Charleston, and has done more to prolong the war than the whole state of Carolina"

(Catton 1981, p. 144). A Congressional committee appointed in 1864 to investigate the trade in contraband between North and South remarked that Union-occupied New Orleans "had helped the Confederacy more than any of the Confederacy's own seaports, with the exception of Wilmington, North Carolina" (Catton 1981, pp. 144–145).

Throughout the war, there were few signs of notable deprivation among the middle class. In a January 1864 letter to her mother, Mary Mallard described the unexpected abundance she had discovered in Atlanta: "You would be amazed to see how full all the stores are at present. They are flooded with calicoes, and light spring worsted goods" (Myers 1972, p. 1134). Colonel Arthur James Lyon Fremantle, an English officer with the elite Coldstream Guards, and a noted chronicler of the war who would later publish a compelling account of the battle at Gettysburg, remarked on the evident lack of hardship at a dance he attended in Galveston, Texas, shortly after entering the country through Mexico in 1863: "[T]he ladies were pretty, and considering the blockade, they were very well dressed" (Fremantle 1957, p. 185).

Those without the resources to pay the exorbitant prices for contraband goods did what they could with what they had, and came up with creative substitutes for articles in short supply. "Confederate needles" were made from the thorns of hawthorn bushes, rope was fashioned out of Spanish moss, and paintbrushes used hog bristles (Ward 1990, p. 166). Coffee substitutes were made out of all manner of things, including peas, corn, beets, and pumpkin seeds. The *Macon Daily Telegraph*, commenting on these improvised brews, declared that "all that is wanted is something to color the water; it is coffee or dirty water, just as you please" (Ward 1990, p. 166).

In the course of the war, blockade-runners brought in approximately 60 percent of the rifles and small arms, 30 percent of the lead needed for bullets, and about 60 percent of the saltpeter (potassium nitrate) needed for the production of gunpowder. Although 92 percent of all attempts to run the blockade were successful, it wasn't enough to satisfy the essential needs of the Confederacy. As the war progressed, the effectiveness of the Union blockade grew, slowly constricting the South's ability to traffic the high seas. The blockade remained in effect until officially lifted by President Andrew Johnson, on June 23, 1865.

BIBLIOGRAPHY

Anderson, Bern. *By Sea and by River: The Naval History of the Civil War*. New York: Alfred A. Knopf, 1962.

Catton, Bruce. *Reflections on the Civil War*, ed. John Leekley. Garden City, NY: Doubleday, 1981.

Fowler, William M., Jr. *Under Two Flags: The American Navy in the Civil War*. New York and London: Avon Books, 1990.

Fremantle, A. J. L. "A Journey across Texas: Three Months in the Southern States: April, June, 1863." In *The Confederate Reader*, ed. Richard B. Harwell. New York: Longmans, Green, 1957.

Luraghi, Raimondo. *A History of the Confederate Navy*. Annapolis, MD: Navy Institute Press, 1996.

Myers, Robert Manson, ed. *The Children of Pride: A True Story of Georgia and the Civil War*. New Haven, CT, and London: Yale University Press, 1972. Letters written by the family of the Rev. Dr. Charles Colcock Jones between 1854 and 1868.

Norris, David A. "Blockade of the CSA." In *Encyclopedia of the American Civil War: A Political, Social, and Military History*, eds. David S. Heidler and Jeanne T. Heidler. New York: W. W. Norton, 2000.

Sears, Stephen W. *To the Gates of Richmond: The Peninsula Campaign*. New York: Ticknor & Fields, 1992.

Simson, Jay W. *Naval Strategies of the Civil War: Confederate Innovations and Federal Opportunism*. Nashville, TN: Cumberland House, 2001.

Sword, Wiley. *Southern Invincibility: A History of the Confederate Heart*. New York: St. Martin's Press/ Griffin, 1999.

Ward, Geoffrey. *The Civil War: An Illustrated History*. New York: Vintage, 1990.

Richard C. Keenan

War Profiteers

War profiteering is the act of an individual or company making an unreasonable financial gain from selling goods or services during wartime. Certainly, suppliers who feed and transport soldiers, dispose of the dead, and produce weapons and clothing for the military are all necessary for the waging of war. Sometimes the paranoia and common mistrust of others that comes with war leads people to confuse the economic realities of war with war profiteering. For example, wartime food shortages result in significantly higher food prices in urban areas, leading city-dwellers to accuse farmers of gauging produce prices (Norton 1919, pp. 546–547). Basic foreign trade with enemy or neutral countries, and protecting intellectual property can be interpreted as profiteering or even treason (Hammond 1931, p. 3). Strong feelings about the moral reprehensibility of war profiteering sometimes provoke general, public accusations that take the form of racial or religious discrimination against certain groups (Korn 1951, pp. 294–295). All of these things did happen during the U.S. Civil War, but war profiteering of the period went beyond these.

Brooks Brothers Clothing Store. Many merchants delivered substandard products to the Union government at inflated prices. After delivering poor quality uniforms to volunteer soldiers from New York, the Brooks Brothers company became symbolic of businesses that sold shoddy goods during the Civil War. *The Art Archive/The Picture Desk, Inc.*

Almost as soon as the Civil War began, rumors of war profiteering began to circulate. The *New York Herald*, for example, claimed that a quarter of the first $200 million spent on the war had been "dishonestly pocketed" (Brandes 1997, p. 67). These accusations were probably exaggerated, but were not completely without merit. In 1861 it was Secretary of War Simon Cameron (1799–1889), whose family owned the rail lines from Washington, DC, to Harrisburg, Pennsylvania, who set the price and policies for soldiers to be transported during the war, despite his clear conflict of interest. To be sure, Cameron's decisions were made under the assumption that the war would not last long—and there were no other rail options for transporting soldiers into Pennsylvania—but it set a precedent for many rail lines to profit heavily from the war (Brandes 1997, p. 73–74).

The technological advances of the nineteenth century contributed to the potential for war profiteering during the Civil War. The need for transportation and weapons is an economic reality of war, and the complexities of the use of war-related technology during the Industrial Revolution led to stock-market speculation, jumps in executives' incomes, and significant corporate profits reaped from intellectual property and patents (Brandes 1997, p. 69). Samuel Colt (1814–1862), the founder of Colt's Patent Fire-Arms Manufacturing Company, had a long history of marking up the price on military-issue weapons during wartime; before the Civil War began he had sold similar weapons to both American civilians and the British government for lower prices. At the beginning of the war Colt expanded his manufacturing plant, and had 1,000 employees with a $50,000 monthly payroll. In 1864 the plant was destroyed by a fire, and the estimated loss was $1.5 to 2 million (Brandes 1997, p. 88).

War profiteering by suppliers with government contracts was widespread; even military uniforms were so badly made that they may have contributed to the low morale of soldiers early in the war. The uniforms of New York's volunteer soldiers—supplied by the Brooks Brothers of New York City—were so cheaply made that the soldiers were mocked (Brandes 1997, p. 71). The term *shoddies* became the euphemism, coined by *Harper's Weekly*, for clothing manufacturers such as the Brooks Brothers, who maximized their profits by supplying poorly constructed garments made of cheap fabrics (Brandes 1997, p. 73). So widespread was the use of this term that a contemporary novel by Henry Morford, *The Days of Shoddy* (1863), dubbed the war profiteers the "shoddy aristocracy" or the "shoddocracy," which became "a metaphor for Civil War business itself" (Brandes 1997, p. 69).

BIBLIOGRAPHY

Brandes, Stuart. *Warhogs: A History of War Profits in America*. Lexington: University Press of Kentucky, 1997.

Hammond, Matthew. "Economic Conflict as a Regulatory Force in International Affairs." *American Economic Review* 21, no. 1 (1931): 1–9.

Korn, Bertram. *American Jewry and the Civil War*. Philadelphia: Jewish Publishing Society of America, 1951.

Norton, J. P. "Industry and Food Prices after the War." *Scientific Monthly* 8, no. 6 (1919): 546–551.

Christopher D. Rodkey

■ Currency

Both the Union and the Confederacy faced major problems in financing the Civil War. The war called for the creation of armies that quickly dwarfed any previously seen on the North American continent. Equipping, supplying, and paying these troops put monumental strains on governmental budgets and on the general economies of both sides.

As the war began, both sides believed it would be a brief conflict. Both greatly underestimated the costs, efforts, and the changes that fighting the war would produce in their respective societies. Historian John Steele Gordon has noted, "While individual battles may be decided by tactics, firepower, courage, and—of course—luck, victory in the long haul of war almost always goes to the side better able to turn the national wealth to military purposes" (Gordon 1997, p. 67). The North had a much larger economy, and had a governmental system already in place for administering the borrowing and taxation that would be needed to finance the war. This was a decided advantage in the Union's favor.

A Union one dollar bill, 1862. Wartime pressures led both the North and the South to print paper money, and both sides eventually saw the destructive consequences of inflation. *HIP/Art Resource, NY.*

The Union and Confederate governments both used a combination of borrowing, taxing, and printing paper money to finance the war. The Union raised about 20 percent of its war financing through taxes, the Confederacy only about 10 to 12 percent (Hughes and Cain 2003, pp. 258–259; McPherson 2001, p. 222). The fact that the Union paid for the war primarily through increased taxes and borrowing, rather than by simply printing paper money, was another important advantage for the North.

Background

When the Civil War began, the only currency in the United States was gold and silver coins, and the paper money issued by state and private banks. Gold and silver money was called "specie." Silver was used only for small-denominations coins. Many people believed that only specie was real money, and distrusted paper money—a distrust that went back to the nation's experience during the American Revolution, when the Continental paper money issued by the government depreciated so badly that the phrase "not worth a Continental" was used to describe something worthless. Earlier in the nineteenth century the banknotes issued by the Second Bank of the United States had functioned as a sound, respected paper currency. However, Andrew Jackson (1767–1845), who had a lifelong distrust of all banks and a special enmity for the Second Bank of the United States, had killed the bank, and no similar institution took its place.

Confederate Currency

The Confederacy borrowed heavily to raise money to finance the war. By the end of the war the Southern government had sold $2 billion in bonds. The first bonds the Confederate government, issued in 1861 in the amount of $15 million, sold quite well because of enthusiastic responses by the Southern people. But the liquid assets—especially the gold assets—of the Southern populace were quickly depleted, and later issues of bonds did not sell as well.

The Confederate government eventually turned to the printing press—printing paper money, backed by nothing. This kind of money is sometimes called "fiat money" because it has value only because of a government decree (or "fiat") that declares it has value. Overall, the Confederacy raised about 10 percent of the war costs by taxes, about 30 percent by borrowing, and about 60 percent by printing money (McPherson 2001, p. 222). Christopher G. Memminger (1803–1888), the secretary of the treasury in the Confederate government, was a "sound money" man who distrusted paper currency, but the Confederate Congress balked at increasing taxes or depending more on loans. One of the major financial problems in the Confederacy was this use of paper money as the primary way to finance the war effort. In many ways, this was unavoidable. Although there was much wealth in the Southern states, a great deal of that wealth was tied up in property: land and slaves. There was not much liquid wealth for the government to tax, and at the beginning of the war, there was no governmental mechanism in place to administer and collect taxes or arrange bond sales or other forms of loans. To further the problem, when the Confederate government did enact taxes, state governments often paid the taxes for their citizens—but the payments were made in state-issued paper currency, which contributed to further inflation.

There was a wide variety of paper money circulating in the South during the war. Paper money was issued not only by the Confederate national government and state governments, but also by cities, towns, and even private businesses, in small denominations. Some of these, called "shinplasters," were for denominations of less than $1. The South did not have printing establishments capable of turning out high-quality banknotes, and in fact, at the beginning of the war some Confederate money was printed surreptitiously by banknote printers in the North. The difficulty of getting these notes delivered to the South finally ended this practice. Currency printed in the Confederacy was generally low quality, on low-grade paper. In a form of economic warfare aimed at disrupting the Southern economy, the North produced counterfeits of the Confederate currency and tried to get these circulated in the South, hoping to further erode the Southern people's confidence in their currency. Even Southern newspapers noted that these Northern counterfeits were generally better quality than authentic Confederate money.

Confederate paper currency depreciated rapidly, especially at times when the war effort was going badly for the South. Consumer prices inflated tremendously in the South due to commodity shortages and the depreciation of the currency. The economist Eugene Lerner believed that the stock of currency in the South increased eleven times over during the war (Lerner 1955, p. 21). Eventually, there was much more currency in circulation than the South's economy really demanded; this is the classic recipe for inflation—too much money chasing too few goods. Memminger estimated that by late 1863 there was $700 million worth of currency circulating in an economy capable of absorbing only $200 million (Thomas 1979, p. 257).

When money began to depreciate rapidly, people had little incentive to hold on to it—the longer one held it, the less it would be worth. So people spent the paper currency rapidly, which in turn contributed further to depreciation and the rising prices of goods. Many businesses refused to take Confederate notes as payment on debts or for purchases. The Confederate government had never made the currency "legal tender," which would have required businesses to accept it. Commodities came to be used in business transactions, sometimes in simple bartering arrangements, and at times in combination with paper currency. Confederate paper money could not be used to pay taxes to the Confederate's national government, or to buy its bonds. As the historian Emory Thomas suggested, "A government which refused to accept its own money did not exactly inspire soaring confidence" (Thomas 1979, p. 82). Economic historians continue to debate the precise rate of inflation in the South during the Civil War, but all agree it was incredibly high. James M. McPherson, one of the preeminent historians of the Civil War era, cites a figure of 9,000 percent (2001, p. 226).

In February 1864 the Confederate congress attempted to deal with the oversupply of currency by passing a currency reform act that required that all existing Confederate currency be redeemed for new notes at a rate of three-to-two. This did reduce the amount of currency in circulation and succeeded in stabilizing prices for a few months, but the fear that such a forced redemption might be required again in the future further eroded people's confidence in the currency.

Union Currency

The notes circulated by private banks and by the U.S. Treasury before the Civil War were supposed to be redeemable in gold on demand. However, in December 1861 banks and private businesses suspended the practice of converting notes into gold. The government soon followed suit, suspending the convertibility of its Treasury notes into specie. In February 1862 Congress passed the Legal Tender Act, allowing the government to issue the first inconvertible currency, which came to be called "greenbacks" because of the color of the paper. As the term "legal tender" implies, businesses were required to accept this money. Although some taxes could be paid with the greenbacks, tariff duties (import taxes) had to be paid in gold, and the government made interest payments on its own bonds only in gold.

However, government bonds could be purchased with the paper money. There was no provision in the law for the ultimate convertibility of the greenbacks into specie, but many people believed that at some future date, after the war ended, the greenbacks would be redeemable in gold. Resorting to the use of paper money was generally seen as an unfortunate emergency measure demanded by the crisis of the war. Like the Confederacy's Memminger, Salmon Chase (1808–1873), the secretary of the treasury in Lincoln's cabinet, distrusted paper money. He believed issuing paper money was immoral and destructive. However, with an eye to getting name recognition that might help in future political endeavors, Chase put his own picture on some of the first issue of greenbacks. After the Civil War Chase became chief justice of the Supreme Court, and ruled in one case that the issuance of the greenbacks had been unconstitutional. Similarly, many of the politicians who had supported the issuance of the greenbacks during the war quickly called for their suspension when the war ended.

The National Banking Acts passed in 1863, 1864, and 1865 were among the clearest examples of the wartime expansion of federal authority during the Civil War. Under the 1863 law federally chartered banks could be created if they met certain standards. These banks could issue banknotes if they held a required percentage of their assets in U.S. government bonds, as guarantees that their banknotes could be redeemed. This provision meant that these banks not only supplied a sound currency, they also constituted a market for the government's own bonds. The 1865 act imposed a 10 percent tax on state banknotes. Because anyone using greenbacks or the notes from the federally chartered banks

Confederate currency. With much of its wealth tied up in land and slaves, the South could not easily raise large sums of money to finance a prolonged conflict. Eventually the South began to simply print money to pay for the war, causing Confederate currency to quickly lose its value. *The Library of Congress.*

could avoid paying this tax, the state banknotes were quickly driven out of circulation.

Greenbacks were not backed by any precious metal; they were valuable only because the government decreed that they were legal tender and must be accepted by creditors and merchants in payment of debts and for purchases. As in the South, these greenbacks depreciated, but never to the extent that Confederate paper money did. Estimates of the rate of inflation suffered by the North range from 80 to 100 percent; it is probably safe to say that the cost of living roughly doubled in the North because of wartime inflation. Greenbacks were preferred to Confederate money by some merchants in the upper tier of Confederate states, and even the Confederate treasury in Richmond held some Union greenbacks as financial assets in its vaults. The first issue of greenbacks was $150 million. By the end of the war a total of $450 million had been issued.

Aftermath

The Fourteenth Amendment included a provision that guaranteed the repayment of the federal war debt, but disallowed the repayment of the Confederate war debt. This meant that all Confederate bonds, as well as all Confederate currency, technically became worthless as soon as the war ended, although some of these documents eventually acquired considerable value as collector's items. In the decades after the Civil War the question of what kind of money the United States should have was debated repeatedly. Groups such as the Greenback Party and later the Populists wanted an expansion of the amount of currency in circulation, in part because this caused inflation that could help debtors pay off debt. The Greenback Party wanted the paper money from the Civil War to stay in circulation, whereas those who advocated a "hard money" or "sound money" policy wanted all the greenbacks to be redeemed and the country to go back to a gold standard as quickly as possible.

BIBLIOGRAPHY

Curry, Leonard P. *Blueprint for Modern America: Nonmilitary Legislation of the First Civil War Congress.* Nashville, TN: Vanderbilt University Press, 1968.

Gordon, John Steele. *Hamilton's Blessing: The Extraordinary Life and Times of Our National Debt.* New York: Penguin Books, 1997.

Hammond, Bray. "The North's Empty Purse, 1861–1862." *American Historical Review* 67, no. 1 (October 1961): 1–18.

Hammond, Bray. *Sovereignty and an Empty Purse: Banks and Politics in the Civil War.* Princeton, NJ: Princeton University Press, 1970.

Hughes, Jonathan, and Louis P. Cain. *American Economic History*, 6th ed. New York: Addison Wesley/Pearson Education, 2003.

Lerner, Eugene M. "Money, Prices, and Wages in the Confederacy, 1861–1865." *Journal of Political Economy* 63, no. 1 (February 1955): 20–40.

McPherson, James M. *Ordeal By Fire: The Civil War and Reconstruction*, 3rd ed. New York: McGraw-Hill, 2001.

Thomas, Emory M. *The Confederate Nation, 1861–1865.* New American Nation Series. New York: Harper and Row, 1979.

Willard, Kristen L., Timothy W. Guinnane, and Harvey S. Rosen. "Turning Points in the Civil War: Views from the Greenback Market." *American Economic Review* 86, no. 4 (September 1996): 1001–1018.

Mark S. Joy

■ Labor

LABOR: AN OVERVIEW

As had been true since the colonial period, American workers during the Civil War, male and female, occupied a continuum from unfree and unpaid to free and paid. Neither slaves nor indentured servants nor apprentices were completely in control of either their work schedules or their labor contracts. The Civil War proved to be the key event that changed the nature of labor in the United States. Not only did the end of the war bring the end of slavery in the form of the Thirteenth Amendment—but the rapid industrialization associated with the war also helped to end apprenticeships in many fields and emphasize the use of larger amounts of semiskilled labor. Finally, the removal of large numbers of workers from industrial or agricultural labor into military service gave the remaining workers temporary leverage to seek higher wages and better working conditions, thus paving the way for the trade union movement of the postwar period.

Labor in the South

In 1861, at the start of the Civil War, approximately four million African Americans remained enslaved in the South. Even after the eleven states that would form the Confederate States of America seceded, four border states remained in the Union, making unfree labor a characteristic of both the Union and the Confederacy. As the slaves had before the Civil War, they continued to perform a vast array of duties during the conflict. These included field work in diverse settings; domestic labor; the performance of artisanal trades; animal husbandry; work in industrial settings, like iron foundries; and coal mining. Although slaves were theoretically unpaid and unwaged, in practice some owners who hired out their slaves did allow them to keep their earnings after paying the master a set fee; or, as in the case of William Weaver's Buffalo Forge, the owners allowed slaves to perform "overwork" for credit that could then be used to buy consumer goods (Dew 1994). Slaves and their masters continually renegotiated their economic relationships during the Civil War.

As the war wore on, many slaves found that the nature of their work was transformed. Lucinda Davis, a young Creek woman from Oklahoma then working on a plantation in Texas, reported that adult male slaves had all slipped away behind Union lines, leaving the women and children to bring in a harvest of green corn in the midst of the battle for the area (Davis 1996, p. 116). John Fields, a slave living in Kentucky, credited the use of slave labor by the South with its ability to earn early victories. He learned of the Emancipation Proclamation's passage in 1864 at the age of sixteen. Fields and his brother ran away to try to join the Union Army only to be refused for being too young. Fields was able to hire out his labor for $7 per month, marking his transition from slave to paid worker (Fields, p. 3).

The Civil War forced a transformation in the nature of work for factory workers. The South had lagged far behind the North in its level of industrialization and manufacturing before the war; however, as soon as the war began, the Confederate government embarked on an ambitious state-led manufacturing program. The Confederacy gave advances of 33 to 50 percent on government contracts to entrepreneurs who thought they would be able to provide essential materials for the use of the army and the states. The Confederate states also regulated the wartime labor market, first by legislating a draft covering all white men between eighteen and thirty-five, and then by exempting industrial workers in those industries that were productive. (Morgan 2004, pp. 4, 11).

The shortage of skilled white workers in some industries in the South elevated the status of workers who had previously been overlooked in a society where slaves and land conferred status. For example, because steel production was in its infancy, iron was a key commodity during the Civil War. As a result, the demand for the services of blacksmiths and farriers (persons who shoed horses) soared in both the North and the South. Some blacksmiths and farriers worked in uniform for army units, but others worked for the government from their own small shops or had their slaves do so. Both the Northern and the Southern armies exempted blacksmiths and farriers from the draft, but used bonuses to entice them into military service.

The Southern labor shortage also brought more white women and children into the manufacturing labor force. Augusta, Georgia, became a center of Southern manufacturing, as one large textile factory named the "Augusta Factory" employed 750 hands. Factory work remained culturally problematic, however. On the one hand, manual labor was associated with slaves, making the status of male factory workers ambiguous; on the other hand, married women and children were supposed to be economic dependents and not work in factories at all. A compromise was struck whereby factories hired almost exclusively single women; only three percent of the Augusta Factory's mill women were married (Whites 1995, p. 82).

The removal of breadwinners from the family circle combined with the lack of paid work opportunities for married women meant destitution for many families. In response, institutions like Augusta's Purveying Association were set up to organize the distribution of charity. The Augusta Purveying Association ended by serving 800 families, including some who had been displaced and were living in railroad cars (Whites 1995, p. 78). The Augusta Factory made a donation of $40,000 to the town's poor in 1863, and also distributed vast amounts of cloth to the poor. The fact that the factory acted paternalistically helped increase the acceptability of factory work in that part of Georgia.

Wartime realities made continued employment in Southern factories uncertain. One such factory, in Bellville, Georgia, supplied not only cloth for clothing and hats for "negroes and laborers" but also tents for soldiers and cloth casings for artillery. When the factory burned in 1862, poor white families were deprived of their only means of support (*Daily Morning News*, February 28, 1862). In 1864 the *Daily Richmond Examiner* reported that 400 young Southern women working in one Roswell, Georgia, factory found their work had been interrupted by Sherman's march; the factory that they had worked in was burned to the ground and they were involuntarily shipped north, away from their families (August 11, 1864).

Southern middle-class families coped with the strains of the war and the absence of male breadwinners by sending into employment many members who had not had to work before. Paid sewing assignments became a major resource for married women, whether they were hired by those few upper-class women who could afford to have dresses made or by the Confederate government in the "sewing manufactories" popping up in many government buildings by 1863.

Other government jobs—including hand-signing Confederate banknotes—became a major source of employment for male and female white workers, but such assignments did not ensure prosperity. Employees of the postal service petitioned the Confederate government to allow their families to shop at military commissaries, since with rising prices their salaries were totally inadequate. J. B. Jones, a Confederate war clerk, noted that meat was scarce and that the price of all groceries had risen; he was thankful that he and his family owned their own furniture, despite the fact that it had probably passed through twenty families before ending up in his own home (Jones 1866, p. 35).

While work in Southern factories and for the Confederate government was noteworthy because it represented change, the majority of white workers in the South who were not incorporated into the army still lived and worked on farms. Women and children did assume new tasks, including the marketing of crops and livestock as well as bookkeeping; however, gender roles died hard. Bad harvests and the commandeering of goods by both Northern and Southern troops kept many Southern families in a perilous state, and as James McPherson has argued, resulted in demoralizing letters begging loved ones to go absent without leave and come home to resume work with the harvest (1997, p. 135).

Labor in the North

The Northern economy suffered through a recession in 1861, as the immediate impact of war was a decrease in the demand for goods and services. By 1862, however, many manufacturing plants were able to shift over to production for the government or the army, and the economy began to recover and then to boom. Prices for necessities escalated as material was diverted from the consumer market to fill army contracts; wages also escalated, albeit less quickly. In many industries, workers took advantage of their temporary scarcity to strike for higher wages and better conditions; one historian, Joseph Rayback, counted 300 new union locals spread over sixty-nine different trades (1966, p. 111).

The fate of free black labor in the North, which had always been controversial, became even more of a flashpoint during the war. There were a few white workers like Alonzo Draper—the leader of a major strike among the shoemakers of Lynn, Massachusetts, in 1860, who then stepped forward to lead a regiment of black troops during the Civil War. But more typical were the hundred white caulkers whose case was reported in the Boston *Liberator*. In April 1863, these men walked away from their jobs at the Navy Yard, refusing to work alongside a skilled black caulker from Baltimore. Frederick Douglass had written of similar discrimination in New

Bedford years before in his autobiography (Douglass, 1963, p. 113).

The relationships among black and white workers became an urgent question as slaves freed themselves by running away to the Northern lines, where they were pressed into largely unpaid service as valets, cooks, ditch-diggers and water carriers for the Union forces. The tension broke into a firestorm in the first few days of July 1863, as mobs of white workers in New York City destroyed the city's central draft recruiting offices, burned black homes and schools, and tortured black people.

While some Northern workers fought for higher pay or quarreled over the question of who deserved work, other workers slipped into the jobs that grew up as a result of the war. Black and white women as well as some men served as nurses in makeshift army hospitals and on hospital ships. The poet Walt Whitman worked in a part-time job in the Army Paymaster's Office during the three years that he visited convalescent wards around Washington, DC, bestowing little gifts of food, tobacco, and time on the wounded soldiers (Price 2004). Others performed volunteer labor with the two great wartime institutions on the Union side: the Sanitary Commission, which provided soldiers in the field and convalescing in hospitals with clean bedding, bandages, letter-writing services, and an improved diet; and the Christian Commission, which provided soldiers with Bibles and religious tracts.

BIBLIOGRAPHY

Daily Morning News (Savannah, GA), February 28, 1862.

Daily Richmond (VA) *Examiner*, August 11, 1864.

Davis, Lucinda, "Creek Freedmen" In *The WPA Oklahoma Slave Narratives*, eds. T. Lindsay Baker and Julie P. Baker. Norman: University of Oklahoma Press, 1996, pp. 107–117.

Dew, Charles. *Bond of Iron: Master and Slave at Buffalo Forge*. New York: W.W. Norton, 1994.

Douglass, Frederick. *Narrative of the Life of Frederick Douglass*. New York: Doubleday and Co., 1963.

Fields, John W., in *WPA Slave Narrative Project*, Indiana Narratives, Volume 5, Federal Writer's Project, United States Work Projects Administration (USWPA); Manuscript Division, Library of Congress, available from www.loc.gov.

Jones, John Beauchamp. *A Rebel War Clerk's Diary at the Confederate States Capital*. Volume 2. Philadelphia: Lippincott, 1866.

The Liberator (Boston, MA), April 10, 1863.

McPherson, James. *For Cause and Comrades: Why Men Fought in the Civil War*. Oxford, U.K.: Oxford University Press, 1997.

Morgan, Chad. "The Public Nature of Private Industry in Confederate Georgia." *Civil War History* 50, no. 1 (2004): 27–46.

Price, Angel. "Whitman's *Drum Taps* and Washington's Civil War Hospitals" (2004), available from http://xroads. virginia.edu/.

Rayback, Joseph. *A History of American Labor*. New York: The Free Press, 1966.

Whites, LeeAnn. *The Civil War as a Crisis in Gender: Augusta, Georgia, 1860–1890*. Athens: University of Georgia Press, 1995.

Jamie Bronstein

CHILD LABOR

Although white children—especially those living in urban areas—were likely to receive at least a few years of organized education, most nineteenth-century Americans felt there was a moral benefit to children's gainful employment. "A certain amount of work is necessary for the proper education of children," the Colorado *Daily Miners' Register* noted in 1865. "Their future independence and comfort depend on being accustomed to provide for the thousand constantly recurring wants that nature entails on them." The extent to which this ideal was met, however, depended on the region of the country in which one lived and the race of the child in question.

Southern Children

For black children living in the South, work was a fact of life. The youngest children watched the babies and did errands; older children often performed a stint of labor as domestic servants before graduating to the fields as quarter- or half-hands at the age of ten or twelve. Except for those black children who were able to flee with their families to Northern battle lines, the Civil War did not change the reality of work. "The times I hated most was pickin' cotton when the frost was on the bolls," a former slave, Mary Reynolds, reported:

> My hands git sore and crack open and bleed. We'd have a li'l fire in the fields and iffen the ones with tender hands couldn't stand it no longer, we'd run and warm our hands a li'l bit. When I could steal a tater, I used to slip it in the ashes and when I'd run to the fire I'd take it out and eat it on the sly. (Reynolds, p. 239)

As the war continued, black child workers faced long days in the fields supported by dwindling food supplies, suffered punishment at the hands of frustrated masters for wartime reverses, did heavy farm labor tasks formerly performed by men, or endured involuntary relocation to areas far from Union control, like Texas. And for children, even the war's end did not mean an end to involuntary servitude—apprenticeship laws forced children to labor on plantations without wages until the age of twenty-one, even without parental consent (Mintz 2004, p. 114).

"Powder monkey." Children contributed to the war effort on both sides of the Mason-Dixon line. Some youths volunteered at home to make extra supplies such as bandages for hospitals or preserved foods to supplement a soldier's rations. Others found action on the front lines, such as the children who earned the nickname "powder monkeys" from carrying ammunition to naval gun crews. *Hulton Archive/Getty Images.*

Poor Southern white children also suffered hardship, assuming childcare responsibilities for younger siblings, foraging in the woods and fields for weeds and berries to supplement meager wartime diets, and peddling small items. With fathers absent, they also assumed larger responsibilities for farming chores alongside their mothers.

Northern Children

In the North, children were more likely to attend school, but those old enough to supplement the family income through paid labor might attend only intermittently. In industrializing Massachusetts, the law required that children under fifteen attend school for eleven weeks out of the year and children under twelve for eighteen weeks; but as the Civil War wore on, this requirement, often disregarded, became even more moot. The scarcity of factory labor attracted children into the workforce who might otherwise have been at school; with fathers and older brothers gone off to the war, these younger children were a crucial support to their families. In the absence of safety covers over mill machinery, disasters could easily happen. The *Dover Gazette* told the sad tale of John Francis Horrocks, a fourteen-year-old boy working in the Portsmouth Steam Factory in New Hampshire in 1863. He found his leg caught in the mill gearing, which stripped his thigh of half its flesh and pulled his femoral artery out of his body.

During the war, young children were encouraged to labor to support the war effort, as well as to bring income to their families. Fourteen-year-old Susie Baker—a former slave—did laundry for a United States Colored Troops (USCT) regiment, taught school, and served as a nurse (Mintz 2004, p. 119). In Ohio, ten-year-old Emma Andrews took to her needle and sewed 229 towels for soldiers in connection with her local aid society. During school vacations, children flocked to the woods to pick fruit, which was used both to make medicinal wine for soldiers and to help them prevent scurvy (Brockett and Vaughn, 1867, p. 82). Children enlisted with both the Confederate and Union armies as drummer boys, or, if they were able to lie about their age, as infantrymen. Adelaide Smith, an army nurse, made one injured and emaciated fifteen-year-old boy her hospital orderly rather than send him back to the Thirty-seventh New Jersey Regiment, where he had enlisted against his parents' wishes (Smith 1911, p. 86).

In contrast with children living in the Northeastern part of the Union, fewer than half of school-aged children living in the West spent their days in school. Thus in the many areas of the West that were untouched by the war, children engaged in work from the time they could be helpful. They planted and harvested, fed animals, rode the range after livestock, sewed clothes, ran errands, cooked and cleaned, and sometimes helped out in retail establishments and mining camps.

Stephen Mintz has described the gradual development over the course of the nineteenth century of two warring concepts of childhood (2004, p. 152). One concept was rooted in the idea that children, whether in farm or factory, should contribute through their work and wages to the success of the family. The other concept regarded childhood as an innocent time during which children should be protected from labor and from other worldly realities and given an education. The Civil War set back the progress of the second concept of childhood, as orphaned children and young war veterans were absorbed into the postwar labor force.

BIBLIOGRAPHY

Brockett, Linus, and Mary C. Vaughan. *Woman's Work in the Civil War.* New York: R.H. Curran, 1867.

Daily Miners' Register, Central City, Colorado, March 4, 1865.

Dover Gazette, Dover, NH, May 1, 1863.

Hindman, Hugh. *Child Labor: An American History.* Armonk, NY: M.E. Sharpe, 2002.

Mintz, Stephen. *Huck's Raft: A History of American Childhood.* Cambridge, MA: Belknap Press of Harvard University Press, 2004.

Reynolds, Mary. *The American Slave*, vol. 5: 236–246, available online at http://xroads.virginia.edu/.

Smith, Adelaide W. *Reminiscences of an Army Nurse during the Civil War.* New York: Greaves Publishing Company, 1911.

West, Elliott. *Growing up with the Country: Childhood on the Far Western Frontier.* Albuquerque: University of New Mexico Press, 1989.

Jamie Bronstein

PAID LABOR

At first, despite the removal of about one-third of the industrially-employed waged workers from the Northern labor market to the Union army, wages for labor in the North during the Civil War were not much different than they had been in the antebellum period. Laborers earned about a dollar a day, while master artisans took account of the cost of their materials and added a standard fee for working the materials into finished products. Prices began to climb as agricultural produce was diverted for army use, and more than one-third of the workforce was diverted into uniform.

In the antebellum period labor activism had been channeled in the direction of land reform, cooperative workshops and stores, and the ten-hour work day. Throughout the Civil War, however, rampant inflation combined with more slowly rising wages brought financial issues to the center; the cost of living index escalated from 100 in 1860 to 176 by 1865. Workers responded to their immediate wage problem by forming union locals; Joseph Rayback reports in his 1966 book *A History of American Labor* that by November, 1865, sixty-nine trades had organized three hundred locals. Also formed during the Civil War were some of the large cross-trade labor associations that would dominate the postwar period: the miners, the train engineers, and the house carpenters among them.

The war did not deter these new locals from striking. Urban artisans demanded a rise in the rates that they were paid for piecework. Laborers on canals and railroads from San Francisco to New York struck for higher wages. The *New York Herald* reported on March 24, 1863, that four hundred tailors at Brooks' Brothers paraded down the streets of the Bowery demanding a pay raise. Miners in Pottsville, Pennsylvania, protested low pay and poor conditions by turning off pumps and allowing mines to fill with water. Other miners withheld coal from the government, a move that their employers argued was tantamount to treason. By the war's second and third years, those workers who remained in the workforce achieved some success using the leverage of the labor shortage to wrest concessions from their employers. In 1864, for example, Pennsylvania miners were receiving $3 to $4 a day in wages, well up from their prewar level.

The need to raise and maintain an army also contributed to conflict between workers and employers. The prevailing wage rate of $13 a month for Union soldiers, plus a $100 bonus, was well under the market rate for paid labor, never mind life-threatening labor—and this resulted in a shortage of volunteers. The government's decision to respond with a draft, yet allow individuals to hire a substitute or pay a commutation fee, helped to convince workers that the Civil War was a "rich man's war but a poor man's fight." Urban workers' resistance to the draft became most patent in July 1863, when mobs attacked black homes and schools and destroyed New York's recruiting office. The denouement of the Draft Riots illustrates that even when workers were not dissuaded from striking by arguments centering on nationalism or patriotism, their attempts could be limited by the large numbers of men in uniform available to put down labor unrest. An 1864 military order, General Order 65, outlawed picketing and protected strikebreakers.

As Northern workers were siphoned away from the labor market and into the army, new categories of workers took their place, at least temporarily. The war attracted many women into paid positions, and wages rose across all classes and grades of labor. Nonetheless, women were still paid less than were men working in the same industries. In 1864 a Contract Labor Law allowed employers to bring European workers into the country—the first step in the major wave of European immigration that would follow the war and begin to make up for the demographic disaster that war had caused.

While labor scarcity during the war had done much to advance the cause of paid labor, demobilization after the war accomplished the opposite—especially as a recession set in between 1866 and 1868. Terence Powderly, later the Grand Master Workman of the Knights of Labor, noted in his 1889 memoir *Thirty Years of Labor* that as soon as the war ended, a dozen men would show up for an advertised position that had lain open an entire week during the war. The National Labor Union, one of the forerunners of the Knights of Labor, was founded in 1866 as a result of workers' perceptions of their declining position.

The South

The South faced an even more intractable labor problem than the North: not an absence of workers, but an absence of industrial production. At the outset of the war the South had 20,600 factories with 111,000 workers, compared with the North's 100,500 factories with 1.1 million workers. Part of the Southern response was to expand its existing factories for wartime production and to fill the factories with unpaid labor of every description: slaves who had

Locomotive engine. The civilian workforce was often directly affected by Civil War hostilities, as evidenced in this picture of train workers righting a locomotive overturned during fighting at the Second Battle of Bull Run. *The Art Archive/National Archives, Washington, DC/The Picture Desk, Inc.*

been impressed from their masters, convict labor, and prisoners of war.

The reliance on various types of slave labor both before and during the Civil War meant that Southern workers lacked the history of labor activism that characterized the antebellum North. Thus despite levels of price inflation that reached 900 percent, strikes were rare. In 1862, as the *Milwaukee Daily Sentinel* reported, journeymen printers at a major Richmond newspaper struck for an increase in wages, taking advantage of the fact that their skills were scarce and that every printer not at work in a newspaper office had been conscripted; but the printers were the exception.

The largest paid-labor question in the South was not the formation of a union movement or any kind of class cohesiveness among white workers, but rather, "Will the freedmen work for wages?" As early as 1862, as soon as some Southern areas were under federal control, former slaves came forward to demand wages for their continued labor on plantations; and plantation owners were forced to pay. Former slaves were also quickly contracted to build roads for the government and to mine coal for mine owners, also for wages.

In the South after the war, while some former slaves were hired directly under labor contracts, the majority worked as sharecroppers. The war had set back the Southern infrastructure—much was destroyed, and nothing could be built during the war. The collapse of banking and the worthlessness of the Confederate dollar also prevented postwar investment. Without capital and infrastructure Southern workers could not be as productive as Northern workers. Southern wages declined from their wartime levels, creating a situation whereby the North and the South were two distinct and separate labor markets: one flourishing, and one poor.

BIBLIOGRAPHY

Alpert, Cady, and Kyle D. Kauffman. "The Economics of the Union Draft: Institutional Failure and Government Manipulation of the Labor Market during the Civil War." *Essays in Economic and Business History* 17 (1999): 89–107.

Craig, Lee A., and Thomas Weiss. "Agricultural Productivity Growth during the Decade of the Civil War." *Journal of Economic History* 53, no. 3 (September 1993): 527–548.

Crews, Edward. "The Industrial Bulwark of the Confederacy." *Invention and Technology* (1992): 7–17.

Hutchinson, William, and Robert A. Margo. "The Impact of the Civil War on Capital Intensity and Labor Productivity in Southern Manufacturing."

Explorations in Economic History 43, no. 4 (2006): 689–704.

Kneller, Pamela. "Welsh Immigrant Women as Wage Earners in Utica, New York, 1860–1870." *Llafur, Journal of Welsh Labor History* 5, no. 4 (1991): 71–79.

Milwaukee Daily Sentinel, August 21, 1862; November 20, 1862.

The New York Herald, March 24, 1863.

Palladino, Grace. *Another Civil War: Labor, Capital and the State in the Anthracite Regions of Pennsylvania, 1840–1868.* Urbana: University of Illinois Press, 1990.

Powderly, Terence Vincent. *Thirty Years of Labor.* Columbus, OH: Excelsior Publishing, 1889.

Rayback, Joseph G. *A History of American Labor.* New York: Free Press, 1966.

Jamie Bronstein

WOMEN LABORERS

During the Civil War, the scale of participation by working men in both North and South meant that women—previously relegated to the domestic sphere by the ideals of the time—were forced to assume greater and more varied work responsibilities. Not only did they continue their unpaid labor at home—unwaged labor that expanded to include home production of textiles in the South—they also engaged in farming, in paid factory labor, and in paid and unpaid positions supporting the armed forces.

Slave women, who found the prospect of running away to Union lines more logistically challenging than did slave men, continued to perform the fieldwork, domestic service, cooking, and childcare they had been doing for generations. Increasingly, this work was done under greater than usual duress: Troops crossed through plantations, commandeering food, while masters who became impoverished were no longer willing or able to provide for their slaves. Mary Chesnut, the wife of a Confederate brigadier general, reported that because the price of raw cotton had sunk to five cents a pound, and finished cloth was thirty-seven cents a yard, masters were hiring out slaves for the price of food and clothing (Martin and Avery 1905, p. 139).

Southern white women who had never been expected to work outside the home took on new economic roles. Because it was impossible to industrialize the Southern economy speedily, the kind of work that was done in factories in the North—like the production of cloth—was often farmed out to white women and slaves working on individual plantations. Virginian Myrta Lockett described sewing for the soldiers:

> Sewing machines had been carried into the churches, and the sacred buildings had become depots for bolts of cloth, linen, and flannel. Nothing could be heard in them for days but the click of machines, the tearing of cloth, the ceaseless murmur of voices questioning, and voices directing the work. Old and young were busy. Some were tearing flannel into lengths for shirts and cutting out havelocks and knapsacks. And some were tearing linen into strips and rolling it for bandages ready to the surgeon's hand. Others were picking linen into balls of lint. (Lockett Avery 1903, pp. 28–29)

The notion that the work was being done in the service of the war effort helped to redirect suspicions about the unladylike nature of manual labor. J. B. Jones, a Confederate war clerk, noted in his memoir, "Everywhere the ladies and children may be seen plaiting straw and making bonnets and hats." He remarked that even Jefferson Davis's wife could be seen with her household sitting on the front porch making straw hats (Jones 1866, p. 16). Young women were also sent from their homes to work in Confederate cotton factories. In 1864 four hundred young Southern women working in one factory in Roswell, Georgia, found their work interrupted by Sherman's march to the sea. The factory that they worked in was burned to the ground and they were involuntarily shipped north (*Daily Richmond Examiner*, August 11, 1864).

In the North as in the South, farmwomen filled the gap when husbands went off to fight. Those sectors of the farm economy traditionally given over to women and children—the production of eggs, chickens, and hogs, for example—boomed as workdays became longer. Women also performed work traditionally relegated to men: They plowed, planted, and harvested crops; mended fences; tended animals; kept household books, and oversaw the work of slaves and servants. Eliminating the traditional gendered division of labor in this way helped to produce a permanent increase in farm production (Craig and Weiss 1993, p. 544).

Northern women also undertook volunteer work with the United States Sanitary Commission and the Christian Commission—sewing tents, rolling bandages, and holding bazaars to raise funds. In the South, although there were no similar overarching organizations, Mary Chesnut recalled writing letters to "sister societies at home," for women's help with nursing and rounding up supplies (Martin and Avery 1905, p. 100). All these activities were seen as extensions of the normal domestic duties of women, as was women's labor in field hospitals and hospital ships.

Nonetheless, the departure of men from the labor force led to a temporary reevaluation of the capabilities of women workers in other sectors of the paid workforce. The San Francisco *Daily Evening Bulletin* reported that the former Massachusetts governor Edward Everett called for women to contemplate work as bookkeepers, clerks, accountants, artists, sales personnel, and "attendants in establishments of every kind where the labor is not too severe for females" (September 13, 1862). Women were hired by the *Milwaukee Daily Sentinel* to set type—a move that precipitated a strike by all of the newspaper's male printers. As

The influence of women. Women in both the North and the South were pushed from the domestic sphere into the fields and factories to fill gaps left by men away at war. This shift in the role of women continued after the war's end, as both women and men reached a greater understanding of women's potential in the workforce. *The Library of Congress.*

H. M. Gitelman (1965) records, the Waltham Watch Company recruited women in Maine and the Massachusetts countryside. In 1864 Waltham's female workforce, its wages lagging far behind those of male workers, threatened to strike, but the company capitulated before a strike became necessary.

Women's wartime participation in the workforce—and the creation during the war of vast numbers of disabled veterans—helped to create permanent changes in the notion of "women's work." In the face of an enormous number of casualties, Northerners reevaluated the concept of the "family wage"—the notion that male breadwinners should earn enough to support their families without their wives working.

BIBLIOGRAPHY

Craig, Lee A., and Thomas Weiss. "Agricultural Productivity Growth during the Decade of the Civil War." *Journal of Economic History* 53, no. 3 (1993): 527–548.

Daily Richmond Examiner, August 11, 1864.

Faust, Drew Gilpin. *Mothers of Invention: Women of the Slaveholding South in the American Civil War.* Chapel Hill: University of North Carolina Press, 1996.

Gitelman, H. M. "The Labor Force at Waltham Watch during the Civil War Era." *Journal of Economic History* 25, no. 2 (1965): 214–243.

Jones, J. B. (John Beauchamp). *A Rebel War Clerk's Diary at the Confederate States Capital.* 2 vols. Philadelphia: Lippincott, 1866.

Lockett Avery, Myrta, ed. *A Virginia Girl in the Civil War, 1861–1865: Being a Record of the Actual Experiences of the Wife of a Confederate Officer.* New York: D. Appleton, 1903. Electronic edition available at http://docsouth.unc.edu/.

Martin, Isabella D., and Myrta Lockett Avery, eds. *A Diary from Dixie, as Written by Mary Boykin Chesnut.* New York: D. Appleton, 1905.

Milwaukee Daily Sentinel, January 29, 1863.

San Francisco Daily Evening Bulletin, September 13, 1862.

Jamie Bronstein

Technological Advances in Agriculture and Industry

The Civil War was the first "modern" war, in terms of its weaponry. Torpedoes, land mines, machine guns, ironclad ships all made their first appearance in the 1860s. But technological advances that helped determine the war's outcome went beyond military innovations. Some technological innovations did help the military effort. Others had no military value but created an economic value that was equally crucial.

It was the North that had the upper hand technologically when the Civil War began in 1861, and the North held that hand throughout the war. Both the North and the South were heavily dependent on agriculture. But in the South, agriculture was by far the key component of the economy. In the North, agriculture was important, but manufacturing was beginning to play a far greater role. By the time the Civil War began, the north had more than 110,000 factories; the South had only 18,000 (Stewart 2000, p. 15).

Cotton and the South's Agrarian Heritage

The South was not bothered by its agrarian character; in fact, it embraced it. In his inaugural address as President of the Confederacy, Jefferson Davis noted with no small amount of pride that Southerners are "an agricultural people—whose chief interest is the export of a commodity required in every manufacturing country" (Davis 1861). That commodity was cotton, and it was cotton more than anything else that determined the South's adherence to slavery.

References to "King Cotton" were no exaggeration: The cotton industry brought $100 million into the South annually (Stewart 2000, p. 45). To cultivate, King Cotton required human energy, and the cheapest and most plentiful form of human energy came in the form of slaves.

Because the South had always relied on cheap slave labor, it never bothered to mechanize its farming production. In the North, the Industrial Revolution had come full force and there was no financial need for slaves. In the largely agrarian South, by contrast, to abandon the slave system would not only break the plantations financially, it would let loose an entire new work force in the form of freed slaves, who might work for less than their white counterparts.

One observer, a writer named Samuel Powell pointed out in *Notes on Southern Wealth and Northern Profits* (1861) a key reason why slavery was never abandoned in the South for more technologically advanced means of farming: "A great secret of the productiveness of slave labor is that the tiller of the soil is nourished with the simplest, the coarsest, and the grossest fare" (p. 7). "The slave system," he continued, "builds no cities, few mills, few ships; it does little for common roads and bridges, canals, manufactures, trade, or commerce of its own—its gifts and its mission do not seem to lie in that way" (p. 8).

A Serious Miscalculation

The South believed—mistakenly, as it turned out—that its dominance of the cotton market would help it in two ways: First, the lack of cotton for Northern textile mills would put them into an economic tailspin and force them to make peace and accept the secession of the Confederacy. Second, countries like the United Kingdom, which used large quantities of cotton, would want to ally themselves with the South to ensure an uninterrupted supply.

What happened instead was that Northern textile mills substituted cotton with wool and began manufacturing woolen goods—which had added the benefit of producing record profits for sheep farmers (Catton 1971, p. 172). Meanwhile, Britain actually had a surplus of cotton at the start of the Civil War and thus had no reason to take sides in another nation's domestic battle (Stewart 2000, p. 16). The cotton surplus did not last, of course, and other countries besides the United Kingdom relied on Southern cotton. But as the war dragged on, the foreign markets decided to look elsewhere for their cotton, and they increased imports from India, South America, and Egypt (Danbom 2006, p. 115). This turn of events was a blow to the South, which simply lacked the means or the knowledge to create its own industrial boom.

Technology's Role in Agriculture

Many of the implements and devices used during the Civil War had been around for some time, but the presence of cheap labor in the North, as well as the South, kept farmers from taking any real interest in automation. As the Civil War drew thousands of young men and boys away from their homes and farms, it

A John Fowler clip drum. With thousands of men fighting in the war rather than working in the fields, labor saving technologies, such as steam-driven farm implements, became an important factor in the industrialized North. Whereas Southern agriculture depended on a labor force made unstable by the Emancipation Proclamation, the North improved their productivity by replacing manpower with machine power. *Hulton Archive/Getty Images.*

became clear that labor-saving devices might turn out to be a necessity.

Cyrus McCormick's reaper was developed in the 1830s and mass-produced beginning in the 1840s. It essentially increased the speed of cutting wheat by as much as fivefold. A farmer could clear a 15-acre field of wheat in a day with a McCormick reaper and just eight men. Using sickles or cradles (the older way), the farmer would need fifteen men (Danbom 2006, pp. 110–111). Because of the vast increase in productivity, farmers were able to satisfy the national need for wheat, and also to cater to a growing overseas demand for grains. Just before the Civil War, the United States was exporting eight million bushels of wheat per year; by the middle of the war, that number had risen to 27 million bushels per year (Danbom 2006, p. 111).

Other devices that were either created or perfected during the Civil War included improved plows, a corn planting machine, steam-driven threshing machines, and a two-horse cultivator (Catton 1971, p. 172). Those machines that had been driven by oxen in the past were now being driven by horses; the streamlined machines called for animals that were themselves more streamlined; faster and more efficient than the reliable but lumbering ox (Danbom 2006, p. 111).

Drawing the Country Closer Together

The Union government was concerned with more than mending the rift with the South. Expanding the nation's boundaries west of the Mississippi was a key concern, and new and existing technology was used to make this goal more reachable. Using relatively new technologies to assist in wartime efforts made those technologies more familiar and also more easy to assimilate into civilian use.

The telegraph had been invented by Samuel F. B. Morse in 1844, and its presence during the war provided something that to that point had been impossible to imagine: the ability to send news quickly from one point to another and, in this case, directly from the battlefield. Telegraph operators would travel with the troops and set up their equipment on the battlefield to send news, which could be reviewed by the government and by the press. A series of drawings in the January 24, 1863 edition of *Harper's Weekly* shows how the telegraph operators would move their equipment and send telegraphic messages once it was set up safely. During the course of the war, some 1,100 telegraph operators accompanied the troops, a number of which lost their lives along with the soldiers (Plum 1882, p. 376).

Photography, still new at the start of the Civil War, proved to be one of the most effective ways of capturing not only the events of the war but also the grim mood of the participants (Mindell 2000, p. 4). Photographers, the best known of which is Mathew Brady, accompanied the troops to the battlefields, often capturing the devastation left behind after particularly brutal fights.

Trains helped carry supplies to the troops during the Civil War, and extending rail service to the Pacific coast was considered essential to the economic expansion of the United States. Congress passed two Pacific Railroad Acts during the Civil War, one in 1862 and one in 1864. These acts extended rail service to Sacramento, California and Portland, Oregon. Without these railroads, it is doubtful that the Great Plains would have become an agricultural resource (Danbom 2006, p. 112).

Less glamorous, but nonetheless important, inventions also proved their value during the war. Signal flares, used by the U.S. Navy, were the invention of Martha Coston, who carried on the work of her late husband in perfecting the flares' performance. She patented the flares and sold the rights to the Union government, also acquiring the contract to manufacture the flares (Macdonald 1992, p. 182).

Although neither side could know it at the time, one legacy of the Civil War was that it served as a catalyst for a new national direction that would increasingly rely on machines and technology for economic growth and expansion.

BIBLIOGRAPHY

"The Army Telegraph: Setting Up the Wire During an Action." *Harper's Weekly*, January 24, 1863, p. 53.

Catton, Bruce. *The Civil War.* New York: American Heritage Press, 1971.

Danbom, David B. *Born in the Country: A History of Rural Life in America.* Baltimore: Johns Hopkins University Press, 2006.

Davis, Jefferson. *Inaugural Address of President Davis, Delivered at the Capitol, Monday, February 18, 1861, at 1 o'clock, p.m.* Montgomery, AL: 1861.

Macdonald, Anne L. *Feminine Ingenuity: Women and Invention in America.* New York: Ballantine Books, 1992.

Mindell, David A. *War, Technology, and Experience Aboard the USS Monitor.* Baltimore: Johns Hopkins University Press, 2000.

Plum, William R. *The Military Telegraph During the Civil War in the United States.* Chicago: Jansen, McClurg, & Company, 1882.

Powell, Samuel. *Notes on "Southern Wealth and Northern Profits."* Philadelphia: C. P. Sherman and Sons, 1861.

Stewart, Gail. *The Civil War: Weapons of War.* San Diego: Lucent Press, 2000.

George A. Milite

Politics

■ Politics Overview

Politics was fundamental to the Civil War. Politics had been the way Americans expressed and dealt with their differences before the Rebels had, in Lincoln's phrase, appealed "from the ballot to the bullet." Even during the war itself, most of the goals the two sides sought were political objectives—the maintenance or the establishment of national sovereignty, preserving or revoking the legal status of slavery. The Prussian militarist Carl von Clausewitz's famous dictum, "War is politics carried on by other means," was never more apt than during the American Civil War.

During the decades leading up to the war, Americans had expressed their growing sectional differences through national politics. Antislavery Northerners strove to gain enough political power to limit the spread of slavery and make at least that very small start toward a time in the distant future when the "peculiar institution" might be rolled back and finally abolished. On the contrary, proslavery Southerners made it the cornerstone and chief goal of their own politics to protect slavery not only in the states where it already existed, but throughout all the territories of the United States. By prevailing politically, they hoped to make slavery safe from all attempts to abolish it, and also to demonstrate that it was above moral reproach, the accepted and universal policy of the United States. When they failed to achieve these goals politically—when in the presidential election of 1860 they suffered a severe setback in the election of a president pledged to halt the further spread of slavery in the territories—proslavery Southerners waged a successful political campaign within the South aimed at persuading a majority of their fellow Southerners to declare their states no longer part of the United States, and to organize a new slaveholding republic, the Confederate States of America.

The average American in the mid-nineteenth century paid more attention to politics than does his counterpart of the early twenty-first. Much of the energy and excitement that modern Americans derive from, for example, spectator sports, their predecessors in the nineteenth century put into politics. They turned out in large numbers to hear political speeches and cheered vociferously for their candidates. During the Lincoln-Douglas debates in 1858, crowds stood to listen to the contending politicians for well over two hours at a stretch, and the debates were not unusual in that respect. The spectators reacted intensely to political speeches, and heckling of speakers was not uncommon.

During the Civil War the North continued to have a functioning two-party system. The Republicans and Democrats had contended for power in the region before the conflict started, and continued to do so throughout its course. The Democrats were in some ways helped by their temporary separation from the Southern wing of the party, which for years had been the tail that had wagged the Democratic dog. Yet, without the voting strength of the South, the Democrats were unable to win national elections or to gain control of Congress, and even though the proslavery fire-eaters of the South were absent from the party during the war years, the Democrats remained divided. War Democrats, as their name implied, favored a vigorous prosecution of the war, and some of them, such as Tennessee senator Andrew Johnson (1808–1875), came to support the Lincoln administration.

Peace Democrats, in contrast, labeled the war both wicked and a failure. Americans ought not to fight other Americans—presumably even if the other Americans had started the shooting—and no one, as far as the Peace Democrats were concerned, ought to fight for the freedom of blacks, whom they preferred to see continue as slaves. In any case, they maintained, the North would never succeed in subduing the South, and therefore the continuance of the conflict was nothing but a waste of life. The government should at once suspend hostilities and open negotiations to make the best deal possible, even if it meant recognizing Confederate independence. Peace Democrats and War Democrats polarized the wartime Democratic Party, and yet members of the party during those years did not always fit neatly into one camp or the other. The views of Civil War Democrats ran the gamut from the Peace to the War camps of their party.

The Republican Party also had its internal divisions. The Radical Republicans, who tended to dominate the party's contingent in Congress, favored abolition of slavery and the passage of laws tending to protect the civil rights of the former slaves and even to establish racial equality. They demanded vigorous and ruthless prosecution of the war and appropriate punishment of the traitors who had launched and supported the rebellion. The Congressional Joint Committee on the Conduct of the War, which the Radicals controlled, kept a wary eye on generals who did not seem to display sufficient zeal for the causes of victory and abolition, or who betrayed an undue tenderness for the rights or property of guilty traitors who, as far as the Radicals were concerned, had forfeited both. Conservative or moderate Republicans were no less committed to winning the war, but were more willing to be magnanimous with Rebels who laid down their arms, and more ready to accept at least some measure of gradualism in the changing status of African Americans. Lincoln, who was himself a moderate, balanced precariously throughout the war between that faction and the hard-liners in Congress. He was as skillful a politician as ever occupied the White House, and he used—and needed—all of his political skill in order to keep Northerners politically unified enough to keep fighting the Rebels and not each other.

The Confederacy, in contrast, was, as historian George Rable calls it, "a revolution against politics" (Rable 1994). As most white Southerners saw it, politics had failed them, had not secured them their rights, and had allowed them to be outvoted in a nation that had less and less sympathy with their "peculiar institution." What was needed, they maintained as they founded the new Confederacy, was a government that would not be moved by political forces, but instead would be governed by men who acted solely on the basis of principle, without regard to the tawdry concerns of politics. The irony that secessionist political leaders had used every political trick in the book to bring their states out of the Union and into the new slaveholders' Confederacy was apparently lost on practically all of them.

No one embodied the new Confederate ideal of the principled leader who disdained politics any more than the man they selected as their first and, as it turned out, only president. Senator Jefferson Davis of Mississippi prided himself on those very qualities. Northern senators who had had to contend with him during the years leading up to the war complained that he was self-righteous, proud, and rigid, and the war had not reached its midpoint before many of his fellow Confederates were making the same accusations. Making matters worse was the fact that from the day he was elected Confederate president, Davis was a lame duck. Hoping to insulate the presidency from politics, the writers of the Confederate constitution had specified that the president was to be elected to a nonrenewable six-year term. As is the case with any lame-duck president, Davis's political clout was weakened by the fact that everyone knew he would never head a party's ticket in any future election.

As a further bulwark against the evils of party politics—and because all good Southerners should be united as one in their determination to repel the "invaders"—politicians of the new Confederacy gloried in the fact that their republic possessed no political parties, and throughout its history the Confederacy never developed a two-party system. Yet this feature, which Southerners at first touted as another of their many advantages over the despised Yankees, turned out to be more of a curse than a blessing. Political parties can serve to channel political disagreement into constructive—or at least survivable—courses. The disintegration of the two-party system in the United States during the 1850s had been a harbinger of the impending crisis of the Union. Within the Confederacy, the absence of political parties actually led to increased acrimony in political debate. Without party loyalties to hold them in line, Confederate politicians resorted to bitter personal rhetoric and gauged their support of legislation according to their personal loyalty to—or hatred of—Jefferson Davis. By the latter years of the war, the supporters and opponents of the Confederate president were on their way to becoming a two-party system of their own, but the added rancor lent by the personal nature of their debates had compounded the Confederacy's difficulties.

Despite the problems caused by the Confederacy's unintentionally chaotic political system and the further problems caused by his own stubborn and undiplomatic nature, Davis succeeded in securing passage of every piece of major legislation he sought, and blocking every one he opposed, up until the closing months of the war. Nonetheless, he could have secured heartier cooperation throughout the Confederate system if he, and it, had used more effectively the methods of politics, distasteful as they could sometimes be. Less than 100 miles north of his capital, Lincoln was even then demonstrating how it could be done.

Steven E. Woodworth

■ Abolitionists

More than 200 years before the first shot was fired during the American Civil War, early Quaker colonists protested against the institution of slavery in the New World. Their struggle to end the practice of human bondage in the colonies and the United States was called the "abolitionist movement," and many of the advocates of the abolitionist cause were opposed to slavery based on their religious beliefs and moral values. In 1693, Pennsylvania Quakers instituted a policy that its citizens should only purchase African slaves in order to set them free because of their view that slavery, in any form, was abhorrent to their religious beliefs (Horton 2001, p. 35). In his antislavery publication "All Slave-Keepers That Keep the Innocent in Bondage, Apostates" (1737), Benjamin Lay (1681–1760) encouraged his fellow Quakers to completely reject the institution of slavery in America. Lay believed that slavery was a morally corrupt institution, and he was vehemently opposed to its continuation in America. Lay declared:

> [Y]ou that practice Tyranny and Oppression for Slave-keeping is such, he that assumes in arbitrary Manner, unjustly, Dominion over his Fellow-Creature's Liberty and Property, contrary to Law, Reason or Equity, He is a wicked sinful Tyrant, guilty of Oppression and great Iniquity: But he that trades in Slaves and the Souls of Men, does so; therefore .... Beside, Friends, the very Name of the Tyrant is odious, to God, to good men, yea to bad Men too; and the Nature and Practice is much worse. And Friends, you that follow this forlorn filthy Practice, do you not consider that you are opening the Door to others, or setting them an Example to do the like by you, whenever it shall please the Almighty to suffer them to have power over us, as a Scourge to us for our Sins, what Reason then shall we have to complain. (Lay 1737, pp. 43–44)

Because of Lay's almost fanatical opposition to slavery and his theatrical stunts that attempted to call attention to the horrors of slavery, many members of Quaker meeting houses banned him from their premises (Soderlund 1985, pp. 14–18). By 1758, Quaker abolitionists condemned slavery at their yearly meeting and decided that any Quakers who participated in the slave trade through buying, selling, or importing slaves would be expelled from the Quaker congregation. Because of the efforts of early abolitionists such as Lay, the Commonwealth of Pennsylvania abolished slavery in 1780 (Horton 2001, pp. 35–36).

One of the earliest African American abolitionists was David Walker (1785–1830), the son of a free black mother and a father who was a slave in North Carolina. Walker was an antislavery advocate who published *David Walker's Appeal to the Coloured Citizens of the World* on September 28, 1829, in Boston. *David Walker's Appeal* was one of the earliest and most important abolitionist writings of the time, and it was smuggled into towns and cities across the country. Walker was considered a dangerous man: He encouraged slaves to rebel against their masters by running away, insurrection, or by whatever means necessary, including outright rebellion and violence, to obtain their own freedom and to bring down the institution of slavery (Hinks 1997, pp. 237–240). He wrote:

> [I]f you commence, make sure work—do not trifle, for they will not trifle with you—they want us for their slaves, and think nothing of murdering us in order to subject us to that wretched condition—therefore, if there is an attempt made by us, kill or be killed. Now, I ask you, had you not rather be killed than to be a slave to a tyrant, who takes the life of your mother, wife, and dear little children? Look upon your mother, wife and children, and answer God Almighty; and believe this, that it is no more harm for you to kill a man, who is trying to kill you, than it is for you to take a drink of water when thirsty; in fact, the man who will stand still and let another murder him, is worse than an infidel, and, if he has common sense, ought not to be pitied. (Walker 1830, pp. 29–30)

Walker warned white slave owners and all white citizens of the United States that it would be better to free the African American slaves than to wait for them to free themselves; slaves eventually would be free, no matter what their white masters did to try to impede their efforts:

> Remember Americans, that we must and shall be free and enlightened as you are, will you wait until we shall, under God, obtain our liberty by the crushing arm of power? Will it not be dreadful for you? I speak Americans for your good. We must and shall be free I say, in spite of you. You may do your best to keep us in wretchedness and misery, to enrich you and your children, but God will deliver us from under you. And wo (sic), wo (sic), will be to you if we have to obtain our freedom by fighting. Throw away your fears and prejudices then, and enlighten us and treat us like men, and we will like you more than we do now hate you. You are not astonished at my saying we hate you, for if we are men we cannot but hate you, while you are treating us like dogs and tell us now no more about colonization, for America is as much our country, as it is yours. (Walker 1830, pp. 79–80)

In his *Appeal*, Walker also encouraged white Americans to end the institution of slavery in a peaceful way so that people of European and African descent could live together harmoniously:

> —Treat us like men, and there is no danger but we will all live in peace and happiness together. For we are not like you, hard hearted, unmerciful, and unforgiving. What a happy country this will be, if the whites will listen ... But Americans, I declare to you, while you keep us and our children in bondage, and treat us like brutes, to make us support you and your families, we cannot be your friends. You do not look for it, do you? Treat us then like men, and we will be your friends. And there is not a doubt in my mind, but that the whole of the past will be sunk into oblivion, and we yet, under God, will become a united and

> happy people. The whites may say it is impossible, but remember that nothing is impossible with God. (Walker 1830, p. 80)

Walker's words were thought to be incendiary and seditious, and a reward was posted for his capture, dead or alive, by Southerners in the slaveholding states. The *Appeal* encouraged slave rebellions and incidents of slaves standing up to their masters, and it is considered to be one of the most important works of antislavery literature written by a black abolitionist.

Impact of Antebellum Abolitionists on the Civil War

During the 200 years that slavery was legal in the American colonies and the United States, European Americans, as well as free and enslaved black people, struggled to bring an end to the institution of slavery. White citizen activists used methods different from blacks', including individual and group protests, legal actions in the courts, or appeals to state and federal governmental actors who were sympathetic to the abolitionist cause. None of these approaches was entirely effective on its own, but in combination with other means, their efforts were the driving impetus that led to the outbreak of the Civil War in 1861, and the eventual abolition of slavery completely after the end of the Civil War in 1865.

The abolitionist movement in the United States included both white and black members, although most historical accounts focus mainly on the efforts of well-known African Americans such as Frederick Douglass (1818–1895), an escaped slave and abolitionist. After his escape from slavery, Douglass became associated with the abolitionist William Lloyd Garrison (1805–1879) and worked with him and other white abolitionists to spread the word about the evils of slavery in the United States. Douglass had a unique perspective as an abolitionist because he was an African American former slave and had personally experienced the horrors of slavery. He was strongly influenced by Garrison's abolitionist newspaper the *Liberator*, and although he preferred a peaceful solution to the slavery problem, he knew that a totally nonviolent approach probably would not be possible in the Southern slaveholding states. Douglass, Garrison, and other antislavery advocates resolved to hold 100 conventions in one year to help spread the abolitionist message. According to Douglass:

> The year 1843 was one of remarkable anti-slavery activity. The New England Anti-Slavery Society at its annual meeting, held in the spring of that year, resolved, under the auspices of Mr. Garrison and his friends, to hold a series of one hundred conventions. The territory embraced in this plan for creating anti-slavery sentiment included New Hampshire, Vermont, New York, Ohio, Indiana, and Pennsylvania. I had the honor to be chosen one of the agents to assist in these proposed conventions, and I never entered upon any work with more heart and hope. All that the American people needed, I thought, was light. Could they know slavery as I knew it, they would hasten to the work of its extinction. (Douglass 1881, p. 229)

In addition to his other abolitionist work, from 1847 to 1863 Douglass published the *North Star* newspaper. Its mission was to work to "abolish slavery in all its forms and aspects, advocate universal emancipation, exalt the standard of public morality, and promote the moral and intellectual improvement of the colored people, and hasten the day of freedom to the Three Millions of our enslaved fellow countrymen" (Douglass 1881, p. 233).

Many of Douglass's and Garrison's writings induced the men and women of America to fight to abolish slavery permanently in the United States, at any cost. Garrison believed that the United States should abolish slavery immediately, and one solution would be to separate the Southern slaveholding states and the Northern antislavery states (Richman 1981, pp. 328–329).

One of the most active abolitionist organizations in the United States during the pre–Civil War period was the American Anti-Slavery Society. Antislavery activists, including Garrison and Arthur and Lewis Tappan, established the American Anti-Slavery Society in 1833 to campaign for the eradication of slavery in the United States. Its members included prominent members of Philadelphia society, and its goal was to end slavery through legal and peaceful methods, though some of its members advocated revolution as a means to end the abominable practice. Article III of the American Anti-Slavery Society provided:

> The objects of this society are the entire abolition of slavery in the United States. While it admits that each State in which slavery exists has, by the constitution of the United States, the exclusive right to legislate in regard to its abolition in said State, it shall aim to convince all our fellow-citizens, by arguments addressed to their understandings and consciences, that slaveholding is a heinous crime in the sight of God, and that the duty, safety, and best interests of all concerned require its immediate abandonment, without expatriation. The society will also endeavor, in a constitutional way, to influence Congress to put an end to the domestic slave trade, and to abolish slavery in all those portions of our common country which come under its control, especially in the District of Columbia, and likewise to prevent the extension of it to any State that may be hereafter admitted to the Union. (Garrison 1833)

Some abolitionists favored the use of any means necessary to end slavery in the United States, including violent slave uprisings and rebellions, and direct confrontation with the proslavery forces in American society. Some of these antislavery advocates planned slave insurrections and collaborations between abolitionist whites,

Famous abolitionist John Brown (1800–1859). John Brown was a religious man who considered slavery immoral and in direct conflict with the Bible. He was one of the most famous of abolitionists who believed in using any means necessary to stop slavery, including violence and confrontations with those who supported the institution. *National Archives & Records Administration.*

free blacks, and African slaves (Higginbotham 1980, pp. 26–30). These actions were partly responsible for precipitating the Civil War, and had a direct and lasting impact on both proslavery and antislavery Americans. One of the most famous proponents of this approach was John Brown (1800–1859), a religious man who vehemently believed that slavery was an abomination that violated biblical precepts. Douglass met Brown in 1847 and later described Brown's mission to fight slavery at any cost, even if he had to kill slave owners:

> He denounced slavery in look and language fierce and bitter, thought that slaveholders had forfeited their right to live, that the slaves had the right to gain their liberty in any way they could, did not believe that moral suasion would ever liberate the slave, or that political action would abolish the system.... An insurrection he thought would only defeat the object, but his plan did contemplate the creating of an armed force which should act in the very heart of the south. He was not averse to the shedding of blood, and thought the practice of carrying arms would be a good one for the colored people to adopt, as it would give them a sense of their manhood. No people he said could have self respect, or be respected, who would not fight for their freedom. (Douglass 1881, pp. 279–280)

Most other religious abolitionists favored peaceful resolution of the issue of slavery. For example, William Henry Furness (1828–1867) was a Philadelphia minister who favored using peaceful methods to hasten the end of slavery and maintaining the union between the slaveholding and free U.S. states. In an 1860 speech he declared:

> [I]f Slavery be peacefully abolished,—and most earnestly do I pray that it may be so abolished, and only so,—for no other than a peaceful abolition of it, would I ever lift a finger or breathe a word, for no other could be really successful: if, I say, Slavery is peacefully abolished, it will only be through the united effort of the whole people of the land. And, being united in the accomplishment of so humane a work, the people will naturally, and almost unconsciously, have a bond of union formed between them all, so strong that no geographical divisions, no diversity of their lesser interests, will be able to break it. (Furness 1860, p. 9)

Some moderate antislavery activists believed that an amendment to the U.S. Constitution would be the best legal method to abolish slavery, but it was an unlikely solution because of the number of proslavery legislators in Congress: It would be impossible to get Congress to vote for its passage and the president to ratify the amendment. The abolitionist Wendell Phillips (1811–1884), a colleague of Garrison's, said that "[t]he distant hope of Constitutional amendment not only allows but makes it necessary that we should remain in The Union, performing its sinful requirements while they continue the law of the land, in order to effect our object" (Richman 1981, p. 328).

Positive Outcomes

The infamous *Dred Scott v. Sandford* Supreme Court case (1857) galvanized the abolitionist movement and helped to precipitate to the Civil War. In the decision, Chief Justice Taney wrote that a black person, whether free or slave, could not be a citizen of the United States, and that blacks were "so far inferior, that they had no rights which the white man was bound to respect." The decision also declared that the Missouri Compromise was unconstitutional, thereby allowing the expansion of slavery into the western territories. The written opinion of Chief Justice Taney, a former slave owner from Maryland, so inflamed both antislavery and proslavery forces that it eventually led to bloody conflicts in Kansas and, in the end, the Civil War (Simon 2006, pp. 1, 9).

On April 16, 1862, President Abraham Lincoln signed the District of Columbia Compensated Emancipation

Act. This law made slavery illegal in Washington, DC. It was the first time that the U.S. government had taken any legislative action to abolish slavery. Lincoln freed the slaves in the slaveholding states when he signed the Emancipation Proclamation on January 1, 1863. Ultimately, after the end of the Civil War, Congress passed the Thirteenth and Fourteenth Amendments to the U.S. Constitution, effectively abolishing slavery in the United States and entitling African Americans to enjoy the rights and privileges of American citizenship.

BIBLIOGRAPHY

Chapman, Maria Weston. "'How Can I Help Abolish Slavery?' or, Counsels to the Newly Converted." Antislavery Tracts No. 14, New York: Office of the American Antislavery Society, 1855. Available from the Antislavery Literature Project of Arizona State University, http://antislavery.eserver.org/tracts/.

Douglass, Frederick. *Life and Times of Frederick Douglass: His Early Life as a Slave, His Escape from Bondage, and His Complete History to the Present Time.* Hartford, CT: Park Publishing, 1881. Available from Documenting the American South, University of North Carolina at Chapel Hill, http://docsouth.unc.edu/neh/douglasslife/.

Foster, Stephen Symons. "Revolution the Only Remedy for Slavery." Antislavery Tracts No. 7. New York: Office of the American Antislavery Society, 1855. Available from the Antislavery Literature Project of Arizona State University, http://antislavery.eserver.org/tracts/.

Furness, W. H. "The Blessings of Abolition: A Discourse Delivered in the First Congregational Unitarian Church." Sunday, July 1, 1860. Philadelphia: C. Sherman and Sons, 1860. Available from the Antislavery Literature Project of Arizona State University, http://antislavery.eserver.org/religious/.

Garrison, William Lloyd. "The Declaration of the National Anti-slavery Convention." *The Liberator*, Philadelphia, December 14, 1833.

Higginbotham, A. Leon, Jr. *In the Matter of Color, Race, and the American Legal Process: The Colonial Period.* New York: Oxford University Press, 1980.

Hinks, Peter P. *To Awaken My Afflicted Brethren: David Walker and the Problem of Antebellum Slave Resistance.* University Park: Pennsylvania State University Press, 1997.

Horton, James Oliver, and Lois E. Horton. *Hard Road to Freedom: The Story of African America.* New Brunswick, NJ and London: Rutgers University Press, 2001.

Lay, Benjamin. "All Slave-Keepers that Keep the Innocent in Bondage, Apostates." Philadelphia: Author, 1737. Available from the Antislavery Literature Project of Arizona State University, http://antislavery.eserver.org/religious/.

Richman, Sheldon. "The Antiwar Abolitionists: The Peace Movement's Split Over the Civil War." *Journal of Libertarian Studies* 5, no. 3 (Summer 1981): 327–340.

Simon, James F. *Lincoln and Chief Justice Taney: Slavery, Secession, and the President's War Powers.* New York: Simon and Schuster, 2006.

Soderlund, Jean R. *Quakers and Slavery: A Divided Spirit.* Princeton, NJ: Princeton University Press, 1985.

Walker, David. *Walker's Appeal, in Four Articles; Together with a Preamble, to the Coloured Citizens of the World, but in Particular, and Very Expressly, to Those of the United States Of America, Written in Boston, State of Massachusetts.* September 28, 1829. Boston: Author, 1830.

Jocelyn M. Cuffee

Civil Liberties and Censorship

Civil liberties is a general term that refers to freedoms protecting individuals from arbitrary interference by government. The phrase itself was first used in England around 1644, but the concept goes back further in English law to Magna Carta (the "Great Charter," 1215), a document that King John (1166–1216) was forced to sign by the barons of England that imposed limitations on his powers as monarch. In particular, the king gave up the power to imprison people without a trial, to seize people's lands as he pleased, or to raise taxes without "the common consent of the kingdom" (*Magna Carta* 1215).

Civil liberties as understood in the twenty-first century includes such freedoms as freedom of speech, freedom of assembly, freedom of religion, the right to bear arms, the right to a speedy and fair trial, and the right of due process. In American law, the Bill of Rights—the first ten amendments to the Constitution, proposed by James Madison in 1789 and ratified by three-quarters of the states in 1791—is considered the foundational document of civil liberties in the United States.

Lincoln's Suspension of *Habeas Corpus*

The Civil War was the first period in American history in which the scope and extent of civil liberties in the United States became a matter of open disagreement between the executive branch of the federal government (the President) and the judicial branch (the Supreme Court). The dispute was precipitated in 1861 by Lincoln's

President Lincoln's secretary of war, E. M. Stanton (1814–1869). E. M. Stanton was the secretary of war for President Lincoln during the time of the Civil War. In this position, he ordered in 1862 that *habeas corpus* be suspended for a variety of crimes for both civilians and soldiers, including Lambdin P. Milligan (1812–1899). *MPI/Hulton Archive/Getty Images*

suspension of *habeas corpus*, which can be briefly defined as a citizen's right to petition for relief from unlawful detention or imprisonment (of themselves or another person).

To make use of *habeas corpus*, the petitioner asks for a writ (a legal order issued by a court) of *habeas corpus ad subjiciendum*, to use the technical legal phrase. The Latin words go back to the Middle Ages and are a command issued in the monarch's name to a lower court or officer holding someone in custody to present that individual before a judge or higher court. Thus *habeas corpus* is essentially a procedure to examine the legality of someone's detention or imprisonment. Articles 36 and 38 through 40 of the Magna Carta are usually considered to be the foundation of *habeas corpus* in English law, although the phrase itself was not used until 1305, in the reign of King Edward I (1239–1307). The customary form of words used in American law for a writ of *habeas corpus* is as follows:

> We command you that the body of [person's name], in your custody detained, as it is said, together with the day and cause of his [her] caption and detention, you safely have before Honorable [judge's name and judicial district], within the circuit and district aforesaid, to do and receive all and singular those things which the said judge shall then and there consider of him [her] in this behalf; and have you then and there this writ.

Habeas corpus is mentioned in the Constitution of the United States in Article One, Section 9, also known as the Suspension Clause: "The privilege of the writ of *habeas corpus* shall not be suspended, unless when in cases of rebellion or invasion the public safety may require it." It was Lincoln's use of the Suspension Clause in 1861 that brought him into conflict with the Supreme Court—in particular, with Chief Justice Roger Taney (1777–1864).

Lincoln suspended *habeas corpus* in Maryland on April 27, 1861, as a response to riots in the city of Baltimore that broke out when the first Union troops arrived in the city in response to Lincoln's call for volunteers. In addition to the breakdown of public order, Lincoln was concerned that Maryland might secede and join the Confederacy, which would leave the federal capital surrounded by enemy territory. He had also received requests from several Union generals to set up military courts in order to deal with Copperhead Democrats and supporters of the Confederacy living in Union states. Lincoln's order of suspension was carried out by General Winfield Scott:

> HEADQUARTERS OF THE ARMY,
> Washington, April 27, 1861.
> The undersigned, General-in-Chief of the Army, has received from the President of the United States the following communication:
> COMMANDING GENERAL ARMY OF THE UNITED STATES:
> You are engaged in repressing an insurrection against the laws of the United States. If at any point on or in the vicinity of the military line which is now used between the city of Philadelphia via Perryville, Annapolis City and Annapolis Junction you find resistance which renders it necessary to suspend the writ of habeas corpus for the public safety, you personally or through the officer in command at the point where resistance occurs are authorized to suspend that writ.
> ABRAHAM LINCOLN.
> In accordance with the foregoing warrant the undersigned devolves on Major-General Patterson, commanding the Department of Pennsylvania, Delaware and Maryland; Brigadier-General Butler, commanding the Department of Annapolis, and Colonel Mansfield, commanding the Washington Department, a like authority each within the limits of his command to execute in all proper cases the instructions of the President.
> WINFIELD SCOTT. (Lincoln 1861a)

In December 1861, Lincoln extended the suspension of *habeas corpus* to Missouri, addressing his order to Major General Henry Halleck (Lincoln 1861c).

Ex parte Merryman (1861)

Ex parte Merryman is a case that came before Chief Justice Roger Taney in his capacity as a Maryland circuit judge in the early summer of 1861, after Lincoln had suspended *habeas corpus* in Maryland. *Ex parte* is a legal term that means "from one party [to the case] only." Among other legal applications, *ex parte* is traditionally used with the names of petitioners for a writ of *habeas corpus.*

John Merryman was an officer in the Maryland cavalry who assisted in ejecting a Union general from Baltimore and in blowing up several railroad bridges to prevent the movement of additional Union troops into the city in April 1861. Merryman was seized by Union troops several weeks later and held in Fort McHenry outside Baltimore. He immediately petitioned for a writ of *habeas corpus.* The following day, Chief Justice Taney, who was sitting as a circuit judge for the Baltimore circuit (Supreme Court justices acted as circuit judges when the Supreme Court was not in session—until 1869, when the practice was abolished), ordered the government to show just cause for Merryman's detention.

When Taney was informed that Lincoln had suspended *habeas corpus* (a decision that had been kept secret at first), he issued a judicial opinion to the effect that the President acting alone does not have the constitutional authority to suspend the right; only Congress can put the Suspension Clause into effect. The question as to whether only Congress has the authority to suspend *habeas corpus,* however, has not been definitively decided as of the early 2000s (Rehnquist 2000b). Using President Andrew Jackson's defiance of a former Chief Justice, John Marshall, as precedent, Lincoln simply ignored Taney's opinion that Merryman was illegally confined.

On July 4, however, Lincoln justified his actions before Congress gathered in special session:

> Soon after the first call for militia it was considered a duty to authorize the commanding general in proper cases according to his discretion, to suspend the privilege of the writ of habeas corpus ... This authority has purposely been exercised but very sparingly. Nevertheless the legality and propriety of what has been done under it are questioned and the attention of the country has been called to the proposition that one who is sworn to 'take care that the laws be faithfully executed' should not himself violate them [but] the whole of the laws which were required to be faithfully executed were being resisted and failing of execution in nearly one-third of the States. Must they be allowed to finally fail of execution, even had it been perfectly clear that by the use of the means necessary to their execution some single law, made in such extreme tenderness of the citizen's liberty that practically it relieves more of the guilty than of the innocent, should to a very limited extent be violated? To state the question more directly, are all the laws but one to go unexecuted and the Government itself go to pieces lest that one be violated? (Lincoln 1861b)

Lincoln's suspension of *habeas corpus* in order to preserve the Union continues to be one of the most controversial executive decisions in American history (Rehnquist 2000a).

Ex parte Milligan (1866)

Ex parte Milligan was another landmark civil liberties case that emerged from the Civil War. Lambdin P. Milligan (1812–1899) was a lawyer and Confederate sympathizer from Indiana who was accused in 1864, along with four other men, of conspiracy to overthrow the government of the United States and conspiracy to aid the Southern rebellion. Part of the plot involved seizing a federal arsenal in order to raid a military camp near Chicago that held Confederate prisoners of war. One of the defendants turned state's evidence against the others, who were sentenced to death by hanging by a military court in the fall of 1864.

The reason why Milligan and his co-defendants had been tried by a military rather than a civil court is that Edwin Stanton had ordered, in his capacity as Secretary of War in 1862, that *habeas corpus* be suspended for people accused of various crimes even if they were civilians. In addition, Stanton's proclamations ordered such persons to be tried before military commissions rather than civil courts. This provision meant not only that the accused could be detained for long periods of time but also that such procedural rights guaranteed by the Constitution as the right to a jury trial would be denied. Stanton justified his actions on the basis of an old Roman maxim, *Inter arma silent leges,* which can be loosely translated as "When the guns speak, the [civil] laws must keep quiet."

If Lincoln had not been assassinated in April 1865, it is highly likely that he would have set aside the death sentence imposed on Milligan and the others by the military court (Rehnquist 1996, p. 8). By the time of the Indianapolis treason trials, as they were known, Sherman was completing his march through Georgia, the end of the war was in sight, and the public mood was shifting toward clemency rather than harshness toward those accused of treason.

Andrew Johnson, who became President on Lincoln's death, intended to have the death sentence imposed in 1864 carried out in May 1865. At this point, however, Milligan and the other defendants petitioned the federal court in Indianapolis for a writ of *habeas corpus.* In January 1866, the case came before the Supreme Court under the title of *Ex parte Milligan.* The defendants were ably represented by a future president, James A. Garfield, who argued that even in wartime civilians should not be tried by military courts as long as the civil courts are open for business. The majority opinion of the Court contained a famous passage:

> The Constitution of the United States is a law for rulers and people, equally in war and in peace, and covers with the shield of its protection all classes of men, at all times, and under all circumstances. No doctrine, involving more pernicious consequences, was ever invented by the wit of man than that any of its provisions can be suspended during any of the great exigencies of government. Such a doctrine leads directly to anarchy or despotism, but the theory of necessity on which it is based is false; for the government, within the Constitution, has all the powers granted to it, which are necessary to preserve its existence; as has been happily proved by the result of the great effort to throw off its just authority. (*Ex parte Milligan*, 71 U.S. [4 Wall.] 2, 120–121, 1866)

Censorship of the Press in the North

Censorship in general refers to the examination of letters, print matter, or other media in order to remove materials considered morally harmful or politically sensitive. The term comes from the period of the Roman Republic (443–22 BC), in which the censors were magistrates of high rank responsible for taking a periodic census and for supervising public morality.

The American Civil War was the first conflict in the nation's history in which some censorship of the press in both North and South was justified on the grounds of military necessity. This necessity in turn was the by-product of changes in technology and communications which had led to the rapid growth of popular newspapers in the 1830s and 1840s. The invention of the electric telegraph in 1838 by Samuel F. B. Morse (who gave his name to the Morse code alphabet devised by his assistant, Alfred Vail) made it feasible—and profitable—for newspaper owners to hire reporters and correspondents in distant cities to write and transmit local news stories via telegrams. By 1858 the construction of a transatlantic telegraph cable made it possible to set up news bureaus overseas, and by 1861 there was a telegraph line from New York to San Francisco, part of a 50,000-mile network crisscrossing the United States (Harris 1999).

In addition to the increased speed of news transmission, the use of woodcut illustrations—direct reproduction of daguerrotypes or photographs was not possible with the printing presses of the 1860s—greatly increased the visual appeal of American newspapers. As the number of subscriptions rose, newspapers began to pay their top-level employees handsome salaries; by 1861, one upper-level manager at the *New York Herald* was paid more than the members of Lincoln's cabinet (Harris 1999, p. 27). The fact that newspapers had become a major industry helps to explain why censorship of the press during the Civil War was a touchy issue. In addition, the nation had no precedents to guide either the press or the government in handling such questions as reporting on troop recruitment or movement (Sears 1994, p. 17). Newspaper correspondents had little experience, let alone training, in discriminating between genuine news and "chin music"—gossip or local hearsay (Sears 1994, p. 18).

There were two major considerations that guided Northern officials in their censorship of the press. The first was the possibility that reporters would assist the enemy by revealing secret military information. One motivation for so doing was financial rather than political, however; some reporters hoped to boost their newspaper's subscription base (and their own salaries) by printing information before their rivals could obtain it. The editor of *Harper's Weekly* commented on economic as well as political motives for publishing military secrets in the spring of 1862:

> A censorship of the press is one of the temporary inconveniences which the present unexampled rebellion has involved. At the outbreak of the war there were throughout the North journals conducted by unprincipled men which were prepared deliberately to afford aid and comfort to the enemy. Ever since then there have been journals which, without the excuse of rebel sympathies, have been willing to betray strategical secrets, in order to outstrip their rivals in the publication of military and naval intelligence. The only means of checking the one and the other was a press censorship, and it is to the credit of Mr. LINCOLN that he did not hesitate to establish it. (May 17, 1862)

A second potential problem was the effect on public morale, were the press to expose some of the government's dirty laundry, so to speak. This concern was not groundless; one of the earliest European war correspondents, William Howard Russell (1821–1907) of the London *Times*, was credited with forcing the resignation of the British government during the Crimean War (1853–1856) by his candid accounts of the poor training and leadership of the British troops sent to the Crimea. As it turned out, the *Times* sent Russell to cover the opening months of the American Civil War in 1861. When Russell's account of the Union defeat at Bull Run as "a miserable, causeless panic" accompanied by "scandalous behavior" reached the Northern public, the British reporter received threatening letters. His press credentials were revoked in 1862 and he returned to London shortly afterward (Sears 1994, p. 18).

Newspaper censorship in the North passed through several stages. At the beginning of the war, General-in-Chief Winfield Scott declared that the Washington telegraph office would no longer carry dispatches related to military information that had not first been approved by the commanding generals or admirals. The Confederate government in Richmond took the

THE GENERAL AND THE JOURNALIST

Although relations between military commanders and newspaper reporters during the Civil War could be disharmonious, few generals were as hostile to the press as William T. Sherman. Newspaper correspondents believed that the First Amendment gave them complete freedom to report whatever they wished; Sherman, on the other hand, was infuriated when newspapers printed Union orders of battle and other sensitive military information prior to combat. In addition to giving away troop movements and positions, some reporters helped to spread rumors that Sherman was mentally ill. A reporter for the *New York Tribune* once remarked that "being a cat in hell without claws is nothing to [being] a reporter in General Sherman's army" (Brown 2004).

On one occasion, a field correspondent for the New York Herald named Thomas Knox published an account of the Union defeat at Chickasaw Bluffs in 1862 in direct defiance of Sherman's orders calling for secrecy. Upon receiving a copy of Knox's article from a Union naval officer, Sherman responded:

> The spirit of anarchy seems deep at work at the North, more alarming than the batteries that shell us from the opposite shore. I am going to have the correspondent of the *New York Herald* tried by court-martial as a spy, not that I want the fellow shot, but because I want to establish the principle that such people cannot attend our armies, in violation of orders, and defy us, publishing their garbled statements defaming officers who are doing their best, and giving information to the enemy. You of the Navy can control all who sail under your flag, whilst we of the Army are almost compelled to carry along in our midst a class of men who on government transports usurp the best accommodations on the boats ... and report their limited and tainted observations as the history of events they neither see nor comprehend. (U.S. Naval War Records 1911, p. 234)

Knox was duly court-martialed and sentenced to banishment from the Union's western theater of operations. He and his newspaper appealed to President Lincoln, who offered to revoke the court's sentence, provided that Grant, Sherman's superior, was willing to allow Knox to return to Union headquarters near Vicksburg. In a letter to Knox, Grant refused permission "unless General Sherman first gives his consent to your remaining" (Bowman 1865, p. 450). Knox then sent Lincoln and Grant's letters to Sherman, along with a written request for permission to remain. Sherman's reply was forthright:

> After having enunciated to me that newspaper correspondents were a fraternity bound together by a common interest that must write down all who stood in their way, and that you had to supply the public demand for news, true if possible, but false if your interests demanded it, I cannot be privy to a tacit acknowledgement of the principle.
>
> Come with sword or musket in your hand, prepared to share with us our fate in sunshine and storm, in prosperity and adversity, in plenty and scarcity, and I will welcome you as a brother and associate; but come as you now do, expecting me to ally the reputation and honor of my country and my fellow soldiers with you, as the representative of the press, which you yourself say makes so slight a difference between truth and falsehood, and my answer is, NEVER. (U.S. Congressional Serial Set 1887, p. 895)

Knox left the Vicksburg theater immediately and never returned.

REBECCA J. FREY

BIBLIOGRAPHY

Bowman, Samuel Millard, and Richard Biddle Irwin. Sherman and His Campaigns: A Military Biography. *New York: Charles B. Richardson, 1865.*

Brown, Dale E. "Sherman and the Reporter." Parameters (Autumn 2004).

U.S. Congressional Serial Set. Miscellaneous Documents. Washington, DC: United States Government Printing Office, 1887.

U.S. Naval War Records. Official Records of the Union and Confederate Navies in the War of the Rebellion. Series 1, vol. 24. January 1–May 17, 1863. Washington, DC: Government Printing Office, 1911.

same step. Scott did not, however, impose direct controls on the reporters' mail or on what they sent back to their editors.

Edwin Stanton (1814–1869), who became Lincoln's Secretary of War in January 1862, moved government censorship of the press to a higher level by putting all telegraph lines in Union territory, not just those coming out of Washington, under the direct control of the War Department. Moreover, war correspondents were required to sign formal pledges not to publish any material on restricted topics. Stanton was criticized heavily by the *New York Times* and other Northern newspapers for his gag orders; in addition, the news blackout undermined the administration's credibility by fueling the growth of wild rumors about plots to overthrow the government in Washington and similar conspiracy theories (Sears 1994, p. 21)

Military Censorship of Journalists

The third stage of press censorship in the North was a series of decisions taken by individual Union commanders to ban newspaper correspondents from their camps. Although General Sherman's hostility to "the set of dirty newspaper scribblers who have the impudence of Satan" is well known, other generals were equally distrustful of reporters (Sears 1994, p. 16).

General Henry Halleck, the senior commander of the Union forces at the Battle of Shiloh, set the precedent of banning newspaper reporters—these "unauthorized hangers-on"—from his camp on May 13, 1862 (Sears 1994, p. 22). And although Sherman's 1863 court martial of Thomas Knox, a reporter for the *New York Herald*, is the best-known instance of the army's suspicious attitude toward the press (Brown 2004), there were other instances of Union generals getting even with reporters who aroused their anger. In 1864, General George Meade not only expelled Edward Crapsey, a correspondent for the *Philadelphia Inquirer*, from his camp, but had the unfortunate reporter mounted on a mule and paraded around the camp wearing a placard that read "Libeler of the Press" while the regimental band played the "Rogue's March" (Finney 2003).

Censorship of the Press in the Confederacy

Most of the conflicts between freedom of the press and strategic military considerations were fought out in the Northern newspapers. There were two reasons for the relatively low level of press censorship in the South: the impact of the war on the size and frequency of publication of Southern newspapers; and consistent support for the Confederate government on the part of newspaper editors. With regard to the first factor, the South had only half as many newspapers as the North in 1861 and only a quarter of the Northern papers' circulation (Harris 1999, p. 12). Several major Southern newspapers ceased publication entirely during the war. The others dwindled from four to two pages per issue as a result of shortages of reporters as well as newsprint, as the South drafted more and more categories of able-bodied men for military service (Sears 1994, p. 19).

With regard to the second factor, few Southern editors took an oppositional stance toward the government in Richmond. Their support stood in sharp contrast to the adversarial attitude of many Northern newspapers toward the Lincoln administration, particularly such stridently Democratic newspapers as the *Chicago Times*, the *Cincinnati Enquirer*, and the *New York World* (Harris 1999, p. 22). As an example of the generally cooperative position of the Southern press, the editor of the *Charleston* (SC) *Mercury* sent the paper's correspondent in Richmond the following instructions in early 1862: "Be therefore, I suggest, as amiable as consistent with truth ... [and present] as much as possible of the bright side of things" (Sears 1994, p. 19).

BIBLIOGRAPHY

Brown, Dale E. "Sherman and the Reporter." *Parameters, U.S. Army War College Quarterly*, Autumn 2004, inside back cover.

"The Censorship of the Press." *Harper's Weekly*, May 17, 1862, p. 306.

Ex parte Milligan, 71 U.S. 2 (1866). Available online at http://caselaw.lp.findlaw.com/scripts/.

Finney, Torin R. "Reporting the American Civil War." First posted 2003; available online at *The Bohemian Brigade* [Civil War re-enactors who portray newspaper correspondents], http://www.bohemianbrigade.com/.

Harris, Brayton. *Blue and Gray in Black and White: Newspapers in the Civil War*. Washington, DC: Brassey's, 1999.

Lincoln, Abraham. Message to Congress, July 4, 1861. In *The Official Records of the Union and Confederate Armies*, Series IV, I, pp. 311–321. Washington, DC: Government Printing Office, 1880–1901. Available online at http://facweb.furman.edu/~benson/docs/lincoln.htm.

Lincoln, Abraham. Suspension of the writ of *habeas corpus* relating to the events in Baltimore. Washington, DC: Headquarters of the Army, April 27, 1861. Available online at http://www.civilwarhome.com/.

Lincoln, Abraham. Suspension of the writ of *habeas corpus* relating to the events in Missouri. Washington, DC: Headquarters of the Army, December 2, 1861. Available online at http://www.civilwarhome.com/.

Magna Carta (1215). Modern English translation with annotations available online at *Sources of English Constitutional Law*, http://www.constitution.org/.

Rehnquist, William H. *All the Laws but One: Civil Liberties in Wartime*. New York: Random House, 2000.

Rehnquist, William H. "Civil Liberty and the Civil War: The Indianapolis Treason Trials." Remarks delivered at the Indiana University School of Law-Bloomington, October 28, 1996. Available online at http://social.chass.ncsu.edu/.

Rehnquist, William H. Remarks at the 100th anniversary celebration of the Norfolk and Portsmouth Bar Association, Norfolk, Virginia, May 3, 2000. Available online at http://www.supremecourtus.gov/.

Sears, Stephen W. "The First News Blackout." *Civil War Chronicles* (Winter 1994): 16–23.

Taney, Roger B. *Ex parte Merryman*, 17 F. Cas. 144 (C.C.D. Md. 1861). Available online at http://www.tourolaw.edu/.

Rebecca J. Frey

■ Election of 1860

The election of 1860 did much to increase the inevitability of civil war. An article published in the *Charleston Mercury* on November 17, 1856, conveyed South Carolina's apprehensions about the new presidential election cycle: "The Presidential contest of 1856 is ended, and that of 1860 has just commenced. The struggle for the Presidency is over, and James Buchanan is elected, but the issues involved in the contest are not yet settled. These are yet in the womb of the future, and what the next four years may bring forth, we must wait and see, hoping for the best while we should be forearmed against the worst." The debates that shaped the election of 1860 comprised a referendum on the nation's past, present, and future. And the election's outcome stood to affect the daily lives of millions of Americans, as the future prospects for a united nation hung in the balance.

Parties and Candidates

On November 6, 1860, approximately 81 percent of eligible voters in America went to the polls to cast their ballot in support of one of four national candidates for president. In reality, none of the four could truly call themselves a national candidate. During the 1850s, congressional debates over the future expansion of slavery had increasingly divided the nation into slaveholding and non-slaveholding sections. At the beginning of the 1860 election, the Democrats were the only party with a national constituency—but they too would soon splinter.

American politics has been dominated by a two-party system throughout most of its history. During the antebellum period, the Whig and Democratic parties vied for national supremacy until the former collapsed during the early 1850s due to sectional strife within the party. Some mourned the Whig Party's demise; for example, the editor of *The Weekly Raleigh Register* (North Carolina) asserted, "The Whig party more than once had saved the country from impending ruin, in 1820, 1832, and in 1850. Without Henry Clay where would we have been?" (March 8, 1854).

As the Democratic Party splintered and the Republican Party gained additional support among Northern voters, former Whig and Know-Nothing Party members formed a new Constitutional Union Party. During their May convention, the delegates nominated John Bell of Tennessee as their presidential candidate. The party's ticket also included the famed orator and former Whig, William Everett of Massachusetts. The Constitutional Union Party had constituents in most Southern communities, but their principal base of support came from Upper South states that longed for the days of Senator Henry Clay of Kentucky and wanted to resolve the nation's sectional tensions. Although the Constitutional Union Party had no chance of seeing its candidate elected, it sill had enough influence to shape the outcome of both the Republican and Democratic Conventions. Republicans sought a moderate candidate who would appeal to former Whigs and Know-Nothing Party members in the North. Southern Democrats, already distrustful of Northern Democrats, wanted to select a candidate who would force Southerners to take a stand on what they considered to be the key election issues. They worried that a more moderate stance might attract additional voters into the Constitutional Union Party fold.

Left without a national party, many Southern former Whigs reluctantly entered into the Democratic fold, whereas in the North, the collapse of the Whig Party gave rise to a new national party, the Republican Party. Founded in 1854, the Republican Party was from its earliest beginnings a sectional party supported by an unprecedented coalition of abolitionists, free-soilers, free laborers, former Northern Democrats, and former Northern Whigs. In 1856 the party ran its first presidential campaign, nominating John C. Frémont, a famed explorer, military officer, and one-time senator and governor of California, as its candidate. While Frémont lost that election, his party's strong showing among the New England and upper Midwestern states, and its victory over the American-Know Nothing-Whig Party candidate, Millard Fillmore, the thirteenth President of the United States, showed that it could successfully attract voters in areas that had once been Democratic Party strongholds.

During the 1858 congressional elections, Abraham Lincoln, a little-known Illinois lawyer, former Whig, and one-term congressman, attracted national attention as the state's Republican Party candidate, running to unseat six-term Democratic Senator Stephen A. Douglas. Lincoln's "House Divided Speech," given following his acceptance as the party's candidate for the Senate, expressed the sentiments of both the party and its growing number of supporters. "I believe this government cannot endure," declared Lincoln, "permanently half *slave* and half free. … Either the *opponents* of slavery will arrest the further spread of it, and place it where the public mind shall rest in the belief that it is in course of ultimate extinction, or its *advocates* will push it forward, till it shall become lawful in *all* states, *old* as well as new—*North* as well as *South*. Have we no tendency to the latter condition?" (Basler, 1953, vol. 2, pp. 461–462). Even though Douglas emerged victorious from that campaign, Lincoln's well-fought challenge attracted the attention of the national Republican Party.

Lincoln's "Cooper Union Speech," delivered in February of 1860, further enhanced his newfound position as party spokesperson. "If [slavery] is right, we cannot justly object to its nationality—its universality; if it is wrong, they cannot justly insist upon its extension—its enlargement. All they ask, we could readily grant, if we thought slavery right; all we ask, they could as readily grant, if they thought it wrong. Their thinking it right, and our thinking it wrong, is the precise fact upon which depends the whole controversy. Thinking it right, as they do, they are not to blame for desiring its full recognition, as being right; but, thinking it wrong, as we do, can we yield to them?" (Basler, 1953, vol. 3, p. 549).

A piece of campaign propaganda from the election of 1860. A former senator from Maine, Hannibal Hamlin served as Abraham Lincoln's vice presidential running mate in the 1860 election. Both men supported the idea that laws for slavery should be consistent throughout the entire United States. *The Library of Congress.*

When the Republican Party met in Chicago in June 1860 to nominate a presidential candidate, the initial frontrunner was New York Senator William H. Seward, but his bid lost momentum as the members began to see the need for a less polarizing figure. Two years earlier, during a speech delivered in Rochester, New York, Seward had referred to the nation's sectional crisis as an "irrepressible conflict." Democrats cast Seward as a radical whose abolitionist zeal would bring the country to war. Northern voters did not see Lincoln as a radical. Indeed, his views on slavery, sectionalism, secession, and numerous other issues, as displayed during the Lincoln-Douglas debates (1858), appeared to be quite amorphous. On the issue of slavery, Lincoln's support of Congress's power to prohibit slavery in the territories permanently alienated Southern voters. Many Northern farmers who saw slavery as a threat to free labor shared Lincoln's views, however. While Northern farmers and industrial workers alike feared that emancipation might drive down wages and create massive unemployment, their anxieties were calmed by Lincoln's assurances that he would uphold the slaveholder's constitutional rights where the institution currently existed. Lincoln's nomination was also the result of the party's pragmatism. Republicans needed to win Illinois, a Democratic stronghold. Lincoln, rather than Seward, most appealed to Midwestern voters.

While the Democratic Party was still a national party at the start of the 1860 election, finding a candidate who could appease its Northern and Southern constituents proved to be an insurmountable obstacle. James Buchanan, the fifteenth President of the United States, did not seek a second term. Illinois Senator Stephen A. Douglas seemed to be the party's leading potential candidate. Douglas had spent the better part of his life preparing to become president. But his popularity had waned among Northern and Southern voters during the late 1850s. In the North, many believed that Douglas's support of popular sovereignty catered to Southern interests. On March 1854 a crowd in Cleveland, angered by Douglas's role in the proposed territorial expansion of slavery, hung "an effigy of Senator Douglas ... with the words, 'Stephen Arnold Douglas, hung for treason,' attached" (*Daily Cleveland Herald*, March 24, 1854). At the same time, statements made by Douglas during the 1858 senate campaign had alienated large segments of Southern voters. During a debate with Lincoln held in Freeport, Illinois, Douglas argued "the people have the lawful means to introduce it [slavery] or exclude it as they please, for the reason that slavery cannot exist a day or an hour anywhere, unless it is supported by local police regulations" (August 27, 1858). His views became known as the Freeport Doctrine. This version of popular sovereignty angered Southerners, who argued that the Constitution protected a slaveholder's right to transport his property anywhere in the country.

National events further divided the Democrats. In October of 1859, the abolitionist John Brown led an attack on a Federal arsenal at Harpers Ferry, Virginia. Brown intended to capture the arsenal's weapons and distribute them to slaves along the Shenandoah Valley, thus inciting a massive slave rebellion. Though his plan failed, Southerners saw the scheme as a product of Northern abolitionism and the Republican Party. Despite Northern Democrats' (as well as many Republicans') condemnation of Brown's actions, large numbers of their Southern counterparts entered the 1860 election season convinced that Northern interests threatened slavery and the Southern way of life.

In February of 1860, two months prior to the scheduled Democratic National Convention, Senator Jefferson Davis of Mississippi prepared a series of resolutions that became the Southern platform. Davis, who later served as the President of the Confederate States of America, called for the adoption of a federal slave code as a means of enforcing the recent *Dred Scott* Supreme Court ruling. Chief Justice Roger Taney's decision argued that Congress lacked the power to restrict slavery in federal territories. Davis now wanted a federal slave code that would ensure slaveholders' right to transport their slaves wherever they pleased. The Southern-sponsored federal slave code was a direct response to Douglas's Freeport Doctrine. Southern Democrats made it clear that if Douglas did not endorse a federal slave code, they would block his nomination.

When the national party convention convened at South Carolina Institute Hall in Charleston, South Carolina, on April 23 through May 3, 1860, Douglas and other Northern Democrats staunchly refused to include a federal slave code in their party platform, asserting that its insertion would alienate their Northern constituents. When Douglas's supporters rejected the Southern platform, a party of Deep South delegates, along with a handful of Upper South members, protested by walking out of the convention. The Alabama delegate and renowned "fire-eater" William Lowndes Yancey declared that the South was as a minority whose rights had been trampled upon by rising industrial powers.

> We have come here, with the twofold purpose of saving the country and of saving the Democracy; and if the Democracy will not lend itself to that high, holy and elevated purpose [,] ... it will be our duty to go forth and make an appeal to the loyalty of the country to stand by that Constitution which party organizations have deliberately rejected.... [The party's Northern leaders who] ask the people to vote for a party that ignores their rights, and dares not acknowledge them ... ought to be strung upon a political gallows higher than that ever erected for Haman. (Walther, 2006, pp. 249–252).

As Yancey led the Southern delegation out of the Charleston Convention, the national Democratic Party perished. Without a uniform platform that appealed to both Northern and Southern constituents, the Democratic Party appeared to be incapable of contending for the office of president in light of the ascendancy of the Republican Party.

On June 18, 1860, the Democratic Party reconvened its nominating convention in Baltimore, Maryland. Initially, only a handful of Southern delegates attended the meeting. Those who had walked out of the Charleston Convention had decided to hold their own meeting in Richmond, Virginia, on June 11. Hoping to somehow reform the national party, most of the Richmond delegates eventually traveled to Baltimore to participate in the Northern convention, but the split proved to be irrevocable. In Baltimore, the issue of endorsing a federal slave code remained the central divisive issue. Consequently, Northern Democrats nominated Stephen A. Douglas as their candidate for president, whereas Southern Democrats formed a Southern wing of the

Democratic Party with Vice President John C. Breckinridge of Kentucky as their presidential nominee. In an effort to appeal to Southern voters, Douglas selected a former Georgia governor, Herschel Johnson, to be his running mate.

The Campaign

The former Louisiana governor and prosecessionist Paul O. Hébert told the readers of *The Weekly Mississippian* that "Mr. Lincoln's election is a foregone conclusion.... 'What will the South do?' ... We have the power to bring these men—this aggressive majority—to rue with sorrow the day they forced us to the wall, and we *should do it*; *now* is the time" (November 7, 1860). Like Hébert, most Americans understood that the election of 1860 would only further aggravate the nation's sectional division. Astute observers understood that if Lincoln and the Republicans managed to win the collective electoral votes of the nation's non-slaveholding states, this gain would be sufficient to secure victory without garnering a single Southern supporter. The key to Lincoln's victory would be defeating Douglas in such pivotal states as Illinois and Pennsylvania, which had supported the Democratic candidate in 1856.

The 1860 election saw the introduction of what would prove to be a significant aspect of American politics. For the first time ever, a presidential candidate, Stephen A. Douglas, actively campaigned in person during a whirlwind tour that included stops in Pennsylvania, Wisconsin, Iowa, Michigan, Illinois, Missouri, Tennessee, Georgia, and Alabama. Typically, electors chosen by the party represented candidates locally, by making a select number of campaign speeches, writing newspaper editorials, or engaging in debate with the opposing party's local elector. Lincoln, Bell, and Breckinridge, the election's other candidates, made few public appearances. By and large, they relied on local electors to promote their campaigns. Douglas's campaign was aided by the nation's expanding railroad network, which allowed him to tour large sections of the country during a short period of time. During his trips, he made numerous campaign stops, frequently addressing a mixed crowd of supporters and critics. His behavior attracted sharp criticism from several newspaper editors who found his campaign to be unpresidential. "The movements of this most stupendous of all demagogues [Douglas] are laughable," wrote an editor for the Atchison, Kansas, newspaper *Freedom's Champion*. "The fellow is a bore. Without an idea that a statesman should be proud of.... It seems as if he feared that if he got hold of a new idea it would choke him to death. If he would only say something new, or even say his old things in a new way, it would be some relief" (September 22, 1860).

In a bold effort to rekindle support among Southern voters, Douglas embarked on a tour of the Deep South states of Georgia and Alabama. While Douglas did not achieve a broad base of support among Southern voters, he did garner significant amounts of local support in select counties. In Cass County, Georgia, for example, the editors of the *Cassville Standard* published several biographical sketches of Douglas in an attempt to convince locals of his southern sympathies. Such portrayals appeared in a few other regional newspapers. Most contained some account of Douglas's Pearl River, Mississippi, plantation home or made reference to his efforts to resolve the nation's sectional divide. When Douglas's Western and Atlantic Railroad train made an overnight stop in Kingston, Georgia, for fuel and water, crowds soon flocked to the town in anticipation of a Douglas speech. Here Douglas's inclusion of Herschel Johnson, a close friend of many locals, helped his cause. While Douglas attracted perhaps the largest crowd in the county's antebellum history, his efforts fell short of producing a local victory in the election. Other stops along the trip found residents less hospitable. In Montgomery, Alabama, an unidentified man hit Douglas with several eggs following a poorly received speech. Most Southern newspaper editors strongly condemned Douglas's campaign. The editor of the *Charleston Courier, Tri-Weekly*, for example, declared: "Keep it before the people that Stephen Arnold Douglas, who is coming South, to divide and distract the sons of the South, and sow discord among brethren, has lately made stumping tours through the leading Free-soil States, and had not one word to say against stealing the property of the South" (October 22, 1860).

Election Results

On November 6, 1860, voters across the nation went to the polls in record numbers to cast their ballots. The results displayed and foretold the nation's impending crisis. Lincoln won the election, receiving 39.8 percent of the popular vote and 180 electoral votes despite not appearing on the ballot in ten slave states. Douglas won the second-largest percentage of the popular vote with 29.5 percent, but managed only a meager twelve electoral votes, winning Missouri and a portion of New Jersey. The nation's slaveholding states, except Missouri, split their votes between Breckinridge and Bell. Perhaps most revealing was the fact that the electoral totals won by Breckinridge, Bell, and Douglas combined were still fifty-seven votes shy of Lincoln's total.

The Southern slaveholding states responded to Lincoln's election in piecemeal fashion. One week after the election, the residents of Aiken, South Carolina, angrily "turned out *en masse* to celebrate the event by a torch light procession.... All the residences along the line were filled with the fair sex, who sanctioned the proceedings.... Midway in the procession ... was the effigy of Abe Lincoln, with the following placard suspended in the right hand: 'Abe Lincoln First President Northern Confederacy.'" *(Charleston Courier Tri-Weekly*, November 15, 1860).

Similar acts occurred throughout the region. On December 20, 1860, the state of South Carolina seceded from the Union. By the time Lincoln delivered his Inaugural Address on March 4, 1861, seven slave states had followed suit. When Alabama seceded on January 11, 1861, their secession ordinance proclaimed that "the election of Abraham Lincoln ... to the office of president ... by a sectional party, avowedly hostile to the domestic institutions and to the peace and security of the people of the State of Alabama ... is a political wrong of so insulting and menacing a character as to justify" secession (Ordinances of Secession of the 13 Confederate States of America, 1861).

While historians remain divided over precisely when the Civil War became an "irrepressible conflict," the results of the election of 1860, as evidenced by the actions of seven slaveholding states, clearly shows that Lincoln's election only further aggravated existing sectional tensions. Even if the election did not directly push the nation into civil war, its results clearly hastened the South's journey toward disunion.

BIBLIOGRAPHY

Barney, William L. *Battleground for the Union: The Era of the Civil War and Reconstruction, 1848–1877.* Englewood Cliffs, NJ: Prentice Hall, 1990.

Basler, Roy P., ed. *The Collected Works of Abraham Lincoln*, vols. 2 and 3. New Brunswick, NJ: Rutgers University Press, 1953.

Donald, David Herbert. *Lincoln.* New York: Simon & Schuster, 1995.

Gienapp, William E. *The Origins of the Republican Party, 1852–1856.* New York: Oxford University Press, 1987.

Johannsen, Robert W. *Stephen A. Douglas.* New York: Oxford University Press, 1973.

Walther, Eric H. *William Lowndes Yancey and the Coming of the Civil War.* Chapel Hill: University of North Carolina Press, 2006.

Keith S. Hébert

Feminism

The word *feminism* is a modern word that came into use in the early twentieth century. It was not a term that individuals used during the Civil War. The ideas of feminism, however, existed during the Civil War era and before. Feminism is a belief in the theory of economic, social, and political equality of the sexes. Thus, anyone who advances equality can be considered feminist. The Civil War provides many examples of individuals and groups exhibiting feminist ideals. The reactions to these ideals show that nineteenth-century society was not ready for a feminist movement to take hold.

A Challenge to "True Womanhood"

In the nineteenth century the "cult of true womanhood" dictated societal expectations for women. According to historian Barbara Welter in her 1966 article "The Cult of True Womanhood: 1820–1860," the "four cardinal virtues" of true womanhood were piety, purity, submissiveness, and domesticity. Pious women acted as moral safeguards and submissive women kept good order in society. The loss of purity in a woman was so unnatural that she became a "fallen woman" unworthy of true womanhood. A true woman's place was in the private domestic sphere of the home, creating a moral haven for her husband and family. Any woman who stepped beyond the boundaries of true womanhood threatened to disrupt the social order, including wreaking havoc in the home. Southern women, both white and black, had additional restraints in a culture dominated by male honor, male power, and slavery.

The emergence of feminist action in the United States dates from the first women's rights convention at Seneca Falls, New York. In 1848 women's rights activist Elizabeth Cady Stanton (1815–1920) proclaimed in *The Declaration of Sentiments* that "all men and women are created equal." She proceeded to list grievances against the "tyranny of men," reproduced by Laura A. Belmonte in her 2007 book *Speaking of America: Readings in U.S. History*, that included obstacles to women's participation in economic independence, education, and the political process. The response to Seneca Falls was mixed. In its 1848 article "Woman's Rights," the Syracuse *Recorder* referred to the meeting as "excessively silly," and the *Oneida Whig* in "Bolting among the Ladies" regarded it as the "most shocking and unnatural incident ever recorded in the history" of womanhood. Abolitionist Frederick Douglass's (1818–1895) Rochester newspaper *North Star* had a favorable opinion of the convention, endorsing it in the article "The Rights of Women" by asserting that "Right is of no sex."

Competing Interests

During the Civil War, feminist activists put the issue of women's rights on hold to focus on the cause of Union and emancipation. The women's rights conventions held annually since 1848 abruptly stopped in 1861. Many women's rights activists who were also involved in the abolitionist movement struggled with which cause should have priority during the war, women's rights or emancipation? The debate over this question was fierce. Although reluctant at first, the most famous women's rights activist Susan B. Anthony (1820–1906) agreed that emancipation should be the first cause, stating in the 1863 "Resolutions and Debate" that "there is great fear expressed on all sides lest this war shall be made a

Susan B. Anthony (1820–1906) and Elizabeth Cady Stanton (1815–1902). After working toward the abolition of slavery, many leading female speakers of the period, such as Susan B. Anthony and Elizabeth Cady Stanton, sought to achieve full rights for women in American society. *Kean Collection/Hulton Archive/Getty Images*

war for the negro. I am willing that it shall be. It is a war to found an empire on the negro in slavery, and shame on us if we do not make it a war to establish the negro in freedom." Others were not so quick to sacrifice the rights of women for the rights of slaves. Ernestine Rose, a Polish immigrant and long-time women's activist, questioned the abandonment of women's rights, claiming in the same debate that while women "desire to promote human rights and human freedom ... in a republic based upon freedom, woman, as well as the negro, should be recognized as an equal with the whole human race."

On May 14, 1863, Stanton and Anthony formed the Woman's Loyal National League (WLNL), dedicated to a constitutional amendment that would end slavery forever. Although there was no mention of women's rights in the final resolution adopted by the WLNL, the organization hoped that debates on emancipation would logically move to debates on women's rights. Stanton and Anthony believed that the WLNL could exert political influence on Republican political candidates to push not only for the issue of emancipation but also later for the issue of women's rights. In many ways the WLNL existed to build an alliance with Republican leaders that could be beneficial to the women's fight for suffrage following the war. When Republican leaders refused to endorse women's suffrage after the war's end, choosing instead to pass a universal male suffrage amendment, Stanton and Anthony were furious. In 1866, they sent a petition for universal suffrage to Congress. When abolitionist Gerrit Smith (1797–1874) refused to endorse it, believing it would hurt the cause of black suffrage, Stanton responded, and William E. Gienapp reproduced in his 2001 edited work *The Civil War and Reconstruction: A Documentary Collection*, that Smith's action revealed that "to demand protection for woman against her oppressors, would jeopardize the black man's chance of securing protection against his oppressors" (p. 361).

Breaking Gender Roles

Some women challenged gender norms during the Civil War by disguising their gender in order to serve as soldiers. It is unclear how many women served in this capacity since neither the Union nor Confederate armies allowed women to legally enlist. It has been noted that the number of such was extremely small, estimated at a little more than 0.01 percent of the total number of soldiers and less than 0.003 percent of the total number of women in America at that time. Many women who served in this capacity were discovered early in their service and discharged. Others like Sarah Emma Edmonds, alias Franklin Thompson, and Albert D. J. Cashier served for years without discovery. Cashier lived as a man throughout much of her adult life before her sex was discovered in 1913. Edmonds left her Michigan unit in April 1863 after contracting malaria, fearful that she would be discovered and discharged. Consequently, her alias Franklin Thompson became a deserter. Following her recovery, Edmonds served as a female nurse for the duration of the war. Years after the war, Edmonds appealed to have "deserter" removed from Franklin Thompson's name and in 1886 was awarded a pension for her service. Reporting on the story, *The Galveston Daily News* in the 1886 article "Romance of the War" seemed more interested in Edmonds's service as a female following the war, what the paper referred to as "her proper character," rather than in her two-year service as a Michigan infantryman.

Women nurses and doctors also challenged nineteenth-century gender norms by caring for men who were strangers, men whose bodies were not only exposed but also violently wounded. For many women, medicine seemed a logical occupation, given that most of the medical care of the sick was done within the home by women. There was, however, a societal aversion to women becoming nurses and doctors, as it directly challenged the true womanhood ideals. Women nurses expressed not only satisfaction in their work but also disappointment at the hostility of male doctors. Gienapp reproduced the feminist sentiments of Cornelia Hancock, a Union Nurse at Gettysburg, describing her satisfaction with her role. Hancock, writing home to her sister in 1863, asserted: "I am as . . . dirty as a pig and as well as I ever was in my life." She added, "there is all in getting to do what you *want* to do and I am doing that" (p. 190). Southern women faced even more adversity, as nursing challenged the expected role of a southern lady. When Phoebe Yates Pember received an offer from the Confederate secretary of war to become a matron in the largest Confederate hospital, Chimborazo, in Richmond, Virginia, she was shocked to find that male doctors treated her with open hostility. Pember, Gienapp noted, claimed that "the natural idea that such a life would be injurious to the delicacy and refinement of a lady—that her nature would become deteriorated and her sensibilities blunted, was rather appalling" (p. 204). Mary Edwards Walker, a graduate of Syracuse Medical College, was unable to secure a military commission as a doctor, forcing her to offer her services as a volunteer. Not only did she receive the cold shoulder from Union men but Confederate as well. In 1864, while serving as a doctor in the field, Walker was captured. Her male attire initially fooled the Confederates but, as Elizabeth D. Leonard recounted in her 1994 book *Yankee Women: Gender Battles in the Civil War*, when they discovered Walker was a "female doctor," one Confederate captain stated that the troops were "amused and disgusted . . . at the sight of a *thing* that nothing but the debased and depraved Yankee nation could produce" (pp. 138–139).

The most famous Civil War battlefield nurse, Clara Barton (1821–1912), expressed feminist sentiments in her writing during and after the war. While motivated by the "patriot blood" of her father, Laura Belmonte reprinted in her 2007 book *Speaking of America: Readings in U.S. History*, Barton initially admitted that she struggled with her "sense of propriety" as a woman (p. 365). She quickly recanted in shame, writing that if nursing was too "rough and unseemly for a woman" it was equally "rough and unseemly for men" (p. 365). In a poem composed years after the Civil War, Barton captured the essence of not only women's expectations based on true womanhood, but also women's challenges to those expectations. The 1892 poem "The Women Who Went to the Field" mocks the true womanhood ideal when Barton notes that the expectation was that women would "scream at the sight of a gun" and "faint at the first drop of blood." The theme of true womanhood continues: "That the place for the women was in their homes, there to wait patiently, wait until victory comes." Barton proceeded to write that these women were "uninvited, unaided, [and] unsanctioned" but through their experiences came knowledge, and according to Barton "knowledge is power."

Women's roles in the workplace and at home significantly changed due to the absence of men. Women moved into the public sphere as paid employees and exercised greater responsibility on plantations and farms all over the North and South. In Cincinnati, Ohio, women workers protested their low wages to President Abraham Lincoln (1809–1865). Showing an astute sense of the market structure, the women requested that their work come directly from the government rather than from independent contractors who, Gienapp notes in his book, "fatten on their contracts by grinding immense profits out of the labor of their operatives" (p. 194). When southern women moved into government jobs they still found themselves bound by the cult of true womanhood. In Gienapp's book, Sally Putnam described the hundreds of "intelligent and deserving women" who sought government work, noting that "none could obtain employment . . . who could not furnish testimonials of intelligence and superior moral worth" (p. 206). In the South, women on the farms and plantations faced enormous hardships as a result of out-of-control inflation that made a loaf of bread unaffordable. On April 2, 1863, several thousand women marched to Richmond and took what they needed from bakers and grocers. When one participant was asked if the crowd was celebrating, Gienapp noted that the woman replied "we celebrate our right to live" (p. 200).

Socially bound by the ideals of true womanhood, some women chose to step beyond those boundaries to exercise feminist action during the Civil War. While suffragists increased their political knowledge, women soldiers, nurses, doctors, and workers challenged not only existing gender roles but also existing racial stereotypes.

BIBLIOGRAPHY

Barton, Clara. "The Women Who Went to the Field," 1892. Available from http://www.nps.gov/.

Belmonte, Laura A., ed. *Speaking of America: Readings in U.S. History*, vol. 1 to 1877, 2nd edition. Belmont, CA: Wadsworth, 2007.

Blanton, DeAnne. "Women Soldiers of the Civil War." *Prologue* 25, no. 1 (Spring 1993). Available from http://www.archives.gov/publications/prologue/.

"Bolting among the Ladies." *Oneida Whig*, August 1, 1848. American Treasures of the Library of Congress: The Seneca Falls Convention. Available from http://www.loc.gov/exhibits/treasures/.

Clinton, Catherine. *Tara Revisted: Women, War & the Plantation Legend*. New York: Abbeville Press, 1995.

Gienapp, William E., ed. *The Civil War and Reconstruction: A Documentary Collection.* New York: W. W. Norton, 2001.

Leonard, Elizabeth D. *Yankee Women: Gender Battles in the Civil War.* New York: W. W. Norton, 1994.

"Resolutions and Debates, Women's National Loyal League Meeting, New York City, May 14, 1863." Available from http://www.sscnet.ucla.edu/.

"The Rights of Woman." *North Star*, July 28, 1848. American Treasures of the Library of Congress: The Seneca Falls Convention. Available from http://www.loc.gov/exhibits/treasures/.

"A Romance of the War: Mrs. S. E. E. Seelye Wishes the Removal of the Charge of Desertion on Record against Her." *The Galveston Daily News*, March 25, 1886. Available from http://infotrac.galegroup.com/.

Tubman, Harriet. "Harriet Tubman's Letter to Abraham Lincoln," 1862.

Welter, Barbara. "The Cult of True Womanhood: 1820–1860." *American Quarterly* 18, no. 2 (Summer 1966): 151–174.

"Woman's Rights." *The Recorder*, August 3, 1848. American Treasures of the Library of Congress: The Seneca Falls Convention. Available from http://www.loc.gov/exhibits/.

Lisa Guinn

■ Lectures and Speeches

LECTURES AND SPEECHES: AN OVERVIEW

Before the first shot was fired on Fort Sumter, the war proved divisive within each side. Whether in drawing rooms or over factory din, Northerners and Southerners argued. They looked to two men, President Abraham Lincoln and Confederate President Jefferson Davis, to galvanize their armies and lead them to victory.

Jefferson Davis's Resignation from the Senate

Jefferson Davis resigned from the U.S. Senate on Monday, January 21, 1861, twelve days after Mississippi, his home state, seceded from the Union. The secession effectively ended his tenure in the Senate and cast the proud and often overbearing Davis into uncertainty (Kagan and Hyslop 2006, pp. 50–51). The noted Civil War historian Shelby Foote observed that Davis's public glory was shadowed by private tragedy and sorrow. Like his adversary, Abraham Lincoln, Davis was born in Kentucky and lived in a log cabin. Though not accomplished as a student, he was liked and admired by his classmates. He graduated from West Point in 1828 still a private, a mere twenty-third out of a class of thirty-four. He was widowed after three months of marriage when his first wife, Knox Taylor, succumbed to a fever that had stricken them both. Davis recovered from the fever but never lost the gaunt, pallid look of a survivor of a near-mortal illness (Foote 1958, vol. 1, pp. 5–8).

Though Davis considered himself more of a military leader than a statesman, he entered politics nonetheless. Contributing to the noisy antebellum rhetoric that deepened the chasm between the North and the South, a defiant Davis declared on the eve of Lincoln's election in November 1860: "I glory in Mississippi's star. ... But before I would see it dishonored I would tear it from its place, to be set on the perilous ridge of battle as a sign around which her bravest and best shall meet the harvest home of death" (Foote 1958, vol. 1, p. 4). Later, when Davis heard the news of Mississippi's secession, he waited and wondered whether he would be arrested as a traitor, which he hoped would give him the opportunity to test the right of secession in the federal courts. He never doubted the right of secession, just its wisdom, as the threat of war became increasingly probable. Thus when Davis rose from his seat in the Senate to declare his resignation and confirm the secession of Mississippi from the Union, his somber demeanor lacked the bluster of his November speech (Foote 1958, vol. 1, pp. 1–2, 4). For now he realized the dangers that lay ahead.

Addressing President Lincoln and the Senate in a voice that faltered at the start but grew stronger, he declared:

> We but tread in the paths of our fathers when we proclaim our independence and take the hazard ... not in hostility to others, not to injure any section of the country, not even for our own pecuniary benefit, but from the high and solemn motive of defending and protecting the rights we inherited, and which it is our duty to transmit unshorn to our children. (Foote 1958, vol. 1, p. 5)

Using the lion as a metaphor for England and a bear as a symbol of the Union, Davis continued: "[W]e will invoke the God or our fathers who delivered them from the power of the lion, to protect us from the ravages of the bear: and thus putting our trust in God and in our own firm hearts and strong arms, we will vindicate the right as best we may." He concluded by stating, "Mr. President and Senators, having made the announcement which the occasion seemed to me to require, it remains only for me to bid you a final adieu" (Foote 1958, vol. 1, p. 5).

First Inaugural Address, Abraham Lincoln

With full understanding of the importance of his inaugural speech, Abraham Lincoln tried to avoid offending Southerners and people in slave states that had not seceded by March 1861, such as Virginia and Maryland. His strategy was not only intended to mollify Southerners but also to make the Confederacy look like the aggressor if it refused to preserve the peace. Thus the North would be more likely to blame the secessionists and then agree to war against them. Accordingly, Lincoln reminded all listeners on Inauguration Day, March 4, 1861, that the Constitution is the supreme law of the land. Thus changing the government established by the Constitution would require either an amendment to the Constitution or a revolution to overthrow it. Lincoln then expressed willingness to accept an amendment to uphold slavery in states where it now existed. But if states insisted on tearing apart the Union, then as President he had the authority to wage war on those in rebellion. He would take no action, however, while a chance of peace existed (Kagan and Hyslop 2006, p. 54). "[T]he government will not assail you, unless you first assail it" (McPherson 1988, p. 262). "The power confided to me will be used to hold, occupy, and possess the property and places belonging to the government" (Faragher et al. 2002, p. 450).

Still, Lincoln sought to assuage disgruntled Southerners: "We must not be enemies. Though passion may have strained, it must not break our bonds of affection." Lincoln continued: "The mystic chords of memory, stretching from every battle-field, and patriot grave, to every living heart and hearthstone, all over this broad land, will yet swell the chorus of the Union, when again touched, as surely they will be, by the better angels of our nature" (McPherson 1988, p. 263).

The reaction to Lincoln's address was mixed. People heard in the speech the ideas they chose to hear. Many Northerners hailed its moderation, firmness, and effort to reach out to the South. On the other hand, many in the South deemed it a declaration of war (McPherson 1988, p. 263). Meanwhile, people across the country waited and watched day by day for the next significant act that would determine whether the country went to war. They had only to wait until the next month; the Confederates opened fire on the Union-occupied Fort Sumter in South Carolina, on April 12, 1861. When Union forces fired back, the American Civil War began.

First Inaugural Address, Jefferson Davis

While the Confederate Constitution drafted in February 1861 copied the U.S. Constitution verbatim in most areas, it permitted the Confederate President only one six-year term. Jefferson Davis appeared to be the ideal candidate—an experienced statesman as a senator and former secretary of war, and most importantly, a secessionist. Davis accepted the candidacy out of a sense of duty and honor, not because he sought it or even wanted it. The elections for the provisional government, a one-chamber congress, and a provisional president, took place in November 1861. Davis was only the provisional president until his inauguration on February 18, 1862 (McPherson 1988, pp. 257–259). Although adult Southern white males were given the right to vote for the Confederate President, it was a feeble attempt at democracy since only one candidate was proposed by the state delegations.

The newly elected Davis, when first introduced to a cheering crowd, imprudently crowed: "The time for compromise has now passed . . . The South is determined to maintain her position, and make all who oppose her smell Southern powder and feel Southern steel" (McPherson 1988, p. 259). The bellicose declaration affected the lives of many people—Northerners and people in the Border States and upper South, who were all easily alarmed and worried by the prospect of war. Though the election of Abraham Lincoln, a Northern Republican, had prompted several Southern states to secede, the threats of the Confederate President made Americans anxious over the possibility of bloodshed.

Not surprisingly, Davis presented a more reserved message in his inaugural address, when he stated that the Confederacy possessed peaceful intentions and welcomed any states that "may seek to unite their fortunes to ours" (McPherson 1988, p. 259). Davis never mentioned slavery in his speech, instead extolling the agrarian life of the South. He asserted, "It is joyous in the midst of perilous times to look around upon a people united in heart, where one purpose of high resolve animates and actuates the whole, where the sacrifices to be made are not weighed against honor and right and liberty and equality." Continuing, he said: "Obstacles may retard, but they cannot long prevent the progress of a movement sanctified by its justice and sustained by a virtuous people. Reverently let us invoke the God of our fathers to guide and protect us in our efforts to perpetuate the principles which by His blessing they were able to vindicate, establish, and transmit to their posterity." He said in closing: "With the continuance of His favor, ever gratefully acknowledged, we may hopefully look forward to success, to peace, and to prosperity" (Foote 1958, vol. 1, pp. 40–41).

The people of the Deep South reacted with pride in their new leader, thankful they had chosen well. Day after day they boasted of his trim, erect figure, his handsome features, his eloquent oration, and his charm and dignity of manner (Foote 1958, vol. 1, p. 40). And Davis worked hard to maintain a connection to the

An illustration of Jefferson Davis's inauguration. During his inauguration speech after winning the presidency of the Confederacy, Davis emphasized the South's desire to peacefully coexist with their Northern neighbors and be allowed the liberty to make decisions that reflected their beliefs. *HIP/Art Resource, NY*

people of the South. He made a point of staying personally accessible and appealing directly to Southerners by addressing crowds in his many visits throughout the South. In the two years after his election he visited all the Confederate states, many of them twice. In contrast, Lincoln rarely left Washington, choosing instead to concentrate on directing military affairs (Foote 1958, vol. 1, p. 826).

The Emancipation Proclamation

President Lincoln harbored strong antislavery sentiments, yet he respected the constitutional rights of slaveholders. Pressure from abolitionists persuaded him to back the emancipation of slaves—if not from a moral standpoint, then as a military strategy to show that the Union stood firm against slavery (*American Presidents* 1992, p. 87). So Lincoln wrote the Emancipation Proclamation, yet waited for a Union victory to declare it. When the Union defeated the Confederacy at the Battle of Antietam in Maryland in September 1862, Lincoln found his opportunity. On September 22, 1862, he issued the proclamation that freed slaves in states still in rebellion as of January 1, 1863 (Faragher et al. 2002, p. 465). The proclamation declared that slaves "shall be then, and thenceforward, and forever free; and the executive government of the United States, including the military and naval authority thereof, will recognize and maintain the freedom of such persons" (Kagan and Hyslop 2006, p. 171).

The Emancipation Proclamation did not apply to Union-occupied areas of the Confederacy or to slave states outside the Confederacy. Though the proclamation affected slaves outside the reach of the Federal armies, the significance of the decree forced Europe to favor the Union for moral reasons and impelled slaves to flee their masters in Confederate states and seek refuge in the North or in Union-occupied areas (Kagan and Hyslop 2006, pp. 170–172). Although Lincoln possessed the power to issue the Emancipation Proclamation, the Civil War historian Bruce Catton asserted that Lincoln knew that the document had to be ratified by "the tacit consent of the people at home and by the active endorsement of the soldiers in the field" (Catton 1960, p. 378). The Thirteenth Amendment made the act of emancipation a part of the Constitution. Although Congress endorsed the amendment, it was not until after Lincoln's death that a sufficient number of states ratified it. On December 6, 1865, Georgia became the twenty-seventh state to ratify the Thirteenth Amendment.

Lincoln relied upon his army to back him. With the exception of some abolitionist regiments, however, most Union soldiers were indifferent to slavery; instead, they fought for the Union. Once the proclamation was issued, some soldiers from the border states and other areas sympathetic to the South opposed the freedom of blacks. Still, by the end of the war, 180,000 black men had fought for the Federals (Catton 1960, pp. 378–379).

The response by the Confederacy was deadly. Confederate President Jefferson Davis responded to the Emancipation Proclamation by telling the Confederate Congress that it was "the most execrable measure in the history of guilty man." Then the Confederacy began to capture black Union officers and soldiers in order to execute them (McPherson 1988, p. 566). It is no wonder that Davis was tried as a criminal after the war and sentenced to prison.

The paramount effect of the Emancipation Proclamation was not just that it freed slaves but that it also provided the North with a dual purpose for fighting—to reunite the nation and to extend human freedom—goals that changed the character of the war (Catton 1960, p. 249). And it was this proclamation that affected so many thousands of lives, none more important than those of liberated slaves. The Emancipation Proclamation also gave Northerners a moral and emotional reason to back the war. Now they knew that lives lost, injured, and absent represented freedom for others as well as preservation of the ideal of a united nation.

The proclamation also affected the South. Southerners previously accustomed to the luxury of commanding forced labor now had to do for themselves. Slaves had provided the foundation of the Southern agrarian economy; without them, the pampered and the oppressive were forced to step into their shoes and provide the lost labor of the slave. Not surprisingly, the Southern economy crashed, not to recover for two more generations. The preservation of the ideal of a Confederate nation faltered with the Emancipation Proclamation, and then died under the weight of the Union battle victories that followed.

Lincoln's Gettysburg Address

Once a hired laborer mauling rails on a flatboat along the Mississippi River, later a shopkeeper and self-taught lawyer, Abraham Lincoln rose from a log cabin to the White House in our country's most divisive and catastrophic time—the Civil War. And amid the turmoil of bloodshed and animosity, he delivered one of the best-known speeches in U.S. history, the Gettysburg Address. The opening lines are unforgettable: "Four score and seven years ago our fathers brought forth, upon this continent, a new nation, conceived in Liberty, and dedicated to the proposition that all men are created equal" (Kagan and Hyslop 2006, p. 244).

The national cemetery in Gettysburg, Pennsylvania, was dedicated on November 19, 1863. The tremendous significance of the Union victory at Gettysburg in July 1863 had garnered national interest and drew crowds to the parade and cemetery site. President Lincoln, who wrote and polished the speech over several weeks, delivered his brief yet powerful message at the dedication after the famous orator Edward Everett had spoken for two hours (Catton 1960, pp. 330–331). With concise eloquence, President Lincoln honored the sacrifices of the soldiers and urged continued support for the war: "The world will little note, nor long remember what we say here, but it can never forget what they did here. It is for us the living, rather, to be dedicated here to the unfinished work which they who fought here have thus far so nobly advanced" (Kagan and Hyslop 2006, p. 244).

Lincoln's speech made clear that the significance of the war went beyond the dispute over slavery—the war had put democracy and the underlying historical values of American society on trial. Lincoln urged renewed commitment to the task of winning the war and reuniting the nation through the sacrifices of the fallen:

> It is rather for us to be here dedicated to the great task remaining before us—that from these honored dead we take increased devotion to that cause for which they gave the last full measure of devotion—that we here highly resolve that these dead shall not have died in vain—that this nation, under God, shall have a new birth of freedom—and that government of the people, by the people, for the people, shall not perish from the earth." (Catton 1960, pp. 331, 437–439)

Lincoln knew that the combined Union victories at Gettysburg and Vicksburg (the latter having taken place on July 4, 1863) had altered the course of the war in favor of the North. Yet if Unionists failed to support the war and withstand the casualties, then the Union battle triumphs would have been in vain. If Lincoln had lost the presidential election the next year, his successor might negotiate concessions to the South. In writing the Gettysburg Address, Lincoln sought to rally the North to fight to preserve the Union (Kagan and Hyslop 2006, p. 245). Many people learned that Gettysburg was the bloodiest and mightiest battle ever waged on American soil, costing the two armies 50,000 casualties, though few understood its importance. The historian Bruce Catton maintained that the deeper significance of Gettysburg was not understood at once by those who heard the president's address; the crowd at the cemetery dedication in 1863 failed to appreciate the full significance of Lincoln's words (Catton 1960, p. 437). Most observers paid more attention to the photographer setting up his equipment than they did to the speech. When Lincoln finished he received only scant polite applause. The initial response by critics and the media was mixed, though it changed to positive in the days after the speech (Foote 1958, vol. 1, pp. 832–833).

Lincoln's second inaugural address. After winning reelection in 1864, Lincoln stressed that at the end of the Civil War, the North and South should look to rebuild a unified nation, as each side had suffered greatly and needed no further punishment. *General Photographic Agency/Getty Images*

Only after some time for reflection did people of the North heed the president's words and understand the importance of sustained daily commitment to the war effort.

Second Inaugural Address, Abraham Lincoln

By early 1865, the territory of the Confederacy had been reduced to North and South Carolina and southern Virginia, with the Confederate army dead, in prison, or otherwise in disarray. President Lincoln won reelection intent on finishing the war by bringing the South to its knees. Yet in his second inaugural address he conveyed a conciliatory and visionary tone. Lincoln surmised that the four years of war could be summarized as one side trying to destroy the Union while the other side tried to hold it together (McPherson 1988, p. 859).

President Lincoln reasoned that both sides had borne the cost of war, had shared the blame for it, and should celebrate the end of it. A humane peace was due both sides—no punishment should be meted out to the South. Likewise, all must accept the fact that slavery no longer existed; by March 1865 Congress had passed the Thirteenth Amendment, which made slavery unconstitutional, and eighteen states had already ratified the amendment.

Lincoln acknowledged the mystery of the cause and the impact of the war: "Neither side," he said, "expected for the war the magnitude or the duration which it has already attained. Neither anticipated that the cause of the conflict might cease with, or even before, the conflict itself should cease." "Both [sides] read the same Bible and pray to the same God, and each invokes His aid against the other.... The prayers of both could not be answered; that of neither has been answered fully. The Almighty has His own purposes" (Catton 1960, pp. 581, 584).

In the shortest inaugural speech since George Washington's second inaugural address, Lincoln, a master of the English language, stated:

> With malice toward none; with charity for all; with firmness in the right, as God gives us to see the right, let us strive to finish the work we are in; to bind up the nation's wounds; to care for him who shall have borne the battle, and for his widow, and his orphan—to do all which may achieve and cherish a just and lasting peace, among ourselves and with all nations. (Foote 1958, vol. 3, p. 813)

As with the Gettysburg Address, initial reaction to the inaugural address was mixed but then turned positive. A Pennsylvania resident said of the address: "While the sentiments are noble, [Lincoln's address] is one of the most awkwardly expressed documents I ever read—if it be correctly printed. When he knew it would be read by millions all over the world, why under the heavens did he not make it a little more creditable to American scholarship?" (Foote 1958, vol. 3, p. 814). On the contrary, reaction in Great Britain was favorable. The Duke of Argyll wrote: "It was a noble speech, just and true, and solemn. I think it has produced a great effect in England." Meanwhile, the London *Spectator* proclaimed: "No statesman ever uttered words stamped at once with the seal of so deep a wisdom and so true a simplicity" (Foote 1958, vol. 3, p. 814).

Lincoln had the awkward, if not contradictory, task of promising that the war would continue to the full extent of Southern stubbornness, yet at the same time promise future peace and unification. He must have succeeded to some extent, as many have compared his second inaugural address to the cogent eloquence of the Gettysburg address. Though Lincoln was assassinated before he could implement his plan for reconstructing the nation, he did experience the satisfaction of Confederate surrender the very next month. Many Americans, though they may have read or heard the words of the president and later rejoiced at the end of the war, were burdened with the loss of fathers, husbands, sons, and brothers. They replanted and rebuilt and recovered, or at least tried to—for the bloody acrimony had devastated the land, its traditions, and the hearts and souls of an entire generation.

BIBLIOGRAPHY

The American Presidents. Danbury, CT: Grolier Incorporated, 1992.

Catton, Bruce. *The American Heritage Picture History of the Civil War.* New York: American Heritage Publishing Co., 1960.

Davis, William C. *Jefferson Davis: The Man and his Hour.* New York: HarperCollins, 1991.

Faragher, John Mack, Mari Jo Buhle, Daniel Czitrom, and Susan H. Armitage. *Out of Many: A History of the American People.* Upper Saddle River, NJ: Prentice Hall, 2002.

Foote, Shelby. *The Civil War: A Narrative.* 3 vols. New York: Random House, 1958.

Kagan, Neil, and Stephen G. Hyslop. *Eyewitness to the Civil War: The Complete History from Secession to Reconstruction.* Washington, DC: National Geographic, 2006.

McPherson, James. *Battle Cry of Freedom.* New York: Oxford University Press, 1988.

Oates, Stephen B. *With Malice toward None: The Life of Abraham Lincoln.* New York: HarperPerennial, 1994.

Sandburg, Carl. *Abraham Lincoln.* New York: Harcourt, 1982.

Judith P. Bruce

GETTYSBURG ADDRESS

On November 19, 1863, President Abraham Lincoln delivered a short oration at the dedication ceremony at the National Cemetery at Gettysburg, Pennsylvania. He had been invited to present "a few appropriate remarks" (Wills 1992, p. 25) "to perform this last solemn act to the soldiers dead on the Battle Field" and his speech was not expected to take long (Boritt 2006, p. 41). The principal oration was to be delivered by Edward Everett (1794–1865), the former president of Harvard and a well-known speaker who had gained fame in his speeches dedicating several Revolutionary War sites. Everett spoke for two hours but his speech is little noted nor remembered; Lincoln's 272 words, delivered in the space of approximately three minutes, have shone for generations across the ensuing century and have had an impact on audiences around the world.

It is difficult to reconstruct the immediate impact of Lincoln's words either upon the crowd at Gettysburg or on those who would read them in the newspapers in the weeks after the ceremony—though not for want of scholarly discussion. William E. Barton, a Lincoln scholar writing in the 1950 edition of his history, *Lincoln at Gettysburg*, observed:

> As to the effect of its delivery, there is equally impressive proof that the address was several times interrupted by applause and that there was prolonged applause at the close; that there was applause at the close only and that it was perfunctory; that there was no applause because people who heard the address were disappointed in it; and that there was no applause because the occasion was so solemn and the address was so impressive that applause would have seemed profane. (1950, p. iii)

In an earlier biography of Lincoln, Barton described the reaction to the speech in similar fashion:

> The address was received without enthusiasm and left the crowd cold and disappointed; it was received in a reverent silence too deep for applause; it was received with feeble and perfunctory applause

An illustration depicting Lincoln's delivery of the Gettysburg Address. To honor the hundreds of war dead, President Abraham Lincoln delivered a speech at the dedication of the Gettysburg National Cemetery. Though just over two minutes long, the address has become one of the most famous in American history. *The Library of Congress.*

> at the end, but it was the man and not the address that was applauded; it was received with applause in several places and followed by prolonged applause. (1925, p. 218)

Positive Press Reactions

The contradictions surrounding the reactions to the speech that Barton identified persist to this day. Accounts in newspapers of the day vary according to the partisanship of the paper. Press reactions would have been of great importance to Lincoln for he realized the press's power. One acknowledgment of this recognition is that several members of the press had been invited to sit on the speakers' platform at Gettysburg (Boritt 2006, p. 57). A professor visiting from England remarked upon the reach of the press and noted that American farmers were avid readers of newspapers; nearly a third of all the newspapers in the world at that time were published in America (p. 59). People would often read papers aloud to others, guaranteeing that the reports in the press would spread to the furthest reaches of the country and even to the illiterate. Lincoln would have been aware of these realities and probably anticipated that his speech would be read or heard by thousands more than were present at Gettysburg.

The spectrum of reaction in the press was wide. The *Boston Herald* reported that the speech had been interrupted five times for applause and that at its conclusion the president received "long continued applause" (November 20, 1863, p. 2). This version apparently circulated in New England papers sympathetic to the president, as a nearly identical description appeared in the *Farmer's Cabinet*, an Amherst, New Hampshire, paper six days later (November 26, 1863, p. 2). The New Hampshire paper added that the crowd then gave three cheers for the president and governors present. This description is nearly identical to the front page story in the November 21 edition of the *Chicago Tribune,* which reported: "The conclusion of the President's remarks was followed by immense applause, and three cheers given for him, as also three cheers for the Governors of the States" (November 21, 1863, p.1).

Barton quotes several papers that were effusive in their praise of the president's speech and recognized its power, elegance, and impact. The *Springfield* (MA) *Republican* wrote on November 20: "... the rhetorical honors of the occasion were won by President Lincoln.

His little speech is a perfect gem; deep in feeling, compact in thought and expression and tasteful and elegant in every word and comma." Similarly, the *Providence Journal* asked, "But could the most elaborate and splendid oration be more beautiful, more touching, more inspiring than those thrilling words of the President?" The *Philadelphia Evening Bulletin* editorialized, "It is warm, earnest, unaffected and touching. Thousands who would not read the long elaborate oration of Mr. Everett will read the President's few words, and not many will do it without a moistening of the eye and a swelling of the heart" (Barton 1925, p. 222). Similarly, the *Chicago Tribune's* reporter wired from Harrisburg, Pennsylvania, "The dedicatory remarks by President Lincoln will live among the annals of man." Barton believes that this simple line is the first written acknowledgment of the power and eloquence of what would come to be known as the Gettysburg Address (p. 116).

Negative Press Reactions

Democratic and Copperhead papers, opposed to Lincoln's administration and the war, were generally bitterly critical when they reported Lincoln's remarks at all. The Harrisburg *Patriot and Union* reported, "We pass over the silly remarks of the President; for the credit of the nation we are willing that the veil of oblivion shall be dropped over them and that they shall no more be repeated or thought of" (Barton 1950, p. 115). The *Chicago Times*, which had been suspended for one day by military order and reinstated by Lincoln, attacked the speech, and of the president's remarks on the front page stated simply, "President Lincoln made a few remarks upon the occasion." In an editorial on November 23, the paper accused the president of mocking the Union dead by misstating the cause for which they had died—the Union—and not freedom or equality for blacks. "How dared he, then, standing on their graves, misstate the cause for which they died, and libel the statesmen who founded the government? They were men possessing too much self-respect to declare that negroes were their equals, or were entitled to equal privileges" (Mitgang 2000, p. 361).

Similarly the *Register* from Springfield, Illinois, Lincoln's hometown, printed only the first two lines of the speech and then attacked the president, saying,

> If the above extract means anything at all, it is that this Nation was created to secure the liberty of the negro as well as of the white race, and dedicated to the proposition that all men, white and black, were placed, or to be placed, upon terms of equality. This is what Mr. Lincoln means to say, and nothing else, and when he uttered the words he knew that he was falsifying history, and enunciating an exploded political humbug (Barton 1925, p. 220).

Curiously, it seems that the Copperhead papers were the first to identify the true political importance of the speech, however vituperatively. The *Chicago Times*, along with the *Detroit Free Press*, the *Indiana State Sentinel*, and the New York *World* recognized the true impact and meaning of Lincoln's words. The speech is a war speech; in it Lincoln must comfort the bereaved, assure them that their dead have not died in vain, and give them courage to continue the struggle. Lincoln accomplishes this eloquently but he also suggests a change in the war's aims and in the true provenance of the country. The war is now undertaken not only to preserve the Union but also to continue a great experiment—to test whether a government can maintain the proposition of equality (Wills 1992, p. 37). Simply put, four score and seven years before the dedication of the cemetery at Gettysburg was 1776; Lincoln is clearly referring to Jefferson's words in the Declaration of Independence. He elevates the self-evident truths of the Declaration over the legal compromises of the Constitution and in three minutes restates the foundation of the country. It is the proposition that all men are created equal that must bind the disparate elements of the nation together. The editors of the Copperhead papers were violently opposed to this interpretation of history, but it is Lincoln's vision that will prevail and the speech marks perhaps the most concise and clearest definition of democracy extant.

Despite some favorable reaction in the press, however, coverage of Lincoln's remarks was not widespread. Most journalists present at the dedication did not offer detailed commentary on the speech, however friendly they may have been toward Lincoln. Their editors back home did the same, mostly contenting themselves with printing the text of the address. Most of the Democratic papers, however, tried to hide or ignore the President's speech (Boritt 2006, pp. 140–141).

Robert Reid, a Civil War historian, examined the files of 260 contemporary newspapers that covered the president's speech and corroborated Barton's earlier conclusion that reaction varied markedly (1967, p. 51). Reid also noted that press reactions were closely correlated to two primary variables: the political stance of the paper and its frequency of publication. According to Reid, weeklies gave little coverage to the ceremony while dailies typically covered the dedication. This difference may have simply been a matter of capacity. Weeklies in the Civil War era averaged four pages in length and half of those were given over to advertisements. It may be that the dailies, large metropolitan papers, simply had more space. In all cases where the event was reported, relatively more space was devoted to Everett's speech. Reid reports that in Republican papers 40 percent placed Lincoln's speech on the front page while 62 percent gave that placement to Everett's speech. In papers classified as anti-administration, 55 percent placed Everett's speech on the front page while only 14 percent placed Lincoln's there (Reid 1967, p. 53).

First page of the second draft of the Gettysburg Address. The Gettysburg Address was given by President Abraham Lincoln at the dedication ceremony at the National Cemetery at Gettysburg, PA. *MPI/Hulton Archive/Getty Images*

Eyewitness Accounts

Reminiscences of people who were present at Gettysburg that day mirror the newspaper reports in their variability. Anna Morris Ellis Holstein, a nurse at a hospital in Gettysburg, described her experience at the ceremony very matter-of-factly: "... we were so fortunate as to have a place directly in front and within a few feet of our martyred President, and there heard distinctly every word he uttered of that memorable speech, which will last while the Republic endures" (Holstein 1867, p. 54). John Russell Young, who had been dispatched to Gettysburg by the *Philadelphia Press* to report on the occasion, recounted in an 1887 letter to the editor that "very few heard what Mr. Lincoln said, and it is a curious thing that his remarkable words should have made no impression at the time." Young repeated the story of the hapless photographer who was positioning his equipment to take the president's photograph and missed his opportunity because Lincoln's speech was so short. According to Young, many on the platform were more entertained by the photographer's evident distress at his failure than were interested in the president's address (Young 1886).

Emory Sweetland, detailed by his Union Army unit to care for the wounded at a military hospital in Gettysburg, was also present for the dedication. In a talk to fellow veterans, he recalled that "I was present and I heard it. It made an impression on my mind that will never be effaced. He continued to speak in the same eloquent manner a few minutes and sat down amid silence like death" (Dunkelman 1994, pp. 48–49). Though there is little doubt that Sweetland was present at Gettysburg, in his talk he confused the dedication of the cemetery with the laying of a cornerstone there, which did not take place until after Lincoln's assassination. This confusion casts some doubt on the accuracy of his remembrance.

On the other hand, Robert Bloom related a less enthusiastic response: "A Gettysburg college student who heard [Lincoln] and remarked to a companion, 'Well, Mr. Lincoln's speech was simple, appropriate, and right to the point, but I don't think there was anything remarkable about it'" (Bloom 1981, p. 773).

The Associated Press reporter present at the dedication, Joseph Gilbert, recalled in 1917 that the audience stood mute, listening reverently while Lincoln spoke. "It was not a demonstrative nor even an appreciative audience. Narratives of the scene have described the tumultuous outbursts of enthusiasm accompanying the President's utterances. I heard none. There was no outward manifestation of feeling. His theme did not invite holiday applause, a cemetery was not the place for it, and he did not pause to receive it" (Barton 1925, p. 214).

Colonel Clark Carr, a member of the Cemetery Commission from Illinois who was also present for the President's speech, remarked that the insertion of applause in newspaper transcripts of speeches was an "invariable custom of the time... Except as he concluded, I did not observe it, and at the close the applause was not especially marked. The occasion was too solemn for any kind of boisterous demonstration" (Carr 1909, p. 60).

In a letter to the editor of the Manchester (New Hampshire) *Mirror*, and reprinted in the *New York Times* on July 3, 1887, twenty-four years after the battle, a writer identified as W. C. K., who claimed to have been present at the speech as part of the "guard of honor," recounted his experience there:

> The speech was not read. Mr. Lincoln held a piece of paper crumpled in his hand, but did not once

> refer to it while speaking ... He spoke without the slightest hesitation, and with an intense earnestness such as I have never heard from any other man ... The speech made a most profound impression upon the audience. Men lowered their voices in discussing it with each other. I may be permitted to add that when the President began speaking I was a Democrat, when he finished I was a Republican—a conversion as sudden as that of St. Paul, and, I trust, as permanent. (July 3, 1887, p. 11)

In his essay on the Gettysburg Address, Glenn La Fantasie concluded that those who heard Lincoln's speech reacted very differently, but emotionally, to the president's words. Some people apparently clapped wildly during the speech while others stood in silent awe of the speaker and his eloquence (1995, p. 81).

But it was perhaps Edward Everett, the occasion's featured orator, who best summarized the importance that the country and world would attach to Mr. Lincoln's words. In a note to the president the day after the ceremony at Gettysburg he commented, "I should be glad, if I could flatter myself that I came as near to the central idea of the occasion, in two hours as you did in two minutes" (Boritt 2006, p. 146).

BIBLIOGRAPHY

Barton, William E. *The Life of Abraham Lincoln*, vol. 2. Indianapolis, IN: The Bobbs-Merrill Company, 1925.

Barton, William E. *Lincoln at Gettysburg: What He Intended to Say; What He Said; What He Was Reported to Have Said; What He Wished He Had Said*. New York: Peter Smith, 1950.

Bloom, Robert L. "The Gettysburg Address." *Lincoln Herald* 83, no. 4 (1981): 765–774.

Boritt, Gabor. *The Gettysburg Gospel: The Lincoln Speech That Nobody Knows.* New York: Simon & Schuster, 2006.

Carr, Clark. *Lincoln at Gettysburg*. Chicago: A.C. McClurg & Co., 1909.

"Dedication of the National Cemetery at Gettysburg." *Boston Herald*, November 20, 1863, p. 2.

Dunkelman, Mark H. "An Impression That Will Never Be Effaced: Emory Sweetland Remembers November 19, 1863." *Lincoln Herald* 96, no. 2 (1994): 44–50.

Farmer's Cabinet, November 26, 1863, p. 2.

Holstein, Anna Morris Ellis. *Three Years in Field Hospitals of the Army of the Potomac.* Philadelphia: J.B. Lippincott, 1867.

La Fantasie, Glenn. "Lincoln and the Gettysburg Awakening." *Journal of the Abraham Lincoln Association* 16, no. 1 (1995): 73–89.

Mitgang, Herbert. *Abraham Lincoln: A Press Portrait.* New York: Fordham University Press, 2000.

Reid, Robert F. "Newspaper Response to the Gettysburg Address." *Quarterly Journal of Speech* 53, no. 1 (1967): 50–60.

"Special Dispatch to the Chicago Tribune." *Chicago Tribune,* November 21, 1863, p. 1.

W.C.K. "Lincoln at Gettysburg." Letter to the editor of the *Manchester* (NH) *Mirror,* reprinted in the *New York Times,* July 3, 1887, p. 11.

Wills, Gary. *Lincoln at Gettysburg: The Words That Remade America.* New York: Simon & Schuster, 1992.

Young, John Russell. "Letter to the Editor." *The New Mississippian,* no. 11, May 18, 1886, col. E.

James C. Onderdonk

JEFFERSON DAVIS'S SPEECH OF RESIGNATION FROM THE U.S. SENATE

Jefferson Davis, long a staunch supporter of the Union and a beloved representative of the state of Mississippi, was the fourth and final Southern senator to announce his resignation from the U.S. Senate on January 21, 1861. As one of the most highly respected and reputable men serving in Washington, Davis received the honor of being the final Southern representative to give a farewell address to the Senate. His speech not only declared Mississippi's severance from the Union, it also specifically warned of the dangers of entering into a civil war.

At the time of his farewell address, Davis was in poor health. Suffering from several ailments, including dyspepsia and facial neuralgia, he had been bedridden for the past week. Acting against the advice of his physicians, Davis arrived at the Senate early on Monday morning to say his final farewell to his fellow senators. Only a few days before, he had received word from Governor Pettus of Mississippi to hastily return home, in order to assist in forming the Confederacy.

During the previous weekend, the city of Washington had been abuzz with anxiety and excitement over rumors of Davis's imminent farewell address. Regarded as one of the great orators of the Senate, Davis was highly respected by both Republicans and Democrats. He had a long record of serving his nation, including posts as secretary of war and as a battlefield officer in the Mexican War. When South Carolina began moving toward succession, Davis recommended that the Southern states secede before Lincoln could be inaugurated. He would not consider any compromise proposals that did not require the Republicans to abandon their elected platform and allow the further spread of slavery in the territories.

In his much-anticipated farewell address, Davis first asserted that there was "satisfactory evidence that the

State of Mississippi, by a solemn ordinance of her people in convention assembled, has declared her separation from the United States." He then expressed strong hopes for "peaceful relations" between the recently seceded states and the rest of the Union (*Congressional Globe* 36th Congress, 2nd Session, January 21, 1861, p. 487).

The nation reacted with little surprise to Jefferson Davis's farewell speech. The states of South Carolina, Georgia, Florida, Alabama, and his own Mississippi had all already voted in state-level conventions to secede from the Union. Representatives of those states who functioned in any capacity in the federal government were resigning their positions and returning to their home states for service (*Mobile Weekly Advertiser*, January 12, 1861). The main reason for excitement over Davis farewell speech was that many Washington representatives viewed Davis as the spokesman for the Southern Democrats. His farewell symbolized a crack in the sovereignty of the nation and the beginning of the Southern states' permanent dissolution from the Union.

In many places throughout the South, the act of state succession was met with public rejoicing. The *Daily Morning News* in Savannah, for example, reported on January 22, 1861, that there was "tremendous enthusiasm" in Montgomery over news of Georgia's succession. Yet when Davis gave his farewell address, newspapers across the country merely viewed his farewell as a footnote. For example, the January 21, 1861, *New Orleans Bee* reported his departure in a single sentence: "The Mississippi Senators have also retired from the Senate of the United States." With many states on the verge of seceding and news of U.S. Army garrisons being commandeered by Southern militias, Davis's speech may have not been considered as newsworthy as it would otherwise have been.

In particular, newspapers were greatly concerned with the recent skirmishes at Fort Sumter. After South Carolina seceded from the Union in December 1860, the federal garrison at the Charleston fort was repeatedly petitioned to surrender by the Confederate militia. With Union reinforcements blocked from assisting the fort, it was only a matter of time before either surrender or conflict would occur. Many major newspapers, including the *Daily National Intelligencer* of Washington, DC, were focused on covering the "impressive incident" that was taking place at the fort and would soon become the staging point for the first conflict of the Civil War (*Daily National Intelligencer*, January 12, 1861).

Although Davis's farewell address expressed hopes for a peaceful break between nation and state, many Northerners felt he should be arrested as a traitor. The January 19, 1861, *Bangor Daily Whig and Courier*, for example, remarked that while the "Great Speech of Jefferson Davis" revealed him as "the eloquent, patriotic and gallant champion of State Sovereignty," his "mouth [was] full of treason." The *New York Herald* noted that Davis was named in an affidavit for the "Wholesale Charge of Treason," along with fifty-two other sympathizers of the secessionist states by a councilor to the Supreme Court (January 25, 1861). As Davis prepared to return to Mississippi, many people across the nation began to wonder if the Union would be able to firmly stand without the recently seceded states.

A few days after his farewell address, Davis left Washington to assume leadership of the Mississippi militia. Along his journey to Mississippi, he was met with both praise and protest, though praise predominated. His arrival prompted public jubilation in many locales, as he was widely viewed as the chief defender of Southern rights. In a letter to his wife Varina, Davis noted that "all along the [train] route, except in Tennessee, the people at every station manifested good-will and approbation by bonfires at night, firings by day, shouts and salutations both" (Strode 1966, p. 59). In Tennessee, Davis ran into trouble from Union sympathizers, who disapproved of his resignation. Several days after his farewell address, Davis gave a speech in Chattanooga, which called for the people of Tennessee to question their allegiance to the Union. One observer, in an uncharacteristic display of incivility, yelled to Davis that "we are not to be hoodwinked, bamboozled, and dragged into your Southern, codfish, aristocratic, tory-blooded South Carolina mobocracy" (Davis 1991, p. 293).

Only a few weeks after Davis resigned from the Senate, he was appointed to the position of president of the confederacy. Although he was not eager to become the political leader of the unified seceded states, he assumed the position nonetheless, and was inaugurated on February 18, 1861. Despite having been a loyal Unionist for many years, and having taken to heart the Jacksonian ideal of "preserving the Union," he now found himself at the helm of a new, Confederate nation that would soon be battling the Union he had formerly cherished.

BIBLIOGRAPHY

Congressional Globe, 36th Congress, 2nd Session, January 21, 1861.

Davis, Varina. *Jefferson Davis: Ex-President of the Confederate States of America: A Memoir by His Wife*. New York: Belford, 1890.

Davis, William C. *Jefferson Davis: The Man and His Hour*. New York: HarperCollins, 1991.

Dodd, William E. *Jefferson Davis*. Philadelphia: G. W. Jacobs, 1907. Reprint, New York: Russell & Russell, 1966.

"Important Proceedings of Congress," *New York Herald*, Column E, January 25, 1861.

Ross, Ishbel. *First Lady of the South: The Life of Mrs. Jefferson Davis*. New York: Harper, 1958.

"Rejoicing at Montgomery,"*Savannah* (GA) *Daily Morning News*, Issue 18, col. D, January 22, 1861.

"South Carolina Convention," Mobile (AL) Weekly Advertiser, Issue 2, col. A, January 12, 1861.

"Southern Discontent," *Bangor (MN) Daily Whig and Courier*, Issue 171, col. A, January 19, 1861.

Strode, Hudson. *Jefferson Davis*, vol. 1: *American Patriot, 1808–1861*. New York: Harcourt, Brace, 1955.

Strode, Hudson. *Jefferson Davis: Private Letters, 1823–1889*. New York: Harcourt, Brace, 1966.

"Succession of Alabama,"*New Orleans Times Picayune*, col. E, January 21, 1861.

Tate, Allen. *Jefferson Davis: His Rise and Fall: A Bibliographical Narrative*. New York: Minton, Balch, 1929.

"Thirty-Sixth Congress, Second Session,"*Washington* (DC) *Daily National Intelligencer*, Issue 15, 108, col. C, January 12, 1861.

Woodworth, Steven E. *Jefferson Davis and His Generals: The Failure of Confederate Command in the West*. Lawrence: University of Kansas Press, 1990.

Matthew M. Mitchell

DAVIS'S AND LINCOLN'S INAUGURAL ADDRESSES

The inaugural ceremonies for Jefferson Davis, the president of the Confederacy, occurred at the Alabama State House in Montgomery on February 18, 1861. Before Howell Cobb, the president of the Montgomery secession convention, administered the oath of office, Davis delivered a brief speech in which he offered humble justification for the new nation. He envisaged successfully meeting the challenges of Confederate nationalism; a permanent, peaceful, and prosperous government would emerge, sustained by the ideological intervention of the Founding Fathers and the legacy of the American Revolution (Crist and Dix 1992, pp. 45–50).

Reaction to Davis's Addresses

Southerners responded with excited praise. "Your speech was telegraphed & gives general satisfaction," Texas senator Louis T. Wigfall wrote to Davis. "It has the ring of the true metal" (Crist and Dix 1992, pp. 51–52). "The Inaugural pleased everybody and the manner in which Davis took the oath of office was most impressive," the outspoken Georgia secessionist Thomas R. R. Cobb reported (Southern History Association 1907, p. 182). One woman who attended the ceremonies wrote to a friend in Montgomery that "[Davis] read a very neat little speech, not making many promises, but hoping, by God's help, to be able to fulfill all expectations." She remarked that never before had she borne witness to such a solemn, impressive scene (*Harper's Weekly*, March 9, 1861).

Many Southern newspapers reproduced the entire speech; some, like the *Charleston Mercury*, noted that the speech "needed few comments": "Brief, clear, pointed, firm, explicit. It is all that could be desired by a bold and patriotic people, resolved upon their freedom and independence, under a new and permanent form of government" (February 22, 1861). Buoyed by the arithmetic of the founders, a Nashville paper reflected that the ceremonies were "the grandest pageant ever witnessed in the South. Davis' inaugural address was chiefly based upon propositions contained in the Declaration of the American Independence" (*Weekly Union and American*, February 19, 1861).

Union editors, despite their opposition to secession, often offered objective commentaries. "Mr. Davis's Inaugural was a temperate and carefully studied document," Horace Greeley, the editor of the *New York Tribune*, later commented. Still, he found Davis' expectation for peace to be less than genuine. "There was an undertone in this Inaugural... which plainly evinced that the author expected nothing of the sort" (Greeley 1866, pp. 415–416). Other Northern papers found evidence of excitement, vindictiveness, and malevolence in Davis's address. Maintaining that the Union was perpetual and secession illegal, one ridiculed the "harangue" of a "bogus President" (*Chicago Tribune*, February 20, 1861).

In February 1862, following outright election by his Confederate constituents, Davis delivered a second inaugural address, furthering the themes of the previous year. As a result, responses were virtually identical. Most notably, Unionist editors parodied Davis's desire for permanent government. "[It] reminds one very much of the sort of speech a desperate and hardened criminal of more than ordinary intelligence would get off while on the scaffold, and just about to swing off into a condition of 'permanent' elevation on a bottomless platform," a San Francisco paper suggested (*Daily Evening Bulletin*, March 29, 1862).

Reaction to Lincoln's Addresses

On March 4, 1861, just weeks after Davis's first address in Montgomery, Abraham Lincoln, the sixteenth president of the United States, delivered his First Inaugural Address in a voice that "rang out over the acres of people before him with surprising distinctness, and was heard in the remotest parts of his audience" (Julian 1884, p. 187). Lincoln's intent, especially in regard to the states in the Upper South that had not yet left the Union, was to dispel Southern apprehension about his administration. "I have no purpose, directly or indirectly, to interfere with the institution of slavery in the States where it exists," he declared (Basler and Basler 1953, vol. 4, pp. 262–263). He appealed for careful reflection, assuring the South that "you can have no conflict, without being yourselves the aggressors." The new president, in the language of conciliation, was determined to uphold the Fugitive Slave Law enacted with in the Compromise of 1850; he also referenced the "safeguards of liberty" in the U.S. Constitution. Yet concurrently, he maintained that the Union was perpetual and that secession was the "essence of anarchy."

Among Northern Republicans, the reaction to the speech was unsurprising. The *Philadelphia North American* wrote, "Its language is so direct, its tone so patriotic, its honesty so unmistakable, that all will feel the earnestness of its author and the significance of his words" (*Philadelphia Inquirer*, March 6, 1861). "I cannot let one day pass without expressing to you the satisfaction I have felt in reading and in considering the Inaugural address," New York Governor Edwin D. Morgan penned to Lincoln. "Kind in spirit, firm in purpose, national in the highest degree, the points are all well made, and the call is fairly stated and most honorably met. It cannot fail to command the confidence of the North, and the respect of the South" (Morgan to Lincoln, March 5, 1861). From Wall Street, H. D. Faulkner noted that his "heart responded 'amen' to every patriotic sentiment" of the speech. After discussing the speech with Republicans and supporters of both the Northern and Southern wings of the Democratic Party, he concluded, "I think the honest portion of the American people are with you, and will hold themselves subject to your direction whether it be storm or sunshine that may follow" (Faulkner to Lincoln, March 5, 1861). Indeed, after the speech, a Virginian in the audience told Lincoln, "God bless you, my dear sir; you will save us" (*New York Times*, March 5, 1861).

African Americans sensed no such guarantee. Frederick Douglass (1818–1895), an escaped slave, leading black newspaper editor, abolitionist, and intellectual, wrote that his race "must declare the address to be but little better than our worst fears, and vastly below what we had fondly hoped it might be" (Foner 1952, vol. 3, p. 72). Citing Lincoln's commitment to courting both the South and the slavecatcher, Douglass expressed disapproval; however, he also found "the presence or something like a heart as well as a head" in Lincoln's suggestions for safeguarding liberty and humane jurisprudence (Foner 1952, vol. 3, p. 75). As an African American advocating a cleansing, apocalyptic civil war to purge the national sin of slavery, Lincoln's address was certainly deemed inadequate by Douglass; however, the contours of an advance by the Lincoln administration to higher, more liberal ground could be vaguely distinguished. Ultimately, for Douglass, Lincoln's First Inaugural was "a double-tongued document, capable of two constructions .... No man reading it could say whether Mr. Lincoln was for peace or war...." (Foner 1952, vol. 3, p. 72).

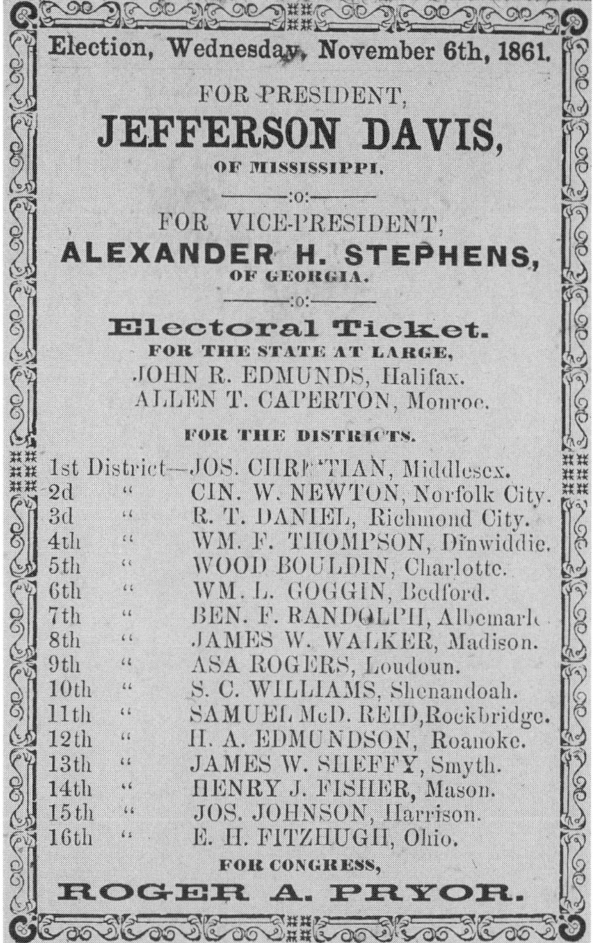

Election, Wednesday, November 6th, 1861.

FOR PRESIDENT,

JEFFERSON DAVIS,

OF MISSISSIPPI.

:o:

FOR VICE-PRESIDENT,

ALEXANDER H. STEPHENS,

OF GEORGIA.

:o:

Electoral Ticket.

FOR THE STATE AT LARGE,

JOHN R. EDMUNDS, Halifax.

ALLEN T. CAPERTON, Monroe.

FOR THE DISTRICTS.

1st District—JOS. CHRE'TIAN, Middlesex.
2d " CIN. W. NEWTON, Norfolk City.
3d " R. T. DANIEL, Richmond City.
4th " WM. F. THOMPSON, Dinwiddie.
5th " WOOD BOULDIN, Charlotte.
6th " WM. L. GOGGIN, Bedford.
7th " BEN. F. RANDOLPH, Albemarl
8th " JAMES W. WALKER, Madison.
9th " ASA ROGERS, Loudoun.
10th " S. C. WILLIAMS, Shenandoah.
11th " SAMUEL McD. REID, Rockbridge.
12th " H. A. EDMUNDSON, Roanoke.
13th " JAMES W. SHEFFY, Smyth.
14th " HENRY J. FISHER, Mason.
15th " JOS. JOHNSON, Harrison.
16th " E. H. FITZHUGH, Ohio.

FOR CONGRESS,

ROGER A. PRYOR.

Electoral ticket for Davis and Stephens, 1861. A copy of an 1861 Confederate States of America electoral ticket, promoting presidential candidate Jefferson Davis. *Kean Collection/Hulton Archive/Getty Images.*

Similarly, many Democratic mouthpieces were confused by a double-tongued document; these partisans dismissed Lincoln's pledge to slavery noninterference, for again, it was coupled with clear condemnation of secession. "If the President selected his words with the view of making clear his views, he was, partially at least, unsuccessful," the *Providence Daily Post* noted (Perkins 1942, vol. 2, p. 645). The *Baltimore Sun* called Lincoln's argumentation "puerile...a shaky specimen of pleading" (March 5, 1861). The *Philadelphia Evening Journal*, perhaps hinting that Lincoln's rural boyhood had not prepared him for the presidency, noted that the speech was, "one of the most awkwardly constructed official documents" it had ever examined (*New York Tribune*, March 7, 1861). Some Radical Republicans even espoused these arguments, arguing in the vein of Frederick Douglass that the speech did not accomplish enough. "Lincoln's message good ... but not conclusive; it is not positive; it discusses questions, but avoids

The starting point of the great war between the states. During his inauguration speech after winning the presidency of the Confederacy, Davis emphasized the South's desire to peacefully coexist with their Northern neighbors and be allowed the liberty to make decisions that reflect their beliefs. *The Library of Congress.*

to assert. May his mind not be altogether of the same kind," reflected Polish immigrant Adam Gurowski (Gurowski 1968, p. 13).

Despite the president's rhetoric averring that the sections were "not enemies, but friends," a line that the *Indianapolis Daily Journal* lauded as "singularly and almost poetically beautiful," some editors predicted that Lincoln's words would lead to war (*New York Tribune*, March 7, 1861). "Blood will stain the soil and color the waters of the entire continent," an Ohio paper editorialized (Perkins 1942, vol. 2, p. 634). Edward Everett, the Massachusetts orator and Constitutional Unionist who would join Lincoln at Gettysburg in 1863, expected bloodshed, despite the president's message being "as conciliatory as possible" (Frothingham 1925, pp. 414–415). Gurowski was sure that a "great drama will be played" (1968, pp. 13–14).

Southern newspapers were readying themselves for the drama; naturally, sharp censure was leveled at a speech they considered at best inconclusive and at worst provocative. "It is not a war message. It is not, strictly speaking, a Black Republican message," noted a Raleigh newspaper, inviting its readership to make individual assessments (*North Carolina Standard*, March 9, 1861). But many Southern editors offered no such invitation. "The Inaugural Address of Abraham Lincoln inaugurates civil war .... The sword is drawn and the scabbard thrown away," the *Richmond Dispatch* declared (March 5, 1861). According to the *Richmond Enquirer*, the lines of the message constituted the language of a fanatic (March 5, 1861).

Editors and diarists would again consider an inaugural address on March 4, 1865, when Lincoln began his second term. In this considerably shorter address, Lincoln tendered an account of the war that refused to ascribe blame. The war to end slavery—slavery was "somehow the cause of the war"—had persisted because God willed it to continue. Calling for "malice toward none" and "charity for all," Lincoln endorsed a binding up of the nation's wounds.

Despite Lincoln's admonishment, Southern newspapers responded sharply. A Petersburg, Virginia, newspaper charged Lincoln with "wholesale murder, robbery and arson" (*Petersburg Daily Express*, March 4, 1865). Even so, after four years of conflict, most Northerners were ready to "strive on and finish the work" they were in. Although some Democratic papers, such as the *Chicago Times*, deprecated the "slip shod" effort, most proffered favorable reviews (Mitgang 1989, pp. 440–441). The *Washington National Intelligencer* noted that the words of Lincoln's final sentence were "equally distinguished for patriotism, statesmanship, and benevolence, and deserve to be printed in gold" (March 6, 1865). The monumental diarist George Templeton Strong accurately predicted the speech's historical acclaim. "It is certainly most unlike the inaugurals of Pierce, Polk, Buchanan, or any of their predecessors; unlike any American state paper of this century," he wrote. "I would give a good deal to know what estimate will be put on it in ten or fifty years hence" (Strong 1952, vol. 3, pp. 560–561).

Perhaps the most emblematic response to the speech emanated from Frederick Douglass. "The whole proceeding was wonderfully quiet, earnest, and solemn. ... The address sounded more like a sermon than a state paper" (Douglass 1882, p. 801). Although substantial tests remained ahead, the Emancipation Proclamation and the enlistment of African American troops had instructed Douglass which construction of Lincoln's first inaugural had been the most readable.

BIBLIOGRAPHY

Baltimore Sun, March 5, 1861.

Basler, Roy P. and Christian O. Basler, eds. *The Collected Works of Abraham Lincoln*. 9 vols. New Brunswick, NJ: Rutgers University Press, 1953.

Charleston Mercury, Charleston, SC, February 22, 1861.

Chicago Tribune, February 20, 1861.

Cobb, Thomas Reade Rootes. *The Correspondence of Thomas Reade Rootes Cobb, 1860–1862.* Washington, DC: Southern History Association, 1907.

Crist, Lynda Lasswell, and Mary Seaton Dix, eds. *The Papers of Jefferson Davis*, vol. 7. Baton Rouge: Louisiana State University Press, 1992.

Daily Evening Bulletin, San Francisco, March 29, 1862.

Douglass, Frederick. *The Life and Times of Frederick Douglass: From 1817–1882, written by himself*, 1882.

Faulkner, H. D. Letter to Abraham Lincoln. March 5, 1861. In *Papers of Abraham Lincoln*, Washington, DC: Library of Congress.

Foner, Philip S., ed. *The Life and Writings of Frederick Douglass.* 4 vols. New York: International Publishers, 1952.

Frothingham, Paul Revere. *Edward Everett, Orator and Statesman.* Port Washington, NY: Kennikat Press, 1925.

Greeley, Horace. *The American Conflict: A History of the Great Rebellion in the United States of America.* Chicago: George and C. W. Sherwood, 1866.

Gurowski, Adam. *Diary from March 4 1861 to November 12 1862.* Reprint. New York: Burt Franklin, 1968.

Harper's Weekly, March 9, 1861.

Julian, George W. *Political Recollections, 1840 to 1872.* Chicago: Jansen, McClurg, 1884.

Mitgang, Herbert, ed. *Abraham Lincoln: A Press Portrait.* Athens: University of Georgia Press, 1989.

Morgan, Edwin D. Letter to Abraham Lincoln. March 5, 1861. In *Papers of Abraham Lincoln.* Washington, DC: Library of Congress.

New York Times, March 5, 1861.

New York Tribune, March 7, 1861.

North Carolina Standard, Raleigh, NC, March 9, 1861.

Perkins, Howard Cecil, ed. *Northern Editorials on Secession.* 2 vols. New York: D. Appleton-Century, 1942.

Petersburg Daily Express, Petersburg, VA, March 4, 1865.

Philadelphia Inquirer, March 7, 1861.

Richmond Dispatch, Richmond, VA, March 5, 1861.

Richmond Enquirer, Richmond, VA, March 5, 1861.

Southern History Association. *Publications of the Southern History Association*, vol. 11. Washington, DC: The Association, 1907.

Strong, George Templeton. *The Diary of George Templeton Strong*, ed., Allan Nevins and Milton Halsey Thomas. 4 vols. New York: Macmillan, 1952.

Washington National Intelligencer, Washington, DC, March 6, 1865.

Weekly Union and American, Nashville, TN, February 19, 1861.

Brian M. Jordan

THE EMANCIPATION PROCLAMATION

One of the most noted accomplishments of Abraham Lincoln (1809–1865), the sixteenth president of the United States, was his Emancipation Proclamation, which led to the end of slavery and earned Lincoln the nickname "The Great Emancipator." While federal forces initially fought the American Civil War as a means to preserve the Union, the Emancipation Proclamation, a part of Lincoln's evolving wartime antislavery policy, redefined the war's objective as ending slavery in order to defeat the Confederacy. The proclamation was a carefully phrased legal document recognizing the fact that attacking slavery would weaken the Confederate war effort. As slaves escaped from plantations and farms in the direction of Union lines, Lincoln's policy offered a last chance for the Confederate states to rejoin the Union and keep the institution of slavery intact.

The preliminary draft of the Emancipation Proclamation, announced on September 22, 1862, outlined the Union policy that would take effect on January 1, 1863. The proclamation freed slaves in Confederate-held territory after that date—although from a practical standpoint, the Union armies actually had to advance into Confederate areas before the terms of the proclamation could be enforced. The Emancipation Proclamation accelerated the debate over slavery among Northerners, strengthened slaves' hopes for freedom, and raised the stakes of the war for Southerners.

Northern Reactions

The preliminary announcement of the Emancipation Proclamation drew public attention from both Lincoln's supporters and his detractors. Citizens in the North pondered the significance and possible consequences of the proposed proclamation. Some citizens believed that the proclamation would simplify the issues of the war. In reference to conservative Northerners, the *Milwaukee Daily Sentinel* declared on September 26, 1862, that "the proclamation calls upon them to choose between the government and slavery, and the choice cannot be delayed."

Many citizens approved of emancipation as a war measure that would bring the conflict to a resolution but were not truly committed to racial equality. These reluctant proponents of freedom were willing to support any policy that would hurt the Southern slaveholders, whom many Unionists considered traitors. Northern abolitionists, however, supported the proclamation on moral grounds, and welcomed the president's announcement. A Northern minister stated that it was the white race "whose emancipation this great act of the president announces," because Northerners would no longer be forced to tolerate the existence of slavery (Furness 1862, p. 9).

Black Unionists were also encouraged by the prospect of emancipation. The *Daily Evening Bulletin* reported on September 27, 1862, that the black citizens of San Francisco, California, were hopeful that all Unionists would embrace the policy. A black newspaper editor remarked of the preliminary Proclamation that "to our race it is the harbinger of so much gratifying." He expressed the hope that it would "help immensely in crushing the rebellion, and saving the Union, and put the nation immeasurable forward of its former self" (*Daily Evening Bulletin*, September 27, 1862). Black communities throughout the North celebrated the news of the proclamation. The final version of the Emancipation Proclamation included a provision for enlisting black men into the Union Army, and black Unionists in turn showed their support by enlisting in large numbers.

Some Unionists were not as enthusiastic about the president's proposal. In the October 3, 1862, issue of the *Newark Advocate*, the editor proclaimed that "the vital interests of the country demand that the proclamation shall be revoked, the sooner the better, and, until it is revoked, every loyal man should unite in vigorously working for its revocation." Protests about the preliminary Emancipation Proclamation often resulted from racist attitudes and the acceptance of stereotypes about blacks. Once the proclamation went into effect on January 1, 1863, opponents to emancipation continued to object to the measure. The *Cincinnati Enquirer* reacted to the official version of the proclamation on January 4, 1863, by claiming that the act encouraged slaves to "massacre white women and children." Those who objected to the proclamation often resurrected the racist claim that African Americans were not able to function independently and would not be able to provide for themselves if freed.

Southern Reactions

The news of the Emancipation Proclamation was met with scorn and resentment in the Confederacy. In Jackson, Mississippi, the *Daily Southern Crisis* remarked on January 24, 1863, that the proclamation "will be an enduring monument of the stupendous wickedness and folly of our enemies." Southerners believed that the proclamation was an effort to incite violent insurrection in the Confederacy. In spite of slaveholders' assertions that loyal slaves would not leave their masters, Southerners took measures to move slaves away from the paths of Union armies. Confederate troops took violent action against slaves who were caught trying to reach the Union lines. In Mississippi, a Confederate officer wrote to his superiors on January 8, 1863, regarding former slaves who had been captured while traveling from Union lines to spread news of the Emancipation Proclamation. The officer asked what to do with the captives, noting that "yesterday a negro was caught armed and killed two dogs in the attempt to catch him." The officer was informed that any armed black men found coming from the Union camps should be hanged (Berlin 1997, pp. 96–97).

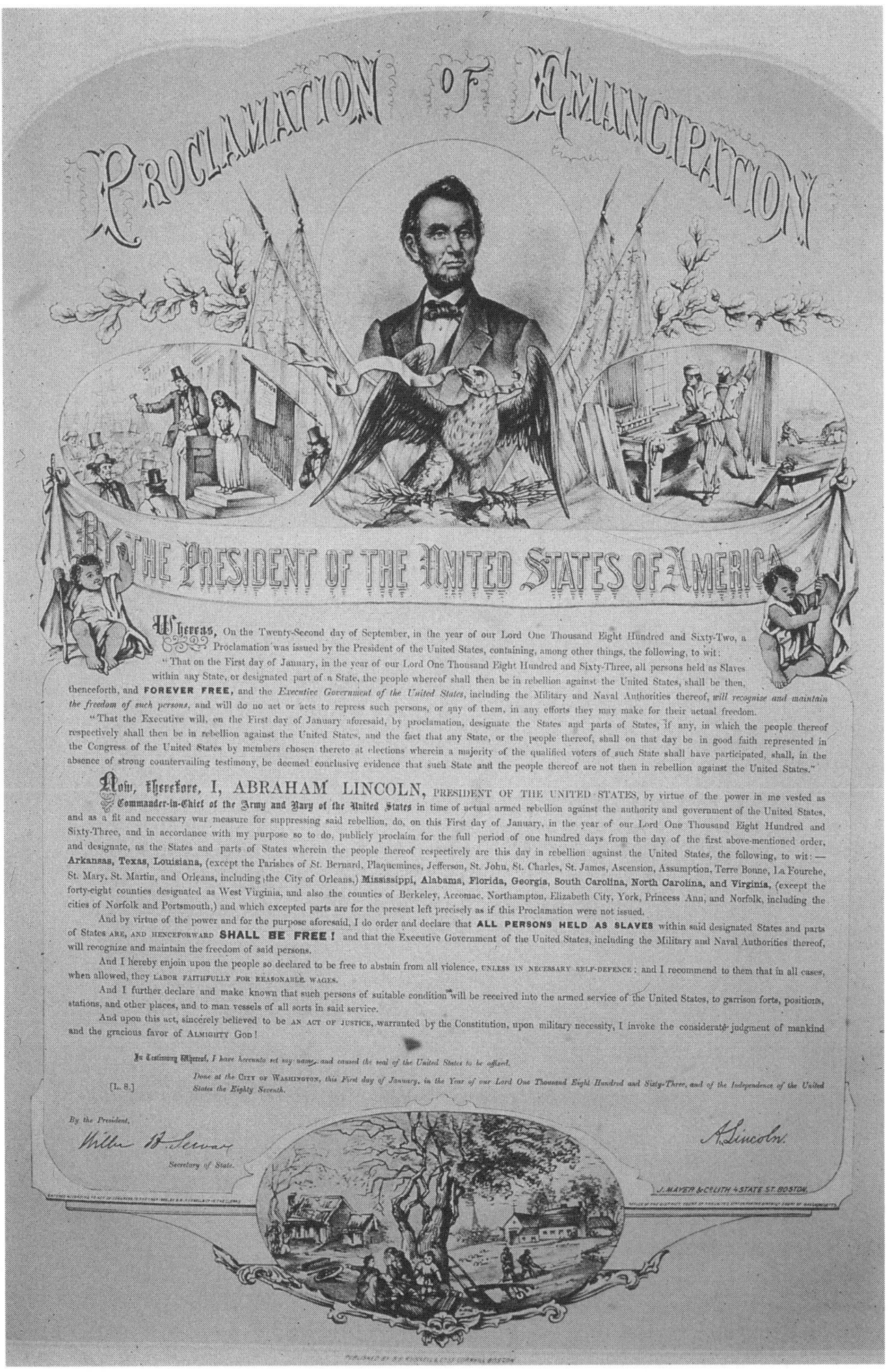

PROCLAMATION OF EMANCIPATION

BY THE PRESIDENT OF THE UNITED STATES OF AMERICA.

Whereas, On the Twenty-Second day of September, in the year of our Lord One Thousand Eight Hundred and Sixty-Two, a Proclamation was issued by the President of the United States, containing, among other things, the following, to wit:

"That on the First day of January, in the year of our Lord One Thousand Eight Hundred and Sixty-Three, all persons held as Slaves within any State, or designated part of a State, the people whereof shall then be in rebellion against the United States, shall be then, thenceforth, and **FOREVER FREE,** and the *Executive Government of the United States,* including the Military and Naval Authorities thereof, *will recognise and maintain the freedom of such persons,* and will do no act or acts to repress such persons, or any of them, in any efforts they may make for their actual freedom.

"That the Executive will, on the First day of January aforesaid, by proclamation, designate the States and parts of States, if any, in which the people thereof respectively shall then be in rebellion against the United States, and the fact that any State, or the people thereof, shall on that day be in good faith represented in the Congress of the United States by members chosen thereto at elections wherein a majority of the qualified voters of such State shall have participated, shall, in the absence of strong countervailing testimony, be deemed conclusive evidence that such State and the people thereof are not then in rebellion against the United States."

Now, therefore, I, ABRAHAM LINCOLN, PRESIDENT OF THE UNITED STATES, by virtue of the power in me vested as **Commander-in-Chief of the Army and Navy of the United States** in time of actual armed rebellion against the authority and government of the United States, and as a fit and necessary war measure for suppressing said rebellion, do, on this First day of January, in the year of our Lord One Thousand Eight Hundred and Sixty-Three, and in accordance with my purpose so to do, publicly proclaim for the full period of one hundred days from the day of the first above-mentioned order, and designate, as the States and parts of States wherein the people thereof respectively are this day in rebellion against the United States, the following, to wit:— **Arkansas, Texas, Louisiana,** (except the Parishes of St. Bernard, Plaquemines, Jefferson, St. John, St. Charles, St. James, Ascension, Assumption, Terre Bonne, La Fourche, St. Mary, St. Martin, and Orleans, including the City of Orleans,) **Mississippi, Alabama, Florida, Georgia, South Carolina, North Carolina, and Virginia,** (except the forty-eight counties designated as West Virginia, and also the counties of Berkeley, Accomac, Northampton, Elizabeth City, York, Princess Ann, and Norfolk, including the cities of Norfolk and Portsmouth,) and which excepted parts are for the present left precisely as if this Proclamation were not issued.

And by virtue of the power and for the purpose aforesaid, I do order and declare that **ALL PERSONS HELD AS SLAVES** within said designated States and parts of States ARE, AND HENCEFORWARD **SHALL BE FREE!** and that the Executive Government of the United States, including the Military and Naval Authorities thereof, will recognize and maintain the freedom of said persons.

And I hereby enjoin upon the people so declared to be free to abstain from all violence, UNLESS IN NECESSARY SELF-DEFENCE; and I recommend to them that in all cases, when allowed, they LABOR FAITHFULLY FOR REASONABLE WAGES.

And I further declare and make known that such persons of suitable condition will be received into the armed service of the United States, to garrison forts, positions, stations, and other places, and to man vessels of all sorts in said service.

And upon this act, sincerely believed to be AN ACT OF JUSTICE, warranted by the Constitution, upon military necessity, I invoke the considerate judgment of mankind and the gracious favor of ALMIGHTY GOD!

In Testimony Whereof, *I have hereunto set my name, and caused the seal of the United States to be affixed.*

[L. S.] *Done at the* CITY OF WASHINGTON, *this First day of January, in the Year of our Lord One Thousand Eight Hundred and Sixty-Three, and of the Independence of the United States the Eighty Seventh.*

By the President,

Secretary of State.

A. Lincoln.

J. MAYER & CO. LITH 4 STATE ST. BOSTON.

Lithograph of Lincoln's Emancipation Proclamation. Effective January 1, 1863, President Abraham Lincoln's memorable Emancipation Proclamation freed slaves living in Confederate states. The practice was not outlawed, however, in proslavery states that remained in the Union, such as Kentucky and Maryland. *Kean Collection/Hulton Archive/Getty Images*

Slaves outside the Confederacy also responded to the proclamation. In the border slave state of Maryland, slaves believed that they would be freed by the proclamation on January 1 and refused to work. The Lowell *Daily Citizen and News*, a Massachusetts newspaper, reported on the situation in Maryland on January 12,

An artist's imagining of Lincoln drafting version of the Emancipation Proclamation. Resistant to outlaw slavery early in his presidency, Abraham Lincoln eventually used the Emancipation Proclamation to rally Northern support and give new incentive to persevere against the Confederacy. *George Eastman House/Hulton Archive/Getty Images*

1863, by stating that "some of the slaveholders, in order to settle matters amicably and preserve peace in the family, have agreed to pay their slaves wages." The Emancipation Proclamation did not apply to slave states that had not seceded from the Union (such as Kentucky and Maryland), but these border states were affected nonetheless. In spite of their owners' attempts to prevent it, Kentucky slaves began enlisting in the Union Army in 1864, wishing to take up arms and assist in securing their own freedom.

Emancipation and the Union Army

Union soldiers had a variety of reactions to the Emancipation Proclamation. Some Union soldiers objected to emancipation because they believed that the war was about restoring the Union and maintaining the Constitution, not freeing slaves. An army surgeon from New York opposed the proclamation because in his opinion, "The negro, for whose emancipation this war is avowedly carried on, has proved itself but a poor auxiliary in its prosecution" (Ellis 1863, p. 11). Other soldiers were relieved that they would not have to return slaves to their disloyal masters. The proclamation promised to hasten the end of the war because it denied the Confederacy the use of slave labor, while allowing former slaves to be employed by the Union Army. A corporal in the Forty-fourth Massachusetts Volunteer Militia outlined the political opinions within his company of ninety-seven men. He remarked that out of the sixty-one Republicans in Company D, "sixty-one sustained the Emancipation Proclamation" (Corporal 1863, p. 26). While Lincoln's proclamation was political in nature and controversial in its implications of freedom and citizenship for black Americans, it was indeed successful in aiding Union victory and redefining the Civil War as a crusade for freedom.

BIBLIOGRAPHY

Berlin, Ira, Barbara J. Fields, Steven F. Miller, et al., eds. *Free At Last: A Documentary History of Slavery, Freedom, and the Civil War.* New York: New Press, 1992.

Cincinnati Enquirer, January 4, 1863.

Corporal [pseud.]. *Letters from the Forty-fourth Regiment M.V.M.: A Record of the Experience of a*

Celebration of freedom. Artist Thomas Nast presents a picture of an optimistic future for freed slaves, contrasting the evils of the past with the hope for a better life. *Illustration by Thomas Nast. The Library of Congress*

Nine Months' Regiment in the Department of North Carolina in 1862–3. Boston, 1863.

Daily Evening Bulletin (San Francisco), September 27, 1862.

Daily Southern Crisis (Jackson, MS), January 24, 1863.

Ellis, Thomas T. *Leaves from the Diary of an Army Surgeon, or, Incidents of Field, Camp, and Hospital Life.* New York: J. Bradburn, 1863.

Furness, William Henry. *A Word of Consolation for the Kindred of Those Who Have Fallen in Battle: A Discourse Delivered September 28, 1862.* Philadelphia: Crissey and Markley, 1862.

Guelzo, Allen C. *Lincoln's Emancipation Proclamation: The End of Slavery in America.* New York: Simon and Schuster, 2004.

Holzer, Harold, Edna Greene Medford, and Frank J. Williams. *The Emancipation Proclamation: Three Views.* Baton Rouge: Louisiana State University Press, 2006.

Lowell Daily Citizen and News (MA), January 12, 1863.

Milwaukee Daily Sentinel (WI), September 26, 1862.

Newark Advocate (NJ), October 3, 1862.

Striner, Richard. *Father Abraham: Lincoln's Relentless Struggle to End Slavery.* New York: Oxford University Press, 2006.

Wood, Forrest. *Black Scare: The Racial Response to Emancipation and Reconstruction.* Berkeley and Los Angeles: University of California Press, 1968.

Stephen Rockenbach

Letters to the President

During the Civil War, writing to the president was not as easy as it is today. The literacy rates in the United States were lower and postage rates were much higher, with delivery taking much longer. But during the Civil War, unlike today, correspondents would likely have received a handwritten reply, either from Lincoln or Davis himself, or from a member of their staffs. An examination of the content of the letters to the two presidents reflects the attitudes of citizens at the time of the Civil War, and demonstrates their attempts to communicate with their government officials.

Writing to Abraham Lincoln

Many of the letters written by Northerners to President Lincoln are known as "open letters," a common form of literature during the nineteenth century. These were published letters written to one or more people. Many unpublished letters are available at archives and libraries across the nation as well. In some cases, these letters reflected racial attitudes still present at the time of the war. Particularly, some writers expressed views sympathetic with the colonization movement to return African Americans to Africa and establish colonies for them there. One such letter, written by James Mitchell, encourages President Lincoln to influence the branches of government to speed up the process, "to produce the separation of those races, the removal of the colored race to a proper locality, and establishment in independence there" (Mitchell 1862, p. 3). Mitchell also expresses his fear of an eventual race war, especially if the Lincoln government does not adopt colonization, and notes the issues that will arise from the 4.5 million persons "who, whilst among us, cannot be of us," reflecting the racism prevalent in the nation at the time (Mitchell 1862, p. 4).

Joseph Scoville also wrote to Lincoln, among other prominent Union leaders, regarding the issue of colonization. In his letter he notes how Union forces began confiscating slaves of Confederates. In addition, Scoville expresses his hope that the Southern people will realize their error and rejoin the Union (Scoville 1862, p. 3). Scoville then launches into a long examination of the question of what ought to be done with confiscated slaves, proffering three possibilities: (1) that the slaves should be re-enslaved; (2) that they should be apprenticed; or (3) that they should all be freed at once. Scoville argues that re-enslavement is not an option because it would be a great mark of shame on the country, and that apprenticing confiscated slaves would maintain the slaves' manhood and prepare them for freedom with education (Scoville 1862, p. 4).

President Lincoln's Emancipation Proclamation prompted some soldiers to write to him, either expressing their opposition to it, or appealing to him to address their grievances over the Union army's confiscation of their slaves. Those affected by the confiscation of slaves often were residents of the border states that had remained loyal to the Union, and in some cases, were themselves serving in the Union army. One such case was of Marcellus Mundy, who was both a Kentucky slaveholder and a commander of a Kentucky regiment of the Union army. Mundy wrote to Lincoln to inform him that he had not only suffered at the hands of the Confederates, but also that a Union regiment from Michigan had taken his slaves and those of his neighbors into their own lines, even while Mundy was in command of Union troops. In his letter Mundy details the personal sacrifices that he made to serve in the army, and declares that although he agrees with the confiscation of the slaves of Confederates, if he were president, he would make sure not to trample on the rights of those who remained loyal to the Union. Finally, Mundy expresses his faith in Lincoln and his willingness, as a soldier, to execute the orders of the president (Berlin, Fields, Miller, et al. 1992, pp. 82–83).

African Americans also wrote letters to President Lincoln. Some were slaves' requests to be freed; others were from black soldiers pressing for equal treatment with regard to pay and usage. Some were pleas from relatives of black Union soldiers over the issue of mistreatment of captured black soldiers by Confederates. For example, several letters were presented to Lincoln by Richard Boyle, a black schoolteacher, on behalf of blacks residing in a contraband camp on Roanoke Island in North Carolina. The letters aired grievances about abuse in Union captivity and pressed for the soldiers' rights. The letters express the willingness of the former slaves to serve the Union cause and work hard, but complain that they do not want to be trampled upon by Union officials (Berlin, Fields, Miller, et al. 1992, pp. 222–224).

President Lincoln's Letters

Lincoln occasionally wrote to Americans, usually about their losses in the war. The most famous example is his letter to Mrs. Bixby, who lost five sons in the war. President Lincoln's letter is as follows:

> Executive Mansion, Washington, November 21, 1864.
> Mrs. Bixby, Boston, Massachusetts:
> Dear Madam: I have been shown in the files of the War Department a statement of the Adjutant-General of Massachusetts that you are the mother of five sons who have died gloriously on the field of battle. I feel how weak and fruitless must be any words of mine which should attempt to beguile you from the grief of a loss so overwhelming. But I cannot refrain from tendering to you the consolation that may be found in the thanks of the Republic they died to save. I pray that our Heavenly Father may assuage the anguish of your bereavement, and leave you only the cherished memory of the loved and lost, and the solemn pride that must be yours to have laid so costly a sacrifice upon the altar of freedom.
> Yours very sincerely and respectfully,
> Abraham Lincoln. (1864)

Although this letter may have been of little comfort to Mrs. Bixby, it illustrates that the president cared enough about the people and the suffering of the nation to express his condolences for their sacrifice to the Union.

Writing to Jefferson Davis

Southerners wrote to their leader as well. William Lee wrote to Jefferson Davis to express his concern about the absence of the men in his area who had large families to support—these families would suffer if the men had to leave to serve in the Confederate army. He also expresses his fear about slaves revolting in his area, and requests that Davis either remove all black men over age seventeen to holding areas (he argues for forting them up), or press them into the army (Berlin, Fields, Miller, et al. 1992, p. 4). Lee's second suggestion is particularly interesting, given the racist views prevalent in the nation and the hesitance to enlist blacks, even in the North.

William Lee was not the only Southerner who argued for the enlistment of blacks into the Confederate army, though his was the earliest written account. Most calls for such measures came when Southerners realized that they were losing the war, and that black soldiers would be one last gamble at success. O. G. Eiland of Mississippi wrote to President Davis only weeks after the fall of Vicksburg in July 1863, arguing that the only chance for the Confederates to succeed was "to call out every able bodied Negro man from the age of sixteen to fifty years old." He added, rather optimistically, that these men would gladly and willingly join the army, and that masters would gladly provide their slaves. Eiland even argued that the slaves would prefer the Confederate army to the Union army (Berlin, Fields, Miller, et al. 1992, pp. 132–133).

Another letter that called for the enlistment of blacks when times became desperate for the Confederacy was written by a Mr. F. Kendall of Georgia. Kendall wrote the letter soon after the fall of Atlanta in September 1864. He wrote the Southern president, exclaiming, "Is it not time now to enlist the negroes?" He notes his support for the idea ever since the Union began the practice of enlisting blacks, arguing that it is the only sure way to augment the army, and warns that many in his area have become so disillusioned with the Confederacy that they would likely vote to return to the Union, even with emancipation of the slaves. Kendall cautions that if blacks are not enlisted in the Confederate army, they will surely join Sherman's force, especially with the promise of freedom and a bounty. Kendall implores Davis to call the Confederate Congress into this issue, and believes that the South could raise a large army of perhaps 100,000 blacks, which, Kendall notes, could affect the Northern election (Berlin, Fields, Miller, et al. 1992, pp. 151–152).

In some cases, when locals formed slave patrols to prevent slaves from escaping to Union lines, the patrols would be drafted into the army, prompting letters to Davis from concerned citizens. Jere Pearsall of North Carolina wrote to his president to request that the local slave patrol in his county, which he helped to oversee, not be conscripted because they had prevented slaves from escaping even as Union forces neared. He expresses his concern that the disbandment of the patrol would cause many of the local slaves to escape, and asks Davis to keep the patrol in the area even if they are conscripted into the army so that they can continue to perform their vital function (Berlin, Fields, Miller et al. 1992, pp. 142–143).

Other Southerners wrote to President Davis to protest Southern governmental officials' impressment of slaves that seemed to benefit planter-heavy counties and neglect the poorer areas. For instance, several citizens from Randolph County, Alabama, signed a letter to Davis appealing to him to review the policy of impressing blacks. They argue that the local officials were taking too many blacks away, leading to food shortages and other negative effects on the agriculture of the county (Berlin, Fields, Miller, et al. 1992, pp. 148–151). Several residents in Sussex County, Virginia, wrote to Davis around the time of the siege of Petersburg, Virginia (June 1864 to March 1865), asking for the suspension of impressments. They argued that for every slave called up by the government, the Union would gain several more by way of escape. In addition, like the correspondents from of Randolph County, Alabama, they note the possibility of agricultural hardships should slaves be impressed into military service (Berlin, Fields, Miller, et al. 1992, pp. 153–154). Overall, these letters illustrate the willingness of Confederate citizens to call on their leader for assistance, as well as the dire situation in the South in the later stages of the war.

President Davis's Letters

Jefferson Davis also occasionally wrote to citizens regarding losses sustained in the war. For instance, in a letter written to James Howry, Davis expresses his appreciation for the sacrifices made by the Howry family in the war. Davis specifically asks that his compliments be presented to Howry's wife "for her patriotic devotion" (Davis 1863). However, it seems that Davis did not write to his people as often as Lincoln did.

BIBLIOGRAPHY

Berlin, Ira, Barbara J. Fields, Steven F. Miller, et al., eds. *Free at Last: A Documentary History of Slavery, Freedom, and the Civil War.* New York: New Press, 1992.

Davis, Jefferson. "Letter to James M. Howry, 27 August 27, 1863." Available from http://jeffersondavis.rice.edu/.

Lincoln, Abraham. "Letter to Mrs. Bixby, 1864." Internet Modern History Sourcebook, Fordham University. Available from http://www.fordham.edu/halsall/.

Mitchell, James. "Letter on the Relation of the White and African Races in the United States: Showing the Necessity of the Colonization of the Latter." Washington, DC, 1862.

Scoville, Joseph Alfred. "What Shall Be Done with the Confiscated Negroes?: The Question Discussed and a Policy Proposed in a Letter to Hon. Abraham Lincoln, Gen." United States, 1862.

Daniel Sauerwein

■ Support for the War

SUPPORT FOR THE WAR: AN OVERVIEW

The view from Northern states was alarming in the winter of 1860 to 1861: following South Carolina into secession was Mississippi, Florida, Alabama, Georgia, and Texas. Congress, now with a Northern Republican majority, moved frenetically to find a political solution. The result was a proposed amendment to the Constitution forbidding the federal government from ending slavery. The senators and representatives hoped their proposed measure would provide security for Southerners who saw Abraham Lincoln's recent election as the beginning of the end for their way of life. But far from assuaging Southern anger over the threat to their rights, the measure generated a rejoinder demanding the permanent legal extension of slavery throughout the American West. This struck at a fundamental plank of the Republican Party, which had consistently advocated the end to slavery's expansion outside the South. There was no compromise, and hostilities commenced.

The Lead-Up to the War

Support for the war on both sides was presaged for more than a decade by political wrangling over the Wilmot Proviso, the Compromise of 1850, and the Kansas-Nebraska Act. Positions sharpened further through fear given life by fiery Southern rhetoric and the action of the zealous abolitionist John Brown (1800–1859). In the North, citizens rightly understood the image drawn in February 1890 by presidential candidate Abraham Lincoln when he spoke of Southern threats upon the possible election of a Republican president. "In that supposed event," he said to the Southern antagonists, "you say you will destroy the Union; and then you say the great crime of destroying it will be upon us! That is cool. A highwayman holds a pistol to my ear, and mutters through his teeth, 'Stand and deliver, or I shall kill you, and then you will be a murderer!'" (Basler and Basler 1953–1955, vol. 3, pp. 546–547). In the South, Mississippi governor John J. Pettus (1813–1867) offered his own metaphor after the election of Lincoln when he claimed, "It would be as reasonable to expect the steamship to make a successful voyage across the Atlantic with crazy men for engineers, as to hope for a prosperous future for the South under Black Republican rule" (Dew 2001, p. 22). Secession commissioner Stephen Hale on his December 1860 mission to bring Kentucky to the Confederacy was direct arguing for support: Lincoln as president was a war declaration. The new president would destroy the South, "consigning her citizens to assassinations and her wives and daughters to pollution and violation to gratify the lust of half-civilized Africans" (Dew 2001, p. 54). The antagonistic spirit of the 1850s sectional crises convinced many their political opponents were unrecognizable, disfigured by evil intent and blind ambition. Unsurprisingly, eager, zealous support for war grew rapidly in the North and South during the secession period.

The siege at Fort Sumter ended in April 1861 with the surrender of the Union troops, but the effort was more a political show for both sides than a strategic military effort. The result was a war fever silencing almost all outward expression for caution. Unionists understood their cause as the preservation of the country—a fight for the flag. They assured themselves it was an effort not to subjugate the South, but to preserve the Constitution. Lincoln, demonstrating his strength as a leader, put the conflict into an easily grasped context:

> "Our popular government has often been called an experiment. Two points in it, our people have already settled—the successful establishing, and the successful administering of it. One still remains—its successful maintenance against a formidable internal attempt to overthrow it .... This issue embraces more than the fate of these United States. It presents to the whole family of man, the question, whether a constitutional republic, or a democracy ... can or cannot, maintain its territorial integrity, against its own domestic foes." (McPherson 1988, p. 309)

Southerners believed their cause was equally righteous and legitimate. They began their fight over issues of racial purity, black subjugation, state sovereignty, and their belief in a Constitution supportive of secession. Confederate leaders encouraged citizens to consider the new nation as the true heir to the Revolutionary generation. This was a fight for the right of self-government.

Support in the South

The need to maintain a defensive posture added further clear ideological goals for Southerners. Whatever one's view on self-government, Southerners knew the war would be an invasion. Home defense proved a powerful incentive early on. Images of marauding Yankees intent on plunder came easily to mind for slaveholders and non-slaveholders alike. Indeed, for many Southerners, their initial support for the war was not in defense of slavery or its expansion, but in anticipation of their community being overrun by Union troops. Slavery nevertheless presented non-slaveholding Southerners with an inescapable paradox. Potential invasion existed because the political disagreement over slavery remained.

The historian Armstead Robinson has argued that the South faced a more significant paradox that explains both its early support and later defeat. "Insurrection anxiety helped create the Confederacy as surely as this same anxiety played a major role in bringing the Southern Republic to its knees" (Robinson 1980, p. 279). The potential for slave rebellion generated by abolitionists and realized in John Brown's insurrection attempt at Harpers Ferry required a martial response, but without a quick resolution, the war would make provisions against insurrection increasingly difficult. The beginning of the war made this apparent as Confederate enlistments drained the South of the white males whose absence allowed slave resistance to grow in new, more threatening directions. Initial enthusiasm for the war crumbled within two years as the social contradictions mounted. Robinson remarked, "the South's ruling elites proved incapable of sustaining their hegemony amidst the radically altered conditions imposed by the War for Southern Independence" (Robinson 1980, p. 280). Two failures in particular set in motion changes that dampened Southerners' support. Initial military success failed to attract European recognition of the Confederacy, and a cotton embargo to Britain and France also did not compel either nation to alter their positions. The inability to provision a fighting force capable of capturing poorly defended Washington, DC, early in the war meant an increasing drain on limited supplies and personnel that would reach deep into the Southern countryside.

The costs of pursuing the fight with the Union was ultimately too high because it required destroying the very social structure Southerners defended. Robinson and other historians point to the Confederate Congress for supportive evidence. Two pieces of legislation stand out as having directly caused open hostility by Southerners against the Confederate government. During April 1862 the Confederate Congress passed a draft law requiring most white men to enlist, but also providing an exception for those who could afford to hire a substitute. The substitute provision generated sharp recriminations among regular Southerners who immediately revived latent class and wealth antagonisms. Lincoln's preliminary issuance of the Emancipation Proclamation on September 22, 1862, spurred Confederate leaders to bolster their home guard in an effort to prevent insurrection efforts that might arise from the U.S. president's declaration. The notorious "Twenty Nigger Law," as it was called, passed on October 11, 1862, provided draft exemptions of one overseer for every twenty slaves. Clearly designed to benefit large plantations, the law once again laid bare stark class, economic, and wealth disparities. The war, interpreted through the implications of the law, was about preserving slavery by using the poor white non-slaveholding majority in the fight. Support for the war withered in the face of such unapologetic privilege.

The consequences of the two laws emerged most obviously in the form of desertions and draft resistance. The six months of protest and wrangling between the two acts proved the undoing of Southern support. Desertion rates jumped after the October law. One Confederate colonel reported that half his troops had deserted by December (Robinson 1980, p. 294). The Confederate leadership knew the measure would be unpopular, but they believed that the dire circumstances required it. Reports came in across the South about the unsettled state of slaves and their increasing potential for violence. Evidence from Louisiana, Alabama, and Mississippi indicate plots were uncovered and others suspected after the news of the Emancipation Proclamation.

Unfair draft laws were not the sole factor in destroying the South's support for the war. Deprivation among the civilian population came quickly and hurt common whites substantially worse than the upper classes. Food shortages were exacerbated by rampant inflation and poor crop yields. Conditions in many areas grew so bad that civilians turned to banditry, violence, and riots. North Carolinians were perhaps the most willing to strike against the conditions under the Confederacy. The governor had to dispatch troops to the Piedmont region on several occasions to manage draft dodgers, deserters, and violent Unionists. Food riots occurred in both ends of the state in 1863. Increasingly, the populace sanctioned illegal activities and ceased viewing perpetrators as criminals. The historians Jeffery Crow and Paul Escott have noted that women began to use their culturally defined roles as caregivers to justify illegal actions: In January 1865 in Yadkin County "A Band of women, armed with axes [made] a raid . . . on Jonesville." They "came down on the place to press [seize] the tithe corn etc [the government's tax-in-kind] brought wagons along to carry it off." Despite initial failure, these female bandits soon succeeded at Hamptonville, taking "as much as they wanted without meeting any resistance" (Escott and Crow 1986, p. 395).

Northern Support

While worsening conditions eroded Southern support for the war until lawlessness gained social sanction, conditions in the North followed a similar pattern. Northerners entered the war with gusto under the impression the fighting would be brief and the Union easily preserved. The Lincoln administration and Congress maintained a neutral stance toward slavery in 1861. Even abolitionists restrained themselves. William Lloyd Garrison

(1805–1879) cautioned his peers to "'stand still, and see the salvation of God' rather than attempt to add anything to the general commotion" (McPherson 1988, p. 312). The first indication the conflict might run a different course occurred on July 21, 1861, with a humiliating rout of Union troops at Bull Run. Shocked by their army's failure, Northerners received torrents of bad news in the coming months. The army was plagued with crippling problems. Many officers were elected to their posts not by a measure of military experience, but for political reasons or in recognition of their local status. They immediately proved highly ineffective. The Northern press called for the military to launch an immediate campaign to take the Confederate capital of Richmond, Virginia, but supply and manpower shortages stalled efforts throughout the summer of 1861. Matters grew grave as thousands of enlisted men who had signed up for the standard ninety-day term walked away at the end of their short service.

Lincoln revised Union strategy immediately after Bull Run, encouraging the navy to redouble their efforts to create an effective blockade, ordering the army to properly train its troops while preparing to move against Richmond, and pressing the Confederacy on the western front under the command of the newly appointed commander, General John C. Frémont (1813–1890). Although Lincoln believed Frémont's reputation as a solidly experienced officer, the general mired himself in controversy. After losses in Missouri, Frémont shocked the North with his August 1861 Missouri proclamation declaring martial law, the death penalty for guerillas, and the freeing of all slaves belonging to Missouri Confederate sympathizers. With a show of gigantic restraint, Lincoln asked Frémont to revise the orders, and the general, with remarkable hubris, refused, sealing his fate. Lincoln removed Frémont from command, but the damage was done. The general had placed slavery back into public view, and antislavery Republicans began to press for shifting war aims to the emancipation of the slaves. Frémont had given them the new argument that such action was a military need. Slaves were aiding the Confederacy with their labor, and Congress responded to the argument by passing the Confiscation Act on August 6, 1861. The legislation made slaves who had been working for the Confederacy and taken into Union lines "contraband," or confiscated property. The question of their freedom was unanswered, but the law opened a breach in what had been a bipartisan war effort.

Northern Democrats found themselves in an increasingly difficult position during the opening years of the war. If they expressed support for their former allies in the South, Republicans branded them "Copperheads"—those who would lead the Union to defeat through disloyalty. Most Northern states had two Democratic factions: those who advocated a negotiated peace with the Confederacy and those who viewed the Confederacy as the enemy, but also opposed Lincoln's policies. Although the positions did not allow much cooperation, the Confederate sympathizers were generally too few in any state to wield power. Connecticut was the exception. There the two groups were of similar size, and the conflict was serious. After the Union defeat at Bull Run, Democratic Confederate supporters in Connecticut celebrated and were met with violent attacks by war supporters (Cowden 1983, p. 543). Protests and violence continued throughout the war, but were most acute when Lincoln issued the Emancipation Proclamation in September 1862. Democrats of both stripes throughout the North were enraged by this shift in war aims.

War support was not an issue only for the Democratic Party. Northerners' support for the war, like civilian Southerners', was built around social and economic interests. The low point came during 1862 and 1863. Protests against Secretary of State William H. Seward's overzealous efforts to jail anyone suspected of aiding the Confederacy marked the closing months of 1861. Lincoln shifted internal security to the War Department in February, and the trampling of constitutional rights eased. The spring appeared to offer an end to the war with the taking of Richmond, but Union efforts went terribly wrong. The Seven Days Battles (June 25 to July 1, 1862) cost the Confederate army dearly, but its effect on Northern morale was devastating. The Army of the Potomac's failure and lucky escape convinced many that the tide had turned for the Confederacy. Only the incentive of bounties—paid in part immediately after enlistment—helped maintain Northern fighting strength.

Lincoln, recognizing the need for total war and the impossibility of gaining support for gradually ending slavery in the border states, began preparations in summer 1862 for the Emancipation Proclamation. The public debate about freeing the slaves was hot during the summer, and it was clear that many Northerners were not supportive. The initial announcement in September of the abolition of slavery and the subsequent official proclamation in January generated significant resistance. Issues of race focused the debate for those who believed that blacks belonged permanently on the mudsill. Working-class whites in major cities believed freed slaves would soon arrive to take their jobs, and they showed their discontent with protests and riots.

The efforts of Peace Democrats—those who favored negotiating with the Confederacy—were gaining traction in the spring of 1863, and Clement Vallandigham (1820–1871) had positioned himself as the leader of their efforts. Raising the temperature of his rhetoric, Vallandigham castigated the administration and called the war an act of despotism. He drew the ire of General Ambrose Burnside (1824–1881), who, without the knowledge of the president, had him arrested for treason. The case drew national attention and laid bare the growing loss of support for the war. A military

Fremont Proclamation. Satirical cartoon criticizing President Abraham Lincoln for nullifying the Fremont Proclamation, an edict from Union General John C. Frémont that emancipated slaves held in Missouri during the Civil War. Many felt the president had given unintentional "aid and comfort" to the enemy and hindered the movement to crush the rebellion by nullifying the unauthorized proclamation, printed October 1861. *The Art Archive/Culver Pictures/The Picture Desk, Inc.*

commission sentenced Vallandigham to prison for the war's duration, immediately making him a martyr for antiwar supporters. Lincoln commuted the sentence to banishment. Although they had averted further disturbance from Peace Democrats for the time being, Lincoln and Congress would face more protests against the war when the Enrollment Act of March 1863 passed.

The new draft was unnecessarily complex and open to fraud. Two exceptions existed to avoid the draft: One could hire a substitute, or pay a $300 commutation fee. Democrats railed against the effort, but they were not alone. The Northern lower class, immediately recognizing that the wealthy could avoid service, mounted strong resistance, and nowhere was this more evident than in New York City. Irish Catholics living in squalor and working for low pay feared job competition from blacks. When enlistment officers entered their neighborhoods it proved enough to start a conflagration. During summer 1863 four days of mob violence gripped the city and left hundreds dead as draft dodgers launched mayhem. The racial implications of the resistance did not pass unnoticed by the administration, but the Union war effort remained a total effort, including the destruction of slavery. Matters might have escalated further had the military not had some significant successes. The early spring was grim with defeat at Chancellorsville, but pressures on the Lincoln administration eased and support for the war rebounded in July with almost simultaneous victories by General Ulysses S. Grant at Vicksburg and General George Meade at Gettysburg. The war had turned in favor of the Union, and although it would grind on for another two years, it was increasingly clear that the Confederacy was broken.

BIBLIOGRAPHY

Basler, Roy P., and Christian O. Basler, eds. *The Collected Works of Abraham Lincoln*. 9 vols. New Brunswick, NJ: Rutgers University Press, 1953–1955.

Cowden, Joanna D. "The Politics of Dissent: Civil War Democrats in Connecticut." *New England Quarterly* 56, no. 4 (December 1983): 538–554.

Dew, Charles B. *Apostles of Disunion: Southern Secession Commissioners and the Causes of the Civil War*. Charlottesville: University of Virginia Press, 2001.

Dupree, A. Hunter, and Leslie H. Fishel, Jr. "An Eyewitness Account of the New York Draft Riots, July, 1863." *Mississippi Valley Historical Review* 47, no. 3 (December 1960): 472–479.

Escott, Paul D., and Jeffrey J. Crow. "The Social Order and Violent Disorder: An Analysis of North Carolina in the Revolution and the Civil War." *The Journal of Southern History* 52, no. 3 (August 1986): 373–402.

Man, Albon P., Jr. "Labor Competition and the New York Draft Riots of 1863." *Journal of Negro History* 36, no. 4 (October 1951): 375–405.

McPherson, James B. *Battle Cry of Freedom: The Civil War Era*. New York: Oxford University Press, 1988.

Robinson, Armstead L. "In the Shadow of Old John Brown: Insurrection Anxiety and Confederate Mobilization, 1861–1863." *Journal of Negro History* 65, no. 4 (Autumn 1980): 279–297.

David F. Herr

PROSECESSIONISTS/SOUTHERN NATIONALISTS

Prosecessionists or Southern nationalists were advocates for the secession of Southern states from the United States government based on the theory that, as the Southern states predated the formation of the union, they had the right to leave the union. Secessionists largely based their argument for secession on the need to protect the institution of slavery, which they felt was increasingly threatened by a free North that would move to stop slavery from expanding into the western territories and thereafter doom the institution to a gradual death in the South. Nonetheless, the constitutional thought they drew on to justify secession had a heritage that predated the crisis over the expansion of slavery.

States' Rights

Thomas Jefferson (1743–1826) and James Madison (1751–1836), as the authors of the Kentucky and Virginia resolutions in 1798, laid the constitutional basis for the doctrine of secession by arguing that states could decide which acts were constitutional. States had the power to interpose themselves between the people and the federal government and argued in the Kentucky Resolution that states could nullify federal acts if they believed them to be unconstitutional. The Virginia and Kentucky resolutions effectively outlined a compact theory of government, which argued that states had formed the national government and were the ultimate authority on what was constitutional and in the best interests of their people. Federalists in New England weighed the option of secession numerous times under the same compact theory after the election of Republican presidents, most notably at the Hartford Convention in 1815. Thus secession as a constitutional option had a history that predated the Southern concerns.

John C. Calhoun (1782–1850), as a senator from South Carolina and vice president to Andrew Jackson (1767–1845) would, in order to combat the Tariff of 1828, use these precedents to argue that nullification was a state's constitutional right. Calhoun argued that a state convention could be called to nullify a law, at which point the law could remain void or a constitutional amendment could be passed to enact it. South Carolina nullified the federal tariff in 1832, which it felt gave advantages to the industrial North while causing higher prices for consumers in the South. Nullification placed South Carolina at odds with federal law and authority under President Andrew Jackson. Ultimately violence failed to break out as Senator Henry Clay (1777–1852) engineered a compromise that lowered the tariff and gave Jackson the power to use force; South Carolina in turn rescinded its nullification of the tariff. The failure to secede despite calls from many leaders in South Carolina was also in part due to the failure of other states to join South Carolina in its protests over the tariff. As a practical matter South Carolinians realized that they could not accomplish secession alone. Still, South Carolina continued to be a nursery for secessionist thought and established a political movement and an intellectual tradition that persevered in ensuing years.

New Territories, Heightened Tensions

The series of political battles that erupted over the territories taken from the Mexican War (1846–1848) transformed secession from a largely elite and theoretical argument into a mass movement in the South. The efforts of Northerners to bar slavery from the territories taken from the Mexican War further exacerbated tensions and calls for secession in the South. The Compromise of 1850 failed to settle the issues at play as rabid secessionists called "fire-eaters" continued to promote the idea. A prominent fire-eater was Robert Barnwell Rhett (1800–1876), a senator from South Carolina and one of the early advocates for Southern secession. Rhett had advocated secession over the tariff and was a delegate to the Nashville Convention in 1850, which contemplated secession if Congress passed legislation barring slavery from the territories, though the convention ultimately failed to support such a course. William Lowndes Yancey (1814–1863) of Alabama and Virginian

Prominent "fire-eater" Robert Barnwell Rhett (1800–1876). Robert Barnwell Rhett was a senator from South Carolina and an early advocate of Southern secession. He was considered a prominent "fire-eater," or a rabid secessionist who continued to champion this cause after the Compromise of 1850 was established. *The Library of Congress*

Edmund Ruffin (1794–1865) similarly were early advocates of secession, opposing attempts by any level of government to limit slavery and supporting Southern cooperation to expand slavery and to protect it where it already existed. Ruffin actually moved to South Carolina given his own state's failure to take the lead among Southern states in the protection of slavery.

The Kansas-Nebraska Act of 1854 further heightened sectional tensions by overturning the Missouri Compromise of 1820 that had barred slavery from territories North of the 36° 30′ parallel. Instead slavery in the territories would now be decided by popular sovereignty, the choice of the majority of the voters in a territory. As a result the North and South now competed to spread their systems to the western territories, resulting in vigilante violence throughout Kansas as Northern and Southern immigrants fought one another. The Kansas-Nebraska Act and the U.S. Supreme Court's 1857 *Dred Scott* decision (*Dred Scott v. Sanford*), which ruled that Congress could not bar slavery from the territories, resulted in Northern fears of an aggressive Southern policy that seemed to have captured the federal government with the intention of spreading slavery. As a result the Republican Party, which opposed the expansion of slavery into the territories, was in an excellent position to play on these Northern concerns and, with the decline of the Whigs, rise to become one of the two dominant political parties. The Republican Party, given its membership and opposition to the expansion of slavery, raised concerns throughout the South, which resulted in significant gains for secessionists throughout the region as the population turned against Republican Party policies.

The Breaking Point

With the election of Republican President Abraham Lincoln (1809–1865) in the election of 1860 a series of Southern states began to hold secession conventions, as South Carolina had in 1832. In 1860 South Carolina was the first state to secede in response to Lincoln's election. Southern states in the Lower South were the first to hold secession conventions, and Mississippi, Florida, Alabama, Georgia, Louisiana and Texas all seceded from the United States. Majorities had voted within these states to nominate the delegates that led them out of the convention. Native-born Americans who were slave-owners were far more likely to support secession, while those from areas of the South that had less of a connection to the institution were more likely to oppose secession, as were first and second generation immigrants in the South. The Upper South similarly appeared far less likely to support secession than its Gulf Coast cousins. The Lower South formed a government and adopted a constitution on February 7, 1861. Once hostilities broke out with the firing on Fort Sumter the Upper South moved to join its Southern brethren. Virginia seceded on April 17 and Arkansas, Tennessee, and North Carolina then followed, joining the Confederate States of America, the capital of which was transferred to Richmond shortly after Virginia left the Union.

The Southern state conventions argued that the election of the Republican Party endangered their constitutional rights. The Convention in South Carolina in its *Declaration of the Immediate Causes which Induce and Justify the Secession of South Carolina from the Federal Union* wrote of the Republican victory in 1860:

> This party will take possession of the Government. It has announced, that the South shall be excluded from the common Territory; that the Judicial Tribunals shall be made sectional, and that a war must be waged against slavery until it shall cease throughout the United States. The Guaranties of the Constitution will then no longer exist; the equal rights of the States will be lost. The slaveholding States will no longer have the power of self-government, or self-protection, and the Federal Government will have become their enemy. (p. 10)

In attempting to persuade Virginia to secede and combine with the Lower South, C. G. Memminger, acting as the commissioner from South Carolina to the authorities of the state of Virginia, noted in his 1860 address the common bonds of the South and the failure of the North to respect Virginia pointing to John Brown's raid into Virginia at Harper's Ferry: "That very North, to whom she had surrendered a territorial empire—who had grown great through her generous confidence—sent forth the assassins, furnished them with arms and money, and would fain rescue them from the infamy and punishment due to crimes so atrocious" (p. 7). Secession commissioners would focus on the aggressions of the North and a common Southern heritage, but slavery remained at the heart of their arguments. As Charles B. Dew points out in his 1861 book *Apostles of Disunion*:

> The commissioners sent out to spread the secessionist gospel in late 1860 and early 1861 clearly believed that the racial fate of their region was hanging in the balance in the wake of Lincoln's election. Only through disunion could the South be saved from the disastrous effects of Republican principles and Republican malevolence. Hesitation, submission—any course other than immediate secession—would place both slavery and white supremacy on the road to certain extinction. (p. 80)

Thus, slavery lay at the heart of the Southern secessionist movement. Despite the long history of the compact theory of government, it was unlikely that without the slavery issue the South would have chosen the course of secession.

Many Southern nationalists and secessionists took up their course reluctantly and saw the Confederacy as far more in line with the original Constitution of the United States than the course they feared the Republicans would pursue once in power. Thomas Ruffin of North Carolina, as a member of the House of Representatives, addressed this point, arguing in an 1861 speech that the issue at hand was whether Southern states and Southern institutions were to be treated as equals:

> They are to decide whether they will tamely and quietly submit to the arrogance, the tyranny, the usurpation of a hostile, unprincipled, and reckless majority, fatally bent on the destruction of their institutions, or whether they will assert their rights, and maintain them by all the means in their power. Devotedly attached to the Constitution and the Union, as the people of the South have ever been, and ardently hoping that a change in the public sentiment of the North would prevent a further persistence in the wrongs practiced upon the minority section, they have exercised the most extraordinary forbearance. (p. 1)

With Lincoln's election many Southerners felt that the rights of individuals were about to be violated—specifically the rights to take their property into the western territories—but more importantly Southern citizens saw the election of Lincoln as leading to their region's movement into a permanent minority status within the nation, a nation that, in Ruffin's view, would be increasingly willing to violate the rights of the minority party.

Contributing Factors

There were other motives for secession. In the 1861 publication *The Effect of Secession upon the Commercial Relations between the North and South, and upon Each*

Virginia planter and "fire-eater," Edmund Ruffin (1794–1865). Known as a "fire-eater" for his outspoken attitudes advocating slavery and secession, Virginia planter Edmund Ruffin became well known for his research to improve Southern agriculture as well as his claim to have fired the opening shot of the Civil War at Ft. Sumter. *The Library of Congress.*

Section, issued shortly before the start of the war, a motive for secession explored the federal government's use of the tariff, which appeared to benefit the North at the expense of the South:

> For nearly half a century South Carolina, the author of the movement, has been dissatisfied with the policy of the General Government as to the mode of raising its revenue. In 1832, this dissatisfaction very nearly broke out in open rebellion, but was awed into submission by the determined attitude of General Jackson then President of the United States; but, the question was not settled—only postponed by the adoption of the compromise of Mr. Clay. (pp. 3–4)

While the issue of expansion of slavery into the territories was the primary issue of the day, the work raises an important point: that the secession movement in the South began not over slavery, but rather the issue of the tariff. As an issue it continued to be of importance for the Southern economy and conceivably to the advantage of Southern consumers if secession could be accomplished.

During the war M. J. Michelbacher's 1863 work *A Sermon Delivered on the Day of Prayer* reiterated Southern fears over how the Northern majority endangered the practice of slavery in the South. Michelbacher expressed the Southern feelings of inequality for their region within the union and how that necessitated secession and the war:

> We have fought, and are now fighting, by reason of a virtuous resolution to live apart from those, who for many years marred our peace and increased our anxiety for the preservation of our institutions and our safety, and, who down to the moment of our separation, derided our solemn protests against their repeated violations of our sovereign rights, and have converted a Federal government into a central one, for the purpose of founding a despotism, that we may more speedily receive the lash of a tyrant. (p. 8)

This Southern impression of the North as an overreaching entity was at the center of secessionism and the increasing sense of Southern nationalism. Given the feared violation of Southern institutions the Southern states believed they could withdraw from the union and have authority devolve to the state governments, which predated the union. The governor of South Carolina, F. W. Pickens in his 1861 statement *The Governor's Message and Correspondence with the Commissioners from Virginia* wrote: "We have been forced to resume our original power of government, and to assert our separate sovereignty as a State, in order to seek that protection which we were compelled to believe would not be given to us and to our people, under the power of such a party and such a Chief Magistrate" (p. 4). Southern nationalism was at first largely state-centered rather than focused on the Southern region. The creation of the Confederate States of America and the war itself would create a stronger sense of Southern nationalism than had existed before the war.

Secessionists and Southern nationalists drew on a rich intellectual tradition in the compact theory of government in order to justify secession. South Carolina's earlier attempt at secession in 1832, in particular, was a turning point in that it created a radical minority that persevered in its calls for secession. It would not be until the series of crises between the North and the South arising out of the lands taken in the Mexican War, however, that secession became a live option for the majority of Southerners. The issue of slavery was the primary incentive for secession, and the Confederacy throughout the war struggled in its efforts to form a strong sense of Southern nationalism, as states' rights doctrines continued to hamper the Southern war effort.

BIBLIOGRAPHY

Dew, Charles B. *Apostles of Disunion: Southern Secession Commissioners and the Causes of the Civil War.* Charlottesville: University of Virginia Press, 2001.

The Effect of Secession upon the Commercial Relations between the North and South, and upon Each Section. [1861] Charlottesville: University of Virginia Press, 2001.

Memminger, Christopher Gustavus. *Address of the Hon. C.G. Memminger, Special Commissioner from the State of South Carolina: Before the Assembled Authorities of the State of Virginia, January 19, 1860.* [U.S., s.n., 1860?] Sources in U.S. History Online: Civil War. Gale. Available from http://galenet.galegroup.com/.

Michelbacher, Maximilian J. *A Sermon Delivered on the Day of Prayer: Recommended by the President of the C.S. of A., the 27th of March, 1863, at the German Hebrew Synagogue, "Bayth Ahabah."* Richmond, VA: Macfarlane and Fergusson, 1863. Sources in U.S. History Online: Civil War. Gale. Available from http://galenet.galegroup.com/.

Pickens, F. W. *The Governor's Message and Correspondence with the Commissioners from Virginia.* Charleston: Evans and Cogswell, 1861. Sources in U.S. History Online: Civil War. Gale. Available from http://galenet.galegroup.com/.

Ruffin, Thomas. *State Rights and State Equality: Speech of Hon. Thomas Ruffin, of North Carolina, Delivered in the House of Representatives, February 20, 1861.* [Washington, DC: H. Polkinhorn's Steam Job Press, 1861.] Sources in U.S. History Online: Civil War. Gale. Available from http://galenet.galegroup.com/.

South Carolina. Convention. *Declaration of the Immediate Causes which Induce and Justify the Secession of South Carolina from the Federal Union: and the Ordinance of Secession.* Charleston: Evans and Cogswell, 1860.

Michael Kelly Beauchamp

PROSLAVERY ADVOCATES

Proslavery advocates defended the institution of slavery from increasing attacks by Northern abolitionists. These advocates vigorously argued for slavery's expansion into the western territories and also into the Caribbean and Latin America, while defending its preservation where it already existed. Proslavery arguments tended to take three different tacks. Some argued for the justness of the institution based on the racial inferiority of African Americans. Under this argument, slavery was justified as natural and a positive good for blacks that lifted them up from a degraded state. Other advocates of slavery chose to contrast the civilization of the South with the abuses of the increasingly industrialized North to illustrate the superiority of a patriarchal civilization based on slavery. Other advocates based their defense of the institution on Christian scripture and history.

The revolutionary generation of the South felt that slavery was an evil that would be eliminated in time, though they themselves failed to deal with the issue. Founders such as Thomas Jefferson (1743–1826) and James Madison (1731–1826), while slaveholders themselves, had little problem acknowledging the detrimental effects of the institution, not just for the slaves but for whites as well. Many Southerners in the first decades after the American Revolution (1775–1783) hoped to gradually abolish the institution in the South and to resettle the former slaves elsewhere, with Africa or Latin America as the most popular choices. This commitment to ending slavery was demonstrated in many members of the elites' decisions to free their slaves either late in life or upon their death. This active antislavery movement in the South in the early nineteenth century began to decline after 1832, when Virginia's state legislature failed to pass a law that would have led to the gradual emancipation of slavery in the state, similar to legislation that had occurred in New York and other states.

Over the course of the 1830s and 1840s, Southern opposition to slavery or even to criticism of the institution began to disappear. This Southern attitude mirrored and was in part a response to a more vigorous abolitionist critique from groups in Northern states. The large corpus of abolitionist literature elicited a response from numerous Southern authors. For instance, Harriet Beecher Stowe's (1811–1896) antislavery novel *Uncle Tom's Cabin*, published in 1852, resulted in responses from numerous Southern writers, most notably, novelist William Gilmore Simms (1806–1870) and his novel *The Sword and the Distaff.* Proslavery advocates across the South made it increasingly difficult for those Southerners who were abolitionists to remain in the South if they expressed their views publicly.

Some proslavery advocates defended the institution as beneficial for the slaves themselves. This argument was based on the supposed inferiority of African Americans. William Henry Holcombe argued that the natural inferiority of African Americans made it acceptable for whites to put them in a state of slavery in order to improve their lot in life. He believed this to be the natural order ordained by providence itself, as he argued in his 1860 book *The Alternative: A Separate Nationality or the Africanization of the South.* In reference to the slave trade, Holcombe wrote: "It was permitted by God in order to teach us the way in which the dark races are to be elevated and civilized. Jamaica and Hayti [*sic*] have also been permitted, as timely and salutary warnings, not to desert the path which was marked out by Providence" (p. 6). Holcombe viewed the inferiority of blacks as a result of natural differences, but differences ordained by God. He illustrates his point by pointing to the failure of black nations such as Haiti to achieve a semblance of stability. Advocates of this view argued that blacks were incapable of taking care of themselves and needed the guidance of their white masters. Thus, slavery not only provided whites with economic benefits but also, in the view of many Southern proslavery advocates, helped to advance the black race. Holcombe, like many other slavery advocates, became as a matter of course a secessionist. Holcombe in the same work wrote that the Republican Party was intent on freeing slaves of the South and thereby allowing them to Africanize the region through natural propagation. The idea of a biracial society based on equality was absurd to Holcombe, as he believed it would degenerate into violence. Earlier Southern leaders had also pointed to this problem, such as Thomas Jefferson, who argued that should the slaves be freed, whites and blacks would be incapable of living peacefully with one another.

Other proslavery advocates defended the institution by contrasting it with what they viewed as the industrial abuses of the North. Lawyer and plantation owner George Fitzhugh (1806–1881) argued that slavery was a far more humane institution than wage labor in factories in that slaves were cared for in their youth, in old age, in sickness, and in health, whereas the industrial workers of the North when elderly or unproductive would be unemployed with no one to care for them. Fitzhugh's 1854 work *Sociology for the South* argued that free market capitalism as a system benefited the strong while degrading the weak. Slavery for Fitzhugh benefited blacks, who otherwise would be exploited by the industrial system, but also poor whites who thereby secured a higher social and economic status while avoiding the perils of an industrial work force. Fitzhugh's second book, the 1857 *Cannibals All*, described Northern industrial society as "wage slavery." Fitzhugh went beyond just a simple defense of the institution of slavery to a critique of the inequalities found in modern industrial society. He believed the South through slavery represented an older and more just agrarian form of civilization when compared to the harsh realities of the capitalistic industrial North.

Many Southern advocates of slavery defended the institution through Christian doctrine. In order to justify the practice they tended to turn to biblical passages in both the Old and the New Testaments that emphasized obedience and respect to masters. In addition, Christian apologists for slavery noted the ancient Israelite patriarchs use of slavery. These Christian defenses of slavery ultimately led to the division of several denominations as abolitionist Christians in the North and proslavery Christians in the South disagreed as to the morality of the institution in the eyes of God. In 1844, the Methodist Episcopal Church split into Northern and Southern branches over slavery. Similarly, the Baptist church in the United States split over the issue of slavery, leading to the formation of the Southern Baptist Convention in 1845. Presbyterians bridged the divide until the onset of the Civil War. When the split did occur, however, Southern Presbyterians explicitly defended slavery. The General Assembly of the Presbyterian Church in the Confederate States of America, in its 1861 *Address to all the Churches of Jesus Christ throughout the Earth*, rejected the notion that slavery could be a sin given the lack of a scriptural condemnation of it, a position its recently-connected Northern brethren had held to until the political separation:

Southern author William Gilmore Simms (1806–1870). Many Southern authors, including William Gilmore Simms, penned novels glorifying the place of slavery in the South in response to Harriet Beecher Stowe's *Uncle Tom's Cabin*. These proslavery works often featured benevolent white masters and gentle wives who cared for their grateful slaves, as a father cares for his young children. *Public Domain*

> Shall our names be cast out as evil, and the finger of scorn pointed at us because we utterly refuse to break our communion with Abraham, Isaac and Jacob, with Moses, David and Isaiah, with Apostles, Prophets and Martyrs, with all the noble army of confessors who have gone to glory from slave-holding countries and from a slave-holding church, without ever having dreamed that they were living in mortal sin, by conniving at slavery in the midst of them. (p. 13)

The Southern Presbyterians made a historical argument that the church and scripture heretofore had not made a judgment as to the evils of slavery, and that for the North or other churches to do so at his moment was extravagantly overreaching, given the history of the church and the words of the scriptures on the issue.

Protestant Southern ministers were among some of the most strident proslavery advocates. Presbyterian ministers such as Benjamin M. Palmer, James Henley Thornwell, and Robert Lewis Dabney, who was also an influential theologian, defended slavery. Benjamin M. Palmer, in an address to his congregation of the First Presbyterian Church of New Orleans entitled *The South: Her Peril and her Duty* on November 29, 1860, explicitly argued that secession was a necessity given the importance of slavery for Southern civilization, an arrangement justified in the Bible: "Need I pause to show how this system is interwoven with our social fabric? That these slaves form parts of our household, even as our children; and that, too, through a relationship recognized and sanctioned in the scriptures of God even as the other?" (p. 8). Augustus Baldwin Longstreet (1790–1870) similarly defended slavery and the Southern cause as a Methodist minister, as did Baptist minister Thornton Stringfellow. Even Northern born Episcopalians such as Samuel Seabury would produce slavery apologias.

British observers of the American Civil War discerned Southern motivations for the war and investigated Southern defenses of slavery. Sidney E. Morse, in his 1863 work *A Geographical, Statistical and Ethical View of the American Slaveholders' Rebellion*, gave the Southern defenders of slavery a sympathetic treatment, taking their religious arguments on slavery quite seriously:

> Not only Abraham and other Jewish patriarchs, but some of the men most distinguished for Christian virtues in the time of Christ and his Apostles, were slaveholders, none of whom were rebuked for holding their fellowmen in slavery, while on one of these slaveholders, who was also an officeholder in the army of an absolute military despot, Christ bestowed the highest eulogy, and that too immediately after this slaveholder had openly avowed that he held and exercised absolute power over his fellow-men in both of these relations. (p. 6)

Thus from a strictly scriptural point of view, outside observers acknowledged the Southern defense of slavery had some validity.

Upon the end of hostilities, many Southern secessionist advocates began to subtly shift their position, attributing secession not to the issue of slavery but to states' rights. Nevertheless, after the Civil War, Southern proslavery apologists in their histories, while concentrating on states' rights far more than slavery, continued to point to slavery as a beneficial institution. Edward Alfred Pollard in one of the first such Southern histories on the war described slavery as a pretext seized on by the North to justify its sectional animosity against Southern civilization. Even so, Pollard in his 1866 work *The Lost Cause* still engaged the Northern argument against slavery on its own merits:

> That system of servitude in the South which was really the mildest in the world; which did not rest on acts of debasement and disenfranchisement, but elevated the Africans, and was in the interest of human improvement; and which by the law of the land, protected the negro in life and limb, and in many personal rights, and, by the practice of the system, bestowed upon him a sum of individual indulgences, which made him altogether the most striking type in the world of cheerfulness and contentment. (p. 49)

Thus, even though Pollard contested that the morality question was really not what the war was about, he notes that it was a beneficial institution. Similarly, Alexander Hamilton Stephens (1812–1883), who at the beginning of the conflict had vociferously identified slavery with the Confederacy in speeches as the vice president of the Confederacy, focused on issues of state sovereignty rather than slavery in his treatment of the issue after the war. Stephens, in his 1868 *A Constitutional View of the Late War Between the States*, wrote how he thought Southerners who opposed Northern centralization were identified with proslavery forces: "By their acts, they did not identify themselves with the Pro-slavery Party (for in truth, no such Party had, at that time, or at any time in the History of the Country, any organized existence). They only identified themselves, or took position, with those who maintained the Federative character of the General Government" (p. 11). Stephens and other Southerners soon after the war's conclusion began the process of revising the Southern cause not as a defense of slavery, but rather as a defense of states' rights. Yet these first revisionists could not avoid making at least a theoretical defense of slavery that shares an intellectual history with the arguments made by earlier proslavery advocates.

BIBLIOGRAPHY

Holcombe, William H. *The Alternative: A Separate Nationality, or the Africanization of the South.* New Orleans: Delta Mammoth, 1860. Sources in U.S. History Online: Civil War. Gale. Available from http://galenet.galegroup.com/.

Morse, Sidney E. *A Geographical, Statistical and Ethical View of the American Slaveholders' Rebellion.* New York: A. D. F. Randolph, 1863. Sources in U.S. History Online: Civil War. Gale. Available from http://galenet.galegroup.com/.

Palmer, Benjamin Morgan. *The South: Her Peril, and Her Duty: A Discourse, Delivered in the First Presbyterian Church, New Orleans, on Thursday, November 29, 1860.* New Orleans: True Witness and

Sentinel, 1860. Sources in U.S. History Online: Civil War. Gale. Available from http://galenet.galegroup.com/.

Pollard, Edward Alfred. *The Lost Cause: A New Southern History of the War of the Confederates: Comprising a Full and Authentic Account of the Rise and Progress of The Late Southern Confederacy.* New York: E. B. Treat and Co., 1866. Sources in U.S. History Online: Civil War. Gale. Available from http://galenet.galegroup.com/.

Presbyterian Church in the Confederate States of America. General Assembly. *Address of the General Assembly of the Presbyterian Church in the Confederate States of America to All the Churches of Jesus Christ throughout the Earth.* [Augusta, GA.]: By order of the Assembly, [1861]. Sources in U.S. History Online: Civil War. Gale. Available from http://galenet.galegroup.com/.

Stephens, Alexander Hamilton. *A Constitutional View of the Late War between the States: Its Causes, Character, Conduct and Results: Presented in a Series of Colloquies at Liberty Hall.* Philadelphia, PA: National Pub. Co., 1868–1870. Sources in U.S. History Online: Civil War. Gale. Available from http://galenet.galegroup.com/.

Michael Kelly Beauchamp

NORTHERN SUPPORT FOR THE WAR

Few scholars would argue today that a moral objection to slavery was the direct cause of the American Civil War. There were those, however, including contemporary Northerners, who supported the war in belief that it amounted to a moral crusade to destroy slavery. In a speech on March 3, 1863, at the Statehouse in Albany, New York, George I. Post of Cayuga castigated those who insisted that slavery was not the cause of the Civil War. Post explained, "Sir, the cause of this controversy [Civil War] is slavery. The cause of the disregard of the obligations of laws and Constitution is slavery. The cause of disrespect of constituted authority has grown out of slavery" (Post 1863, p. 2). Peter Cooper, a Christian patriot, was highly disturbed that conditions in the South would require the Federal Government to use its power and authority to maintain slavery. He believed that "... the enslavement of human beings has so far infused its insidious poison into the very hearts of the Southern people [and] that they have come to believe ... the evil of slavery to be a good ..." (Cooper 1863, p. 2).

Some who supported the war on a moral basis were abolitionists who filtered their views through a prism of religion and righteous indignation. Other abolitionists in the North, black and white, viewed the war effort from a more practical basis. They noted the contradiction between the declaration of the equality of all men in the preamble to the United States Constitution and the nation's toleration of the existence of a large slave population. In addition, these abolitionists believed that it was impossible for the United States to continue to exist as a half-slave and half-free polity. Their support in waging war against the South was both moral and pragmatic. While the moral legitimacy of slavery was not the direct cause of the Civil War, as Peter Cooper believed it was, slavery affected and poisoned the moral, economic, social, cultural, and political climate of the United States. Had slavery not existed, it is unlikely that there would have been an American Civil War.

Concept of the Union

There were other issues of significance for some Northerners who had pragmatic reasons for supporting the war. Much of the white Northern population in general cared less about the abolishment of slavery than about the breakup of the federal union of the states. They were willing to compromise on the question of abolition provided that the South rejected secession as a political solution to the issue of slavery. Furthermore, many Northern industrialists and businessmen thought that slave labor was inefficient and hindered industrial development. They too would have preferred a compromise that involved monetary compensation for slaveholders in exchange for abolishing slavery. After all, a large pool of low-paid black industrial workers would have been profitable for Northern capitalists.

Slavery and Westward Expansion

Slavery also became a highly charged political issue relating to sectional development as immigrants crossed the Mississippi River and settled in the Western Territories. Neither the North nor the South wanted the other to gain a political advantage in Congress. Therefore, the question of the extension of slavery into the West became a political issue of the highest order. To a number of both antislavery and proslavery politicians in the North, the issues related to slavery in the Western Territories were as much about political power as they were about the moral dimension of slavery. If Congress had allowed the unrestricted expansion of slavery into the Western lands, the balance of power would have favored the slaveholding Southern states and likely would have resulted in the establishment of a permanent slavocracy. The Western Territory remained important to Northerners after the beginning of hostilities due to the number of Southern sympathizers living there. An 1864 Army intelligence report noted that "... it has been generally known ... that a secret treasonable organization affiliated with the Southern Rebellion, and chiefly military . . . has been rapidly extending itself throughout the West" (U.S. War Department 1864, p. 1).

The political crises precipitated by the Missouri Compromise (1820), which allowed slavery in Missouri while Maine entered the Union as a free state; the Compromise of 1850, which permitted slavery in the New Mexico and Utah Territories while California became a free state; and the Kansas-Nebraska Act (1854), which based the existence of slavery in Kansas and Nebraska on popular sovereignty, were efforts to maintain political parity between the antislave North and the proslave South. However, the bloody internecine war in Kansas ("Bleeding Kansas") in 1856 between proslave and antislave factions; the brutal beating that Radical Republican leader Charles Sumner (1811–1874) received in 1856 at the hands of a Southern representative, Preston Brooks (1819–1857), on the floor of the Senate; and the decision in the *Dred Scott* case (1857), declaring slaves chattel, exacerbated fears in the North of a Southern conspiracy to make slavery legal supported by then-President James Buchanan (1791–1868). Northern papers and other publications frequently published what they purported to be Southern outrages against antislavery Northerners in the South and West. Conversely, John Brown's antislavery activities in Kansas and ultimate raid on the federal arsenal in Harpers Ferry, Virginia (1859), and abolitionist fervor in the North made Southerners fear a pro-black Republican conspiracy to abolish slavery and subjugate Southern whites. In fact, William H. Holcombe, a Southern physician, went so far as to accuse the North of purposely Africanizing the South. Holcombe contended that "If the Republican Party is permitted to get into power, the Africanization of the South will be gradual, but it will be sure" (1860, p. 9).

Harriet Tubman (1820–1913), escaped slave and liberator. A slave who escaped from bondage, Harriet Tubman made numerous return trips to the South, helping nearly seventy slaves escape, including members of her own family. Unlike other Northern Civil War supporters who fought the South to preserve the Union, Tubman believed the primary focus of the war should be the abolition of slavery. *The Library of Congress.*

Northern Attitudes toward Abolition

Abraham Lincoln, who came to national prominence in 1858 after the famous Lincoln-Douglas debates with Senator Stephen A. Douglas (1813–1861), was not a fervent abolitionist bent on destroying the "evil" system. Lincoln was a pragmatist whose first priority as president was to find common ground between the North and the South to prevent fragmentation of the Union. When castigated by the journalist and abolitionist Horace Greeley (1811–1872) for his timidity in denouncing slavery, Lincoln replied in a public letter to Greeley that "My paramount object in this struggle is to save the Union, and is not either to save or destroy slavery" (Rhodes 1907, p. 74). After the Civil War began in April 1861, abolitionists continued to press Lincoln to abolish slavery but he refused to do so. Furthermore, most Northern Democrats did not support war with the South for any reason. These so-called Copperheads accused President Lincoln of violating the Constitution and claimed, with some justification, that the Civil War was a poor man's war. Others were against secession. For example, a Northern Democrat, in a letter to W. G. Brownlow, the Whig editor of a Knoxville newspaper, praised Brownlow's proslavery but antisecessionist views by saying that "The classes of Northern people have no feelings but the most friendly toward their brethren of the South and are ready to concede to them all their rights" (Ash 1999, p. 56).

There were in fact many Northerners who had little sympathy with or interest in abolitionism and the problems of either slaves or free blacks. A Democratic Pennsylvania state senator, Hiester Clymer (1827–1884), for example, adamantly opposed a bill in Congress during the Civil War to emancipate slaves in the District of Columbia. Clymer insisted that its passage would "... afford a place for harboring and concealing free Negroes and runaway slaves [and] . . . where arms can be put into the hands of slaves . . . from which tumult, rebellions and insurrections may be—and will be—incited in the State of Maryland" (Clymer 1862, p. 4). One popular slogan of the time was "We Won't Fight to Free the Nigger." Recent immigrants in particular tended to support the views of antiwar Copperheads. Northern Democrats who supported Lincoln were interested in restoring the Union and were adamantly against emancipating the slaves. They petitioned Lincoln often in an attempt to obtain equal consideration of their views as an alternative to those of the Radical Republicans and free blacks who urged the President to abolish slavery outright. Quite simply, many white Northerners did not want to wage a war for the benefit of African Americans.

Northern and Southern racists fueled the flames of Negrophobia in the North with wild stories about hordes of emancipated slaves arriving in the North and posing a threat to the safety of white women. Moreover, many Northern Democrats feared that emancipation would result in competition for jobs, housing, and other resources at the expense of whites. Like Democrats, Northern Republicans were not unified on the issue of emancipation. Conservative Republicans did not favor the emancipation of slaves or providing assistance for their welfare. In addition, they were against arming blacks and recruiting them into the Northern army. The Radical Republicans, on the other hand, advocated the confiscation of Southern land for the use of freed slaves and supported their participation in the military in defense of the nation. In the end, President Lincoln's issuance of the Emancipation Proclamation in 1863, applicable to those Southern states in rebellion against the Union, occurred when the war was not going well for the North.

Costs of the War

As is the case for any war, the longer it lasts the more support for it dwindles. The Civil War proved to be a hardship for Northern soldiers and civilians alike. It was the most costly war in terms of lost lives in the nation's history. The North suffered 140,414 battle deaths; 224,097 deaths as a result of disease, poor medical care, accidents, and other causes; and 281,881 nonfatal casualties out of a total population of only 22 million in 1861 (*World Almanac*, 1996, p. 166). Understandably, the high casualty rate caused disenchantment with the war.

Further, the 1863 draft in the North was not applied equally; the law allowed some men to hire substitutes, including mercenaries, for the draft. Wealthy Northerners could pay a $300 exemption fee and skip military service. These practices further eroded support for the war in the North and led to violent antidraft riots in New York in the summer of 1863. In addition, as a result of increased resentment of blacks, the rioters, primarily Irish immigrants, assaulted, burned and even lynched a number of black New Yorkers.

African Americans in the North came closest to giving President Abraham Lincoln's policies unconditional support and backing. However, while Frederick Douglass, Sojourner Truth, Harriet Tubman, and other black abolitionists supported war against the South, their emphasis was on destroying the institution of slavery. They were less concerned about the criticism of Lincoln as a tyrant for suspending civil liberties in violation of the Constitution. They understood that Lincoln's critics were not talking about the rights of African Americans. Chief Justice Roger Taney (1777–1864) had articulated the majority view about blacks in the *Dred Scott* decision when he said that blacks had no rights that whites are bound to respect. Furthermore, Douglass himself on many occasions had referred to the Constitution as a proslavery document.

Senator James A. Bayard, Jr. (1799–1880) of Delaware, a border state, apparently agreed with Douglass. In protest against the emancipation of slaves in the District of Columbia, Bayard reminded his Senate colleagues of the Fifth Amendment, which states in part that no person should "... be deprived of life, liberty, or property [slaves] without due process of law; nor shall private property [slaves] be taken for public use without just compensation" (Bayard 1862, p. 9). In light of such views, black support for Lincoln and waging war against the secessionist states was predicated on the abolition of slavery.

African Americans in general wanted to participate in the war to abolish slavery. There was, however, widespread resistance in the North relating to the recruitment of so-called colored troops. While much of this resistance was based on pure racism—the belief that blacks were inferior, undisciplined, and prone to running in the face of danger, there was also alarm and fear in the North about arming large numbers of African Americans. Nonetheless, the political reality of the North's tenuous military position was apparent by the late summer of 1862, and the military began to recruit colored soldiers. Following the issuance of the Emancipation Proclamation in January 1863, Lincoln authorized the recruitment of colored troops with white leadership in Connecticut, Rhode Island, and Massachusetts. The Fifty-fourth Massachusetts Infantry Regiment was among the first black regiments to be formed in the North. In July 1863, the regiment launched a courageous but ultimately ill-fated attack against Confederate forces at Fort Wagner in South Carolina. Nevertheless, even in defeat the black soldiers achieved a victory in demonstrating their courage, effectiveness, and patriotism.

The support in the North for war against the Confederate States reflected the bitter divisiveness of the Civil War. While a majority of the Northern populace approved of the war to save the Union, a significant number were ambivalent about the abolition of slavery and the cause of African Americans. Nonetheless, the support of blacks was a crucial factor in the ultimate victory of the North. Ironically, participation in a largely segregated Northern military did not bode well for African Americans in achieving full equality in either military or civilian life. Some 200,000 blacks served in the Union Army during the Civil War but still faced pervasive racism (*World Almanac*, 1996, p. 162). Black soldiers were most critical about receiving less pay than white soldiers. A soldier from Pennsylvania expressed black sentiment on the issue eloquently in a letter to the *Christian Recorder* in February 1864. He stated, "I am a soldier, or at least that is what I was drafted for in the 6th USCT . . . and it made me feel proud to fight for Uncle Sam . . . our officers tell me now that we are not soldiers . . . that the government just called us out to dig and drudge, that we are to get but $7.00 per month" (*The Christian Recorder*, 1864). Nonetheless, African American soldiers supported the North during the Civil War and would continue to fight in the nation's wars. They served primarily in racially segregated units until President Harry S. Truman (1884–1972) signed an Executive Order in 1948 outlawing racial discrimination in the military.

BIBLIOGRAPHY

American Anti-Slavery Society. *A Fresh Catalogue of Southern Outrages upon Northern Citizens.* New York: American Anti-Slavery Society, 1860.

Ash, Stephen V., ed. *Secessionists and Other Scoundrels: Selections from Parson Brownlow's Book.* Baton Rouge: Louisiana State University Press, 1999.

Bayard, James A. *Abolition and the Relations of Races: Speech of Hon. James A. Bayard: Delivered in the Senate of the United States, April 8, 1862.* Washington, DC: 1862.

The Christian Recorder. Philadelphia: February 20, 1864.

Clymer, Hiester. "Is Emancipation the Object of the Present War, or Is It to Sustain the Constitution as It Is, and Restore the Union as It Was?" *Speech of Hon. Hiester Clymer of Berks County.* Philadelphia: Statehouse, March 11, 1862.

Cooper, Peter. *Letter of Peter Cooper on Slave Emancipation in Loyal Publication Society,* No. 23. New York: William C. Bryant & Co., Printers, 1863.

Holcombe, William H., M. D. *The Alternative: A Separate Nationality or the Africanization of the South.* New Orleans, LA: Delta Mammoth Job Office, 1860.

Johnson, Michael. P. *Reading the American Past, Selected Historical Documents: Volume I: To 1877.* Boston: Bedford/St. Martin's, 2005.

Post, George I. *Cause of the War-Proclamation-Arbitrary Arrests: Speech of Honorable George I. Post of Cayuga, In the House of Assembly.* Documents from the New York State Union Central Committee, No. 14, March 3, 1863.

Rhodes, James Ford. *History of the United States from the Compromise of 1850 to the Final Restoration of Home Rule at the South in 1877.* New York: The Macmillan Company, 1907.

United States Army, Judge Advocate General's Department. *Report of the Judge General on the "Order of American Knights" or "Sons of Liberty:" A Western Conspiracy in Aid of the Southern Rebellion.* Washington, DC: War Department, 1864.

Yetman, Norman R., ed. *Voices From Slavery: 100 Authentic Slave Narratives.* Mineola, NY: Dover Publications, Inc., 1970.

The World Almanac and Book of Facts, 1996. Mahwah, New Jersey: World Almanac Books, 1996.

Donald Roe

Opposition to the War

OPPOSITION TO THE WAR: AN OVERVIEW

As in all armed conflicts—and particularly in regards internal national conflicts—public opinion on both sides of the Civil War was acutely divided on how the war should be conducted and even over whether it should be waged at all. Opposition existed at all strata of society and at all levels of intensity, passive and active, and would manifest itself in a variety of ways. It may be fair to say that the actual combat was waged by a relative few and, though almost everyone would have been at least indirectly affected, the vast majority of individuals wished to avoid being in harm's way, to cope and survive, and to continue with their lives. The rationale that drove individuals or groups into opposition were varied and complex. To many, the outcome of the war was a matter of indifference; others openly or secretly sympathized with the other side, but chose not to make the trip—either north or south—to enlist. For many, it was personal. Some opposed war on principle or religious conviction; others were scared of dying or saw no compelling reason to risk themselves for emancipation, states' rights, slavery, sectional particularism, or the concept of an "indivisible" Union. The ways in which they expressed their dissent could be as divergent as their motives for opposition. Some deserted, some protested, others sympathized with the other side or expressed their opposition in the political arena.

Pockets of Resistance

Within the Confederacy there were large areas where the majority of the population was pro–Union: eastern Tennessee; western North Carolina; half of Missouri, Kentucky and Arkansas; and most of the counties of western Virginia (which branched off to form the separate Loyalist state of Kanawa and in 1863 evolved into West Virginia). In those regions plantation slavery had not established and indeed could not have established, a dominant economic profile; the quality of the agricultural land simply did not allow it. Consequently, most of the population had little or no stake in preserving the Southern way of life. Though most resisted passively, some did supply intelligence and support to occupying Union troops when the situation allowed, and a much smaller minority engaged in sporadic guerrilla raids.

Within the United States the most tender spots also lay along the border regions: eastern (Tidewater) Maryland was a hotbed for Confederate sympathizers, espionage, and smuggling. It was this network of Southern sympathy that John Wilkes Booth (1839–1865) tried to capitalize on to make his escape into Virginia after he assassinated President Abraham Lincoln (1809–1865). New York City, whose mayor Fernando Woods (1812–1881), had tried to have it declared a neutral area, and the Midwestern border region around the Ohio River also functioned as cradles for antiwar advocacy.

The Knights of the Golden Circle (KGC), a secretive fraternal organization with trappings and rituals reminiscent of Freemasonry, had been in existence since 1854, but after 1861 its membership was widely feared as a Southern "fifth column" bent on undermining the Union war effort. Though branches were rumored to exist in every state from the Eastern Seaboard to the California coast, most of its lodges were located provocatively close to the border in southern Illinois, Ohio, and Indiana. The nature and extent of the Knights' activities remain obscure. Allegedly they were involved in sending money and supplies to the Confederacy, in stoking sentiment for peace and resistance to the draft and war taxation, and (much less substantiated) in espionage and sabotage in various parts of the country.

More substantial was the threat posed by the Copperheads, because it was through them that the antiwar threat was translated into its most effective political terms. The Democratic Party had split into pro- and anti- war factions, and the peace advocates were pejoratively labeled "Copperheads." Congressman Clement Laird Vallandigham (1820–1871) of Ohio was certainly the loudest and most visible of this group. His outspokenness led General Ambrose Burnside (1824–1881) to order his arrest on May 5, 1863, imprisonment, and subsequent exile to the Confederacy. Though the Copperhead "Heartland" at first approximated that of the Knights of the Golden Circle, primarily in the regions in which it operated, sentiment for the movement gained strength in the East, particularly in New York City and other major urban hubs. Continuing Union defeats and mounting casualty rolls fueled the tide of discontent, which came to a climax in the 1864 elections with the defeat of Copperhead-supported presidential candidate George B. McClellan (1826–1885) at the hands of Lincoln's Republican Party.

Pacifism and the Draft

Some opposers of the war were forced to assume combat roles. George Hylton, a farmer from southwestern Virginia, was a member of the pacifist Dunker faith who could not pay the necessary $500 tax required for draft exemption on religious grounds. He was compelled by a Southern press gang to join the Confederate cavalry on pain of imprisonment and dispossession of his family's house and land. Hylton was pressed into the cavalry as a teamster and on the occasions that he was caught up in combat, he simply fired his gun into the air and managed to avoid direct confrontation with Federal soldiers.

Conscription had not been in the American military tradition; it was identified with Napoleonic Europe, and with despotism rather than democracy. Yet the length, intensity, and cost in manpower of the conflict were such that both sides felt compelled to initiate conscription in the face of sometimes fierce opposition. Draft resistance in the South, though it manifested itself less often in violence, was nevertheless widespread and pervasive, and in the end the conscription laws were irregularly enforced and became ineffectual. What was seen as innate unfairness in the exemption clauses that advantaged the wealthier echelons of society contributed to a passive resistance that proved to be extremely effective simply because it was quiet and non-confrontational. In the United States, as it became more obvious that volunteer enlistments were inadequate to cope with the demands of a war that had no end in sight, the president and congress resorted, in August 1862, to a draft law that proved only minimally effective but which aroused a great deal of resentment over its exemption clauses and over the fact that draftees who had money could hire "substitutes" to serve in their stead. Corrupt manipulation of the system by doctors who provided untruthful medical certificates, draft officials who could be bribed, and by "professional substitutes" who would sell themselves as draft substitutes several times, employing fake names and deserting, only to later re-enlist, were widespread.

Slavery and Emancipation

The issue of emancipation proved very divisive in the North. The Emancipation Proclamation, limited though

Riot in Baltimore, Maryland, April 19, 1861. Secessionists in Baltimore, Maryland, fired upon troops from the 6th Massachusetts Infantry Regiment during a prosecession riot on April 19, 1861. © *Corbis*

it was to freeing only those slaves located in areas still under Confederate control as of January 1, 1863, engendered resentment. This was in part for fear of excessively alienating slave owners and slavery supporters in the border states and in regions of the Confederacy recently—and in some cases only tentatively—under Federal occupation. Northern majority sentiment certainly adhered to the idea that African Americans were inferior to whites, and many considered the conflict to be a white man's war to be waged for the primary goal of preserving the Union rather than for abolishing slavery. Racism and war opposition could combine, with disastrous results, as witnessed during the New York Draft Riots of July 13–16, 1863, when African Americans were prime targets for the insurgents.

In the Confederacy race and slavery were also issues among many lower class whites, particularly among what was termed the yeoman farmer class. Many knew, slave holding being the expensive proposition that it was, that they would never own slaves and that they would never be of the planter class that many of them thus came to despise. Though most did not oppose the institution, they saw themselves as having a limited or even no stake in a war they considered was being waged to preserve the planter interests that dominated both the state and Confederate governments.

The Civil Liberties Issue

Infringements on civil liberties were put into effect in both the United States and the Confederacy, with the governments invoking necessity and the risk of threats to the national security. In each case the right of *habeas corpus* was suspended, and printing presses and newspaper offices were shut down or were subject to government censorship—editors and reporters were liable to be arrested and/or indefinitely detained. The first of these incidents occurred in the initial weeks of the conflict as a result of the Baltimore Riot of April 19, 1861, and the uncertainty of the state of Maryland's adherence to the Union—which threatened to cut off the Federal capital at Washington, DC. These events motivated Lincoln's government to suspend the right of *habeas corpus* and to shut down the entire Maryland state legislature. In certain instances, notably in the border states of Maryland, Kentucky, and Missouri, there were claims that Union troops patrolled the voting precincts in order to intimidate, arrest, or turn away known dissidents. On September 24, 1862, only one day after signing the preliminary emancipation proclamation, Lincoln mandated the suspension of *habeas corpus* throughout all the United States and all areas under the control of the United States (Neely 1991, pp. 51–53, 56–57, 72–74). Official handling of security matters was at first placed under the jurisdiction of the State Department (this occasioned Secretary of State William Henry Seward's (1801–1872) remark to the effect that he could arrest anyone in the nation by simply pushing the button to the bell on his desk. In February 1862 these tasks were transferred to the War Department. Although of Secretary of War Edwin M. Stanton (1814–1869) operated in a more restrained style, arrests, detentions, and interrogations continued. The majority of these covert activities were carried out by the National Detective Police (NDP) under Colonel Lafayette Baker, who was accountable only to Secretary Stanton.

Privation and Desertion

Some opposition to the war developed over time, fueled by hardship and privations which pushed resentment to the limit, sometimes with violent results, as in the Richmond Bread Riots of April 2, 1863. This was particularly true for the South, where the Union blockade, exactions from the Confederate government, a scarcity of younger, able-bodied men at work on the farms, and Union commanders' destructive policies had appreciably sapped the South's will to resist by late 1864. This proved decisive throughout the winter of 1864–1865. Desertion is the most pervasive form of antiwar protest, and though the consequences for being caught were severe, it remained endemic at all phases of the war in both sides' armies. After July 1863, and particularly during the declining months of the Confederacy, the specters of starvation and military defeat created such an atmosphere of despair that desertion rates soared. Communities of deserters, clustering in remote, usually mountainous regions, defied all attempts at retrieving them. During 1864–1865, with hopes fading for the Confederacy, desertion proved so horrendous in the trenches around Petersburg for the Army of Northern Virginia that it weaken General Robert E. Lee's (1807–1870) already overextended lines to such an extent that Union general Ulysses S. Grant's (1822–1885) forces were able to force the final breach on April 2, 1865.

BIBLIOGRAPHY

Lesser, W. Hunter. *Rebels at the Gate: Lee and McClellan on the Front Line of a Nation Divided.* Naperville, IL; Sourcebooks, 2004.

Marvel, William. *Mr. Lincoln Goes to War.* Boston: Houghton Mifflin Company, 2006.

Neely, Mark E., Jr. *The Fate of Liberty: Abraham Lincoln and Civil Liberties.* New York; Oxford University Press, 1991.

Palludan, Philip. *A People's Conflict.* 2nd ed. Lawrence: University Press of Kansas, 2007.

Steele, Philip W., and Steve Cottrell. *Civil War in the Ozarks.* Gretna, LA; Pelican Publishing Co., 2003.

Raymond Pierre Hylton

NORTHERN COPPERHEADS

The American Civil War divided the nation, but it also split communities in the North along political lines. At the beginning of the war, some Democrats opposed the decision of President Abraham Lincoln, a Republican, to go to war to preserve the Union. Whereas other Democrats, who became known as War Democrats, united with Republicans to support the war, these so-called Peace Democrats criticized Lincoln's policies and the conduct of the war. Republicans reacted to the Peace Democrats' antiwar agitation by calling them Copperheads, after the poisonous snake. This name stuck, and the Peace Democrats, who preferred to be called Conservatives, eventually embraced the title—but insisted that it was a reference to the U.S. penny (also known as a copperhead), which then depicted Lady Liberty. Although Republican critics often bitterly claimed that the Copperheads were disloyal to the point of conspiring to aid the Confederacy, these Democratic political dissenters actually opposed the war itself and simply disagreed with Republican objectives. Peace Democrats gained political power as the war dragged on, even gaining influence over the Democratic Party's nomination for the 1864 presidential election. Union military successes and Republican efforts to silence the Copperheads, however, eventually ended significant political opposition.

Political Beliefs

The Copperheads' political viewpoint was based on opposition to the war and a belief that the country could be united peacefully. These peace advocates urged compromise during the secession crisis; however, their efforts were fruitless. After Lincoln called for volunteer troops to put down the rebellion, the Copperheads insisted that Lincoln had overstepped his authority by pursuing the war without allowing Congress to vote on the matter. Antiwar Democrats considered themselves strict constructionists and believed that the president's powers were limited to those actions expressly indicated in the Constitution. Peace Democrats were not pacifists; rather, they claimed that they were upholding the principles of America's third president (1801–1809), Thomas Jefferson (1743–1826). Jefferson favored a relatively weak central government that relied on the states for support over a strongly centralized political structure.

As conservative theorists, some Copperheads supported secession. Others, however, simply opposed the expansion of federal authority to wage a war against disunion. Copperheads considered Lincoln's suspension of habeas corpus, which allowed federal authorities to seize and hold citizens without a hearing, to be unconstitutional. This conviction led to the adoption of their motto, "The Constitution as it is, the Union as it was." The nature of Lincoln's exercise of presidential authority was a matter of perspective, but most avid Copperhead leaders believed that Lincoln's interpretation of the Constitution was too loose and therefore a threat to liberty.

Regionalism

The peace movement involved more than simply displeasure with the war. Peace Democrats believed that a

Copperhead menace. Said to be named after the poisonous snake, Copperheads believed that President Abraham Lincoln had neither the Constitutional right to declare war nor the right to prevent Southern states from seceding from the Union. Copperhead ideas were strong among poor whites who feared that newly-freed African Americans would flood the labor force, depressing wages in the North. *MPI/Hulton Archive/Getty Images*

small minority of abolitionists and industrialists in the East had an unfair degree of influence on national politics. Copperhead activity in Indiana, Illinois, and Ohio was an outgrowth of Western sectionalism and reflected resentment of an administration that some thought too beholden to East Coast capitalists and manufacturers (Klement 1960, p. 6). Many Western Peace Democrats lived in rural areas, and some were either Southern-born or had parents who had migrated from the South. Consequently, Republicans dubbed these Western Democrats Butternuts. Although the nickname was originally used derogatorily to describe the poorer residents of the lower Northwest who used butternuts to dye their clothing a light brown color, Western Copperheads eventually embraced this term too. In Indiana, Ohio, and Illinois, some rural folk wore butternut pins to express their opposition to the war.

Politics and Race

The peace faction of the Democratic Party was popular in border regions, where citizens sympathized with, did business with, or were related to their slave-state neighbors. Border cities like Cincinnati, Ohio, were known for having significant Copperhead populations, and these Peace Democrats had considerable social and political influence. Some white working-class citizens feared that former slaves would move to their communities and compete for jobs. This tension resulted in several riots throughout the Ohio Valley during the summer of 1862, including two riots in Ohio by white workers in Toledo and Cincinnati, and another in New Albany, Indiana. A letter printed in an Ohio newspaper, *The Defiance Democrat,* on July 26, 1862, attributed the actions of white rioters in Toledo to "the tide and flood of Negroes poured on this city for the last six months" (Dee 2007, p. 80). The editors of the *New Albany Daily Ledger* published an editorial on July 22, 1862, that blamed the violence in their community on Republicans in Congress who initiated debates over issues that instilled in African Americans an "exalted idea of their own importance" (p. 2).

The fear of job competition and black migration caused a surge of support for the Peace Democrats, who declared that President Lincoln was controlled by abolitionists who wanted to use the war to end slavery and elevate the status of African Americans.

The peace faction gained further attention after Lincoln announced his preliminary Emancipation Proclamation in September 1862. In a December 12, 1862, editorial in the *Cincinnati Enquirer*, James J. Faran, the paper's editor and a former congressman, encouraged readers to oppose President Lincoln's wartime policies. Faran claimed that abolitionists were behind the measure, and were obviously influencing a president who had previously taken a conservative stance on emancipation. Faran's editorial relied heavily on racial stereotypes and promised that "butchery and rapine upon women and children would be the fell work of the degraded and brutal African, whose instincts are even lower and more bestial than those of the Indian" (p. 2).

Arrest of Clement L. Vallandigham

Public outcry against the Emancipation Proclamation, combined with a year of military disappointments for the Union Army, caused the peace supporters within the Democratic Party to gain power via state elections in the late fall of 1862. Critics of Lincoln and the Republican Party grew bolder in their attacks on the war effort and the Lincoln administration. One of the most ardent Copperhead politicians was Clement L. Vallandigham (1825–1879), who served as an Ohio congressman from 1858 to 1862. Vallandigham made a bid for the state's governorship in 1863 but did not have the support of the Ohio War Democrats. On May 1, 1863, he gave a speech in Columbus criticizing the president and testing a previously announced order by Major General Ambrose E. Burnside, Commander of the Department of the Ohio, which allowed for the arrest of anyone who expressed sympathy for the Confederacy. Burnside's men burst into Vallandigham's home in the middle of the night on May 5 and arrested him. A military commission tried Vallandigham, who stated during the proceedings that he believed the war was "for the liberation of blacks, and for the enslavement of the whites" (Dee 2007, p. 136).

Congressman Clement L. Vallandigham (1820–1871). Vallandigham was a congressman and leader of the Copperheads during the Civil War. *Public Domain.*

Vallandigham contended that it was his constitutional right to speak out against the war, regardless of "civil or military authority" (Dee 2007, p. 137). The military commission banished the Ohio politician to territory held by the Confederacy, but Confederate military authorities did not officially accept him. Union troops then escorted Vallandigham through the lines of the warring armies to Tennessee and left him there in February 1864. Vallandigham subsequently traveled by blockade runner to Bermuda and then to Canada.

Democrats were appalled at the use of military authority against an American citizen, and this act not only strengthened opposition to the war, it also won Vallandigham the Democratic nomination for governor of Ohio. This was a bittersweet accomplishment, because Vallandigham was in exile and unable to personally campaign for office; he conducted his campaign from a hotel in Windsor, Ontario. Although the Confederacy did not officially recognize Vallandigham, some Confederate officers did extend their hospitality to him. A British observer visiting the Confederate Army, Lieutenant Colonel Arthur James Lyon Fremantle, noted that Confederates expressed to Vallandigham their belief that reunion was no longer possible. Yet Vallandigham responded that a "scheme of a suspension of hostilities is the only one that has any prospect of ultimate success" (Fremantle 1863, p. 207). The Copperheads' goal to end the war and reunite the states was not compatible with the Confederate goal of independence.

Union Soldiers' Reactions

Vallandigham lost the Ohio gubernatorial election to a War Democrat, John Brough, by more than 100,000 votes. Ohio soldiers were almost unanimous in their opposition to the Copperhead candidate, as they were very concerned that their fellow Buckeyes at home did not support their efforts. In a letter to his sister in Marietta, John Chase lamented, "I understand that my father is a Copperhead, a Butternut, a Traitor, a Vallandigham Peace-Maker" (Dee 2007, p. 159).

A petition by members of the Forty-fourth Ohio Infantry summed up the political opinions of the men by stating that "no better evidence do we want of disloyalty than to hear a man speak in favor of Vallandigham" (Dee 2007, p. 152). Ohio soldiers, like many others, longed to return home and likely agreed with Chase, who declared, "I want peace as much as anyone, but I want it brought about by the rebels laying down their arms and returning to allegiance" (Dee 2007, p. 159). The character of Philip Nolan, the protagonist of Edward Everett Hale's 1863 short story, "The Man without a Country," is based on Vallandigham.

Copperhead Conspiracies

The Republican response to the expansion of Copperhead influence included accusations of disloyalty. Some Republican politicians and military officials advanced theories about widespread Copperhead support for the Confederacy. Most Peace Democrats believed in using political means to bring the war to an end and reunite the Union. The activities of a few militant Copperheads, however, added to the spread of Republican conspiracy theories. Evidence of such secret societies as the Knights of the Golden Circle and the Sons of Liberty led Union officials to suspect that there was a widespread organization planning to form a Northwest confederacy and ally with the Southern Confederacy. When Indiana authorities uncovered a plot to free and arm Confederate prisoners, military men overestimated the threat. Official Union documents reported that in Indiana the organization consisted of 75,000 to 125,000 members who were "well-armed men, constantly drilled and exercised as soldiers" (United States Army Judge Advocate General's Department 1864, p. 5). In reality, Indiana Copperheads did not have a large disciplined army; at most they could muster a few thousand draft resisters and agitators who demonstrated, sometimes violently, in their communities.

Opposition to the Draft

On a local basis, Copperheads were civilians who felt the economic burden of war and refused to support or participate in the war. The draft riot in New York City in July, 1863, was the most infamous example of violent resistance to the war effort in the North. White working-class rioters, many of them Irish, lashed out at wealthy whites who could afford to avoid military service, and at black residents, whom the rioters considered competitors for jobs. Resistance to the draft was widespread on the Union side; provost marshals in the Midwest had difficulty enforcing the draft. Enforcement led to violence, including an incident in Van Wert County, Ohio, in which protestors fired on two deputy provost marshals. The July 11, 1864, edition of the *New Albany Daily Ledger* reported that a man in Harrison County, Indiana, shot and killed a former lieutenant colonel of the Eighty-first Indiana Regiment after an argument among several women devolved into a frenzied shouting match. The Republican women noticed a woman wearing a butternut emblem in church and tried to take it from her. Passionate disagreements about the war were not confined to the political arena. Instead, war-weary citizens throughout the North took out their anger on one another.

Presidential Election of 1864

Copperhead political influence reached its peak during the presidential election of 1864. At the Democratic convention in Chicago, delegates agreed to nominate a former Union general, George B. McClellan, for president, but also chose George Pendleton as the vice-presidential candidate. Pendleton was a notorious Copperhead politician from Ohio who had voted against every major bill supporting the war effort. Consequently, the Democratic ticket running against Lincoln attempted to unite both

Peace Democrats and War Democrats. Hard-line Copperheads resisted this compromise because they believed that War Democrats would not work for an immediate peace. Even the Copperheads who supported McClellan later regretted it. Union victories during the summer of 1864 increased public support for Lincoln and rekindled many people's hopes that the war would soon end. McClellan distanced himself from the Peace Democrats, unwilling to advocate peace when the Union appeared to be winning the war.

In October 1864, stalwart peace advocates met in Cincinnati to organize the last-minute creation of a Peace Party. Delegates from Northern states, including Indiana, Illinois, Pennsylvania, and Ohio, decreed that "the Chicago Convention has distinctly repudiated Democratic principles, and nominated General McClellan, who has responded to the platform by his war record, but the Peace and State Rights Democracy scouting the whole proceedings, have no idea of surrendering their doctrines" (Peace Convention 1864, p. 2). Regardless of several staunch declarations against McClellan, the Cincinnati convention failed to produce any nominations. Peace Democrats had to settle for voting for McClellan, who lost the election to Lincoln in November 1864.

Politically, the Copperheads were unable to steer the nation toward a peaceful path to reunion. In part their inability resulted from their failure to articulate a clear plan for ending the fighting and reuniting the country. At the local level, Copperheads voiced their concern for their future livelihoods, occasionally resorting to violent protest. The career of the Northern Copperheads demonstrates that the war was fought not only on the battlefield but also within communities back home.

BIBLIOGRAPHY

Bernstein, Iver. *The New York Draft Riots: Their Significance for American Society and Politics in the Age of the Civil War.* New York and Oxford: Oxford University Press, 1990.

Dee, Christine, ed. *Ohio's War: The Civil War in Documents.* Athens: Ohio University Press, 2007.

Fremantle, Arthur James Lyon, Sir. *Three Months in the Southern States, April–June, 1863.* Edinburgh and London: William Blackwood & Sons, 1863.

Klement, Frank L. *The Copperheads in the Middle West.* Chicago: University of Chicago Press, 1960.

Klement, Frank L. *Dark Lanterns: Secret Political Societies, Conspiracies, and Treason Trials in the Civil War.* Baton Rouge: Louisiana State University Press, 1984.

Klement, Frank L. *The Limits of Dissent: Clement L. Vallandigham and the Civil War.* Lexington: University Press of Kentucky, 1970.

Lincoln, Abraham. *President Lincoln's Views: An Important Letter on the Principles Involved in the Vallandigham Case: Correspondence in Relation to the Democratic Meeting at Albany, N.Y.* Philadelphia: King & Baird, 1863.

Neely, Mark E., Jr. *The Divided Union: Party Conflict in the Civil War North.* Cambridge, MA: Harvard University Press, 2002.

Peace Convention. *Cincinnati Convention, October 18, 1864: For the Organization of a Peace Party upon State-Rights, Jeffersonian, Democratic Principles and for the Promotion of Peace and Independent Nominations for President and Vice-President of the United States.* Cincinnati, OH: 1864.

Rosecrans, William S. *Letters from General Rosecrans: To the Democracy of Indiana: Action of the Ohio Regiments at Murfreesboro, Regarding the Copperheads.* Philadelphia: King & Baird, 1863.

United States Army. Judge Advocate General's Department. *Report of the Judge Advocate General on the "Order of American Knights," or "Sons of Liberty:" A Western Conspiracy in Aid of the Southern Rebellion.* Washington, DC: Government Printing Office, 1864.

Weber, Jennifer L. *Copperheads: The Rise and Fall of Lincoln's Opponents in the North.* New York and Oxford: Oxford University Press, 2006.

Stephen Rockenbach

SOUTHERN UNION LOYALISTS

The secession movement that preceded the Civil War was not completely supported by the population of the Confederacy. There remained a sizable portion of the citizenry that continued to support the "old flag," as they called the flag of the United States. On many occasions, their support went beyond just moral support, but also translated into material aid to the Union war effort. In many instances, Southern Union loyalists aided the Federal war effort by providing comfort to Union prisoners of war, giving military information to Union regiments, and disrupting Confederate authority within their communities.

Beginning of Union Loyalist Opposition

After reaching a low point during the secession crisis, the strength of Unionists began to re-emerge as the weaknesses of the Confederacy began to come to the surface in 1862. The first of several Confederate conscription acts brought the class divisions of the war effort out into the open. Unionists had been a part of the initial wave of volunteers for the state regiments; however, the reality of the costs of the war and the conscription of large numbers of the Southern yeomanry revealed the failure of the new republic. Long causality lists affected the makeup of local communities that had a large number of white males fighting in the war. Conscription efforts to bring the remaining white male population into the

William G. Brownlow (1805–1877). The South was not unanimous in their support of secession. Southern Unionists, such as William G. Brownlow of Tennessee, advocated slavery but fought against Confederate rule once his home state joined the war against the North. *The Library of Congress.*

conflict brought the Unionists out to resist the Confederate government. In 1863, another Confederate conscription act dealt the outlying communities another blow with the introduction of the twenty-slave rule, which now exempted owners of farms that employed twenty or more slaves. This exemption further intensified the class divisions of Southern society. Unionists and other segments of Southern society now saw the war as an instrument of the rich. The Confederacy also instituted a new tax known as the tax-in-kind to generate funds for the war by taxing crop production at a rate of ten percent and taxing such other valuables as watches and slaves.

Many Unionists began to resist the Confederate government by hiding men from the conscription officers. They hid draft-age men in woods and caves and provided food for them. A number of farmers refused to turn over ten percent of their crops to the Confederacy, choosing instead to hide their harvests from local justices of the peace and Confederate commissary officers. They encouraged their family members and friends to avoid enlisting in Confederate service or to resist calls to report to the county courthouse for enrollment for conscription. They also wrote to relatives and friends to encourage them to desert by giving information about the destitute condition of their families and friends.

Unionist Secret Societies

In addition to this resistance, Unionists began forming secret societies to communicate with one another without attracting the attention of Confederate authorities. Organizations like the Heroes of America were formed in small communities to communicate information to fight against the Confederate government. The Heroes were also known as the Red Strings because the members wore red strings on their lapels to denote their membership. They conducted secret meetings in locations away from attention in their towns. Entry to the meetings was governed by secret handshakes and passwords that were very similar to Masonic rituals. Through this type of organization, the resistance of Unionists began to grow in various parts of the Confederacy.

In addition to these Unionist societies, a number of individuals began to emerge as leaders of Union loyalist activities within the Confederacy. William G. Brownlow (1805–1877), the editor of a newspaper in Knoxville, Tennessee, and later governor of the state, promoted the ideals of Unionism through his editorial columns as his son served as an officer of a loyal Tennessee regiment (Coutler 1937, pp. 262, 402–403; Evans 1996, pp. 17–18). William Woods Holden (1818–1892) led the development of the peace movement in the Old North State as editor of a Raleigh newspaper, the *North Carolina Standard.* Holden promoted Zebulon Vance as the anti-Confederate government candidate in the gubernatorial election of 1862. Despite threats to his editorial business, Holden became the candidate of the Peace Party in North Carolina and challenged Governor Vance in the statewide elections in 1864 (Harris 1987, pp. 12–18, 116–121, 127–155). Senator Andrew Johnson (1808–1875) remained as U.S. Senator from Tennessee despite his state's seceding from the Union, and did return as military governor of the Volunteer State in 1862. Johnson was inaugurated as Abraham Lincoln's vice president in March 1865 and succeeded to the presidency little more than a month later following Lincoln's assassination in April 1865 (Trefousse 1989, pp. 143–151, 152–175, 189, 194–195).

Armed Resistance

Early on in the war, gangs composed of draft dodgers and conscript age men armed themselves and fought against the abuses committed by conscription officers and Confederate regiments on detached service. Many communities became armed camps with men providing security and supported by their family and relatives. The increase of violence against wives and daughters of conscript age men forced the communities to react violently against the Confederacy. In the mountain regions, much of the violence followed family lines, with Unionist families fighting pro-Confederate families. Abuses were committed by both sides, with the taking of no prisoners and the abuse of women.

Helping the Union Army

Southern Unionists also took their support to the war through enlistment in the Union Army. A number of Unionist regiments were formed in the South in 1862 to help stop the rebellion. In Virginia, the First Virginia Volunteers were formed by Unionists from all parts of the state; the unit was assigned to the Army of the Potomac. Other Southern states had such Unionist regiments formed for service as the First Tennessee Volunteers, the First Alabama Cavalry, and the First and Second Texas Cavalry, United States Army. In addition, a number of Unionists traveled to areas under federal control to enlist in Union regiments. A number of Northern regiments contained a sizable contingent of Southerners within their ranks. One Federal prisoner of war noted the discovery of an Alabamian as a member of the Sixteenth Illinois Volunteers at the Confederate prison near Andersonville, Georgia. The Twenty-first Indiana Volunteers contained a number of North Carolinians and Virginians within its companies. One North Carolinian became a recruitment officer for a Michigan regiment serving in Tennessee.

Unionists began to recruit and form military units within the Confederacy for serving in the Union Army. Wilkes County, North Carolina, was a county that had voted overwhelmingly for William W. Holden for governor in 1864. Unionists began to gather men for the beginning steps of forming companies for regiments. Once enough men had volunteered to form a company, a Union officer would swear them into service, and then the men marched westward to Tennessee to receive equipment. Through this method, the majority of the Third North Carolina Mounted Infantry was formed for service in the mountains. The Thirteen Tennessee Cavalry, U.S.A., also included within its troops a large number of Unionist North Carolinians who had traveled through the Great Smokey Mountains to enlist in the Union Army.

Besides these overt methods of serving the Union, Southern Unionists also worked as spies and scouts for the "old flag." During the Carolinas Campaign of 1865, Southern Unionists served as scouts for the Union Army because they could blend in with the local communities and obtain information on Confederate movements. Loyal Southerners also provided food and clothing to Union prisoners, and if able, guided escaped prisoners back to Union lines. Unionists were also able to pass along information to advancing Federal armies through slaves or direct contact with the U.S. Army's Bureau of Military Intelligence. An example was Elizabeth Van Lew (1818–1900), who passed along information to the Federal forces surrounding Richmond through a complex network of spies (Varon 2003, pp. 77–106). Major General William T. Sherman's Union armies benefited by intelligence passed via slaves from Union spies within the defenses of Atlanta.

After the capture of Atlanta, Sherman planned to evacuate the city and issued Special Order No. 67 to remove the civilian population. A number of Unionists in the city took steps to find a way for them to remain with their homes and businesses. Several of these families approached three Union army surgeons who had been imprisoned in the city. They asked these surgeons to write General Sherman for an exception to their expulsion, due to their assistance of food and medicine to Union prisoners. Sherman granted an exception for fifty families to stay in the city based on the testimony of the former Federal prisoners, but warned the families that their homes might still be destroyed due to the building of new entrenchments. The Unionist families that actually did leave Atlanta numbered around 1,500 persons. The majority of these families traveled northward to such states as Connecticut, Iowa, New Jersey, New York, and Pennsylvania. Some families also traveled to Washington, DC, and New York City to join a number of other exiled families from Georgia (Dyer 1999, pp. 202–212).

After the end of the war, many Southern Unionists became the base of support for the Republican Party in the South. Along with former slaves, the Unionists constituted the base of a new political party that was nearly destroyed by President Rutherford B. Hayes's abandonment of this wing of the Republican Party in 1876. Other Unionists returned home from either being exiled or serving in the Union Army. Jesse Dobbins returned home to Yadkin County, North Carolina, after serving for three years in an Indiana regiment. He was immediately arrested for murdering a conscription officer in 1863. He beat up the deputy sheriff and escaped to the woods. He contacted the closest United States Army detachment for protection, and after a lengthy court case, he was eventually acquitted of the crime (Casstevens 1997, pp. 86–96, 107, 117–118).

BIBLIOGRAPHY

Barrett, John G. *The Civil War in North Carolina.* Chapel Hill: The University of North Carolina Press, 1963.

Bynum, Victoria. *The Free State of Jones: Mississippi's Longest Civil War.* Chapel Hill: The University of North Carolina Press, 2001.

Casstevens, Frances. *The Civil War and Yadkin County, North Carolina.* Jefferson, N.C.: McFarland, 1997.

Crofts, Daniel W. *Reluctant Confederates: Upper South Unionists in the Secession Crisis.* Chapel Hill: The University of North Carolina Press, 1989.

Coutler, E. Merton. *William G. Brownlow: Fighting Parson of the Southern Highland*. Chapel Hill: University of North Carolina Press, 1937.

Dyer, Thomas G. *Secret Yankees: The Union Circle in Confederate Atlanta*. Baltimore, MD: John Hopkins University Press, 1999.

Evans, David. *Sherman's Horsemen: Union Cavalry Operations in the Atlanta Campaign*. Bloomington, IN.: Indiana University Press, 1996.

Fishel, Edwin. *The Secret War for the Union: The Untold Story of Military Intelligence in the Civil War*. Boston: Hougton Miffin Co., 1996.

Freehling, William A. *The South vs. The South: How Anti-Confederate Southerners Shaped the Course of the Civil War*. New York: Oxford University Press, 2001.

Grimsley, Mark. *The Hard Hand of War: Union Military Policy toward Southern Civilians, 1861–1865*. New York: Cambridge University Press, 1995.

Harris, William C. *William Woods Holden: Firebrand of North Carolina Politics*. Baton Rouge: Louisiana State University Press, 1987.

Moore, Albert L. *Conscription and Conflict in the Confederacy*. New York: Macmillan, 1924.

Paludan, Phillip S. *Victims: A True Story of the Civil War*. Knoxville: University of Tennessee Press, 1981.

Ryan, David D. *A Yankee Spy in Richmond: The Civil War Diary of "Crazy Bet" Van Lew*. Mechanicsburg, PA.: Stackpole, 1996.

Sarris, Jonathan Dean. *A Separate Civil War: Communities in Conflict in the Mountain South*, Charlottesville: University of Virginia Press, 2006.

Sutherland, Daniel E., ed. *Guerrillas, Unionists, and Violence on the Confederate Home Front*. Fayetteville: University of Arkansas Press, 1999.

Tatum, George L. *Disloyalty in the Confederacy*. Chapel Hill: The University of North Carolina Press, 1934.

Trefousse, Hans Louis. *Andrew Johnson: A Biography*. New York: Norton, 1989.

Varon, Elizabeth. *Southern Lady, Yankee Spy: The True Story of Elizabeth Van Lew*. New York: Oxford University Press, 2003.

Wiley, Bill I. *The Plain People of the Confederacy*. Baton Rouge: Louisiana State University Press, 1943.

William H. Brown

PACIFISM AND CONSCIENTIOUS OBJECTORS

Pacifists and conscientious objectors refused to serve in the military or engage in combat during the Civil War for a variety of reasons. While pacifism was not new within America, the Civil War was the first time that the federal government had to deal actively with the issue because of the innovation of the military draft. The Confederacy first adopted conscription on April 16, 1862. This legislation required all able-bodied white men between the ages of eighteen and thirty-five to enter the Confederate Army. Later acts expanded the age range to seventeen years at the lower end and fifty at the upper. In addition, those already serving had their contracts extended for another three years. Many Southerners were angered by exceptions for those who could pay five hundred dollars or provide a substitute, as well as a series of exemptions for certain offices and professions—including an exemption for owners of plantations with twenty slaves or more.

The Union followed suit, adopting a conscription law in 1863 that called up able-bodied men between the ages of twenty and forty-five. Similar to Southern practice, exemptions were given to men in specific offices or jobs or men who were only sons. Exemption from the draft could also be purchased for three hundred dollars.

Religious Pacifists

Several small religious sects in the United States in both North and South subscribed to pacifism as part of their understanding of Christianity. The Society of Friends (Quakers) and such Anabaptist groups as the Mennonites had significant populations in some Northern states, particularly Pennsylvania and Indiana. There were also smaller groups like the Amanists (members of the Amana Society, who purchased land in Iowa and formed six communal villages in 1859), Dunkards, and Schwenkfelders, who also maintained a pacifist stance. Both the Confederacy and the Union had pacifist religious sects, though the Union had a far larger population of religious pacifists.

In October 1862 the Confederacy adopted another draft act that exempted members of pacifist sects from service but still required them to furnish a substitute or pay the five-hundred-dollar fee. Because the South was gradually worn down by the war, however, it became nearly impossible for pacifists to avoid military service, given the decline in both Southern manpower and money. The Confederacy could ill afford to take action against pacifists that could be better directed toward the war effort, however. Consequently, as the situation worsened pacifists were left to their own devices. Any action to enforce conscription against Southern pacifists was left to the discretion of local officials and the Confederate Army. Some states mandated exemptions but required pacifists to work in other fields. North Carolina, for instance, used pacifists as workers in salt mines and in hospitals. Nevertheless, pacifists living near combat areas were subject to abuse and the seizure of their property, particularly in the South.

The North, which never faced the same crisis in manpower, tended to grant better treatment to members of pacifist sects, though the Union never formally exempted them from service by a formal act of Congress. There was no clear policy within the North for dealing with those who refused to serve. Generally, pacifists who could not afford to pay the exemption fee would report for duty, express their religious opposition to war, and then request assignment to hospitals or service in logistical fields. These exemptions were generally granted by the Union and supported by Lincoln, who wished to avoid formal Congressional legislation on pacifist sects.

Most mainstream Protestant and Catholic bodies embraced the war effort, justifying both the Union and the Confederate causes with religious arguments. Indeed, the Christian churches before the war counted as members the some of the most vociferous critics and defenders of the institution of slavery. An Episcopalian priest, Noah Hunt Schenck (1825–1885), who ministered in the border state of Maryland, was one of the few church leaders who called for reason and moderation at the beginning of the conflict rather than encouraging volunteers. He counseled patience and understanding rather than describing the Civil War as a moral crusade. Schenck clearly chose to separate the kingdom of God from the kingdom of man in his arguments:

> The servant of Christ has an office in an hour like this when the elements of storm have combined, as in days when the skies above him are clear and clean. He lies under special obligation as a follower of "the Prince of Peace" to avert by "the soft answer" and the life of "moderation" the threatened disasters which the madness of his brethren have invited. (Schenck 1861, p. 20)

For Schenck, despite his colleagues' bromides on the subject, war was out of line with the message of the Gospel. Regardless of the sins of the Confederacy, Schenck believed that punishment was best left to God, while political problems could be resolved through the exercise of reason and moderation.

Constitutional Objections to Conscription

In contrast to previous wars involving the United States, the Civil War depended on armies formed through conscription. To many Americans, however, the military draft violated traditional constitutional rights at the heart of the American republic, for which both Northerners and Southerners believed they were fighting. As a consequence, many who chose not to fight gave conscription as a violation of individual rights as their objection to the war effort. Southerners who had opposed secession and felt that the chances of a Confederate victory were unlikely were especially opposed to the war on these grounds. George Adams Fisher, who considered himself a Union man, was a citizen of Texas that was conscripted into the Confederate Army. Fisher thought that there was no legal basis for secession, and was particularly outraged by the Confederate government's use of force against its own troops in the cases of Southerners who chose to leave the army or who refused to have their contracts extended after the conscription act of 1862. After describing an incident in which a Confederate officer threatened his own men with grapeshot after they decided that they had fulfilled their contract and chose not to reenlist, Fisher wrote: "This is a specimen of the devotion of the Southern soldiers to the cause in which they are engaged, and of the means made use of to keep their armies together. These statements produced a wonderful excitement among the Union citizens of Texas. Many solemnly vowed they would never submit to the conscription law" (Fisher 1864, p. 61).

Josephine Clare, a woman from Natchitoches, similarly opposed secession. The Confederacy's use of conscription motivated her husband to flee with his family to the North, given the undemocratic methods used to support the Southern war effort. Clare wrote, "In the Spring of 1862, the rebel authorities conscripted every man between the ages of eighteen and thirty-five. Their opinions were not consulted, but at the point of the bayonet they were compelled to obey the tyrannical orders of their oppressors" (Clare 1865, p. 3).

Conscription produced significant opposition within the Confederacy, even among Southerners who in principle supported secession. Governor Joseph E. Brown of Georgia (1821–1894) wrote in his message to the state's legislature on the subject of conscription, "Not only the rights and the sovereignty of the States have been disregarded, but the individual rights of the citizen have been trampled under foot, and we have by this policy been reduced, for a time at least, to a state bordering upon military despotism" (Brown 1862, p. 4). Conscription in both the North and South was widely viewed as unconstitutional and out of keeping with the tradition of a voluntary military in United States history that dated back to the American Revolution.

Many Northerners also objected to conscription, most spectacularly in the draft riots that took place in New York City from July 13 to July 16, 1863. The riots were a direct response to conscription on the part of Irish and German Americans, who targeted the wealthy and African Americans. Ultimately, federal troops had to be called in to end the violence. The New York City draft riots resulted in the deaths of 119 people, serious injury to another 300, and significant property damage (Paludan 1988, pp. 190–191). The riots indicated that the North too had significant opposition to conscription. Many Democrats, even some who supported the war effort, considered the draft to be unconstitutional. Border state populations and recent immigrants like the Irish and the Germans were also more likely to oppose the draft as a violation of their civil rights; these groups also objected to the war effort on these constitutional grounds.

In sum, pacifists and conscientious objectors in the North and the South opposed the Civil War for both religious and constitutional reasons. Because of the scope of the conflict and the resort to a military draft, the Confederacy and the Union had to deal with the problem that pacifists and conscientious objectors pose in a war between two mobilized societies for the first time in American history.

BIBLIOGRAPHY

Brown, Joseph E. *Special Message of his Excellency Joseph E. Brown, to the Legislature.* Milledgeville, GA: Boughton, Nisbet & Barnes, 1862.

Clare, Josephine. *Narrative of the Adventures and Experiences of Mrs. Josephine Clare.* Lancaster, PA: Pearson & Geist, 1865.

Fisher, George Adams. *The Yankee Conscript, or, Eighteen Months in Dixie.* Philadelphia: J. W. Daughaday, 1864.

Paludan, Phillip. *A People's Contest: The Union and the Civil War, 1861–1865.* Lawrence: University Press of Kansas, 1988.

Schenck, Noah Hunt. *Christian Moderation, the Word in Season, to the Church and the Country*, 2nd ed. Baltimore: Entz & Bash, 1861.

Michael Kelly Beauchamp

DRAFT RIOTS AND DRAFT RESISTERS

Resistance to conscription acts in both the Union and the Confederacy was the strongest and most violent form of activism on the home front to the national policies of the respective combatants. Draft resistance showed the rising level of discontent with losses on the battlefields, food shortages at home, and racial tensions in local communities. In the North, draft resistance showed that federal policies were not completely supported by the country and that the President's conduct of the war was seriously questioned in some quarters. In the Confederacy, draft resistance revealed the open wounds of class divisions. In addition, the resistance forced the Confederacy to pull badly needed troops from the various theaters of war to enforce its conscription acts within its states. To enforce those acts, Confederate troops committed war crimes against the civilian population to enforce the authority of the national government.

Both sides of the conflict realized by 1862 that there would not be enough volunteers to sustain their armies in the field. As a result, both governments turned to conscription to maintain and strengthen their armies. In April 1862 the Confederacy passed the first of three conscription acts to bring more men into its armies and to prevent the massive mustering-out of twelve-month volunteers. The South concentrated on men who fell within the militia age of eighteen to thirty-five with exceptions for those in business and government jobs. As expected, battlefield losses forced the Confederacy to institute additional conscription acts in 1863 and 1864. The last act was the most severe; it called up all able-bodied men between the ages of seventeen and forty-five with only a few exemptions.

Draft Resistance in the North

By 1862, the federal government began to look for new ways to increase enlistments in the Union Army. The Militia Act of 1862 was expected to provide roughly 300,000 men for military service; however, widespread opposition prevented the federal government from fully implementing its provisions. The Northern states used a bounty system to increase recruiting to fulfill their quota of state regiments for military service. By March 1863, the Enrollment Act was signed. This act provided for the enrollment of all households within a congressional district by government agents. A lottery was held to see which men would be called up for military service. If enough men to meet the quota volunteered in a district, then the lottery was not held. Drafted men could obtain the services of a substitute to go in their place or pay $300 to exempt themselves from military service.

Northern citizens did not respond positively to President Lincoln's initial call for recruits in 1862. Local opposition to the Militia Act grew into violence in several states. In many cases, the citizens' outrage was not directed toward the state governments but rather toward the national government that had forced the issue on the states. A month after the Union victory at Sharpsburg (Antietam), Maryland, in September 1862, a massive riot occurred in Port Washington, Wisconsin, in October. A crowd marched through the streets of the town under a banner protesting the draft. They proceeded to attack the courthouse and destroyed the local enrollment papers for the county. A battalion of infantry had to be deployed to restore order in the town.

New York City Draft Riots

These disturbances were minor skirmishes compared to the major protests that occurred over the Enrollment Act of 1863. The potential conscription of poor whites who did not have the financial means to hire substitutes for the draft became a major point of contention. In addition, the anger over the conscription lottery became tied to labor issues in Northern cities. African Americans were beginning to compete with immigrants for lower-wage work, thereby destroying the labor monopoly of German and Irish workers. By the spring of 1863, violence was erupting throughout the North over the Enrollment Act. Violence occurred in places as distant from each other as Detroit, Michigan, and Rutland, Vermont. The draft lottery was disrupted in Chicago and local police were attacked when they attempted to stop the crowd.

On July 11, 1863, the first names of the lottery were drawn in New York City without incident. At the same

New York City draft riots, 1863. On July 13, 1863, riots broke out in New York City over the second lottery drawing and the opening of the draft office. The mob mostly consisted of poor immigrants who sought those they felt were taking their jobs. Soon, African Americans became the target, resulting in lynching and fires. *The Art Archive/Culver Pictures/The Picture Desk, Inc.*

time, nearly all of the New York State Militia had been deployed to Pennsylvania to cover portions of that state during the Gettysburg campaign. On July 13, riots broke out in response to the second drawing of lottery numbers and the opening of the draft office. A large mob burned the office and looted stores and the homes of the wealthy on Lexington Avenue. The bottom floor of the office of the *New York Tribune* was burned, and Brooks Brothers' store was attacked and looted by the crowd. Up to that point, the mob consisted of the poor of the city, mainly German and Irish. On the following day, the mob was primarily composed of Irish immigrants. The rioters quickly focused on those minorities who they believed were taking their jobs and were the cause of the war itself. In short order, African Americans were being targeted within the city. Soon, individual African Americans were being attacked and lynched on the street. Businesses that employed African Americans were also attacked and burned by the mob. The Colored Orphan Asylum was also burned; however, all the children except one were able to escape.

The New York City police, seriously outnumbered, attempted to control the crowds, but they were also attacked by mobs of men and women. Republicans, policemen, wealthy individuals, and African Americans were assaulted on the streets by the mobs. The crowd overran one armory and gained weapons to fight police barricades and assault additional blocks of the city. In Pennsylvania, the deployed militia regiments were ordered back to the city. U.S. Army regulars from Governor's Island were set over to clear the streets with muskets with fixed bayonets. The provost marshal even requested the U.S. Navy to station an armed steamer near the business district and send ashore a contingent of U.S. Marines to assist the police.

The arrival of the militia regiments, as well as volunteer Union regiments from Michigan and Indiana, soon spelled the end of rioting in the city. The regiments were sent into the street to clear away barricades and return law and order. As a measure to calm the crowds, the draft lottery was ordered suspended within the city. By July 17, 1863, law and order was completely restored. The next day, regiments from the Union Army of the Potomac arrived to help patrol the city. Over 1,000 fatalities occurred during the period of July 12 through July 17, 1863, along with $2 million dollars of property damage. It was later determined that the actual toll was 105 killed and 193 seriously wounded (Cook 1974, pp. 194–195). During this period, other Northern cities experienced rioting over the proposed lottery for the Enrollment Act of 1863. A Federal armory was attacked in Boston, Massachusetts, on July 14, 1863. Other disturbances erupted throughout the mid-Atlantic states, and in Ohio and Wisconsin in the Midwest.

Despite the fears over another riot, conscription officials made plans to hold another draft lottery for New York City in mid-August 1863. On August 17, the mayor and police commissioner requested that thirteen militia regiments be deployed to protect the draft locations and parts of the city. No violence occurred during this draft, and the regiments remained until mid-September 1863.

Draft Resistance in the Confederacy

Within the Confederacy, resistance to the draft grew as a response to class discrimination in the conscription acts and the growing burden imposed on the poor by the Confederate government. Initially, the First Conscription Act of 1862 was passed in order to deal with the potential mustering-out of twelve-month volunteers just before the season of active campaigning in the spring and summer of 1862. The act specified a large number of exemptions for a number of jobs and government positions. The burden fell upon the small farmers and mechanics to fulfill the manpower quotas of the act. Throughout May 1862, large numbers of men volunteered to prevent having to be conscripted by the government.

After this initial wave of volunteers, however, the enrollment of additional conscripts began to fall off in the South. Many communities had sent large numbers of their white male population off to war, and they were soon greeted with long casualty lists from the battles of late 1862, including Antietam and Stones River. To fill the ranks, Confederate conscription officers became more ruthless in ferreting out men who had not been exempted from service. Abuses were committed against families by Confederate troops looking for draft evaders and private property was destroyed. Conscription officers and their troops kicked in doors of private dwellings and ransacked houses, barns, and storage bins. Soldiers tied up women to force them to reveal the locations of their male relatives. (Barrett 1963, pp. 188–189, 193–194)

Beginning in late 1862, resistance grew into violence in a number of counties toward conscription officers and their military companies. Officers were beaten up by gangs of men or shot during roadside ambushes. Justices of the peace, who were required to compile lists of men to be drafted, were threatened by citizens in their counties of residence. By 1863 violence was regularly occurring in a number of locales in the South. Randolph County, North Carolina, home to a number of Quakers and Unionists, was considered to be in open rebellion by the governor of North Carolina. In mountain regions, the draft was seen as the tyrannical reach of a government founded by large plantation owners. Draft resisters and deployed state regiments murdered citizens on a regular basis in Southern mountain counties.

Second Conscription Act

The Confederate Congress passed the Second Conscription Act in the spring of 1863. This act was notable for the inclusion of the so-called twenty-slave rule. According to this provision, masters of twenty slaves or more were now exempted from military service. This exemption drove an even greater division between the rich and poor in Southern society. Many saw this exemption as a way to ensure that poor Southerners would fight the war while the rich would be unaffected. In addition, the number of exemptions was increased for those individuals working in government and higher levels of businesses.

Not surprisingly, draft resistance grew in the South. The desertion rate rose in frontline regiments, and deserters from those regiments joined up with draft resisters to form gangs to fight against Confederate troops. In Yadkin County, North Carolina, a number of local men fought a pitched battle and succeeded in driving off a conscription officer and his detachment. Men also avoided military service by hiding in the woods and the mountains, which forced the Confederacy to send troops needed at the front to search for these men in the backwoods.

Women related to the draft resisters often left food for them at certain locations. Consequently, conscription officers began to target and follow the women as they traveled through the countryside to locate groups of deserters. State governors were pleading with the national government in Richmond to send regular troops to deal with the growing threat within the mountain counties.

Increasingly, the Confederate government was forced to deploy regiments and brigades to bring these regions back under central authority. General Robert E. Lee had to send regiments back to their native states to assist in reestablishing Confederate authority in a number of counties. In several cases, battle-weary and numerically reduced regiments were sent back to assist conscription officers and to recruit additional soldiers to bring their units back up to full strength. These troops would bring a local area under control and bring in conscripts to send to camps of instruction. As soon as the regiment was sent back to its parent army, the local population would rise back up again to fight the conscription officers and their detachments. In several cases, men of conscript age and deserters formed improvised groups to protect their communities from the intrusion of Confederate soldiers. Toward the end of the conflict, many local communities were not under Confederate control, and only the arrival of Union soldiers ensured the return of law and order.

In summary, attempts to raise recruits for both the Union and Confederate Armies were met with violence and social unrest. In Northern states, mob violence affected the entire system of using a lottery to pick men for military service. The increase of bounties offered by the states and the timely deployment of military troops enabled the system to function despite the lowered quality of men being brought into the armies. In the Confederacy, draft resistance played a major role in the breakdown of the government's influence in outlying communities. In addition, the nature of conscription itself divided the Confederacy along class lines, and damaged the nation internally. This breakdown in authority coupled with losses on the battlefield served to doom the Confederacy in short order.

BIBLIOGRAPHY

Barrett, John G. *The Civil War in North Carolina.* Chapel Hill: University of North Carolina Press, 1963.

Bernstein, Iver. *The New York City Draft Riots: Their Significance for American Society and Politics in the Age of the Civil War.* New York and Oxford, UK: Oxford University Press, 1990.

Coakley, Robert W. *The Role of Federal Military Forces in Domestic Disorders, 1789–1878.* Washington, DC: Center of Military History, 1988.

Cook, Adrian. *The Armies of the Streets: The New York City Draft Riots of 1863.* Lexington: University of Kentucky, 1974.

Gallman, J. Matthew. *The North Fights the Civil War: The Home Front.* Chicago: I.R. Doe, 1994.

Geary, James W. *We Need Men: The Union Draft in the Civil War.* DeKalb: Northern Illinois University Press, 1991.

Leach, Jack. *Conscription in the United States: Historical Background.* Rutland, VT: Tuttle, 1952.

Moore, Albert L. *Conscription and Conflict in the Confederacy.* New York: Macmillan, 1924.

Murdock, Eugene C. *One Million Men: The Civil War Draft in the North.* Madison: State Historical Society of Wisconsin, 1971.

Paludan, Phillip S. *Victims: A True Story of the Civil War.* Knoxville: University of Tennessee Press, 1981.

William H. Brown

Propaganda

PROPAGANDA: AN OVERVIEW
David F. Herr

RALLIES, LECTURES, AND SPEECHES
Carol Brennan

POLITICAL HUMOR AND CARTOONS
Carol Brennan

BIASED NEWSPAPER REPORTING
Stephen Rockenbach

PARTY POLITICS
George A. Milite

PROPAGANDA: AN OVERVIEW

The American Civil War gave rise to rich and diverse propaganda, although in neither the Union nor the Confederacy was much of this propaganda generated by the government directly, aside from speeches by their respective presidents. Unlike governments in subsequent wars, both sides dedicated the bulk of their attempts at persuasion to international lobbying, rather than focusing on the home front. There was, however, no shortage of propagandistic rhetoric from politicians seeking election, newspaper editors and reporters, and assorted public speakers. The South's changing fortunes during the war limited the amount of propaganda it produced. Whereas there were close to 800 daily papers published in the South in 1860, there were at best twenty by the end of the war.

The influence of nongovernmental propaganda was complex and significant. During the 1863 New York City draft riots, for example, Republican newspapers played a pivotal role when they fixed blame for the riots on New York Governor Horatio Seymour, who had delivered a series of speeches attacking emancipation and conscription. In the South during the closing years of the war, Jefferson Davis, the Confederate president, increasingly became a reviled figure once Southern editors turned their vitriol against him. They repeatedly accused him of choosing poor generals and meddling in military affairs.

Newspaper editorialists both North and South were perhaps the most significant contributors to wartime propagandizing. At the same time, they also criticized the practice: "It is impossible to condemn too strongly," the Newark, New Jersey, *Daily Advertiser* exclaimed in January 1861, "the pestiferous inventions and exaggerations of reckless political gossips and paid letter-writers, whom the times have hatched into being." The problem was not merely the dishonesty of the propaganda, but its results. The stories had, the *Advertiser* asserted, "a tendency to take the bread out of the mouths of thousands, and in the end to endanger the Union everywhere and bring anarchy itself in their train" (Smith 1948, p. 1,043). *The Daily Picayune* of New Orleans spoke in equally harsh terms against anti-Confederate propaganda, labeling some newspapers, "atrabilious sheets, whose columns are blackened by detraction and scandal—whose mission is to misrepresent and slander" (Dumond 1964 [1931], p. 487).

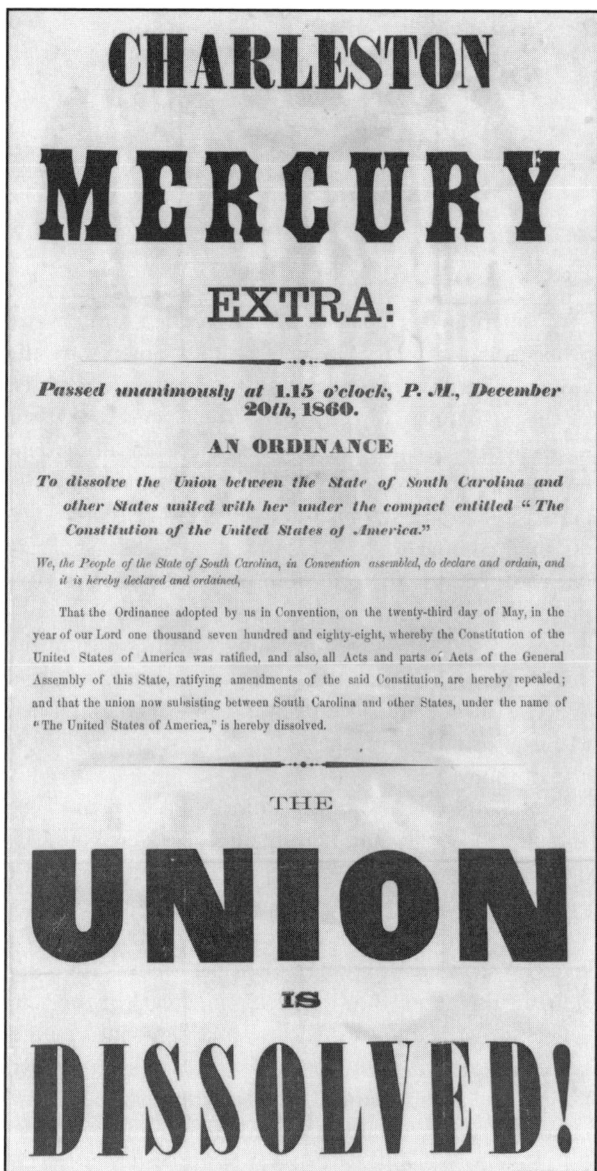

CHARLESTON

MERCURY

EXTRA:

Passed unanimously at 1.15 o'clock, P. M., December 20th, 1860.

AN ORDINANCE

To dissolve the Union between the State of South Carolina and other States united with her under the compact entitled "The Constitution of the United States of America."

We, the People of the State of South Carolina, in Convention assembled, do declare and ordain, and it is hereby declared and ordained,

That the Ordinance adopted by us in Convention, on the twenty-third day of May, in the year of our Lord one thousand seven hundred and eighty-eight, whereby the Constitution of the United States of America was ratified, and also, all Acts and parts of Acts of the General Assembly of this State, ratifying amendments of the said Constitution, are hereby repealed; and that the union now subsisting between South Carolina and other States, under the name of "The United States of America," is hereby dissolved.

THE

UNION

IS

DISSOLVED!

Broadside from the *Charleston Mercury*, December 20, 1860. Technological advances in printing presses allowed for an inexpensive way to quickly spread ideology to the reading public. Much of the propaganda disseminated throughout the Civil War came not from Union or Confederate governments but rather through the efforts of newspapers, by way of editorial essays and political cartoons. *© The New York Public Library/Art Resource, NY*

Diverse Expression

The unexpected ferocity of the fighting during the war's early stages and the conflict's profound implications quickly gave rise to an abundance of varied propaganda. Newspapers were by far the most common medium. Nineteenth-century papers were overtly political and built their readership through allegiance to specific party politics. Their appeal to the masses was limited until the 1830s. Reliable steam-powered cylinder presses helped create the era of the "penny press" by the late 1830s. The inexpensive papers' new audience was less interested in political diatribe, and newspapers, including the *New York Herald*, responded by beginning to publish sensational stories about crimes and scandals. The Civil War proved a desirable topic and the papers provided coverage of the fighting, as well as editorials on the actions of both governments. Many papers also included poetry from poets and amateurs alike, as well as directly propagandistic political cartoons. Readership was large in urban regions. Hundreds of thousands of Americans subscribed to *Harper's Weekly*, for example. Although Southern subscriptions rates are more difficult to determine, many Confederates regularly read *Southern Illustrated News* and the *Magnolia Weekly*.

One reason the warring governments may not have felt compelled to produce their own domestic propaganda was the effort of private citizens. Historian George Winston Smith (1948) argues that the various clubs and organizations in New England that reproduced editorials for wide dissemination as broadsides played a significant role shaping public opinion. Boston businessman John Murray Forbes, for example, began in 1862 to have newspapers reprint editorials at his expense for distribution to Massachusetts troops and residents. Northern pamphleteering was also significant. Union Leagues and pamphlet societies distributed millions of propaganda pamphlets throughout the war. The South had a tradition of outspoken public speakers, and many of these men employed their rhetoric skills during the sectional conflict. These "fire eaters" were wealthy, powerful men who took every opportunity to disseminate their propaganda. They included large planters like Robert Barnwell Rhett and Edmund Ruffin, and the newspaper editor and lawyer William Lowndes Yancey.

Literature was another popular form of war propaganda. New fiction genres focused on the war included stories of women defending the home front, tales of boy's adventures supporting the war, and stories about the opposing side. Harriet Beecher Stowe introduced what proved to be the most enduring of the fictional works used propagandistically almost a decade before the fighting: *Uncle Tom's Cabin*, published in 1852. Stowe effectively captured the inhumanity of slavery, and her book became wildly popular; more than three hundred thousand copies were printed between 1852 and 1853 alone. Almost 8,000 more were printed during the war.

Poetry and music were also effective media for propaganda and may have surpassed newspapers and broadsides in their reach. Easily learned and passed on orally, songs and poetry about the war were enormously popular on both sides. The message was rarely subtle, as reflected in the opening lines of a poem by George H. Miles:

> God save the South!
> God save the South!

Her altars and firesides—
God save the South!
Now that the war is nigh—
Now that we arm to die—
Chanting—our battle-cry,
Freedom or Death! (Miles 1866)

Northern poetry was similarly direct, as evidenced by these lines from Caroline A. Mason's poem, "God Bless Abraham Lincoln":

God *bless* him—with a large increase,
With righteousness that shall not cease,
With wisdom and His "perfect peace." (Mason 1864)

While much of the most famous poetry and song from the Civil War years may not be overtly propagandistic, authors nonetheless frequently tried to convey that the cause they championed was great and its heroes admirable. Sidney Lanier's poem "The Dying Words of Stonewall Jackson" paints a heroic image, as does Walt Whitman's homage to Abraham Lincoln, "O Captain! My Captain!" John Savage's "Dixie" takes the Confederate song and makes it a Union cheer, with such lines as, "Oh, the Starry flag is the flag for me; 'Tis the flag of life, 'tis the flag of the free" (Hill 1990, p. 222). People on both sides drew from a wealth of similar material as they sought to apprehend their place in the conflict.

The Meaning of Propaganda

Propagandists of all stripes invoked a wide range of emotionally charged topics in their attempts to incite or persuade, including nationalism, nation-making, the Constitution, the fighting, race, gender, and patriotism. While almost every aspect of the war was the subject of propaganda, the most popular forms were driven in part by the desires of the audience and the context of the moment. Shortly after Southern troops fired on Fort Sumter, the focus of propaganda shifted to addressing the implications of war. Following the Union retreat at Shiloh, Confederate propagandists began to crow about imminent victory. Each battle or political move generated the next wave of propagandistic material.

Studies of newspaper editorials during the period leading to war reveal that the most divisive issue was slavery. Slavery was either seen as a challenge to the notion of liberty, or as an institution that needed to be protected if the rights of individuals (individual property owners, that is) were to be affirmed. On both sides of the argument, propagandists placed the survival of the country in the balance. Both sides turned to the Revolutionary generation for inspiration. Increasingly, propagandists claimed that their side was the true inheritor of the American Revolution, whereas their opponents desired a society antithetical to the values the Revolution embodied.

During the war, both sides experienced a shift away from blind public support. New debates arose as a result of wartime deprivation and, for the South, the increasing uncertainty of victory. Peace movements launched their own propagandistic efforts and the press in North and South freely criticized the policies of their respective governments. While there was some government censorship, the trend was more toward restraint. War correspondents were a new type of journalist, and enjoyed almost unlimited access to the military. In fact, correspondents were often present when commanders discussed strategy. Some reporters were even used by the military to communicate orders. Despite this unfettered access, the quality of war reporting was often poor. The style of reporting was propagandistic, not objective. Southern reporters tended to exaggerate the size of the enemy forces, whereas Northern reporters sometimes claimed victory even when the Union lost. The press on both sides was fond of evaluating the performance of prominent generals. Reporters praised their victories or castigated them for losses. One of the Confederacy's most unpopular generals, Braxton Bragg, was notorious for his dislike of war reporters.

The absence of extensive government propaganda efforts and the proliferation of organized civilian efforts make Civil War propaganda quite different from that seen in later conflicts. Rather than centralized control aimed at shaping ideas about a conflict, the Civil War period featured many voices and little repression of critical views.

BIBLIOGRAPHY

Cullop, Charles P. *Confederate Propaganda in Europe, 1861–1865.* Coral Gables, FL: University of Miami Press, 1969.

Dumond, Dwight Lowell. *Southern Editorials on Secession.* New York and London: Century Company, 1931. Reprint, Gloucester, MA: Peter Smith, 1964.

Fahs, Alice. *The Imagined Civil War: Popular Literature of the North and South, 1861–1865.* Chapel Hill: University of North Carolina Press, 2001.

Freidel, Frank, ed. *Union Pamphlets of the Civil War, 1861–1865.* Cambridge, MA: Belknap Press of Harvard University Press, 1967.

Hill, Lois, ed. *Poems and Songs of the Civil War.* New York: Gramercy Books, 1990.

Mason, Caroline A. "God Bless Abraham Lincoln." In *Personal and Political Ballads*, ed. Frank A. Moore. New York: G. P. Putnam, 1864. Available on-line from http://hdl.loc.gov/umich.dli.moa/.

Miles, George H. "God Save the South." In *War Poetry of the South*, ed. William Gilmore Simms. New York: Richardson & Company, 1866. Available online from http://www.gutenberg.org/dirs/.

Mott, Frank Luther. *American Journalism: A History, 1690–1960.* 3rd ed. New York: Macmillan, 1962.
Perkins, Howard Cecil. *Northern Editorials on Secession,* vol. 2. New York and London: D. Appleton-Century Company, 1942. Reprint, Gloucester, MA: Peter Smith, 1964.
Smith, George Winston. "Broadsides for Freedom: Civil War Propaganda in New England." *New England Quarterly* 21, no. 3. (1948): 291–312.
Stevenson, Louise L. "Virtue Displayed: The Tie-Ins of *Uncle Tom's Cabin.*" In *Uncle Tom's Cabin and American Culture: A Multi-Media Archive.* Available from http://www.iath.virginia.edu/utc/.
Winship, Michael. "Uncle Tom's Cabin: History of the Book in the Nineteenth-Century United States." In *Uncle Tom's Cabin and American Culture: A Multi-Media Archive.* Available from http://www.iath.virginia.edu/utc/.

David F. Herr

RALLIES, LECTURES, AND SPEECHES

During the American Civil War, both the Union and Confederate sides actively marshaled support for their respective cases through rallies, lectures, and speeches. At these frequently well-attended events, impassioned orators either condemned slavery and the treasonous secession of the Confederate states, or affirmed the South's moral justifications for slavery and its right to secede in order to continue its way of life. Celebrated orators such as Edward Everett and Frederick Douglass drew large crowds, but so too did various politicians, ministers, and other notables.

Edward Everett

In the cities and towns of the Union side, mass meetings were frequently held to rally patriotic support for the war. The famed orator Edward Everett—a former governor of Massachusetts, president of Harvard College, and one of the most respected Whig Party politicians of his era—was the most sought-after speaker at such events. In November 1863, Everett spoke at the dedication of a Soldiers' National Cemetery at Gettysburg, Pennsylvania, the site of terrible Union losses earlier that year:

> And now, friends, fellow-citizens, as we stand among these honored graves, the momentous question presents itself, Which of the two parties to the war is responsible for all this suffering, for this dreadful sacrifice of life, —the lawful and constituted government of the United States, or the ambitious men who have rebelled against it? … I call the war which the Confederates are waging against the Union a "rebellion," because it is one, and in grave matters it is best to call things by their right names. I speak of it as a crime, because the Constitution of the United States so regards it, and puts "rebellion" on a par with "invasion." The constitution and law, not only of England, but of every civilized country, regard them in the same light; or rather they consider the rebel in arms as far worse than the alien enemy. To levy war against the United States is the constitutional definition of treason, and that crime is by every civilized government regarded as the highest which citizen or subject can commit. (Everett 1864, p. 61)

His speech was two hours in length, but was followed by President Abraham Lincoln's far briefer, yet also eloquent, the Gettysburg Address. Everett's words, however, were characteristically forceful and stirring, and widely reprinted in Union newspapers of the day.

Frederick Douglass

One of the most popular figures on the Northern lecture circuit was Frederick Douglass, a former slave and America's most famous abolitionist in the years leading up to the war. Douglass published a series of newspapers and journals, and during the war his editorial writings took up the Union cause and advocated for the abolition of slavery. These writings also shaped his lectures, including one event at the Brooklyn Academy of Music in May 1863, titled "What Shall Be Done with the Negro?" This speech gives a sense of Douglass's stirring oratorical powers:

> Our answer [to the question of what should be done with the slaves] is, do nothing with them; mind your business, and let them mind theirs. Your doing with them is their greatest misfortune. They have been undone by your doings, and all they now ask, and really have need of at your hands, is just to let them alone. … Let us stand upon our own legs, work with our own hands, and eat bread in the sweat of our own brows. When you, our white fellow-countrymen, have attempted to do anything for us, it has generally been to deprive us of some right, power or privilege which you yourself would die before you would submit to have taken from you. (Douglass 1975, p. 164)

Following the Emancipation Proclamation of 1863 and the authorization of new Union Army regiments for black soldiers, Douglass became an ardent recruiter of blacks for the Union side.

Recruitment Rallies

Recruitment rallies in general—such as those occurring during a massive recruitment drive in Boston, Massachusetts, during the spring and summer of 1862—were a commonplace event in many cities during the first years of the war (O'Connor 1997, p. 101). The Boston effort, a response to President Lincoln's call for 600,000 more troops, kicked off in August with a major rally at Faneuil

Frederick Douglass (1817–1895), escaped slave and author. Born a slave in Maryland, Frederick Douglass escaped to the North in 1838 and wrote of his experiences in bondage in his first autobiography, *Narrative of the Life of Frederick Douglass, an American Slave.* On account of his public speaking talents, he became well regarded as an abolitionist orator, relating his story to audiences throughout the United States. *The Library of Congress.*

Hall, during which a brass band playing military marches and hymns. This was followed by a weeklong drive in which recruiters canvassed the city and set up recruiting tents on busy street corners. During the final week of the August drive, all stores and businesses closed at 2 p.m. and a festive atmosphere overtook the city. Large crowds turned out for the daily rallies in which local politicians and military officials urged the men of Massachusetts to join the Union fight. The jubilant mood of the city got a bit out of control at times, as when crowds pumped up with patriotic fervor tossed bricks through the windows of businesses that had not closed promptly at 2 p.m.

Southern Ministers

In the Confederate states, lectures were a popular draw in cities, many of which were suffering severe economic hardships, including a lack of food. In the final year of the war, these speeches increased in number as local officials and church pastors sought to bolster the spirits of an increasingly hard-pressed civilian population. Often, the ideals of the American Revolution were invoked, because patriotic sentiment in the Confederacy rallied around the belief that the secessionist states were battling the tyranny of a larger power, much as the original thirteen colonies had fought for their independence from England. In a somewhat ironic twist, some members of the British aristocracy supported the Confederate cause.

Sermons were also an occasion to provide justification for the preservation of slavery. In Savannah, Georgia, a minister named Stephen Elliott delivered a sermon on September 18, 1862, which Jefferson Davis had proclaimed as a day of thanksgiving throughout the Confederacy for battlefield victories at Manassas, Virginia, and Richmond, Kentucky. He was the Episcopal bishop of Florida and subsequently, during the war, the first and only presiding bishop of the Protestant Episcopal Church in the Confederate States of America. "It is very curious and very striking, in this connexion, to trace out the history of slavery in this country, and to observe God's providential care over it ever since its introduction," Elliott noted in his sermon. "Strange to say, African slavery, upon this Continent, had its origin in an act of mercy. The negro was first brought across the ocean to save the Indian from a toil which was destroying him, but while the Indian has perished, the substitute who was brought to die in his place, has lived, prospered and multiplied" (Elliott 1862, pp. 11–12).

BIBLIOGRAPHY

Boston Daily Advertiser, August 28, 1862.

Douglass, Frederick. *The Life and Writings of Frederick Douglass.* Edited by Philip S. Foner. New York: International Publishers Company, Inc., 1975.

Elliott, Stephen. *Our Cause in Harmony with the Purposes of God in Christ Jesus.* Savannah, GA: Power Press of John M. Cooper, 1862.

Everett, Edward, and Abraham Lincoln. *Address of Hon. Edward Everett, at the Consecration of the National Cemetery at Gettysburg, 19th November 1863.* Boston: Little, Brown, 1864.

Fahs, Alice. *The Imagined Civil War: Popular Literature of the North and South, 1861–1865.* Chapel Hill: University of North Carolina Press, 2003.

New York Times, May 16, 1863.

O'Connor, Thomas H. *Civil War Boston: Home Front and Battlefield.* Boston: Northeastern University Press, 1997.

Sutherland, Daniel E. *The Expansion of Everyday Life, 1860–1876.* New York: Harper & Row, 1989.

Carol Brennan

POLITICAL HUMOR AND CARTOONS

The American Civil War witnessed the rise of searing political humor featured on the pages of scores of new newspapers founded in the mid-nineteenth century. Much of the humor took the form of cartoons, which merged opinion with visual artistry and, in the North, helped shape public opinion against the war. In an era entirely devoid of electronic media, such propaganda-tinged images were crucial to marshalling public sentiment.

Thomas Nast

In 1857 the New York publishing house Harper and Brothers launched a new illustrated publication called *Harper's Weekly*, which was modeled after the highly successful British publication, the *Illustrated London News*. Though *Harper's Weekly* was focused on New York City, it was also widely read in cities such as Boston, Philadelphia, and Washington; and in the first months of the war it experienced circulation peaks as high as 115,000 copies per issue (Fahs 2003, p. 42). In 1862 *Harper's Weekly* rehired a young German-born illustrator named Thomas Nast (1840–1902), who had spent the past three years working for other publications. Considered the father of American political cartooning, Nast produced scores of images for *Harper's Weekly*, many of which appeared on its cover.

Just twenty-two years old in 1862, Nast, as an immigrant, had experienced difficulties in school during his early teen years. He was believed to be functionally illiterate, at least in English, his second language. He was, however, a talented artist, and his pictorial illustrations of Civil War battles and the evils of slavery spoke to a nation of new immigrants like himself, many of whom possessed the same limited English-language skills. Nast was an ardent supporter of President Abraham Lincoln and the Republican Party, and was committed to the Union cause—personal beliefs that were reflected in his illustrations. These often delivered scathing indictments of Confederate policies, as with two multi-image prints from 1863: "The War in the West," which depicted the suffering of civilians in border states, including starving women and children, and "Southern Chivalry Dedicated to Jefferson Davis," which showed a Confederate soldier holding the severed head of a Union soldier and Confederate wagons tossing wounded soldiers out onto the roadside to die. Nast was also known for producing battlefield scenes that were epic in scope and rich in detail, such as "Grand Review of the Army of the Potomac" from 1863, in which the line of soldiers appears to stretch on into infinity. Such images stirred patriotic sentiment and helped boost public support for the war, despite the terrible death toll that was rising daily by that time, and they thus became invaluable tools of wartime propaganda.

Famous political cartoonist, Thomas Nast (1840–1902). Perhaps the best known political cartoonist of the Civil War era, Thomas Nast encouraged support for the Union cause through his unsympathetic illustrations of antiwar Copperheads, Southern slave holders, and Confederate soldiers. *The Library of Congress.*

Railing against Copperhead Perfidy

Nast produced scathing satirical images critiquing Northern opponents of the war, who were known as Copperheads, and also as Peace Democrats. This faction—considered somewhat allied with their Democratic Party brethren in the South—advocated an immediate end to the war. One famous image by Nast was used for a much-circulated anti-Copperhead leaflet called *A Traitor's Peace*. Published by the Congressional Union Committee of Washington, DC, its front page featured Nast's illustration of Confederate States of America President Jefferson Davis standing triumphant on a Union grave, accepting the bowing gratitude of a Union Army soldier who was missing part of his lower leg. Underneath Nast's image were conditions for peace taken directly from a Richmond newspaper, which called for the withdrawal of all troops from Confederate states, and the warning, "so surely shall we make [the North] pay our war debt, though we wring it out of their hearts" (Wagner 2006, page for April 20).

The Union General Ulysses S. Grant, who in later years would become a close personal friend of Nast, once famously described him as the one person most

Hercules of the Union. Political cartoons enjoyed enormous popularity during the Civil War as competing factions in the North and South attempted to garner public support for their cause by mocking the beliefs of their opponents. *The Library of Congress.*

responsible for the preservation of the Union. President Lincoln also spoke highly of Nast and his work, once calling him "our best recruiting sergeant. His emblematic cartoons have never failed to arouse enthusiasm and patriotism, and have always seemed to come just when these articles were getting scarce" (Heidler 2002, p. 1,390). During Lincoln's 1864 bid for reelection, Nast's pen produced several images for *Harper's Weekly* that derided the Copperheads, who were Lincoln's most important political opponents, and who were exerting their influence on the presidential campaign of Lincoln's Democratic Party challenger, a Union Army general named George McClellan. In one of Nast's most famous cartoons of the era, "How Copperheads Obtain Their Votes," Nast depicted Copperheads in a cemetery at night copying names from the headstones onto voting ballots. The Copperhead peace movement in the North incited such forceful public opposition that McClellan was eventually forced to recant his position on the matter of ending the war before a Union victory.

Union Abolitionist Sentiment

Another well-known work of Nast's was "Emancipation," from 1865. In this multi-image piece, vignettes juxtapose African American life in the slave-owning Confederate South with hopes for a life of freedom and dignity in the North. The anchor image is a multigenerational family scene in which several blacks gather around a wood-burning stove marked *Union*. A portrait of Lincoln is visible in the home, and is repeated elsewhere on the page. Scenes depicting the barbarity of bondage, such as fugitive slave hunts and slave auctions, contrast with images of a former slave in the North being paid wages and a black mother sending her children to school.

Nast was not the only political cartoonist who gained prominence during the war years, though he remains the best known. Besides *Harper's Weekly*, another publication that published strong pro-Union cartoons was the *New York Illustrated News*. The New York City printing house of Nathanial Currier and James Merritt Ives also produced scores of propagandistic images. Currier and Ives's immense factory turned out hundreds of hand-colored lithographs that were the mid-nineteenth-century version of poster art for the home. During the war years these lithographs often contained strongly pro-Union imagery, as with one from 1861, *The Dis-United States, Or the Southern Confederacy*, which shows prominent figures from the first six states to secede from the Union. The figures representing Alabama, Mississippi, and Georgia are seated on bales of cotton, while the one representing Louisiana sits astride a barrel of liquor, the one representing Florida sits in a canoe, and, most prominently, Francis Pickens, representing South Carolina, the initiator of secession, is seated atop the back of a kneeling slave (Wagner 2006, page for January 19).

Southern Political Humor

Political humor was far less developed in the Confederate states than in the North. Wartime shortages meant a drastically reduced stock of ink and newsprint, and many publications struggled to stay afloat. Because of this scarcity, few publishers had funds to pay established professional writers and artists. Many publications, such as the *Southern Illustrated News* and *Magnolia Weekly*, relied on reader submissions to fill their pages, and, indeed, in the first half of the war thousands of war poems and hymns to Dixie were sent in every week.

The only Confederate artist to equal Nast's success was Adalbert J. Volck (1828–1912), who like Nast was a German immigrant. Volck, a dentist in Baltimore, produced artwork that was intensely critical of antislavery advocates and of Lincoln. Many of these images were reproduced under Volck's pen name, "V. Blada." One example of Volck's work is *Under the Veil—Mokana* (1863), which caricatures Lincoln as a female dancer in an Arab harem, and gives him obviously African facial features. This image reflected a belief found in the South that Lincoln was of mixed ancestry. Another of Volck's works was copied from a widely circulated Northern print of Lincoln writing the Emancipation Proclamation, but in Volck's version allegorical details reveal the president to be doing the work of the devil. Volck's *Worship of the North* (1863) shows Lincoln and several other figures, including a young man who is a sacrificial victim, surrounded by such phrases as "free love," "negro worship," and "socialism." Volck's works, many of which were published via subscription series throughout the South, also included less ferocious, but nevertheless patriotic images. These include *Offer of Bells to Be Cast into Cannon* (1863), which showed Roman Catholic and Protestant clergy bringing their dismantled church bells to the local forge so that the metal could be used for Confederate Army field weapons.

During the war years, the *Atlanta Constitution* published regular letters that were the work of the journalist Charles Henry Smith (1826–1903), writing under the pen name "Bill Arp." This weekly feature, which allowed Smith to poke fun at the North using the voice of a typical Confederate, was written in a common Southern vernacular form. The first of these appeared quite early in the war as a letter to "Abe Linkhorn" written by the fictional Arp in response to Lincoln's order for the Southern rebels to disperse. From Rome, Georgia, Arp writes:

> Mr. Linkhorn: Sur: These are to inform you that we are all well, and hope these lines may find you in statue ko. We received your proklamation, and as you have put us on very short notis, a few of us have conkluded to write you, and ax for a little more time. The fact is, we are most obleeged to have a few more days, for the way things are happening, it is utterly onpossible for us to disperse in twenty days. Old Virginny, Tennessee, and North Callina, are continually aggravatin us into tumults and carousements, and a body can't disperse until you put a stop to sich onruly conduct on their part. (Smith 1903, p. 7)

Smith continued to write a regular feature as Bill Arp even after the war, which permitted him to voice opinions he might not have otherwise been able to express in his position as the mayor of Rome, Georgia.

In New York City, Nast went on to further distinguish himself with cartoons that called attention to the rampant municipal corruption in the city under a notorious figure, William Marcy "Boss" Tweed.

BIBLIOGRAPHY

Fahs, Alice. *The Imagined Civil War: Popular Literature of the North and South, 1861–1865.* Chapel Hill: University of North Carolina Press, 2003.

Heidler, David Stephen, Jeanne T. Heidler, and David J. Coles. *Encyclopedia of the American Civil War: A Political, Social, and Military History.* New York: W. W. Norton, 2002.

Smith, Charles Henry. *Bill Arp from the Uncivil War to Date, 1861–1903.* 2nd ed. Atlanta, GA: Hudgins Publishing Company, 1903.

Streitmatter, Rodger. *Mightier Than the Sword: How the News Media Have Shaped American History.* Jackson, TN: Westview Press, 1997.

Sutherland, Daniel E. *The Expansion of Everyday Life, 1860–1876.* New York: Harper & Row, 1989.

Wagner, Margaret E. *The American Civil War: 365 Days.* New York: Harry N. Abrams/Library of Congress, 2006.

Carol Brennan

BIASED NEWSPAPER REPORTING

Newspapers performed the vital task of providing civilians and soldiers with information about military events, politics, and the home front. Most small rural communities had at least one newspaper, and large cities, such as New York, had several. Civil War-era newspapers, however, were quite forthright about their biases. Many editors were politicians or had political aspirations. Editors usually supported a particular political party, resulting in the reporting of most news from a single political view. A few editors considered their newspapers to be neutral, but the common practice of the day was to editorialize on recent events instead of simply conveying the facts. The political impact of newspapers was most evident during the secession crisis, but throughout the Civil War editors fought their own rhetorical battles over the war's conduct. Although there were fewer newspapers in the South, newspapers both North and South fueled political debates and offered social commentary. During the war people in the Union and the Confederacy read newspapers not only to become informed, but also to form their own opinions on controversial topics such as emancipation, military strategies, and political leadership.

The bias in newspaper reporting often resulted from editors establishing newspapers with the purpose of representing a particular political or social perspective. There were abolitionist newspapers, such as William Lloyd Garrison's (1805–1879) *Liberator*, foreign language newspapers, including German newspapers in most Northern cities, and papers that supported various political parties. During the war most Northern newspapers aligned with either the Republican and Democratic parties. With their particular points of view, newspapers served as a forum for political debate. Many editors were more concerned about shaping public opinion than on reporting what happened.

Newspapers varied in size and circulation. Horace Greely's (1877–1970) *New York Tribune* boasted a circulation of 55,000, whereas a typical rural newspaper would have only a few hundred. All newspaper editors, however, read and printed news from other papers, often responding to other editorials. They would also sometimes print unsubstantiated information or rumor, correcting any errors later, if at all.

Wartime Correspondents

The desire for information led larger newspapers to hire correspondents to travel in search of newsworthy information. Some of these men followed the armies, and on several occasions these reporters, or "specials" as they were called, witnessed battles firsthand and wrote reports. Correspondents, however, could only report on what they witnessed or were told, which often caused the newspapers to print misinformation. A reporter who witnessed the First Battle of Bull Run on July 21, 1861 (also known as First Manassas) returned to Washington, DC, before the battle had ended, mistakenly spreading the news of a Union victory. Based on these early reports, New York newspapers announced the "glorious Union victory" the day after the battle. As J. Cutler Andrews relays in his 1955 work *The North Reports the Civil War*, other newspapers were able catch the error before they went to press and were then able to print the correct account of the disastrous Union defeat. Even correspondents who took the time to check their facts often gave overly optimistic and ingratiating accounts of the Union army and its officers. Because reporters relied on officers as a source of information, some newsmen found that they could gain access to the armies if they frequently spoke well of military men in their articles.

Union Newspapers

In addition to providing the public with information, newspapers could also affect shape public opinion and affect politics. Horace Greely, editor of the *New York Tribune*, initially supported President Abraham Lincoln (1809–1865), but as the war continued Greely went on to criticize Lincoln's leadership and the military situation. He condemned Lincoln for taking so long to develop an emancipation policy, but also rebuked Lincoln for not seeking a peace treaty with the Confederacy.

Masthead of *The Liberator*. *The Liberator*, published by William Lloyd Garrison, was a paper that called for the abolition of slavery as an institution. Its slogan was "Our Country Is the World—Our Countrymen Are Mankind." *The Library of Congress.*

Greely's criticism was not consistent or along party lines, but may be attributed to the Lincoln's decision to appoint one of Greely's political enemies, William H. Seward, as Secretary of State.

Lincoln understood that editors played an important role in politics and public opinion. He made a concerted effort to correspond with James Gordon Bennett (1795–1872), the editor of the *New York Herald*. Bennett's newspaper had a wide circulation, including overseas subscriptions, and its large professional staff meant that the *Herald* often had better intelligence than the Union Army. On one occasion the newspaper printed the Confederate Army's muster roll, which the staff meticulously gathered from Confederate newspapers. Unlike Greely, however, Bennett resisted infusing the news with his own political agenda.

Bias was most evident among those editors who opposed the war, known collectively as the *Copperhead press*. Copperheads were members of the peace faction of the Democratic Party, which opposed Lincoln's wartime policy, especially emancipation, and called for a peaceful restoration of the Union. Some of these editors were simply opposed to the president's decisions, but a few editors made unsubstantiated claims to turn public opinion against the Republican Party. The best example of this political bias occurred after Lincoln announced the Emancipation Proclamation. On October 10, 1862, the *Cincinnati Enquirer*, considered a Copperhead newspaper by local Republicans, declared that "the President's Negro Proclamation, if it can be enforced, will bring hundreds and thousands of negroes into Ohio to compete with the white laboring men." This was a scare tactic aimed at convincing readers to vote for Democrats in upcoming state elections. A New York Copperhead newspaper, the *Weekly Caucasian*, also used race as a way to sway opinion against emancipation. On October 11, 1862, as Andrew S. Coopersmith recounts in his 2004 work *Fighting Words: An Illustrated History of Newspaper Accounts of the Civil War* the paper warned readers that if the defenders of slavery were defeated "and the negro distorted into the status of the white man, then liberty and Republican institutions, and civilization itself, will be overthrown" (pp. 106–108). Editors eager to criticize Lincoln also allowed false information to be printed. In 1864 the *New York World* ran a phony proclamation that indicated President Lincoln was calling for four hundred thousand additional volunteers. The announcement implied that the war was not going well and, in response, military officials temporarily stopped publication of the newspaper.

Newspapers and Secession

Southern newspapers played an important role in the establishment of the Confederacy. During the winter of 1860–1861, southern newspapers provided a forum for the debate over secession. After Abraham Lincoln won the 1860 election, prosecession editors published heated editorials warning that Lincoln's presidency would result in abolition and violence against white southerners. These editors used fear to convince undecided southerners that secession was the only viable course of action. On October 30, 1860, South Carolina's *Charleston Daily Courier* declared that "if Lincoln is elected there is an end to cotton and all the various advantages that result from it." The editor based his conclusion on the assumption that Lincoln would end slavery and because no free black farmer had been known to grow cotton, the crop would perish.

Secessionist editors openly criticized southern editors who believed that the Union could be preserved or that secession should be organized and gradual. In several cases secessionist editors called for Unionist papers in the south to be banned. South Carolina secessionist William Lowndes Yancey (1814–1863) sent a threatening letter to Unionist editor William G. Brownlow, which Brownlow printed in his paper, the *Knoxville Whig*. The letter indicated that Yancey believed someone would hang Brownlow in 1861. Brownlow's reply, reprinted by Donald E. Reynolds in his 2006 book *Editors Make War: Southern Newspapers in the Secession Crisis*, says "come what may, through weal or woe, in peace or war, no earthly power shall keep me from denouncing the enemies of my country" (p. 172). Confederate authorities did eventually capture Brownlow, but he was released and did not return to Knoxville until Union forces occupied the city in 1863.

Confederate Newspapers

In the Confederacy, newspapers reported the progress of the war to people on the home front who were desperate to hear news of Confederate victories. As with Union correspondents, Southern journalists tended to write what they believed people wanted to hear or, rather, what would sell papers. Confederate newspapers often printed stories about how Union soldiers abused southern civilians, although reporters witnessed few of these accounts. Printing stories about the greed or incompetence of "Yankees" helped build morale, so editors freely printed rumors and second-hand stories for the good of the war effort. After the Confederate victory at Fredericksburg, Virginia, in December 1862, the *Knoxville Daily Register* exaggerated the odds against the Confederate troops by claiming, as J. Cutler Andrews reprints in 1970's *The South Reports the Civil War*, that the Union "had 200,000 soldiers participating in the battle while the Confederates had only 20,000" (p. 230). In fact, during the battle an estimated 78,000 Confederate soldiers faced approximately 120,000 Union troops, a much smaller disparity than the *Register*'s ten to one odds. Over-exaggerating reports of victories and downplaying defeats did raise morale in the Confederacy, but it also meant that citizens were often misinformed about the prospects for ultimate victory.

The Southern press could also be critical of Confederate political and military leaders. Editors freely commented on the character and performance of generals, especially when these commanders restricted reporters' access to the news. In early 1862 Confederate general Braxton Bragg issued an order excluding correspondents from accompanying his army after he read newspaper accounts that he believed depicted him in a negative way. Bragg's unsuccessful invasion of Kentucky in September 1862 only drew additional criticism from the press. Editor John M. Daniel of the *Richmond Examiner* wrote about Bragg on November 19, 1862. Andrews reproduces Daniel's words in *The South Reports the Civil War*: "with an iron heart, and iron hand, and a wooden head, his failure in a position where the highest intellectual facilities were demanded was predestined" (p. 253). The negative press coverage drew the attention of Confederate president Jefferson Davis (1808–1889), who took action to reduce the extent of Bragg's command. Confederacy newspapers also scrutinized Davis's actions. Although there were no competing political parties in the Confederacy, some editors blamed Davis for military losses by claiming that Davis made poor choices when appointing generals.

The Civil War-era press held a substantial amount of influence, but publishing standards of the time also allowed editors to take liberty with the facts. In spite of some efforts by both Union and Confederate governments to censure newspapers, editors openly voiced their opinions about the war. This allowed people access to a wide range of perspectives and created a national forum for discussion of major issues. The extent of bias in Civil War newspaper reporting, however, often contributed to controversy and political division.

BIBLIOGRAPHY

Andrews, J. Cutler. *The North Reports the Civil War*. Pittsburgh, PA: University of Pittsburgh Press, 1955, reprinted 1985.

Andrews, J. Cutler. *The South Reports the Civil War*. Pittsburgh, PA: University of Pittsburgh Press, 1970, reprinted 1985.

Coopersmith, Andrew S. *Fighting Words: An Illustrated History of Newspaper Accounts of the Civil War*. New York: New Press, 2004.

Douglas, George H. *The Golden Age of the Newspaper*. Westport, CT: Greenwood Press, 1999.

Harris, Brayton. *Blue and Gray in Black and White: Newspapers in the Civil War*. Washington, DC: Brassey's, 1999.

Ratner, Lorman A., and Dwight L. Teeter Jr. *Fanatics and Fire-Eaters: Newspapers and the Coming of the Civil War*. Urbana: University of Illinois Press, 2003.

Reynolds, Donald E. *Editors Make War: Southern Newspapers in the Secession Crisis*. Carbondale: Southern Illinois University Press, 2006.

Stephen Rockenbach

PARTY POLITICS

By the election of 1860, the wheels of secession had been set in motion, and the disputes and rivalries among the major political parties reflected this starkly. The Democratic and Republican parties represented camps that seemed diametrically opposed (with the Republicans opposing slavery and the Democrats accepting it), but within each party were rifts that would grow as the Civil War progressed. Lincoln, the presidential victor, represented the conservative (moderate) Republicans, who wanted to end slavery but favored a gradual end as a means of preserving the Union. The radical Republicans, who counted staunch Northern abolitionists among their ranks, wanted an immediate end to slavery across the nation. The Democrats were split into Northern and Southern factions, with the Southern faction more steadfastly opposed to any government action that could curtail the rights of white citizens to hold slaves as personal property.

Southern and Northern Politics

For the duration of the war the Southern Democrats remained fairly unified, with their key focus on maintaining the Confederacy and the slave economy. The states that made up the Confederacy were not a monolithic entity, however; indeed, little unified them but their commitment to maintaining slavery. President Jefferson Davis led the new government with a strong hand and helped create a centralized government to hold the seceded states together (Catton 1971, pp. 220–221). Moreover, because the Confederate constitution called for the president to serve a single six-year term, Davis had no need to worry about running for reelection.

In the North, politics were different. The Republican National Convention of 1860 in Chicago made the party's position on slavery quite clear: "[W]e brand the recent re-opening of the African Slave Trade, under the cover of our national flag, aided by perversions of judicial power, as a crime against humanity, and a burning shame to our country and age" (Halstead 1860, p. 139). The radical Republicans saw Lincoln as ineffective and they made their disapproval quite plain. Led by politicians, including Thaddeus Stevens of Pennsylvania, Charles Sumner of Massachusetts, and Ohio's James A. Garfield (later President in his own right), they worked both openly and behind the scenes to push their agenda. Aided by prominent individuals such as the abolitionist Wendell Phillips and *New York Tribune* editor Horace Greeley, the radical Republicans sought to exert their influence on the president.

Lincoln, however, was not about to allow the radicals to dictate policy. A practical man who looked toward the longer term, he allied himself with other conservative Republicans, most notably William Seward, who served as his secretary of state. The president wisely chose both radical Republicans and Northern Democrats to fill various cabinet and other government positions. Salmon P. Chase, a radical Republican and self-avowed rival of Lincoln's, was named treasury secretary and later chief justice of the United States. George B. McClellan, a young and brilliant general, was named commander of the Union Army. Edward M. Stanton, who had served in James Buchanan's cabinet, was named Lincoln's secretary of war in 1862.

Pro- and Anti-War Forces Clash

The tensions between pro- and anti-war politicians continued to grow throughout the war. Many political leaders were opposed to slavery, but equally opposed to the bloodshed that seemed to be increasing daily. Moreover, while among the general public the sentiment was decidedly antislavery, many Northerners viewed blacks as an inferior race nonetheless, just as their Southern counterparts did. As the war continued, many white Northerners began to question whether freedom for the slaves was worth the destruction of so many lives. The sentiments expressed by Maine legislator Moses Page in a speech before the state's house of representatives in 1863 were not uncommon: "I think this country was destined for one people, and would have remained ok, had not the fell spirit of abolition crept in and overturned the work of our fathers" (Stout 2006, pp. 279–280).

Democrats split into two factions: the "War Democrats," who supported Lincoln's aims of reunifying the nation, and the "Peace Democrats" (called *Copperheads* because they wore copper Indian Head pennies on their lapels), who wanted an immediate end to the war—at any price. The Copperheads produced anti-Lincoln propaganda in the form of pamphlets, articles, newspaper advertisements—even songs. One example was a booklet titled *The Lincoln Catechism, Wherein the Eccentricities and Beauties of Despotism Are Fully Set Forth*, printed in time for the 1864 election. It offered such question-and-answer couplets as, "What did the Constitution mean by freedom of the press? / Throwing Democratic newspapers out of the mails.... What is the meaning of the word 'traitor'? / One who is a stickler for the Constitution and the laws" (pp. 4–5).

The 1864 presidential election was viewed as a critical juncture for a country that was war-weary and cynical. Abraham Lincoln was chosen as the candidate for what was dubbed the "Union Party"—made up primarily of Republicans and War Democrats. (Andrew Johnson, his running mate, was a Democrat from Tennessee.) The Copperheads chose General McClellan as their candidate. McClellan, despite his brilliance, had failed to live up to his reputation while on the battlefield and Lincoln had removed him from his command in 1862.

Partisan Activity and the Public

Both sides printed massive quantities of posters, pamphlets, and other documents stating their case and asking the public for support. In Pennsylvania, an estimated 280,000 pieces of political literature were printed (Neely 2006, p. 74). People from all walks of life had strong political opinions and had no trouble making them known. Poet Walt Whitman wrote about visiting a Brooklyn pub in 1864 and seeing a barmaid wearing a McClellan pin. He "called her and asked if the other girls there were for McClellan too—she said yes every one of them, and that they wouldn't tolerate a girl in the place who was not, and the *fellows* were too" (Neely 2006, p. 1).

"Great Copperhead Jubilee!" Anti-Democratic Party political cartoon. During the presidential election of 1864, Republican supporters often lampooned the views of anti-war Copperheads and their candidate, the demoted General George B. McClellan. © *Corbis*

In addition to posters, pamphlets, and buttons, Americans could purchase a variety of political memorabilia, either to show support for a particular group or to build up collections. The printing industry was more than accommodating when it came to meeting this need; for example, copies of the Emancipation Proclamation were produced for display in homes. *Cartes de visite* (small collectible cards not unlike today's baseball cards or postcards) depicting various political figures proved popular collectors' items as well. People purchased cards with portraits of Lincoln, his cabinet, members of Congress, and other leading figures of the war years (Neely 2006, p. 27).

After the election, conservative and radical Republicans continued to attack each other, but the business at hand was now bringing the war to a conclusion and political intrigue was largely kept behind the scenes. When the war ended in April 1865, the radical Republicans wanted strong punitive action taken against the Confederacy, but Lincoln planned for a more moderate approach. His assassination on April 14 made the question moot.

BIBLIOGRAPHY

Catton, Bruce. *The Civil War.* New York: American Heritage Press, 1971.

Gallagher, Gary W., and Alan T. Nolan, eds. *The Myth of the Lost Cause and Civil War History.* Bloomington: Indiana University Press, 2000.

Halstead, Murat. *Caucuses of 1860: A History of the National Political Conventions of the Current Presidential Campaign.* Columbus, OH: Follett, Foster & Company, 1860.

The Lincoln Catechism, Wherein the Eccentricities and Beauties of Despotism Are Fully Set Forth: A Guide to the Presidential Election of 1864. New York: J. F. Feeks, 1864.

Neely, Mark E, Jr. *The Boundaries of American Political Culture in the Civil War Era.* Chapel Hill: University of North Carolina Press, 2006.

Schouler, James. *Eighty Years of Union, Being a Short History of the United States, 1783–1865.* New York: Dodd, Mead & Company, 1903.

Stout, Harry S. *Upon the Altar of the Nation: A Moral History of the Civil War.* New York: Viking, 2006.

Williams, T. Harry. *Lincoln and the Radicals.* Madison: University of Wisconsin Press, 1941. Reprint, 1969.

George A. Milite

Effects of the War on Slaves and Freedpeople

■ Effects of the War on Slaves and Freedpeople Overview

In no respect was the complexity of the Civil War more apparent than in the experiences of African Americans. Their status as slaves was the war's only significant cause, but their welfare was far from being the chief concern of the majority in either North or South. Nor was it clear what their status would or should be if they were no longer to be slaves. In a complex interplay of their own actions with the actions of whites who supported their rights, opposed them, or just did not care, the war brought about their freedom but did not finally secure for them the full rights of citizenship.

The stage was set for the complexity of the Civil War's effects on African Americans by the multiplicity of attitudes toward them among whites in both sections of the country. In the South, about one-fourth of white families owned slaves at any given time, and about half of southern heads of household would do so at some time during their lives. Those who owned slaves and those who had an expectation of doing so obviously wished to preserve the institution of slavery because of the economics benefits they gained or hoped to gain by it. The vast majority of the South's capital was invested in human chattels and would be lost if slavery were ended.

Southern whites with no direct economic interest in slavery might have been expected to oppose the institution, since it constituted economic competition for their own labors. This was the argument of Hinton Rowan Helper, a North Carolinian who in 1857 published *The Impending Crisis of the South*, in which he urged his fellow non-slaveholding white Southerners to oppose slavery for just that reason. Unfortunately, Helper's own racism was as virulent as that of any slaveholding planter, and his concern was solely for the good of his fellow non-slaveholding Southern whites. They shared his racism but not the conclusion he drew from it. For them, slavery was to be preserved as the best way to maintain white supremacy. It was an attitude the planters assiduously cultivated: the curious belief that all whites were elevated to a level of equality by the fact that most blacks were held in slavery.

Northern whites were even more divided in their views about African Americans. Abolitionists generally favored full civil rights for the newly freed or soon-to-be-freed slaves and substantial racial equality, but abolitionists did not comprise a majority in most parts of the North. Moderate antislavery men like Abraham Lincoln were still contemplating colonization of the freedpeople to Central America or the Caribbean as late as 1863 and were moving only slowly toward positions such as advocacy of voting rights for the former slaves. Some of the "Free Soil" support for the Republican Party before the war had come from Northerners who were as committed to racism as any of their Southern brethren and simply wanted the western territories reserved for white settlers with no blacks present. And of course a large minority of the Northern electorate was comprised of Democrats, who had voted against even the limitation of slavery's spread. Many of them had as their wartime slogan: "The Union as it was. The Constitution as it is. The Slaves where they are"—in which they often substituted a racial epithet for the word "Slaves." The war itself transformed some Northerners' attitudes about slavery and race. Even Democrats or racist-minded Republicans might come to the view that if slavery was trying to destroy the Union, then the institution of slavery must die. What status that meant for those who had once been slaves, was a very confused question.

Beyond all this, African Americans in a number of ways were participants in the struggle that brought such momentous change to their role in American society. The Fugitive Slave Act of 1850, more than almost any other single element, helped turn Northerners against slavery, and it was the persistence of a small minority of slaves in escaping and seeking refuge in the North (or passage across the North to ultimate safety in Canada) that kept bringing the act's onerous provisions before the eyes of Northerners, making slavery real to them in all of its ugliness.

Once the war started, slaves were not slow to seize the chances for escape presented to them by the presence of Union armies. Their appearance in Federal camps forced Northern soldiers to make decisions that many of them would rather have avoided. Official Union policy early in the war, driven by the desire to maintain the allegiance of proslavery Northerners or citizens of such Union-loyal slave states as Missouri, Kentucky, and Maryland, was that runaways who entered Union lines should be returned to their owners. Regiments with abolitionist leanings frequently defied such orders, harbored escaped slaves, and forwarded them to freedom farther north. Even Federals of a more racist bent often found that an escaped slave made a handy personal servant to cook, wash clothes, or perform other menial functions that helped make soldiering tedious. The slaves, for their part, seemed eager to help the cause that they correctly sensed was ultimately fighting for their freedom.

It was Union Major General Benjamin Butler, a pre-war Massachusetts lawyer and politician, who found a legal solution to the demands of proslavery persons, even those loyal to the enemy, that the U.S. forces were bound by the Fugitive Slave Law to return escaping slaves to Rebel owners. When a pro-Confederate slaveholder came to his headquarters demanding the return of escapees believed to have entered Butler's lines, the general replied that the slaves had no doubt previously been used for the benefit of the Confederacy and were therefore, like any property in the use of the enemy, subject to military confiscation as contraband of war. Thereafter few slaves were ever returned to Rebel masters, and all escaped slaves within Union lines came to be referred to as contrabands. With the issuance of the final Emancipation Proclamation on January 1, 1863, the Union army became explicitly the force for liberating the slaves, but the name "contraband" stuck throughout the rest of the war.

The life of the contrabands varied a great deal. In a Union-controlled enclave on the South Carolina coast and in the Federal-held Mississippi Delta country below Memphis, Union commanders set up various arrangements for the former slaves to work abandoned plantations for wages, but these success stories came to an end when the war ended and the absconded erstwhile Rebel owners of the lands returned and were permitted by federal authorities to reclaim their acres. In many cases, former slaves who fled to Union lines had nowhere to go but the squalid contraband camps set up behind the lines by a Union army that was much at a loss to know how to handle its new charges. Life could be hard in the contraband camps, disease rampant and deaths frequent. This situation was ameliorated somewhat when Congress established the Freedmen's Bureau for the care and supervision of the former slaves.

Sometimes the army's need to fight the war and inability to serve as a refugee-aid organization was brought into conflict with blacks' desire to escape from slavery as soon as possible at almost any price. Fast-moving Union expeditions that penetrated deep into Southern territory quickly gained long tails of escaping slaves—thousands of men, women, and children that might string out for miles behind the Federal rearguard. They included both the very young and the very old, and they came on foot and on every kind of beast or conveyance they could lay hold of on the plantations from which they were fleeing. Their presence could be a nuisance to Union commanders, who often lacked the means of feeding their new followers or of protecting them from re-capture by marauding Confederate cavalry. Yet the blacks could not be dissuaded from following the army, despite the Union officers' advice that they would be better off patiently awaiting their liberation on their plantations. Conditions for the freedpeople in the wake of the army could be very hard; they lacked adequate food and shelter and were sometimes left entirely behind by troop columns who could not afford to wait for them.

By the end of the war it was clear that slavery was finished in the states that had comprised the Confederacy. A few months later the Thirteenth Amendment abolished slavery in the remaining slave states. The status of the former slaves remained to be fought out in the long, twilight conflict of the Reconstruction Era, however. White Southerners were united in their continued determination to maintain white supremacy in the South, despite their defeat on the battlefield. A U.S. Congress dominated by Republicans, and especially those of a fairly radical stripe, desired to see the freedpeople accorded substantial civil rights and full citizenship. They worked toward that end, despite an uncooperative President Andrew Johnson and, later, with the aid of a like-minded President Ulysses S. Grant. Ultimately they fell short. America has never excelled at waging low-intensity wars or at persevering in conflicts that last more than four or five years. More than eleven years after Appomattox—and more than fifteen years after Fort Sumter—the remaining pro-civil rights contingent in the North had grown weary of the long battle, while white Southerners, increasingly seconded by the more racist elements in the North, stood as staunchly as ever for white supremacy. The result was that when Reconstruction ended in 1877, African Americans were left in a sort of limbo. The war had brought them freedom, which was an accomplishment that would have seemed almost impossible a quarter-century before, yet they were consigned for the most part to a status of peonage that would continue for another three-quarters of a century.

Steven E. Woodworth

■ Slave Markets

Perhaps nothing symbolized the dehumanizing effects of slavery more than slave markets. Abolitionists saw them as the evil apotheosis of the Southern economic system where human beings literally became livestock to be prodded and inspected like prized cows and bulls on the eve of a sale. For the enslaved, the markets raised a legion of uncertainties, fears, and terrors; something to avoid at all costs. To many Southerners, the marts were necessary evils—unpleasant, but vital for the production of cotton. Finally, for the merchants, the sales served as placed where one, if savvy, could make a fortune.

The quintessential image of the slave market shows a bewildered, shivering, and nearly nude slave on an auction block, humiliated before a host of broad-brim-hatted, silver-caned planters. And while that scene certainly played out at various slave markets in the United States, it was not the only method for selling slaves. Natchez, Mississippi, home of the Forks of the Road slave mart (the second largest in the South) on the outskirts of the town, consisted of a series of shops and corrals—much like a modern strip mall—where planters went to view the various slave merchants's offerings (Barnett and Burkett 2001, pp. 169–187). New Orleans slave traders operated in a similar manner. A British traveler to the Crescent City in the 1850s recorded how the well-dressed slaves loitered in courtyards "not doing any work" like so many mannequins, awaiting potential buyers. The dealer, thinking her a potential customer, lined the slaves up in two rows "and began to describe and extol his wares" (Pfeiffer 1856, pp. 403–404).

In some communities, the slave depots became so squalid and disease ridden that city officials forbade them from conducting business within the city limits. In Natchez the final straw came when a dealer got caught dumping the bodies of cholera-infected slaves in a ravine. Rather than give them proper burials, he treated them in death like he did in life—as livestock (Deyle 2005, p. 326).

Prior to the sales, the traders housed the slaves in anything from small tents, to barns, to large pens. Sometimes they languished for months on end, waiting for a buyer to take them. To make them more attractive the traders tried to make them as youthful and healthy looking as possible. William Wells Brown (d. 1884), a former slave, recalled his chore of making older slaves look younger prior to a sale:

> I was ordered to have the old men's whiskers shaved off, and the grey hairs plucked out where they were not too numerous, in which case he had a preparation of blacking to color it, and with a blacking brush we would put it on. These slaves were also taught how old they were by Mr. Walker, and after going through the blacking process they looked ten or fifteen years younger. (Brown 1849, p. 39)

Slave block at the St. Louis Hotel in New Orleans, Louisiana, 1906. Much like animals at a livestock auction, slaves were put on display for a degrading examination and inspection prior to their purchase. *The Art Archive/Culver Pictures/The Picture Desk, Inc.*

An illustration of a slave auction. Slaveholders gave little concern to keeping slave families intact at auctions. Slaves were frequently separated from their children and spouses, as buyers had little regard for purchasing and preserving entire families. *The Art Archive/Culver Pictures/The Picture Desk, Inc.*

A Yankee clergyman, Joseph Holt Ingraham (1809–1860), described a similar scene where slaves were "made to shave and wash in greasy pot liquor to make them look sleek and nice; their heads combed and their best clothes put on." Next, the dealer ordered the slaves to stand in a double line, segregated by sex, after which the customers were taken into a private room for a more thorough examination, which disgusted the transplanted Yankee (Ingraham 1835, pp. 234–241). "See a large, rough slaveholder, take a poor female slave into a room, make her strip, then feel of and examine her, as though she were a pig, or a hen, or merchandise. O, how can a poor slave husband or father stand and see his wife, daughters and sons thus treated" (Anderson 1857, p. 14). Such were the humiliations experienced daily in the slave markets.

Of the stories that emerged from the slave marts, the separation of loved ones are among the most heart-rending. In another scene at another auction, Brown recalled the selling of a husband and wife—separately. The auctioneer sold the husband first, who immediately began lobbying his new owner to purchase his wife, pleading, "Master, if you will only buy Fanny, I know you will get the worth of your money. She is a good cook, a good washer, and her last mistress liked her very much. If you will only buy her how happy I shall be." Although the new owner did not want her, he relented, and began bidding on her. The couple's hearts rose and sank with each bid until, finally, the hammer dropped and someone else purchased her. They both broke down into tears and the husband bade farewell, "Well, Fanny, we are to part forever, on earth; you have been a good wife to me . . . I hope you will try to meet me in heaven. I shall try to meet you there" (Brown 1849, pp. 39, 127–128).

In addition to trying to get potential masters to purchase family members, the enslaved, at times, actively tried to influence a sale to their own advantage. During the inspection process, slaves often faced untenable situations. If they were sick, had runaway in the past, or in some manner could not work efficiently, they ran the risk of beatings if they did not tell their potential owner. On the other side, if they revealed too much information, they risked the ire of the slave trader. In some cases, the slaves could not resist gaming the system, especially if they could gain significant advantage or avoid greater hardship by marketing themselves to a planter or shop owner. If they knew a potential buyer liked to beat his slaves, work them too hard, or abuse them in other ways, then they would often influence the sell. If the master lived in a location where the potential for escape was good, that too could influence the slave's behavior during the inspection. But such gaming only worked in the marts where individual masters shopped for new slaves. In auctions, unless the enslaved had opportunity to talk with a potential buyer beforehand, gaming was much more difficult.

As a symbol of the evils of slavery, auctions served as an effective propaganda tool for the abolitionists. In the years leading up to the war, abolitionists published reams of first-person accounts describing humiliation and heartbreak on the auction blocks of the South. But it was a white female abolitionist from the North who made the greatest impact among Northern readers. Harriet Beecher Stowe's (1811–1896) fictional composite account of the auctions in *Uncle Tom's Cabin*, which she based on stories she had read in the abolitionist press and through her encounters with runaway slaves, reached people who normally did not read abolitionist literature. Only the coldest of hearts remained unmoved after reading of Tom's sale at an auction, followed by his humiliation at the hands of Simon Legree.

Such was the power of slave market imagery that near the conclusion of the war, the sign and steps of the slave auction block in Charleston, South Carolina, were sent to the Eleventh Ward Freedman's Aid Society of Boston, Massachusetts, as a trophy of war. There, William Lloyd Garrison (1805–1879), and others, gave triumphant speeches. One speaker called "the relics of the Great Barbarism" a symbol "of the worship of the Anti Christ" and requested that it be preserved alongside the "racks of the Inquisition and the keys of the Bastille," as symbols of oppression. The highlight of the evening, however, came when Garrison climbed the steps to put "the accursed thing under his feet" as a symbol of abolitionism victory over slavery (*The Liberator*, March 17, 1865).

BIBLIOGRAPHY

Anderson, William J. *Life and Narrative of William J. Anderson, Twenty-four Years a Slave.* Chicago: Daily Tribune Book and Job Printing Office, 1857.

Barnett, Jim, and H. Clark Burkett. "The Forks of the Road Slave Market at Natchez." *The Journal of Mississippi History* 63, no. 3 (2001): 169–187.

Brown, William W. *Narrative of William W. Brown, an American Slave.* London: Charles Gilpin, 1849.

Deyle, Steven. *Carry Me Back: The Domestic Slave Trade in American Life.* New York: Oxford University Press, 2005.

Ingraham, Joseph Holt. *The South-West, by a Yankee.* Two vols. New York: Harper and Brothers, 1835.

The Liberator (Boston, MA), "An Immense Meeting in Music Hall (The Charleston Slave Auction–Block)" March 17, 1865, issue 11, col. B.

Pfieffer, Ida. *A Lady's Second Journey Around the World.* New York: Harper and Brothers, 1856.

David H. Slay

Slaves

According to Alexander Stephens, the Confederate vice president, slavery and the inequality of the races were the cornerstones of the new republic known as the Confederate States of America. The desire to preserve slavery was the singular reason for the creation of the Confederacy and the eruption of the American Civil War. Other complex reasons for regional secession were only an extension of the public effort to protect the institution of slavery, which drove the economic engine of Southern states. Upon secession, Southern political leaders were committed to preserving the full array of legal and social controls that had underpinned slavery. Despite their

Lynching in 19th-century literature. An illustration from *The White Slave; or, Memoirs of a Fugitive*, by Richard Hildreth. The picture depicts an African American man standing atop a barrel with a noose around his neck, while a Caucasian man below him starts to kick the barrel. *The Library of Congress.*

efforts, the conservative rebellion to protect slavery began to change the institution into a form that would be unrecognizable by 1865.

Slavery and the Confederate Government

The primary focus of the new Confederate constitution was protecting the institution of slavery. The document the delegates produced contained a defense of slavery, and recognition of its value to the new nation. In other respects, the Confederate constitution closely mirrored the U.S. one. For example, the three-fifths clause was retained. Originally added to the U.S. Constitution as a compromise between the North—which did not want slaves counted at all when determining state representation in the House of Representatives—and the South, which wanted each slave to be counted, this stated that each slave would be counted as three-fifths of a white or freed black person. The importation of slaves from foreign countries remained illegal, as it had been in the U.S. Constitution, but the expansion of slavery either south or west was now justified by the formation of a new nation, and thereby protected as a point of national policy. Finally, the U.S. Constitution's fugitive-slave provision was also adopted into the Confederate constitution. Unlike the United States' version of the law, however, responsibility for the enforcement of the fugitive-slave law was now established on the state level, rather than the national level.

On the surface, the life of free blacks and slaves did not initially change with the creation of the Confederate States of America. They remained the property of their white owners, legally considered no different than livestock or tools. Their value was found in their role as laborers for the South's cash agricultural system, and they were bought and sold as major tools of that economy. Slaves were often bred like livestock to produce stronger and more valuable workers. Older slaves were allowed to live out their days on farms, or in some cases, they were simply abandoned in local towns. The latter practice forced the care of elderly slaves on county and state governments, and caused state legislatures to pass legislation outlawing slave abandonment.

Slaves continued to live under oppressive restrictions within their local communities, as the fear of slave rebellions was ever-present. African Americans' religious and social relationships were monitored. On farms, the overseer regulated their work habits, and adjusted their schedules based on the season and crop production goals. In urban areas, slaves were hired out to generate income for their masters, but were still restricted in their movements. The large number of slave insurrections, such as those led by Denmark Vesey in Charleston, South Carolina (1822), and by Nat Turner in Courtland, Virginia (1832), increased white fears over possible violence by their slaves. Each unsuccessful rebellion prompted the white community to introduce further restrictions on their slave population. John Brown's 1859 raid on the federal arsenal at Harpers Ferry, West Virginia, convinced many Southern citizens that their slaves needed to be controlled and monitored daily.

In the new Confederacy, many preexisting laws designed to safeguard white citizens from slaves and freedpeople were left in place. Various laws limited the ability of African Americans to travel, as a way to stop the spread of insurrection. Other laws prevented slaves from learning basic literacy skills, as an additional hedge against possible violence. At the county level, the superior court became the main regulatory force used to control African Americans, coupled with the use of armed slave patrols. Before slaves could carry out some of the basic functions of life and enterprise, these courts had to grant their approval. For example, slave masters had to petition the superior court to allow their slaves to travel across county lines or to other cities and towns to conduct business. In rural areas, slaves needed approval from the court to carry firearms or to carry weapons to protect livestock. These laws were passed to restrict movement, prevent assemblies of individuals, and to monitor the presence of possible abolitionists in slave communities.

Slave patrols were created out of local militia units and patrolled both urban and rural areas, looking for signs of possible rebellions. Many patrols were under the authority of the local sheriff, who in turn acted under orders issued by either the county superior court or the local justices of the peace. Membership was drawn from the population of white male property owners within a particular township. These patrols looked for slaves or freedpeople moving about individually or in groups, seeing such activity as a possible indication of a slave insurrection. If rumor identified an individual or a group of slaves as a threat, the local reaction was to quell the potential revolt swiftly and cruelly. Many whites believed that a firm hand was needed to keep their African American communities in check.

Slaves and Southern Communities

As the war progressed, Southern communities and the life of the South's slave population began to change due to the conflict's effect on the civilian population's social composition. Starting in 1862, the Confederacy passed three conscription acts designed to bring additional men into the army. These concentrated on white men between the ages of eighteen and thirty-five. The drafting of these men removed the main controlling influence on Southern farms. Slaves found themselves being directed by new overseers, who were not of conscript age. Some of these overseers turned to increased levels of violence to control slaves on farms. Southern wives also found themselves in the new role of having to enforce the obedience of slaves. Some used merciless beatings to enforce order. In other cases, wives and new overseers alike had difficulty imposing their authority, and their orders were not followed. In the latter circumstance, many slaves took the opportunity to escape, particularly with the approach of Union armies.

Conscription also caused the effectiveness of slave patrols to wane. The mass conscription of white males gutted local militia companies, particularly as many previously exempted older males were pressed into service. As a result, patrols were not able to completely maintain order in many communities. This lack of control enabled slaves to begin moving freely between farms and towns. In North Carolina, Governor Zebulon Vance created the "Home Guard" in 1863 to increase the military presence in counties and thus control the movement of slaves. Toward the end of the war, runaway slaves joined with deserters to form criminal gangs roaming through Southern communities. The *Fayetteville Observer* reported on March 6, 1865 that gangs were robbing farms along the North Carolina-South Carolina border. Union prisoners liberated from camps in South Carolina, the *Observer* claimed, had formed gangs, and had been joined by a number of runaway slaves, after the disappearance of Confederate authority before the advance of Major General William T. Sherman's Union armies.

During the war, Southern cities and towns experienced a great surge in population. Businesses sprung up to meet the military production needs of the Confederate government. Military supply depots and hospitals were set up in towns connected by rail to the major urban centers of the Confederacy. Along with workers for these businesses, refugee families also moved into cities and towns. These families brought their slaves with them, and soon those slaves were being incorporated into the urban workforce. Large numbers of freemen and slaves moved about cities like Atlanta and Richmond, working in government departments, tending wounded in hospitals, and assisting in the movement of supplies. Their presence in the workforce was viewed as competition by poor whites and immigrants, who had historically comprised the urban labor force. When white workers went on strike for better wages, they often found themselves replaced by either slaves or freedpeople. White workers frequently attacked these African Americans workers, in an effort to drive them off and regain their jobs. As the war progressed, and the Southern economy rapidly collapsed, blacks and working class whites found themselves increasingly in competition for scarce jobs.

Slavery and Confederate Conduct of the War

Slave communities were subjected to the harsh realities of the war more severely than were white communities. Unfortunately, both sides of the conflict committed abuses against African Americans. The Confederate army committed numerous crimes against blacks in the midst of military operations. Farm hands or traveling craftsmen were shot by roving bands of Confederate cavalry and partisans. It was not uncommon for local militia companies to hang randomly selected African Americans as a lesson to runaway slaves in a community. During the Carolinas Campaign of 1865, one Confederate cavalry brigade shot slaves working in the field while patrolling the flanks of the army in North Carolina. Soldiers raped African American women while on the march or after deserting their units in the field. Most often, soldiers were not prosecuted for committing these rapes, even though crimes against white women were usually met with severe punishment.

Roughly 180,000 Southern blacks enlisted in the U.S. Army (Thomas 1979, p. 237). If an African American soldier was taken captive on the battlefield, death was the probable outcome. Many black soldiers, along with their white officers, were shot during the process of surrendering, or while lying wounded in field stations behind the lines. If a soldier were lucky enough to survive his initial capture, he might be sent to a Confederate military prison like the one in Andersonville, Georgia. Once there, he would become a laborer for the Confederates, tasked with the construction of military projects and with burying the numerous dead.

The Confederate army was based on the Provisional Army of the Confederate States, which was created from the gathering together of state militia units on the South's initial separation from the United States. In most states, African Americans could not serve as members of a county militia unit, in part because militia privates were generally required to be tax-paying property owners. One exception was the Louisiana Native Guards, a militia unit of color that offered its services to the Confederacy. This unit was similar to African American and Creole militia units that had protected Louisiana before the territory was sold to the United States. The Native Guards' offer to be absorbed into the Confederate Army was rejected by Louisiana, however.

Nonetheless, there were cases in which African Americans served as soldiers in Confederate units. Most of these men were light-skinned, and were thus not perceived as being "black" at the time of their enlistment. In several cases, African Americans who had successfully enlisted were eventually discovered and discharged from military service. Others managed to escape notice throughout the course of their service.

The greatest contribution slaves made to the Confederate war effort was as laborers for the Confederate army. President Jefferson Davis and other politicians saw slave labor as a valuable resource that could free up significant numbers of white soldiers for combat duty. The practice of impressing slaves for manual labor first developed during 1861 and 1862, when large numbers of slaves were impressed from their masters to help build fortifications to protect the Confederate capital. Slave owners were always compensated for the time spent by their slaves in performing military labor, and if a slave were killed, his master would receive restitution from the government based on the slave's market value. This ready source of labor soon became widely used in those localities where trenches and fortifications were needed to impede possible Federal advances.

In addition, President Davis persuaded the Confederate Congress to authorize the use of freemen and slaves for noncombatant military duties then performed by soldiers, such as transporting supplies, cooking, and serving as hospital assistants. As a result, additional white soldiers were freed up to reinforce battered Confederate regiments in the field. Beginning in 1862, Confederate armies began to employ large numbers of African Americans as support personnel. With the failure of the first conscription act to provide a steady supply of manpower for the Confederate armies, the idea of impressing more slaves began to be discussed in the Confederate Congress. Several states were opposed to the idea because impressments would pull slaves from crop production and harvesting. In addition, many members of Congress were opposed to impressments of what was still considered private property. By the time of the third Confederate conscription act of February 1864, the Confederate Congress had agreed to set the number of impressed freemen and slaves at 20,000. By December 6, 1864, the Confederate Congress was ready to double the number of impressed slave laborers. The February 28, 1865, law left the final number of slaves that could be impressed up to the War Department, which could raise or lower totals depending on the need at hand.

The failure of the conscription acts to provide enough soldiers for regiments in the field convinced several officers that African Americans were a ready source of men for the front. On January 2, 1864, one officer in the Army of Tennessee saw that it was time to tap into this potential manpower source. Major General Patrick Cleburne proposed to a group of fellow officers of his division that slaves be asked to enlist as soldiers in exchange for the promise of freedom for them and their families upon victory. Several of the other officers were shocked by the Irish-born Cleburne's idea, and the army's commander, General Joseph E. Johnston, decided to ignore the suggestion. In an effort to discredit Cleburne, Major General William H. T. Walker sent a copy of Cleburne's proposal to President Davis. No action was taken against Cleburne, but he was never elevated beyond division commander throughout the remainder of the war.

On November 7, 1864, President Davis asked the Confederate Congress to authorize the purchase of 40,000 slaves for use by the Confederacy. He did not specify how these slaves would be used, but the stage was set for the beginning of African American enlistment. On February 10, 1865, legislation was introduced that called for the arming of slaves as Confederate soldiers. Several days later, in his new role as the commanding general of all Confederate armies in the field, General Robert E. Lee endorsed the idea of African American enlistment. The support of General Lee provided enough political capital for the legislation to pass. Several weeks later, General Order Number Fourteen was issued, to authorize the recruitment of African American soldiers by the Confederate War Department. On March 25, 1865, the *Richmond Enquirer* reported the appearance of an African American infantry company drilling in the Confederate capitol. That same day, General Lee launched his final attempt to break the Union lines at Fort Stedman. This attempt failed, and several weeks later the Union's spring offensive forced the evacuation of the Confederate capitol.

BIBLIOGRAPHY

Brewer, James H. *The Confederate Negro: Virginia's Craftsmen and Military Laborers, 1861–1865.* Durham, NC: Duke University Press, 1969.

Davis, William C. *Jefferson Davis: The Man and His Hour.* New York: HarperCollins, 1991.

Franklin, John Hope, and Loren Schweninger. *Runaway Slaves: Rebels on the Plantation.* New York: Oxford University Press, 1999.

Genovese, Eugene D. *Roll, Jordan, Roll: The World the Slaves Made.* New York: Pantheon Books, 1974.

Halasz, Nicholas. *The Rattling Chains: Slave Unrest and Revolt in the Antebellum South.* New York: D. McKay, 1966.

Johnson, Guion G. *Ante-Bellum North Carolina: A Social History.* Chapel Hill: University of North Carolina Press, 1937.

Levine, Bruce. *Confederate Emancipation: Southern Plans to Free and Arm Slaves during the Civil War.* New York: Oxford University Press, 2006.

Morris, Thomas D. *Southern Slavery and the Law, 1619–1860.* Chapel Hill: University of North Carolina Press, 1996.

Roark, James L. *Masters without Slaves: Southern Planters in the Civil War and Reconstruction.* New York: Norton, 1977.

Robinson, Armstead L. *Bitter Fruits of Bondage: The Demise of Slavery and the Collapse of the Confederacy, 1861–1865.* Charlottesville: University of Virginia Press, 2005.

Thomas, Emory M. *The Confederate Nation, 1861–1865.* New York: Harper & Row, 1979.

Wiley, Bell Irvin. *Southern Negroes, 1861–1865.* New Haven, CT: Yale University Press, 1938.

Yearns, Wilfred Buck. *The Confederate Congress.* Athens: University of Georgia Press, 1960.

William H. Brown

Freedpeople

The Union army went to war with no real plan for dealing with slaves that entered their lines. Often, the fate of slaves who had escaped from their masters depended on the political leanings of the commander of whichever Union regiment they happened to encounter first. It finally took the lawyer-general, Benjamin Butler (1818–1893), to solve the problem. In May 1861 three slaves escaped to the Union-held Fortress Monroe at Hampton Roads, Virginia, where they encountered Butler's men. Rather than return them to their masters and work on the Confederate fortifications, Butler declared them contraband of war. The definition held, for it enabled Union authorities to deny slave labor to the Confederacy while simultaneously keeping the faith with more radical Northerners who wanted slavery abolished.

With the battle of Antietam, Lincoln had a victory that permitted him to issue the Emancipation Proclamation from a position of strength. When it took effect on January 1, 1863, the term *contraband* no longer applied to black refugees in the South; they became freedpeople and they became a top priority for the Lincoln administration. Given the progress of Union forces up to 1863, the issue of caring for the freedpeople became an all-important problem. The Army and Navy had liberated tens of thousands of people of African descent along the coasts and waterways of the south, but only in central Tennessee had Union forces advanced very deep into Confederate territory east of the Mississippi River. With no place to put the refugees, the army established freedmen camps along the southern coast and waterways—and the call went out for help.

In the West, along the Mississippi River, General Ulysses S. Grant (1822–1885) assigned army chaplain, John Eaton Jr. (1829–1906) as Commissioner of Contrabands (a title that did not reflect the changed status of freedpeople) in his department. Eaton's duties consisted of seeing to it that the freedpeople received food, health care, religious instruction, education, and work. Toward that end, Northern church organizations aided him tremendously, sending missionaries and other necessities. The obstacles they faced were daunting, for the hundreds of thousands of freedpeople huddled in camps around the country often left the plantation with the clothes on their back, with no provision for the future. In cases where they did bring possessions with them, it was often completely useless items pilfered from their former masters's abandoned homes.

Colonel Herman Lieb of the United States Colored Troops (USCT) recalled the procession of freedpeople who followed General William T. Sherman's (1820–1891) column to Vicksburg at the conclusion of the Meridian raid in early 1864:

> Their arrival caused a general turnout of citizens and garrison which through the endless cortege passed. Such a sight was never seen since the exodus of the Jew from Egypt. Hundreds of vehicles of the most varied description, from the mule cart to the family equipage of their former masters, loaded promiscuously with women and children, household and kitchen furniture, while their male protectors, not so naked as you saw them in Omdurman, but just as dirty and uncivilized, marched in file on both sides of the caravan. In apparel they presented a most laughable spectacle, the majority in bedraggled plantation clothing, some with boots, some in shoes, most barefoot, in parts of Confederate and Union uniforms, a few here and there with stovepipe hats, caps or colored handkerchiefs on their heads." (Johns 1912, pp. 138–139)

The periodic deluges of freedpeople taxed the resources of both government and private charities. Elkanah Beard (1833–1905), a missionary working among the freedpeople at various islands and landings on the Mississippi wrote to his supporters that "several in the week past have frozen to death, and others were so chilled that they are not likely to survive long. Hundreds of women and children are barefoot, and have nothing but cotton clothing, which has been worn for months." Beard's supporters responded with books, seeds, and other sundries (Association of Friends of Philadelphia and Its Vicinity, for the Relief of Colored Freedmen 1864, p. 10). The camps existed as a temporary measure, for the government ultimately wanted the freedpeople to become Christian, hardworking, self-reliant, citizen farmers. As one missionary summarized, their mission was to make sure "that the freed people are treated as free, and encouraged to respect and observe the institutions of religion, marriage, and all the customs of virtuous and civilized society, and to become worthy of the blessings of a Christian civilization" (Forman 1864, p. 120).

While the missionaries saw to it that the freedpeople kept their spiritual houses in order, the government looked to finding them physical shelter. The task was daunting, for by the spring of 1864 some 20,000 freedpeople lived in the vicinity of Norfolk and Portsmouth, Virginia; 10,000 at Fortress Monroe; and 8,000 at Yorktown. Across the country, in the Mississippi Valley, the government seized Jefferson Davis's (1808–1889) plantation and deposited up to 5,000 freedpeople on the property, while Memphis, Tennessee; Natchez, Mississippi; and New Orleans, Louisiana, took in 5,000 to 6,000 each (Association of Friends of Philadelphia and Its Vicinity, for the Relief of Colored Freedmen 1864, pp. 7–9). The Treasury Department attempted to relieve the pressure on the cities and towns by leasing abandoned plantations. Ideally, the plan provided incomes for the former slaves, put them in healthier environments, and settled them in communities where they learned how to become good citizens; but it did not always work out. Rebel raiders often struck the plantations and camps, taking both livestock and freedpeople to resell in the interior of the Confederacy. Unscrupulous opportunists leased plantations,

Civil War "contrabands." In the opening months of the Civil War, the North lacked procedures to deal with Southern slaves escaping to Union camps; they were afraid of upsetting proslavery states still in the Union by granting the runaways freedom and of angering abolitionists by returning slaves to their owners. A lawyer in civilian life, General Benjamin Butler decided to consider the escaped slaves "contraband," thereby keeping them in the possession of the Union army and paying them for their labor. *Hulton Archive/Getty Images*

harvested a crop, then left without paying their workers. The government had to come up with a better plan by the time the war ended or it would have faced hundreds of thousands more freedpeople to care for in addition to the ones already liberated by advancing armies.

In March 1865, Congress established the Bureau of Refugees, Freedmen, and Abandoned Lands which operated until December 1868 under the leadership of General Oliver O. Howard (1830–1909). The Freedmen's Bureau, as the agency was commonly known, brought all of the government's efforts on behalf of freedpeople under one umbrella organization. It supervised humanitarian efforts by feeding and clothing destitute blacks, establishing schools, and founding hospitals. In the legal realm it

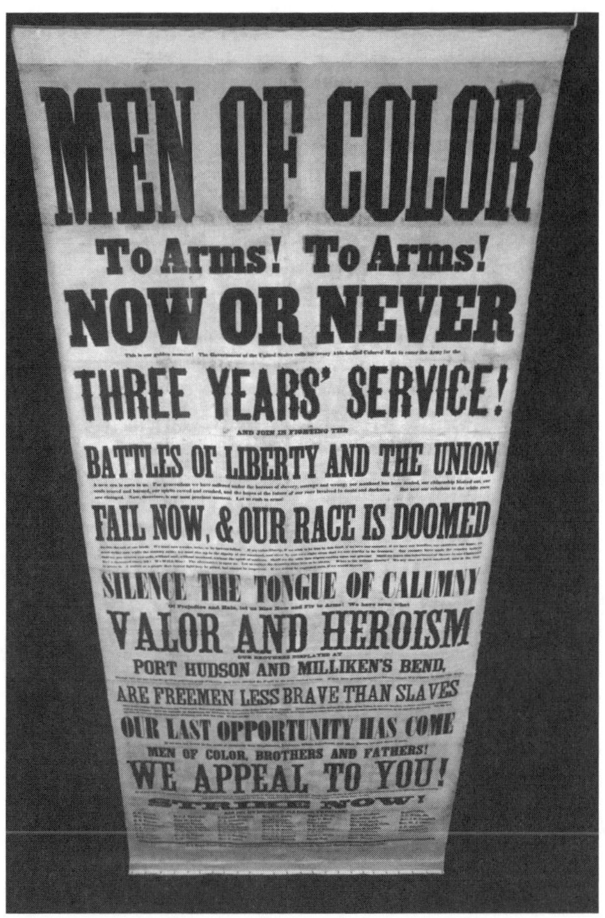

Poster exhorting blacks to arms. Black abolitionists encouraged free black men to volunteer for military service, suggesting that they should prove their bravery on the battlefield and fight to ensure that their freedom remains permanent. *© Louie Psihoyos/Corbis*

established courts to mediate disputes between black laborers and white planters, while in the financial realm it established banks to teach frugality to newly liberated African Americans. The Bureau had its detractors. Many white Southerners, ever sensitive about their own personal freedom, felt that the Bureau violated their rights, as it established its own courts and legal framework. In 1872 the Bureau passed out of existence. Within five years the Bourbon Redeemers had retaken control of the Southern governments, virtually ending government efforts on behalf of freedpeople. Nevertheless, in the short time between the Emancipation Proclamation and the end of Reconstruction, the ratification of the Thirteenth, Fourteenth, and Fifteenth Amendments to the Constitution changed the status of blacks once again, that from freedpeople to American citizens (Bentley 1955).

BIBLIOGRAPHY

Association of Friends of Philadelphia and Its Vicinity, for the Relief of Colored Freedmen. *Statistics of the Operations of the Executive Board of the Friends' Association of Philadelphia and Its Vicinity, for the Relief of Colored Freedmen.* Philadelphia: Inquirer Printing Office, 1864.

Bentley, George R. *A History of the Freedmen's Bureau.* Philadelphia: University of Pennsylvania Press, 1955.

Forman, Jacob Gilbert. *The Western Sanitary Commission; A Sketch of Its Origin, History, Labors for the Sick and Wounded of the Western Armies, and Aid Given to Freedmen and Union Refugees, with Incidents of Hospital Life.* St. Louis, MO: R. P. Studley, 1864.

Johns, Jane Martin. *Personal Recollections of Early Decatur, Abraham Lincoln, Richard J. Oglesby and the Civil War.* Decatur, IL: Decatur Chapter, D.A.R., 1912.

David H. Slay

Family

In a world filled with uncertainty, many slaves and freedpeople placed a high value on family. For slaves, having families provided a sense of normalcy and the illusion of control over their own lives. For freedpeople, emancipation became a time to reestablish contact with lost loved ones, start new families, or pilot their existing families into a safe harbor. Both groups met with soul-wearying obstacles. Slaves faced the ever-present threat of separation, while freedpeople found that liberty created new challenges for which they were unprepared. Ultimately, many affirmed the place of family in African American life by either bringing their families through the transition from slave to citizen intact, or picking up the pieces and creating new families.

For many slaves, forming a family provided them with a connection to the past as well as provided them roots in the present. The new families created in slavery replaced the old kinship networks of Africa, while the slave quarters on the larger plantations simulated villages. Within these villages hierarchies developed as individual slaves exercised their talents in medicine, preaching, and hunting. Depending on the plantation owner's wishes, slaves could court one another in the quarters or visit with members of the opposite sex from other plantations, with the view of marriage as the ultimate goal.

On some plantations marriage simply consisted of the planter telling a couple that they were married, sometimes whether they wanted to be or not. On others, the male slave had to ask the master's permission. In cases of interplantation courtship, the individual masters had to work out agreements—if they were inclined to do so. Depending on the wealth of the master, his affection for the couple, or his religiosity, the wedding ceremony could range from the very simple to the more elaborate, complete with music and feasting (*The Daily National Intelligencer,* February 15, 1858).

With marital bliss often followed by the birth of children, relationships on the plantations became complex. Unlike most of white America in 1861, where the father headed the household, slave families answered to the white masters and overseers. This proved emasculating for many black men, for their owners could punish the slave's children, abuse his wife, or humiliate the slave by punishing him in front of his family. J. T. Tims, who was just ten years old when Union forces entered his area of Mississippi, recalled the train of events that led his family to flee the plantation. Upon getting into trouble for a wrong he did not commit, J. T. bit his mistress on the thigh when she scissored his head between her legs to hold him still and get better aim at his backside. That only enraged her further, and she ordered another slave to beat J. T., at which time his mother intervened when "she come out with a big carving knife and told him, 'That's my child and if you hit him, I'll kill you.'" The mistress then ordered her son to whip J. T.'s mother, which he did lightly for show. The next day the master asked J. T.'s father, Daniel, why he was appeared so upset. To which he replied, "You'd be lookin' glum too if your wife and chile had done been beat up for nothin" (Tims 1941). Infuriated, the master smacked Daniel on the head with a cobbler's hammer. Humiliated at seeing his wife and child beaten by whites, and brutalized himself for standing up for his family, Daniel took his family and fled to Natchez, Mississippi. There, he joined the United States Colored Troops (USCT).

Even if slave families managed to carve out some kind of stability, a bad crop, poor management, or the death of the owner could change everything and force them onto the auction block. If fortunate, the family remained together, but as often as not they ended up among different owners where, if the distance was great, they started over and formed new families. Even the mere threat of Union invasion of a region could force the dissolution of families, which is precisely what happened to many in the Mississippi Valley when General Ulysses S. Grant (1822–1885) began his campaigns for Vicksburg. Many planters, not wishing to see their slaves liberated, sent them hundreds of miles away from their homes. In the case of one slave family, it was a matter of discipline that separated them. "The father (Daniel) left home in a fit of anger because one of his children had been whipped." The master, knowing how much Daniel loved his family, put the man's wife and infant child in jail as bait. The authorities allowed him to visit his family, but on his final visit they locked him in a cell. "The next day, he and his son Johnny were sold to some speculators who promised to carry them so far away that they could not return" (Huff 1941, p. 239). As Daniel left he promised his wife Harriet that he would return one day. Although she despaired, Harriet remained committed to Daniel's promise, which he kept, returning several months after the war's end.

After liberation, many freedpeople could not go looking for their evacuated family members, for to pass out of Union-held territory ensured death or re-enslavement. In many cases all they had to go on were rumors of where their family members ended up. Therefore, when the end of the war came, hundreds of miles separated families, distances the freedpeople did not have the time or resources to cross. Men looked for their wives, wives looked for their husbands, and children looked for their parents.

Many freedpeople, therefore, chose to re-family, or start over afresh. They found new spouses, got legally married by Union officials, and established new communities in the freedmen's camps and plantations that dotted the South. Others chose the less moral route of living with members of the opposite sex outside of marriage. Orphaned children, either through the death of their parents, abandonment, or having gotten separated from them, ended up in orphanages. If too young to remember their given names, the staffers gave them new ones; the names were primarily generic, but in some cases cruel, as in the cases of Mary Lincoln, Wade Hampton, and Major Kirby Smith, all black children who passed through the Vicksburg orphanage (Vicksburg Orphans Report, June 30, 1865).

Families that survived slavery, too, faced perils. In the confusion of the passage or because of armies, they often became separated and unable to find one another later on. Work oftentimes took them away from one another, especially if the father signed on as a laborer with the army. If a father or brother enlisted in the USCT, then the family may have lived on the borders of the camp in a nearby freedmen's colony, or have never seen them again if the regiment received orders to go on a campaign. The families that did survive the transition to freedom found advantages in their new status. They sometimes pooled their resources to purchase property or a mule, took care of one another during sickness, and, in the still dangerous days after the war ended, provided safety in numbers. Thus, in the end, the family enabled the former slaves to enter freedom with many advantages.

BIBLIOGRAPHY

The Daily National Intelligencer (Washington, DC), "Plantation Wedding," February 15, 1858, col. B.

Huff, Bryant. *Georgia Narratives.* In *Born in Slavery: Slave Narratives from the Federal Writers' Project, 1936–1938,* vol. 4, part 2, Library of Congress, Washington, DC, 1941.

Tims, J. T. *Arkansas Narratives.* In *Born in Slavery: Slave Narratives from the Federal Writers' Project, 1936–1938,* vol. 2, part 6, Library of Congress, Washington, DC, 1941.

"Vicksburg Orphans Report." In *Records of the Mississippi Freedmen's Department ("Pre-Bureau Records"), Office of the Assistant Commissioner, Bureau of Refugees, Freedmen, and Abandoned Lands, 1863–1865: Roll 4, Miscellaneous Records 1863–1865.* National Archives and Records Administration, Washington, DC, June 30, 1865.

David H. Slay

Plantation Life

Life on an American antebellum plantation was framed by social forces such as one's race and social caste; by environmental forces such as the plantation's region, the season of the year, the plantation owner's choice of crop or dominant economic activity; and by the nature of the interaction between the owners, managers, and laborers. Winthrop Jordan offers sound footing for understanding the national context of plantation slavery: "The major factor making for sectional division in the U.S. was the proportion of Negroes in the population" (1968, p. 315). As Jordan points out, the "very tone of society" on plantations differed between the Upper South and the Lower South, based upon the proportion of enslaved Africans and the profitability of slave-based agriculture in the regions (1968, p. 316).

The Owners

The etiology of American antebellum plantation life lies within a western European worldview framed and informed by a mercantilist economic vision. John Locke's ideas on labor, liberty, and natural rights provide a context for understanding the structure of plantation culture—a way of life informed by the dialectic between the owners and enslaved, yet overdetermined by the ideological superstructure of Enlightenment-era political economy. One of the rights that Locke prefigured was the right to own enslaved Africans. Antebellum South Carolina benefited greatly from Locke's involvement in the slave trade. In Charleston Harbor are two rivers, the Ashley and Cooper, which take their names from Locke's employer—the Earl of Shaftesbury, Anthony Ashley Cooper (1621–1683). The Earl of Shaftesbury and Locke were among nineteen founding stockholders in the Royal Africa Company. Locke's ideas about the suitability of enslaving Africans are described in his *Second Treatise on Government*: "A king of a large and fruitful (non-European) territory ... feeds, lodges, and Is clad worse than a day-laborer in England" (Carruthers 1999, p. 49). Locke held that Africans were primitive men who did not deserve "unrestrain'd Liberty, before [they] had Reason to guide them..." (Blackburn 1997, p. 263). As Carruthers clarifies, Locke's ideas about Liberty are grounded in his notion of the work ethic (the management of labor), its connection to wealth, and the notion of noblesse oblige and virtue: "The labor of (a man's) body and the work of his hands ... are properly his. Whatsoever ... he removes out of ... nature ... is his own ... it is his Property" (Carruthers 1999, p. 47). Locke declared that the English alone were possessed of true freedom, based on the Protestant ideal rather than Catholicism, which he deemed a form of religious slavery. And in effect, English values were the values of antebellum plantation owners.

The most important aspect of the planter's life on the plantation was his—or more seldom, her—relationship with employees and property. The overwhelming sense of paternalism described by Eugene Genovese (1974) connects Locke's Enlightenment ideas on labor and liberty to the plantation life experienced by the planter. Paternalism required that order be maintained from the upper echelon of the plantation through three functions: meting out basic provisions, directing labor in a sensible manner, and punishing infractions of the order. The ability to operate as a local autocrat was supported by prohibitions against educating the enslaved, and by the Southern state legislatures, which by the antebellum period had developed a web of laws pioneered by Virginia and South Carolina to secure the dominance of white over black.

The lives of the owners were determined by a number of factors, including the primary crop under cultivation and the requisite labor system, what may be described as the management style of the owner, the relationship with the enslaved Africans and the white drivers, and the season of the year. Mark Smith (1997) provides an interesting discussion of the slave owner's plantation life relative to the concept of clock time, which he and his class copied from their Northern capitalist peers. Smith quotes a writer in the *Southern Agriculturalist* describing the habits of a Southern plantation owner in 1832 who drew up a schedule and

> strictly enjoined its observance upon his people. He ordained that the cook should have breakfast at a suitable hour to which the people were to be punctual in attendance.... The hour of attendance was to be declared by the sound of the horn, and the time for taking their last meal, was so regulated, that the workers always had ample space for completing their tasks before the call. If any one had not finished at the appointed hour, he was disgraced and went without his dinner for that day. (Smith 1997, p. 93)

Of course, this schedule was determined by the labor system forced upon the enslaved, which was either gang-based (for tobacco and cotton) or task-based (for rice). In both labor systems, most planters hired poor whites and forced some enslaved Africans to encourage efficiency amongst the enslaved. The manufactured distance provided by these managers allowed the planter to direct his attention to a social life for his family or to the pursuit of more gain.

Five slave generations. Entire families generally lived in slave quarters: small, one room houses with a minimal amount of furniture and necessities for everyday life. *The Library of Congress*

The Enslaved

Plantation life for the enslaved was shaped by several factors, including their birthplace, living conditions, and work regimen. Although Michael Conniff and Thomas Davis are correct in their assertion that "by 1720 more blacks were being born in the colonies than were being imported there, and by 1740 most blacks there were American-born," there is no direct correlation between the percentage of the enslaved population born in America and either the strength of resistance to oppression or the Africanity of the cultures practiced in those regions (Conniff and Davis 1994, pp. 132–133). This assertion, held aloft by Frazierians old and new, has contributed to great distortions and omissions in African American historiography (Frazier 1930; Park 1918; Mintz 1992; Sidbury 2007). In fact, newly imported Africans often were viewed as links to an ancestral heritage offering a way of life and set of values different from the antebellum American South (Stuckey 1987; Gomez 1998). At least one observer of the day noted that enslaved Africans were advocates of an animistic type of religion that included goblins, godlings, witches, and "supernatural agencies generally" (*Boston Emancipator and Republican*, December 5, 1850).

This description was stereotypical, of course, but plantation life for slaves was dominated by the effort to create a meaningful culture despite the duress of the world of work. In cotton- and tobacco-growing regions, the gang-labor system dictated a community unified in its drudgery, sharing the burden of the collective rising upon the sounding of the conch or bell. The primacy of the enslaved community was the result of this forced unity. Although being sold "down the river" in the internal slave trade has been discussed in terms of its effect on the slave family, the enslaved African community was affected significantly as well. The laboring class that an enslaved person was assigned or born into dictated the course of his or her day. John Blassingame's account of the daily routine of the enslaved is instructive. He maintains that field laborers "rose before dawn, prepared their meals, fed the livestock, and then rushed to the fields before sunrise" (Blassingame 1972, p. 155). Often, those who were late would be whipped. After working in the fields, the slaves performed other tasks to support the cultivation of the crop and maintain the plantation, such as building fences, cutting down trees, constructing dikes, and clearing new land. In the evening enslaved Africans had to care for "the livestock, put away tools, and cook their meals before the horn sounded bedtime in the quarters" (Blassingame 1972, p. 155). One correspondent for the *Boston Emancipator and Republican* in 1850 described the yearly ration of clothing for the enslaved African as consisting of a pair of shoes, two shirts, a pair of pantaloons, and one jacket. The lives of house slaves were little better. House slaves "ate better food and wore better clothes than the field slaves," but were completely at the beck and call of the slave master and his family. They rose before the slavemasters and went to bed after them (Blassingame 1972, pp. 155–156).

White Managers and Drivers

The class of white overseers was primarily comprised of poor whites, some mulattos, and very few middle-class whites. The role of these whites was prescribed by the laws of the Old South. For example, A. Leon Higginbotham discusses a 1705 amendment to the Virginia House of Burgesses 1669 Slave Act that created clear racial lines by deputizing all Christians (i.e., whites) to police and intimidate the servile African population (Higginbotham 1996, pp. 30–31). This was the legal and social context for poor whites in the antebellum South: They were dragged along into a political economy that devalued labor through the very nature of slavery, and they could not expect to share in the planter class's bountiful profits derived from plantation agriculture. Blassingame records that poor whites who made up the overseer class were in a degraded state: "Better fed, housed, and clothed than the poor whites, the slaves considered them far from superior beings. Instead, [the whites] were the objects of ridicule, pity, and scorn in the quarters" (1972, p. 202). Blassingame also quotes Henry Bibb, a former slave who became an eloquent and effective abolitionist and who viewed poor whites as "generally ignorant, intemperate, licentious, and profane" (1972, p. 202). One news correspondent of the day concurred, describing "the uneducated lower class of whites" as "the most indolent, ignorant, and degraded class of beings I have ever seen. They lead a kind of Gipsy (sic) life; here to-day and gone to-morrow" (*Boston Emancipator and Republican*, December 5, 1850). The relationship between the poor whites and enslaved Africans is observable in the commerce they pursue: "The negroes steal from their masters and traffic with (the poor whites), and are not a whit beneath them in their condition or sphere of life. This miserable and degraded people form no inconsiderable part of the population of Carolina, and this state" (*Boston Emancipator and Republican*, December 5, 1850).

Antebellum plantation life represented a give-and-take relationship between African slaves, the degraded class of poor whites, and the white planter class. Although this relationship largely depended upon a form of patriarchy described aptly by Genovese, it was hardly a peaceful hegemony. Violence was encoded in the slave law of the antebellum South, and periodic rumors and actual outbursts of rebellious violence bloodied the scene of slavery. The warped social fabric of antebellum plantation life provided the backdrop for both the defenders and detractors of slavery. Both groups saw in it the root cause of their complaint and the catalyst of their convictions.

BIBLIOGRAPHY

Blackburn, Robin. *The Making of New World Slavery: From the Baroque to the Modern, 1492–1800.* London: Verso, 1997.

Blassingame, John. *The Slave Community: Plantation Life in the Antebellum South.* New York: Oxford University Press, 1972.

Boston Emancipator and Republican, December 5, 1850.

Carruthers, Jacob H. *Intellectual Warfare.* Chicago: Third World Press, 1999.

Conniff, Michael L., and Thomas J. Davis. *Africans in the Americas: A History of the Black Diaspora.* New York: St. Martin's Press, 1994.

Frazier, E. Franklin. "The Negro Slave Family." *Journal of Negro History* 15, no. 2 (1930): 62.

Genovese, Eugene. *Roll, Jordan, Roll: The World the Slaves Made.* New York: Vintage Books, 1974.

Gomez, Michael. *Exchanging Our Countrymarks: The Transformation of African Identities in the Colonial and Antebellum South.* Chapel Hill and London: University of North Carolina Press, 1998.

Higginbotham, A. Leon. *Shades of Freedom: Racial Politics and Presumptions of the American Legal*

Process. New York and Oxford: Oxford University Press, 1996.

Jordan, Winthrop. *White over Black: American Attitudes toward the Negro, 1550–1812*. Baltimore: Penguin Books, 1968.

Mintz, Sidney, and Richard Price. *The Birth of African-American Culture: An Anthropological Perspective*. Boston: Beacon Press, 1992.

Park, Robert E. "The Conflict and Fusion of Cultures with Special Reference to the Negro." *Journal of Negro History* 4, no. 2 (1918): 23.

Sidbury, James. *Becoming African in America: Race and Nation in the Early Black Atlantic*. New York: Oxford University Press, 2007.

Smith, Mark M. *Mastered by the Clock: Time, Slavery, and Freedom in the American South*. Chapel Hill: University of North Carolina Press, 1997.

Stuckey, Sterling. *Slave Culture: Nationalist Theory and the Foundations of Black America*. New York: Oxford University Press, 1987.

Kwasi Densu
Samuel Livingston

Culture and Leisure

At the outbreak of the Civil War, there were about four million enslaved African American people in the United States. Cut off from the wider American society by ideological constructions of racial inferiority and the legal constraints of perpetual bondage, the slave population developed a distinct culture and a counter-ideology that supported their communities in brutal oppression.

Slave culture finds its roots both in the ideas, beliefs, and customs brought from Africa, and in the European milieu in which enslaved Africans found themselves in the New World (with Native American influences that should not be overlooked). The mix that resulted affected white American culture as well as black, but gave rise to a distinctive slave culture that included a deep sense of solidarity and community.

Slave culture emerged at a time when the assumption of white supremacy was ubiquitous. Every leader of thought and every institution in American society—laws, governments, courts, churches, clerics, universities, books, newspapers, academies of science, and so forth—were unanimous in the assertion that black people were not, and could never be, full members of the human family. Slaves, therefore, were regarded as inferior persons to whom ordinary moral considerations did not apply. This attack on black humanity left slaves profoundly isolated existentially, socially, economically, politically, and ideologically.

Culture of Defiance

Under such circumstances, the fundamental project of slave culture was to resist dehumanization, assert black humanity, and convince enslaved people of their own self-worth. Historian Cornel West suggests that the primary challenge of the culture was "to ward off madness and discredit suicide as a desirable option" (West 1996, p. 81). The slave culture that developed in response to this challenge was intense and compelling, characterized by an animated orality, tense physicality, covert intellectual musing, nimble improvisation, deep secrecy, coded communication, and defiant spirituality. Slave culture, by the time of the Civil War, was in all its aspects focused on the problem of black suffering and the appropriate response to it. West suggests that "the 'ur-text' of black culture is neither a word nor a book, not an architectural monument or a legal brief. Instead, it is a guttural cry and a wrenching moan ..." (West 1996, p. 81). Such shouts and moans were found omnipresent in slave song and religious practice, in musical performance, and in folktales—even in everyday speech.

The slave response to suffering and injustice was not to deny it, but rather to defy it. That is, slave culture consistently demanded that suffering be acknowledged and that life be celebrated in all its aspects in spite of such suffering. The words of one slave spiritual illustrate such defiance: "Nobody knows the trouble I've seen. / Nobody knows but Jesus. / Nobody knows the trouble I've seen. / Glory, hallelujah!"

The shift of mood in the last line of the lyric from mournful grief to joyful exultation is typical of the sudden mood shifts found in black cultural performance. Another slave spiritual, cited by W. E. B. Du Bois in *The Souls of Black Folk*, illustrates this same defiance: "You may bury me in the East, / You may bury me in the West, / But I'll hear the trumpet sound in the morning ..." ("You May Bury Me in the East," or "I'll Hear the Trumpet Sound," Du Bois [1903] 2005, p. 180).

Such defiance is masked and coded, however. As much as slave culture was universally a culture of resistance to the dehumanization that lay at the foundation of slavery, it had to accommodate itself to the realities of bondage and white domination. The culture recognized the need for slaves to masquerade in the presence of masters as dull, crude, foolish, childlike, or jovial. Nonetheless, the study of slave life has revealed a culture of great subtlety, strength, and introspection. The African American poet Paul Lawrence Dunbar (1872–1906) acknowledged this painful masking in the poem "We Wear the Mask," published in 1896, well after the end of slavery:

> We wear the mask that grins and lies,
> It hides our cheeks and shades our eyes,
> This debt we pay to human guile;
> With torn and bleeding hearts we smile,
> And mouth with myriad subtleties.
> Why should the world be over-wise,
> In counting all our tears and sighs?
> Nay, let them only see us, while
> We wear the mask.... (Dunbar 1997, p. 896)

Leisure Time

Slave life was dominated by long hours of toil and unpaid labor. But slaves were given some time for leisure and recreation, and their culture could be expressed most fully during these periods. Almost all masters observed Sunday as a day of rest, because it was a religious obligation, and slaves were left to themselves. Saturday was often only a partial work day, with Saturday evening a time for gathering and partying. The Christmas holiday, the week from December 25 to January 1, was usually observed as period of no work, for field workers at least. Other holidays, such as Thanksgiving, Easter Monday, and the Fourth of July, might also be given to slaves as holidays, depending on the practice of each master. Work was usually suspended on rainy days, when fieldwork became impossible. Impromptu holidays might also be declared by masters after planting was done, during slow periods of the agricultural cycle, and in association with weddings, birthdays, and funerals of the master's family.

Naturally, slaves might create other opportunities for recreation. Illicit nighttime gatherings, for worship and for socializing, were a regular part of slave life. Though they might be broken up by slave patrols, they usually went undetected. More risky options for taking leisure were pretending to be sick or simple truancy—leaving the plantation without permission.

During such periods of rest, slaves spent most of their time in parties with music and dancing, in worship services, hunting and fishing, lounging, storytelling, drinking, or visiting wives, girlfriends, and family on other plantations. Slave codes in the South usually outlawed certain other leisure activities, such as cards or dice, gambling, or playing any game of chance for money—indicating that such games were popular pastimes among slaves.

Religious Worship

Sunday was a day of worship, of course, at least for enslaved Christians. However, most African Americans slaves resisted conversion right up until the Civil War. Michael A. Gomez suggests that by 1860, only 22 percent of slaves may have been converted to Christianity (1998, pp. 260–261). John Blassingame supports this estimate, suggesting that about one million slaves—a quarter of the slave population—were Christians by 1860 (Blassingame 1979, pp. 97–98). The former slave Charles Ball claimed that his African-born grandfather "never went to church or meeting, and held that the religion of this country was altogether fake, and indeed, no religion at all; being the mere invention of priests and crafty men, who hoped thereby to profit through the ignorance and credulity of the multitude" (Ball 1837, p. 21). So, contrary to popular belief, Christian slaves probably remained in the minority until the end of the war.

Christians might hold secret prayer meetings at night in secluded areas they called "hush harbors." Clandestine night gatherings were a regular feature of slave life, in any case. Mary Reynolds recalled one of these meetings many years later:

> Once my maw and paw taken me and Katherine [her sister] after night to slip to 'nother place to a prayin' and singin'. A nigger man with white beard told us a day am comin' when niggers only be slaves of God....We prays for the end of Trib'lation and the end of beatin's and for shoes that fit our feet. We prayed that us niggers could have all we wanted to eat and special for fresh meat. Some the old ones say we have to bear all, cause that all we can do. Some say they was glad to the time they's dead, cause they'd rather rot in the ground than have the beatin's. (Rawick 1972–1979, pp. 240–241)

Slave Christian gatherings consisted of singing, praying, and preaching; they lacked formal services, rituals, or sacred objects. In the ring shout, a form of Christian worship, believers formed a circle and shuffled counterclockwise while singing, shouting, dancing, and praying. Others stood outside the circle and sang and clapped. Eventually, some dancers would become possessed by the spirit and fall. The ring shout probably combines African forms of worship with Christian practice.

The slave's theology rejected the slaveholders' Bible teachings that supported slavery and justified their mistreatment. Enslaved Christians believed that they were the people of God. Slaves were convinced that they were going to heaven and that their masters were not. Frederick Douglass (1818–1895) remembered that crowds watched his master's dramatic conversion to Methodism. The white congregants celebrated, saying: "Capt. Auld had come through." But the slaves secretly believed otherwise, according to Douglass: "...The slaves seldom have confidence in the piety of their masters. 'He cant go to heaven with our blood in his skirts,' is a settled point in the creed of every slave; rising superior to all teaching to the contrary and standing forever as a fixed fact" (Douglass [1855] 1969, pp. 195–196).

Slave Christianity also included a covert theology of liberation, at least by the antebellum period. In June 1850 a white slaveholder in South Carolina accidentally overheard a slave named George sharing a Christian message with other slaves, that they:

> ... ought not to be discouraged on account of their difficulties. There was no reason why they were in the situation they were, only that God permitted it to be so. That God was working for their deliverance. He was working by secret means, and would deliver them from their bondage as sure as the children of Israel were delivered from the Egyptian bondage....[They] did not know exactly how long it would be before they

> would be set free. There was no doubt that it would be soon. That they ought to pray for [it], and their prayer would go up before God and be answered. (Harris 1985, p. 41)

George was arrested, charged with sedition, tried, and sentenced to thirty-nine lashes plus deportation from the state. It is clear that, as with other aspects of slave culture, slave theology had to be kept strictly secret.

Nonetheless, cultural attitudes and beliefs can be discerned in slave music, and especially in spirituals and other slave songs. The Bible story most often found in spirituals is that of God delivering the Israelites from bondage in Egypt. Moses is one of the most often mentioned figures in these songs. Others include Noah, Daniel, and Jonah—all rescued from tribulations by God. Jesus appears as the innocent child, the victim of whipping, and the powerful King Jesus, who cannot be defeated. Bible stories are conflated, with episodes from the Old and New Testaments lumped together. Salvation was universal for slaves; God would save anyone who believed in him. Slaves spent little time singing about hell or damnation. Whites seldom appear in these spirituals, as the songs invoke the autonomous world of African American cultural imagination.

Besides Christianity, enslaved Africans preserved their ancestors' beliefs as "conjure" or "hoodoo." This was a rich mixture of European and African magical practices that included herbal medicine, love potions, ghost lore, witchcraft spells, protection from evil, and divination. Such practices remained important in the slave community even after conversion to Christianity.

Storytelling

The cultural values of the slave community were also embodied in storytelling, which was an important part of slave life. African American folktales were widely known before the Civil War. They amused and entertained generations of Americans—white and black. But one of the of the persistent misunderstandings of these stories is that they were told as mere foolishness—that they are light and nonsensical stories that slaves told one another just to pass the time, or to provide a source of amusement. On the contrary, contemporary scholars have argued that this folklore represents the serious oral literature of slave culture. Charles Joyner has suggested, for example, that the same role that the novel played in twentieth-century European culture was carried by the folktales in slave culture (Joyner 1984, p. 172).

Although the tales can be quite humorous, enslaved African Americans used folktales to explore the most central and urgent issues that their culture faced. They used folktales to inspire and educate others, to socialize children to the norms and realities of slavery, to maintain solidarity within their communities, to rebuke and satirize their masters, to protest their condition of bondage, to resist the dehumanization of the slave system, to accommodate to the injustices of slavery and make them bearable, to communicate encoded messages to one another, to suggest solutions to common dilemmas, to explain how things came to be as they are, and so forth.

It is one of the most profound achievements of African American culture that the animal tales, at least—the stories about Br'er Rabbit, Br'er Fox, Br'er Bear,and so on—could achieve all of these purposes with such perfect subtlety and ambiguity that they could be told openly and freely—in full view of white society, without attracting suspicion or condemnation. This in itself gives insight into the nature of slave culture and black consciousness in the antebellum South. Although it pretended to be clumsy and foolish, slave culture was consistently subtle and indirect. It was a culture that was extremely careful with words, and it crafted its literature with delicate nuance and shrewd complexity. It was also a secretive culture, but one that tended to hide its secrets in plain sight.

Most of the animal stories are trickster tales. These are consistently the stories of how a small, weak, but cunning creature (such as a rabbit) outsmarts a much larger, more powerful, but actually rather stupid animal (a fox, perhaps) who in the natural course of things should be eating the smaller creature. The little trickster animal is marked by his capacity for bragging, lying, and trickery, and by his strutting, egotistical, and self-assured personality. The larger animal is portrayed in these stories as dull, slow, rather unsure of himself, and easily tricked. The identification of the smaller animals with the slave and the larger ones with the slave master must have been obvious to the black community, but it seems not to have occurred to slave-owning whites.

The cultural productions of African American people during the centuries of slavery in the United States are indeed remarkable. Their creativity seems to have reached its peak during the years just before the Civil War. By then, the culture included a rich musical tradition, a new form of Christianity, a remarkable dance tradition, a vast and subtle oral literature, and a counter-ideology to prevailing attitudes of white supremacy. In addition, the slave community developed unique patterns of extended family relationships, styles of dress, and styles of work that both resisted and accepted the limitations and intrusions of slavery. They developed a full and expressive language that, although it was regarded as an ignorant and broken form of English at the time, is now recognized by scholars as a full and legitimate language system that is, in some ways, more expressive than Standard English. The culture also provided slaves with amusements, games, and pastimes for leisure hours.

Slave culture was a fully developed system that provided its people with tools with which they could protect themselves, especially psychologically, from the brutal ravages of racial oppression. Beyond that, it has had a profound influence on all aspects of American life and has influenced white society and culture in every aspect.

BIBLIOGRAPHY

Ball, Charles. *Slavery in the United States: A Narration of the Life and Adventures of Charles Ball.* New York: John S. Taylor, 1837.

Blassingame, John W. *The Slave Community: Plantation Life in the Antebellum South.* Rev. ed. New York: Oxford University Press, 1979.

Douglass, Frederick. *My Bondage and My Freedom.* [1855]. New York: Dover Publications, 1969.

Du Bois, W. E. B. "The Sorrow Songs." In *The Souls of Black Folk.* [1903]. New York: Barnes and Noble, 2005.

Dunbar, Paul Lawrence. "We Wear the Mask." In *The Norton Anthology of African American Literature*, eds. Henry Louis Gates, Jr. and Nellie Y. McKay. New York: W. W. Norton, 1997.

Gomez, Michael A. *Exchanging Our Country Marks: The Transformation of African Identities in the Colonial and Antebellum South.* Chapel Hill: University of North Carolina Press, 1998.

Harris, J. William. *Plain Folk and Gentry in a Slave Society: White Liberty and Black Slavery in Augusta's Hinterlands.* Middletown, CT: Wesleyan University Press, 1985.

Joyner, Charles. *Down by the Riverside: A South Carolina Slave Community.* Urbana: University of Illinois Press, 1984.

Rawick, George P., ed. *The American Slave: A Composite Autobiography*, vol. 5. Westport, CT: Greenwood Press, 1972–1979.

West, Cornel. "Black Strivings in a Twilight Civilization." In *The Future of the Race*, eds. Henry Louis Gates Jr. and Cornel West. New York: Alfred A. Knopf, 1996.

Anthony A. Lee

■ Spirituals

Many of the West Africans who were forced into slavery in America came from cultures in which music played an important role in everyday life. Thus it is not surprising that the slaves continued to make music in their new surroundings. At work, at play, and at worship they sang, often mixing sacred with secular songs. While settlers of European origin were accustomed to singing hymns during worship as written in hymnals, the slaves were much more flexible in their use of music, singing hymns whenever they pleased.

Some plantation owners did not want their slaves to sing songs—religious or secular—while they worked because they believed that the slaves might be communicating secret messages via the songs. In this regard, the owners were correct. Former slave Wash Wilson once commented, "When de niggers go round singin' 'Steal Away to Jesus,' dat mean dere gwine be a 'ligious meetin' dat night" (Rawick 1977–1979, p. 198). Such songs as "Swing Low Sweet Chariot," "Canaan, Sweet Canaan," and "Ride on King Jesus, No Man Can Hinder Thee" depict a future in which God would deliver them from slavery and thus were thought to promote efforts at escape. Although some plantation owners forbid singing by their slaves, others were either unconcerned or found that when slaves were allowed to sing, they worked more productively and were generally more accepting of their lot. Repetitive and rhythmic tasks especially lent themselves to singing, and the bulk of slave work was just this kind.

Where permitted, some slaves attended religious services at their owner's place of worship, where their boisterous singing was not always appreciated. Some religious leaders objected to what they called the nonsensical lyrics the slaves created for their songs, which were often improvised. The slaves readily mixed secular and sacred lyrics and more often than not found inspiration in stories from the Old Testament, which they would have heard in oral readings from scripture or in sermons, since they were forbidden to learn to read. The runaway slave and author, William Brown, described a black woman selling strawberries in Norfolk, Virginia, in 1855. She sang:

> I live fore miles out of town,
> I am gwine to glory.
> My strawberries are sweet an' soun',
> I am gwine to glory.
> I fotch 'em fore miles on my head,
> I am gwine to glory.
> My chile is sick, and' husban' dead,
> I am gwine to glory.
> Now's de time to get em cheap,
> I am gwine to glory.
> (Brown 1880, p. 211)

Another observer of slave spiritual singing, writing in the November 23, 1867 issue of the *Daily Evening Bulletin*, found this mixture of sacred and secular imagery startling:

> King Jesus, he was so strong *(er,)* my Lord,
> That he jarred down the walls of hell.
> Don't you hear what de chariot say? *(bis,)*
> De fore wheels run by de grace of God,
> An' de hind wheels dey run by faith.

Rather than conform to white notions of propriety during worship, some groups of slaves held their own services on the plantation. The freedom to worship varied from plantation to plantation. Some sympathetic owners built special buildings, called praise houses, in which the slaves might worship, while at other locations, slaves had to meet in the woods on a Sunday or at 2 or 3 a.m. another night in order to worship. As the unnamed author of the 1859 article "Songs of the Blacks" commented, "[It] is in religion that the African pours out his whole voice and soul. . . . All the revelations of the Bible have to him a startling vividness, and he will sing of the Judgment and the Resurrection with a terror or a triumph which cannot be concealed" (September 9, 1859). This type of emotive display certainly ran counter to white Protestant notions of worship.

Many whites did not understand so could not appreciate the complexities of slave singing, which incorporated African rhythms, tonalities, and vocal embellishments. Rhythms were often syncopated and set against each other in complicated patterns. The tonality, or scale on which the music was based, might only include five notes (pentatonic) or microtones (half or quarter steps between pitches). The vocal embellishments might include yodeling, bending a pitch up or down, and singing several notes to one syllable of lyrics. In addition, grunts, yells, cries, or moans were common forms of musical expression. It is no small wonder that non-Africans were baffled by such original musical displays.

Although African music was incomprehensible to many, some whites were impressed by slave singing. Describing slaves at a camp meeting in 1856, a correspondent for *Dwight's Journal of Music* wrote that when hundreds of blacks "join[ed] in the chorus of such a hymn as 'When I can read my title clear, / To mansions in the skies,' the unimpassioned hearer is almost lifted from his feet by the volume and majesty of the sound" (p. 178–180). A *Liberator* writer thought that freemen could learn from this music, particularly to praise the Creator. "Americans are the most favored people on earth, and yet they are the least expressive of their joy.... Let us not be ashamed to learn the art of happiness from the poor bondmen of the South. If slaves can pour out their hearts in melody, how ought freemen to sing!" Over time, the African songs did become an integral part of American society, developing into such popular styles of music as blues, jazz, and pop.

BIBLIOGRAPHY

Boston Daily Advertiser (Boston, MA), September 14, 1864, issue 63, col. B.

Brown, William Wells. *My Southern Home: or, The South and Its People.* Boston: A.G. Brown, 1880.

Daily Evening Bulletin (San Francisco), November 23, 1867, issue 41, col. H.

Dwight's Journal of Music 15, (1859): 178–80.

Fayetteville (NC) Observer, January 20, 1862, issue 2329, col. F.

Rawick, George P., ed. *The American Slave* Series 1 and 2, vol. 5, Texas Narratives, part 4. Westport, CT: Greenwood Press, 1977–1979.

"Songs of the Blacks." *The Liberator* (Boston, MA), September 9, 1859, issue 36, col. D.

"War Songs of the South" *The Charleston Courier Tri-Weekly*, May 31, 1862, col. C.

White, Shane and Graham White. *The Sounds of Slavery.* Boston: Beacon Press, 2005.

Jeanne M. Lesinski

■ Religion Practiced by Slaves

The religious life of slaves in antebellum America was shaped by and varied according to a number of factors. These included, but were not limited to, slaves' African region of origin, the section of the United States slaves lived in, the predominant local plantation labor system, the European American and Native American religious cultures slaves were exposed to, and the historical moment under consideration. Three significant regions will be considered in this brief discussion of religion and slavery: the Carolina-Georgia Low Country, the Chesapeake, and the Gulf Coast. Each is considered in terms of its African-influenced religious life and in terms of the form of Christianity that took hold.

Understanding the religious life of the enslaved requires that clear distinctions be made between the way the sacred and secular were experienced in European American and African Diasporic societies and cultures. By the antebellum period, both the sacred and secular realms of Euro-American society were increasingly subject to church dictates concerning the daily life of congregants. Despite the vibrant culture of worship brought about by the Second Great Awakening, Christian churches failed to completely control the daily lives of whites, and exerted even less control over the spiritual life of enslaved African Americans. This latter population (a majority in some locations), harboring resentment toward the master population, possessed of a completely different cultural worldview, and retaining their own spiritual values resisted the reality of white control through an alternate religious culture (Gomez 1998, pp. 247–248). The great majority of the African captives imported into America came directly from Africa or with only transitory stops in the Caribbean. These people—primarily the Bakongo, Ovimbundu, Igbo, Ibibio, Akan, Mandinka, and Bambara—faced with the social death of slavery, chose to create a cohesive unified religious community in which ethnic differences enriched the collective religious experience, but were subsumed by central religious institutions: the ring shout, baptism, root-work, hoodoo, funeral rites, and the exhortative priest (Patterson 1982). Each of these institutions was drawn from the African cultural imagination and then integrated into African American religious culture (Gomez 1998, pp. 12–16; Stuckey 1987, ch. 1; Thompson 1984).

Scholars disagree on the impact American religious movements had on slave worship practices during the eighteenth and early nineteenth centuries. Some, such as Sterling Stuckey (1987), maintain that even if reform

HOODOO: AFRICAN FOLK MAGIC AMONG SOUTHERN SLAVES

Hoodoo is a term that refers to a collection of folk magical practices used in the South before the Civil War and still practiced today. The English word *hoodoo* is derived from the Ewe word *hudu*; hoodoo is also known as *conjuration, conjure, or rootwork* (from the practice of chewing and spitting out plant roots as part of some hoodoo rituals). Hoodoo is not a separate religion; it was practiced by slaves who had become Christian as well as by those who had not. Hoodoo in the nineteenth-century rural South was primarily West or Central African in origin, though some spells or rituals were borrowed from Native American peoples such as the Chickasaw and Cherokee. Slaves practiced hoodoo in order to gain some control over their lives—to avoid being whipped, to attract love, to cure disease, to foretell the future, or to contact the spirits of their ancestors.

Henry Bibb (1815–1854) was a former slave from Kentucky who obtained his freedom by fleeing northward, first to Detroit and later to Canada. In 1849–1850 he published an autobiography in which, among many other things, he described hoodoo spells and rituals. Although Bibb discusses his early use of hoodoo in order to inform the reader that he has outgrown "superstition," his autobiography is considered an accurate source of information about Southern folk magic. Below are some excerpts:

> There is much superstition among the slaves. Many of them believe in what they call "conjuration," tricking, and witchcraft; and some of them . . . say that by it they can prevent their masters from exercising their will over their slaves. . . . The remedy [to prevent a flogging] is most generally some kind of bitter root; they are directed to chew it and spit towards their masters when they are angry with their slaves. (Bibb 1849, p. 25)

Bibb describes an instance in which he paid another slave for a hoodoo recipe to keep his master from beating him:

> After I had paid him his charge, he told me to go to the cow-pen after night, and get some fresh cow manure, and mix it with red pepper and white people's hair, all to be put into a pot over the fire, and scorched until it could be ground into snuff. I was then to sprinkle it about my master's bedroom, in his hat and boots, and it would prevent him from ever abusing me in any way. After I got it all ready prepared, the smallest pinch of if scattered over a room, was enough to make a horse sneeze from the strength of it; but it did no good. (Bibb 1849, p. 27)

Later on, Bibb paid another "conjurer" for a love charm, which also failed:

> After I had paid him, he told me to get a bull frog, and take a certain bone out of the frog, dry it, and when I got a chance I must step up to any girl whom I wished to make love me, and scratch her somewhere on her naked skin with this bone, and she would be certain to love me and would follow me in spite of herself. . . . So I got me a bone for a certain girl, whom I knew to be under the influence of another young man . . . [and] when I got a chance, I fetched her a tremendous rasp across the neck with this bone, which made her jump. But in place of making her love me, it only made her angry with me. She felt more like running after me to retaliate on me for thus abusing her, than she felt like loving me. (Bibb 1849, pp. 30–31)

REBECCA J. FREY

SOURCE: *Bibb, Henry.* Narrative of the Life and Adventures of Henry Bibb, an American Slave, Written by Himself. *New York: Author, 1849.*

movements initiated a gradual transition from the "Africanized" Christianity of the slave quarters and the "hush harbor" to more Western conventions of worship within churches, most slaves still favored the more lively and outdoor settings of the ring shout and John Kunering ceremonies (Stuckey 1987, p. 167). Others argue that the impact of Euro-American culture, society, and worship practices was much more fundamental. In *Roll Jordan Roll* (1976), for example, Eugene Genovese claims that by the nineteenth century Afro-Caribbean religious practices had almost completely given away to the religion of the master class.

According to Lawrence Levine (1977), while enslaved Africans brought no unified "African" culture with them, they did create a new and unique African American religious culture (pp. 3–5). Likewise, Stuckey and Michael Gomez (1998) argue that Africans developed a religious life of their own, largely independently of whites, by developing (1) religious institutions based on African patterns; (2) an Africanized version of Christianity; and (3) a quasi-Islamic religious life.

Spirituality in the Low Country

The Low Country is a coastal region of Southeastern North America stretching from Wilmington, North Carolina, to Northern Florida, and including South Carolina and Georgia. Its original inhabitants—the Chicora, Cherokee, Creek, and other Native American cultural groups—were displaced by the Spanish, French, and British and the enslaved Africans they brought to the region. By 1830 in South Carolina as a whole, Africans (slave and free) outnumbered whites 323,000 to 258,000 (Gomez 1998, p. 295), with the greatest concentration being along the Atlantic coast. Having a numerical advantage—annually reinforced by "fresh saltwater" captives who brought with them their own religious ideas from West Central Africa, the Gold Coast, Sierra Leone, and Senegambia—enslaved African Americans developed a new spiritual gestalt that focused on two major religious institutions: root-work and the ring shout. Both of these practices were most likely first introduced during the colonial period by Bakongo and other Congo-Angolans practicing close variations of Western Bantu traditions (Gomez 1998, p. 250; Stuckey 1987; Thompson 1984, p. 107). Root-work, a spiritual practice that originated out of the Bakongo reverence for *minkisi*—the sacred medicines embodied in certain roots, herbs, and minerals—functioned as an amalgam of medical and spiritual practices (Thompson 1987, p. 108). The ring shout simultaneously expressed Bakongo reverence for the quartered circle as a symbol of the totality of life, various complicated intersections, particularly of the living with the ancestral realm (*Pemba/Mpemba*), and the motion of the sun, as recorded in the counterclockwise dance of its practitioners. By 1810, the ranks of ring shouters had been strengthened by captive men and women from Sierra Leone, organized into variants of Poro (male) and Sande (female) initiation societies, allowing the enslaved African American community to preserve spiritual agency in a rich cultural context. These institutions were most clearly preserved by the Gullah culture, from Georgetown to Hilton Head, South Carolina, and to a lesser extent by the Geechee culture of the Ogeechee River area in Georgia and North Florida; they were also found in the Congaree Swamp area outside of Columbia, South Carolina.

The Chesapeake of Virginia and Maryland

Virginia had a history of close cross-cultural contacts between African Americans, Native Americans, and Euro-Americans during the early colonial period, as evidenced by the records of the House of Burgesses. Africans and Scottish bondsmen ran away together, Africans and Native Americans rose up in revolt together, and Africans and Englishmen joined forces to suppress these uprisings. The result was a division during the antebellum period between the religious culture of slaves and the religious culture of free African Americans, the latter being much more patterned on Eurocentric Christianity. The slave culture that developed in the Tidelands was, however, weakened by an internal slave trade that arose to meet a demand for labor caused by the spread of cotton culture into the Louisiana Territory.

The Great Awakening brought about by the missionary efforts of George Whitfield, among others, from 1740 to 1790 led to the freeing of hundreds of enslaved Africans, largely by white converts (Gomez 1998, p. 251). Still, during this period no more than 4 percent of the African American population (slave and free) converted to Christianity (Gomez 1998, p. 254). By 1830, one in every seventeen Africans had converted, bringing the percentage to six. From 1790 to 1830 black church life in Virginia developed along lines that mirrored class distinctions within the black community. Field slaves were largely excluded from proselytizing efforts, while free blacks organized their own churches largely along white Christian lines. By the first decade of the nineteenth century, poor whites were showing the influence of African American forms of worship during revival meetings that featured outdoor worship, shouting, dancing, and other "ecstatic" manifestations.

During the antebellum period, the predominant African ethnicities found in the Chesapeake region were the Igbo and Ibibio (Bight of Biafra), followed by the Asante and Fante (Gold Coast/Akan), and Mandinka and Bambara of Senegambia. Gomez and other scholars suggest that slaves of Igbo origin had an unusually strong connection to their homeland that led to heightened psychological stress and despair, manifested at times in suicidal behavior (Gomez 1998, pp. 250–251). Slaves of Igbo origin resided primarily in the Tidewater region, where tobacco cultivation employing the gang labor system predominated. Although the region had a large concentration of black labor, the gang system mitigated the development of a strong cultural community comparable to that of the Gullahs or Geechees in the Low Country. Nonetheless, a local religious community did develop among slaves. This was weakened, however, when many slaves from the Tidewater region were sold "down the river" during the spread of cotton into the Louisiana Territory.

Forced into the Gulf region and other parts of the Louisiana Territory, Chesapeake slaves, unable to take much of their material culture with them, held onto their beliefs and crossed their Igbo-Akan-Mande religion with their new region's Fon-Ewe-Yoruba-Bakongo traditions to create a new religious subculture. After the Bakongo, the Bambara were the most dominant cultural presence among slaves in the Gulf region. Their African-influenced spiritual worldview is indicated by their prominent use of amulets. With the importation of increased numbers of captives from Congo-Angolan and Fon-Ewe Yoruba regions, a synthesis of African religious culture known popularly as *voodoo*—or *vodun* in its Haitian variant—developed in the region.

Christianity and the Pursuit of Freedom

In the antebellum period, the free black population developed an emancipatory form of Christianity most strikingly proclaimed by David Walker (1785–1830), advocated by Maria Stewart (1803–1879) and Henry Highland Garnet (1815–1882), and practiced by Denmark Vesey (1767–1822). In his 1829 *Appeal to the Coloured Citizens of the World*, Walker, an African American abolitionist from Wilmington who made Boston his base, argued that slavery and true Christianity were incompatible:

> I ask O ye *Christians !!!* who hold us and our children, in the most abject ignorance and degradation.... If you will allow that we are MEN ... does not the blood of our fathers and of us their

children, cry aloud to the Lord of Sabaoth [*sic*] against you, for the cruelties and murders with which you have, and do continue to afflict us? (Walker 1994 [1829], p. 16)

Walker's *Appeal* is significant, as it signaled a reaction against biblically based claims of African inferiority. Walker identified historical events as the cause of enslaved African Americans' debasement. He wrote of "Our Wretchedness in consequence of Slavery" (p. 17), "Our Wretchedness in consequence of Ignorance" (p. 29), and "Our Wretchedness in Consequence of the Preachers of the Religion of Jesus Christ" (p. 46).

Many blacks demanding immediate freedom based their appeal in part on Christianity. In 1857 two black Christians from Cleveland, John Malvin and the Reverend Robert Johnson, writing in *The Liberator*, condemned a biracial man who supported slavery and black inferiority. Malvin and Johnson wrote that "we do not love him, but hate him as an apostate from the religion of Jesus Christ, and a traitor and disgrace to his people" (Aptheker 1971, vol. 1, p. 391). Christianity, thus, had been transformed from solely being the belief system of the slave master into a part of the insurgent culture of those seeking freedom.

BIBLIOGRAPHY

Aptheker, Herbert. *A Documentary History of the Negro Peoples in the United States*, vol. 1. New York: Citadel Press, 1951.

Berry, Mary Frances, and John W. Blassingame. *Long Memory: The Black Experience in America.* New York: Oxford University Press, 1982.

Genovese, Eugene D. *Roll, Jordan, Roll: The World the Slaves Made.* New York: Vintage Books, 1976.

Gomez, Michael A. *Exchanging Our Country Marks: The Transformation of African Identities in the Colonial and Antebellum South.* Chapel Hill: University of North Carolina Press, 1998.

Levine, Lawrence. *Black Culture and Black Consciousness: Afro-American Folk Thought from Slavery to Freedom.* New York: Oxford University Press, 1978.

Patterson, Orlando. *Slavery and Social Death: A Comparative Study.* Cambridge, MA: Harvard University Press, 1982.

Stuckey, Sterling. *Slave Culture: Nationalist Theory and the Foundations of Black America.* New York: Oxford University Press, 1987.

Thompson, Robert Farris. *Flash of the Spirit: African and Afro-American Art and Philosophy.* New York: Vintage Books, 1984.

Walker, David, and Henry H. Garnet. *David Walker's Appeal and Henry Highland Garnet's Address.* 1848. Reprint, Nashville, TN: James C. Winston, 1994.

Wood, Peter H. *Black Majority: Negroes in Colonial South Carolina from 1670 through the Stono Rebellion.* New York: W. W. Norton, 1974.

Kwasi Densu

■ Dance among Slaves

Dance was an integral part of daily life among African American slaves. Observations of slave culture, particularly on the Southern plantation, yield evidence of a layering of traditional African tribal dance practices shared, blended, and reinvented in the New World. For this reason, dance practices among African American slaves represent a narrative of resistance and survival.

In *Black Dance in the United States from 1619 to 1970* (1972), Lynne Fauley Emery discusses the slave owners' practice of what they called "dancing the slaves." This activity occurred on board the ships transporting the slaves from Africa to America, the voyage American history records as the Middle Passage. She notes, "Dancing was encouraged for economic reasons; slaves who had been exercised looked better and brought a higher price" (Emery 1972, p. 6). Noting the physiological benefits of exercise, slave owners forced slaves to exercise to maintain their health. Alexander Falconridge, a white surgeon on board one of the slave ships, recalled "Exercise being deemed necessary for the preservation of [the slaves' health], they are sometime obliged to dance, when the weather will permit their coming on deck. If they go about it reluctantly, they are flogged" (Emery 1972, p. 8). "Dancing the slaves" continued beyond the slave ships, permeating America's Southern plantation culture.

On the plantations, slave owners forced slaves to dance "under the lash," both for economic reasons and for entertainment. Slaves were danced to maintain a healthy appearance, though, given the often-meager conditions in which they lived, they appeared anything but. Emery concludes, "[The African slave] danced not for love, nor for joy, nor religious celebration [as he had done in his native African home]; he danced in answer to the whip. He danced for survival" (1972, p. 12). Dancing provided a mask for what were sad, dismal living conditions, despite the slaves' happy and healthy façades. The process of "dancing the slaves" demonstrates the way slave owners made negative a practice that, for many African slaves, had been culturally redeeming. But many slaves were able to recast many of these same movements in a positive light simply by using similar movements and gestures to create a common language and use it for the good of community and culture-building.

Dance was an integral part of slave plantation culture. Some of the more popular dances involved types of animal mimicry. A common form mentioned was the

Buzzard Lope. In *Slave Songs of the Georgia Sea Islands* (1942), the song collector, Lydia Parrish, described this dance as she witnessed it in the Georgia Sea Islands: "March aroun' / Jump across! / Get the eye! .... / Get the guts! / Go to eatin'! .... / Look aroun' for mo meat" (1942, p. 111). Other animal mimicry dances included the Fish Tail, Pigeon Wing, Snake Hip, and Turkey Trot. Dances such as these were similar to the

An example of the Cakewalk, 1903. In some areas of Africa, heavy loads were often carried on one's head, inspiring American slaves to dance while balancing a bucket of water. Couples who spilled the least amount of water earned a cake for a prize, hence the dance, minus the bucket of water, became known as the Cake-Walk. *Hulton Archive/Getty Images*

African tribal dances celebrating a successful hunt. As such, these slave dances represented a survival of African tribal culture on the plantation in the American South.

Other dances containing elements of African tribal culture were ring dances. In *Drums and Shadows: Survival Studies Among the Georgia Coastal Negroes* (1986), the Savannah Unit of the Georgia Writers' Project of the Works Project Administration cites Hettie Campbell of St. Mary's Island, Georgia, who described these ring dances: "We does plenty uh dances in those days. Dance roun' in a ring. We has a big time long bout wen crops come in an everybody bring sumpm tuh eat wut they makes an we all gives praise fuh the good crop an then we shouts an sings all night. An wen the sun rise, we stahts tuh dance" (pp. 186–187). Ring dances provided a form of communal fellowship in which slaves recalled their tribal customs of praising the gods for a successful crop.

The Ring-Shout was a type of ring dance marking sacred occasions. This dance was particularly observed among the Mohammedans of West Africa. On the slave plantations, the ring-shout offered a means for African slaves to maintain their fervent religious customs while adhering to the American Protestant church's ban on dancing of any kind. In the *Slave Narratives* of the Federal Writers' Project, Louisiana slave Wash Wilson explained, "Us longed to de church, all right, but dancin' ain't sinful iffen de foots ain't crossed. Us danced at de arbor meetin's but us sho' didn't have us foots crossed" (1941, p. 198). One of the earliest accounts of the ring-shout comes from Laura Towne, a Northern teacher sent by the Freedman's Bureau to teach the Negroes in the Sea Islands. In her book, *Letters and Diary of Laura M. Towne*, a letter to her family describes:

> Tonight I have been to a "shout," which seems to me certainly the remains of some old idol worship. The Negroes sing a kind of chorus,—three standing apart to lead and clap,—and then all the others go shuffling around in a circle following one another with not much regularity, turning round stamping so that the whole floor swings. I never saw anything so savage. (1969, p. 20)

To the outside observer, such dancing appeared savage, but in fact it represented retention of African cultural practices in America.

In his book *Slave Culture* (1987), Sterling Stuckey notes this very distinction between African slave and European cultures. He states, "The division between the sacred and the secular, so prominent a feature of modern Western culture, did not exist in black Africa in the years of the slave trade, before Christianity made real inroads on the continent" (1987, p. 24). This type of dancing was a concept foreign to the European powers, in whose culture existed a distinct boundary between sacred and secular. Whereas such dancing perpetuated a conception of savagery in the minds of European Americans viewing these acts, it sustained a central element of African tribal culture among the slaves.

BIBLIOGRAPHY

Emery, Lynne Fauley. *Black Dance in the United States from 1619 to 1970.* Palo Alto, CA: National Press Books, 1972.

Federal Writers' Project, Works Progress Administration. "Wash Wilson." In *Slave Narratives*, vol. 14, part 4: *Louisiana Narratives.* Washington, DC: Library of Congress, 1941.

Georgia Writers' Project, Works Progress Administration. *Drums and Shadows: Survival Studies among the Georgia Coastal Negroes.* Athens: University of Georgia Press, 1986.

Parrish, Lydia. *Slave Songs of the Georgia Sea Islands.* New York: Creative Age Press, 1942.

Stuckey, Sterling. *Slave Culture: Nationalist Theory and the Foundations of Black America.* New York: Oxford University Press, 1987.

Towne, Laura M. *Letters and Diary of Laura M. Towne.* New York: Negro Universities Press, 1969.

Ondra Krouse Dismukes

Race and Racial Tensions

After Nat Turner's (1800–1831) rebellion in 1831, Southern fears of servile insurrections increased exponentially. Southern legislatures passed laws further prohibiting the already limited movement of slaves, slave patrols became more serious in the exertions, and the slightest hint of servile plotting brought swift and brutal retribution. Free blacks found themselves subjected to deeper scrutiny, while some states debated whether to allow blacks—free or enslaved—within their borders.

Events of the 1850s did nothing to lesson Southern concerns of a race war. In early 1855 several counties in Maryland experienced a scare, while later that year rumors of a Christmas insurrection stoked fears in a number of Southern states. The following year slaves rebelled in New Iberia, Louisiana; Hopkinsville, Kentucky; and Columbus, Texas (Wish 1937, pp. 314–320). Moreover, events in *Bleeding Kansas* threatened to spill over into the rest of the country. The Brooks-Sumner Affair; the sacking of Lawrence, Kansas; and John Brown's Pottawatomie Massacre—all occurring within a seven-day period—increased tensions to a fever pitch. The guerilla war in Kansas threatened to spread into other states. Southerners suspected abolitionist plots everywhere; and in the North, the concept of *Slave Power* as a malevolent force began to take hold.

Already strained race relations in the South reached their breaking point on the night of October 16, 1859, when John Brown (1800–1859), along with a small party of white men and five free blacks, seized the

United States arsenal at Harpers Ferry, Virginia. Intent on leading a servile insurrection, Brown had exhibited a penchant for murder at Pottawatomie Creek that horrified Southerners. His sudden violent appearance in Virginia terrified the South. Captured, and sentenced to die, Brown wrote on the day of his execution that he had become "quite certain that the crimes of this guilty land will never be purged but with blood," which many Southerners took as a prediction of a race war (Bancroft 1900, p. 497). In attempt to forestall such a future, many Southern states, believing free blacks were an unholy influence on otherwise content slaves, debated the idea of expelling free blacks from their boundaries. Rumors of insurrections persisted well into the Civil War. In the spring of 1861 several black coach drivers in Adams County, Mississippi, concocted a plan to murder their white masters and rape their female kin. Whites discovered the plan and executed an untold number of slaves suspected of participating in it. A year later the provost marshal of Natchez, Mississippi, wrote, "within the last 12 months we have had to hang some 40 for plotting an insurrection, and there has been about that number put in irons" (Farrar 1862).

Indeed the war placed a new set of strains on race relations. In the Black Belt region of the South, mobilization further changed an already dangerously skewed ratio of blacks to whites. In the North, white troops began marching south, encountering people of African descent in significant numbers for the first time. The troops's attitudes varied according to their political stripes and ethnicity. Hardened Democrats, as a general rule, did not care for blacks, considered the war a contest for the Union, and wanted no part of abolition. Rank and file Republicans, for the most part, remained ambivalent about slavery during the first half of the war, but gradually swung toward the radical position of abolitionism as they advanced farther into the South and saw the evil side of slavery for themselves. Irish soldiers—and civilians for that matter—had little love for blacks, free or slave. They considered them economic competition and at times lashed out violently, most notably during July 1863 when Irish civilians rioted in New York City, murdering blacks as they encountered them. About that same time, at freedmen camps and leased plantations along the Mississippi River, abuse in the shape of rape, murder, and robbery became so prevalent that General Ulysses S. Grant (1822–1885) had to issue orders promising the summary dismissal of any officers who tolerated such behavior in their commands (U.S. War Department Series I, vol. 24, part, p. 571).

The year 1863 also saw the widespread recruitment of black soldiers into the Union army—which was abhorred by men in both armies. The average Union soldier was rather ambivalent about it, so long as they did not have to serve side by side with a black regiment. They believed a black soldier could stop a bullet as well as a white, and that blacks should fight for their freedom. Not all Union officers agreed. General Andrew Jackson Smith (1815–1897) expressed his disgust with Adjutant General Lorenzo Thomas's (1804–1875) recruitment of black soldiers, claiming he would

> hang old Thomas if he comes into his camp making such a speech. Says he hates abolitionists worse than he does the Devil. If Jesus Christ was to come down and ask him if he would be an abolitionist if he would have him to heave, he answers that "I would say NO! Mr. Christ, I beg to be excused. I would rather go to hell than be an abolitionist." (Hass 1961, p. 71)

Later, in 1864, General William T. Sherman (1820–1891), wrote that in response to the question of

> 'Is a negro as good as a white man to stop a bullet?' Yes, and a sand-bag is better; but can a negro do our skirmishing and picket duty? Can they improvise roads, bridges, sorties, flank movements, &c., like the white man? I say no. Soldiers must and do many things without orders from their own sense, as in sentinels. Negroes are not equal to this. (U.S. War Department series 1, vol. 38, part 5, p. 793)

Questions of racism in the Union high command again came to the fore in December 1864 when Major General Jefferson C. Davis (1828–1879) ordered his men to remove a pontoon bridge over Ebenezer Creek in Georgia. The small army of freedpeople trailing Davis's corps fond themselves trapped between Confederate cavalry and the stream. Many desperate blacks, terrified at being captured or killed by the Rebels, drowned trying to swim the creek (Grimsley 1995, p. 199).

The recruitment of black troops by Union forces posed a major policy question for the Confederacy—should they be treated as prisoners of war, escaped slaves, or insurrectionists? Initially the Davis and the Confederate high command proscribed execution as the penalty for any Union officers caught in command of black troops. For black enlisted men captured under arms, it depended on who captured them. In some cases Confederates murdered captured black troops, but most ended up sold back into slavery. The most blatant example of Confederate disgust of black troops came in April 1864, when General Nathan Bedford Forrest's (1821–1877) troops overran Fort Pillow on the Mississippi River forty miles north of Memphis, Tennessee. In the melee that followed the attack, Forrest's men killed nearly 300 Union soldiers, many of whom were trying to surrender.

A year later, at Fort Blakely near Mobile, Alabama, the Confederates found themselves in an earthen fortification with their backs to a major waterway, outnumbered by a mixed force of white Union regiments and United States Colored Troops (USCT)—Fort Pillow in reverse. Like Fort Pillow, the attackers worked themselves into a rage

Church scene, Nashville, Tennessee. Instilling fear and intimidating were ways to maintain control over both slaves and free blacks throughout the South. Whites fearful of slave rebellions looked to eliminate any opportunity African Americans had to organize acts of resistance, including disrupting church services where people of color worshipped. *Kean Collection/Hulton Archive/Getty Images*

before the final assault. Walter A. Chapman, a newly commissioned white officer in the USCT wrote "As soon as our niggers caught sight of the retreating figures of the rebs the very devil could not hold them, their eyes glittered like serpents and with yells & howls like hungry wolves, they rushed for the rebel works." The sight of the howling, charging black troops struck fear into the white Mississippians in the Confederate line. Some threw down their arms and made for the river in their rear, hoping to swim their way out of the fight. Chapman wrote that the "others threw down their arms and ran for their lives over to the white troops on our left, to give themselves up to save being butchered by our niggers. The niggers did not take a prisoner. They killed all they took to a man" (April 11, 1865). While most historians believe that Chapman exaggerated to a certain extent, other Union accounts support the belief that the black soldiers at Blakely raised the cry of Fort Pillow, and came very close to visiting their wrath on the Confederates but for the efforts of a few brave Union officers (Fitzgerald 2001, pp. 248–251).

As the last major action of the Civil War, the battles around Mobile, Alabama, marked the end of organized combat. But the conflict between the races did not end. Confederate soldiers, who had spent most of the war campaigning, came home to a transformed society that afforded as much legal protection to a black laborer as it did to a white planter. Many Confederates found the situation intolerable and immediately set about to change things; if not to the way they were before the war, then at the very least, to something similar. White-led race riots broke out in Memphis, Tennessee in 1866; Colfax, Louisiana in 1873; and in a host of other Southern towns between 1874 and 1876, when whites finally restored their control over the former Confederate states. Thus, while the Civil War changed the legal status of race in America, it did not change people's hearts.

BIBLIOGRAPHY

Bancroft, Frederic. *The Life of William H. Seward*. Two vols. New York: Harper and Brothers, 1900.

Chapman, Walter A. Walter A. Chapman Papers, Manuscripts and Archives, Yale University Library.

Farrar, A. K. "Provost Marshal A. K. Farrar to Governor John J. Pettus, Natchez, July 17, 1862." *Records of the Office of the Governor*. Jackson: Mississippi, Department of Archives and History, 1862.

Fitzgerald, Michael W. "Another Kind of Glory: Black Participation and Its Consequences in the

Campaign for Confederate Mobile." *Alabama Review* 54 (2001): 243–275.

Grimsley, Mark. *The Hard Hand of War: Union Military Policy toward Southern Civilians, 1861–1865.* New York: Cambridge University Press, 1995.

Hass, Paul H., ed. *The Diary of Henry Clay Warmouth, 1861–1867.* Master's Thesis, University of Wisconsin, 1961.

U. S. War Department. *The War of Rebellion: A Compilation of the Official Records of the Union and Confederate Armies.* Washington, DC, 1880–1901.

Wish, Harvey. "American Slave Insurrections before 1861." *Journal of Negro History* 22, no. 3 (1937): 299–320.

David H. Slay

■ Free Blacks

Free blacks occupied a precarious position in American society on the eve of the Civil War. Southerners, for the most part, distrusted them; and in the North, many states refused to recognize their civil rights. While considered free, they were free in name only in most regions of the country, for one misstep and they could find themselves enslaved, exiled, or imprisoned. Yet despite those handicaps, some free blacks found prosperity within the limbo, acquiring land, businesses, and, ironically enough, slaves of their own.

In 1846, the Jackson *Mississippian* complained that free blacks "continued to saunter about the streets of our cities, engaging in acts of petty larceny, gambling in secret, and lounging about as fops and dandies, corrupting the slaves and rendering them disobedient and discontented with their lots in life" (September 3, 1846). In neighboring Louisiana, a state with a population of nearly nineteen thousand free blacks in 1860, the distrust of free blacks was so great after John Brown's (1800–1859) raid on Harpers Ferry, Virginia, that the state legislature passed a law in 1859 prohibiting them from entering the state (*The Weekly Mississippian*, September 7, 1859). That same year, a New York newspaper noted that since John Brown's raid, many Southern states sought to restrict the travel of free blacks on Southern railroads (*New York Herald*, November 3, 1859). In St. Landry Parish, Louisiana, whites passed a resolution calling for the enslavement of any free black "convicted of any offence against the laws" (*The Liberator*, March 18, 1859, p. 43). So great was Southern paranoia over Brown's raid that three states legislatures passed measures expelling free blacks, and nine others seriously considered it (Atkins 2005).

Yet some free blacks managed to find prosperity between slavery and complete freedom. William Johnson, a free black barber in Natchez, Mississippi, amassed enough wealth to build a three story brick home and purchase several slaves (Davis and Hogan 1954, pp. 1–24). In New Orleans, which had a long tradition of civically-active free blacks, over 900 free black members of the Louisiana Native Guard volunteered their services to the Confederacy in the fall of 1861—though not out of any great love for the Confederacy, but rather for the protection of their livelihoods and families. They never saw active duty on behalf of the Confederacy and were disbanded until Union forces captured the Crescent City in early 1862 (Hollandsworth 1995, pp. 1–12). Free black women, too, could attain some financial standing in the community, for in Natchez a significant number of free black and mulatto women acquired slaves of their own (Ribianszky 2005, pp. 217–245). Nevertheless, the vast majority of free blacks in the south eked out a living on the peripheries of society, working as woodchoppers, domestics, and other menial tasks—their freedom dependent solely on the goodwill and honesty of local whites.

Free blacks in the North often faced similar obstacles as their Southern counterparts, for many Northerners feared competition between black and white labor. In 1858 in Baltimore, Maryland, conflict broke out when white workers attempted to break the monopoly free black caulkers held in the shipyards—the very same yards where Frederick Douglass (1818–1895), America's most prominent free black man, worked during his younger days (Douglass 1845, p. 118). The perception of unfair competition between the races came to a head in July 1863 during the New York City Draft Riots, in which a mob consisting predominantly of Irish immigrants rampaged through sections of the city, torturing and murdering any black men, women, and children they encountered.

Despite such difficulties, many free blacks worked tirelessly to abolish slavery. A number of escaped slaves living in the North and in Canada published narratives of the captivity, often providing lurid and sensational details of their lives in bondage. For those escaped slaves, however, freedom was fleeting because the passage of the Fugitive Slave Act of 1850 made it the duty of all law officials to arrest escaped slaves. The law also established a low threshold for proof of ownership—a claimant's word. Since the legislation prohibited accused runaway slaves from testifying on their own behalf, a number of free blacks had no recourse after they were arrested and were sold into slavery. Others fell prey to criminal whites, as in the case of Solomon Northup (b. 1808), a free black man from Saratoga, New York, who fell in with a couple of smooth-talking criminals who promised him high wages to play his violin on tour with them. It took him twelve years to recover his freedom.

Once the war began, the status of free blacks changed on both sides of the Mason-Dixon Line. In the South, the position of free blacks eroded even more, with frequent calls to enslave them all. Many, however, rather than becoming legally enslaved, became de facto slaves through impressment as laborers in support of Confederate arms, usually felling trees, digging ditches, and building fortifications. In the North, new opportunities arose for free blacks. The army and navy opened their ranks to free blacks, and perhaps just as importantly, the masses of freed

Black dock workers in a federally occupied port. Many free blacks were distrusted in the South, and some Northerners refused to acknowledge their civil rights. Yet some free blacks managed to do well by buying land, starting businesses, and even owning slaves. *National Archives/Time Life Pictures/Getty Images*

slaves in the South needed their assistance. Once the Union army began to organize its policies for the care of freedpeople, as the former slaves were called, many free blacks went South to teach and provide political leadership for their kin. Indeed many of the black political figures elected to state and national officer after the Civil War, were free blacks who established themselves in areas occupied by the Union army during the conflict. Moreover, as some of the more affluent free blacks had received quality education at some point in their lives, they were equipped to take on administrative positions during Reconstruction. By the time the firing stopped, they had built up enough of a constituency to make the leap to elected office.

BIBLIOGRAPHY

Atkins, Jonathan M. "Party Politics and the Debate over the Tennessee Free Negro Bill, 1859–1860." *Journal of Southern History* 71, no. 2 (2005): 245–278.

Davis, Edwin Adams and William Ransom Hogan. *The Barber of Natchez.* Baton Rouge: Louisiana State University Press, 1954.

Douglass, Frederick. *Narrative of the Life of Frederick Douglass, an American Slave.* Boston: Anti-Slavery Office, 1845.

Hollandsworth, James G., Jr. *The Louisiana Native Guard.* Baton Rouge: Louisiana State University Press, 1995.

The Liberator (Boston, MA), March 18, 1859, issue 11, col. G.

Mississippian, "Free Negroes—Outrage," September 23, 1846, issue 39, col. B.

The New York Herald, "Free Negroes on Railroads," November 3, 1859, col. F.

Northup, Solomon. *Twelve Years a Slave: Narrative of Solomon Northup, a Citizen of New York.* Auburn, NY: Derby and Miller, 1853.

Ribianszky, Nikki. "'She Appeared to be Mistress of Her Own Actions, Free From the Control of Anyone:' Property Holding Free Women of Color in Natchez, Mississippi, 1779–1865." *Journal of Mississippi History* 48, no. 3 (2005): 217–245.

The Weekly Mississippian, "The Law in Louisiana on Free Negroes," September 07, 1859, issue 38, col. C.

David H. Slay

Emancipation

The arrival of 1863 changed the legal status of people whom the U.S. government had previously labeled as contraband: subject to seizure like any other Confederate property such as horses, mules, and cows. Their long journey to freedom suffered from many fits and starts. When General John C. Frémont liberated the slaves of disloyal owners in Missouri in August 1861, Lincoln, recognizing the country was not quite ready for emancipation, ordered him to retract the order. In April 1862, slavery was abolished in Washington, DC, with money set aside to reimburse loyal owners and remove any slaves who wished to leave the United States. Finally, in September 1862, after the Union victory at Antietam, Lincoln issued the Emancipation Proclamation as a war measure to go into effect on New Years Day, 1863.

In the North and occupied regions of the South, January 1, 1863, arrived with fanfare beyond the usual New Year celebrations. Abolitionists, free blacks, and freedpeople around the country rejoiced. Slaves in Kentucky, Missouri, Maryland, Delaware, and West Virginia had to wait, for the document did not apply to them, but only covered the states in rebellion. Furthermore, it only had teeth in areas occupied by Union forces, otherwise the Confederates thumbed their noses it at. In Union occupied Hilton Head, South Carolina, thousands of freedpeople journeyed to the camp of the First South Carolina Regiment of African Descent to listen to speeches, give speeches, and otherwise have a good time.

One eyewitness said the crowd "constituted one of the most motley assemblages of which it is possible to conceive." Present, eager for a speech, and some barbecue from the ten oxen roasting over a fire, the crowd consisted of "young and old, of all shades, sizes, and costumes; ancient domestics . . . antiquated aunties, done up in turbans, tickled and curtseying to everyone they met; gay and gaudy yellow girls, decorated with superabundant jewelry, smiling profusely at the gay and gallant youths around them." Also present were "toothless crones, sucking on black pipes, and young mothers violently hushing their babies, while here and there gleamed the red bayonet and glowed the red breeches of a South Carolina volunteer" (*New York Herald*, January 7, 1863).

Others had to wait on the Union army to liberate them before they could celebrate, and even then concern for the future tempered some of their celebrations. Booker T. Washington, who at the close of the war lived

Freed African Americans crossing Union Line after the Emancipation Proclamation. In September of 1862, Lincoln issued the Emancipation Proclamation, freeing slaves in the Confederate states, effective on New Years Day, 1863. The proclamation covered only the areas occupied by the Union in states that were part of the Confederacy. Those who could rejoiced. *© North Wind Picture Archives*

on a tobacco farm near Roanoke, Virginia, recalled how a Union officer rode up, read the Emancipation Proclamation, and told the assembled slaves that they were free. His mother broke into joyful tears and kissed her children, explaining to them what it meant. After a short celebration, the weight of responsibility sank in. "The great responsibility of being free, of having charge of themselves, of having to think and plan for themselves and their children, seemed to take possession of them. It was very much like suddenly turning a youth of ten or twelve years out into the world to provide for himself." Washington explained that to dream of freedom was one thing, but to actually have "freedom was a more serious thing than they had expected" (Washington 1901, p. 21–22).

Former slave Caroline Richardson stated that they had "been teached dat de Yankees will kill us, men women an' chillun." So, when the Union army came, "de drums wus beatin', de flags a wavin' an de hosses prancing' high. De whole hundret of us runs an' hides." They eventually came out of hiding to hear what the Union soldiers had to say. Many freedpeople left the plantation, but Caroline's family stayed on and worked for wages which was quite common at war's end (*Born in Slavery*, Richardson, p. 201). Mattie Gilmore recalled a similar experience in Athens, Texas, when after the announcement sunk in, her master invited her family to stay on and work for wages (*Born in Slavery*, Gilmore, p. 73). Some heard the news of emancipation from their masters, without ever had come into contact with Union soldiers. G. W. Pattillo a former slave who lived on a plantation near Griffin, Georgia, heard the news from his master. The master, having called the slaves together, told them that "Mr. Lincoln whipped the South and we are going back to the Union. You are as free as I am and if you want to remain here you may. I am not rich but we can work together here for both our families, sharing everything we raise equally," which Pattillo's family did for five years after the conclusion of the war (*Born in Slavery*, Pattillo, p. 170). William Black of Hannibal, Missouri, recalled that "when we was freed our master didn't give us nothing, but some clothes and five dollars. He told us we could stay if we wanted to, but we was so glad to be free dat we all left him. He was a good man though" (*Born in Slavery*, Black, p. 33).

In her interview with the Works Progress Administration writer during the 1930s, Mattie Gilmore, commented on how unprepared the freedpeople were for liberty, recalling that they "never done no managin' and didn't know how." Some, in the rush to get away from their masters, or preserve their freedom by following the Union army, did not fully understand the dangers that faced them. Along the Mississippi River they fled from plantations in the interior by the thousands, overwhelming the infrastructure of the river towns. Union Brigadier General Joseph Stockton, upon observing the cavalcade of freedpeople that followed William T. Sherman's army into Vicksburg after the raid on Meridian, felt pity for the freedpeople. He wrote that "the men were held at the Big Black River and recruited into regiments while the women and children were permitted to come into Vicksburg where they were furnished such quarters as could be found. Most of them had to take the open air for their cover and take such food as they could get. Poor things, they will die off rapidly" (Stockton Diary, March 4, 1864). Unable to feed themselves or even find shelter, they languished until the U.S. organized relief efforts and set up a bureaucracy to address their needs.

For those who remained on the plantations far removed from the Union army's line of march, and unwilling to flee, emancipation came later rather than sooner. For black in Galveston, Texas, freedom came when Union General Gordon Granger's troops landed on June 19, 1865. Today it is celebrated around the country as *Juneteenth.* Some Confederates resisted emancipation as late as July 1865. Samuel Glyde Swain, a Union officer who served in Mississippi during the latter half of the war, wrote to his brother the summer after the war ended, remarking that "it will require the presence of troops through the country for some time yet to make the citizens through the country respect the Emancipation Proclamation." He based his opinion on the fact some Southerners were engaging in violence against freedpeople, "trying to keep up slavery by force, practicing greater cruelties upon the negroes than ever before the war" (July 26, 1865).

BIBLIOGRAPHY

General Joseph Stockton Diary, Chicago Historical Society.

Library of Congress, *Born in Slavery: Slave Narratives from the Federal Writers' Project, 1936–1938,* Georgia Narratives, vol. 4, part 3, "A Talk with G. W. Pattillo, Ex-Slave." Available from http://memory.loc.gov/ammem/snhtml/snhome.html.

Library of Congress, *Born in Slavery: Slave Narratives from the Federal Writers' Project, 1936–1938,* Missouri Narratives, vol. 10, William Black. Available from http://memory.loc.gov/ammem/snhtml/snhome.html.

Library of Congress, *Born in Slavery: Slave Narratives from the Federal Writers' Project, 1936–1938,* North Carolina Narratives, vol. 11, part 2, Caroline Richardson. Available from http://memory.loc.gov/ammem/snhtml/snhome.html.

Library of Congress, *Born in Slavery: Slave Narratives from the Federal Writers' Project, 1936–1938,* Texas Narratives, vol. 16, part 2, Mattie Gilmore. Available from http://memory.loc.gov/ammem/snhtml/snhome.html.

New York Herald, January 7, 1863.

Samuel Glyde Swain Papers, Wisconsin Historical Society.

Washington, Booker T. *Up From Slavery: An Autobiography*, Garden City, NY: Doubleday & Company, Inc., 1901.

David H. Slay

Reconciliation and Remembrance

■ Reconciliation and Remembrance Overview

By the early twentieth century, the United States had experienced a significant degree of sectional reconciliation. The scenes of aged veterans of the opposing sides greeting one another amicably on the battlefields over which they had once fought were touching, and the nation reveled in its burgeoning strength and returning unity of spirit. Yet the reunion was gained at the price of granting the South a negotiated half-victory despite its complete defeat on the battlefields of the Civil War.

White Southerners had launched their bid for independence in 1861 with the goal of preserving slavery. Though only about 25 percent of white Southern families owned slaves at any one time, far more than that percentage had actively and enthusiastically supported the Confederacy and the cause of slavery because the slave system offered more than mere economic benefits for those wealthy enough to own slaves. Its added dividend for white Southerners, frequently touted in political speeches throughout the prewar era, was that it kept blacks in an inferior position and assured a status of social superiority for whites, along with an imaginary equality among all whites. Many a non-slaveholding white farmer soldiered four long years in the Confederate army at least in part because he feared that Union victory and emancipation would bring him into a position of social equality with an ethnic group he feared and despised.

Union victory did indeed bring emancipation, finally cemented and made national by the Thirteenth Amendment, but the white Southerners who had just surrendered on the battlefield set out immediately afterward to insure that the demise of their slaveholders' republic did not bring about the black social and civil equality they had feared. The conventional war that had just ended now was re-born as a low-intensity conflict, with night-riding groups such as the Ku Klux Klan waging a long, wearying terrorist campaign against blacks and their white allies. The struggle, known as Reconstruction, dragged on for three times as long as the conventional war had lasted. The Northern populace grew tired of political conflict. First there had been the long decades of strife over slavery that had led to the Civil War, then the blood-drenched years of the war itself, and finally this twelve-year twilight struggle waged against foes who went about wearing the cloak of state-rights, local control, and self-determination by day—and sheets by night.

Meanwhile, Southern writers, beginning with Richmond newspaper editor Edward A. Pollard, started building the mythology of what Pollard was first to call "the Lost Cause." Within the Lost Cause myth, the Confederacy, though defeated, had fought for truth, justice, and righteousness—the cause of God and of Robert E. Lee, if the latter two were to be differentiated at all. Slavery had been a benevolent institution, according to the myth, but the Confederacy had not fought for slavery but rather for state-rights, or agrarian virtues, or, most vaguely of all, for the Southern "way of life." The North, in contrast, was the lair of low-flung, money-grubbing oppressors who lusted for the economic destruction of their virtuous and genteel betters in the South.

For its part, the North had never been politically unified and now found itself much more divided than the South. Some Northerners had been opposed even to waging a war to preserve the Union, and a still larger Northern minority had dissented from emancipation. Such consensus as there had ever been in favor of full civil rights for the newly freed slaves was even more fragile. During the years of Reconstruction, Southern resistance finally overcame the North's tenuous commitment to racial equality. In 1877 Reconstruction formally ended with the withdrawal of the last federal troops from the Southern states.

During the decade that followed, blacks disappeared from government in the Southern states as well as from the congressional delegations of those states. Black voting rights and civil rights winked out, and by the 1890s the former slaves and their descendents faced a system of second-class citizenship known as "Jim Crow." Southern whites had regained uncontested supremacy within their states, and the threat of black social equality was safely banished for the foreseeable future.

It was no coincidence that the 1890s was also the decade that saw the great surge of sectional reconciliation. The movement was based on the tacit willingness of Northerners, who had already, as a group, abandoned the political fortunes of African Americans, to accept key elements of the Lost Cause Myth. In the new Reconciliationist version of the Civil War, both sides had fought nobly for their own equally noble causes; Southern troops had, perhaps, been somewhat braver and more heroic than their Northern conquerors; Robert E. Lee was a great American; and slavery had had nothing whatever to do with the war. White Southerners, for their part, would allow that it was for the best, all things considered, that the United States had remained united. It was on these terms that veterans in the 1890s began to hold joint reunions and other graphic expressions of sectional reconciliation. With the causes of the war forgotten, its bitterness could fade as well.

There were additional reasons for the upsurge of reconciliation and remembrance during the 1890s. Many of the war's senior participants were coming to the end of their lives. Jefferson Davis died in 1889, and his funeral and celebrated re-interment several years later were the occasions of massive outpourings of Southern devotion to the memory of the Confederacy. General Philip H. Sheridan had died in 1888, his fellow general William Tecumseh Sherman in 1891, Joseph E. Johnston a few weeks later, and Pierre G. T. Beauregard in 1893. The deaths reminded veterans of the great events they had been through and of their own mortality. More of them became interested in marking and preserving the battlefields where they had fought a quarter of a century before. In a country in which fewer and fewer people could remember the momentous events of the 1860s, men who had been soldiers in those years found that they had strong bonds in common with others who had marched in the ranks during the war, even if they had fought for the other side.

Still more reasons for reconciliation were provided by the Spanish-American War. The country pulled together to defeat a foreign foe. Evidence of the new unity could be found among the generals of the volunteer troops who went to fight in Cuba in 1898, two of whom had previously been generals in the Confederate army. One of them, the dashing cavalry leader Joseph Wheeler, on seeing Spanish troops falling back before his advancing soldiers momentarily so far forgot himself as to shout to his men, "Come on, boys! We've got the d—— Yankees on the run!" Even after the Spanish-American War a ripening popular awareness of America's growing power and prominence in a world that seemed both exciting and dangerous encouraged Americans to embrace nationalism, even at the expense of forgetting what their fathers had fought for in the Civil War.

Steven E. Woodworth

■ The Lost Cause

While the Civil War occupies a central place in U.S. history and culture, the legacies of the war have been the subject of considerable debate. The cultural memory of the war, or the ways in which people collectively have understood and represented the Civil War, have never been homogenous, static, or inextricable from the politics of the present (Blight 2002, p. 1). Over the years, multiple and often conflicting interpretations of the war have battled to dominate Americans' understanding of the ultimate meaning of this climactic event in their nation's past (Blight 2001, p. 2).

Confederate Mythology

In an atmosphere of demoralization in the years immediately following the war, former Confederates sought to justify the South's secession and defeat in a catastrophic war. Nearly every aspect of this so-called Lost Cause account of the war has been refuted by contemporary scholars, with the exception of the fact that the Union fielded a higher number of soldiers than the Confederacy (Waugh 2004, p. 17; McPherson 2004, p. 73; Gallagher 2004, p. 58). Yet with its white supremacist underpinnings, the myth of the Lost Cause thrived in the era of Jim Crow. And well into the twentieth century, the myth eclipsed the emancipationist interpretation of the war, which can be defined as understanding the conflict as the reestablishment of the American republic and the admission of black people to citizenship and political equality (Blight 2001, p. 2).

Adherents of the Lost Cause hold that the Southern states seceded and waged war in defense of states' rights, not slavery; that despite being vastly outnumbered and undersupplied, the Confederate Army fought heroically in the face of overwhelming odds and inevitable defeat; that despite the loss, the integrity of the struggle is preserved through the veneration of military leaders, especially Robert E. Lee. Variants of the Lost Cause myth also recycled antebellum defenses of slavery. While maintaining that slavery was neither the cause nor the central political issue of the war, Lost Cause ideologues insisted that slavery had been a benevolent institution (Nolan 2000, pp. 11–31; Waugh 2004, pp. 15–16).

The latter item of propaganda was and remains impossible to reconcile with the personal testimonies of former slaves and the well-documented history of slave rebellions, fugitive escapes, and smaller-scale forms of

Horace Greeley (1811–1872), editor of *The New York Tribune* and author of *The American Conflict.* As later generations revisited Civil War history, many Southerners tried to explain their defeat by refocusing the purpose of the war. Perhaps the primary reason for the conflict, the abolition of slavery, was downplayed in favor of remembering the Civil War as a battle over states' rights. *AP Images.*

day-to-day resistance by enslaved people before the Civil War. It likewise fails to account for the masses of bondspeople who freed themselves during the war by fleeing to Union lines and joining the service of the army that fought their enslavers. According to the historian Alan Nolan, the Lost Cause version of the war is a caricature largely made possible by its misleading picture of slavery and of African Americans. This caricature, he continues, removes African Americans from their central role in the war and makes them historically irrelevant (Nolan 2000, p. 27). Nolan highlighted three issues that he considered the ultimate stakes of the Civil War: the nation's territorial and political integrity; the "survival of the democratic process"; and human freedom (p. 27).

Northern Histories of the War

The third point is what emancipationist interpreters understood to be the most important result of the war, the most significant memory of the war, and the central subject of African American celebrations of Emancipation Day after the war. But by that time, however, the contest over the meaning of the war had already begun to take shape. Several multivolume war histories sold on subscription during the 1860s were marketed as keepsakes that provided a more "permanent" history than newspapers. The first of these was written by John S. C. Abbott (1805–1877), a Congregationalist minister and historian. It was distributed in April 1863, roughly halfway through the war it purported to commemorate (Fahs 1998, p. 118). The editor of the *New York Tribune*, Horace Greeley (1811–1872), followed Abbott's work with his own history in 1864. Both Abbott and Greeley understood the Civil War to be about slavery, but their histories, particularly the second volumes published soon after the war's end, offer a preview of the way in which the Lost Cause interpretation would ultimately combine with other forces to stake its claims to the memory of the war. In the first volume of his *History of the Civil War in America,* John Abbott writes:

> From the commencement of our government there have been two antagonistic principles contending for the mastery—Slavery and Freedom ... But freedom has outstripped slavery in this race. And consequently, the slaveholders, unreconciled to the loss of supremacy, strive to destroy the temple of liberty ... This conflict in which our nation is now involved, is simply a desperate struggle, on the part of the slaveholders, to retain by force of arms that domination in the government of the Republic, which they had so long held, and which, by natural operation of the ballot box, they were slowly but surely losing ... This slaveholding rebellion is the greatest crime on earth. (Abbott 1863, pp. iii–iv)

Personally, Abbott rejected biological arguments about racial difference, which placed him toward the radical end of the era's racial thought (Fahs 1998, p. 116). And Abbott's introduction casts the war in terms that would resonate in the emancipationist memory of the war. Indeed he cited emancipation as the most important outcome of the war. But Abbott largely relegated the history of slavery, emancipation, and black military service to the end of his text.

The literary historian Alice Fahs suggests that Abbott curbed his own radicalism in order to sell more books to a wider audience (Fahs 1998, p. 116). These same market imperatives may have led Abbott to apply his characteristically florid language to describe Lee's surrender as a sentimental reunion of the opposing sides. A scene of Union troops saluting passing Confederate soldiers as they stacked arms concludes with the assurance that former animosities would be set aside and that "the Union was secured for ages to come ... we had emerged from the conflict with an established nationality ... " (p. 593). Already in Abbott's work emancipationist themes receive less emphasis, with greater evidence of a reconciliation theme that would grow in Civil War memory of the war. But exactly who was included in this reunion and national identity that Abbott praised would become another contested aspect of Civil War memory.

Like Abbott, Horace Greeley understood slavery as the cause of the conflict. Unlike Abbott, however, Greeley made the history of slavery in the United States the focus of the first volume of his Civil War history. Greeley's text argues that the Civil War was the inevitable result of slavery and emancipation the inevitable result of the war. Arguments of inevitability are poor substitutes for attention to historical process and should almost always be regarded with suspicion. But even more curious is Greeley's treatment of Lee's surrender. Though more matter-of-fact about the event than Abbott, Greeley writes, "The Rebel Army of Virginia had *not* failed." They had rather, fought "sternly against the Inevitable" and "proved unable to succeed where success would have been a calamity..." (Greeley 1867, p. 745). That Greeley tempers the defeat with a valorization of Confederate soldiers anticipates a trend in war remembrance literature that acquired new prominence in the 1880s.

In *The American Conflict* (1864–1867), Greeley may have been motivated by the philosophy of reunification that he espoused at the end of the war, which he summarized as "magnanimity in triumph" (Fahs 1998, p. 119). According to Greeley, "What we ask is that the President say, in effect, 'Slavery having, through rebellion, committed suicide, let the North and the South unite to bury its carcass and then clasp hands across the grave.'" (Fahs 1998, p. 119). Greeley might also have had in mind the farewell speech Lee gave his troops in General Order No. 9, which begins, "After four years of arduous service, marked by unsurpassed courage and fortitude, the Army of Northern Virginia has been compelled to yield to overwhelming numbers and resources" (Gallagher 2005, p. 40). In the years that followed, purveyors of the Lost Cause would seize upon arguments based on "overwhelming numbers and resources" and inevitability to justify their defeat, just as they would fetishize the Southern soldiers' valor to mitigate their loss.

Southern Histories of the War

While Abbott's and Greeley's histories showed signs of reconciliationist impulses, the Southern journalist Edward A. Pollard (1832–1872) urged the necessity of Southerners writing their own histories of the conflict. Pollard, who published his own multivolume series during the war, wrote in his fourth volume of the *Southern History of the War* that "the very fact that the war has gone against them makes it more important that [the South's] records should not fall entirely to the pens of [its] enemies" (Pollard 1866, p. 4). Later the same year, Pollard published *Lost Cause: A New Southern History of the War.* Part popular history, part manifesto, the book comprehensively stated the Confederate perspectives of the war. David Blight has argued that the Lost Cause was initially a byproduct of grief but that the ideology soon sought to gain control of the nation's collective memory (Blight 2002, p. 261).

As Pollard's writings illustrate, that desire to control the historical memory of the Civil War was inextricably bound to the politics of race and Reconstruction. Pollard conceded that the war decided emancipation and restoration of the Union but also insisted that the war did not decide issues of racial equality or African American suffrage. In the supplement to the second edition of *The Lost Cause*, Pollard seethed against the extension of full citizenship rights to African Americans, which occurred at the same time that Reconstruction policies banned former Confederates from voting. In his 1868 political tract *The Lost Cause Regained*, Pollard prescribed limited reconciliation with Northerners but on the condition of "securing the supremacy of the white man" (Blight 2001, p. 260).

Search for Historical Neutrality

While Lost Cause spokespersons espoused their ideology in a bid to control cultural memory, white Northerners grew increasingly weary of the war and the political battles of Reconstruction. By 1881, when the federal government published the first installment of *Official Records of the War of the Rebellion*, the series was notable not only for its sheer volume but also for the official editorial policy that aimed for a balanced nonpolitical representation (Waugh 2004, pp. 21–22). This decision by the War Records Office to include the offical records of both Union and Confederate armies and to employ veterans from both sides in the compilation signaled a growing tendency to interpret the war in the least controversial way (Waugh 2004, p. 22). More and more, the idea that Confederates went to war in defense of slavery and that the Union army was an instrument of liberation for four million slaves became an embarrassment to white Southerners and thus a hindrance to sectional reconciliation. Consequently, the presence and the roles of African Americans were minimized or ignored entirely in cultural representations of the war (Waugh 2004, p. 22).

As popular remembrance increasingly stripped the Civil War of its ideological contexts, the focus shifted to celebrations of the heroic soldier. In 1884 *Century*, a general-interest magazine of the period, launched its "Battles and Leaders of the Civil War," an enormously popular series of battle narratives submitted by veterans of the conflict. The announcement of the series, which appeared in the October 1884 issue, pledged that most articles would be written by the generals who had commanded troops in the featured battles. The publishers expected that the series would "prove of lasting value to the history of the most eventful period of our national life." But to avert the appearance of sectional partisanship and avoid offending subscribers, the *Century*'s readers were assured that "it is not a part of the plan of the series to go over the ground of the official reports and campaign controversies, but ... to clear up cloudy questions with new knowledge and the wisdom of cool reflection" (October 1884, p. 943).

For such a publication, declared the editors' announcement of the series, "No time could be fitter ... than the present ... when the passions and prejudices of the Civil War have nearly faded out of politics, and its heroic events are passing into our common history where motives will be weighed without malice, and valor praised without distinction of uniform" (October 1884, p. 943). David Blight maintains that the *Century* editors had structured the series as a celebration of the valor of soldiers on both sides in order to further reconciliation; the articles were silent on the causes and consequences of the war or the subjects of race and slavery (Blight 2001, p. 175). If the "passions and prejudices," which the editors had implicitly defined in sectional terms, had faded, it was due to a growing tendency to remember the Civil War apart from its ideological context and to put aside the still-divisive issues of race, slavery, emancipation, and African American civil rights. All in all, the *Century* series indicated that the "common history" was increasingly interpreted from the perspective of white males—not an inclusive interpretation but it was becoming increasingly masculine and increasingly white (Fahs 2004, pp. 84–85).

Alternative Views

The abolitionist orator and newspaper editor Frederick Douglass (1818–1895), who had escaped from slavery in Maryland, had always conceived the Civil War to be a war of emancipation, and what he recognized as a dismissal of the emancipationist view of the war deeply offended his sense of justice, as it threatened the fruits of his life's work. Douglass noted the national tendency to forget slavery and secession as well as the side effects of devotion to the Lost Cause, which prompted him to declare, "It may be said that Americans have no memories ... We look over to the House of Representatives and see the Solid South enthroned there; we listen with calmness to eulogies of the South and of traitors and forget Andersonville ... We see colored citizens shot down and driven from the ballot box, and forget the services rendered by the colored troops in the late war for the Union" (Blight 1989, p. 232).

There were exceptions to the trends that so incensed Douglass regarding the cultural memory of the Civil War—notably in the *Personal Memoirs* of Ulysses S. Grant, published in two volumes in 1885 and 1886. Not surprisingly, Grant devoted much of the work to his military experience, and he did conclude with a prophecy of sectional reunion. But he also stated unequivocally in his conclusion to the second volume, "The cause of the great War of the Rebellion will have to be attributed to slavery" (Grant 1886, p. 539). Rejecting the popular narrative that depicted the motivations of both sides as equally honorable, Grant insisted on the rightness of Northern action against slavery. He described the Fugitive Slave law, which required the return of fugitives to their former bondage, as a "degradation," and maintained that "the National government ... had to be enlisted in the cause of this institution" (Grant 1886, p. 544; Waugh 2004, p. 27).

Writing History in the 1880s

But the most widespread depictions of the war in the 1880s borrowed from the mythology of the Lost Cause. The strategy of sectional reconciliation through mutual acknowledgment of the soldiers' valor echoed the South's esteem of the soldier. And the growing willingness to forget emancipationist politics reflected the Lost Cause's denial of the evils of slavery and the reality of African Americans' roles in the war. These tendencies were not the natural effects of passing time, as the *Century* editors suggested, tempered by the "cool wisdom of reflection." Rather, as the purveyors of the Lost Cause expressed their own version of the Civil War through literature, public monuments, Memorial Day ceremonies and the like, they also attempted to influence the production and adoption of school textbooks. Letter-writing campaigns persuaded Northern publishers to excise content objectionable to Southerners (McPherson 2005, pp. 64–78). The criteria for what these activists found acceptable is reflected in a guide to textbook adoption committees that advised the rejection of any book that "says the South fought to hold her slaves," "speaks of the slaveholder of the South as cruel and unjust," "glorifies Abraham Lincoln and vilifies Jefferson Davis," or "omits to tell of the South's heroes and their deeds" (McPherson 2005, p. 72).

The long reach of the Lost Cause narrative is evidenced in an 1896 article in *Century* that departed from the editorial policy reflected in the "Battles and Leaders of the Civil War" series. The piece, which was written by the son of a Confederate veteran, attempts to answer the question posed by its title: "Why the Confederacy Failed." The apparently novel answer posed by the author was the "excessive issue of paper money" and misuse of the Confederate cavalry. But having been schooled in the romance of the Lost Cause, the author felt compelled to acknowledge the widely held answer he was attempting to revise. The probable response to the question he had undertaken was either that "America was designed by almighty Providence for one great nation" or "if he is a Southerner, that the South was overpowered by the superior numbers and resources of the North" (November 1896, p. 33).

The effect of the Lost Cause on family experience was recalled by a Southern writer, Katharine Du Pre Lumpkin (1897–1988), whose father had served in the Confederate army at the age of 15 and indoctrinated his children in the mythology of the Lost Cause. He often invoked a popular phrase that suggested the Lost Cause was a kind of secular religion. According to Lumpkin, "his wife taught the children prayers, he taught them to revere the Lost Cause... we were certainly reared, each of us in turn, to revere the veterans of that period and to do everything we could to help them" (Lumpkin 1975, pp. 3–4).

But Lumpkin's early education later affected her study of Southern social history, particularly the history of slavery, which had been "unknown" to her. "I had to—by reason of my upbringing . . . really go back and re-do, for myself," she recalled. "I had to relearn from the sources, because my picture is the one . . . that I was reared in" (Lumpkin 1974, p. 66).

When asked to characterize her father in a 1974 interview, Lumpkin replied, "I would say he was a man torn between the past and the present, perhaps. Never having given up the past" (Lumpkin 1974, p. 3). For Lumpkin's father, as with many others of its devotees, the Lost Cause was a refuge from the stresses of military defeat and social change (Blight 2001, p. 266). But at the same time the Lost Cause also provided ammunition for those determined to prevent black people from obtaining equality (Blight 2002, p. 266).

In Richard Wright's autobiography *Black Boy,* first published in 1945, eighty years after the war, the author recalled his grandfather, who escaped from a slaveholder during the Civil War, then joined the Union Army, and stood military guard as the newly enfranchased freedmen cast their first ballots during Reconstruction. According to Wright, when radical Reconstruction ended and the freedpeople were "driven from political power" by the efforts of white supremacists, "his [grandfather's] spirit had been crushed" (Wright 1993 [1945], p. 40). Wright also suggested a link between the politics of white supremacy and the memory of the Civil War. The litany of tabooed subjects that Southern white men did not like to discuss with African Americans, according to Wright, included "the entire northern part of the United States; the Civil War; Abraham Lincoln; U.S. Grant; General Sherman . . . the Republican party; slavery; social equality... .the 13th, 14th, and 15th Amendments to the Constitution; or any topic calling for positive knowledge or manly self-assertion on the part of the Negro" (p. 231).

As the United States commemorated the war's centennial in the 1960s, the writer Robert Penn Warren observed, "The Civil War is, for the American imagination, the greatest single event of our history (Grow 2003, p. 77). But even as he wrote, the observances assumed the character of a racially divided country in the midst of another political revolution. And though the discredited Lost Cause has lost much of its former influence, it still persists, along with disputes over the memory of the war. Not the least of these battles concerned the display of Confederate flags, many of which were raised over Southern capitols during the centennial observances but not lowered afterward (Wiener 2004, pp. 237–253).

BIBLIOGRAPHY

Abbott, John S.C. *History of the Civil War in America*, 2 vols. Springfield, MA: G. Bill, 1863–1866.

"Battles and Leaders of the Civil War." *Century: A Popular Monthly.* October 1884, 943–944.

Blight, David W. *Beyond the Battlefield: Race, Memory and the American Civil War.* Amherst: University of Massachusetts Press, 2002.

Blight, David W. *Frederick Douglass' Civil War: Keeping Faith in Jubilee.* Baton Rouge: Louisiana State University Press, 1989.

Blight, David W. *Race and Reunion: The Civil War in Cultural Memory.* Cambridge, MA: Belknap Press of Harvard University Press, 2001.

Fahs, Alice. "The Market Value of Memory: Popular War Histories and the Northern Literary Marketplace, 1861–1868." *Book History* 1, no. 1 (1998): 107–139.

Fahs, Alice. "Remembering the Civil War in Children's Literature of the 1880s and 1890s." In *The Memory of the Civil War in American Culture,* eds. Alice Fahs and Joan Waugh. Chapel Hill: University of North Carolina Press, 2004.

Gallagher, Gary W. "Shaping Public Memory of the Civil War: Robert E. Lee, Jubal A. Early, and Douglas Southall Freeman." In *The Memory of the Civil War in American Culture,* eds. Alice Fahs and Joan Waugh. Chapel Hill: University of North Carolina Press, 2004.

Grant, Ulysses S. *Personal Memoir of U. S. Grant*, 2 vols. New York: C. L. Webster & Company, 1885–1886.

Greeley, Horace. *The American Conflict: A History of the Great Rebellion in the United States of America, 1860-65*, 2 vols. Hartford, CT: O.D. Case & Company, 1864–1867.

Grow, Matthew. "The Shadow of the Civil War: A Historiography of Civil War Memory." *Nineteenth Century History* [Great Britain] 4, no. 2 (2003): 77–103.

Lumpkin, Katharine Du Pre. Interview conducted by Jacquelyn Hall, August 4, 1974. *Documenting the American South*, University Library, University of North Carolina at Chapel Hill. Available online at http://docsouth.unc.edu/sohp/G-0034/.

McConnell, Stuart. "Epilogue: The Geography of Memory." In *The Memory of the Civil War in American Culture,* eds. Alice Fahs and Joan Waugh. Chapel Hill: University of North Carolina Press, 2004.

McPherson, James M. "Long-Legged Yankee Lies: The Southern Textbook Crusade." In *The Memory of the Civil War in American Culture,* eds. Alice Fahs and Joan Waugh. Chapel Hill: University of North Carolina Press, 2004.

Nolan, Alan T. "The Anatomy of a Myth." In *The Myth of the Lost Cause and Civil War History*, eds. Gary W. Gallagher and Alan T. Nolan. Bloomington: Indiana University Press, 2000.

Pollard, Edward A. *The Lost Cause: A New Southern History of the War of the Confederates.* New York: E. B. Treat and Company, 1866.

Pollard, Edward A. *Southern History of the War: Last Year of the War*, 4 vols. New York: Charles B. Richardson, 1863–1866.

Waugh, Joan. "Ulysses S. Grant, Historian." In *The Memory of the Civil War in American Culture,* eds. Alice Fahs and Joan Waugh. Chapel Hill: University of North Carolina Press, 2004.

"Why the Confederacy Failed." *The Century: A Popular Quarterly,* November 1896, 33–38.

Wiener, Jon. "The Civil War Centennial in Context, 1960–1965." In *The Memory of the Civil War in American Culture*, eds. Alice Fahs and Joan Waugh. Chapel Hill: University of North Carolina Press, 2004.

Wright, Richard. *Black Boy: (American Hunger): A Record of Childhood and Youth.* New York: Harper Perennial, 1993 [1945].

Christina Adkins

■ The Reconciliation Movement

The American Civil War ended in April 1865, but the debate over the political, social, and economic repercussions of the war continued well into the next century. The devastating effects of the war and questions regarding the status of former slaves divided Northerners and Southerners, often resulting in further bloodshed. Even during Reconstruction, white Americans began to seek common ground on which they could unite and forget the pain and loss of war. The reconciliation movement was an effort to obscure the legacy of emancipation and black participation in the war in favor of remembering the conflict as a fight between white Americans, Northern and Southern, which ultimately proved the honor and dignity of both sides.

Reconciliation downplayed the violence of battle, the failure to secure civil rights for former slaves, the centrality of slavery to the conflict, and the opposition to the war in both the Union and the Confederacy. White veterans of both sides embraced this movement in the 1880s and 1890s, after the responsibility of enforcing Reconstruction had been turned over to the Southern state governments. Reconciliation hid the true nature and meaning of the war for many Americans for decades to come, at the cost of creating a narrative of the war that almost eliminated the emancipationist legacy that African American citizens valued.

The Lost Cause

Reuniting the nation was a difficult task, hampered by the changes to Southern society caused by emancipation and by continued white Southern resentment of Northern influence and the imposition of federal authority. The popular postwar song, "Oh, I'm a Good Ole Rebel," epitomizes the bitter feelings of some defeated Confederates. In the song, the former Confederate soldier laments that he can no longer fight, but proclaims, "I don't want no pardon for what I was and am, I won't be reconstructed and I don't care a damn!" (Silber 1995, pp. 256–257).

The process of crafting an acceptable Southern version of the war's meaning began the moment the conflict ended. In 1866, Edward Alfred Pollard wrote an account of the Civil War that emphasized the Southern perspective and coined the term "The Lost Cause." Pollard described North and South as being separate "civilizations" and downplayed the issue of slavery by describing it as "a convenient line of battle between the two sections" (Pollard 1866, p. 46). His argument avoided questions regarding the immorality of slavery and the legality of secession. Pollard's book was mainly a narrative of military events, in which he underscored the bravery and chivalry of the Confederates, especially Virginians.

The Lost Cause myth was solidified in 1873, when former Confederate Lieutenant General Jubal A. Early (1816–1894) became president of the Southern Historical Society. Early wrote several articles that attributed Confederate defeat to the numerical superiority and industrial might of the North instead of the waning support for war among Confederate civilians or the effects of the Emancipation Proclamation. Both Pollard and Early were advocates of forgetting the war's unpleasantness and reuniting as a nation—provided white Northerners accepted the Southern version of the war.

Published Reminiscences

The process of reconciliation was greatly accelerated by a wave of publications on the Civil War in the 1880s and 1890s. The war was far enough in the past by that time that Americans became interested in reading about the conflict. Union and Confederate veterans wrote about their experiences, often filtering their memories through the lens of time and popular concepts of war. Some of the first widely read accounts appeared in newspapers, but were later compiled into such volumes as the Philadelphia *Weekly Times*'s 800-page collection of articles by soldiers and civilians titled *Annals of the War*, which was published in 1879. *Century Magazine* also compiled articles into a volume of reminiscences published in 1887 called *Battles and Leaders of the Civil War.*

A leading historian of the reconciliation movement observed that the authors of these accounts "unabashedly declared their own pursuit of impartial 'truth' and 'facts'" (Blight 2001, p. 164). White Northerners and Southerners were equally complicit in rewriting the history of the war in such a way that African Americans were included in only the most peripheral roles. This literature began a national healing process but also perpetuated the myth of the loyal slave and the Lost Cause's

Jubal Anderson Early (1816–1894). Many white Americans preferred to focus on the battlefield exploits of both Union and Confederate troops and ignore the eventual end result of the conflict, abolition of slavery. President of the Southern Historical Society and a Lieutenant General for the South, Jubal Anderson Early promoted the practical reasons for Northern success, including greater manpower and manufacturing capabilities, over moral ones, such as the concept that all people should be free. *The Library of Congress.*

insistence that the war was not about the continuation or abolition of slavery.

The rise in public interest in the war caused some veterans to write regimental histories that emphasized bravery, heroics, and adventure, often leaving out the grim and gory details of battle. Oliver Christian Bosbyshell (b. 1839) documented his recollection of the war in his regimental history of the Forty-eighth Pennsylvania Infantry. Bosbyshell admitted that his memories "may be somewhat twinged with partiality . . . , but remember, it is the way that it came under my own observation" (Bosbyshell 1895, p. 14). R. M. Collins, a lieutenant in the Fifteenth Texas Infantry, recorded his wartime experience in 1893. The Confederate veteran's reminiscence featured a description of a singing contest between Union and Confederate soldiers, commenting that, "for the time Federals and Confederates were all one" (Collins 1893, p. 72). Like many veterans, Collins described white soldiers, Northern and Southern, as a brotherhood who would pass away and "answer to roll-call with Lee, Johnston, Bragg, Hood, Grant, Meade, Hancock, and the long unnumbered list of soldiers brave, who quit this life" (Collins 1893, p. 93). Collins's list of famous Union and Confederate generals indicates his belief that all soldiers had a common bond regardless of the side for which they had fought. This simplified understanding of soldiers' motivations glossed over the fact that resentment, condescension, and hatred often fueled the violence that had occurred on the battlefield.

Civilians also recounted their experiences and often used their stories to romanticize the war without placing any blame or fostering antagonism. Adelaide Smith (b. 1831) volunteered as a nurse during the war and published her story in 1911. Smith's first chapter, "A View of the Situation," contained the same simplistic explanation of the war's causes as many other Northern reminiscences. The former nurse began her narrative with the Confederates firing on Fort Sumter, without mentioning the events leading up to that day. To Smith the war was a tragic accident, which "caused the separation of hitherto devoted families" (Smith 1911, p. 11). The portrayal of the war as a family squabble, intense yet easily patched up, became popular in the writings of the reconciliation movement. Just like the war veterans who had seen battle, Smith was proud of the part she played in the conflict and declared, "I had done at least what I could in that fearful struggle to save our Union and glorious country" (Smith 1911, p. 263).

White Veterans' Reunions

Veterans played an essential role in reconciliation in the 1880s and 1890s, when white Union and Confederate veterans began to talk about forgiveness and unity. These veterans recognized one another's bravery and devotion, while conveniently forgetting the actual causes of the war. The Grand Army of the Republic (GAR), an organization of Union veterans, held meetings featuring speakers who promoted reconciliation. In Chicago, Illinois, the *Daily Inter Ocean* printed a summary of a GAR meeting on January 29, 1880. A GAR official summed up the reconciliationist sentiment growing within white veterans by stating that "long before the northern troops had marched back over the imaginary Mason and Dixon's Line, they had forgiven the soldiers of the South." The speaker continued by telling his fellow Union veterans that politicians were slow to forgive, but soldiers "did not wish to shake hands over a bloody chasm, but over a saved country" (January 29, 1880).

During the reconciliation movement, white Union and Confederate veterans gathered in major cities to remember past battles and celebrate the role they played in the fighting. In Atlanta, Georgia, exposition organizers invited 300 Union veterans to attend a reunion of the blue and gray on Kennesaw Mountain in 1887. *The*

Advertisement for a Civil War reunion, 1888. As the events of the Civil War became more distant, Confederate and Union veterans looked to remember the common experiences all soldiers shared during the war. Veterans' organizations hosted many such reunions at the end of the nineteenth century, inviting soldiers both Blue and Gray to celebrate their bravery on the battlefield. *© Corbis.*

Daily Inter Ocean informed its readers on August 28, 1887, of the event, pointing out that the day would include barbecues, fireworks, and tributes to both Union and Confederate generals (August 28, 1887). Many of the white veterans in Chicago who listened to the call for reconciliation from their brothers-in-arms found their former adversaries willing to return the sentiment. The news of these reunions spread across the nation, informing citizens of the results of these events. The *Wisconsin State Register* printed an article on September 24, 1887, that declared a blue and gray reunion in Evansville, Indiana, to be a huge success, with 10,000 Union and 3,000 Confederate veterans in attendance. Indiana's governor was present and expressed his feelings about the reunion's significance, stating that "the issues upon which that unfortunate struggle were based are buried" (September 24, 1887). As the news spread about veterans forgiving their former enemies, some Americans began to look at the war differently. White Americans could conveniently forget the causes of the war and the continuation of inequality in the South, but other Americans could not.

Black Veterans' Reunions

Black veterans also gathered in 1887, but their assemblies did not share the laudatory tone of the blue and gray reunions. In Boston, black veterans gathered and drafted statements declaring it "to be the duty of the government to remedy the evils, until the colored man shall have equal protection under the law." These statements were printed in *The Daily Inter Ocean* on August 3, 1887, shortly before the paper ran the article about the white veterans' reunion in Atlanta (August 3, 1887). Black Union veterans didn't ignore the efforts in the 1880s to rekindle the memories of the war, but they organized separate reunions that advanced their own understanding of the war's legacy. On June 18, 1887, the *New York Freeman* announced the meeting of black veterans and declared that, "it will do these noble survivors of the tremendous conflict which brought the race freedom and citizenship a vast deal of good to meet again in precious times of peace" (June 18, 1887). In spite of African American efforts to draw attention to black participation in the war, however, the reconciliation movement eventually rewrote the history of the war, omitting the centrality of slavery to the conflict and neglecting to mention the sacrifices of black soldiers.

Reconciliation and Segregation

As the movement for reconciliation strengthened among white veterans, black veterans were excluded from reunions and commemorations. The most prominent example is the fiftieth anniversary celebration of the Battle of Gettysburg, which organizers named the "Peace Jubilee." In 1913, around 53,000 white veterans attended this function, which celebrated the bravery of both Union and Confederate soldiers while ignoring the causes or consequences of the conflict. Although some participants claimed that there were black veterans present, there is no evidence of black GAR members in attendance. Instead, the event, like the nation at the time, was segregated. The only documented black participation was that of the hired laborers who distributed blankets and erected tents for the white veterans. On

July 3, 1913, Union and Confederate veterans of Pickett's charge reenacted the pivotal moment on the third-day of the Battle of Gettysburg by meeting at the infamous stone wall and shaking hands. This commemoration of the anniversary of the unsuccessful Confederate charge that ended the battle signaled the success of reconciliation and the establishment of the war as an apolitical moment in American history of which Southerners and Northerners could both be proud.

Reconciliation dictated that white Americans selectively remember the war, leaving out the aspects that contradicted the myth of the Lost Cause or invoked the legacy of emancipation and the struggle for civil rights. During the Peace Jubilee at Gettysburg, then-President Woodrow Wilson (1856–1924) gave a speech to the assembled veterans and spectators that reiterated the meaning of reconciliation. Wilson praised the healing brought about by peace, and proclaimed that "We have found one another again as brothers and comrades in arms, enemies no longer, generous friends rather, our battles long past, the quarrel forgotten—except that we shall not forget the splendid valour, the manly devotion of the men then arrayed against one another, now grasping hands and smiling into each others eyes" (Brown 2004, p. 21). Wilson was quick to proclaim an end to the feelings of hostility, but the event did not properly reflect the feelings of African Americans who had experienced the war.

It was no coincidence that so many white veterans embraced Gettysburg as a symbol of reconciliation. The battle was a Union victory but was also considered the high-water mark of the Confederacy because it was the most ambitious of the few Confederate offensives into Union territory. Moreover, the recently raised black Union regiments played no role in the fighting, enabling Southerners to emphasis the struggle between white Northerners and white Southerners, thereby conveniently forgetting that emancipation had been a major objective of the war. The agreement to celebrate Gettysburg as the ultimate battle of the war has led to the conclusion that the battle was the turning point upon which the war's conclusion ultimately hinged. The war continued for almost two years after Gettysburg; however, and the lengthy sieges of Vicksburg, Mississippi, in 1863 and Petersburg, Virginia, in 1864 and 1865 were arguably more decisive in bringing the war to a close. Nonetheless, Confederate veterans commemorated Gettysburg as the crucial moment of the war when rebel troops advanced against overwhelming odds and courageously stood their ground against a larger force.

Monuments and Memorials

Reconciliation was also a visible process that changed the American landscape, often paying homage to famous generals and important battles while glossing over the war's devastation and the lack of equality and freedoms for black Southerners. Monuments were initially placed on battlefields by veterans and community groups to commemorate the participation of soldiers from a particular state or locality. As the reconciliation movement grew, state and local governments also built monuments to commemorate the soldiers. On April 7, 1898, the *Milwaukee Sentinel* announced the completion of a bronze monument depicting Wisconsin soldiers charging into battle, with one soldier taking up the regimental colors from a fallen comrade. Like most monuments, this show of pride in the soldiers who fought and died was not a threat to reconciliation but rather a depiction of the shared glorification of the war. The newspaper article noted that in order to raise the $30,000 needed to pay for the monument, a collection of autographs, sketches, and quotes would be available for purchase. This commemorative album included comments from Southern officials, and the *Milwaukee Sentinel's* editor commented that "It is certainly a sign of the times when ex-Confederates are contributing to the success of a monument to Union soldiers." A Virginia congressman wrote in that album that "a soldier of the Old Dominion in the war between the states, a representative of the suffering and heroic people of Richmond, Va., wishes you success in commemorating your heroic slain." When Northerners celebrated battlefield heroics, they were acknowledging the Southern contention that the war was primarily a military event without any political or social dimensions. The Virginia veteran asserted the legitimacy of the Confederacy by referring to the conflict as "the War between the States" instead of using the name Northerners preferred—"the War of Rebellion." As white Northerners and Southerners reconciled by remembering the war as a disagreement between Northern and Southern states, the debate over the roles of slavery and secession was effectively silenced.

White Southerners made a conscious effort to recast the meaning of the war by celebrating Confederate military leadership as the embodiment of Southern honor and sense of duty. Proponents of reconciliation chose General Robert E. Lee (1807–1870) as the representative of the Confederacy instead of former Confederate President Jefferson Davis (1808–1889), whose prewar career as a planter and slave owner undermined the Lost Cause interpretation of the war's origins. Although some white Northerners scorned Confederate commemorations as romanticizing treason, many white Northerners accepted and admired commemorations of Lee. When the city of Richmond, Virginia, unveiled a prominent equestrian statue of Lee, Northern newspapers commented on the significance of the event. The *New York Times* reported that although Lee chose loyalty to his state over loyalty to his country, "There is no question at all that his conduct throughout the war, and after it, was that of a brave and honorable man" (Brown 2004, p. 98). The *Minneapolis Tribune* used the opportunity to criticize Lee because "at the time when his services were most needed he deserted his post and took up arms against his country." The editors of the *Tribune*, however, admitted that "the Lee cult is much in vogue, even in the North, in these days" (Brown 2004, p. 97).

The movement for reconciliation met resistance, but those who sought to romanticize and depoliticize the Civil War eventually won the battle for the war's meaning. Most of the nation forgot the sacrifices of black soldiers and the efforts of slaves to realize their freedom. For white Northerners, the failures of Reconstruction faded away and the Civil War became a renewed source of pride. Meanwhile, white Southerners took satisfaction in the fact that despite technical defeat, the reconciliationist history of the war and its causes had been written by the Confederacy.

BIBLIOGRAPHY

Blight, David W. *Race and Reunion: The Civil War in American Memory.* Cambridge, MA: Belknap Press of Harvard University Press, 2001.

Bosbyshell, Oliver Christian. *The 48th in the War: Being a Narrative of the Campaigns of the 48th Regiment, Infantry, Pennsylvania Veteran Volunteers, during the War of the Rebellion.* Philadelphia: Avil Printing Company, 1895.

Brown, Thomas J. *The Public Art of Civil War Commemoration: A Brief History with Documents.* New York: Bedford/St. Martin's, 2004.

Collins, R. M., Lieut. 15th Texas Infantry. *Chapters from the Unwritten History of the War between the States, or, the Incidents in the Life of a Confederate Soldier.* St. Louis: Nixon-Jones Printing Co., 1893.

"Colored Veterans The Boston Convention—Southern Outrages on Negro Citizens Deplored" in *The Daily Inter-Ocean*, (Chicago, IL) Wednesday, August 3, 1887, pg. 7, Issue 132, col. C.

"The Colored Veterans' Reunion" in *The New York Freeman*, Saturday, June 18, 1887, issue 31, col A.

Fahs, Alice, and Joan Waugh, eds. *The Memory of the Civil War in American Culture.* Chapel Hill: University of North Carolina Press, 2004.

"Feds and Bonfeds Fraternizing: Great Success of the Evansville Blue and Gray Reunion" in *The Wisconsin State Register*, (Portage, WI) Saturday, September 24, 1887, issue 32, col. E.

Foster, Gaines M. *Ghosts of the Confederacy: Defeat, the Lost Cause, and the Emergence of the New South, 1865 to 1913.* New York: Oxford University Press, 1987.

"Milwaukee's Monument to be Erected in Memory of her Sons Fallen in the Civil War" in *The Milwaukee Sentinel*, Thursday, April 7, 1898, issue 9, col. A.

Pollard, Edward Alfred. *The Lost Cause: A New Southern History of the War of the Confederates.* New York: E. B. Treat & Co., 1866.

Reardon, Carol. *Pickett's Charge in History and Memory.* Chapel Hill: University of North Carolina Press, 1997.

"Reunited Veterans Annual Encampment of the Illinois Department of the Grand Army of the Republic" in *The Daily Inter Ocean*, (Chicago, IL) Thursday, January 29, 1880, pg. 3, issue 257, col. A.

Shackel, Paul A. *Memory in Black and White: Race, Commemoration, and the Post-Bellum Landscape.* Walnut Creek, CA: Altamira Press, 2003.

Silber, Irwin, ed. *Songs of the Civil War.* New York: Dover, 1995.

Smith, Adelaide W. *Reminiscences of an Army Nurse during the Civil War.* New York: Greaves Publishing Company, 1911.

"The South to the North: Piedmont Exposition Directors Invite Old Soldiers to a Reunion of Blue and Gray" in *The Daily Inter Ocean*, (Chicago, IL) Sunday, August 28, 1887, issue 157, col. E.

Stephen Rockenbach

■ Veterans

Fighting in the U.S. Civil War drew to a close during the spring and early summer months of 1865. By June 1865 all Confederate armies had surrendered. General Ulysses S. Grant wrote, "The surrender of the rebel armies and the collapse of the rebellion rendered a large part of our military force unnecessary" (Simon 1967, vol. 15, p. 357). Hundreds of thousands of Union soldiers and their Confederate counterparts were demobilized and disbanded in a matter of months. Never before in U.S. history had an army been comprised of so many volunteers; at the end of hostilities, troops needed immediate, efficient release and safe transport home. As one Union soldier wrote in a May 1865 diary entry, "the dismantling of this mighty engine of war; of returning this 'citizen army' to its legitimate and proper field of action ... is an Herculean task" (Lane 1905, p. 264).

Establishment of Veterans' Organizations

Ulysses S. Grant, general-in-chief of all U.S. armies, reported to Secretary of War Edwin Stanton in October 1865 that an impressive 800,000 Union troops transitioned "from the army to civil life so quietly that it was scarcely known, save by the welcomes to their homes, received by them" (Simon 1967, vol. 15, pp. 357–358). One officer's wife observed that "in a few brief weeks the thousands who had followed the life of soldiers laid aside their accoutrements of war and took up the implements of peace, dissolving into citizens as rapidly as they had become soldiers" (Logan 1913, p. 200). "It became necessary to dissolve all organization in a few days," a Confederate surrendering at Appomattox remarked, and although his brigade "kept somewhat together, for a day or two, we

A Civil War veterans parade, Washington, DC. Citizens of the North honored their veterans at the end of the Civil War by organizing parades and homecoming celebrations. *The Art Archive/Culver Pictures/ The Picture Desk, Inc.*

soon broke apart, each brigade taking the nearest route towards home" (Caldwell 1866, p. 244).

As former soldiers transitioned into civilian life, many encountered financial hardships. The average Union soldier returned from the war was in his mid-twenties, and most likely had lacked a steady occupation before the war. Many Confederate veterans returned to their farms only to find them ruined by warfare. One Southerner wrote that her "part of the country has suffered more heavily than any other from the war," and veterans went to great lengths "in order to keep themselves and their families from starvation" (Leigh 1883, p. 119).

Confederate and Union veterans alike sought to recapture that sense of military camaraderie in the postwar years. Early Confederate groups were organized primarily on the local or county-wide level; the Confederate veterans' movement proved "sketchy and poorly coordinated," but "its course of organization was logically adapted to the environment and the troubled times" (White 1962, p. 25). Still, these organizations laid the groundwork for the rejuvenation that forged the largest Confederate veterans' group, the United Confederate Veterans (UCV).

The UCV, formed in Louisiana in 1889, was "designed as an association of all bodies of ex-Confederate soldiers and sailors throughout the Union" (*News and Observer*, September 6, 1889). It was organized in the military tradition. The UCV elected Confederate general John B. Gordon as its first leader. In an address to the veterans, Gordon addressed its purposes, to "succor the disabled, help the needy, strengthen the weak and cheer the discontent" (*Milwaukee Sentinel*, September 8, 1889). At its height, the UCV boasted over 150,000 members.

The UCV's federal counterpart was the Grand Army of the Republic (GAR). Dr. Benjamin Stephenson, veteran surgeon of the Fourteenth Illinois Infantry, saw the daily "neglect of the solider and the soldier's widow and orphans" at his medical practice, and quickly became "convinced that something must be done" (Stephenson 1894, p. 41). After various discussions with Union generals John A. Logan and Richard Oglesby, Stephenson devised the outline and regulations for the GAR; the organization extended membership to "all those who served under the federal flag and who received an honorable discharge," and held as its main objectives to "perpetuate those ties of friendship which had been formed in the smoke of battle and to secure the interests of those who had suffered for the Union" (*Macmillan's Magazine*, November 1891). April 6, 1866, saw the establishment of "the first encampment of the Grand Army of the Republic, Post No. 1, of Decatur, District of Macon, Department of Illinois" (Stephenson 1894, p. 43).

The *Indianapolis Journal* deemed the new organization "full of spirit" and "destined to become immensely popular" (*Harper's Weekly*, December 29, 1866). The GAR called upon "every honorably discharged soldier and seaman of the Union army and navy, whose heart yet stirs with the fraternal feeling which scenes of death and danger inspired" to "rally once again . . . for peaceful communion and pleasant intercourses" (*Chicago Tribune*, September 3, 1871). Upon the conclusion of wartime activities, "it was natural . . . that while such citizens ceased to be soldiers they should still seek to cherish the feeling of old comradeship and the memories of a common cause and a common peril" (*Harper's Weekly*, August 10, 1889).

The GAR adopted, appropriately, an organizational system in the military tradition. Local units were divided into various "posts," the state levels into "departments," and a "commander-in-chief" was in charge of the entire operation. Its primary objectives involved promoting camaraderie, providing for disabled veterans and their dependants, and fighting the pension battle. "If the majority is ready to make the Grand Army a pension-reform organization, well and good; it can be a very powerful one, and can do much to purify the pension list" (*Harper's Weekly*, June 10, 1893).

The GAR spanned the entire breadth of the United States. On a trip to the George H. Thomas Post in San Francisco, California, GAR commander-in-chief John Kountz called it "the grandest army of the grandest Republic the world has ever seen" (*Los Angeles Times*, April 24, 1885). *Harper's Weekly* acknowledged that "the Grand Army of the Republic stands practically without parallel in this country" (August 31, 1889). Determining the actual membership numbers proved almost impossible, yet most estimates placed membership around 500,000 Union veterans by 1891 (Blight 2001, p. 171). "The idea of the G.A.R. seemed to take right hold of the hearts of the soldiers," and as an immediate consequence, "posts sprang up rapidly" (Stephenson 1894, p. 45).

The GAR officially endorsed egalitarianism, unlike many other nineteenth-century fraternal organizations. Some 178,000 African American troops had served during the Civil War (Schaffer 2003, p. 11). Although the national level of the GAR boasted a color-blind membership, individual posts had notorious reputations of discrimination. GAR members accepted new members to a post based on a vote. In 1870, a Worcester, Massachusetts GAR post rejected the membership of an African American veteran on three consecutive ballots, even after the post leaders reemphasized the GAR's nondiscriminatory policies (Shaffer 2004, p. 144). In the lower South, GAR posts were often segregated. As a result of such prejudice, many African Americans opted to create their own veterans' organizations, such as the Colored Soldiers' and Sailors' League and the Colored Veterans Association, to celebrate the contributions of African American soldiers.

Wielding Political Power

As the GAR reached its pinnacle in the late 1880s and early 1890s, no one could deny the veteran organization's sheer force in the world of politics. Members firmly believed the GAR could "create a public sentiment in this country. . . . The Grand Army can force Congress to pass such laws" (*Los Angeles Times*, April 14, 1885). The staunchly Republican organization played a pivotal role in presidential elections for more than thirty years, until the turn of the twentieth century. No president could secure an election without first receiving GAR support. Union veterans wielded political power unmatched by any other veterans' organization.

Some viewed the GAR's vast political influence as a severe abuse of power and misappropriation of trust. One writer to *Harper's Weekly* raved that "nothing could be more unworthy and illegitimate than to convert such an association into a political society," and that the Grand Army of the Republic had transformed into "a machine to extort advantages of every kind for themselves and their kind by promising their continued political support." Rather than the fraternal organization in its original form, the GAR had taken "a course which necessarily covers the association with discredit, and alienates the sympathy of patriotic and intelligent citizens everywhere. . . . It disgraces the name of Union soldier" (August 10, 1889).

President Grover Cleveland, the first Democrat elected since the Civil War, personally witnessed the GAR's partisan potential. Cleveland was scheduled to attend the annual GAR encampment in St. Louis, Missouri, in 1887. Upset by his consistent vetoes of pension legislation, and further angered by his suggestion to return captured Confederate flags, livid members of the GAR sent hostile mail and "threats of personal violence and harm" to Cleveland. The attitude of many GAR members, according to Cleveland, indicated "such prevalence of unfriendly feeling and such menace . . . that they cannot be ignored" (*News and Observer* [Raleigh, NC], July 8, 1887). Cleveland cancelled his planned visit to the GAR National Encampment for fear of personal harm.

Veterans Pensions

Such incidents underscored the highly charged issue of veteran pension legislation. Veterans of the Civil War witnessed, and in most cases caused, massive changes in the federal pension system. In 1862, President Abraham Lincoln had signed into law a pension act that provided payment to all disabled veterans of the war. After the war, the definition of pension eligibility grew even broader. The Dependent Pension Act of 1890, which extracted the wartime service disability qualification, allowed eligibility for any disabled veteran who served at least ninety days in uniform; nevertheless, the burden of demonstrating pension eligibility rested with the veteran. As a result, many veterans enlisted the aid of newspaper editorials, veterans' organizations, and lobbyists. Cognizant of the challenges of establishing entitlement, the clerk Thomas J. Brown made repeated pleas to the pensions' bureau to tabulate veterans' vital statistics. Frustrated by the government's lack of fervor for veterans but its pronounced intervention on behalf of mortgage debtors, Brown noted that "it is supremely sad to reflect that the worthy desire to know the average life of a mortgage ... is tenfold more potent to put the wheels of government into rapid and beneficial revolution than the equally worthy, if not worthier, desire to know the number and age-expectations of veterans of the Civil War" (p. 8).

Pension laws did not overtly discriminate. Many African American veterans applied for and received benefits from the U.S. government. Still, former slaves had a particularly difficult time providing proof of service, often were illiterate, and sometimes did not know their birthplaces and birthdates. Difficult as it was for white soldiers to prove eligibility, African Americans faced even tougher circumstances.

Confederate veterans, in contrast, had no such pension system. Due largely to the distressed conditions and "wide-spread ruin" of the individual Southern states at the war's end, and the political turbulence and military occupation of Reconstruction (1865–1877), Confederate veterans would not see a pension system in effect until the late 1880s. They relied on a less satisfactory system of pensions managed by the state. Southern pension eligibility was limited solely to disabled veterans and widows.

Pension legislation did have its share of opponents. Criticism of the pension system often emanated from the higher economic strata of society. The veteran Benjamin F. Scribner wrote that "the laws granting pensions to soldiers have undergone much hostile criticism from those whose lines were cast in pleasant places during the war" (Scribner 1887, p. 307). When both armies instituted drafts, wealthy citizens were able to pay for men to replace them on the battlefield. As a result, many members of the more affluent classes never saw a day in uniform, and therefore were ineligible for pensions. Some were unwilling to spend tax dollars on benefits for others. Scribner continued, "if these objectors would reflect a moment and try to estimate the sum of money that would induce them to stand up within a range of a line of muskets and take the chances of one volley therefrom, I do not think they would consider the pittance so enormous which has been granted" to veterans (Scribner 1887, p. 307). In addition to such complaints, the pension system was steeped in fraud. News pieces such as the *Cleveland Herald*'s "Audacious Forgeries," which claimed fraud in the pension claims offices, appeared frequently (November 29, 1882).

Disabled Veterans

Not only did veterans face pecuniary, political, and pension battles, but thousands suffered permanent battle scars and disabilities. Ever-present reminders of the carnage of war caused them daily pain and difficulty. As the war came to a close, local populations began "turning their attention to the question of how best to provide permanently for those soldiers who have been disabled in the service" (*New York Times*, May 9, 1865). Concern for disabled veterans frequently made its way into national discussion. In his second inaugural address, President Lincoln made clear his desire "to care for him who has borne the battle." On March 21, 1866, Congress passed legislation chartering the National Asylum for Disabled Volunteers, later renamed the National Home for Disabled Volunteers. These "Soldiers' Homes," as they were commonly known, provided "the care and protection of the ... maimed veterans of the late bloody strife" (*Milwaukee Daily Sentinel*, June 8, 1874).

General Benjamin F. Butler filled the role of president of the organization, and immediately began scouting cities and towns across the country for potential Soldiers' Home branch locations. Butler and various board members did "invite proposals for sites by donation or sale," the stipulations being that sites "must be situated in loyal States; they must contain not less than two hundred acres, must be in healthy locations and easily accessible by railroad or otherwise" (*Lowell Daily Citizen and News*, May 19, 1866). Over the next forty years, Soldiers' Home branches appeared all across the country, from Maine to California. As with pension laws, the Soldiers' Homes had no explicit racial restrictions, yet, African American veterans comprised only an average of 1 percent of the Soldiers' Home population (Shaffer 2003, p. 137). These institutions received funding via military fines and forfeitures, rather than by direct taxation. As one resident of the National Military Asylum in Dayton, Ohio, explained, "it is not a 'charity,' but a contribution of soldiers to soldiers; nor is it an almshouse, but a home in every sense of the word" (*Vermont Watchman and State Journal*, July 20, 1870). The *Daily Arkansas Gazette* reported that in 1875 alone, "reports from the several homes showed 6,651 disabled soldiers were cared for" (December 18, 1875).

The National Home for Disabled Soldiers provided care solely for Union army veterans. The postwar devastatation of the Southern states and tumultuous years of Reconstruction prevented any such organization from developing in the former Confederate states. Upon a visit to a hospital in 1874, ex-Confederate president Jefferson Davis wrote to his wife, Varina, "the veterans in many stages of decay and disability came in, each bearing a smart tricolor and many with military orders on their breasts.... It was a spectacle which could but painfully remind me of our neglected braves and their unprovided orphans. It is well that virtue is its own reward, for sometimes it would otherwise be without compensation" (Hudson 1966, p. 393). Institutions similar to Soldiers' Homes for Confederate veterans finally came to fruition in the 1880s and 1890s, but remained the responsibility of organizations such as the United Daughters of the Confederacy and United Confederate Veterans.

Veterans' Publications

Contending with these problems and maintaining contact with comrades became easier with the publication of veterans' newspapers. William O. Bourne's *The Soldier's Friend* and the GAR–endorsed *The Great Republic* hit the presses in 1864 and 1866, respectively. *Confederate Veteran* magazine became the official organ of the United Confederate Veterans, and remained in publication until 1932. Sometimes, publications were intended to settle old scores from the battlefield. The Southern Historical Society Papers aimed to promote a strictly Confederate version of the history of the war; under the tutelage of Jubal Early, president of the Southern Historical Society, many of the papers contributed to the canonization of Robert E. Lee (1807–1870) at the expense of Richard S. Ewell (1817–1872), James Longstreet (1821–1904), and other subordinates. Other publications simply strove to help their readers, promoting events and holding contests: Left-handed penmanship contests for veterans who had lost a right arm proved particularly popular. The wounded veteran Seth Sutherland, a yearly contestant, wrote to the *Soldier's Friend* editor that the contest "will infuse new life and vigor into the heart of many a wounded soldier, and be another evidence to him that his services ... are not forgotten" (Sutherland to Bourne, July 22, 1865). The *Soldier's Friend* attracted loyal readers such as veteran George N. Dale: "I think every true American ought to patronize the *Soldier's Friend*" (Dale to Bourne, March 18, 1868).

The most influential and lasting newspaper, however, was the *National Tribune.* Founded by George B. Lemon, a Washington, DC, pension claims agent and veteran of the One Hundred Twenty-fifth New York Volunteer Infantry, the *National Tribune* featured articles written by veterans describing their wartime experiences. The paper provided veterans an ideal forum for debate, and an opportunity to reminisce. In 1884, Lemon hired veteran John McElroy as another editor for the *Tribune.* Until the turn of the twentieth century, articles written by veterans describing their wartime experiences appeared regularly; Lemon and McElroy devoted large amounts of space in the paper to various news pieces from veterans' organizations (e.g., the GAR, the Women's Relief Corps, etc.). The paper provided veterans an ideal forum for debate and opportunity to reminisce. As time progressed, the *Tribune* attempted to appeal to a wider audience, and it grew popular with veterans of the Spanish-American War. The GAR stopped publication around the outbreak of World War I, but a private corporation continued the paper, changing its title to *Stars and Stripes.*

Veterans Reunions

These papers also announced hundreds of reunions beginning in the 1880s and continuing until the final meeting of the Blue and Gray at Gettysburg in 1938. Large organizations such as the GAR and the UCV held yearly national encampments, drawing thousands of veterans from across the country. Reunions involving both Union and Confederate veterans gained popularity, becoming "not only a pleasant custom, but a gratifying indication of the gradual passing away of the passions and prejudices of the war" (*Harper's Weekly*, July 19, 1884). A culture of romantic reunion had emerged. *Chicago Daily Tribune* coverage of one early Union Army of the Potomac banquet indicated "the greetings were hearty and affectionate, for there were vacant chairs, and the members ... knew not if they would meet again," a sentiment commonly shared in veterans' reunions (January 7, 1891). These reunions were often accompanied by the erection of monuments on the battlefields. One of the most famous of these episodes occurred on July 2, 1887, when members of the Philadelphia Brigade invited former Confederates of General George Pickett's division to attend a monument dedication at Gettysburg. What once had been the site of fierce combat, death, and destruction became a place of reunion where former enemies shook hands and celebrated a common, united future.

For the rest of their lives, veterans "continued to set themselves above 'civilians' as a class by virtue of their military service" (McConnell 1992, p. 34). These battle-hardened veterans, by recalling and celebrating the conflict, encouraged the late-nineteenth-century emergence of the vigorous manhood and athleticism movements. At the outbreak of the Spanish-American War, these concepts were coupled with a new, virile patriotism. Often, these sensibilities encouraged the idea that veterans were of a higher caliber. According to one colonel, although most assumed that a veteran's lifespan would be less than those "who have not been exposed to the shock of battle and the hardship and privation of field, camp, and prison ... by the operation of the law of the survival of the fittest ... the survivors have become a selected class, where average duration of life is likely to be greater than that of an equal number of nonveterans" (memorandum quoted in Brown Papers). The *New York Times* wrote that veterans, "the defenders of their country in time of war, are its best citizens in every walk of life now that the war is over" (August 12, 1872). Veterans placed themselves on a different, and higher, level of society due to their wartime experiences. As Oliver Wendell Holmes orated in a speech delivered before a New Hampshire GAR post in May 1884, "the generation that carried on the war has been set apart by its experience. Through our great good fortune, in our youth our hearts were touched with fire" (Holmes 1884).

BIBLIOGRAPHY

Blight, David. *Race and Reunion: The Civil War in American Memory.* Cambridge: Belknap Press of Harvard University Press, 2001.

Brown, Thomas J. "The Census and the Soldier and the Census and the Mortgage: A Parallel." Papers of Thomas J. Brown. Library of Congress, Washington, DC.

Caldwell, J. F. J. *The History of the Brigade of South Carolinians.* Philadelphia: King and Baird, 1866.

Chicago Daily Tribune, September 3, 1871; January 7, 1891; December 7, 1892.

Cleveland Herald, Cleveland, OH, November 29, 1882.

Daily Arkansas Gazette, Little Rock, AR, December 18, 1875.

Dale, George N. Letter to William O. Bourne, March 18, 1868. Papers of William O. Bourne. Library of Congress, Washington, DC.

Davies, Wallace Evan. *Patriotism on Parade: The Story of Veterans and Hereditary Organizations in America, 1793–1900.* Cambridge, MA: Harvard University Press, 1955.

Dearing, Mary R. *Veterans in Politics: The Story of the G.A.R.* Baton Rouge: Louisiana State University Press, 1952.

Harper's Weekly, December 29, 1866; August 10, 1889; August 31, 1889; June 10, 1893; July 19, 1884.

Holmes, Oliver Wendell. "Dead Yet Living," address delivered May 30, 1884. Boston: Ginn, Heath, & Company, 1884.

Hudson, Strode, ed. *Jefferson Davis: Private Letters, 1823–1889.* New York: Harcourt Brace Jovanovich, 1966.

Lane, David. *A Soldier's Diary: The Story of a Volunteer, 1862–1865.* Jackson, MI: 1905.

Leigh, Frances Ann Butler. *Ten Years on a Georgia Plantation since the War.* London: Bentley and Son, 1883.

Logan, Mary Simmerson. *Reminiscences of a Soldier's Wife: An Autobiography.* New York: Charles Scribner's Sons, 1913.

Logue, Larry M., and Michael Barton, eds. *The Civil War Veteran: A Historical Reader.* New York: New York University Press, 2007.

Los Angeles Times, April 14, 1885; April 24, 1885.

Lowell Daily Citizen and News, Lowell, MA, May 19, 1866.

Macmillan's Magazine 65 (November 1891–April 1892).

Marten, James. *Civil War America: Voices from the Home Front.* Santa Barbara, CA: ABC-CLIO, 2003.

McConnell, Stuart. *Glorious Contentment: The Grand Army of the Republic, 1865–1900.* Chapel Hill: University of North Carolina Press, 1992.

Milwaukee Sentinel, June 8, 1874; September 8, 1889.

New York Times, May 9, 1865; August 12, 1872.

News and Observer, Raleigh, NC, July 8, 1887; September 6, 1889.

Rosenburg, R. B. *Living Monuments: Confederate Soldiers' Homes in the New South.* Chapel Hill: University of North Carolina Press, 1993.

Scribner, Benjamin F. *How Soldiers Were Made; Or, The War as I Saw it Under Buell, Rosecrans, Thomas, Grant, and Sherman.* New Albany, IN: George S. MacManus, 1887.

Shaffer, Donald R. *After the Glory: The Struggles of Black Civil War Veterans.* Lawrence: University Press of Kansas, 2004.

Simon, John. *Papers of Ulysses S. Grant.* Carbondale: Southern Illinois University Press, 1967.

Stephenson, Mary Harriet. *Dr. B. F. Stephenson.* Springfield, IL: H.W. Rokker Printing House, 1894.

Sutherland, Seth. Letter to William O. Bourne, July 22, 1865. Papers of William O. Bourne, Library of Congress, Washington, DC.

Vermont Watchman and State Journal, Montpelier, VT, July 20, 1870.

Wagner, Margaret E., Gary W. Gallagher, and Paul Finkelman, eds. *Civil War Desk Reference.* New York: Simon and Schuster, 2002.

White, William W. *The Confederate Veteran.* Tuscaloosa, AL: Confederate Publishing Company, 1962.

Allison E. Herrmann

■ Memorial and Decoration Days

Memorial Day is a special time for Americans. Few patriotic events conjure up the emotion, commemoration, and gratitude of the nation like the remembrance events on the last Monday of May each year, when all across the United States, and even abroad, Americans set aside time to remember those who have fallen in defense of our nation. But few citizens stop to think of the history of the day, which appeared shortly after the Civil War as an effort to remember the dead of that conflict.

One newspaper summed up the historic role of Memorial Day in 1869 as "a memorial day as useful and suggestive to the living as it is significant and grateful to the dead," and went on to describe the effort: "To strew flowers on the graves of the heroes is at once a pious and patriotic tribute, done in the simplest and most touching way. This right of affection, not too public for the most modest and retiring woman in her own secluded way to celebrate, yet not too lowly for the loftiest citizen to disdain, is one of those very few customs which a nation may be proud to have originated and maintained" ("Decoration Day," p. 4). Moreover, this decoration activity at cemeteries across the United States, both North and South, played a major role in the eventual reconciling of the two sections after the war.

Historians are hard pressed to pinpoint the exact date of the first Memorial Day. Some argue that it began haphazardly even during the war, while others point to a period

Veterans on parade at war's end. In the late 1860s, veterans' organizations pressed for the observation of a holiday to honor the nation's fallen soldiers. Americans celebrated with solemn parades and floral wreaths not only for the troops who perished in the Civil War, but also those who died serving the United States in previous conflicts. *The Library of Congress.*

immediately after the conflict ended (Blight 2001, pp. 65–70; Neff 2005, 136–137). One of the earliest mentions of an actual day termed "Memorial Day" came in 1868, when on May 30 the town of Lafayette, Indiana, decorated the graves of its Civil War dead. Even this early, however, there was some crossing of the sectional lines and a desire to reconcile the North and South. The *New York Times* reported that the decorators of the Indiana cemetery received a wreath and a note from a little girl which read, "Will you please put this wreath upon some rebel soldier's grave? My dear papa is buried at Andersonville, and perhaps some little girl will be kind enough to put a few flowers upon his grave" ("An Incident of Memorial Day," p. 3). The officials did so, laying the wreath on the only Confederate grave in the cemetery.

Most sources point to 1868 as the actual birth of the yearly Memorial or Decoration Day tradition, however. The Grand Army of the Republic was a leader in the effort, one story saying its commander was given the idea by a Philadelphia woman who had traveled around the South and "had noticed the Southern women decorating the graves of their dead, fallen in battle" ("Memorial Day," p. 4). Another story stated that an anonymous member recommended the idea (Neff 2005, p. 137). By 1869, however, numerous events were held across the nation, in both North and South, and in that year the tradition was referred to by the New York Times as being "introduced into the national calendar" ("Decoration Day," p. 4). The paper described the 1869 event in New York: "there was no lack of attendance at the cemeteries, where thousands participated in the beautiful and appropriate ceremony of decorating our heroes['] graves with flowers" ("Decoration Day," p. 4).

Throughout the Reconstruction era as well as the 1880s, most Memorial Day observances were localized efforts to decorate soldiers' graves in local cemeteries, and not just the Civil War dead. William T. Sherman gave an address at a St. Louis Memorial Day event in 1875 and also mentioned other veterans buried in that particular cemetery: "men who fought for the honor of our common country against the foreign foe before most of us were born; others who brought from Mexico and our Indian borders seeds of disease which caused their death" ("Gen. Sherman on Memorial Day," p. 2). There was also an effort by the Grand Army of the Republic to make this effort both national and permanent in scope, and success would ultimately come when Congress made the day an official holiday for both sides in 1889. To be sure, the effort to memorialize the dead had crossed the sectional lines by that time. "Both Union and Confederate graves decorated in Maryland," read the Washington Post in 1879, with the practice becoming more common as the years passed ("A Day of Remembrance," p. 1). "Speeches were delivered and the graves of the Confederate and Union dead were decorated," read another newspaper in reference to ceremonies in Charleston, South Carolina, in 1888 ("Memorial Day in the South," p. 1).

Not surprisingly, the national cemeteries across the land were special favorites for Memorial Day observances, especially those that sat on or near the developing national military parks in the 1890s and beyond. Special observances were held each year at places such as Shiloh, Tennessee, Vicksburg, Mississippi, Antietam, Maryland, and Gettysburg, Pennsylvania. At Shiloh each year in the 1890s and early 1900s, the local Grand Army of the Republic post placed flags on the Union and Confederate graves, despite several years of rain on the specific day, prompting park officials to refer to their "customary rain" (Smith 2004, pp. 14, 102). Each year at Gettysburg, one newspaper reported, "the children of the public schools covered with flowers the thousands of graves" ("Triumphant March of G.A.R.," p. 10).

Since the official holiday was declared, Memorial Day has become a part of almost every American's yearly remembrance, and today is no different. Whether Americans watch on television the elaborate ceremonies at Arlington National Cemetery where the President of the United States lays a wreath at the Tomb of the Unknowns or attend the local ceremonies at one of the many national cemeteries across America, they do so for the same purpose: to remember, honor, and commemorate, just like those first pioneers of the Memorial Day tradition did immediately after the Civil War.

BIBLIOGRAPHY

"A Day of Remembrance." *Washington Post*, May 31, 1879, p. 1.

"An Incident of Memorial Day." *New York Times*, June 7, 1868, p. 3.

Blight, David. *Race and Reunion: The Civil War in Memory and Reunion*. Cambridge, MA, 2001.

"Decoration Day." *New York Times*, May 31, 1869, p. 4.

"Gen. Sherman on Memorial Day." *New York Times*, June 4, 1875, p. 2.

The Golden Age of Battlefield Preservation: The Decade of the 1890s and the Establishment of America's First Five Military Parks. Knoxville, TN, 2008.

Holt, Dean W. *American Military Cemeteries: A Comprehensive Illustrated Guide to the Hollowed Grounds of the United States, Including Cemeteries Overseas*. Jefferson, NC, 1992.

"Memorial Day." *Washington Post*, August 27, 1889, p. 4.

"Memorial Day in the South." *New York Times*, May 12, 1888, p. 1.

Neff, John R. *Honoring The Civil War Dead: Commemoration And The Problem Of Reconciliation*. Lawrence, KS, 2005.

Piehler, G. Kurt. *Remembering War the American Way*. Washington DC, 1995.

Smith, Timothy B. *This Great Battlefield of Shiloh: History, Memory, and the Establishment of a Civil War National Military Park*. Knoxville, TN, 2004.

"Triumphant March of G.A.R." *New York Times*, May 31, 1894, p. 10.

Timothy B. Smith

■ Battlefield Sites

BATTLEFIELD SITES: AN OVERVIEW

The battle sites of the Civil War are some of the most hallowed pieces of ground in the United States. Shiloh National Military Park's first historian, the Iowa veteran David W. Reed, remarked, "There is nothing in this broad land of ours more sacred than the soil which has been wet with the blood of its patriotic sons" (Reed 1898, p. 374). In the early twenty-first century literally millions of visitors to the various military parks tramp along trails and roads and drive along tour routes in search of information on what happened at the various sites or the places where their ancestors once stood. Books, maps, Internet sites, and photographs can aid a visitor and inform them about what happened at specific sites, but none of those media are equal to walking on a Civil War battlefield and feeling a connection to what happened there. Fortunately, throughout our history Civil War veterans and others have worked to preserve some of these historic sites for visitors, allowing us of later generations the opportunity to connect to a former time.

Civil War battlefield preservation has gone through four stages since the Civil War. The first was a disjointed early attempt at erecting monuments and preserving individual areas, with a few monuments going up during the war itself and more built immediately after the conflict ended. The vast majority of the preservation that was achieved was inadvertently realized through the medium of national cemeteries, which were normally located on historic ground. The second phase, the golden age of Civil War battlefield preservation, took place in the 1890s, when the biggest and best-preserved battlefields were placed under protection. Unfortunately, the next wave of protection did not occur until the late 1920s and 1930s, when it was already too late to properly save many fields of conflict. Nevertheless, these parks of the New Deal era saved what could be preserved at the time. The most recent phase is a century later than the golden age; nonetheless a new generation of preservationists is doing what it can to protect the sites. Recently, efforts have gathered more momentum, with the Civil War Preservation Trust leading the way.

Early Battlefield-Preservation Efforts: The Veteran Generation

During the Civil War and up until 1890, veterans and local citizens marked several important sites. During the war itself, several soldiers and units marked such famous places as the Round Forest at Stones River, the Vicksburg surrender site, and the Henry House Hill at Manassas. The oldest extant example of these monuments is the Hazen Brigade monument at Stones River, which called the nation "to greater deeds" (Brown 1985, pp. 5–8). These commemorative features were individually and independently erected by sponsors with no Federal government involvement beyond the fact that those performing the work were primarily soldiers.

Although not specifically built for preservation purposes in most cases, silent national cemeteries established during the war—"for the soldiers who shall die in the service of the country," in the words of the enabling legislation—also marked the sites of many battlefields, such as Chattanooga, Antietam, and Gettysburg (Holt 1992, pp. 2–3). For example, Major General George Thomas, commander of the Union Army of the Cumberland, ordered the establishment of the cemetery at Chattanooga "in commemoration of the Battles of Chattanooga, November 23–27, 1863" (Holt 1992, p. 65). Many other national cemeteries also marked the locations of hospitals, prison camps, and camping areas.

After the war, preservation activity began to increase. In the period up until 1889, several veterans placed monuments and markers at such various sites as Antietam and Pea Ridge, but these were likewise privately funded with no government subsidization. The Federal government did, however, continue the building of national cemeteries on historic land. Desiring to build these cemeteries with the least amount of trouble, the government often took the nearest possible land to where the soldiers had been buried, which inadvertently was battlefield land in most cases. Among the resulting cemeteries were the national cemetery at Pittsburg Landing on the battlefield of Shiloh, the national cemetery on the banks of the Mississippi River on the Vicksburg battlefield, and the national cemetery within the confines of the Fort Donelson defense area. These refuges were established primarily to allow a place of decent and honorable individual burial for U.S. soldiers. One builder commented that such individual recognition "accords with our intense individualism as a people, and with the value we attach to individual life; and it is demanded by the eminent worth of those for whom historic notice would thus be secured" (U.S. Army Quartermaster Corps 1865–1871, no. 11, p. 12). These national cemeteries also inadvertently yet opportunely preserved crucial areas of each battlefield site.

Not surprisingly, in the pre-1890 period by far the most significant battlefield preservation activity was at Gettysburg, Pennsylvania, where the Gettysburg Battlefield Memorial Association emerged to provide oversight. The state of Pennsylvania appropriated money for the use of the association, the legislature directing that the money "be applied to the purchase of portions of the battle-grounds" (Vanderslice 1899, p. 360). Made up of prominent Northern officials and Gettysburg citizens, the association was nevertheless underfunded despite several infusions of money from other Northern states. Observing the apparent inactivity of association officials, the Grand Army of the Republic took over the association by garnering sufficient stock to attain a controlling interest. Thereafter the association was on better footing and oversaw a myriad of such preservation attempts as buying key areas of the battlefield, marking troop positions, and working with individual states to erect monuments on the site. Nevertheless, there never seemed to be enough money and the work was somewhat disorganized and irregular. Most importantly, the activity at Gettysburg was primarily non-Federal, non-Confederate, and non-reconciliatory. It was a Union venture through and through.

Golden Age of Battlefield Preservation

America turned a major corner in its preservation activity in 1890. This shift from the Gettysburg style of commemoration, which was neo-Union, non-reconciliatory, and haphazard to say the least, ushered in the "Golden Age" of Civil War battlefield preservation (Smith, in press).

During the 1890s, several factors came together to generate a strong impetus to save the battlefields. One was that veterans who could return to the fields to document what had happened there were rapidly aging. David W. Reed, the first historian at Shiloh, remarked, "The work of restoring these battlefields has not been undertaken too soon. Those who have personal knowledge of positions and movements are rapidly passing off the stage" (Reed 1898, p. 373). To mark specific sites, the veterans building these parks often relied not only on official records and papers but also on the testimony and memories of other veterans. Such testimonies were a very important component of the process; while there were some areas of disagreement, for the most part the veterans were amazingly consistent in their memories.

One factor that made the 1890s the golden age of preservation activities was the ability to preserve almost pristine battlefields. Reed observed that soon veterans would "find it difficult to visit these old fields, or when there to fully comprehend the changes that have been made" (Reed 1898, p. 373). While there had been some change at the sites, they had not yet undergone the rapid development brought on by the second industrial revolution, during which massive industrialization, urbanization, and mobilization forever altered the face of American culture and society. It would be only a little over a decade after the 1890s before the Chickamauga commission would complain that "the roads [passing through the Chickamauga Battlefield] are in a section of country ... [experiencing] rapid increase of populations and development of varied industries, and extensive use is made of them by farmers, merchants, contractors, and others, who haul material or merchandise over them" (*Annual Report of the Secretary of War: 1907*, p. 316). Urbanization and industrialization brought the loss of battlefields. Yet, in the 1890s most sites were still primarily pristine, and thus the veterans' generation was able to preserve some important battlefields.

Another factor making the 1890s the optimal time to preserve Civil War battlefields was the participation in politics of large numbers of veterans, which translated into strong support for preservation in Congress and in state legislatures dominated by veterans. At the same time, the presence of veterans in government went into a steady decline after 1890. Researching the members of

Marker at the site of the Vicksburg surrender. The Vicksburg surrender site was marked while the war was still raging. The monument on this site and others were sponsored without any aid from the Federal government. *The Library of Congress*

Congress in the years between 1890 and 1899, in fact, shows a decline of some 20 percent in the percentage of members who were veterans—from around 50 percent in 1890 to around only 30 percent in 1899. Thus the best opportunity to fund military parks was the 1890s, when veterans who were interested in their old battlefields were there to pass the needed legislation.

These factors all worked together within the context of a reconciliation process that took place in the 1890s. After a war fueled by decades of heated debate over slavery and states' rights, the nation had again been divided by years of animosity-ridden reconstruction. Lasting in many cases into the 1880s, this anger was primarily related to racial issues. In the 1890s, however, whites in both the North and South began to move away from the conflict over racial issues that had so divided them in the past. This change, of course, meant less commitment to supporting the gains made by African Americans in the Civil War and during Reconstruction. As a result, segregation and Jim Crowism developed in the 1890s as whites in the North and South turned away from the divisive issues of race to issues on which both sides could agree. One of the major ways this reconciliation was achieved was through a focus on the bravery, courage, and honor of the aging Civil War generation, both North and South. The battlefield preservationist Henry Boynton remarked that a "quarter of a century has brought this [reconciliation] about, a period which is but a day in the life of a nation. He would indeed be impatient who looked for more speedy progress" ("Camping on Chickamauga," *Washington Post*, September 16, 1892; Blight 2001).

The four battlefields set aside as parks during the 1890s—Chickamauga-Chattanooga, Antietam, Shiloh, and Vicksburg—are, together with Gettysburg, the largest and best preserved. Unlike the one-sided effort at Gettysburg, the 1890s parks were created with Federal monies for *both* sides, with Confederate battle lines receiving just as much attention as the Union positions, and with legislation even mandating that some of the commissioners be former Confederate soldiers.

Two distinct styles of parks developed during this golden age of preservation. One reflected the ideas espoused by Henry Boynton, the founder of the first national military park at Chickamauga. His aim was to preserve entire battlefields, even those that covered thousands of acres, as was done at Chickamauga and Shiloh. A second style of preservation sought to preserve key features of a battlefield rather than the entire acreage. Where it was not possible to set aside large tracts of land, roadways and prominent points could be secured, as at the urbanized battlefield at Chattanooga, the first to be preserved in this manner. This second style of preservation, however, was also used for battlefields away from urbanized areas, most famously at Antietam. The Antietam Board President George B. Davis espoused the idea of buying small sections of battlefields and interpreting the action from those points. The "Antietam Plan" was thus much cheaper and would actually be used for the next several decades on other battlefields (Lee 1973, p. 40).

The physical construction of the five parks (including Gettysburg) was only half the work, however. As each of the parks was being established through land purchases, monument and tablet placements, and artillery positioning, a historiographical account of each battle was also being constructed. The commissions published books and generally promoted what they believed to be the correct history of their respective sites through drawing attention to key locales and such events as the Hornet's Nest at Shiloh, Snodgrass Hill at Chickamauga, and Pickett's Charge at Gettysburg (Reed 1902 passim). Their version of events largely became the accepted history of each battle, and has remained dominant even until the early twenty-first century although some scholars are beginning to dispute the older accounts.

Yet, just as many had feared, Civil War veterans did begin to pass away in large numbers soon after the turn of the twentieth century. There were so many deaths, in fact, that Congress revised its method of appointing individual commissioners for each battlefield park. In 1912 Congress passed a law that gradually discontinued the commission system. No commissioners would be put out of a job, but when they died or resigned, their position would not be filled (Lee 1973, p. 45). The five flagship parks were thus soon turned over to civilian superintendents who were not veterans and who operated within the War Department. A few old veteran commissioners lived into the 1920s, but by 1930 none of the original parks had a veteran commissioner.

Although only five battlefields had been preserved by the end of the 1890s, the Federal government had nevertheless laid the groundwork for future battlefield preservation work. Unfortunately, it would be several decades before any more battlefields were preserved (Lee 1973, p. 51).

Parks of the 1930s and the Modern Period

The next wave of preservation did not occur until the late 1920s and 1930s, when it was already too late to fully save the fields of conflict. The result was a series of much smaller, less well marked, and highly urbanized parks such as Fort Pulaski, Petersburg, Fredericksburg and Spotsylvania, Kennesaw Mountain, Stones River, Fort Donelson, Tupelo, and Brices Crossroads (Lee 1973, pp. 51–52).

Each of these parks, being patterned after the Antietam Plan, was not nearly as extravagantly constructed as most of the original parks preserved during the 1890s. Whereas most of the earlier parks were thousands of acres in size, the 1920s-era parks were at most only hundreds of acres large. Brices Crossroads and Tupelo, for example, were about an acre each, whereas Stones River and Fort Donelson were in the five hundred-acre range. This relatively small size reflected not only the methodology of the Antietam Plan but was also a result of the fact that the battlefields were no longer pristine and whole, due to urbanization and the industrialization of the World War I (1914–1918) era. Preservation of the land that was left cost large amounts of money, and a Congress no longer dominated by Civil War veterans would not appropriate the sums necessary to buy expensive urban tracts. Furthermore, the parks that were created in the 1920s were not marked with the detail of the 1890s parks, as most Civil War veterans had died by that time or were aged men with fading memories.

A major change came in 1933, however, when President Franklin D. Roosevelt transferred all the War Department parks from that entity to the National Park Service. The system also gained new parks during the New Deal era, when a significant amount of federal funding was put into the park system, as part of the government's public works approach to lowering Depression-era unemployment. The parks at Appomattox, Richmond, and Manassas were established in the years prior to World War II, though these were on the minimal scale of the 1920s-era parks.

The post–World War II era saw the further development of Civil War parks; however, in this period the initiative for preservation largely shifted from the federal to the state and private level. Around the time of the war's centennial, Congress did establish several new parks, such as those at Fort Sumter, Harpers Ferry, Wilson Creek, Pea Ridge, Arkansas Post, and Andersonville, some of which were transferred from other government agencies. On the other hand, numerous other battlefields that could have been preserved—such as those at Franklin, Nashville, Perryville, Mansfield, and Champion Hill—were not. The Federal preservation effort reached its nadir in the 1970s and 1980s, which saw very little activity. Fortunately, the various states assumed responsibility for preservation and created state parks out of battlefields ignored by the federal government, such as the parks at Perryville, Sailors Creek, Bentonville, Olustee, Fort Blakely, Mansfield, Fort Pillow, and Pickett's Mill.

During the 1990s, however, the national battlefield preservation effort was suddenly revived with the establishment of several preservation entities, most notably the mammoth Civil War Preservation Trust. And even the Federal government became involved again through the American Battlefield Protection Program (ABPP) within the National Park Service. The ABPP has saved thousands of acres of battlefield land since its establishment in 1996.

In the early twenty-first century, there are still hundreds of unpreserved battlefields, most admittedly small, though a few large battle sites have seen very little preservation work. Many groups are attempting to preserve these battlefields, from small local commissions struggling to purchase land to large national organizations that lend considerable weight to the preservation effort. None of these contemporary efforts, however, can ever equal what was done in the 1890s, when all the factors lined up to produce a "Golden Age" of Civil War battlefield preservation.

BIBLIOGRAPHY

American Battlefield Protection Program Web site. Available from http://www.nps.gov/history/hps/.

Blight, David W. *Race and Reunion: The Civil War in American Memory.* Cambridge, MA: Belknap Press of Harvard University Press, 2001.

Brown, Daniel A. *Marked for Future Generations: The Hazen Brigade Monument, 1863–1929.* Murfreesboro, TN: National Park Service, 1985.

Civil War Preservation Trust Web site. Available from http://www.civilwar.org.

Civil War Sites Advisory Commission Report on the Nation's Civil War Battlefields. Washington, DC: Government Printing Office, 1993.

Friends of the Mansfield Battlefield Web site. Available from http://www.mansfieldbattlefield.org/.

Holt, Dean W. *American Military Cemeteries: A Comprehensive Illustrated Guide to the Hallowed Grounds of the United States, Including Cemeteries Overseas.* Jefferson, NC: McFarland, 1992.

House Committee on Military Affairs, House Report No. 1139. "National Military Park at the Battlefield of Shiloh." In *House Reports*, 53rd Congress, 2nd Session, June 22, 1894. Washington, DC: House of Representatives, 1893–1895.

Lee, Ronald F. *The Origin and Evolution of the National Military Park Idea.* Washington DC: National Park Service, 1973.

"Pickett's Mill History." Available from http://gastateparks.org/net/content/.

"Preservation at Bentonville." Available from http://www.ah.dcr.state.nc.us/sections/hs/bentonvi/.

Reed, David Wilson. "National Cemeteries and National Military Parks." In *War Sketches and Incidents: As Related by the Companions of the Iowa Commandery Military Order of the Loyal Legion of the United States*, ed. Military Order of the Loyal Legion of the United States, Iowa Commandery. 2 vols. Des Moines, IA: Kenyon, 1893–1898.

Reed, David Wilson, ed. *The Battle of Shiloh and the Organizations Engaged.* Washington, DC: Government Printing Office, 1902.

Sellars, Richard West. *Pilgrim Places: Civil War Battlefields, Historic Preservation, and America's First National Military Parks, 1863–1900.* Fort Washington, PA: Eastern National, 2005.

Smith, Timothy B. *The Golden Age of Battlefield Preservation: The Decade of the 1890s and the Establishment of America's First Five Military Parks*. Knoxville, TN, in press.

United States Army Quartermasters Corps. *Roll of Honor: Names of Soldiers Who Died in Defence of the American Union, Interred in the National [and Other] Cemeteries*. 27 nos. in 9 vols. Washington, DC: Government Printing Office, 1865–1871.

Unrau, Harlan D. *Administrative History: Gettysburg National Military Park and Gettysburg National Cemetery, Pennsylvania*. Denver, CO: U.S. Department of the Interior, National Park Service, 1991.

Vanderslice, John M. *Gettysburg, Then and Now: The Field of American Valor: Where and How the Regiments Fought, and the Troops They Encountered; An Account of the Battle, Giving Movements, Positions, and Losses of the Commands Engaged*. New York: G. W. Dillingham Company, 1899.

Timothy B. Smith

WARTIME COMMEMORATION AND MONUMENTS

Civil War battlefield preservation is a popular effort today, but the foundations of this phenomenon stretch back almost a century and a half. Indeed, the very first monumentation and commemoration of Civil War events occurred as early as 1861, the year the war began. Today, these initial efforts, some of which no longer exist in full form, are among the most distinguished commemorative features on any battlefield and serve as the foundations of present Civil War preservation and commemoration initiatives.

Early Civil War Monuments

During the course of the Civil War, soldiers placed monuments on several fields to commemorate what had taken place and to eulogize the dead. In September 1861, Confederate soldiers in Colonel Francis Bartow's brigade placed a monument on the Bull Run battlefield to mark the site of Bartow's death on July 21, 1861. Soldiers of the 8th Georgia erected a white marble slab shaped in the form of an obelisk to commemorate their leader. Over one thousand people attended the dedication. Unfortunately, the monument is no longer in existence; it disappeared after the Confederates left the area and its fate was never determined.

Hundreds of miles to the west, soldiers of Colonel William B. Hazen's Union brigade erected a monument on the battlefield of Stone's River, near Murfreesboro, Tennessee, in the spring and early summer of 1863. Hazen's brigade had repelled numerous assaults by the Confederates in the Round Forest and had buried their dead where they had fallen. As the Army of the Cumberland moved southward, Hazen's men remained to garrison the Murfreesboro area. That summer, they built a memorial to their dead on the spot where they had been buried. A burial vault patterned after an Egyptian mastaba, the monument has the following inscription: "The blood of one third of its soldiers twice spilled in Tennessee crimsons the battle flag of the brigade and inspires to greater deeds" (Brown 1985, pp. 5–8; Abroe 1996, p. 90). The oldest surviving Civil War monument, it still stands at Stone's River National Battlefield.

Also during the summer of 1863, Federals in Vicksburg, Mississippi, marked the "surrender interview" site at which Grant and Pemberton had met to discuss terms of Confederate surrender (Abroe 1996, p. 92). The Federals took from a local stonecutter's shop a marble shaft that had originally been intended to memorialize Vicksburg's Mexican War dead. The monument's hurriedly carved inscription read: "The Site of Interview between Major General U. S. Grant USA & Lieut. General Pemberton July 4, 1863." Unfortunately, the date given for the meeting was incorrect; it had actually occurred on July 3. Nevertheless, this monument was somewhat different than earlier memorials: It marked the site of a significant event only; there was no memorialization of the dead.

Though put up as the war was ending, the two still-intact monuments at Manassas, erected in June 1865, must be mentioned in relation to wartime commemorative efforts. Federal veterans placed two sandstone obelisks to commemorate the two battles fought on that ground. One placed on Henry House Hill commemorated the first battle, while another placed near the famous railroad cut memorialized the second and larger engagement. Each honored fallen soldiers, and marked the most significant points on the respective battlefields (Abroe 1996, pp. 92–93).

National Cemeteries

The major act of preservation and remembrance during the Civil War was the establishment of national cemeteries. The War Department began the process of burying the dead and enumerating burial plots when the war began. Department and army commanders simply buried the dead, particularly battle casualties, on the ground where they had fought or had been stationed in camps or hospitals. Primarily located on private land, these burial grounds had to be bought or condemned. The 37th Congress of the United States passed legislation that allowed for national cemeteries as deemed necessary by the president, and Abraham Lincoln signed the bill into law on July 17, 1862. Section 18 gave him the "power, whenever in his opinion it is expedient, to purchase cemetery grounds and cause them to be securely enclosed, to be used as a national cemetery for the soldiers who shall die in the service of the country" (Holt 1992, pp. 2–3).

As a result of this legislation, the Lincoln administration created fourteen national cemeteries in 1862, and many others followed throughout the war. Most were set up around Washington, DC, and other troop induction and care centers. Alexandria and Soldiers' Home near the capital, and cemeteries at Annapolis, Maryland; Camp Butler, Illinois; and Philadelphia held more soldiers who died of disease and accident than of battle wounds. Perhaps the most famous cemetery in the United States, Arlington National Cemetery, was also a product of the war. Established by Quartermaster General Montgomery Meigs on the estate of Confederate General Robert E. Lee, Arlington became the site of burial for thousands of soldiers over the years (Holt 1992, pp. 2–3; Piehler 1995, p. 52).

Several of the fourteen original cemeteries, as well as many of the later burial areas, were on battlefields, marking the first time actual sites of conflict were preserved to commemorate the fallen. Although intended primarily to honor and commemorate the dead, they inadvertently preserved some of the core areas of battlefields for posterity. Still in embryonic form in the 1860s, these cemeteries would eventually form the backbone of the park system established by a national military park movement during the 1890s, when massive tracts of land were preserved to commemorate what had happened at various sites.

The early national cemeteries also at times made larger statements about the war itself. When asked if he wanted soldiers buried by state at the Chattanooga National Cemetery, Major General George H. Thomas was reported to have replied, "No, no. Mix them up; mix them up. I am tired of state-rights" (Van Horne 1882, p. 213).

The War Department erected a small cemetery at the site of the January 1862 battle of Mill Springs in eastern Kentucky, and other national cemeteries were created at Chattanooga, Tennessee; Sharpsburg, Maryland; Murfreesboro, Tennessee; and Gettysburg, Pennsylvania. These cemeteries were established primarily to honor the dead, but also to preserve a portion of the historic landscape. There was also new attention to honoring soldiers as individuals. For example, Thomas B. Van Horne, the chaplain in charge of the Chattanooga National Cemetery, noted that extreme care would be taken to:

> secure a short military history of every officer and soldier interred in the cemetery whose remains have been identified. . . . It seems eminently fitting that this should be done. It accords with our intense individualism as a people, and with the value we attach to individual life; and it is demanded by the eminent worth of those for whom historic notice would thus be secured. (U.S. Army Quartermaster Corps 1865–1871, no. 11, p. 12)

The war's most celebrated remarks on the commemoration of the dead, however, came from President Abraham Lincoln during the establishment of the Gettysburg cemetery in 1863. "We have come to dedicate a portion of that field as a final resting place for those who here gave their lives," Lincoln proclaimed, before calling on the nation to continue the fight, so that "these dead shall not have died in vain" (Wills 1992, p. 21).

Even if honoring the dead was their primary focus, the original cemetery builders also had preservation and commemoration of the historic landscape in mind as well. The War Department report on Gettysburg noted that the cemetery "embraces that portion of the ground occupied by the center of the Union line of battle on the 2d and 3d of July, 1863," and called this position "one of the most prominent and important . . . on the field" (U.S. Army Quartermaster Corps 1865–1871, no. 16, p. 76). In establishing the Chattanooga National Cemetery in 1863, Major General George H. Thomas ordered that the memorial cemetery be established "in commemoration of the Battles of Chattanooga, November 23–27, 1863" (U.S. Army Quartermaster Corps 1865–1871, no. 11, pp. 11–13).

There was one great distinction made in the building of these wartime sites, however. By and large, only Union dead were reinterred in the cemeteries; the Confederate dead were left on battlefields or moved to local cemeteries. Regulations required that only U.S. military personnel could be buried in national cemeteries, and Confederates were technically not U.S. personnel. Some exceptions occurred, however, such as at Arlington National Cemetery and Shiloh National Cemetery. Following the war, one Confederate veteran wrote bitterly of this one-sided policy:

> We admit that we fought to destroy the old Union, and to establish a new government for ourselves, but you refused to let us go. You said you forgave us and would take us back into full fellowship, with all our former rights and privileges. We accept in good faith your offer and are willing at all times to prove our loyalty to our country, but we feel that if we have been restored to our places in the Union on equal terms with you, that it is hardly just that the bones of these, our brothers who wore the gray, should be left scattered upon the fields, while those who wore the blue are cared for and honored. (Reed 1893–1898, pp. 369–370)

Whereas the federal government made little effort to memorialize or honor Confederate dead during the war, viewing Confederates as traitors, revolutionaries, and enemies, African American soldiers were increasingly commemorated. This wartime commemoration at national cemeteries evidenced the growing standing of African

A dedication of the battle monument at Bull Run, VA, June 10, 1865. Before the end of the Civil War, Federal veterans installed an obelisk honoring the fallen soldiers of the First Battle of Bull Run. *The Library of Congress.*

Americans in the United States, particularly in the armed forces. Many national cemeteries that would not allow the burial of white Confederates contained United States Colored Troops. Although segregation was the norm even in burial, United States Colored Troops nonetheless received the same recognition that white soldiers gained by being buried in a national cemetery. In addition Quartermaster General Montgomery Meigs remarked that the "colored soldiers buried now together give evidence of the death of many of their race in the struggle for their freedom" (Neff 2005, pp. 197–198). That African Americans, considered property by both governments at the beginning of the war, were being buried in national cemeteries by the end of the war reveals just how much the nation had changed.

While the vast majority of the commemoration and monumentation did not begin until after the war ended, there were some early efforts at marking positions, commemorating actions, and memorializing those who had given their lives. And these early efforts can mostly still be seen today, giving a critical glimpse into the war years and showing that those who fought it were already thinking about the legacy of their actions.

BIBLIOGRAPHY

Abroe, Mary Munsell. " 'All the Profound Scenes:' Federal Preservation of Civil War Battlefields, 1861–1990." Ph.D. diss., Loyola University, Chicago, 1996.

Brown, Daniel A. *Marked for Future Generations: The Hazen Brigade Monument, 1863–1929.* Murfreesboro, TN: National Park Service, 1985.

Holt, Dean W. *American Military Cemeteries: A Comprehensive Illustrated Guide to the Hallowed Grounds of the United States, Including Cemeteries Overseas.* Jefferson, NC: McFarland, 1992.

Krick, Robert E. L. "The Civil War's First Monument: Bartow's Marker at Manassas." *Blue and Gray* 8, no. 4 (1991): 32–34.

Neff, John R. *Honoring the Civil War Dead: Commemoration and the Problem of Reconciliation.* Lawrence: University Press of Kansas, 2005.

Piehler, G. Kurt. *Remembering War the American Way.* Washington, DC: Smithsonian Institution Press, 1995.

Reed, David Wilson. "National Cemeteries and National Military Parks." In *War Sketches and Incidents: As Related by the Companions of the Iowa Commandery*

Military Order of the Loyal Legion of the United States, ed. Military Order of the Loyal Legion of the United States, Iowa Commandery. 2 vols. Des Moines, IA: Kenyon, 1893–1898.

Sellars, Richard West. *Pilgrim Places: Civil War Battlefields, Historic Preservation, and America's First National Military Parks, 1863–1900.* Fort Washington, PA: Eastern National, 2005.

Smith, Timothy B. *The Golden Age of Battlefield Preservation: The Decade of the 1890s and the Establishment of America's First Five Military Parks.* Knoxville, TN: in press.

United States Army Quartermaster Corps. *Roll of Honor: Names of Soldiers Who Died in Defence of the American Union, Interred in the National [and Other] Cemeteries* 27. 9 vols. Washington, DC: Government Printing Office, 1865–1871.

Van Horne, Thomas B. *The Life of Major-General George H. Thomas.* New York: C. Scribner's Sons, 1882.

Wills, Garry. *Lincoln at Gettysburg: The Words That Remade America.* New York: Simon & Schuster, 1992.

Timothy B. Smith

CHICKAMAUGA

Roughly twenty years after the end of the American Civil War, veterans and citizenry began to focus on memorializing the events of the late war to commemorate the soldiers' bravery and the lives lost. These efforts also focused on attempts to heal the wounds from the conflict and the political crisis that caused the bloodshed. In doing so, these veterans and citizens laid the foundation of historical preservation in the United States.

In 1880 the United States Congress passed legislation to allocate funds to preserve an American battlefield to commemorate past conflicts. $50,000 was disbursed to survey and develop maps detailing troop movements at the site of the Battle of Gettysburg in Pennsylvania. Once that mapping was completed, additional funds were set aside to mark the positions of the Army of the Potomac on the battlefield. While this work was being done, historical patrons from the South were requesting that a battlefield in the Southern United States be similarly marked.

Society of the Army of the Cumberland

After the late conflict of 1861 to 1865, various veterans' organizations were formed to remember comrades past and present. Organizations were created that focused on the victorious Federal armies that had existed during much of the war. One example was the Society of the Army of the Cumberland, an organization made up of veteran officers of the Army of the Cumberland, which had served in the Western Theater of the American Civil War, primarily in Tennessee and Georgia. In 1881, the organization held its annual reunion in Chattanooga, Tennessee. Many of the veterans were concerned that their old battlefields might be become unrecognizable over time without the placement of markers at key locations. Upon arrival at the old Chickamauga battlefield, a number of the older veterans were unable to pinpoint the locations of their regiments and brigades.

In May 1888, two former officers of the Army of the Cumberland visited the old battlefield. While examining the terrain, the two former officers developed the notion of turning the old Chickamauga battlefield in Georgia into a military park. The two officers were both brigadier generals, Henry Van Ness Boynton (1835–1905) and Ferdinand Van Derveer (1823–1892). Both Boynton and Van Derveer had served together in the Thirty-fifth Ohio Volunteer Infantry. Van Derveer, a lawyer in civilian life, had commanded a brigade in the engagement at Chickamauga, while Boynton had been rewarded the Congressional Medal of Honor at Missionary Ridge during the Battle of Chattanooga in November 1863. Boynton used his position as a reporter with the Cincinnati *Commercial Gazette* to write columns to promote the idea of a military park in Chickamauga. In those columns, Boynton advocated a need for a "Western Gettysburg" for the veterans of the Western battles. Initially, he directed his editorial focus to the members of the Society of the Army of the Cumberland. Unlike the plans for the military park at Gettysburg, however, Boynton proposed that both Confederate and Union veterans participate in the establishment of the Chickamauga site:

> The survivors of the Army of the Cumberland should awake to great pride in this notable field of Chickamauga. Why should it not, as well as eastern fields, be marked by monuments, and its lines be accurately preserved for history? There was no more magnificent fighting during the war than both armies did there. Both sides might well unite in preserving the field where both, in a military sense, won such renown. (Boynton 1895, p. 219)

During the early development of the Gettysburg battlefield, only monuments to the regiments of the Union Army of the Potomac had been erected and not to the men of the Confederate Army of Northern Virginia.

During the society's reunion in September 1888, in Chicago, the organization adapted a resolution to appoint a committee to develop a plan for purchasing land encompassing the Chickamauga battlefield site. The society chose its former commander, Major General William S. Rosecrans (1819–1898), to appoint the members of the committee. The committee was named the Chickamauga Memorial Association and was made up of former officers who had served in the engagement in September 1863. Invitations were sent to the governors of the states that had had troops serving in the battle to be members of the committee.

Battle of Chickamauga. Nearly two decades after the end of the Civil War, veterans laid out plans to commemorate soldiers who fought in the West by establishing a military park on the grounds of the Battle of Chickamauga. Unlike the early parks in the East, the one at Chickamauga honored the efforts of Union and Confederate troops alike. *Hulton Archive/Getty Images.*

The War Department and Congressional Approval

While this initial planning was being done, the U.S. War Department also became involved in the early planning stages at Chickamauga. Captain Sanford C. Kellogg, a veteran of the battle, was assigned to research troop positions for maps to be included in the *Official Records of the War of the Rebellion*. Kellogg conducted interviews of veterans and became a part of the research efforts to establish this new military park.

On February 13, 1889, the Chickamauga Memorial Association met in Washington, DC, with five members of the U.S. Congress who were from the South and had served as Confederate generals during the Battle of Chickamauga. These former generals agreed to cooperate with the Association and to assist with the formation of a joint memorial battlefield association. At the same time, Captain Kellogg agreed to assist the association by contacting additional parties who might be interested in serving as incorporators of a joint association.

The organizational meeting of the joint memorial association occurred during the annual reunion of the Society of the Army of the Cumberland in Chattanooga in September 1889. The reunion, which was a festive occasion, also hosted an assembly of Confederate veterans to participate in the creation of the memorial organization as well as local representatives from Georgia and Tennessee. The members of the Association proposed purchasing a tract of land that would encompass the battlefield from Rossville Gap to Crawfish Springs. It was hoped that the city of Chattanooga would also participate so that the future visitors would be able to examine the battlefields from Georgia to the northernmost points of Missionary Ridge in Tennessee. Twenty-eight former officers from both the Union and Confederate armies were selected to serve as a board of directors for the Chickamauga Memorial Association, with John T. Wilder as president and Joseph Wheeler as vice president.

The charter of the Chickamauga Memorial Association was registered with the Superior Court of Walker County, Georgia on December 4, 1890, and the incorporation was to last for twenty years until 1910. The organization consisted of the general membership, incorporators, the governors of various states, president and secretary of the Southern Historical Society, and the Secretary of War. General membership was open to all veterans for a lifetime membership fee of $5.00.

Congressmen Charles H. Grosvenor (1833–1917), who had served as a colonel of the Eighteenth Ohio Volunteer Infantry at Chickamauga, introduced H.R. 6454, "An Act to Establish a National Military Park at the battle-field of Chickamauga" on the floor of the U.S. House of Representatives in May 1890. The legislation served quick approval in the House Committee, and passed both houses of the U.S. Congress. President Benjamin Harrison (1833–1901), himself a Union veteran, signed the bill into law on August 19, 1890. The federal government would obtain roughly 7,600 acres through condemnation, while roads to the park would be ceded to the federal government by the states of Georgia and Tennessee. Soon after the incorporation of the Association, the Secretary of War appointed a national commission to oversee the work at the site of the military park. Joseph S. Fullerton was to serve as chairman, Alexander P. Stewart was placed in charge of construction, and Captain Kellogg would serve as secretary of the commission.

Construction of the Park

Work began on converting the property into a military park with markers and a museum. Underbrush was cleared away, roads were built to connect various portions of the site, and research was done to pinpoint the locations of regiments and batteries during the engagement. In some cases, Boynton and Kellogg worked together to gather information on troop positions and compose maps to aid in construction. Veterans were also interviewed to help locate landmarks that indicated where a particular unit fought during the battle. In 1890, the United Confederate Veterans held an encampment at the battlefield site and helped to locate Confederate regimental positions for Boynton and Kellogg. The members attempted to work through controversies dealing with these fighting positions between veterans of companion units. In addition to setting up memorials to the volunteer units, Boynton made an effort to place markers to commemorate the United States Army Regulars, which had also fought at Chickamauga in September 1863.

As the work continued on the site, the grounds of the park itself became training grounds for local militia and regular troops. In 1890, the Georgia State Guard used the old battlefield for encampments and training. With the start of the Spanish-American War in 1898, the United States Army created Camp George H. Thomas, named for Rosecrans's successor as the commander of the Army of the Cumberland, on the grounds of the military park. This site continued to be used by the U.S. War Department and became the town of Fort Oglethorpe, Georgia. The military use of this portion of the park continued throughout the turn of the twentieth century and up through World War I (1914–1918). The site was beneficial because the location of the battlefield was near the major north and south railroad lines running through Chattanooga. It was an ideal location for troops to be encamped during their training and possible deployment overseas. In addition, the park commission saw the military as an excellent way to increase use of the park and to justify its continued funding as an educational tool to citizens and the military.

The role of the commission in a leadership role with the park continued until 1921. By this date, the various commissioners who had taken an active role in the development of the site began to pass away. Joseph Fullerton died in 1897, and his chairmanship was passed down to Boynton. Boynton himself died on June 3, 1905, and his successor was Ezra Carman, who had commanded a New Jersey regiment during the Civil War. Former Confederate general Alexander P. Stewart passed away in 1908, and another former Confederate general, Joseph B. Cumming, replaced him. Captain Kellogg was reassigned from the park commission because of friction between himself and the civilian commission members. Much of the controversy came from the fact that a U.S. Army captain was trying to tell former generals what to do, which was not very conducive to career advancement. The park continued with its construction plans, and the hiring of staff to maintain and interpret portions of the military park.

In 1912, legislation was passed to allow the Secretary of War to assume the duties of commission members upon their deaths or resignations. By May 1922, Joseph B. Cumming passed away; with his death, the sole commission member remaining was the Secretary of War, at that time John W. Weeks of Massachusetts. By 1930, the staff of the National Military Park fluctuated with the additions and removals of permanent staff and the introduction of numbers of temporary personnel. At the same time, discussions were afoot to transfer jurisdiction over the Chickamauga-Chattanooga National Military Park and the other national military parks to the U.S. Department of the Interior. Many persons were opposed to the transfer due to the belief that Fort Oglethorpe would remain open, and the U.S. military and National Guard units would need the park property for conducting military education and training. Despite these objections, the Chickamauga-Chattanooga National Military Park was transferred to the U.S. Department of the Interior in August 1933. As of the early twenty-first century, the Chickamauga battle site is under the care of the National Park Service.

BIBLIOGRAPHY

Boynton, Henry V. *The National Military Park, Chickamauga-Chattanooga: A Historical Guide, With Maps and Illustrations.* Cincinnati, OH: Robert Clarke, 1895.

Kaser, James A. *At the Bivouac of Memory: History, Politics, and the Battle of Chickamauga.* New York: P. Lang, 1996.

Paige, John C., and Jerome A. Greene. *Administrative History of Chickamauga-Chattanooga National Military Park.* Denver, CO: National Park Service, 1983.

Robertson, William Glenn [et al.]. *Staff Ride Handbook for the Battle of Chickamauga, 18–20 September 1863.* Fort Leavenworth, KS: Combat Studies Institute, U.S. Army Command and General Staff College, 1982.

Sauers, Richard A. "From Hallowed Ground to Training Ground: Chickamauga's Camp Thomas, 1898." *Civil War Regiments*, vol. 7, no. 1, (2000): 129–143.

Sullivan, James R. *Chickamauga and Chattanooga National Military Park, Georgia–Tennessee.* Washington, DC: Government Printing Office, 1961.

United States Chickamauga and Chattanooga National Park Committee. *Legislation, Congressional and State, Pertaining to Establishment of the Park, Regulations Original and Amended, Governing the Erection of Monuments, Markers and Other Memorials.* Washington, DC Government Printing Office, 1897.

United States Congress. Joint Committee to Represent the Congress at the Dedication of Chickamauga and Chattanooga National Military Park. *Dedication of the Chickamauga and Chattanooga National Military Park, September 18–20, 1895.* Washington, DC: Government Printing Office, 1896.

William H. Brown

SHILOH

Shiloh National Military Park, established by Congress in 1894, preserves one of the most crucial battlefields of the Civil War. Containing some 96 percent of the actual fighting area, the Tennessee park is the best-preserved major battlefield of the war. It allows visitors and historians alike to glimpse what a Civil War battlefield looked like and to follow the movements of troops throughout the battle. More profoundly, it offers visitors a chance to connect with the traumatic events that occurred there.

National Context

The original establishment of the park was a product of several factors that came together in the 1890s to create a national preservation movement. In that decade, white Northerners and Southerners began to reconcile with each other after decades of grueling animosity, war, and reconstruction. In 1892 battlefield preservationist Henry Boynton wrote of the reconciliation, "[a] quarter of a century has brought this about, a period which is but a day in the life of a nation. He would indeed be impatient who looked for more speedy progress" (Boynton 1892, p. 4). Backing away from divisive racial issues, the veterans of the Civil War began to find common ground by focusing instead on the bravery, courage, and honor shown by Civil War soldiers on both sides during the 1860s. Thus, America began a process of reconciliation through memorialization, commemoration, and preservation. Statues went up all over the nation during this time—on almost every courthouse lawn, and in the two capitals that had once directed war against each other. No more vivid example of this reconciliation through commemoration is available than Shiloh National Military Park.

In the 1890s, the "Golden Age" of Civil War battlefield preservation, the federal government began a process of saving battlefields, and secured five of the war's major sites to varying degrees. Shiloh National Military Park was the third of the five battlefields preserved, following the Chickamauga and Chattanooga site and Antietam, and preceding Gettysburg and Vicksburg.

Establishment

The impetus for preserving Shiloh dated back to 1893, and can be traced to several sources. Veterans of the Army

"Last Line" at Pittsburg Landing. Encompassing almost the entire site of the actual battlefield, the Shiloh National Military Park commemorates the early Union victory in this Tennessee city which helped secure Northern control of the Mississippi.

of the Tennessee, who felt their army needed to be memorialized as others had been, began to lobby for Shiloh's establishment and passed a resolution "heartily favor[ing]" making Shiloh a park (Society of the Army of the Tennessee 1894, pp. 124–126). One of the author's of this resolution, Representative David Henderson, addressed fellow members of Congress on the subject, stressing that the creation of a park at Shiloh would "meet the wishes of the Western armies" (*Congressional Record*, p. 21). On a more personal level, veterans who returned to the battlefield were appalled to hear local farmers tell of unearthing battlefield graves while plowing or digging ditches or roadways. As late as 1893, one veteran remarked, farmers were "ploughing up ... [soldiers'] bones all over the field" (Society of the Army of the Tennessee 1893, pp. 8, 60–61). These veterans wanted their former comrades to rest in peace, and the way to do that was to preserve the entire battlefield.

These men soon established the Shiloh Battlefield Association, out of which came the idea of lobbying Congress to create the park. Congress did agree to do so in 1894, with the president signing the bill into law on December 27, 1894. The act declared the importance of having "the history of ... memorable battles [fought by the Army of the Tennessee] preserved on the ground where they fought" (*Congressional Record*, p. 19).

The founding legislation stipulated that "the affairs of the Shiloh National Military Park shall, subject to the supervision and direction of the Secretary of War, be in charge of three commissioners, ... each of whom shall have served at the time of the battle in one of the armies engaged therein" (*Congressional Record*, p. 19). Secretary of War Daniel S. Lamont appointed Colonel Cornelius Cadle, a veteran of the 11th Iowa Infantry of the Army of the Tennessee, as chairman of the commission. To represent the Army of the Ohio, Lamont chose that army's commander at Shiloh, Major General Don Carlos Buell. Former Confederates were also included in the process, befitting the era's move toward reconciliation; the secretary appointed Colonel Robert F. Looney of the 38th Tennessee Infantry as the Confederate representative. These men, along with such figures as Josiah Patterson, Basil Duke, David W. Reed, and James H. Ashcraft, who gradually replaced the original commissioners as deaths and resignations occurred, were the primary people responsible for what is today America's best-preserved Civil War battlefield. Reed, in addition to later becoming a full commissioner, served as the park's historian from its inception and has gained the title "Father of Shiloh National Military Park" for the work he did physically on the ground, as well as historiographically in print (Smith 2006, pp. 139–155).

Building the Park

The commission began its work early in 1895. Engineer Atwell Thompson and his crew surveyed the battlefield and mapped the area and its plots of land in what veterans described as an effort to convert "mere land into a park" (Smith 2004, p. 45). Only after this process was completed could the commission begin to buy the property. Land agent James W. Irwin found it difficult to sort out land titles in the rural area, and the commission was further hampered by a rogue veteran who obtained options on some of the land in hopes of blackmailing the government into giving him an appointment as a commissioner. The commission reported to the secretary of war in 1897 that "[m]uch difficulty has been experienced in obtaining sufficient titles to the land negotiated for, but this is gradually being overcome" (United States War Department 1897, p. 59). Eventually, the commission purchased some 3,600 acres of land; only about 500 acres have been added since, illustrating the comprehensiveness of their original work. With the land purchase, the history of the battle could be, in the words of the enabling legislation, "preserved on the ground" (*Congressional Record*, p. 19).

Once the land purchases went into effect, the commission was able to begin the process of marking the history of the battle" (Smith 2004, p. 62). The commission itself paid for the hundreds of iron tablets marking troop positions and campsites and giving direction that went up over the next few years, and also paid for replica iron cannon carriages on which they placed several hundred original Civil War cannon tubes that had been donated by the War Department. The commission also erected headquarters and monuments marking specific locations where general officers camped or were killed. These markings allowed, in the words of the park's superintendent DeLong Rice, "the seeker after history ... [to] start at the tablet where the first volley was fired and follow every movement of the divisions, brigades, and regiments through all the evolutions of the battle" (United States War Department 1915, p. 885).

The major monumentation, however, was paid for by other entities. Congress appropriated money to erect monuments to several regular army units that had fought at Shiloh. Most notably, the various states that had troops at Shiloh began to erect monuments all over the battlefield. The enabling legislation stated that "it shall be lawful for any State that had troops engaged in the battle of Shiloh to enter upon the lands of the Shiloh National Military Park for the purpose of ascertaining and marking the lines of battle of its troops engaged there" (*Congressional Record*, pp. 19–20).

The various states went about monumentation in different ways. Some erected one monument to all their units, whereas others placed different monuments dedicated to each of the units. Some erected both types of monuments. No matter the process, however, each state shared the same goal, stated succinctly by Ohio's legislature: "ascertaining and marking the positions occupied ... by each regiment, battery, and independent organization ... which were engaged there" (Lindsey 1903, p. 152). By no means the most heavily monumented park of the 1890s, Shiloh National Military Park is nevertheless beautiful in its simplicity (Smith 2004, pp. 137–138).

By 1908 the park was relatively complete—just in time for a thrashing in 1909 when, in the words of the commission chairman Cornelius Cadle, "a cyclone visited the Park" (Shiloh National Military Park Daily Events, October 14, 1909, pp. 274–277). The damage caused by the cyclone necessitated extensive repair and reconstruction. Following this, the physical building of the park was complete. It would not be until the 1930s that major work at the park began again.

Just as important as the physical building of the site was the development of an accepted historiographical analysis of the battle. As Ulysses S. Grant, the Army of the Tennessee commander at Shiloh, remarked, the "Battle of Shiloh ... has been perhaps less understood, or, to state the case more accurately, more persistently misunderstood, than any other engagement" (Grant 1884–1888, p. 465). Careful examination of all available written records was an important first step, as the recollections of elderly veterans were often unreliable and contradictory. As Reed remarked, "occasionally ... some one thinks that his unaided memory of the events of 50 years ago is superior to the official reports of officers which were made at [the] time of the battle. It seems hard for them to realize that oft-repeated campfire stories, added to and enlarged, become impressed on the memory as real facts" (United States War Department 1912, pp. 195–196). One of the park sponsors in Congress had promised that the park itself would "put at rest once and for all time to come the uncertainties and misrepresentations surrounding the battle," but that turn of events of course failed to materialize (*House Reports*, pp. 1–5). The park commission disseminated its own version of the battle, however, through the marking of the battlefield and in its official history, *The Battle of Shiloh and the Organizations Engaged* (1902).

The commissioners themselves soon died away, leaving the park in the hands of non-veterans such as DeLong Rice and Robert A. Livingston. Rice, who was very much attuned to what the veterans had done, took over in the 1920s. Unfortunately, he died as a result of an explosion on the park in 1929. Park clerk Robert A. Livingston then became superintendent. Life at Shiloh was relatively quiet in the 1920s and early 1930s (Smith 2006, pp. 157–170).

The Modern Era

President Franklin D. Roosevelt transferred Shiloh, and the other parks, from the War Department to the National Park Service in 1933, the same year he began implementing the New Deal, which sent many workers to Shiloh. In the 1940s, however, much of this labor force went off to war, leaving Shiloh with an almost perpetual shortage of funds and workers (Smith 2004, p. 127). The late 1990s and early twenty-first century saw an upswing in activity at the park, with a new unit opening twenty miles to the south at Corinth, Mississippi. Its state-of-the-art visitor center focuses not only on Corinth's relevance to Shiloh, but also on the siege of Corinth and the subsequent battle there (*Special Resource Study: Corinth Mississippi 2003*). As of 2007, several entities are continuing efforts to preserve more battlefield ground at Shiloh, as well as at Corinth. Their efforts will continue to carry out the desires of its founders: to commemorate and memorialize those who fought on those hallowed fields of combat.

BIBLIOGRAPHY

Blight, David W. *Race and Reunion: The Civil War in American Memory.* Cambridge, MA: Belknap Press of Harvard University Press, 2001.

Boynton, Henry. "Camping on Chickamauga." *Washington Post*, September 16, 1892.

Congressional Record, 53rd Congress, 3rd Session, 27, 1

Eisenschiml, Otto. *The Story of Shiloh.* Chicago: Civil War Round Table, 1946.

Grant, Ulysses S. "The Battle of Shiloh." In *Battles and Leaders of the Civil War*, ed Robert Underwood Johnson and Clarence Clough Buel. 4 vols. New York: The Century, 1884–1888.

House Reports, 53rd Congress, 2nd Session, Report No. 1139.

Lee, Ronald F. *The Origin and Evolution of the National Military Park Idea.* Washington, DC: National Park Service, 1973.

Lindsey, T. J. *Ohio at Shiloh: Report of the Commission.* Cincinnati, OH: C. J. Krehbiel, 1903.

Reed, David Wilson, ed. *The Battle of Shiloh and the Organizations Engaged.* Washington, DC: Government Printing Office, 1902.

Shiloh National Military Park Daily Events. Shiloh National Military Park Archives, October 14, 1909.

Smith, Timothy B. *The Golden Age of Battlefield Preservation: The Decade of the 1890s and the Establishment of America's First Five Military Parks.* Knoxville, TN: in press.

Smith, Timothy B. *This Great Battlefield of Shiloh: History, Memory, and the Establishment of a Civil War National Military Park.* Knoxville: University of Tennessee Press, 2004.

Smith, Timothy B. *The Untold Story of Shiloh: The Battle and the Battlefield.* Knoxville: University of Tennessee Press, 2006.

Society of the Army of the Tennessee. *Report of the Proceedings of the Society of the Army of the Tennessee at the Twenty-Fifth Meeting Held at Chicago, Ills. September 12th and 13th, 1893.* Cincinnati, OH: Author, 1893.

Society of the Army of the Tennessee. *Report of the Proceedings of the Society of the Army of the Tennessee at the Twenty-Sixth Meeting Held at Council Bluffs, Iowa. October 3rd and 4th, 1894.* Cincinnati, OH: Author, 1895.

Special Resource Study: Corinth, Mississippi. National Park Service: Washington, DC, 2003.

United States War Department. *Annual Report of the Secretary of War—1897.* Washington, DC: Government Printing Office, 1897.

United States War Department. *Annual Report of the Secretary of War—1912.* Washington, DC: Government Printing Office, 1912.

United States War Department. *Annual Report of the Secretary of War—1915.* Washington, DC: Government Printing Office, 1915.

Timothy B. Smith

VICKSBURG

The first efforts by Civil War soldiers to mark sites where blood was spilled, comrades fell, and lives were sacrificed began before the reverberations of fire faded from the scene of the conflict's battlefields. The earliest known monument on a Civil War battlefield was erected within the first four months of the war. Confederate soldiers of the Eighth Georgia infantry erected a monument on the battlefield of first Manassas to their brigade commander, Col. Francis Stebbins Bartow, who was killed during that engagement. Private William H. Maxey, of the Eighth Georgia described the occasion in a September 5, 1861, letter to his father: "I will now tell you of our yestodays work. Our whole brigade went to the Battlefield to place a stone for signal whare Bartow fell. We had prare and then had a speech from Mr. Striklin. On the stone it had the words that Bartow spoke it was on the stone 'they have killed me boys but never give up the fight'"(September 5, 1861). In 1863, surviving troops of Col. William B. Hazen's brigade placed a memorial in the Round Forest to commemorate comrades who fell on the battlefield at Stone's River. Similarly, in July, 1864, Federal soldiers marked the site on the Vicksburg battlefield where barely a year before, Union Major General Ulysses S. Grant met Confederate Lieutenant General John C. Pemberton to discuss surrender terms for the Southern forces.

Attempts to set aside battlefield lands as a remembrance of those who struggled and died over them were made on a provincial level even before the conclusion of hostilities. The most well known instance is that of Gettysburg where local citizens formed the Gettysburg Battlefield Memorial Association. In 1864, the association was given the authority, by the Pennsylvania legislature, "to hold and preserve, the battle-grounds of Gettysburg . . . and by such perpetuation, and such memorial structures as a generous and patriotic people may aid to erect, to commemorate the heroic deeds, the struggles, and the triumphs of their brave defenders" (Unrau 1991, pp. v–vi). Although the prosecution of the war prevented much progress until after the end of the hostilities, what was accomplished at Gettysburg served as the example for what were to become the first five Civil War battlefields preserved as National Parks. Localized and parochial efforts to commemorate specific contributions made during the Civil War continued after the conflict ended.

The final three decades of the nineteenth century witnessed the gathering of Civil War veterans at numerous reunions across the United States. The earliest of these were partisan, based strictly on previous Union or Confederate affiliation. In 1875, Confederate veterans journeyed to Boston to join with their Union counterparts for the 100th anniversary celebration of Bunker Hill. It was not until then that the past adversaries came together publicly. As reunions increased they became more frequent and widespread. The former opponents began to interact on an increasingly regular basis. As years passed and interaction between the one-time combatants grew the hostilities and passions of the conflict faded. This is reflected in the comments of Confederate General William B. Bate: "I note with inexpressible pleasure that the lapse of more than thirty years has mitigated the passions, allayed the excitement, and disposed the minds of all surviving contestants of these great battles to look back at the past with those moderated convictions which are due to a contest in which each party held principles and convictions to justify

View of the Vicksburg battlefield. As wounds of war slowly healed, Civil War veterans from both sides reunited in 1890 at the site of the Battle of Vicksburg. Disappointed with the battlefield's lack of preservation, the veterans formed a campaign to construct Vicksburg National Military Park at the turn of the twentieth century. *The Library of Congress.*

the contention" (Boynton 1896, pp. 45–46). A similar comment was expressed by Union veteran. J. S. Fullerton, "Never before has such harmonious work been possible" (Boynton 1896, p. 25).

The fiery sentiments and hostilities of the past were replaced by the soldiers' recognition of their shared experiences. Whether North or South, the aging warriors realized a common bond of sacrifice, suffering, struggle and loss as veterans of the Civil War. "We meet today upon this sacred spot to celebrate the heroism of the American soldier, the great results of battles, and the greater victories of peace. We do not come with words of crimination or with memories charged with bitterness or envy" (Boynton 1896, pp. 68–69). Bate aptly expressed the soldiers' experience:

> Here, within sight of this stand, we and they—the living and the dead, Confederate and Federal—fought for the right as each understood it, for the Constitution as each construed it, and for liberty as each interpreted it. With sheathless swords in sinewy hands we, Confederate and Federal, fought that great battle of duty, and now, thirty-two years after, we again obey the assemble call, we respond to the long roll and fall in line, not to renew the battle nor to rekindle the strife, nor even to argue as to which won the victory, but to gather up the rich fruits of both the victory and defeat as treasures of inestimable value to our common country."(Boynton 1896, pp. 45–46)

Out of that common knowledge grew a desire to commemorate their service. Nationwide interest was generated among the aging veterans to set aside battlefield lands as a remembrance of the common struggle they endured and sacrifices they gave. Bate continues to define the reason of being for the first National Military Park: "We have assembled on these glorious battlefields for the preservation and perpetuation of sacred memories; to treasure the recollections of heroic deeds; to compare in friendly criticism our past action; and to advance by lessons to be learned here the common glory of our common country" (Boynton 1896, pp. 45–46). Union General J. S. Fullerton reiterated the sentiments: "But little over thirty years have passed since this most desperate of battles was fought, and now survivors of both sides harmoniously and lovingly come together to fix their battle lines and mark the places now and forever to remain famous as monuments to the valor of the American soldier" (Boynton 1896, p. 25).

What began as individual attempts in small pockets across the country to commemorate on the local level became a cohesive coordinated effort supported on a national scale. Those efforts to preserve Civil War battlefields as a memorial to the soldiers who fought over their grounds in turn fostered reconciliation.

Union General John M. Palmer conveyed the understanding that exists between the former combatants who shared the common experiences of the battlefield:

> We are here today 'with malice toward none and charity for all;' we meet as citizens of a common country, devoted to its interests and alike ready to maintain its honor, wherever or however assailed. To my comrades, you who were Confederate soldiers during all the weary struggle of the civil war, I beg to say I was proud of your gallantry and courage. I never allowed myself to forget that you were Americans, freely offering your lives in the defense of what you believed to be your rights and in vindication of your manhood. You are now satisfied that the result of the civil war established the unity of the powerful American Republic; you submitted your controversies with your fellow-citizens to the arbitrament of the battlefield, and you accepted the result with a sublime fortitude worthy of all praise; and your reward is that peace and order are restored, and 'the South' which you loved so well and for which you fought so bravely now blossoms with abundant blessings. (Boynton 1896, p. 37)

"Indeed," remarked General Fullerton, "this celebration—the inauguration of this park and commemoration of the grand and noble idea—marks the beginning of a regenerated national life" (Boynton 1896, p. 25).

These efforts calumniated in the establishment of the first Civil War battlefield set aside as a National Park. Chickamauga and Chattanooga were preserved as a National Park by an act of Congress in 1890. Evidence that battlefield preservation was national in scope is exhibited by the addition of Shiloh, Gettysburg, and Vicksburg as national battlefields in 1894, 1895, and 1899, respectively. The establishment of grounds at Vicksburg, Mississippi as a National Military Park perhaps best exemplifies the strides taken toward national reconciliation by the widespread support that effort garnered. Veterans from across the country gathered at Vicksburg in the late spring of 1890, to attend a grand reunion held May 25–30. An association of veterans was formed to prepare for the expected magnitude of the event. The Blue and Gray Association was organized by charter in November, 1889, complete with a board of directors. The scale of the expected event is indicated by the approval to raise $100,000 in capital stock. Attendees of the reunion participated in a parade, field trips to outlying battlefields and visits to the interment sites of both Union and Confederate dead. The reunion was considered a success. Many veterans, however, noticed that the grounds over which they fought, bled and many had died, were ignored. The battlefield was virtually devoid of markings indicating the struggle that occurred there. Veterans left the reunion feeling that the grounds "deserved more and must be properly marked and preserved by our government" (Bearss, p. 3).

Over the course of the next five years veterans returned sporadically to Vicksburg for a number of events. The desire for good will and reconciliation that existed and motivated the interactions between the former combatants is aptly expressed by Union veteran Charles Longley. In a February, 1895, letter to fellow Iowa veteran William T. Rigby, Longley notes,

> I appreciate fully your kindness in telling me of Gen Lees good opinion and for two reasons. 1st I like to have friends. 2d I wanted to make a lasting good impression as a soldier on our friends in the South. You and I were representing the Federal Army and preaching a gospel of Peace and Goodwill to representatives of the Confederate Army their wives and children—increasing or decreasing their heart loyalty to the United States. It is not a small thing that we succeeded and it is not a small thing to have the assurance of the fact from such as Gen Lee and Colonel Floweree. (Files VNMP, Longley letter, February 19, 1895, p. 1)

In the fall of 1895, many of the aged soldiers who participated in the Blue and Gray Association again joined forces to form the Vicksburg National Military Park Association. It was organized at a veterans' meeting on October 22 and 23. According to the Iowa department of the Grand Army of the Republic, "The object of this organization, as indicated by its title, is to secure as a National Park the site of the siege and defense of Vicksburg." (Files VNMP, Department of Iowa Circular, p. 1). The Vicksburg National Military Park Association was chartered as a corporation by the State of Mississippi on November 19, 1895, and conferred with the authority to

> ...purchase, acquire by donation or otherwise, and to hold and dispose of real and personal property, and also to raise a fund either by subscriptions to the capital stock of this association, or by voluntary donation for the purpose of establishing a national military park in and around Vicksburg and to perpetually mark and designate the battlefields and other places of historic interest around said city. (Files VNMP, Charter of Incorporation, p. 1)

Former high ranking officers of both the Union and Confederate armies were represented among the officers, executive committee, and board of directors of the newly formed organization. Union Generals Moritmer Leggett, George McGinnis, and Lucius Fairchild joined Confederate Generals Stephen D. Lee, John B. Gordon, and Thomas Waul among the membership, which was indicative of the reconciliatory nature and work of the organization. The work of the association progressed rapidly. The first meeting of the Board of Directors produced an outline of grounds for inclusion in the park. According to Rigby, who was secretary of the association, "On motion of General Fairchild it was decided that 'the proposed Park should include the lines of the earthworks of the opposing armies and the land included within these lines, with such additions as are necessary to include the Headquarters of Generals Grant and Pemberton. Such of the water batteries as it may be desirable to designate, and other historical spots, the whole not to exceed four thousand acres'" (Files VNMP, Rigby, Brief History of Vicksburg National Military Park Association, p. 4).

The board's executive members appointed a committee charged with framing and presenting a bill for the establishment of a National Military Park at Vicksburg to Congress. The proposal of General Fairchild was incorporated into the bill with a modification to the recommended acreage. Based on an estimated cost of thirty-five dollars an acre, land acquisition of twelve hundred acres as opposed to the desired four thousand was suggested. The bill garnered the support of thirteen different states. By joint resolutions of their legislatures, Mississippi, Iowa, New York, Massachusetts, Rhode Island, Minnesota, Wisconsin, Michigan, Illinois, Indiana, Pennsylvania and Tennessee all endorsed passage of the bill. Numerous veterans' organizations including Department Encampments of the Grand Army of the Republic and Commanderys of the Loyal Legion encouraged passage of the bill. After three successive years in which members of the association traveled to Washington to urge passage of the bill, success was achieved early in 1899. The bill was passed by the Houses of Representatives on February 6, followed the Senate on the tenth, and became law with the signature of President McKinley on the twenty-first. Many aging warriors passed from this world to the next before realizing their dream of establishing a park over the siege and defense lines at Vicksburg. During the early years of the twentieth century, many of those veterans that remained returned to the scene of battle to mark their positions. Union Major D. W. Reed, a veteran of the Vicksburg campaign, stated the purpose behind the tireless efforts of the old soldiers:

> It is not intended that these parks will be ornamental pleasure grounds. The real object is to restore these historic fields to substantially the conditions they were in at the time of the battles; and, in harmony with that idea, these parks will be devoted strictly to the illustration of the great struggles which rendered them famous. In these parks every incident of the battle will be treated from an impartial standpoint of history, without sectional animosity or bias, and in all markings or monuments justice will be shown alike to vanquished and victors. On one or the other of these fields the most distinguished generals of North and South have commanded, and troops from nearly every state and section fought; so that by securing and preserving these fields intact as representative examples of the war, the Government will be able to perpetuate their history, so that they may serve as permanent object lessons of American courage and valor, and each constructed on a grand scale not to be found elsewhere in the world. (Iowa Commandery 1898, pp. 372–373)

The desires for commemoration, preservation and reconciliation among Civil War veterans were inextricably intertwined and naturally evolved from one another. The gathering of veterans in reunions across the country sowed the seeds of reconciliation and resulted in the desire to commemorate and memorialize common experiences. The desire for and accomplishment of preservation on a national level followed. Reconciliation was thus achieved in a communal sense and reunion came full circle. It was the veterans themselves, those who fought and bled over the grounds of numberless Civil War battlefields across the country that worked tirelessly to see that the park was established, marked their lines and positions, and provided for the erection of monuments for the purpose of honoring the sacrifices made over those grounds.

Vicksburg National Military Park is a memorial that tells of the devotion of soldiers and their shared experiences of sacrifice that transcended the boundaries of North and South. It also tells us of the commitment of a grateful citizenry in their efforts to honor unto posterity those sacrifices, and finally the park tells us of a deeply wounded nation and its desire for reconciliation. Vicksburg National Military Park tells the story of the Vicksburg Campaign and a shared experience. It commemorates the devotion of soldiers and their common experience of sacrifice, the commitment of a grateful citizenry, and the desire for reconciliation of a deeply wounded nation. In this one succinct inscription, "Here brothers fought for their principles, here heroes died for their country and a united people will forever cherish the precious legacy of their noble manhood" (Programme Pennsylvania Day, p. 1).

BIBLIOGRAPHY

Bearss, Edwin C., *Administrative History.* Unpublished Manuscript. Files of Vicksburg National Military Park Archives, Vicksburg, Mississippi.

Boynton, H. V., compiler. Joint Committee to represent the Congress. *Dedication of the Chickamauga and Chattanooga National Military Park, September 18–20, 1895.* Washington: Government Printing Office, 1896.

Files of Vicksburg National Military Park Archives. Administrative Series, box 7, folder 158, Vicksburg, MS.

Iowa Commandery Military Order of the Loyal Legion of the United States. *War Sketches and Incidents.* vol. 2. 1898. Reprint, Wilmington: Broadfoot Publishing Company, 1994.

Longley, Charles. Letter to William T. Rigby. February 19, 1895. Files of Vicksburg National Military Park Archives, Vicksburg, Mississippi.

Maxey, William H. Letter to Father. September 5, 1861. Files of Manassas National Battlefield Park Archives, Manassas, Virginia.

Programme Pennsylvania Day, 1906. Irving Press, New York. Files of Vicksburg National Military Park Archives, Monumentation Series, box 3, folder 94. Vicksburg, MS.

Rigby, William, T. Brief History of Vicksburg National Military Park Association. December 7, 1899. Files of Vicksburg National Military Park Archives, Vicksburg, Mississippi.

Unrau, Harlan D. *Administrative History: Gettysburg National Military Park and National Cemetery.* Washington: National Park Service, 1991.

Robbie C. Smith

GETTYSBURG

The battle of Gettysburg, July 1–3, 1863, fought in Adams County, Pennsylvania, was the largest and bloodiest military engagement of the Civil War. Over 160,000 men from the Confederate Army of Northern Virginia, commanded by General Robert E. Lee (1807–1870), and the Federal Army of the Potomac, commanded by Major General George Gordon Meade (1815–1872), had struggled over the hills, woods, ridges, and fields around the small town. The fighting was as fierce as any that took place during the war, and on several occasions, the outcome of the conflict hung narrowly in balance. When the battle ended, however, the Union army still held its position, and the Rebels were forced to admit defeat.

According to Stephen Sears in his 2003 book *Gettysburg*, Lee lost 22,625 men over the course of the battle, while Meade's losses were 23,049 men. Combined casualties for the two armies over the course of the campaign equaled 50,674 men, including 7,691 dead (Sears 2003, p. 498). Almost from the moment the last weapon was fired, Northern troops and civilians sensed that Gettysburg was uniquely important. This feeling grew in part from the staggering scale as well as the death toll of the battle. But in large measure, it came about because the battle was an unquestioned victory for the Army of the Potomac, ending a string of embarrassing defeats dealt it by Lee's Rebels. Initially, many Northerners thought the victory at Gettysburg, combined with Union triumphs in the West, might herald the end of the war. It did not. Two more years of bloody fighting remained before the conflict would close.

Regardless of the disappointing aftermath of the campaign, however, the feeling that this battle was special prevailed. Northerners felt compelled to memorialize the battle, even while the outcome of the war remained uncertain.

Commemorating a Fallen Leader

In the summer of 1863, Major General John F. Reynolds (1820–1863) was one of the most capable officers in the Army of the Potomac. Offered command of the army in the days leading up to the battle of Gettysburg, Reynolds, disdainful of meddling by politicians in the army's management, refused the job. The post went instead to Meade. Thus it was Reynolds who rode into Gettysburg at midmorning of July 1, 1863, at the head of the Union I and XI Corps. Approving the decision of Brigadier General John Buford (1826–1863) to provoke a fight at Gettysburg, Reynolds ordered his troops into the battle, determined to buy time for the rest of the army to reach the field and occupy the high ground south of town. This quick-thinking decision was critical to the outcome of the contest. Even though the Federal I and XI Corps were eventually routed by attacking Confederates, their resistance bought Meade time to get most of his army onto the heights it would successfully defend on July 2 and 3.

John Reynolds did not live to see the fruits of his decisiveness. As Federal infantry rushed forward to meet attacking Confederates, Reynolds was killed instantly when a Rebel bullet struck him in the back of the neck.

The Federal position in Gettysburg. The extreme left flank of the Union army was positioned on Little Round Top, whose elevation afforded the army a strategic advantage. Confederate troops attempted to overrun Little Round Top and split the Union defense, but could not defeat Colonel Strong Vincent's brigade. *The Library of Congress*

He was the first Union general lost in the battle and one of the most talented (Sears 2003, p. 170).

The death of their commander was a painful blow to the men of the I Corps. Shortly after the battle, the idea of building a memorial to the fallen general surfaced. Colonel Charles Wainwright (1826–1907) was the commanding officer of the I Corps's artillery. He noted in his diary, edited by Allan Nevins and reprinted in 1998 under the title, *A Diary of Battle: The Personal Journals of Colonel Charles S. Wainwright, 1861–1865*, that it was Major J. M. "Ben" Sanderson, who initially proposed the erection of a monument to Reynolds.

"At the time we were on the march and could do nothing in the matter," Wainwright recorded on August 29, 1863. But once the rival armies paused along the Rappahannock River in Virginia, the opportunity arose for Reynolds's former staff to discuss the issue. Several of them agreed upon a plan, and Wainwright went to the camp of the Pennsylvania Reserves, whom Reynolds had once led, and proposed an effort to raise money for constructing a proper monument. "All seem anxious to carry out the matter," the colonel happily informed his journal (Nevins 1998, p. 278).

The enthusiasm was real and the intent sincere. Officers and men contributed the first funding for the proposed monument. But the effort quickly slipped into the background as the immediate realities of an unfinished war took precedence. Many of those who subscribed to the cause would join Reynolds in death before the first anniversary of the battle of Gettysburg.

Despite the hopes and plans of Wainwright, Sanderson, and others, the conflict would have to end and time would need to pass before the memorial they envisioned could be funded, designed, and built. Not until 1871 would the idea born in July 1863 see fruition. Nonetheless, the statue of John Reynolds would be the first monument raised on the battlefield to a specific individual.

Dedicating a Cemetery

Even as civilian volunteers and medical personnel strove to deal with the tens of thousands of wounded scattered in temporary hospitals all around Gettysburg, the first steps were taken to preserve the scene of action as a monument. Learning that weather was exposing the bodies of soldiers buried in temporary graves immediately after the fighting, the governor of Pennsylvania, Andrew Gregg Curtin (1817–1894), authorized David Wills (1831–1894), a Gettysburg lawyer, to purchase land for the construction of a permanent soldiers' cemetery. The site selected by Wills was adjacent to the existing Evergreen Cemetery, which gave Cemetery Hill, a key geographic feature of the battle, its name. Now it would become the final resting place for more than 3,600 Union troops killed in the battle (Davis 2002, p. 12).

The landscape architect William Saunders (1822–1900) of the Department of Agriculture was given the mission of designing the cemetery. Saunders produced a simple but elegant plan for the 17-acre site. A "soldiers' monument" would form the center of the cemetery, with graves extending from it in semicircular rows. The dead would be grouped together by state; the size of each state's "lot" in proportion to the number of its fallen. No Confederate dead would be included. Saunders's design was quickly approved by a hastily appointed board of commissioners (Davis 2002, p. 12).

Work on the cemetery began promptly, spurred by the necessity of retrieving already decaying bodies from shallow graves. Even as this task was carried on, however, the commissioners decided to hold an official dedication ceremony for the site. The event took place on November 19, 1863—a mere 139 days after the end of the battle. Some 15,000 people watched as a military procession escorted dignitaries from Gettysburg to the as-yet unfinished cemetery. In his beautifully illustrated 2003 work, *Gettysburg Battlefield: The Definitive Illustrated History*, David Eicher notes that the honored guests included President Abraham Lincoln, Governor Curtin, three members of Lincoln's cabinet, and the French ambassador to the United States. Also included was David Wills, in whose home the president stayed the night before the ceremony (2003, pp. 256, 264).

Several thousand spectators followed the procession to the cemetery. Here they heard the famous orator Edward Everett (1794–1865) give a flowery 117-minute-long speech recounting the history of the battle and the campaign that led to it. Following Everett, Lincoln was given an opportunity to make a few remarks. The president spoke for only two minutes. In that brief span, Lincoln uttered his most famous words—the Gettysburg Address (Eicher 2003, p. 262).

The ceremony over, the work of reinterment continued. Ultimately, 3,629 Federal dead were laid to rest within the cemetery boundaries. Names could be attached to only 1,965 of the men whose remains reside there—1,664 headstones merely read "unknown" (Eicher 2003, p. 262; Davis 2002, p. 16).

Work on the cemetery continued into 1864. The last bodies were buried, the grounds beautifully landscaped, and a stone wall erected around the site. On July 4, 1865, amid another ceremony, the cornerstone of the envisioned Soldiers' Monument was laid in the cemetery grounds. This final piece of Saunders's original plan was finished four years later and dedicated in 1869 (Davis 2002, p. 16; Eicher 2003, p. 271).

Saving the Battlefield

While Governor Curtin and David Wills worked to build the soldiers' cemetery, others conceived additional means to commemorate the battle. As William C. Davis explains in the 2002 edition of *Gettysburg: The Story behind the Scenery*, David McConaughy (1823–1902) was the prime mover in the effort to preserve the battlefield. On August 14, 1863, in an address to Gettysburg's leading citizens, he proposed the town acquire as much of the battleground as possible, and that the field along with its breastworks, fences, and buildings, be "preserved and perpetuated in the exact form and condition they presented during the battle." The good people of Gettysburg concurred. The battlefield, they felt, should become a lasting monument to "perpetuate the great principles of human liberty and just government." Union soldiers had fought to preserve and would help instill those virtues to "all men who in all time" should visit the battleground (Davis 2002, p. 12).

McConaughy was pleased with the response but disinclined to wait for community action. Before the war was over, he had purchased Culp's Hill and the eastern slope of Cemetery Hill—both anchors for Meade's right flank during the battle—as well as parts of Big Round Top and Little Round Top, scenes of heavy fighting on the Union left flank. McConaughy paid for these properties out of his own pocket, anticipating reimbursement by the government of Pennsylvania when the battlefield became an official monument (Davis 2002, p. 12).

On April 30, 1864, the state of Pennsylvania formally chartered the Gettysburg Battlefield Memorial Association (GBMA). Its purpose was to "hold and preserve the battlegrounds of Gettysburg," and care for "such memorial structures as a generous and patriotic people may aid to erect to commemorate the heroic deeds, the struggles and the triumphs of their brave

Little and Big Round Top in Gettysburg, scenes of heavy battle. The battle of Gettysburg was fought in Adams County, PA, July 1–3, 1863. It was the largest and most gruesome battle of the Civil War, where 22,625 Confederate soldiers and 23,049 Union soldiers perished. *The Library of Congress.*

defenders." Membership required a ten-dollar donation and bestowed the right to vote in annual elections for the association's president and twenty-one-member board of directors. In 1866 Pennsylvania's legislature gave the association power to buy land relevant to the battle, build roads, construct monuments, and seize land when owners would not sell. Association property was declared tax-exempt in perpetuity (Davis 2002, p.16).

David McConaughy became the association's legal counsel and was tasked with raising money for the project, hopefully from the legislatures of Northern states whose men had fought at Gettysburg. As an inducement, the governor of any state whose legislature donated funds to the association automatically became a member of the board of directors. Pennsylvania was the first to contribute, granting $4,000 to the association in 1864. To the disappointment of McConaughy and the GBMA, however, other states failed to follow suit. The war would be long over before the vision of the association and the foresight of David McConaughy would truly bear fruit (Davis 2002, p. 17).

Temporary Failure, Ultimate Triumph

Beyond the creation of the soldiers' cemetery, little was done to physically commemorate the battle during and immediately after the war. Although Northerners, particularly those in the Northeastern states, continued to perceive Gettysburg as an important victory, two more horrible years of war remained after July 1863. The necessity of carrying on the conflict, the growing unpopularity of the war, the divisiveness it entailed, the real possibility of Northern defeat, and the seemingly endless flood of casualties produced by the final campaigns shoved Gettysburg into the background. During the remaining years of the war, there were more important things to do. After the war, the rancor of Reconstruction and the settlement of the West captured the public's attention. The nation's wounds remained raw as the enormous cost of the war was digested. Most people wanted to forget the recent horror and get on with their lives.

By the late 1870s the worst aftereffects of the war were wearing off. The dormant impulse to honor fallen leaders and their troops began to reemerge. As the twenty-fifth anniversary of the battle neared, there was an outburst of activity. Time had begun to heal the conflict's wounds; aging veterans were eager to preserve the scene and the story of what they had done; and the nation as a whole had started to come to grips not only with the cost of the war but also its meaning.

Gettysburg would ultimately become the symbol of the entire conflict. As the site of the largest and bloodiest battle of the war, it seemed the natural place for the principal memorial to the struggle. Lincoln's famous speech on the battlefield, which so concisely encapsulated what Northerners believed the war and the battle were about, added weight to this point of view. Even the South, initially barred from commemorating the service and loss of its sons, was invited and willing to tell its side of the battle at Gettysburg.

When the nation was finally ready to use the battlefield to remember and teach what had happened there, to honor those who had fallen and participated in the titanic struggle, the ground was found well prepared by the wartime efforts of Gettysburg's citizens. Their foresight in preserving the physical battleground and providing a final resting place for some of its victims proved the foundation for what is today the nation's most famous and most frequently visited national battlefield park.

BIBLIOGRAPHY

Davis, William C. *Gettysburg: The Story behind the Scenery.* Las Vegas, NV: KC Publications, 2002.

Eicher, David J. *Gettysburg Battlefield: The Definitive Illustrated History.* San Francisco: Chronicle Books, 2003.

Nevins, Allan, ed. *A Diary of Battle: The Personal Journals of Colonel Charles S. Wainwright, 1861–1865.* New York: Da Capo Press, 1998.

Sears, Stephen. *Gettysburg.* Boston: Houghton Mifflin, 2003.

Jeffrey William Hunt

ANTIETAM

Antietam National Battlefield, first preserved by Congress in 1890, is one of the most pristine battlefields in the United States. Situated in rural western Maryland near the small town of Sharpsburg, the battlefield has not been subject to the same urbanization and industrialization that have compromised so many other Civil War fields of conflict. As a result, Antietam is unspoiled, giving visitors a glimpse back in time at famous sites such as Bloody Lane, Burnside Bridge, and Miller's Cornfield, where many historians say the fate of the United States hung in the balance and was decided in favor of unity (Trail 2005).

National Context

Antietam's establishment in 1890 was part of a national movement to preserve battlefields. In the last decade of the nineteenth century, the U.S. government preserved five battlefields in varying degrees: Chickamauga and Chattanooga National Military Park was established first; Antietam second, in the same year; then Shiloh, Gettysburg, and Vicksburg in later years. Thirty years after the war, when tempers had cooled and old age had mellowed many of the veterans, white Northerners and Southerners began to reconcile through memorialization, commemoration, and preservation at, among other places, their old battlefields.

Antietam did not fit the national mold, however. The four other battlefields established during the 1890s were much larger parks, run by permanent commissions made up of veterans. Moreover, the intent, particularly at Chickamauga and Shiloh, and to a lesser degree at Gettysburg and Vicksburg, was to preserve entire fields of conflict, or at least the most important parts of them. This view of preservation was promoted by the United States's chief preservationist of the time, Henry V. Boynton (1835–1905), who served first as the historian and then as the commission chairman at the Chickamauga and Chattanooga National Military Park (Smith 2008). An alternate plan of preservation was adopted for Antietam, promoted by the other major preservationist of the day, Major George B. Davis of the U.S. Army. Davis believed preserving entire battlefields was unnecessary, and that limited purchase of land along roads and lines of battle would suffice, leaving the bulk of the battlefields, particularly those in rural areas, in private farmers' hands. Secretary of War Daniel S. Lamont (1851–1905) agreed, arguing that buying the entire battlefield would necessitate "operations of agriculture," which would be costly and was "outside the ordinary and usual scope of governmental endeavor" (*Annual Report of the Secretary of War—1894*, pp. 29, 255–256). Davis led major effort at Antietam in the 1890s, and that battlefield therefore was much smaller and less monumented than the others. Moreover, Davis's "Antietam Plan," as it was called, was the model for more battlefields throughout the twentieth century as the United States tried to save money and balance the competing effects of preservation and urbanization (Lee 1973).

Establishment

Veterans had placed monuments at Antietam as early as 1887, but the major effort to create a park did not develop until 1890, when a veterans' association and local congressman, Louis E. McComas (1846–1907), proffered a bill to establish a major park like that being contemplated at Chickamauga. McComas was never able to get his bill passed, but according to the local Keedysville *Antietam Wavelet*, he was able to get, "by a short cut," a limited appropriation rider for a board of veterans to mark lines of battle at Antietam (*Antietam Wavelet*, June 21, 1890). In 1891, the secretary of war appointed this board, which consisted of Union colonel John C. Stearns of the Ninth Vermont Infantry and Confederate major general Henry Heth (1825–1899). Right away, all could see that the Antietam project was not as well supported as the other parks then under development. Rather than a three-man commission like the others, Antietam battlefield was governed by a two-man board that did not have nearly the authority or the resources the other commissions had. Likewise, Antietam was not established as a park like the others, but was left simply as an agricultural area with battle lines marked thereon. "Had we been placed on the same footing with the Chickamauga Commission," Stearns and Heth wrote on January 13, 1894, "we would have been able to report greater progress" (Antietam Board to R. N. Bachelder, RG 92, E 707, box 1).

Building the Park

Stearns and Heth began their work in August 1891, but made little progress for the next three years. They managed to locate the lines of battle for the armies and began to mark some of them, but old age, sickness, and limited governmental support caused delay after delay. Heth wrote on August 1, 1894, that "it is hardly necessary to add that in consequence of Col. Stearns' bad health, the work has not progressed as rapidly as it would otherwise have done" (Henry Heth to R. N. Bachelder, RG 92, E 707, box 1). Thus, little was accomplished in the first years of the board's existence.

Secretary of War Lamont soon tired of the lack of progress at Antietam:

> While fully aware of the difficulties that attend upon undertakings of this kind, at Antietam and elsewhere, I cannot resist the conclusion that the Board as organized under the order of June 17, 1891, is less expeditious in its operations than Congress and the

> Department have a reasonable right to expect .... Over three years have passed since the scheme was undertaken, and the Board has so little to show in the way of accomplished results as to lead to the belief that difficulties have been encountered which are either insurmountable, or cannot be overcome by the Board as at present constituted. (Daniel S. Lamont to Quartermaster General, July 14, 1894, RG 92, E 707, box 1)

In summer 1894 Lamont thus called Stearns and Heth to account for their work. Stearns immediately resigned, whereupon Lamont sent George B. Davis to take over the effort.

Davis was then head of the board publishing the Official Records, and would later become the army's judge advocate general. As president of the Antietam board, Davis oversaw the effort, constantly pushing to get the work done. "It is only by constantly pushing in these small ways that we can keep the whole project in motion," Davis wrote (George B. Davis to E.A. Carman, November 27, 1894, RG 92, E 707, box 1). In addition to Davis, a board was still needed to actually do the work. The secretary of war appointed Ezra Carman of the Thirteenth New Jersey Infantry to be the Union representative on site at Antietam, and reappointed Heth to the Confederate side. Lamont also appointed Jed Hotchkiss, Stonewall Jackson's famous cartographer during the war, as the engineer tasked with making maps of the battle and battlefield.

Heth, Hotchkiss, Davis, and particularly Carman then went to work with a vengeance, producing in eleven months more results than Stearns and Heth had produced in three years. The board first began to create maps of the battlefield, but this task was plagued with problems, and even led to Hotchkiss's eventual removal from the project. Davis wrote that Hotchkiss's work "well nigh proved a failure" (George B. Davis Memorandum, August 2, 1895, RG 92, E 707, box 2). Gettysburg National Military Park's engineer, Emmor B. Cope, assisted the board thereafter.

More tangibly, Davis, Heth, and Carman began working on the battlefield itself. They bought a few acres of land, mostly where roads needed to be opened to allow access to the entire battlefield, but endured some opposition from landowners. At one point, Davis told Carman that he would come to Antietam "chiefly to have a show-down about land" (George B. Davis to E. A. Carman, November 6, 1894, RG 92, E 707, box 1). The veterans also began writing text for the several hundred tablets that would be placed along the roadways the government had bought. A few artillery pieces went up, as did fencing and a few monuments to mark where general officers had been killed. The board also built an observation tower at the Bloody Lane, and individual states erected monuments to their troops.

The majority of the work was completed by August 1895, when Davis resigned as president of the board to

Antietam National Battlefield in rural western Maryland. Antietam National Battlefield was first preserved by Congress in 1890. Due to the lack of urbanization at the location of the battlefield, it is left unblemished. This is a photograph of deceased Confederate soldiers by a fence on Hagerstown Road at this site. *Photograph by Alexander Gardner. The Library of Congress.*

become a professor at West Point. He argued he would be "too great a distance to direct the work to advantage" (George B. Davis memorandum, August 1, 1895, RG 92, E 707, box 2). In his place, to tie up the loose ends, was army officer George W. Davis (no relation to George B. Davis). He managed to finish a majority of the work before he, too, left to lead troops during the Spanish-American War. Heth and Carman worked periodically on the site for a few years; with Heth's death in 1899, Carman became the chief historian of the battle and battlefield.

With the board's demise and Carman's eventual appointment as chairman of the Chickamauga and Chattanooga National Military Park Commission, the government property at Antietam fell solely to the local cemetery superintendent, but it proved to be far too much work for him. The quartermaster general even told the secretary of war that "complaint is made that there is no supervision and no responsible authority who may guard the tablets erected by the government and the monuments erected by states and regimental organizations" (J. M. Ludington, May 3, 1900, RG 92, E 89, file 109863). The War Department then appointed a series of superintendents, but had bad luck with a few of them. One was murdered, and one was fired for drunkenness when a War Department inspector reported he was "whiskey crazy and that he is a dangerous man to have as superintendent of the Battlefield (C. P. Spence to Depot Quartermaster, April 14, 1913, RG 92, E 89, file 371906). By the mid-1910s, however, Antietam came under the care of a series of superintendents with little fanfare, and this governance lasted until 1933.

Modern Era

Antietam became part of the National Park Service in 1933, when President Franklin D. Roosevelt transferred the battlefields from the War Department to the Department of the Interior. Thereafter, Antietam became a full-fledged park, a status it had never been given under the War Department.

A major change has come to Antietam in recent years that is as ironic as it is appropriate. Since the 1980s, the National Park Service has begun to acquire large amounts of land at Antietam—land purposefully left in private ownership in the 1890s to save the government money. The so-called "Antietam Plan," has been thrown on the scrap heap of history in favor of total preservation. In the years after the 1890s, most Civil War parks such as Petersburg, Stones River, Kennesaw Mountain, Manassas, and Richmond had been developed along this "Antietam Plan." Now, entities such as the National Park Service, the Conservation Fund, and particularly the Civil War Preservation Trust have swung the pendulum of preservation theory back to Boynton's idea of total preservation. Of course, the results have been beneficial to the park that is considered one of the most beautiful sites in America's historic landscape (Smith 2008).

BIBLIOGRAPHY

Annual Report of the Secretary of War—1894. Washington, DC: Government Printing Office, 1894.

Antietam Wavelet, Keedysville, Maryland, June 21, 1890.

Blight, David. *Race and Reunion: The Civil War in Memory and Reunion.* Cambridge, MA: Harvard University Press, 2001.

"General Correspondence, 1890–1914." E 89, RG 92, Records of the Quartermaster General. National Archives, Washington, DC.

Lee, Ronald F. *The Origin and Evolution of the National Military Park Idea.* Washington, DC: National Park Service, 1973.

"Records of Cemeterial Commissions, 1893–1916, Antietam Battlefield Commission, Letters and Reports to Secretary, 1894–1898." E 707, RG 92, Records of the Quartermaster General. National Archives, Washington, DC.

Smith, Timothy B. *The Golden Age of Battlefield Preservation: The Decade of the 1890s and the Establishment of America's First Five Military Parks.* Knoxville: University of Tennessee Press, 2008.

Snell, Charles W., and Sharon A. Brown. *Antietam National Battlefield and National Cemetery.* Washington, DC: National Park Service, 1986.

Trail, Susan W. "Remembering Antietam: Commemoration and Preservation of a Civil War Battlefield." Ph. D. diss. University of Maryland, 2005.

Timothy B. Smith

National Cemeteries

There are perhaps no more hallowed locations in the United States than the various national cemeteries. These quiet reserves are the final resting places of thousands and thousands of soldiers who served in the U.S. military. While to be sure many soldiers died in America's wars prior to the 1860s, it was not until the Civil War that the United States set aside specific places to bury and honor its military heroes.

Wartime Cemeteries

The burial of the Civil War dead began as soon as the conflict erupted. With more pressing matters to attend to, army units normally buried their dead, particularly battle casualties, on the ground where they had fought. In addition to battlefields, there were other locations where large numbers of soldiers died, such as hospitals and prisons, and in these places too soldiers were buried nearby. The sites where mass burials took place were normally on private land that had to be bought or condemned by the government. In order to legitimize national burial sites on private land, the 37th Congress passed legislation allowing for the establishment of national cemeteries as deemed necessary by the president. Abraham Lincoln signed the bill into law on July 17, 1862. Section 18 gave him the "power, whenever in his opinion it is expedient, to purchase cemetery grounds and cause them to be securely enclosed, to be used as a national cemetery for the soldiers who shall die in the service of the country" (Holt 1992, pp. 2–3).

With the power granted by this legislation, the Lincoln administration created fourteen national cemeteries in 1862. Many were near the Northern capital, such as the one at Soldiers' Home, but other troop induction and care centers also gained national cemeteries, such as those at Annapolis, Maryland; Camp Butler, Illinois; and Philadelphia. In the early days of the war, these cemeteries held more soldiers who had died of disease than of battle wounds (Holt 1992, pp. 2–3).

A few of the fourteen original 1862 cemeteries were located on battlefields. One was on the small battleground of Mill Springs in eastern Kentucky, the site of a January 1862 battle. More famous cemeteries at Chattanooga, Tennessee; Sharpsburg, Maryland; and Gettysburg, Pennsylvania, soon developed as well, as did a cemetery just outside Washington, DC, destined to become America's most enduring symbol of valor: Arlington National Cemetery (Holt 1992, pp. 2–3, Piehler 1995, p. 52).

One of the most famous national cemeteries was begun at Gettysburg, Pennsylvania, site of a titanic battle in July 1863. According to the War Department report *Roll of Honor*, the cemetery "embraces that portion of the ground occupied by the center of the Union line of battle on the 2d and 3d of July, 1863, ... [this being] one of the most prominent and important positions on the field" (U.S. Army Quartermaster Corps 1865–1871, no. 16, p. 76). Following the battle, a corporation charged with honoring its dead was formed, led by a local Gettysburg attorney, David Wills. Its board of directors, made up of representatives from every state who had dead interred there, bought some seventeen acres in August 1863 and began the reburial of Union soldiers. This new cemetery commanded "an extensive view of the surrounding country, which is highly picturesque" (U.S. Army Quartermaster Corps 1865–1871, no. 16, p. 76). By November 1863, some 3,512 Union soldiers from seventeen states had been laid to rest in a semicircular pattern around a central hub. On November 19, 1863, luminaries assembled for the "appropriate and imposing ceremonies" (U.S. Army Quartermaster Corps 1865–1871, no. 16, p. 76). President Abraham Lincoln made "a few appropriate remarks," and in doing so defined for the nation not only why they were fighting, but also why this certain section of land on Cemetery Hill had been preserved and why it was so important. "We have come to dedicate a portion of that field as a final resting place for those who here gave their lives," Lincoln said, calling on the nation to continue the fight "that these dead shall not have died in vain" (Wills 1992).

Alexandria, Virginia, Soldiers' Cemetery. The Civil War marked the first time in the United States that specific cemeteries were constructed to honor fallen soldiers. Planners built many of these early national cemeteries on actual battlegrounds and allowed for individual burial sites instead of common graves. *The Library of Congress.*

In the years after the dedication, the cemetery took on the form of many national cemeteries. It was "enclosed by a well-built stone wall, surmounted with heavy dressed capping stone, with a gateway of ornamental iron-work" (U.S. Army Quartermaster Corps 1865–1871, no. 16, p. 76). In 1869 the corporation marked the site of Lincoln's speech. In 1872, following claims that the corporation was not providing proper oversight for the venture, the Commonwealth of Pennsylvania transferred the cemetery grounds to the Federal government (U.S. Army Quartermaster Corps 1865–1871, no. 16, p. 76).

Another early burial site was the Chattanooga National Cemetery, established by general order of Major General George H. Thomas on December 25, 1863. Demonstrating the era's desire to simultaneously preserve and honor, Thomas wrote that the memorial cemetery was be established "in commemoration of the Battles of Chattanooga, November 23–27, 1863" (U.S. Army Quartermaster Corps 1865–1871, no. 11, pp. 11–13). In his effort to preserve part of the Chattanooga battlefield, Thomas directed that a small knoll near Orchard Knob be used as the burial ground. The knoll, rising a few feet above the plain of Chattanooga, was "the most suitable ground for the purpose contemplated that I have ever seen" and offered "a view of unsurpassed loveliness," testified the chaplain in charge of the cemetery (U.S. Army Quartermaster Corps 1865–1871, no. 11, pp. 11–13). The grounds would eventually receive the standard stone wall, lodge, avenues, and decorations of most national cemeteries. Comprising some seventy-five acres originally, the cemetery received the dead not only from Chattanooga, but also from Chickamauga, numerous local burial sites in the vicinity, and even the Atlanta Campaign. By 1870, more than 12,000 Union soldiers were interred at Chattanooga National Cemetery (Holt 1992, p. 65; U.S. Army Quartermaster Corps 1865–1871, no. 11, pp. 11–13).

The Antietam National Cemetery also began as a nongovernmental effort. Established by the Antietam National Cemetery Association, which was organized under the laws of the state of Maryland in March 1865, it was "composed of members from the different loyal States whose dead are represented in the Cemetery" (U.S. Army Quartermaster Corps 1865–1871, no. 15, p. 2). The association bought land, built an encircling wall, and erected a lodge. The corporation soon found itself in debt, however, and "a large share of this work was undertaken by the General Government" (U.S. Army Quartermaster Corps 1865–1871, no. 15, p. 2). Soon, the buried numbered 4,695, from nineteen different states. A third of the dead were disinterred from the Antietam battlefield, but others came from the battlefields at Monocacy, South Mountain, and Harpers Ferry, and also from several hospital sites in the area. The War Department completed the burial of bodies at Antietam National Cemetery on September 4, 1867, and a dedication was held later that month. The cemetery itself was a beautiful 9.5 acres situated inside what had been Confederate lines on a tall hill just east of Sharpsburg, Maryland. Its grounds are "handsomely laid off, partly in a semicircular form, with a twenty-foot avenue surrounding the whole, and numerous smaller paths intersecting the graves" (U.S. Army Quartermaster Corps 1865–1871, no. 15, p. 2). Because the Antietam National Cemetery Association was unable to remain free of debt even with federal money infused into the project, Congress directed the Secretary of War to take control of the cemetery in 1870, although it was not until 1877, when Congress appropriated money to pay the debt of the original commission, that the cemetery became a completely federal project (U.S. Army Quartermaster Corps 1865–1871, no. 15, p. 2).

These wartime national cemeteries, and many others located primarily on battlefields, inadvertently preserved a portion of these fields during the war itself. They also reflected a transition in the American mindset regarding the dead, particularly Union military dead. For decades prior, military dead from a battlefield were normally buried as a group with one large central monument or memorial to mark the location. Occurring simultaneously with the development of manicured, park-like civilian cemeteries emphasizing individual gravesites, the national cemetery phenomenon brought a new focus on commemorating individual soldiers (Piehler 1995, p. 51). Perhaps Thomas B. Van Horne, the chaplain in charge of the Chattanooga National Cemetery, best summed up this developing attitude. Van Horne noted that extreme care would be taken at Chattanooga to

> secure a short military history of every officer and soldier interred in the cemetery whose remains have been identified.... It seems eminently fitting that this should be done.... It accords with our intense individualism as a people, and with the value we attach to individual life; and it is demanded by the eminent worth of those for whom historic notice would thus be secured. (U.S. Army Quartermaster Corps 1865–1871, no. 11, p. 12)

Postwar Cemeteries

These patterns of individual memorialization and inadvertent preservation of Civil War battlefields spread to other cemeteries after the war ended. Many battlefields were in the Deep South, where the war had precluded any burial work at such places as Pittsburg Landing, Tennessee, and Andersonville, Georgia. Some areas under secure Federal control, such as Chattanooga, received national cemeteries during the war, but it was not until after the war that many other burial grounds on Southern battlefields were established (Smith 2004, p. 10).

For example, the cemetery at Vicksburg, Mississippi, was established in 1866. Vicksburg National Cemetery originally comprised some forty acres and was terraced and landscaped on bluffs overlooking the Mississippi

River, the same bluffs "upon which stood the rebel batteries that offered most effective resistance to the passage of our gunboats past the city" (U.S. Army Quartermaster Corps 1865–1871, no. 24, p. 7). By 1869, over fifteen thousand Union dead had been removed to the cemetery from such nearby battle sites as Champion Hill and Port Gibson, as well as from far away places such as Meridian and even sites across the river in Louisiana. The identity of many of the bodies was impossible to determine, however, and the problem of identifying bodies after five years soon became increasingly obvious. As the *Roll of Honor* observed, "it must soon become impossible, if it is not already so, to distinguish the remains of a soldier from those of a citizen" (U.S. Army Quartermaster Corps 1865–1871, no. 24, p. 7). Nevertheless, the cemetery received the customary lodge and encircling wall, as well as walks and avenues to allow easy access to each grave (U.S. Army Quartermaster Corps 1865–1871, no. 24, p. 7).

The ten-acre cemetery at Pittsburg Landing, Tennessee, was also established in 1866. It came to contain more than 3,500 dead from that battlefield as well as from other areas along the Tennessee River, such as Fort Henry. The unique Pittsburg Landing National Cemetery contains "numerous Regimental Groups, of which there are no less than twenty-nine" (U.S. Army Quartermaster Corps 1865–1871, no. 20, p. 119). These groupings were facilitated by the soldiers' previous burial together in "scattered graves through that wild and desolate country" (U.S. Army Quartermaster Corps 1865–1871, no. 20, p. 119). "On no other battle-field through the entire South and Southwest," the *Roll of Honor* observed, "does there seem to have been so great care and pains taken in the burial of the dead and in providing for their future identification" (U.S. Army Quartermaster Corps 1865–1871, no. 20, p. 119). The grounds of the cemetery contained "a rough stone wall of the most substantial character" and a "flag-staff . . . overlooking the river, from which the Union flag is kept constantly floating" (U.S. Army Quartermaster Corps 1865–1871, no. 20, p. 119). One 1867 visitor described the cemetery as "the handsomest cemetery in the South" (Smith 2004, p. 11).

With the war ended and the need for hasty burial removed, and as other cemeteries were established, it soon became apparent that new legislation to legitimize what had already been done would be required. In many cases, such as Shiloh and Chattanooga, the dead had been placed on private land. As a result, in 1867 Congress passed an act to establish and protect national cemeteries (Meyers 1968, pp. 200–201). The act took the 1862 enabling legislation one step further by allowing and mandating certain measures. Specifically, the bill required that each cemetery be enclosed by a wall and have a lodge. Additionally, the legislation required each cemetery to have "a meritorious and trustworthy superintendent, who shall be selected from enlisted men of the army disabled in service," and that each be inspected annually. The bill also required each cemetery to keep rolls of the dead with military information. Perhaps most importantly, the act allowed the Secretary of War to "enter upon and appropriate" needed land if the owners were not willing to sell (Meyers 1968, pp. 200–201). These measures thus insured that each cemetery would be protected and that each deceased soldier would be honored and remembered. Practically, the bill also took care of the growing problem of private ownership of cemeteries and legitimized condemnation, which would be a major stepping-stone toward future federal control of battlefields. Because of this act, the tracts of land on which the Shiloh and Chattanooga cemeteries stood were condemned, allowing for complete federalization.

As time passed, more and more national cemeteries were established as more veterans died. With the more recent wars of the twentieth century, national cemetery populations have mushroomed, with new cemeteries being developed even in the twenty-first century. These recent wars have added the new phenomenon of national cemeteries being established abroad, such as the American Cemetery in Normandy, France. Still, as the system has grown and developed, it has kept its roots firmly planted in the Civil War era.

BIBLIOGRAPHY

Holt, Dean W. *American Military Cemeteries: A Comprehensive Illustrated Guide to the Hallowed Grounds of the United States, Including Cemeteries Overseas.* Jefferson, NC: McFarland, 1992.

Meyers, Richard. *The Vicksburg National Cemetery: An Administrative History.* Washington DC: National Park Service, 1968.

Neff, John R. *Honoring the Civil War Dead: Commemoration and the Problem of Reconciliation.* Lawrence: University Press of Kansas, 2005.

Piehler, G. Kurt. *Remembering War the American Way.* Washington, DC: Smithsonian Institution Press, 1995.

Smith, Timothy B. *This Great Battlefield of Shiloh: History, Memory, and the Establishment of a Civil War National Military Park.* Knoxville: University of Tennessee Press, 2004.

United States Army Quartermaster Corps. *Roll of Honor: Names of Soldiers Who Died in Defence of the American Union, Interred in the National [and Other] Cemeteries.* 27 nos. in 9 vols. Washington, DC: Government Printing Office, 1865–1871.

Wills, Garry. *Lincoln at Gettysburg: The Words That Remade America.* New York: Simon & Schuster, 1992.

Timothy B. Smith

■ Veterans' Organizations

The American Civil War, like many other wars, created a bond of brotherhood between the men who fought it. Comradery formed from shared privation, fear of battle, and the boredom of camp life helped soldiers cope with the war. Understandably, when the conflict ended former soldiers formed veterans' organizations to remember the fallen, record their history, and support one another during the peace. Eventually two levels of organizations were formed: local groups that usually focused on participation in a local regiment during the war, and national organizations.

Veterans began to establish regimental associations for the purpose of "strengthening and preserving those kind and fraternal feelings which bound soldiers together" (Wittenberg 2007, pp. 238–239). These associations also were intended to help former comrades-in-arms who needed "help and protection, and to extend needful aid to the widows and orphans of our comrades who have fallen in the discharge of our duties" (Wittenberg 2007, pp. 238–239). In addition to these local organizations, a national, centralized organization was needed to bring veterans together and serve as a political tool for veterans' benefits.

The largest and best-known Union veterans' organization was the Grand Army of the Republic. In 1866, the former army surgeons Benjamin Franklin Stephenson and William Rutledge founded Post 1 of the Grand Army of the Republic (GAR) in Decatur, Illinois, to reunite men who formed the "greatest comradeship that ever knit men together" (Wilson 1905, pp. 9–15). Unlike regimental associations, which tended to be in a particular city or county, chapters of the GAR could be found coast to coast, allowing veterans who had relocated since the end of the war to join a veterans' organization. The GAR quickly became the largest veterans' group in the country, necessitating the formation of state departments and a national head (a structure similar to the Union army's). The large influx of members was due to the GAR's role in veterans' affairs. Since its formation, the GAR had kept tabs on state and national legislation affecting veterans' pensions. Its large membership commanded the attention of savvy politicians, and as a result GAR proposals were "adopted by Congress to a very great extent" (Miller 1911, pp. 294–296).

Veterans in the National Soldiers' Home dining room. Local and national veterans' organizations raised funds to care for former soldiers unable to provide for themselves due to advanced age or injury. *© Corbis.*

In addition to the GAR, there was a national veterans' organization made up of former Union officers. Like the Order of Cincinnati, which was formed by American officers immediately after the Revolution, the Military Order of the Loyal Legion of the United States (MOLLUS) was formed just days after the assassination of President Lincoln, amid rumors of conspiracies to destroy the federal government. The original purpose of MOLLUS was to thwart any attempts to overturn the government, but over time, the organization evolved to promote the same objectives advanced by the regimental associations and the GAR. Membership was restricted to commissioned officers who had served honorably in the war, their sons or heirs, and "gentlemen who, in civil life, during the Rebellion, were specially distinguished for conspicuous and constant loyalty to the National Government" (Military Order of the Loyal Legion 1909, p. 11).

There was no national organization for former Confederate soldiers until 1889. Confederate veterans in some states, most notably Virginia, Tennessee, and Louisiana, had formed state-level organizations but like their regimental counterparts, these organizations had little influence except in particular geographic areas. In addition to state organizations, Confederate veterans had created associations based on the regiments in which they had served. In order to meld all these local units into a national organization, Colonel J. F. Shipp proposed "a general organization of Confederates on the order of the Grand Army of the Republic" (Miller 1911, p. 296). Shipp's proposal circulated all over the South, and at a meeting in New Orleans on June 10, 1889, it was agreed to create the United Confederate Veterans (UCV). All pre-existing organizations were folded into the UCV, which was modeled after the GAR and had the same organizational objectives—fraternity and help with veterans' benefits. The first national encampment of Civil War veterans occurred July 3–5 in Chattanooga,

The three cardinal principles of the Grand Army of the Republic. After the end of the Civil War, surviving solders organized to preserve the memories of their lost comrades. Inspired by the principles of fraternity, loyalty, and charity emblazoned on its seal, the Grand Army of the Republic quickly became one of the preeminent national veterans' organizations. *The Library of Congress*

with "reunion invitations extended 'to veterans of both armies and to citizens of the Republic,' and the dates purposely included Independence Day (Miller 1911, p. 298). The UCV's constitution forbade "discussion of political or religious subjects nor any political action shall be permitted in the organization, and that any association violating that provision shall forfeit its membership" (Miller 1911, p. 298).

Aside from the UCV, another, informal, national Confederate organization existed. In 1893 Sumner A. Cunningham established the *Confederate Veteran*, a monthly journal that was "intended as an organ of communication between Confederate soldiers and those who are interested in them and their affairs" (*Confederate Veteran Magazine* 1988, p. 1). The journal provided a forum in which Confederate veterans could relate stories from the war and also read about the successes and failures of other Confederate veteran groups across the South. Publication of the *Confederate Veteran* was discontinued after 1932 because there were few veterans still living.

As the early twentieth century progressed there were fewer and fewer Civil War veterans left. The GAR, which had more than 400,000 members at its height in the decade 1880–1890, by 1910 had been reduced to just over 200,000 members. It finally faded out of existence in 1956. Sensitive to their own mortality, GAR members believed that someone should continue to honor Civil War soldiers after they had passed on, so in 1881 the GAR had established the Sons of Union Veterans of the Civil War, which evolved into the present-day Sons of Union Veterans of the Civil War (SUVCW). Likewise, the UCV, which faded into history in 1951, had created in 1896 an organization similar to the SUVCW to carry on their memory, the Sons of Confederate Veterans (SCV). Both the SUVCW and SCV are the direct descendents of the Civil War veteran organizations.

BIBLIOGRAPHY

Beath, Robert B. *History of the Grand Army of the Republic.* New York: Bryan, Taylor, 1889.

The Confederate Veteran Magazine: Volume I, January 1893–December 1893. Wilmington, NC: Broadfoot, 1988.

Military Order of the Loyal Legion of the United States. *Constitution and By-laws.* Philadelphia: Author, 1909.

Miller, Francis Trevelyan, ed. *The Photographic History of the Civil War in Ten Volume*, vol. 10. New York: Review of Reviews, 1911.

Phillips, Sydney A. *Patriotic Societies of the United States and their Lapel Insignia.* New York: Broadway, 1914.

Wilson, Oliver M. *The Grand Army of the Republic under its First Constitution and Ritual: Its Birth and Organization.* Kansas City, MO: Franklin Hudson, 1905.

Wittenburg, Eric J. *Rush's Lancers: The Sixth Pennsylvania Cavalry in the Civil War.* Yardley, PA: Westholme, 2007.

William Backus

Blue-Gray Reunions

The Civil War caused a deep and wide chasm of animosity between the people of the North and the South. Years of Reconstruction widened that gap even farther as the two regions recovered from war and vied for power over the future of the former slaves. As a result, not surprisingly, it took the United States many years to recover from the war, and the united nation only began to rise from the ashes in the mid- to late-1870s. As noted by one Civil War veteran, however, reconciliation took time: "He would indeed be impatient who looked for more speedy progress" ("Camping on Chickamauga," September 16, 1892). But by the 1880s and on into the

1890s, when the federal government turned its back on racial issues and the gains made in the Reconstruction years, mollifying the South through segregation, Northerners and Southerners were growing friendlier toward one another. Evidence of this reconciliation can be seen best in the Blue-Gray reunions that brought veterans of the North and South together to remember and commemorate their war (Blight 2001).

Despite the popularity of Decoration Day in both regions, few if any joint veterans' reunions took place in the early and middle Reconstruction years. By the mid-1870s, however, there were some joint observances, but these were few and far between. One of the earliest was in Vicksburg, Mississippi, in 1874, when veterans of both sides, the *New York Times* reported, formed "an association known as 'The Order of Blues and Grays,' its avowed purpose being the encouragement of kindly and frank relations between the survivors of both armies" ("Editorial Article No. 5," September 12, 1874). With the official end of Reconstruction in 1877, the proverbial chains of animosity were removed, allowing the two sides to begin reconciling. The 1876 national centennial celebration helped foster this common feeling of oneness (Piehler 1995, pp. 75–76).

By the late-1870s and certainly in the 1880s, joint reunions had become fairly common. Many were on the small scale of local reunions, but there were an impressive number of national joint reunions held as well. One took place at Atlanta in 1880; a headline in the *Washington Post* read, "Opening Day of the Reunion of the Boys in Blue and Gray" ("The Atlanta Celebration," October 19, 1880). Another was at Wilson's Creek, Missouri, in 1883: "Throughout the reunion the most cordial feeling has existed between the old Union and Confederate soldiers," the *Washington Post* reported, "and the most courteous and generous sentiments have been expressed. Not a single unpleasant word has been uttered to mar the general harmony and enthusiasm. The men have camped together as though there had never been a difference between them" ("Blended Blue and Gray," August 12, 1883). An event at Gettysburg—virtually the only marked battlefield park in the 1880s—received a lot of attention because it was "the occasion of a reunion both of Northern and Southern veterans" ("The Blue and the Gray," August 12, 1883).

Gettysburg reunion. After the end of Reconstruction in 1877, relations warmed between former soldiers in the North and South, and joint reunions began to be held in the 1880s. Many of these early gatherings took place at Gettysburg, one of the first national military parks commemorating Civil War soldiers. *The Library of Congress.*

By the 1890s, these reunions were fairly commonplace. With the establishment of the national military parks, numerous gatherings were held in connection with the famous sites. A joint reunion took place in 1889 to promote the idea of a national park at Chickamauga, and a similar joint veterans' reunion of Shiloh soldiers was held at that battlefield on April 6 and 7, 1894. One participant, George W. McBride, remembered the Shiloh reunion and the park were "the offering of those who fought, of a fraternal brotherhood to the future" (McBride [1896] 2003, p. 227). The dedication of the Chickamauga and Chattanooga National Military Park in 1895 brought as many as 75,000 attendees, many of them veterans from North and South. Vice President Adlai Stevenson I (1835–1914) spoke to the 1895 Chickamauga crowd about the veterans: "They meet, not in deadly conflict, but as brothers, under one flag—fellow citizens of a common country" ("Cementing the Union," September 20, 1895).

In later years, the battlefields also served as gathering places for the dwindling number of Civil War veterans. Anniversaries were special times of joint commemoration, such as the fiftieth anniversaries of Gettysburg and Chickamauga in 1913. Both those battlefields observed special ceremonies attended by both sides, with President Woodrow Wilson speaking to the Gettysburg veterans, saying: "We have found one another again as brothers and comrades, in arms, enemies no longer, generous friends rather, our battles long past, the quarrel forgotten—except we shall not forget the splendid valor, the manly devotion of the men then arrayed against one another, now grasping hands and smiling into each other's eyes" (Pennsylvania at Gettysburg 1914, vol. 3, p. 174). A similar joint reunion took place in Vicksburg in 1917. Even as late as the 1930s, veterans were still returning to their fields of conflict to commemorate their deeds. At the seventy-fifth anniversary of the Battle of Gettysburg in 1938, some of the few remaining veterans of both sides reenacted Pickett's Charge and shook hands across the famous stone wall.

With the passing of the veteran generation, so also passed the joint reunions, but for a brief few decades the veterans had come together and remembered their old times. Certainly, the veterans themselves gained a lot of satisfaction from these reunions, but the service they provided to their united nation in fostering reconciliation and promoting reunion between the sections was also extremely important. Although not all the old soldiers were reconciled, it is fitting that significant reconciliation started with the veterans, for it was their generation that was at the helm when the nation split apart.

BIBLIOGRAPHY

"The Atlanta Celebration." *Washington Post*, October 19, 1880.

"Blended Blue and Gray." *Washington Post*, August 12, 1883.

Blight, David. *Race and Reunion: The Civil War in Memory and Reunion*. Cambridge, MA: Harvard University Press, 2001.

"The Blue and the Gray." *New York Times*, July 2, 1888.

"Camping on Chickamauga." *Washington Post*, September 16, 1892.

"Cementing the Union." *Washington Post*, September 20, 1895.

"Editorial Article No. 5." *New York Times*, September 12, 1874.

McBride, George W. "Shiloh, after Thirty-Two Years." *Under Both Flags: A Panorama of the Great Civil War as Represented in Story, Anecdote, Adventure, and the Romance of Reality* [1896]. New York: Lyons Press, 2003.

Neff, John R. *Honoring the Civil War Dead: Commemoration and the Problem of Reconciliation.* Lawrence: University Press of Kansas, 2005.

Pennsylvania at Gettysburg: Ceremonies at the Dedication of the Monuments Erected by the Commonwealth of Pennsylvania to Major-General George G. Meade, Major General Winfield S. Hancock, Major General John F. Reynolds, and to Mark the Positions of the Pennsylvania Commands Engaged in the Battle. 3 vols. Harrisburg, PA: W. S. Ray, 1914.

Piehler, G. Kurt. *Remembering War the American Way.* Washington, DC: Smithsonian Institution Press, 1995.

Smith, Timothy B. *The Golden Age of Battlefield Preservation: The Decade of the 1890s and the Establishment of America's First Five Military Parks.* Knoxville: University of Tennessee Press, 2008.

Timothy B. Smith

■ African American Commemorations

During the Civil War much occurred that gave African Americans cause for excitement. In April 1862 Congress passed the District of Columbia Emancipation Act, which was celebrated as far away as San Francisco by August of that year. African Americans also honored the announcement of the Emancipation Proclamation and the date it became official in 1863; and in 1865 they commemorated the effective date of freedom in Texas, Juneteenth. They remembered comrades lost in individual battles, such as Milliken's Bend; celebrated electoral victories when Lincoln won another term as president; and in the final tragedy of the war, commemorated Lincoln's death. Some commemorations dropped by the wayside over the years, while others such

Civil War banner. African American soldiers serving in the United States Colored Troops took pride in their accomplishments on the battlefront when the Union government finally granted them permission to fight in 1863. *© North Wind Picture Archives*

as Decoration Day, which eventually became Memorial Day, have endured.

Commemorated on the anniversary of its passage, the District of Columbia Emancipation Act became the first of many milestones that African Americans would eventually celebrate. African American society attended that first celebration, which was held at the Fifteenth Street Presbyterian Church. Elizabeth Keckly (1818–1907), Mary Todd Lincoln's (1818–1882) seamstress, showed up in her capacity as president of the Ladies' Contraband Relief Association, while African Methodist Episcopal minister Thomas H. C. Hinton delivered the first speech of the evening, declaring that "slavery which had been maintained by a legion of political devils . . . has been partially done away with" (*The Liberator*, May 8, 1863).

The final speaker of the evening, William E. Matthews, however, captured the spirit of the future of African American commemoration when he noted that "Jews celebrate Passover; England the birthday of her Queen. All the great powers of the earth, including Hayti and Liberia, (applause) have a day of their own. The white Americans celebrate the Fourth of July. But it is an unhappy fact that the colored people of the United States have no day of their own." He "hope[d] the 16th of April [would] ever be a day of rejoicing in the District" and "likes these anniversaries. They inspire me with a manhood I do not feel on other occasions." He did not have to wait long for the next one, for a series of events during 1863 provided a number of red-letter days (*The Liberator*, May 8, 1863).

After the Emancipation Proclamation became official, New Year's Day held special meaning for African Americans. On the third day of 1865, Benjamin Marshall Mills, an officer in the Forty-ninth United States Colored Troops (USCT) regiment stationed in Vicksburg, Mississippi, wrote, "yesterday the black people of this place had a grand time celebrating the anniversary of their Freedom. They marched through town in a long procession and then proceeded to a place a little way out of the city and then they had a glorious old time" (Mills, January 3, 1865). A chaplain in the Fifty-first USCT stationed in another part of town recalled a more serene scene: "At two o'clock went with my regiment to the court house where the Division was assembled to listen to some remarks from Maj. Gen. Washburn in commemoration of this the Anniversary of their Freedom. In the evening held a service in my regiment in the barracks which I enjoyed very much" (Carruthers, January 1, 1865).

The initial battles of the USCT, all within two months in 1863, provided even more days of commemoration. Black troops saw real combat for the first time at Port Hudson on May 27, 1863; Milliken's Bend on June 6; and Fort Wagner on July 18. A year later, in Natchez, Mississippi, Colonel Herman Lieb, who was wounded in the battle of Milliken's Bend, memorialized their baptism of fire with a special supper and a dance (June 7, 1864).

April 1865, brought on a series of short-lived celebrations. With the surrender of the Army of Northern Virginia on April 9, 1865, African Americans had another reason to celebrate, but within a week John Wilkes Booth (1838–1865) changed it to despair. Across the nation, blacks went into mourning. At Jefferson Davis's former plantation on the Mississippi River, Major Samuel Denham Barnes of the Fiftieth USCT observed "All the colored people, men women and children have crape and black string as mourning of some kind for as the Uncle Sam, Marse Lincoln is dead" (Barnes, April 23, 1865). A year later—and a sign of the future for African Americans—blacks celebrating in Richmond felt compelled to parse their reason for celebrating in a handbill that they circulated among whites in the city. It read, "that they do not intend to celebrate the failure of the Southern Confederacy, as it has been stated in the papers of this city, but simply as the day on which God was pleased to liberate their long oppressed race." During the parade, a white man opened fire with a pistol but did not hit anyone, while blacks who participated in the celebration were informed that blacks "who left their work to engage in the jubilee will not be employed again by their old masters" (*The Boston Daily Advertiser*, April 7, 1866).

By the 1890s African Americans had to be even more cautious with how they chose to remember the Civil War. In 1889 a letter to *The Daily Picayune*, a New Orleans newspaper, outlined that the citizens of Vicksburg, Mississippi, would welcome members of the Grand Army of the Republic on Decoration Day, so long as they were white Union veterans, "but that they did not care to aid in an affair with great masses of negroes" (April 10, 1889). In 1897 a concerned white citizen in Henderson, North Carolina, pointed out that "April 9th, the anniversary of Lee's surrender, was observed by the negroes of Henderson... as a day of rejoicing" and "if the negro persists in this he is no true North Carolinian; but an alien. And as an alien let him be treated" (*The Daily Picayune*, April 18, 1897). Thus, by the end of the nineteenth century, African Americans found themselves on the defensive when it came to commemorating their participation in the Civil War.

BIBLIOGRAPHY

Barnes, Samuel Denham. Papers of Samuel Denham Barnes, (1839–1916), The Library of Congress, Washington, DC.

Boston Daily Advertiser (Boston, MA). "The Civil Rights Bill," April 7, 1866, issue 83, col. C.

Carruthers, George North. Papers of George North Carruthers, 1863–1969, The Library of Congress, Washington, DC.

The Daily Picayune (New Orleans, LA). "Decoration Day at Vicksburg," April 10, 1889, issue 76, col. G.

The Liberator (Boston, MA)." Grand Emancipation-Celebration." May 8, 1863, p. 75, issue 19, col. C.

Mills, Caleb. Caleb Mills Family Papers, 1834–1880, Indiana Historical Society, Indianapolis.

The News and Observer (Raleigh, NC). "Negro Celebration of the Anniversary of Appomatox," April 18, 1897, issue 40, col. D.

David H. Slay

Souvenirs and Relics

When any major event, like a war, involves large numbers of soldiers, they are bound to lose or throw away various items. Whether in the heat of battle or on the march, items related to Civil War soldiers were left on battlefields and roads, waiting for someone else to take them or for an archaeologist to find them years later.

Many people may be aware of the growing trade in Civil War era items in countless stores and on the auction circuit as well as online, but fewer are aware of the practice of scouring the battlefield shortly afterward for relics, or the ways in which items were lost or left behind by soldiers. It is through these practices that many items relating to daily life of soldiers and battle began their journey from the soldiers' hands to museum collections, private family holdings, stores, and the auction circuit.

The first leg of the journey is the soldier receiving his equipment, usually in camp. Leander Stillwell (1843–1934), a Union soldier who served as a lawyer, judge, and member of the Kansas legislature after the war, described receiving his clothing when he enlisted:

> The clothing outfit consisted of a pair of light-blue pantaloons, similar colored overcoat with a cape to it, dark blue jacket, heavy shoes and woolen socks, an ugly, abominable cocky little cap patterned after the then French army style, gray woolen shirt, and other ordinary under-clothing. Was also given a knapsack, but I think I didn't get a haversack and canteen until later. (Stillwell 1920, p. 15)

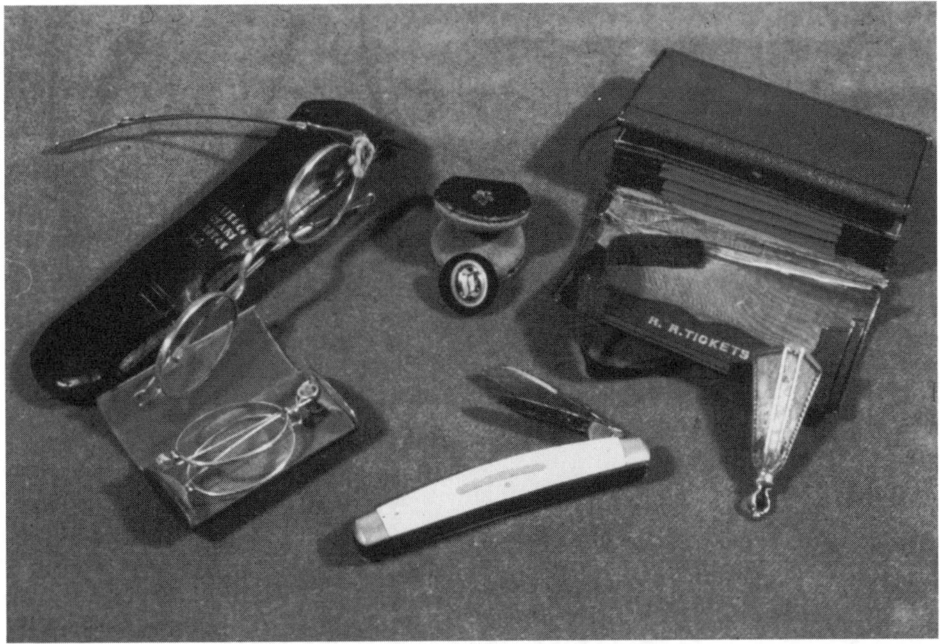

"The Things He Carried." The above picture details objects President Abraham Lincoln carried on his person the evening he was shot by John Wilkes Booth at the Ford Theater. *MPI/Hulton Archive/Getty Images.*

As the soldiers ventured into the field, they often lost equipment on the march or purposely discarded it prior to a battle. Edmund Stedman (1833–1908), a poet and essayist who was one of the first seven members elected to the American Academy of Arts and Letters, remarked that "Coats and knapsacks were thrown to either side, that nothing might impede their work ..." in his account of the Battle of Bull Run (Stedman 1861, p. 26). Other soldiers described similar incidents. For instance, Robert Newell, a Massachusetts soldier, wrote to his brother that, "Before we reached the battlefield, there was not a knapsack left, the men threw away everything to lighten themselves and I finally followed their example ..." (Newell 1864). The purposeful abandonment of items to lighten a soldier's load before battle and the possible loss of items while in the field presented an opportunity for other persons to obtain a souvenir of the war.

In addition, soldiers often sent home letters to loved ones to serve as souvenirs. A Confederate soldier named John Street sent his wife a letter that he had written before the Battle of Shiloh and asked her "to keep it as a sacred relic" (Street 1862). These letters and many others have ended up in manuscript collections in various libraries and archives across the nation.

While many items from soldiers reside in museum collections, many have also been sold through various antique stores and other shops around the country. They have also appeared in auctions, both traditional and online. The sale of such relics presents issues of preservation and ethics, as while most people would cherish such items, the prospect for making money from a dead soldier's property presents an ethical dilemma. Such materials belong in museums for everyone's benefit, or in the possession of the descendants of the soldier who owned the item.

Overall, the issue of souvenirs and relics is one of mystery. It is true that soldiers lost or dropped equipment over the course of their service, which presented opportunities for persons to obtain souvenirs of the war. What is less certain, however, is whether people scoured the battlefield soon after the event looking for items or stole from the dead. Rules at some historic sites that prohibit the use of metal detectors as well as recent incidents involving persons being arrested for digging up artifacts on battlefield sites suggest that the hunt for souvenirs and relics is alive today. An effort must be made to safeguard these treasures of our past for archaeologists and other qualified individuals to find and study so that everyone will benefit.

BIBLIOGRAPHY

Newell, Robert R. Letter to his brother Will, March 9, 1864. Available online at http://www.soldierstudies.org/.

Stedman, Edmund Clarence. *The Battle of Bull Run.* New York: Rudd & Carleton, 1861.

Stillwell, Leander. *The Story of a Common Soldier of Army Life in the Civil War, 1861–1865*, 2nd ed. Erie, KS: Franklin Hudson Publishing Co., 1920.

Personal effects of soldier J. E. B. Stuart. In the heat of battle, many soldiers' personal effects became lost or misplaced. After fighting concluded, civilian men and women would frequently scavenge the battlefield, searching for souvenirs or other objects of value. *William F. Campbell/Time Life Pictures/Getty Images.*

Street, John. Letter to his wife, April 12, 1862. Available online at http://www.soldierstudies.org/.

Daniel Sauerwein

■ Unit and Regimental Histories

After the end of the American Civil War, a time of healing occurred for former combatants scattered across the Southern United States. The wounds from which these men suffered were both physical and mental. Soldiers reflected on the losses they had witnessed, or attempted to forget the pain. After a period of roughly ten to twenty years, soldiers began to record their wartime experiences.

Soldiers wanted to create a record of their experiences for their families, and also hoped to reconnect with fellow veterans. For some officers, writing a memoir was a way to question war decisions or to defend a brother officer who might have been slighted during the war. Collectively, this recording of wartime experiences comprised a historical record of the regiments, brigades, divisions, corps, and armies of the war.

One type of reminiscence was a presentation of the experiences of an individual soldier. Such recollections provided the first glimpse into the workings of a regiment. As these memoirs were often intended for family members, some of the horrors of war might be edited out. An example of this type of memoir is the one by Leander Stillwell, a Union soldier in the Sixty-First Illinois. Stillwell's memoir conveys both the terror of battle and the humor of everyday soldiering. Another example is a memoir by Sam Watkins of the First Tennessee Volunteers. He recalls a visit from General Robert E. Lee to his camp, writing that "He was a fine looking gentleman, and wore a moustache. He was dressed in blue cottonade and looked like some good boy's grandpa. I felt like going up to him and saying, good evening Uncle Bob! I am not certain at this late date that I did not do so" (Watkins 2003 [1865], p. 11).

As reminiscences began to grow in number, groups of veterans formed organizations to compile and publish histories of their unit, regiment, or brigade. Veterans gathered letters, wrote down stories of their own soldiering, and collected photographs of their particular military unit. Veterans' organizations generally chose an admired officer to produce the history. This person would compile the information into book form, and the veterans would then pool their monies to have the work printed. Such works ranged from detailed histories to mere annotated rosters of soldiers with photographs. One example of a carefully assembled regimental history is *History of the Thirty-Sixth Regiment Illinois Volunteers* (1876), by Lyman G. Bennett and William M. Haigh. A classical example of a memoir from the Confederate perspective is D. Augustus Dickert's *History of Kershaw's Brigade* (1866). Unfortunately, there were also cases in which diaries, letters, and photographs were gathered, but no memoir was ever created, as happened with the 154th New York Volunteers. Today, histories of regiments and units continue to be popular; one notable twentieth-century example is John J. Pullen's *The Twentieth Maine* (1957).

Reminiscences were sometimes written to defend the actions of an officer or his command. Thomas Van Horne's *History of the Army of the Cumberland* (1875), for example, was more than a memoir of the Army of the Cumberland; it was also an attempt to defend the record of Major General George H. Thomas, who had been slighted by other general officers toward the end of the conflict.

States also contracted with individuals to produce a record of the contribution made by their regiments. Such histories generally include rosters and brief histories of regiments formed in the 1860s. In addition, they could be drawn into the competition between states to prove which had provided the greatest number of men and officers to their side of the war. For example, Walter Clark's *Histories of the Several Regiments and Battalions from North Carolina* (1901) sought to substantiate North Carolina's claim that it had provided the most troops to the Confederacy. Clark renumbered several regiments, giving them high numbers, and thereby increased the apparent number of North Carolina regiments.

Early unit and regimental histories played a role in the creation of the postwar historiography of the American Civil War. They provide valuable insight into the thoughts of soldiers, both right after the conflict and some twenty years afterward.

BIBLIOGRAPHY

Bennett, Lyman G., and William M. Haigh. *History of the Thirty-Sixth Regiment Illinois Volunteers during the War of the Rebellion.* Aurora, IL: Knickerbocker & Hodder, 1876.

Catton, Bruce. *Mr. Lincoln's Army.* Garden City, NY: Doubleday, 1951.

Clark, Walter, ed. *Histories of the Several Regiments and Battalions from North Carolina, in the Great War 1861–65.* Raleigh, NC: E. M. Uzzell, 1901.

Connelly, Thomas L. *Autumn of Glory: The Army of Tennessee, 1862–1865.* Baton Rouge: Louisiana State University Press, 1971.

Dickert, D. Augustus. *History of Kershaw's Brigade.* Newberry, SC: E. H. Aull, 1899.

Dunkelman, Mark H. *Brothers One and All: Espirit de Corps in a Civil War Regiment.* Baton Rouge: Louisiana State University, 2004.

Freeman, Douglas Southall. *Lee's Lieutenants: A Study in Command.* New York: C. Scribner's Sons, 1942–1944.

Pullen, John J. *The Twentieth Maine: A Volunteer Regiment in the Civil War.* Philadelphia: J. B. Lippincott, 1957.

Stillwell, Leander. *The Story of the Common Soldier in the Civil War, 1861–1865.* Erie, KS: Franklin Hudson Publishing Company, 1920.

Van Horne, Thomas B. *History of the Army of the Cumberland: Its Organization, Campaigns, and Battles.* Cincinnati, OH: Robert Clarke, 1875.

Watkins, Samuel R. *"Co. Aytch:" A Confederate Memoir of the Civil War.* New York: Simon & Schuster, 2003.

Wiley, Bell Irvin. *The Life of Billy Yank.* Indianapolis, IN: Bobbs-Merrill, 1952.

Wiley, Bell Irvin. *The Life of Johnny Reb.* Indianapolis, IN: Bobbs-Merrill, 1953.

Worsham, John H. *One of Jackson's Foot Cavalry: His Experience and What He Saw During the War, 1861–1865.* New York: Neale Publishing Company, 1912.

William H. Brown

■ Obituaries and Local Memorials to the Dead

Most of the monuments to the dead constructed during the Civil War appeared in the Northeast, with considerably fewer in the Midwest and the South. The monuments generally adhered to two styles: a statue of a uniformed soldier standing at parade rest (holding the barrel of a rifle that rests upright on the ground in front of him) or an obelisk. In the years after the Civil War, the soldier replaced the obelisk as the dominant type of monument. Americans only began to commission statues of common soldiers during the Civil War.

Public notions about death and the dead changed during the Civil War. At the beginning of the nineteenth century, the rise of evangelicalism led to a softer, sentimentalized imagination and religious sensibility (Hume 2000, p. 36). Concern over the fate of the soul helped give sentimental memories of the deceased a place in the collective memory of early-nineteenth-century Americans.

Obituaries in mass-circulation newspapers in the early years of the war provide evidence of the sentimental and religious aura surrounding death. The February 19, 1862, *New York Times* obituary of Joseph Vignier de Monteil, lieutenant colonel of the Fifty-third New York State Volunteers (d'Epineuil Zoaves) noted:

> There is something truly touching in the manner of his death. When the order to charge was given, he ran at the head of the column until the fatal bullet came which instantly deprived him of life. Even in this dying moment, amid the triumphant

CIVIL WAR OBITUARIES

The obituary for Samuel Marcy (1820–1862), which appeared in the February 23, 1862, *New York Times*, is typical of the flowery tributes of the Victorian era, particularly those written for deceased members of prominent families. According to official Navy records, Marcy, the son of a former Secretary of State, had been successful in pursuing and seizing several blockade runners in the summer of 1861. At this early point in the Civil War, Americans had not become matter-of-fact about the deaths of their men.

DEATH OF SAMUEL MARCY, U.S.N., LATE LIEUTENANT-COMMANDER UNITED STATES SHIP *VINCENNES*

The costly tribute which the country is daily rendering to the National cause cannot be counted in contributions to the Treasury. Thousands of loyal lives must be added to make up the fearful aggregate. We read of brilliant victories and the National heart is made glad. Rejoicings pervade the land. With our tears we express sympathy in the sad loss of human life, and we place the names of the dead, and dying, and suffering heroes, one the records of the National gratitude. Having done this, we turn our thoughts to new fields, which victory gives an added luster to the National Party.

It is only when some isolated case is presented to our notice that we can appreciate the sacrifices of loyal blood, and the unspeakable sorrow of bereaved hearts, which are the consequences of this disastrous war....

Samuel Marcy [commanded] the sloop-of-war Vincennes, *one of the blockading squadron off the mouths of the Mississippi. To his zealous devotion and earnest sense of duty in this responsible situation, his life became the sacrifice. He was determined that, so far as his ship could maintain the blockade, no vessel should escape. He had already made several captures, when, on the morning of the 23rd of January last, two vessels were seen apparently on fire, having grounded near the outlet after vainly attempting to run the blockade. With the view to secure possession of the vessels and cargos, Lieut. Marcy instantly dispatched two boats from his ship, in one of which was placed a heavy pivot gun. While, with characteristic energy and activity, he had entered personally upon this duty, and was engaged in directing the operations of firing, the gun recoiled, fell upon, and fatally crushed his body and limbs.*
Words of condolence are vainly uttered to soften such bereavements; but sorrow for the dead should find alleviation in the respect and affection which follows the good and true to their last resting-place.

CARYN E. NEUMANN

shouts and steady rush of the charge, his soldier's instinct, we gladly believe, told him that victory was assured. (*New York Times*, February 19, 1862)

A December 1861 resolution passed by the commissioned officers of the Illinois First Regiment Douglas Brigade in commemoration of the death of Colonel W. A. Webb resolved "that to his relatives and friends we tender our sincere sympathy and crave of them the sad privilege of mingling with their sorrow a soldier's tear" ("Death of Col. William A. Webb," December 26, 1861, p. 4).

Newspapers, in a time before death became routine, often provided considerable detail about the manner of death. When Charles E. Zellar, the foreman of the job press rooms of the *Chicago Tribune* died in an accident at work, the newspaper reported that "in some way his hand became entangled between the belt and the drum, and he was drawn up in an instant, his head striking the ceiling with fearful force and dashed down to the floor again, falling upon his face." The obituary further revealed that the coroner found that Zellar's spinal column had been dislocated between the second and third vertebrae ("A Melancholy Accident," January 3, 1862, p. 4).

Throughout the Civil War era, far more men than women were mentioned in obituaries. Because women's lives generally were centered on the home, they were not public figures. Mrs. Isaac Funk was mentioned in an obituary in the February 5, 1865, edition of the *Chicago Tribune* only because she died within hours of her husband, a hog farmer who during his life had risen to considerable wealth and prominence. An obituary for Mrs. H. C. Conant concludes with, "The literary and religious public loses in Mrs. Conant one of its brightest ornaments, but her death falls as a heavy and almost unsupportable blow upon the home where she was conspicuous for feminine virtues, and is mourned as a wife and mother" (*New York Times*, February 20, 1865). Women were noted for their religious faith, fortitude in the face of death, sweet character, and dedication to their families.

During the war, however, the style of obituaries shifted from sentimental tributes to matter-of-fact accounts of a notable life, and by the war's end, they reflected a near indifference toward dying. The obituary for Episcopal Reverend Thomas Brownell of Connecticut, presumed to be the oldest Protestant bishop in the world, might be expected to have included religious rhetoric, but it did not. Instead, Brownell's life is sketched straightforwardly from his education to his public achievements (*New York Times*, January 16, 1865). Men generally were noted for their bravery, patriotism, and public-spiritedness. The obituary of composer and journalist W. H. Fry notes that "it was his privilege and pride to lend a helping hand to younger men who were striving in the cause of art. No one, with a good purpose, sought Mr. Fry in vain" (*New York Times*, January 19, 1865). Death notices were less likely to list specific causes of death, instead mentioning "lingering illness" or sudden death.

Obituaries of African Americans were rare in mass-circulation newspapers. Other forms of commemoration of the dead in black communities also received little public notice, but freed slaves did uniquely remember the deceased. One of the more unusual remembrances of the dead occurred on February 23, 1865, when Union

Massachusetts State Memorial in Vicksburg, Mississippi. In 1963, monuments dedicated to those who died in the Civil War started to appear. These monuments and local obituaries were demonstrations of heroic lives and heroic deaths. Those commemorated were to be examples for the living. *The Library of Congress.*

troops arrived at Middleton Place Plantation outside of Charleston, South Carolina. As the Union soldier Henry Orlando Marcy reported in his diary, while the Union officers burned the main house and numerous outbuildings, the newly freed slaves ransacked the Middleton marble mausoleum, opened the caskets, and threw the "decayed remnants of humanity outside" (Brown 2004, p. 75).

By 1865, the war had diminished the shock value of death. The tremendous numbers of dead, missing, and maimed soldiers accelerated the turn to a greater admiration for emotional and intellectual detachment from the body. Over the course of the fighting, the adoption of a remote attitude toward the physical remains of the dead became a reasonable sensibility. Though Americans honored the memory of their dead after the war, they no longer focused on the corpse or the act of dying.

BIBLIOGRAPHY

Brown, Thomas J. *The Public Art of Civil War Commemoration: A Brief History with Documents.* Boston: Bedford/St.Martin's, 2004.

Chicago Tribune, February 5, 1865.

"Death of Col. William A. Webb," *Chicago Tribune*, December 26, 1861.

Fowler, Bridget. *The Obituary as Collective Memory.* New York: Routledge, 2007.

Hume, Janice. *Obituaries in American Culture.* Jackson: University Press of Mississippi, 2000.

Hunt, Judith Lee. "'High with Courage and Hope': The Middleton Family's Civil War." In *Southern Families at War: Loyalty and Conflict in the Civil War South*, ed. Catherine Clinton. New York: Oxford University Press, 2000.

"A Melancholy Accident," *Chicago Tribune*, January 3, 1862.

New York Times, February 19, 1862.

New York Times, January 16, 1865.

New York Times, January 19, 1865

New York Times, February 20, 1865.

Caryn E. Neumann

Annotated Bibliography

The following resources, which provide overviews of the American Civil War, are recommended for their broad scope and availability.

GENERAL READING

Ash, Stephen. *When the Yankees Came: Conflict and Chaos in the Occupied South.* Chapel Hill, NC: University of North Carolina Press, 1999. A comprehensive and thoughtful account of life in areas of the South that experienced Union military occupation.

Davis, William C. *A Taste for War: The Culinary History of the Blue and Gray.* Mechanicsburg, PA: Stackpole Books, 2003.

Gallman, J. Matthew. *The North Fights the Civil War: The Home Front.* Chicago: I. R. Dee, 1994. A useful overview of the Northern home front during the Civil War.

Gallman, J. Matthew, ed. *The Civil War Chronicle: The Only Day-by-Day Portrait of America's Tragic Conflict as Told by Soldiers, Journalists, Politicians, Farmers, Nurses, Slaves, and Other Eyewitnesses.* New York: Crown Publishers, 2000.

Marten, James. *Civil War America: Voices from the Home Front.* Santa Barbara, CA: ABC-CLIO, 2003.

Paludan, Phillip Shaw. *A People's Contest: The Union and Civil War, 1861–1865.* New York: Harper & Row, 1988. An examination of the impact of the Civil War on Northern society, especially in connection with the growth of industrialization.

Rubin, Anne Sarah. *A Shattered Nation: The Rise and Fall of the Confederacy, 1861–1868.* Chapel Hill: University of North Carolina Press, 2005.

Selby, John G. *Virginians at War: The Civil War Experiences of Seven Young Confederates.* Wilmington, DE: Scholarly Resources, 2002. A study of four Virginia soldiers and three women on the home front (who nevertheless sometimes experienced the passing of armies), this fascinating work seeks the reasons that a generation of Virginians supported the Confederacy and the war.

Sutherland, Daniel E. *The Expansion of Everyday Life, 1860–1876.* New York: Harper & Row, 1989. A popularly written overview of daily life in America during the era of the Civil War and Reconstruction, built on the testimony of those who lived through the period and emphasizing the quest for middle-class status.

Volo, Dorothy Denneen, and James M. Volo. *Daily Life in Civil War America.* Westport, CT: Greenwood Press, 1998.

Williams, David. *Rich Man's War: Class, Cast, and Confederate Defeat in the Lower Chattahoochee Valley.* Athens: University of Georgia Press, 1998. An examination of the impact of the Civil War in southwestern Georgia and southeastern Alabama, with particular emphasis on class divisions.

Woodworth, Steven E., ed. *Cultures in Conflict: The American Civil War.* Westport, CT: Greenwood Press, 2000. A collection of first-person accounts of Civil War life in both the North and the South.

A SOLDIER'S LIFE

Barton, Michael. *Goodmen: The Character of Civil War Soldiers.* University Park: Pennsylvania State

University Press, 1981. A quantitative analysis of the collective personality of Civil War soldiers on the basis of their writings.

Barton, Michael, and Larry M. Logue. eds. *The Civil War Soldier: A Historical Reader.* New York: New York University Press, 2002. Excerpts from some of the memoirs of the Civil War soldiers.

Billings, John D. *Hardtack and Coffee; or, The Unwritten Story of Army Life.* Boston: G. M. Smith, 1887. Reprint, Alexandria, VA: Time-Life Books, 1982. A description of the soldier's life written by a soldier.

Davis, William C. *Rebels and Yankees: The Fighting Men of the Civil War.* New York: Smithmark Publishers, 1991.

Glatthaar, Joseph T. *The March to the Sea and Beyond: Sherman's Troops in the Savannah and Carolinas Campaigns.* New York: New York University Press, 1985.

Grimsley, Mark. *The Hard Hand of War: Union Military Policy toward Southern Civilians, 1860–1865.* New York: Cambridge University Press, 1997. An excellent account and analysis of the behavior of Union troops toward Confederate civilians.

Kennett, Lee B. *Marching through Georgia: The Story of Soldiers and Civilians during Sherman's Campaign.* New York: HarperCollins, 1995.

Marvel, William. *Andersonville: The Last Depot.* Chapel Hill: University of North Carolina Press, 1994. A good account of the worst prison camp of the Civil War.

McPherson, James M. *What They Fought For, 1861–1865.* New York: Anchor Books, 1995. A preliminary to McPherson's *For Cause and Comrades*, this book is nevertheless eminently readable and useful.

McPherson, James M. *For Cause and Comrades: Why Men Fought in the Civil War.* New York: Oxford University Press, 1997. The definitive examination of the motivations of Civil War soldiers.

Mitchell, Reid. *Civil War Soldiers: Their Expectations and Their Experiences.* New York: Viking, 1988. A study of the thought and motivations of the Civil War soldiers.

Mitchell, Reid. *The Vacant Chair: The Northern Soldier Leaves Home.* New York: Oxford University Press, 1993. A discussion of the emotional and psychological effects of the separation entailed by the war, both for Civil War soldiers and their families. Informed by modern scholarly ideas of gender.

Moore, Albert Burton. *Conscription and Conflict in the Confederacy.* New York: Macmillan, 1924. Reprint, New York: Hillary House, 1963.

Murdock, Eugene C. *One Million Men: The Civil War Draft in the North.* Madison: State Historical Society of Wisconsin, 1971. An investigation of how the Civil War draft worked—or failed to work—and why.

Power, J. Tracy. *Lee's Miserables: Life in the Army of Northern Virginia from the Wilderness to Appomattox.* Chapel Hill: University of North Carolina Press, 1998. An outstanding analysis of the devolution of morale within the Army of Northern Virginia during its last year of existence.

Robertson, James I., Jr. *Soldiers Blue and Gray.* New York: Warner Books, 1991.

Silber, Nina, and Mary Beth Sievens, eds. *Yankee Correspondence: Civil War Letters between New England Soldiers and the Home Front.* Charlottesville: University Press of Virginia, 1996. A selection of interesting letters between New England soldiers and their families back home.

Wert, Jeffry D. *A Brotherhood of Valor: The Common Soldiers of the Stonewall Brigade, C.S.A., and the Iron Brigade, U.S.A.* New York: Simon & Schuster, 1999.

Wiley, Bell Irvin. *The Life of Johnny Reb: The Common Soldier of the Confederacy.* Indianapolis, IN: Bobbs-Merrill, 1943. By making extensive use of soldiers' diaries and letters, this book pioneered the modern literature of the Civil War's common soldier.

Wiley, Bell Irvin. *The Life of Billy Yank: The Common Soldier of the Union.* Indianapolis, IN: Bobbs-Merrill, 1952. A highly successful sequel to Wiley's groundbreaking *The Life of Johnny Reb.*

Wiley, Bell Irvin. *The Common Soldier in the Civil War.* New York: Grosset & Dunlap, 1958.

Williams, David. *Johnny Reb's War: Battlefield and Homefront.* Abilene, TX: McWhiney Foundation Press, 2000. A brief but helpful overview of the common Confederate soldier.

Woodworth, Steven E., ed. *The Loyal, True, and Brave: America's Civil War Soldiers.* Wilmington, DE: SR Books, 2002. A collection of writings by and about soldiers.

FAMILY AND COMMUNITY

Attie, Jeanie. *Patriotic Toil: Northern Women and the Civil War.* Ithaca, NY: Cornell University Press, 1998. A study that shows how localism and individualism continued to be characteristic of relief work for the soldiers, despite the efforts of the leadership of the United States Sanitary Commission to impose order and central control.

Campbell, Edward D. C., Jr., and Kym S. Rice, eds. *A Woman's War: Southern Women, Civil War, and the*

Confederate Legacy. Charlottesville: University Press of Virginia, 1996. A collection of six essays examining the wartime experiences of Southern black women as well as white women of various social classes.

Cashin, Joan E., ed. *The War Was You and Me: Civilians in the American Civil War.* Princeton, NJ: Princeton University Press, 2002. A collection of essays dealing with the interconnections between the war and the home front in the North, the South, and on the western frontier.

Clinton, Catherine, ed. *Southern Families at War: Loyalty and Conflict in the Civil War South.* New York: Oxford University Press, 2000. A collection of twelve essays dealing with Southern families and family ties during the Civil War.

Clinton, Catherine, and Nina Silber, eds. *Divided Houses: Gender and the Civil War.* New York: Oxford University Press, 1992. A collection of eighteen essays by different authors examining various aspects of the Civil War from the perspective of modern scholarly ideas of gender.

DeCredico, Mary A. *Mary Boykin Chesnut: A Confederate Woman's Life.* Madison, WI: Madison House, 1996. A biography of the highly perceptive diarist whose husband was a Southern planter, U.S. senator, and Confederate staff officer.

Edwards, Laura F. *Scarlet Doesn't Live Here Anymore: Southern Women in the Civil War Era.* Urbana: University of Illinois Press, 2000.

Faust, Drew Gilpin. *Mothers of Invention: Women of the Slaveholding South in the American Civil War.* Chapel Hill: University of North Carolina Press, 1996. A highly acclaimed account of how upper-class Southern women tried to hold their world together in the midst of the upheavals and dislocations brought on by war and emancipation.

Gallman, J. Matthew. *Mastering Wartime: A Social History of Philadelphia during the Civil War.* New York: Cambridge University Press, 1990. A study of how the war affected Philadelphia socially, economically, and psychologically.

Inscoe, John C., and Gordon B. McKinney. *The Heart of Confederate Appalachia: Western North Carolina in the Civil War.* Chapel Hill: University of North Carolina Press, 2000.

Karamanski, Theodore J. *Rally 'Round the Flag: Chicago and the Civil War.* Rowman & Littlefield Publishers, 2006. A wide-ranging narrative examining the impact Chicagoans had on the war and how the war affected Chicago.

Leonard, Elizabeth D. *Yankee Women: Gender Battles in the Civil War.* New York: W. W. Norton, 1994. A study focusing on three Northern women and their roles within the Union war effort. Leonard argues that the war was a major watershed that changed ideas about women's role in society.

Marten, James. *The Children's Civil War.* Chapel Hill: University of North Carolina Press, 1998.

Marten, James. *Lessons of War: The Civil War in Children's Magazines.* Wilmington, DE: SR Books, 1999.

Marten, James. *Children for the Union: The War Spirit on the Northern Home Front.* Chicago: Ivan R. Dee, 2004. An account of how the war was presented to children in literature and popular culture and of how children reacted and remembered the war.

McCaslin, Richard B. *Tainted Breeze: The Great Hanging at Gainesville, Texas, 1862.* Baton Rouge: Louisiana State University Press, 1994. An excellent account of the hanging of a number of Texas Unionists in one North Texas town.

Moore, Frank. *Women of the War: Their Heroism and Self-Sacrifice.* Chicago: R. C. Treat, 1866. Reprint, Alexander, NC: Blue Gray Books, 1997. One of the first books to be written about the role of women in the Civil War. Moore stresses women's roles in caring for suffering soldiers.

Noe, Kenneth W., and Shannon H. Wilson, eds. *The Civil War in Appalachia: Collected Essays.* Knoxville: University of Tennessee Press, 1997.

Rable, George C. *Civil Wars: Women and the Crisis of Southern Nationalism.* Urbana: University of Illinois Press, 1989. A comprehensive account of the impact of the Civil War on Southern women, showing how traditional roles quickly reestablished themselves after the upheaval of war.

Rose, Anne C. *Victorian America and the Civil War.* New York: Cambridge University Press, 1992. Looking at seventy-five upper-middle-class Victorians in America, this study examines their attitudes on an array of subjects and argues that the war changed them little but did enhance their self-confidence.

Rosen, Robert H. *Confederate Charleston: An Illustrated History of the City and People during the Civil War.* Columbia: University of South Carolina Press, 1994. A brief but profusely illustrated account of wartime life in the city where the Civil War began.

Silber, Nina. *Daughters of the Union: Northern Women Fight the Civil War.* Cambridge, MA: Harvard University Press, 2005.

Spann, Edward K. *Gotham at War: New York City, 1860–1865.* Wilmington, DE: SR Books, 2002. This excellent examination of many facets of wartime New York provides a case study in the impact of wartime pressures on civilian society.

Sutherland, Daniel E. *Seasons of War: The Ordeal of a Confederate Community, 1861–1865.* New York: Free Press, 1995. A highly readable account of the impact of the Civil War in Culpeper County, Virginia, told from the viewpoint of and based on the accounts of the many soldiers and civilians who either lived in the county or passed through it during the war.

Taylor, Amy Murrell. *The Divided Family in Civil War America.* Chapel Hill: University of North Carolina Press, 2005.

Werner, Emmy E. *Reluctant Witnesses: Children's Voices from the Civil War.* Boulder, CO: Westview Press, 1998.

RELIGION

Bailey, David T. *Shadow on the Church: Southwestern Evangelical Religion and the Issue of Slavery, 1783–1860.* Ithaca, NY: Cornell University Press, 1985.

Bennett, William W. *A Narrative of the Great Revival Which Prevailed in the Southern Armies during the Late Civil War between the States of the Federal Union.* Philadelphia: Claxton, Remsen & Haffelfinger, 1877. A Southern minister draws on the reports of his fellow ministers to describe the upsurge in piety that occurred in the Confederate armies. Along with Jones's *Christ in the Camp* (below), this is a favorite of Lost Cause apologists seeking to present the Confederacy as morally superior to the Union.

Blied, Benjamin J. *Catholics and the Civil War.* Milwaukee, WI: Author, 1945.

Boles, John B. *The Irony of Southern Religion.* New York: Peter Lang Publishing, 1994. A brief but fascinating exploration of the multiple ironies involved in the way in which Christianity was adapted to the purposes of antebellum Southern society and, along with this, used to defend slavery.

Brinsfield, John W., William C. Davis, Benedict Maryniak, and James I. Robertson Jr., eds. *Faith in the Fight: Civil War Chaplains.* Mechanicsburg, PA: Stackpole Books, 2003.

Brown, William Young. *The Army Chaplain: His Office, Duties, and Responsibilities, and the Means of Aiding Him.* Philadelphia: Martien, 1863.

Farmer, James O., Jr. *The Metaphysical Confederacy: James Henley Thornwell and the Synthesis of Southern Values.* Macon, GA: Mercer University Press, 1999. A discussion of the shift in religious philosophy behind secession and the Confederacy.

Jones, Rev. J. William. *Christ in the Camp or Religion in Lee's Army.* Richmond, VA: B. F. Johnson, 1888. An account of religious revivals in the Army of Northern Virginia. Along with Bennett's *Great Revival* (above), this is a favorite of Lost Cause apologists seeking to present the Confederacy as morally superior to the Union.

Miller, Randall M., Harry S. Stout, and Charles Reagan Wilson, eds. *Religion and the American Civil War.* New York: Oxford University Press, 1998. A collection of essays exploring various aspects of American religion during the Civil War.

Moorhead, James H. *American Apocalypse: Yankee Protestants and the Civil War.* New Haven, CT: Yale University Press, 1978. Moorhead uses pamphlet sermons and nineteenth-century religious periodicals to argue that Northern Protestant denominations too readily identified the Union war effort with the Christian apocalypse and the ushering in of the millennium—leading to a religious crisis after the war.

Moss, Rev. Lemuel. *Annals of the United States Christian Commission.* Philadelphia: J. B. Lippincott, 1868. An early history of this organization, which was founded as an offshoot of the YMCA for the purpose of bringing both Christian witness and material comfort to the Union soldiers in the field.

Owen, Christopher H. *The Sacred Flame of Love: Methodism and Society in Nineteenth-Century Georgia.* Athens: University of Georgia Press, 1998. An interesting account of the growth of Methodism in Georgia and of the efforts of Georgia Methodists to reconcile their religion with slavery.

Rhodes, Elisha Hunt. *All for the Union: The Civil War Diary and Letters of Elisha Hunt Rhodes.* Ed. Robert Hunt Rhodes. New York: Orion Books, 1985. Made famous by the 1990 Ken Burns PBS Civil War series, Rhodes was a devout Christian who had much to say on the subject of religion in the Civil War armies.

Shattuck, Gardiner H., Jr. *A Shield and Hiding Place: The Religious Life of the Civil War Armies.* Macon, GA: Mercer University Press, 1987. A brief comparative study of religion in the Union and Confederate armies, which suggests that the individualistic nature of Southern religion made it less able to sustain the South in war.

Smith, Edward Parmelee. *Incidents of the United States Christian Commission.* Philadelphia: J. B. Lippincott, 1869.

Smith, Timothy L. *Revivalism and Social Reform: American Protestantism on the Eve of the Civil War.* Baltimore, MD: Johns Hopkins University Press, 1980. An account of the revival of 1857, with a focus on its contribution to reform movements.

Trumbull, Henry Clay. *The Sunday-School: Its Origins, Mission, Methods, and Auxiliaries.* Philadelphia: John D. Wattles, 1888. An account by the chaplain of the 10th Connecticut, discussing the birth and growth of a popular nineteenth-century religious institution.

Trumbull, Henry Clay. *War Memories of an Army Chaplain.* New York: Charles Scribner's Sons, 1898.

Wilson, Charles Reagan. *Baptized in Blood: The Religion of the Lost Cause, 1865–1920.* Athens: University of Georgia Press, 1980. A broad examination of civil religion in the post–Civil War South.

Woodworth, Steven E. *While God Is Marching On: The Religious World of Civil War Soldiers.* Lawrence: University Press of Kansas, 2001. An account of religion within the Civil War armies, focusing on what soldiers thought, said, and did.

POPULAR CULTURE

Abel, E. Lawrence. *Singing the New Nation: How Music Shaped the Confederacy, 1861–1865.* Mechanicsburg, PA: Stackpole Books, 1999. A popularly written account of music as it was performed, published, and composed in the Confederacy, along with an examination of the experiences of bandsmen in the Confederate army.

Bernard, Kenneth A. *Lincoln and the Music of the Civil War.* Caldwell, ID: Caxton Printers, 1966. An account of the music of wartime Washington, DC, focusing on songs related to Lincoln—songs Lincoln heard, songs about Lincoln, songs he liked—including his favorites, "Dixie" and "La Marseillaise."

Bode, Carl. *The American Lyceum: Town Meeting of the Mind.* New York: Oxford University Press, 1956.

Burnham, John C. *Bad Habits: Drinking, Smoking, Taking Drugs, Gambling, Sexual Misbehavior, and Swearing in American History.* New York and London: New York University Press, 1993. This excellent and thought-provoking study of "minor vices" in American history places such activities in the Civil War era within a broader context.

Cornelius, Steven H. *Music of the Civil War Era.* Westport, CT: Greenwood Press, 2004.

Epstein, Dena J. *Sinful Tunes and Spirituals: Black Folk Music to the Civil War.* Urbana: University of Illinois Press, 1977. Documents period accounts of African American music and its development before and during the Civil War.

Gac, Scott. *Singing for Freedom: The Hutchinson Family Singers and the Nineteenth-Century Culture of Reform.* New Haven, CT: Yale University Press, 2007. Tells the story of the Hutchinson Family, America's most popular singing group of the era leading up to the Civil War. Rooted in revival meetings, the Hutchinsons specialized in songs promoting temperance and abolition.

Kirsch, George B. *Baseball in Blue and Gray: The National Pastime during the Civil War.* Princeton, NJ: Princeton University Press, 2003. A brief, popular account of how baseball, already the national pastime, survived and developed during the Civil War.

Lott, Eric. *Love and Theft: Blackface Minstrelsy and the American Working Class.* New York: Oxford University Press, 1993. A history of blackface minstrelsy from its beginnings around 1830 through the Civil War.

Mead, David C. *Yankee Eloquence in the Middle West: The Ohio Lyceum, 1850–1870.* East Lansing: Michigan State College Press, 1951. A detailed study of the lyceum movement in Ohio, focusing on the fifteen most popular lecturers in the state.

Meer, Sarah. *Uncle Tom Mania: Slavery, Minstrelsy, and Transatlantic Culture in the 1850s.* Athens: University of Georgia, 2005. An analysis of the intersections among minstrelsy, abolitionism, American literature, and British-American relations in the nineteenth century.

Morgan, Jo-Ann. *Uncle Tom's Cabin As Visual Culture.* Columbia: University of Missouri Press, 2007. A study of how the various illustrations associated with Harriet Beecher Stowe's famous abolitionist novel influenced popular conceptions.

Ray, Angela G. *The Lyceum and Public Culture in the Nineteenth-Century United States.* East Lansing: Michigan State University Press, 2005.

Reynolds, David S. *Walt Whitman's America: A Cultural Biography.* New York: Vintage Books, 1995.

Silverman, Jerry. *Songs and Stories of the Civil War.* Brookfield, CT: Twenty-First Century Books, 2002.

Sullivan, George. *In the Wake of Battle: The Civil War Images of Mathew Brady.* Munich and New York: Prestel Verlag, 2004. A collection of Brady's photographs, along with helpful explanations.

Toll, Robert C. *Blacking Up: The Minstrel Show in Nineteenth-Century America.* New York: Oxford University Press, 1974. Relates minstrelsy, the most popular entertainment form of the mid-nineteenth century, to American society.

Zeller, Bob. *The Blue and Gray in Black and White: A History of Civil War Photography.* Westport, CT: Praeger Publishers, 2005.

HEALTH AND MEDICINE

Adams, George Worthington. *Doctors in Blue: The Medical History of the Union Army in the Civil*

War. New York: Henry Schuman, 1952. Reprint, Dayton, OH: Press of Morningside, 1985. One of the early pioneering studies of Civil War surgeons, Adams's book is still a classic.

Alcott, Louisa May. *Hospital Sketches*. Boston: J. Redpath, 1863. Published in a local newspaper during the war, these accounts, which originated as letters home, describe the future author of *Little Women*'s service as a volunteer nurse in the District of Columbia's Union Hotel Hospital.

Apperson, John Samuel. *Repairing the "March of Mars": The Civil War Diaries of John Samuel Apperson, Hospital Steward in the Stonewall Brigade, 1861–1865*. Ed. John Herbert Roper. Macon, GA: Mercer University Press, 2001.

Bollet, Alfred Jay. *Civil War Medicine: Challenges and Triumphs*. Tucson, AZ: Galen Press, 2002. A lengthy (475-page), highly documented study encompassing all aspects of Civil War medical practice.

Brinton, John H. *Personal Memoirs of John H. Brinton, Major and Surgeon U.S.V., 1861–1865*. New York: Neale Publishing Company, 1914.

Cumming, Kate. "A Nurse's Diary." In *A Journal of Hospital Life in the Confederate Army of Tennessee, from the Battle of Shiloh to the End of the War: With Sketches of Life and Character, and Brief Notices of Current Events during That Period*. Louisville, KY: John P. Morgan, 1866.

Cunningham, H. H. *Doctors in Gray: The Confederate Medical Service*. Baton Rouge: Louisiana State University Press, 1958. Along with Adams's *Doctors in Blue*, this was one of the early pioneering studies of Civil War surgeons.

Denney, R. E. *Civil War Medicine: Care and Comfort of the Wounded*. New York: Sterling Publishing, 1994. A compilation of first-person observations of Civil War medical care, arranged in an almost day-by-day chronological order.

Dyer, J. Franklin. *The Journal of a Civil War Surgeon*. Ed. Michael B. Chesson. Lincoln: University of Nebraska Press, 2003. Dyer, who served from 1861 to 1864, started the war as surgeon of the 19th Massachusetts and rose to be chief medical officer of the Second Division, Second Corps.

Ellis, Thomas T. *Leaves from the Diary of an Army Surgeon; or, Incidents of Field, Camp, and Hospital Life*. New York: J. Bradburn, 1863.

Flannery, Michael A. *Civil War Pharmacy: A History of Drugs, Drug Supply and Provision, and Therapeutics for the Union and Confederacy*. New York: Pharmaceutical Products Press, 2004. A comprehensive history of pharmaceuticals and the practice of pharmacy in both the Union and Confederate armies.

Freemon, Frank R. *Gangrene and Glory: Medical Care during the American Civil War*. Madison, NJ: Fairleigh Dickinson University Press, 2001. This lavishly illustrated book is organized into twenty-four brief chapters, each dealing with a particular aspect of Civil War medical care.

Giesberg, Judith Ann. *Civil War Sisterhood: The United States Sanitary Commission and Women's Politics in Transition*. Lebanon, NH: University Press of New England, 2006. Giesberg argues that women took an active role in directing the activities of the U.S.S.C. and thus advanced the cause of women fulfilling previously male roles during the years that followed.

Hart, Albert G. *The Surgeon and the Hospital in the Civil War*. Palmyra, VA: Old Soldier Books, 1987.

Parsons, Emily Elizabeth. *Civil War Nursing: Memoir of Emily Elizabeth Parsons*. Boston: Little, Brown, 1880. Reprint, New York: Garland, 1984.

Powers, Elvira J. *Hospital Pencillings: Being a Diary While in Jefferson General Hospital, Jeffersonville, Ind., and Others at Nashville, Tennessee, as Matron and Visitor*. Boston: Edward L. Mitchel, 1866.

Reed, William Howell. *Hospital Life in the Army of the Potomac*. Boston: W. V. Spencer, 1866.

Rutkow, I. M. *Bleeding Blue and Gray: Civil War Surgery and the Evolution of American Medicine*. New York: Random House, 2005. A comprehensive history of Civil War medical care, focusing on the progress made during the course of the war.

Schroeder-Lein, Glenna R. *The Encyclopedia of Civil War Medicine*. Armonk, NY: M. E. Sharpe, 2008. A comprehensive reference guide to all aspects of Civil War medicine.

Smith, Adelaide W. *Reminiscences of an Army Nurse during the Civil War*. New York: Greaves Publishing Company, 1911.

Straubing, Harold Elk, ed. *In Hospital and Camp: The Civil War through the Eyes of Its Doctors and Nurses*. Mechanicsburg, PA: Stackpole Books, 1993. A compilation of eyewitness accounts of medical care during the Civil War.

Woolsey, Jane Stuart. *Hospital Days: Reminiscences of a Civil War Nurse*. New York: D. Van Nostrand, 1870.

WORK AND ECONOMY

Ball, Douglas B. *Financial Failure and Confederate Defeat*. Urbana: University of Illinois Press, 1991. Ball suggests that the Confederacy suffered from an unwillingness to face financial reality, in particular an unwillingness to raise taxes to a level sufficient to finance the war.

Dew, Charles B. *Ironmaker to the Confederacy: Joseph R. Anderson and the Tredegar Iron Works.* New Haven, CT, and London: Yale University Press, 1966. An examination of the business career of the director of the Confederacy's largest and most important industrial concern, showing how Anderson favored the Confederacy but favored his own profits even more.

Dew, Charles B. *Bond of Iron: Master and Slave at Buffalo Forge.* New York: W. W. Norton, 1994. A study of a small iron-making establishment near Lexington, Virginia, demonstrating that although slaves could be used successfully in such industrial work, the system of slavery inhibited technological innovation and placed limits on productivity.

Dublin, Thomas. *Women at Work: The Transformation of Work and Community in Lowell, Massachusetts, 1826–1860.* New York: Columbia University Press, 1979. A study of the social origins and motivations of the young women who made up the work force of one of America's first textile mills during the decades leading up to the Civil War.

Fite, Emerson David. *Social and Industrial Conditions in the North during the Civil War.* New York: Macmillan, 1910.

Gates, Paul W. *Agriculture and the Civil War.* New York: Alfred A. Knopf, 1965. While the war stimulated rapid growth in agricultural mechanization in the North, in the South government policies led to a decline in agricultural production, handicapping the Confederate war effort.

Hareven, Tamara K., and Randolph Langenbach. *Amoskeag: Life and Work in an American Factory-City.* New York: Pantheon Books, 1978. A history of the workers in the Manchester, New Hampshire, textile mills.

Johnson, Russell L. *Warriors into Workers: The Civil War and the Formation of Urban-Industrial Society in a Northern City.* New York: Fordham University Press, 2003. A study of the culture and society of Dubuque, Iowa, during the Civil War.

Massey, Mary Elizabeth. *Ersatz in the Confederacy: Shortages and Substitutes on the Southern Homefront.* Columbia: University of South Carolina Press, 1952. Massey discusses not only the shortages, which were severe and endemic within the Confederacy, but also analyzes their causes, of which Confederate government policies such as impressment and the tax-in-kind were chief.

Otto, John Solomon. *Southern Agriculture during the Civil War Era, 1860–1880.* Westport, CT: Greenwood Publishing Group, 1994. A brief overview of Southern agricultural developments during the Civil War era.

Palladino, Grace. *Another Civil War: Labor, Capital, and the State in the Anthracite Regions of Pennsylvania, 1840–1868.* Urbana: University of Illinois Press, 1990.

Thornton, Mark, and Robert B. Ekelund Jr. *Tariffs, Blockades, and Inflation: The Economics of the Civil War.* Wilmington, DE: SR Books, 2004. An examination of government fiscal policy during the Civil War, showing that the Confederate government pursued policies that ultimate hurt its cause.

Wilson, Mark R. *The Business of Civil War: Military Mobilization and the State, 1861–1865.* Baltimore, MD: Johns Hopkins University Press, 2006.

POLITICS

Abrahamson, James L. *The Men of Secession and Civil War, 1859–1861.* Wilmington, DE: SR Books, 2000. A brief narrative and analysis of the secession crisis, emphasizing that it was not a spontaneous popular outburst but rather a carefully engineered revolution for which secessionist leaders had worked long and hard.

Bernstein, Iver. *The New York Draft Riots: Their Significance for American Society and Politics in the Age of the Civil War.* New York: Oxford University Press, 1990.

Boritt, Gabor. *The Gettysburg Gospel: The Lincoln Speech That Nobody Knows.* New York: Simon & Schuster, 2006.

Cooper, William J. Jr. *Jefferson Davis, American.* New York: Alfred A. Knopf, 2000.

Davis, William C. *Jefferson Davis: The Man and His Hour.* New York: HarperCollins, 1991.

Davis, William C. *A Government of Our Own: The Making of the Confederacy.* New York: Free Press, 1994.

Dew, Charles B. *Apostles of Disunion: Southern Secession Commissioners and the Causes of the Civil War.* Charlottesville: University of Virginia Press, 2001. This study of the rhetoric of commissioners sent by seceding states to other wavering slave states reveals that the overriding motive for secession was the preservation of slavery.

Guelzo, Allen C. *Abraham Lincoln: Redeemer President.* Grand Rapids, MI: W. B. Eerdmans, 1999. This award-winning book looks at Lincoln's thought and sees him as an heir to the classical liberalism of John Locke.

Guelzo, Allen C. *Lincoln and Douglas: The Debates That Defined America.* New York: Simon & Schuster, 2008.

Harris, Brayton. *Blue and Gray in Black and White: Newspapers in the Civil War.* Washington, DC: Brassey's, 1999. An overview of how Civil War newspapers reported and often attempted to influence the course of events.

Holzer, Harold. *Lincoln at Cooper Union: The Speech That Made Abraham Lincoln President.* New York: Simon & Schuster, 2004. A fascinating account of one of Lincoln's greatest speeches. Holzer describes the circumstances leading up to the speech, its delivery, and its reception, and also provides a profound discussion of its meaning, showing Lincoln's eagerness to "think as the Founders thought, and act as the Founders acted."

Jaffa, Harry V. *Crisis of the House Divided: An Interpretation of the Issues in the Lincoln-Douglas Debates.* Garden City, NY: Doubleday, 1959.

Jaffa, Harry V. *A New Birth of Freedom: Abraham Lincoln and the Coming of the Civil War.* Lanham, MD: Rowman & Littlefield Publishers, 2000. A challenging and profoundly thought-provoking meditation on Lincoln's commitment to the truth that "all men are created equal."

Neely, Mark E., Jr. *The Fate of Liberty: Abraham Lincoln and Civil Liberties.* New York; Oxford University Press, 1991. Dispels the myth that the Lincoln administration was unduly harsh or unmindful of the importance of civil liberties.

Neely, Mark E., Jr. *Confederate Bastille: Jefferson Davis and Civil Liberties.* Milwaukee, WI: Marquette University Press, 1993. Dispels the myth that the Confederate government strictly respected civil liberties.

Neely, Mark E., Jr. *The Divided Union: Party Conflict in the Civil War North.* Cambridge, MA: Harvard University Press, 2002.

Rable, George C. *The Confederate Republic: A Revolution against Politics.* Chapel Hill: University of North Carolina Press, 1994. An exploration of Confederate politics. It points up the irony that while many Southerners expressed a desire to get away from politics as they had known it in the old Union, they nonetheless recreated it in a more corrosive form in their new republic.

Walther, Eric H. *The Fire-Eaters.* Baton Rouge: Louisiana State University Press, 1992.

Walther, Eric H. *The Shattering of the Union: America in the 1850s.* Wilmington, DE: Scholarly Resources, 2004. An account of the political struggles of the 1850s that lead the country to the brink of secession and Civil War.

Walther, Eric H. *William Lowndes Yancey and the Coming of the Civil War.* Chapel Hill: University of North Carolina Press, 2006.

Waugh, John C. *Reelecting Lincoln: The Battle for the 1864 Presidency.* New York: Crown Publishers, 1997.

Waugh, John C. *On the Brink of Civil War: The Compromise of 1850 and How It Changed the Course of American History.* Wilmington, DE: Scholarly Resources, 2003. A fascinating and thoughtful narrative of the struggle for passage of the Compromise of 1850, which may have delayed the Civil War by a decade.

Weber, Jennifer L. *Copperheads: The Rise and Fall of Lincoln's Opponents in the North.* New York and Oxford: Oxford University Press, 2006. An account of Northerners who opposed the Union war effort.

White, Ronald C., Jr. *The Eloquent President: A Portrait of Lincoln through His Words.* New York: Random House, 2005. A discussion of Lincoln as one of history's most skillful practitioners of the art of using the English language to communicate with and motivate the American people.

Yearns, Wilfred Buck. *The Confederate Congress.* Athens: University of Georgia Press, 1960.

EFFECTS OF THE WAR ON SLAVES AND FREEDPEOPLE

Bentley, George R. *A History of the Freedmen's Bureau.* Philadelphia: University of Pennsylvania Press, 1955.

Berlin, Ira, Joseph P. Reidy, and Leslie S. Rowland, eds. *Freedom's Soldiers: The Black Military Experience in the Civil War.* New York: Cambridge University Press, 1998. A collection of documents relating to the service of black troops in the Union army. Includes a collection of photographs and a lengthy introductory essay.

Berlin, Ira, and Leslie S. Rowland, eds. *Families and Freedom: A Documentary History of African-American Kinship in the Civil War Era.* New York: New Press, 1997.

Cornish, Dudley Taylor. *The Sable Arm: Negro Troops in the Union Army, 1861–1865.* New York: Longmans, Green, 1956. Reprint, New York: W. W. Norton, 1966. The classic account of black troops in the Union army. Cornish discusses the policy debates leading to black enlistment, the raising and equipping of black units, and their impressive operational performance, including in combat.

Durden, Robert F. *The Gray and the Black: The Confederate Debate on Emancipation.* Baton

Rouge: Louisiana State University Press, 1972. An account of one of the most curious incidents of the war, the tentative (and ultimately stillborn) decision by the Davis administration to attempt to induce slaves to fight for the Confederacy.

Foner, Eric. *Nothing but Freedom: Emancipation and Its Legacy.* Baton Rouge: Louisiana State University Press, 1984. A discussion of emancipation and its effects.

Forbes, Ella. *African American Women during the Civil War.* New York: Garland, 1998.

Frankel, Noralee. *Freedom's Women: Black Women and Families in Civil War Era Mississippi.* Bloomington: Indiana University Press, 1999.

Franklin, John Hope. *The Emancipation Proclamation.* Garden City, NY: Anchor Books, 1965. A discussion of the purposes and impact of the Emancipation Proclamation.

Glatthaar, Joseph T. *Forged in Battle: The Civil War Alliance of Black Soldiers and White Officers.* New York: Free Press, 1990.

Guelzo, Allen C. *Lincoln's Emancipation Proclamation: The End of Slavery in America.* New York: Simon & Schuster, 2004. A study of Lincoln's cautious progress toward emancipation, which balanced his desire to free the slaves with his respect for constitutional limitations.

Hansen, Joyce. *Between Two Fires: Black Soldiers in the Civil War.* New York: Franklin Watts, 1993.

Hargrove, Hondon B. *Black Union Soldiers in the Civil War.* Jefferson, NC: McFarland, 1988.

Levine, Bruce. *Confederate Emancipation: Southern Plans to Free and Arm Slaves during the Civil War.* New York: Oxford University Press, 2006.

McPherson, James M. *The Negro's Civil War: How American Negroes Felt and Acted during the War for the Union.* New York: Pantheon Books, 1965. An early but classic work on the subject by one of the most respected Civil War historians.

Robinson, Armstead L. *Bitter Fruits of Bondage: The Demise of Slavery and the Collapse of the Confederacy, 1861–1865.* Charlottesville: University of Virginia Press, 2005. This long-awaited book, published posthumously from the notes and manuscripts of the late University of Virginia professor, argues that "class conflict based on defense of slavery eroded the Southern will to national independence" (p. 10).

Smith, John David, ed. *Black Soldiers in Blue: African American Troops in the Civil War Era.* Chapel Hill: University of North Carolina Press, 2002. A collection of fourteen essays exploring various aspects of the African American military experience during the Civil War.

Taylor, Susie King. *A Black Woman's Civil War Memoirs.* Ed. by Patricia W. Romero and Willie Lee Rose. Princeton, NJ: Markus Wiener, 1988.

Wiley, Bell Irvin. *Southern Negroes, 1861–1865.* New Haven: Yale University Press, 1938.

Wilson, Keith P. *Campfires of Freedom: The Camp Life of Black Soldiers during the Civil War.* Kent, OH: Kent State University Press, 2002. Wilson not only relates the experiences of black soldiers in military camps, but also places those experiences within the broader setting of the political and social transformation that took place during the Civil War years.

RECONCILIATION AND REMEMBRANCE

Adams, Jessica. *Wounds of Returning: Race, Memory, and Property on the Postslavery Plantation.* Chapel Hill: University of North Carolina Press, 2007.

Blight, David W. *Race and Reunion: The Civil War in American Memory.* Cambridge, MA: Belknap Press of Harvard University Press, 2001.

Blight, David W. *Beyond the Battlefield: Race, Memory, and the American Civil War.* Amherst: University of Massachusetts Press, 2002. Both this book and the one above discuss shifting memories of the war along with ways in which the late-nineteenth-century movement toward reunion had an impact on issues of race.

Brown, Thomas J. *The Public Art of Civil War Commemoration: A Brief History with Documents.* New York: Bedford/St. Martin's, 2004.

Fahs, Alice, and Joan Waugh, eds. *The Memory of the Civil War in American Culture.* Chapel Hill: University of North Carolina Press, 2004.

Foster, Gaines M. *Ghosts of the Confederacy: Defeat, the Lost Cause, and the Emergence of the New South, 1865 to 1913.* New York: Oxford University Press, 1987. A thought-provoking study of Confederate veterans groups and memorial associations.

McConnell, Stuart. *Glorious Contentment: The Grand Army of the Republic, 1865–1900.* Chapel Hill: University of North Carolina Press, 1992. A social history of the great Union veterans' organization.

Neff, John R. *Honoring the Civil War Dead: Commemoration and the Problem of Reconciliation.* Lawrence: University Press of Kansas, 2005. A thoughtful discussion of the commemoration of war dead and how it reflected the difficulties of reconciliation.

Reardon, Carol. *Pickett's Charge in History and Memory.* Chapel Hill: University of North Carolina Press,

1997. An examination of how one of the most famous incidents of the Civil War has evolved in popular memory.

Shaffer, Donald R. *After the Glory: The Struggles of Black Civil War Veterans.* Lawrence: University Press of Kansas, 2004.

Smith, Timothy B. *This Great Battlefield of Shiloh: History, Memory, and the Establishment of a Civil War National Military Park.* Knoxville: University of Tennessee Press, 2004. A history of the Shiloh battlefield, showing its significance to public memory of the war.

Smith, Timothy B. *The Golden Age of Battlefield Preservation: The Decade of the 1890s and the Establishment of America's First Five Military Parks.* Knoxville: University of Tennessee Press, 2008. A fascinating account of the process that led to the creation of the first and most important National Military Parks at battlefields, including Chickamauga, Shiloh, Vicksburg, and Antietam.

Index

This index is sorted word-by-word. Bold page locators indicate main essays. Italic page locators indicate images. Page locators with a *t* indicate tabular material.

A

B

C

D

E

F

G

H

I

J

K

L

M

N

Q

R

S

V

Y

Z